*This book is dedicated to our families:
Shulamit, Naama, and Noga
Jay
Nurit, Sharon, Gill, and Adi*

Contents

	PREFACE	xiii
	ABOUT THE AUTHORS	xvi
CHAPTER 1	THE EVOLUTION OF COMPUTERS	1

    1.1 Overview   1
Historical Perspectives, 2

    1.2 Mechanical Calculators   2

    1.3 Evolution of Electronic Computer Systems   6
*The First Generation: Circa 1943–1956, 7
Summary of First-Generation Computers, 10
The Second Generation: 1957–1964, 11
Summary of Second-Generation Computers, 12
The Third Generation: 1965–1971, 14
Summary of Third-Generation Computers, 15
The Fourth Generation: 1972–circa 1989, 16*

    1.4 The Future   18

CHAPTER 2	NUMBER SYSTEMS, ARITHMETIC OPERATIONS, AND CODES	21

    2.1 Data Representations   21

    2.2 Number Systems   22
*Conversion between Bases, 23
Binary-coded Decimal (BCD) Representation, 27*

v

2.3 Fixed-Point Number Representation   29
   Sign Notations, 30
   Signed Binary Numbers, 33
   Fixed-Point Arithmetic, 35
   Addition and Subtraction Using Complements, 37
   Multiplication and Division, 41

2.4 Floating-Point Number Representation   42
   Floating-Point Arithmetic, 44

2.5 Binary Codes   46
   Decimal Codes, 47
   Alphanumeric Codes, 50
   Error Detection Codes, 53
   Instruction Codes, 55

2.6 Interpretation of Binary Data   55

Problems   56

CHAPTER 3   LOGIC DESIGN PRINCIPLES AND DEVICES   59

3.1 Boolean Algebra   59

3.2 Boolean Functions   62

3.3 Logic Design Example   65

3.4 Simplification of Boolean Functions   67

3.5 Sequential Logic Circuits   70

3.6 Combinational Logic Components   72
   Standard Gates, 73
   MSI and LSI Combinational Devices, 75

3.7 Sequential Logic Components   82
   Flip-Flops, 82
   MSI and LSI Sequential Devices, 85

3.8 Memory Devices   90
   Programmable Arrays, 90
   Random-Access Memory, 94

Problems   95

CHAPTER 4   BASIC COMPUTER ORGANIZATION   99

4.1 System Components   99

4.2 Micro-Operations   100
   Register Transfer Language, 101

4.3 A Simple Computer Example   104
   SIC Machine Structure, 104
   Instruction Set for the SIC, 106
   Timing and Control, 108

Contents

    Functional Units, 113
    System Startup, 114

  4.4 Execution Trace of an SIC Instruction 114
    Execution without Interrupt, 115
    Execution with Interrupt, 117

  Problems 119

CHAPTER 5 THE CENTRAL PROCESSING UNIT (CPU) 121

  5.1 Fundamental Parts of a Computer 121

  5.2 The Register Set 123
    Program Counter Register, 123
    Instruction Register, 123
    General-Purpose Registers, 124
    The Intel 8085 Register Set, 124

  5.3 Instruction Formats 125
    Address Formats, 125
    Address Modes, 127

  5.4 Arithmetic and Logic Unit (ALU) 131
    Arithmetic Functions of an ALU, 133
    Logic Functions of an ALU, 136
    Shifter, 137

  5.5 Control Logic Unit (CLU) 139
    Arithmetic Processor, 141
    Decimal Arithmetic Unit, 144

  5.6 CPU Configuration 147
    Single-Bus Organization, 147
    Triple-Bus Organization, 148

  5.7 Reduced Instruction Set Computers (RISC) 149

  5.8 Summary 150

  Problems 150

CHAPTER 6 INPUT/OUTPUT PROCESSING 153

  6.1 The Input/Output System 153

  6.2 I/O Accessing 154
    Programmed I/O, 155
    Interrupt I/O, 157
    Direct Memory Access (DMA), 162

  6.3 Data Transfer 165
    Data Transfer Formats, 165
    Data Transfer Modes, 165
    Principles of Data Transfer Operations, 168

6.4 Device Interfacing   169
   Structure of a Device Interface, 170

6.5 System-Resident I/O Processors   172
   I/O Channels, 173
   Multiprocessor Configurations, 175
   I/O Processor (IOP), 177

6.6 Summary   180

Problems   181

CHAPTER 7   MEMORY   183

7.1 Aspects of Computer Storage   183

7.2 Stack Memory   184
   Hardware Implementation, 185
   The HP3000 Stack, 188

7.3 Modular Memory   189

7.4 Associative Memory   191
   Key Register, 193
   Reading and Writing, 195

7.5 Cache Memory   196
   How a Cache Works, 197
   Hardware Organizations, 197

7.6 Auxiliary Memory   201
   Magnetic Tape, 201
   Magnetic Disk, 202
   Floppy Disk, 205
   Magnetic Drum, 205
   Magnetic Bubble Memory, 205

7.7 Virtual Memory   208
   Evolution, 208
   Principle, 208
   Implementation, 209
   Virtual Memory Management, 213

7.8 Summary   214

Problems   215

CHAPTER 8   MICROPROGRAMMING   217

8.1 The Control Logic Unit   217

8.2 Hard-wired Control   218

8.3 Microprogrammed Control   221
   Microprogrammed CLU Organization, 221

Microinstruction Formats, 222
Microinstruction Sequencing, 226

8.4 Emulation   227

8.5 Bit Slices   228

8.6 Microprogram Support Tools   229
Microassemblers, 229
Formatters, 230
Development Systems, 230
Hardware Simulators, 230

8.7 Costs and Benefits of Microprogramming   230

Problems   232

CHAPTER 9   PIPELINED COMPUTERS   233

9.1 The Pipeline Concept   223

9.2 Synchronization of Pipelines   234

9.3 Efficiency of Pipelines   236

9.4 Classification of Pipelines   238
Functional Classification, 238
Configurational Classification, 239

9.5 Stage Cascading   241

9.6 General Pipelining Principles   242
Reservation Tables, 242
Scheduling and Collision Prevention, 245
Delay Insertion for Optimum Throughput, 251

9.7 Multifunction Pipeline Example   252

9.8 Recurrence Problem Pipeline   254

9.9 Summary   257

Problems   257

CHAPTER 10   PARALLEL PROCESSING   260

10.1 Need for Parallel Processing   260

10.2 Parallel Processing Techniques   261

10.3 Speedup of Parallel Computers   262

10.4 Classification of Parallel Computer Architectures   263
Flynn's Classification, 263
Shore's Classification, 265

Feng's Classification, 266
Comparison of Classifications, 266

10.5 Vector Processing   266
Characteristics of Vector Instructions, 267
Typical Hardware Architectures, 269
Vector Addressing Considerations, 269

10.6 Array Processors   272
Organization of Array Processors, 273
SIMD Interconnection Networks, 275
Associative Array Processors, 278

10.7 Multiprocessor Systems   278
Private-Memory and Shared-Memory Systems, 279
Multiprocessor Hardware Organizations, 280
Multicaches in Multiprocessor Systems, 283

10.8 Parallel Organizations in General   284

Problems   285

CHAPTER 11   MICROCOMPUTER ORGANIZATION   287

11.1 The Microcomputer Revolution   287

11.2 Technological Developments   287

11.3 General Overview of a Microcomputer System   289

11.4 Single-Chip Processing Unit (MPU)   291
Register Set, 291
Arithmetic and Logic Unit (ALU), 293
Control Logic Unit (CLU), 294

11.5 Instruction Set   295
Instruction Types, 296

11.6 Addressing Modes   299

11.7 Timing Issues   300

11.8 Bit-sliced Microprocessor   301
Bit-sliced Organization, 302

Problems   304

CHAPTER 12   COMPUTER COMMUNICATION NETWORKS   307

12.1 The Evolution of Computer Communication Networks   307
Classification of Computer Communication Networks, 308
Computer Communication Issues, 309

12.2 Computer Communication Network Architecture 310
Open System Interconnection (OSI) Reference Model, 310
Protocol Functions, 314
Classification of Network Protocols, 316

12.3 Computer Communication Network Topologies 316
Network Topologies, 317

12.4 Data Transmission Techniques 319
Link Topologies, 319
Transmission Modes, 320
Multiplexing, 320

12.5 Transmission Media 324

12.6 Network Switching Techniques 325
Circuit Switching, 325
Message Switching, 326
Packet Switching, 327

12.7 Summary 329

APPENDIX: LOGIC GRAPHIC SYMBOLS **330**

A.1 IEEE Standard 330

A.2 Symbol Composition 330

A.3 Dependency Notation 336
G (AND) Dependency, 336
C (Control) Dependency, 336
M (Mode) Dependency, 337

A.4 Concluding Example 337

BIBLIOGRAPHY **339**

INDEX **343**

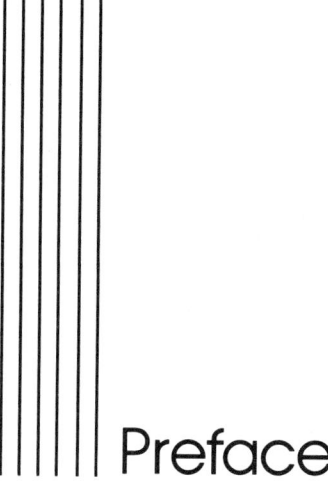

Preface

This text is intended for a first course in computer organization, at the junior or senior level, for electrical engineering, computer engineering, and computer science programs, as well as for a number of other disciplines such as mathematics and physics. The book can also be used for self-study or for review by practicing engineers and computer scientists not intimately familiar with the conventional and modern aspects of computer organization.

No specific background is a prerequisite for this text other than a good grasp of computing fundamentals. The text is self-contained, but prior knowledge of digital design principles would be advantageous.

The book can be covered in a one-semester course, but in a quarter course, the instructor must be selective in the material covered and the emphasis placed on some of the topics. For example, in a program where a digital logic design course is a prerequisite to a course in computer organization, the instructor can skip Chapters 2 and 3. Similar options exist with regard to some of the more advanced topics included in Chapters 9, 10, and 12. We have used this built-in flexibility in numerous courses in computer organization that we have taught in electrical engineering, computer engineering, and computer science programs. After completing this text, the student should be prepared for a second (advanced) course in computer organization, microcomputers, or microprocessors.

We believe that the student should study and understand thoroughly the fundamental concepts of computer organization in a first course. To do so requires a coordinated and integrated treatment of the material that maintains a balance between theory and practice. Hence this text covers practical aspects of computer organization developed gradually from basics. But since the level of presentation is intended to provide the student with a firm understanding of the underlying principles used in computer organization, we have selectively omitted a variety of details that are not necessary at this level and would otherwise have served only to obscure the picture.

We also present in the book a view of both conventional and modern approaches to computer systems organization. The advanced material appears in Chapters 9, 10, and 12. We have included this material so that students participating in programs where a second computer organization course is not provided would be exposed to some of the recent advances in computer organization. For students continuing in a second course, the material in Chapters 9, 10, and 12 will provide a solid base from which to continue.

Computer organization is concerned with the study of the structure, behavior, and design of computers. Although the text concentrates on the hardware aspects of digital computers, it nevertheless provides sufficient details to entice the interested student to probe the impact of software on the organization of a computer system. The book is divided into 12 chapters. Chapter 1 traces the evolution of computers from a historical perspective and the various kinds of computing devices and machines developed to date. This chapter should be read twice: first at the beginning of the course and again after completing the course and having assimilated the ideas and concepts. This way, the evolution of digital computers will be seen in perspective.

Chapter 2 presents various number systems and codes used to represent information in a digital computer. We emphasize the representation of numbers used in arithmetic computations and binary coding of symbols. Chapter 3 introduces tools and devices that are essential to understanding how computers are designed. We introduce Boolean algebra, present the concepts of combinational and sequential circuits, and discuss a variety of MSI and LSI combinational and sequential devices.

Chapter 4 considers the functional organization of a computer. We define a register transfer language, which is used to express in symbolic form sequences of micro-operations among the various registers of the computer. To explore the basic concepts we use a simple computer example.

The three major components of a computer are discussed in Chapters 5, 6, and 7. Chapter 5 presents a detailed exposition of the fundamental building blocks of the central processing unit of the computer. We introduce the register set and discuss instruction formats, addressing modes, the arithmetic logic unit, and the control logic unit. Chapter 6 considers the second major unit of the computer, the input/output system. It explains the various configurations for input/output transfers such as priority interrupt and direct memory access. Other topics covered in Chapter 6 include data transfer formats and modes, device interfacing, and input/output processors. Chapter 7 introduces the third major component of the computer, the main memory unit. We explain the details of a variety of memory organizations such as stack, cache, and associative memory and present the principles and implementation of virtual memory. Also considered in Chapter 7 are a number of auxiliary memory systems such as disks, tapes, and bubble memory.

Chapter 8 presents the concept of microprogramming. It explains the construction of a microprogrammed controller and introduces available microprogramming support tools. The last section in this chapter introduces the concept of bit slices.

Advanced computer organization concepts are introduced in Chapters 9 and 10. Chapter 9 presents the notion of pipelined computers. Pipeline processing is a technique used to improve the throughput of a computer system. The topics covered in this chapter include pipelining principles, synchronization, efficiency, and classification. Chapter 10 introduces parallel processing. We consider some of the organizations used to effect parallel processing and present the details of vector processing, array processing, and multiprocessor systems.

Chapter 11 provides an overview of microcomputer organization. It can be used to review the material in earlier chapters and also features topics that complement previous discussions.

Chapter 12 deals with the important topic of computer communication networks. We present the details of the open-system interconnection reference model, which serves as a conceptual framework for defining standards for interconnecting heterogeneous computer systems. Other topics covered in this chapter include network topologies, data transmission techniques, and the principles of circuit, message, and packet-switching techniques.

The various principles discussed are illustrated by means of examples in the text and a variety of problems at the end of each chapter. The problems range from the routine to the moderately difficult and are intended to promote understanding of, and provoke thought about, computer organization. A *Solution Manual* containing answers to the problems is available for the instructor directly from the publisher.

We would like to acknowledge our indebtedness to the many people who contributed to this book. We owe much to our colleagues and students, from whom we have learned and by whom we have been encouraged. In particular, we appreciate the advice, discussions, and very helpful comments provided by our colleagues Usha Chandrasekaran, Larry Hall, Lois Hawkes, Chris Lacher, Ilan Itzkovich, Jamal Rassoul, and Orit Shacham. We thank the reviewers for many constructive and helpful comments, and John Sulzycki for his support and advice. Last, but not least, we express our appreciation to our editor, James F. Fegen, Jr., our production editor, Patrice A. Fraccio, and the Prentice Hall staff for their encouragement and cooperation.

G.L.
J.F.
A.K.

ABOUT THE AUTHORS

Gideon Langholz received his Ph.D. in Electrical Engineering from the University of London. He is a Professor at Tel Aviv University, and at Florida State University in the Department of Electrical Engineering. Dr. Langholz has co-authored a book on digital logic design and is currently engaged in writing another book on robotics. Additionally, he has published over 45 scientific papers in the areas of digital systems, control systems, and telecommunication networks.

Joan Francioni received the B.S. degree in Mathematics from the University of New Orleans in 1977, and the M.S. and Ph.D. degrees in Computer Science from Florida State University in 1979 and 1981, respectively. Since 1985 she has been an Assistant Professor at Michigan Technological University. She has taught computer organization at both the undergraduate and graduate levels, and has led seminars in parallel processing. Her current research interests are in the area of operating systems for parallel processing machines. Recent publication topics include load balancing techniques for hypercube multiprocessors, virtual memory for distributed memory systems, and operating system support for parallel program debuggers. Dr. Francioni is a member of the IEEE, ACM and Sigma Xi organizations, and is an avid bicyclist and cross-country skier.

Abraham Kandel is Professor and Chairman of the Computer Science Department at Florida State University in Tallahassee. He is also the Director of the Institute for Expert Systems and Robotics at F.S.U. and the Director of the State University System Center for Artificial Intelligence. He received his Ph.D. in EECS from the University of New Mexico, his M.S. from the University of California, and his B.Sc. in EE from the Technion-Israel Institute of Technology. Dr. Kandel is a senior member of the Institute for Electrical and Electronics Engineering and a member of the Association for Computer Machinery, as well as an advisory editor to the international journals *Fuzzy Sets and Systems*, *Information Sciences*, and *Expert Systems*. He has written several books as well as more than 150 research papers for numerous professional publications in Computer Science and Engineering.

CHAPTER 1

The Evolution of Computers

1.1 OVERVIEW

The main function of a digital computer is to process input data and produce results that can be used in a specific application environment. The physical devices used to implement a computer system and manage the storage and flow of data and instructions along its internal communication lines constitute the **hardware** component of the system. The processing hardware is programmed to perform computations according to some set of rules, the **algorithm** (a logical sequence of steps) used to solve the particular problem. The algorithm is translated into a **program**—a set of instructions—that the hardware follows in solving the problem. The collection of programs constitute the **software** component of the system.

The study of software is concerned with programming languages, data representations, creation of efficient programs, software evaluation, and compiler development. Hardware involves the understanding of computer organization and the study of the physical components used for the design of a computer system. Hardware and software are intimately related, and software cannot be fully understood without some understanding of hardware, since a substantial part of software is hardware dependent.

The viewpoint assumed in this book is, for the most part, hardware oriented. Among the components (resources) that we will consider at this functional organization level are these:

    Processors
    Input/output controllers
    Memory units
    Buses (communication paths, data highways)
    Registers, adders, shifters, and multipliers

Data representations
Addressing modes
Machine language instructions
Instruction fetching, executing, and decoding

The terms *computer architecture* and *computer organization* are often used interchangeably at this level. However, they do not mean the same thing. **Computer architecture** refers to the characteristics of a computer as seen by the programmer. **Computer organization** relates to the physical resources of a computer and is concerned with their organization, their integration into a functional system, and the control of communication and data flow among them. It is in this latter context that we view a computer system in this text.

Throughout the book, a **computer** is assumed to be a system having one or more **processors** capable of interpreting and executing instructions. The instructions to be executed, as well as the data to be operated on, are held in **memory**. Interfacing both processors and memory with external data sources or with peripheral hardware, such as terminals and printers, is done through **input/output (I/O)** subsystems. Communication among the various units is accomplished by means of one or more system **buses.**

The basic principles of computer organization involve the structure and organization of the various computer units and their interfaces to other subsystems. The computer designer makes decisions regarding the form in which programs are represented to and interpreted by the underlying computer, the methods by which these programs address or name their data, and data representations. These decisions include aspects such as the size of storage, types and formats of data, instruction sets, storage addressing and protection, and I/O and interface considerations.

Historical Perspectives

The designer of a complex system, such as a computer, must possess a global outlook of the various system functions and be familiar with their corresponding software/hardware trade-offs. However, before proceeding with a detailed description of the building blocks associated with the design process, a historical perspective of the evolution of computing devices is in order. We will focus on some key historical periods and trace the different kinds of computing devices developed during these periods. We recount their evolution and follow through the inventions and discoveries that culminated in the development of the electronic computers available today.

1.2 MECHANICAL CALCULATORS

Circa 4000 B.C. One of the earliest known computational devices, the **abacus,** was developed. This is a mechanical device composed of a slab (*abax* in Greek) with pebbles (*calculi* in Greek) strung on wires. The position of the pebbles on each wire determines the value of a digit. The abacus (also known as the Chinese *suan pan*

Sec. 1.2 Mechanical Calculators

and the Japanese *soroban*) can be used to add, subtract, multiply, and divide. In the hands of a skilled operator, it can produce results as fast as a modern desktop calculator.

A.D. 1623. Machines capable of automatically performing the four basic arithmetic operations first appeared in Europe in the early seventeenth century. The earliest such machine seems to have been designed and built in 1623 by Wilhelm Schickhard at the University of Tübingen. Schickhard's machine was little known in his day.

1645. Blaise Pascal, the French philosopher, mathematician, and physicist, developed the first real **mechanical calculator.** This was a rotating wheel that used a series of eight gears with automatic carry generation between digits for addition and subtraction of decimal numbers.

Mid-1600s. John Napier, a Scot, invented the concept of logarithms and implemented it on a set of ivory rods, known as **Napier's bones,** which were used to perform multiplication and division through repeated additions and subtractions.

Circa 1650. Robert Bissaker extended Napier's work with logarithms and invented the **slide rule,** using sliding pieces of wood.

1671–1694. The Prussian mathematician Baron Gottfried Wilhelm von Leibniz extended Pascal's adding machine to perform multiplication and division through the use of additional gears.

1725. Basile Bouchon introduced a simple draw-loom for weaving figured silks. The silk designs were controlled by patterns of holes punched on a roll of paper. When the coded paper was pressed against a row of needles, those that lined up with the holes remained in place while the others moved forward. The loom's action, controlled by the selected needles, formed the pattern of the fabric.

1728. The French inventor Falcon designed a loom using **punched cards** to make various pattern-weaving operations automatic. This technique was later adopted by the first successful machine to operate with punched cards.

1741. A watchmaker named Jacques de Vaucanson built an automatic loom for weaving figured silks. The designs were established by patterns of holes punched on a **metal drum.** The holes controlled the selection of threads by raising and lowering the treadles.

1801. One of the interesting results of the industrial revolution was the Jacquard loom. Joseph Marie Jacquard, a silk weaver from France, built in 1801 an attachment to the weaving loom that resulted in automated pattern weaving. This was a step toward the development of **programmable instructions** since the loom was controlled by a series of punched cards. The cards had holes in them and functioned just like a **program,** providing sets of instructions that were read by the machine as they passed over a series of rods. By 1812 there were over 11,000 Jacquard looms in France.

1821. The next major advance is associated with the English inventor Charles Babbage. The device, called the **difference engine,** implemented finite difference operations. In 1854 a Swede named Georg Scheutz was able to build a working version of Babbage's difference engine.

Meanwhile, Babbage developed the idea of the **analytical engine,** which contained many features similar to twentieth-century **stored-program** digital computers. It was designed around two types of cards: **operating cards,** which indicated specific functions to be performed, and **variable cards,** which indicated actual data. The machine itself had a store—an area within the device in which instructions and variables were maintained—and a mill—an **arithmetic unit** that performed the operations. Instructions and data were fed into the device by means of punched cards, and output was produced automatically.

An interesting story is indirectly related to Babbage's analytical engine. The Countess Augusta Ada Lovelace, the only daughter of Lord Byron, learned of Babbage's work while attending the London Mechanics Institute and later worked with Babbage in developing some ideas for the analytical engine. She translated into English a treatise on Babbage's work, written by the French mathematician Menabrea in 1842, and wrote a program for the device, promoting many to categorize her as the world's first programmer. The U.S. Department of Defense has recently developed a programming language specifically designed for large applications in real time embedded computer environments and ideally suited for coding programs using the **structured approach.** This language, called Ada, is named after Countess Lovelace.

1822. Many attempts were made to improve the reliability of the machines invented by Pascal and Leibniz, but the engineering techniques available could not produce the precisions required. The first machine to perform the basic arithmetic operations suitable for commercial use was the **Arithmomèter** built by Charles Xavier Thomas in 1822. Only about 1600 Thomas machines were actually constructed.

1850. The inventor D. D. Parmalee developed a **key-driven** adding machine to add single columns of numbers at a time. It was quite unreliable and thus never produced commercially.

1876. An American engineer named George Grant demonstrated a working difference engine. He actually sold a number of these machines, which he called **rack-and-pinion calculators.**

1884. An American bookkeeper named William Seward Burroughs invented the first commercially practical **adding-listing machine.** To build the device he formed a company, which later became the Burroughs Corporation (now part of Unisys).

1885. Dorr Eugene Felt built an experimental key-driven calculating machine using a wooden macaroni box with keys made from meat skewers, key guides made from staples, and rubber bands used for springs. In 1887 Felt formed a partnership with Robert Tarrant to produce the **Comptometer.** This calculating machine was so successful that no other comparable machine was placed in competition until 1902.

1887. Léon Bollée of France designed the first machine to perform multiplication directly rather than by repeated additions. The device had a multiplying piece consisting of a series of tongued plates representing the ordinary multiplication table up to multiples of 9. The **milliner,** a popular commercial calculating machine based on the principles developed by Bollée, was manufactured in Switzerland. It required only one turn of the handle for each figure of the multiplier and provided for automatic shift to the next position.

Dr. Herman Hollerith, a statistician with the U.S. Bureau of the Census developed in 1887 a reliable tabulating machine that used the punched-card concept. Based on his **machine-readable card** concept, he designed a device known as the **census machine.** The census taken in 1880 had required some $7\frac{1}{2}$ years of manual calculations to tabulate; tabulation time with Hollerith's methods was considerably faster, so his techniques were adopted for use in the 1890 census. Although the population had increased from 50 to 63 million in the decade after 1880, the 1890 count was completed in less than three years. After the 1890 census, Hollerith converted his equipment to commercial use and founded, in 1896, the Tabulating Machine Company to produce and sell his invention. Later this firm merged with others to form what is now the International Business Machines Corporation (IBM).

1910. James Powers, a Census Bureau machine shop expert, developed a punched-card system with 240 keys. Its success in the 1910 census encouraged Powers to form the Powers Tabulating Machine Company in 1911, the principal competitor for many years of Hollerith's Tabulating Machine Company. Through a series of mergers, this company later became part of the Remington Rand organization, as the Univac Division of the Sperry Rand Corporation. (The Sperry Corporation has since merged with Burroughs to form Unisys and the Univac name is no longer being used.)

1934. The first prototype **electronic computer,** with vacuum tubes replacing electromagnetic relays, was conceived in 1934 by Dr. John Vincent Atanasoff at Iowa State University. After concluding that none of the ten available calculating devices was adequate for his needs, Atanasoff decided to build his own machine. He teamed up with Clifford Berry, his graduate assistant, and began the task of building the first electronic computer. This computer, called the **Atanasoff-Berry computer (ABC),** was completed five years later.

Atanasoff's attempts to get either IBM or Remington Rand interested in his invention and to obtain patent rights for himself failed. Although he conceived and designed the first electronic digital computer, his invention was for many years credited to others. In 1974 a federal judge ruled that Atanasoff was the true inventor of the concepts required for a working electronic digital computer. It is now generally agreed that the design of the ABC and the use of electronics in that computer provided the foundation for the developments of electronic digital computers.

1937. Howard Aiken of Harvard University began working on an automatic calculating machine called the Mark I, a relay machine. With the help of graduate students and IBM engineers, Aiken's automatic machine was completed in 1944. The Harvard Mark I was 51 feet long and 8 feet high, contained 760,000 parts, used 500 miles of wire, and weighed about 5 tons. It used a program to guide it through long series of calculations. It could add, subtract, multiply, divide, compute trigonometric functions, and perform other complicated calculations. Addition and subtraction were accomplished in 0.3 seconds, multiplication in less than 6 seconds, and division in less than 16 seconds.

1938. Several early electromechanical computers using relays for switching purposes were built at Bell Telephone Laboratories, starting in 1938. These **special-purpose computers** were based initially on the work of Dr. George R. Stibitz. The first one, called the **complex calculator,** is said to be the first computer to employ **binary** components. This machine, put into operation in 1940, could be remotely controlled and performed arithmetic operations on two numbers. Models II and III were built to solve military problems and were placed in operation in 1943 and 1944, respectively. Model IV could handle trigonometric functions, such as sine and tangent. Model V contained 9000 relays and 50 pieces of Teletype equipment, weighed 10 tons, and occupied 1000 square feet of floor space. Model VI, the last of the family, was built for Bell Laboratories' own use and featured many improvements, including **magnetic tape** storage units.

1941. A relay computer was built in Germany in 1941 by Konrad Zuse. Called the Z_3, its logical operations were alterable by changing the interconnections among the relays. The Z_3 was the world's first working **general-purpose program-controlled** computer.

1.3 EVOLUTION OF ELECTRONIC COMPUTER SYSTEMS

Mechanical computers had two serious drawbacks: computer speed was limited by the inertia of the moving parts, and the transmission of information by mechanical means (gears, levers, etc.) was cumbersome and unreliable. In electronic computers, by contrast, the "moving parts" are electrons, and information can be transmitted by electric currents at speeds approaching the speed of light (300,000 km/s). The triode vacuum tube, invented in 1906 by Lee de Forest, enabled the switching of electrical signals at speeds far exceeding those of any mechanical device. The use of vacuum tube technology marked the beginning of the electronic era in computer design.

In the five decades since 1940, the computer industry has experienced four generations of development. Each computer generation is marked by a rapid change in the implementation of its building blocks: from relays and vacuum tubes (1940s–1950s) to discrete diodes and transistors (1950s–1960s), through small-scale and medium-scale integrated (SSI/MSI) circuits (1960s–1970s) to large-scale and very

Sec. 1.3 Evolution of Electronic Computer Systems

large scale integrated (LSI/VLSI) devices (1970s–1980s). Increases in device speed and reliability and reductions in hardware cost and physical size have greatly enhanced computer performance. However, better devices are not the sole factor contributing to high performance. The division of computer system generations is determined by the device technology, system architecture, processing mode, and languages used. We are currently (1989) in the fourth generation; the fifth generation has not materialized yet, but researchers are working on it.

The First Generation: Circa 1943–1956

First-generation computers were extremely large and had poor reliability. They used vacuum tubes to control internal operations, generated considerable heat, and required a lot of floor space. Although first-generation computers were much faster than earlier mechanical or electromechanical devices, they were very slow compared to today's computers, and their internal storage capacity was limited.

Punched cards were used to enter data into the computer. The holes were punched according to a coding scheme (much like Hollerith's cards), and a special-purpose machine (card reader) was used to translate them into **machine language** for the computer. The machine language information was often stored on **magnetic drums,** cylinders coated with magnetizable material, rotating at high speeds. **Read/write heads** suspended just above the rotating surface of the drum either wrote on the drum by magnetizing small spots or read from it by interpreting the already magnetized spots. Numbers were manipulated by the computer according to the instructions, or program, given to it. The results of these operations were punched on blank cards, which could then be read by humans.

Only binary-coded machine language was used in early computers. With hardware costs dominating the developments of first-generation computers, the use of system software to relieve the user of low-level programming was just beginning.

1943. During 1940 and 1941, Atanasoff and Berry met with John W. Mauchly and showed him their work. Mauchly, working at the Moore School of Electrical Engineering of the University of Pennsylvania, then began formulating his own ideas on how a **general-purpose computer** might be built. Mauchly's ideas came to the attention of J. Presper Eckert, Jr., a graduate engineering student at the Moore School, and the team of Mauchly and Eckert was formed. In 1943 they designed their first electronic computer, **ENIAC** (Electronic Number Integrator and Calculator). It used 140 kilowatts of electricity and contained about 18,000 vacuum tubes, 70,000 resistors, and 10,000 capacitors, occupied a space of 1500 square feet, and weighed about 30 tons. The computing elements consisted of many components linked by close to a million hand-soldered connections. The I/O system consisted of modified IBM card readers and punches. ENIAC had a limited storage capacity of only 20 ten-digit numbers (it took 12 vacuum tubes to store one decimal digit), used a 100-kilohertz clock, and could perform 5000 additions or 300 multiplications per second. By today's standards, ENIAC was very slow; however, when delivered in 1946, it represented a major advance in computational power. It was instrumental, for better or worse, in bringing the world into the atomic age.

1944. The Harvard Mark I was delivered.

1945. Dr. John von Neumann recommended in a research report that the binary number system, employing only the digits 0 and 1, be applied in computer design. He also proposed that instructions to control the computer, as well as data, should be stored *within* the computer. The **EDSAC** (Electronic Delay Storage Automatic Calculator), built at Cambridge University in 1949, was the first computer to incorporate these ideas. It was not faster than ENIAC, but it did use the binary number system, and its instructions were stored internally. These instructions were called a program; hence the name **stored-program.**

A similar computer, called **EDVAC** (Electronic Discrete Variable Automatic Computer), was initiated at the University of Pennsylvania. It was the second machine designed by the Mauchly-Eckert team. Completed in 1952, the EDVAC was smaller, more versatile, and more flexible than ENIAC. EDVAC was designed to be a true stored-program machine using binary numbers for both instructions and data. Occupying 140 square feet and containing about 5900 vacuum tubes, it could perform an addition in 854 microseconds and a multiplication in 2.9 milliseconds.

At about the same time, the Massachusetts Institute of Technology (M.I.T.) was assigned to build an aircraft simulator for flight operations. This project resulted in the construction of a computer called **Whirlwind,** completed in 1951. Whirlwind was probably the first computer designed with eventual **real time** applications in mind. Containing about 5000 vacuum tubes, it could perform addition in 3 to 4 microseconds and multiplication in 17 to 18 microseconds. Whirlwind proved to be a reliable machine, and many of the ideas embodied in it are found in most modern computers. The most important was its **magnetic core memory.**

1946. Another machine based on the von Neumann architecture was the **IAS** computer started at Princeton in 1946 but not completed until 1952. This machine, developed under the personal direction of von Neumann, was a stored-program machine containing 2300 vacuum tubes. It could perform an addition in 62 microseconds, a multiplication in 720 to 990 microseconds, and a division in 1.1 milliseconds. Many machines have been patterned after the IAS computer, including the **ILLIAC** (University of Illinois) and the **WEIZAC** (Weizmann Institute in Israel).

1947. The **SSEC** (Selective Sequence Electronic Calculator) was installed at IBM New York World Headquarters in 1947 and was used through 1952. This machine was 100 times faster than the Harvard Mark I. At about the same time, IBM built a machine that could multiply six-digit numbers by counting electronic pulses. This machine, which was simply a tabulating machine connected to some vacuum tubes, was known as the IBM 603 electronic multiplier.

1948. The IBM 604 Electronic Calculating Punch Card machine became available. It could read punched cards, perform arithmetic operations, and punch the results on cards. The machine was programmed with a plugboard and was not a stored-program machine. It had over 1400 vacuum tubes to perform arithmetic operations using electronic registers.

Sec. 1.3 Evolution of Electronic Computer Systems

1950. The **SEAC** (Standards Eastern Automatic Computer) was the first stored-program computer to be put into operation in the United States. Built by the National Bureau of Standards in Washington, D. C., it used **mercury delay lines** for memory and was operational for more than a decade.

The **ERA 1101,** built by Engineering Research Associates of St. Paul, Minnesota, was the first computer to use a **magnetic drum** for main memory instead of mercury delay lines. It had 16,384 words of storage. Many different computers using magnetic drums for main memory were constructed during the period 1950–1955.

1951. The first **UNIVAC** (Universal Automatic Computer) was delivered. This machine was contracted by the National Bureau of Standards and delivered to the Census Bureau for use with the data of the 1950 census. It was designed by the Mauchly-Eckert team, used mercury delay lines for memory, and was the first commercially available stored-program electronic digital computer. A total of 48 of the UNIVAC-1 were built. Before UNIVAC-1 appeared, 60 other electronic computers had been built. No two were alike, and none of the programs developed for one were compatible with any of the others without major modification, or even redesign, of the computer.

Up to this point, computers were used almost exclusively for scientific purposes. Computers entered the business world when a UNIVAC-1 was delivered to the General Electric Company in 1954. With UNIVAC-1, the possibility of applying rapid, extensive computing capability to other than scientific problems became a reality. The UNIVAC-1 received a large amount of publicity in 1952 when it was used to predict—correctly—the victory of Dwight D. Eisenhower in the presidential elections on the basis of incomplete early returns.

1953. The IBM 701 computer, a large-scale scientific computer using a Williams electrostatic memory tube backed up by a magnetic drum, was delivered. This machine had **parallel** binary arithmetic capability and was much faster than the UNIVAC for scientific computations.

The IBM 650 magnetic drum computer was announced. The drum stored 2000 ten-digit words and rotated at 12,500 revolutions per minute. It had IBM cards for input and output but used stored programs, which were read from cards. Because IBM dominated the card market, over 1000 IBM 650 computers were placed in service.

1955. IBM introduced the IBM 702, the first large-scale computer designed for business purposes. The 702 weighed 24,600 pounds, contained approximately 5000 vacuum tubes, and required powerful air conditioning to cool the room where it operated. Actually, only a few of these computers were ever installed. As soon as IBM announced its newer, more powerful machine, the IBM 704, the 702 was withdrawn from the market—obsolete before it was even delivered.

1956. The IBM 704, first offered in 1956, achieved a near-monopoly for IBM in the large-scale scientific computer field. It could handle 91 instructions, add in 24 microseconds, and perform either multiplication or division in 240 microseconds.

Summary of First-Generation Computers

First-generation machines of the early 1950s were mostly programmed in **machine language.** Machine language consists of strings of zeros and ones that act as instructions to the computer, specifying the desired electrical states of its internal circuits and memory banks. Obviously, writing a machine language program was extremely cumbersome, tedious, and time consuming. To make programming easier, **symbolic languages** were developed. Such languages enable instructions to be written with symbolic codes (called **mnemonics,** or memory aids) rather than strings of ones and zeros. The symbolic instructions are then translated into corresponding binary codes (machine language instructions). The first set of programs, or instructions, telling the computer how to do this translation was developed in 1952 by Dr. Grace M. Hopper at the University of Pennsylvania. (She was also instrumental in making COBOL the "official" language of U.S. government computing.) After this breakthrough, most first-generation computers were programmed in symbolic language.

First-generation computers had a **central processing unit (CPU)** that contained a set of high-speed registers used for temporary storage of data, instructions, and memory addresses. The **control unit** decoded the instructions, routed information through the system, and provided timing signals. Instructions were fetched and executed in two separate consecutive steps called the **fetch cycle** and **execution cycle,** respectively. Together they formed the **instruction cycle.**

First-generation computers had numerous design shortcomings, including these:

- Inefficient control of I/O operations resulted in poor overall system performance.
- Address modification schemes were inefficient.
- Because the instruction set was oriented toward numeric computations, programming of nonnumeric and logical problems was difficult.
- Facilities for linking programs, such as instructions for calling subroutines that automatically save the return address of the calling program, were not provided.
- Floating-point arithmetic was not implemented, mainly due to the cost of the hardware needed.

CHARACTERISTICS OF FIRST-GENERATION COMPUTERS

- Use of vacuum tubes in electronic circuits and mercury delay lines for memory
- Magnetic drum as primary internal storage medium
- Limited main storage capacity (1000–4000 bytes)
- Low-level symbolic language programming
- Heat and maintenance problems
- Applications: scientific computations, payroll processing, record keeping
- Cycle time: milliseconds
- Cost: $5 per floating-point operation
- Processing speed: 2000 instructions per second

The Second Generation: 1957–1964

Scientists at Bell Telephone Laboratories, led by John Bardeen, Walter Brattain, and William Shockley, developed in 1948 the first **junction transistor.** The potential advantage of the transistor over the vacuum tube was almost as great as that of the vacuum tube over the relay. The invention of the transistor made computers more widespread because of its dependability, small size, and lower power requirements. Therefore, the second generation was characterized mainly by the change from vacuum tube to transistor technology. Several other important developments also occurred.

Second-generation computers were faster, had increased storage capacity, and required less power to operate. Cathode ray tube and delay line memories of first-generation computers were replaced by **ferrite cores** as the primary internal storage medium. Cores are very small doughnut-shaped rings of magnetic material on which thin wires are wound. An electrical current passing through the wires magnetizes the core to represent either an ON or OFF state. In this way, groups of cores store instructions and data that can be located and retrieved for processing in a few milliseconds—much faster than with magnetic drum storage.

In many second-generation systems, the main memory of the computer was supplemented by using magnetic tapes for **external,** or **auxiliary,** storage. Substituting magnetic tapes for punched cards or punched paper tapes increased I/O processing speeds by a factor of at least 50. Other significant changes that occurred during this period were the development of **magnetic disk** storage, modular hardware, and improved I/O devices. The main advantage of disk storage is that it enables the user to locate a particular record on a set of disks, rotating at high speeds, in a fraction of a second. Unlike a magnetic tape, records on a disk do not have to be processed sequentially. The computer can go directly to the record it needs without having to read everything that comes before it. Thus disks provide direct, or random, access to records in a file.

The modular hardware concept involved using a building-block approach to the design of electronic circuits. With this approach, complete modules (breadboards) could be replaced, thus simplifying maintenance tasks. The improvement in I/O devices could be seen in faster printing speeds and automatic detection and correction of I/O errors. These advances allowed the devices to be connected directly **(online)** to the computer without significantly lowering the overall efficiency of the system. Special **I/O processors** were introduced to supervise I/O operations, thus freeing the CPU from many time-consuming bookkeeping functions. The use of an **index register** and **floating-point arithmetic** hardware became widespread.

Along with the refinements in hardware, second-generation computers were also characterized by further refinements in programming languages. Second-generation computers often used **high-level languages** to instruct the computer on how to perform processing tasks. High-level languages resembled English much more than symbolic languages and hence were easier to use. The first high-level language to achieve widespread acceptance was **FORTRAN** (Formula Translator), developed in the mid-1950s by IBM. The version of the language known as FORTRAN IV was standardized in 1963 and is still used extensively for scientific applications. Because FORTRAN lacked many features desirable for business data processing, another language, called **COBOL** (Common Business-Oriented Language), was developed in 1961. This language was geared toward processing large numbers of business transactions easily. **ALGOL** (Algorithmic Language) and **APL** (A Programming Language) were developed in 1960 as scientific languages. With these languages, computer manufacturers began to provide system software such as compilers, subroutine libraries, and batch monitors.

1954. The first transistorized digital computer, **TRADIC,** was built by Bell Laboratories.

1958. The National Cash Register computer NCR 304 was delivered. It was the first commercial transistorized digital computer.

1960. The IBM 1401 was delivered, and many thousands of this small transistorized computer were sold. IBM also delivered the 7090, a transistorized scientific computer using magnetic core memory with over 32,000 36-bit words of storage.

The TRANSAC S-2000 was manufactured by Philco Corporation. This was a large-scale, scientific, stored-program, transistorized digital computer with magnetic core storage. The CDC 1604 was delivered by Control Data Corporation. This was a transistorized machine with a 48-bit word length.

The ATLAS computer system, built at the University of Manchester in England, was introduced. It incorporated a technique for performing program overlays automatically, which is known today as **virtual memory.** With main memories becoming larger and cheaper, the concept of virtual memory was expanded to facilitate **multiprogramming.**

1960–1961. The UNIVAC **LARC** (Livermore Atomic Research Computer) and IBM 7030 (**STRETCH**) computers were delivered. These rival machines were very large transistorized computers for their time. Only two LARC and seven STRETCH machines were delivered, serving as test vehicles for many features found in third-generation computers.

1964. The CDC 6600 computer was delivered to the Livermore AEC Laboratory. This machine was more than three times as powerful as the IBM 7030 computer. It could execute, on the average, more than 3 million instructions per second and achieved this effective speed by its parallel architecture, which had multiple arithmetic and logical units and used ten small computers for I/O operations.

Summary of Second-Generation Computers

Second-generation computers featured early applications of concepts such as **interleaving** (the distinction of addresses among several independent memory modules) in direct addressing and **effective addressing** schemes. They had relatively large instruction sets, including these:

Sec. 1.3 Evolution of Electronic Computer Systems

1. Instructions for transferring information between the CPU and memory or between CPU registers
2. Fixed-point as well as floating-point arithmetic instructions
3. Logical (nonnumeric) instructions
4. Instructions for modifying index registers
5. Conditional and unconditional branching and related control instructions
6. Input/output operations for transferring data between I/O devices and main memory

An important feature of second-generation machines was the provision of special branch instructions to facilitate the transfer of control between different programs, as in calling subroutines. I/O processors supervised the flow of information between main storage and I/O devices. They did so by executing special **I/O programs,** which were composed of I/O instructions and were stored in main memory.

Another important improvement of second-generation computers was **batch processing.** In first-generation systems, each user's job was run separately, and the computer had to be halted and prepared manually for each new program. With the improvements in I/O equipment that came with second-generation computers, it became feasible to prepare a batch of jobs in advance, store them on a magnetic tape, and then have the computer process them in one continuous sequence, placing all the results on another magnetic tape. This mode of operation is termed batch processing. A small auxiliary computer was used to process the input and output magnetic tapes offline.

Second-generation systems also provided **parallel processing** techniques in two forms:

1. Overlapping the fetching and execution of instructions within a single program
2. Overlapping the execution of different programs—a single CPU system capable of concurrent execution of more than one program (*multiprogramming*)

CHARACTERISTICS OF SECOND-GENERATION COMPUTERS

- Use of transistors for internal operations
- Magnetic core as primary internal storage medium
- Increased main storage capacity (4K–32K bytes)
- Faster I/O; tape orientation
- High-level programming languages (COBOL, FORTRAN, ALGOL)
- Great reduction in size and heat generation
- Increased speed and reliability
- Batch-oriented applications: billing, payroll processing, updating inventory files
- Cycle time: microseconds
- Cost: 50 cents per floating-point operation
- Processing speed: 1 million instructions per second (mips)

The Third Generation: 1965–1971

The year 1965 may be considered as marking the beginning of the third computer generation, but the distinction between the second and third generations is not clear cut. The following developments are frequently singled out:

1. **Integrated circuits (ICs)** began to replace the discrete transistor circuits used in second-generation machines, resulting in a substantial reduction in size and cost.
2. **Semiconductor** (IC) **memories** began to augment, and ultimately replace, ferrite cores in main memory designs.
3. A technique called **microprogramming** came into widespread use to simplify the design of processors and increase their flexibility.
4. A variety of techniques for concurrent, or parallel, processing were introduced, including **pipelining, multiprogramming,** and **multiprocessing.** These had the objective of increasing the effective speed at which a set of programs could be executed.
5. Methods for automatic sharing of facilities and resources of a computer system (e.g., its processors and memory space) were developed. These were intended to improve the use of resources, particularly memory space.
6. The first digital computer for less than $10,000, the DEC PDP-8, became available.

The early 1960s witnessed the introduction of ICs, which incorporated hundreds of transistors on a single silicon chip. The chip itself was small enough to fit on the end of a finger. With ICs, computers could be made even smaller, less expensive, and more reliable. **Small-scale integration (SSI)** techniques indicated the starting point of the third generation, soon to be followed by **medium-scale integration (MSI)** circuits, as well as **multilayered** printed circuit boards.

In the late 1960s, ICs began to be used for main memory. Today, IC memory has completely replaced magnetic core memory (except in some older machines that are still in use). Also, **magnetic disks** began to replace magnetic tapes for auxiliary memory. Today, magnetic disks are the dominant technology for auxiliary memory, and another auxiliary memory technology, **magnetic bubbles,** has appeared on the market.

The most recent advance in computer technology came with the introduction of **large-scale integrated (LSI)** circuits. Whereas the older ICs contained hundreds of transistors, the new ones contained thousands, tens of thousands, or even hundreds of thousands.

In 1964 IBM announced a series of six new computers called System 360 and has since delivered thousands of these machines. With the IBM 360, microprogramming was introduced to assure instruction set compatibility among these machines. Shortly afterward, RCA announced its Spectra 70 series of machines, which were almost completely compatible with the IBM 360 line. In 1971, however, RCA Corporation abandoned the commercial general-purpose digital computer market after having lost many millions of dollars in trying to compete with IBM.

Another third-generation line of computers, the GE 600 series, was manufactured by the General Electric Company. Since these scientific computers were not very successful financially, the GE computer division was sold in 1970 to the Honeywell Computer Division to form Honeywell Information Systems.

Burroughs Corporation, which had produced second-generation machines, now offered a line of computers topped with its 5500, 6500, 7500, and 8500 machines. Univac, which had lost its initial lead in the computer industry to IBM, produced a scientific computer, the UNIVAC 1108. In 1968 National Cash Register (NCR) announced its Century System of business computers

Many smaller companies also announced successful third-generation computers. In particular, Digital Equipment Corporation (DEC) delivered many thousands of **minicomputers.** The first commercial minicomputer was the DEC PDP-5, produced in 1963. It was superseded in 1965 by the very successful PDP-8.

The design of large, powerful computers that began with the LARC and the STRETCH machines continued. The Control Data Corporation (CDC) produced a series of large machines beginning with the CDC 6600 in 1964 and continuing with the 7600, delivered in 1969, and the subsequent CYBER series. These machines are characterized by the inclusion of many peripheral processors, each with a high degree of autonomy. In addition, each CPU is subdivided into a number of independent processing units that can be operated simultaneously. A CPU organization called **pipelining** was used to achieve very fast processing in several computers such as the CDC STAR-100 (String Array Computer) and the Texas Instruments ASC (Advanced Scientific Computer). Another notable computer, the ILLIAC IV (Illinois Automatic Computer), was designed at the University of Illinois. The ILLIAC IV had 64 separate arithmetic-logic units (called processing elements), all supervised by a common control unit and all capable of operating simultaneously.

In 1970 IBM announced a new series of computers called System 370. These machines used ICs and were compatible with System 360 programs. Burroughs Corporation introduced a new line of machines, the 5700, 6700, and 7700 computers. Univac announced a new machine, the UNIVAC 110, and CDC introduced its CYBER 70 series of computers. Honeywell Information Systems announced a successor to the GE line of machines, the 6050, 6060, 6070, and 6080 systems.

Summary of Third-Generation Computers

Important improvements in third-generation computers included:

- Greater storage capacity
- Versatile programs that automated many tasks previously handled by human operators
- Greater compatibility of components, allowing easier expansion of computer systems

- Ability to perform several operations simultaneously
- Ability to perform more sophisticated processing than simple batch processing. **Time-sharing** operating systems became available in the late 1960s. **Virtual memory** was developed by using hierarchically structured memory systems
- Capability to handle both business and scientific applications in the same machine

Another third-generation innovation involved **remote terminals,** placed at various geographic locations and used to communicate directly with a central computer. Through terminals, many users could interact with the central computer at the same time and receive almost instantaneous results in what was called a time-sharing environment.

CHARACTERISTICS OF THIRD-GENERATION COMPUTERS

- Use of integrated circuits
- Magnetic core and solid-state main storage (32K–3M bytes)
- More flexibility with I/O; disk orientation
- Smaller size, better performance and reliability
- Extensive use of high-level programming languages
- Emergence of minicomputers
- Remote processing and time sharing through communication
- Availability of operating system software to control I/O and do many tasks previously handled by human operators
- Applications: airline reservation systems, market forecasting, credit card billing
- Cycle time: nanoseconds
- Cost: 5 cents per floating-point operation
- Processing speed: 10 mips

The Fourth Generation: 1972–circa 1989

In 1971 IBM began delivering its System 370 computers. This family of computers, and others developed by other large computer manufacturers in the 1970s, incorporated refinements such as semiconductor memories, self-diagnostic operating systems, widespread use of virtual storage techniques, and further miniaturization through LSI circuits.

Fourth-generation computers offered significant performance and price improvements over third-generation machines. They have gradually become smaller, as evidenced by the emergence of **microcomputers,** with LSI circuits being replaced by **VLSI** (very large scale integration) circuits and **VHSIC** (very high speed integrated circuits).

Performance improvements in present-day computer systems include increased speeds, greater reliability, and storage capacities approaching billions of characters. The emphasis is on ease of use and application, with the machines often called *"user friendly."* Most systems have communication capabilities; they permit remote input

Sec. 1.3 Evolution of Electronic Computer Systems

and output via communication channels such as ordinary telephone lines. The use of TV-like display screens has become increasingly common.

Data recording equipment to capture data at its point of origin in a form directly suitable for computer processing has been developed; common examples are magnetic ink character readers (MICRs) and optical character recognition (OCR) devices. The former are especially suited for applications like check processing for banks; the latter include point-of-sale (POS) terminals that record data about sales transactions as they occur.

A real computer revolution occurred in 1971, when Intel Corporation produced the first **microprocessor,** or computer on a chip, the 4004 chip. It was a crude, expensive device that was used primarily in commercial settings. In 1972 and 1973 Intel produced the 8008 and the 8080 chips, which soon became the foundation for a whole new industry—**personal computers.** Costing several hundred dollars in 1974 and difficult to obtain, the 8080 can be ordered today for under $6.00. Other, similar chips are Zilog's Z-80 and Intel's own 8085 and 8088.

At about the same time Intel was developing microcomputer hardware, another important ingredient in the personal computing movement was emerging. A simple computer language called **BASIC** (Beginners All-Purpose Symbolic Instruction Code) was developed by John Kemeny and Thomas Kurtz at Dartmouth College. The creation of BASIC made computers easy to use for many people who had no previous contact with them.

Both the microcomputer product and its market changed in 1974 when Micro Instrumentation and Telemetry Systems (MITS) produced its first microcomputer kit, **Altair.** MITS shipped 1500 such units in the first 60 days of production at $398 apiece. The Altair was the first commercially successful microcomputer, but as its demand increased, so did the time between placing an order and receiving the kit. These long delays at MITS created an opportunity for other companies, among them IMSAI, Southwest Technical Products Corporation, Processor Technology, and the Digital Group. Since then, several large manufacturers and retailers have brought mass merchandising to personal computing. Radio Shack, Commodore, Apple, Atari, DEC, IBM, Xerox, NEC, Sharp, Canon, Hitachi, and others offered microcomputers designed specifically for beginners in personal computing—people with neither the electronics background nor the knowledge of computers that characterized many buyers of second-generation machines. The IBM personal computer (PC) was introduced in 1981, followed by Apple's Macintosh.

With the increase in the number of components on a chip, microcircuits can be characterized by the following properties:

1. The complexity, or scope, of the functions performed by the chip increases.
2. The speed at which a given function is performed tends to increase.
3. The power required to perform a given function decreases.
4. The manufacturing cost per finished, mass-produced chip decreases.

The 1980s also marked the beginning of the **supercomputer** era. Supercomputers are characterized by very high processing speeds, of the order of 20 million floating-point operations per second (Mflops), and are mainly used for solving very complex, computationally intensive problems. High-level languages are being extended to handle both scalar and vector data. Most operating systems are time-sharing and use virtual memories. Vectorizing compilers have appeared in the second generation of vector machines, like the Cray-1 (1976) and the CYBER-205 (1982). High-speed mainframes and supercomputers are being designed as multiprocessor systems, like the UNIVAC 1100/80, Amdahl 570, Intel 8748, Fujitsu M 382, IBM 370/168 MP, IBM 3081 (1980), Burroughs B-7800, and Cray X-MP (1983). Pipelining and multiprocessing are greatly emphasized in commercial supercomputers such as the ETA[10] supercomputer (1988).

CHARACTERISTICS OF FOURTH-GENERATION COMPUTERS

- Use of large-scale integrated circuits
- Increased storage capacity (more than 3 Mbytes) and speed
- Increase in modular design and compatibility between equipment (hardware) provided by different manufacturers
- Availability of sophisticated programs for special applications
- Greater versatility of I/O devices
- Extensive usage of minicomputers, microprocessors, and microcomputers
- Applications: mathematical modeling and simulation; electronic funds transfer; computer-aided design, manufacturing, and instruction; home computers
- Cost: 1/100 to 1 cent per floating-point operation
- Processing speed: 100 mips to 1 bips (billion instructions per second)

1.4 THE FUTURE

In the early 1980s there had been a great deal of discussion of the growing need for a new generation of computers. In April 1981 a research project, known as the **Fifth-Generation Computer Systems (FGCS)** project, was announced in Japan by the Institute for New Generation Computer Technology (ICOT) to further the research and development of next-generation computers.

The main conjecture is that the computers of the 1990s will be used increasingly for nonnumeric data processing such as **symbol manipulation** and applied **artificial intelligence.** Conventional system applications, such as scientific calculations, will continue to be performed by the evolving supercomputers, with current database and mainframe systems being improved for use in worldwide networks.

Although current computer systems differ significantly from their predecessors in terms of cost, speed, reliability, internal organization, and circuit technology, the architecture of most present systems has not advanced beyond the concepts of the 1950s. While notions such as microprogramming, instruction pipelining, cache memories, and VLSI indicate advances in the implementation of particular architectures, they are organizational advances rather than new concepts in computer architecture. Therefore, fundamental changes in computer architecture and software are now re-

Sec. 1.4 The Future

quired to support the computers of the 1990s. To carry-out nonnumeric computations, these machines must evolve according to technical goals, which include these:

1. Implementation of basic mechanisms for **inference, association,** and **learning** in hardware, making these capabilities the core functions of fifth-generation systems
2. Preparation of basic **artificial intelligence** software in order to make use of the full power of these functions
3. Implementation of basic mechanisms for retrieving and managing a **knowledge base** in both hardware and software
4. Advantageous use of **pattern recognition** and artificial intelligence research achievements in developing user-oriented human-machine interfaces

Developing viable products from these goals is dependent on the continued evolution of VLSI technology, software engineering, and artificial intelligence, especially the areas of **expert systems** and **knowledge-base engineering.** VLSI chips will be used along with high-density modular designs, with more than 1 billion floating-point operations per second anticipated in these future supercomputers.

We still face significant problems, such as the high cost of software development, software unreliability, execution inefficiency, excessive program size, and compiler and operating system complexity, all of which contribute negatively to the economics of computing. It is quite possible that the basic reasons for the existence of these problems in current systems is that their architectures do not differ substantially from the von Neumann model derived in the 1940s. This remains true even though technological advances in the past half-century have given rise to architectures capable of reconfiguring available resources into variably sized computers, as well as to different types of architectures such as array, pipeline, and multiprocessor.

In the future we will see more new architectures that may differ significantly from the conventional ones. One is the **data flow architecture** now emerging. Although knowledge-based machines to handle the relatively limited mathematical calculations needed for everyday life will be the most widely used of these computers, heavy scientific calculations will require supercomputers. Besides these two classes of machines, there will also be conventional computers with vastly improved technology for business applications, as well as a class of industrial computers for process control, robotics, and automation.

At present, the basic technology developed for ICOT's fifth-generation system is comprised of an **inference** subsystem, which can learn, associate, and infer much as human beings do, and a **knowledge** subsystem, which can store information in a large relational database and manipulate it in parallel as knowledge. Both subsystems would have **intelligent** interfaces. Software for the ICOT systems will be written in an extended version of **PROLOG** (Programming in Logic), a language invented at the University of Aix-Marseille in France and nurtured by researchers at the University of Edinburgh in Scotland. Among the major PROLOG extensions considered are concurrent processing, modularization mechanisms, relational database interfaces, and metastructures to realize high-level inferences. ICOT's extended PROLOG, the kernel language for their fifth-generation computers, will be used to write the operating system and to prepare modules related to four areas:

1. Problem solving
2. Knowledge-base management
3. Intelligent interfaces
4. Intelligent programming

Similar key functions will be adopted from **LISP** (List Processing Language), the language preferred by the U.S. artificial intelligence community.

Although the goal for large computers is a non–von Neumann parallel inference machine, the personal computer will have a microprocessor-based architecture. In fact, the future personal computer will be designed with today's architecture, realized in VLSI, because of its cost and adequate throughput, and will speed programs through at no less than 20 Klips (one logical inference per second, or lips, equals 100 to 300 instructions per second).

In summary, then, what does the future hold? A new generation of computing technology will evolve over the next decade, based on high-performance multiprocessor systems. Elegant ways to express parallelism and concurrency will emerge, and intelligent systems will begin to make their way into the world. The fundamental problems of deep reasoning and understanding will become better defined but will probably continue to elude attempts to solve them. Expert systems of many kinds will become available, and a limited form of computer expertise will begin to be sold in the marketplace.

Communication networks will play an increasingly important role in connecting people and machines. Increased exploitation of knowledge in machine-processable form will occur, and strategic knowledge banks will be established for the retention of critical information. Software technology will continue to mature, with emphasis on large-scale systems and multiprocessor programming. Information management will play a key role in these systems, with emphasis on distributed databases and interoperability.

Completely new applications will emerge; systems with sensory capabilities and elementary reasoning abilities will find widespread initial use in industry and the military. Expert systems will also aid in more sophisticated industrial and military applications, while myriads of powerful microcomputer systems will continue to find their way into every nook and cranny. And all of that will merge with the expanded role of communication, local area networks (LANs), and distributed systems of all types.

CHAPTER 2

Number Systems, Arithmetic Operations, and Codes

2.1 DATA REPRESENTATIONS

Computers use and manipulate data for arithmetic computations, data processing, and logic operations. Data is binary numbers and other binary-coded information that is operated on to achieve some computational results. Binary information is stored in the computer memory or processor registers and is interpreted as either data or control information.

Data types used in digital computers can be classified as follows:

1. **Numeric data,** representing fixed-point integers and fractions, floating-point real numbers, and binary-coded decimals
2. **Logical data,** used by operations such as OR, AND, COMPLEMENT, COMPARE, and SHIFT and to set or test conditions such as those required for conditional branch instructions
3. **Single-bit data,** used by operations such as SET, CLEAR, and TEST
4. **Alphanumeric data,** used for string manipulations by instructions such as MOVE and SEARCH

We begin by considering numeric data representations. The binary number system is the most natural to use; however, it is sometimes more convenient to employ other number systems, such as decimal, octal, hexadecimal, or binary-coded decimal (BCD). Arithmetic operations are introduced to provide a basis for understanding how computers use numbers in arithmetic computations. We shall discuss unsigned and signed binary number representations and consider the four basic arithmetic operations: addition, subtraction, multiplication, and division.

Computer arithmetic differs from real arithmetic in the fundamental issue of number precision. Only **finite precision** computations can be performed with a computer, whereas real arithmetic may produce results of arbitrary precision with no restriction on length. Computer arithmetic can therefore be considered as approximating real arithmetic subject to appropriate rounding mechanisms.

Binary coding is another important issue. Numbers can be represented in a variety of codes and can be operated on. Some of the codes are more useful than others in particular situations. Nevertheless, since numeric data is not the only data type used, we also discuss codes for representing nonnumeric (alphanumeric) data: ASCII (American Standard Code for Information Interchange) and EBCDIC (Extended Binary Coded Decimal Interchange Code), the two most common codes used for data transmission.

We conclude this chapter by introducing the fundamentals of data protection against transmission errors and the principles of coding control instructions in a computer. The other data types, logical data and single-bit data, will be considered in subsequent chapters.

2.2 NUMBER SYSTEMS

A **positional number system** is characterized by a **base** (or **radix**) r, which is an integer greater than 1, and a set of r digits. Any integer $(N)_r$ can be represented by a finite sequence of digits (symbols) concatenated to form a digit (symbol) string:

$$(N)_r = (b_{n-1}b_{n-2} \ldots b_1b_0)_r \qquad (2.1)$$

where each b_i is an integer such that $0 \leq b_i \leq r - 1$. Each b_i is a digit of the number N, and n is referred to as the **length** of the string.

The **decimal** ($r = 10$) number system is comprised of ten digits represented by the symbols 0, 1, 2, 3, 4, 5, 6, 7, 8, 9. The **binary** number system is base 2 and consists of two digits, 0 and 1. An abbreviated word for a binary digit is *bit*. The **octal** (base 8) number system has eight characters, represented by the digits 0 through 7. The **hexadecimal** system is base 16 and is comprised of 16 characters represented by the symbols 0, 1, 2, 3, 4, 5, 6, 7, 8, 9, A, B, C, D, E, F. In the hexadecimal system, A stands for decimal 10, B for 11, C for 12, D for 13, E for 14, and F for 15. Another system, the **binary-coded decimal (BCD)** system, will be considered later in this section.

Each digit in a number has a special meaning, depending on its position. In particular, the leftmost digit in string (2.1), b_{n-1}, is referred to as the **most significant digit,** and the rightmost digit, b_0, is called the **least significant digit.** In the binary number system, these are termed, respectively, the **most significant bit** (abbreviated *msb*) and the **least significant bit** (abbreviated *lsb*). In general, a bit string is referred to as a **word,** but some bit strings have special names: A string of four bits is called a **nibble,** and a string of eight bits is referred to as a **byte.** Most computers have a word length of one or more bytes. For example, the DEC VAX 11/780 is a 4-byte (32-bit) machine, and the Apple II is a single-byte computer.

Sec. 2.2 Number Systems

The **numeric value** of the integer represented by digit string (2.1) is given by

$$b_{n-1}r^{n-1} + b_{n-2}r^{n-2} + \cdots + b_1 r^1 + b_0 r^0 = \sum_{i=0}^{n-1} b_i r^i \quad (2.2)$$

Equation (2.2) is a **weighted sum.** The weights are successive powers of r, and each digit is weighted according to its position in the digit string. The use of other weights is also possible and is considered in Section 2.5.

So far we have considered integer numbers only. What about fractions and mixed integer-fraction numbers? To distinguish between integers and fractions we use the **radix point** convention. The integer part of a number is located to the left of the radix point, while its fraction appears to the right of the radix point. (If the number is an integer, we can dispose of the radix point.) Just as the digits to the left of the radix point are the coefficients of a polynominal of *decreasing positive* powers of the base, the digits to the right of the radix point are the coefficients of a polynominal of *increasing negative* powers of the base. Therefore, the numeric value of the number represented by the digit string

$$(N)_r = (b_{n-1} b_{n-2} \ldots b_1 b_0 . b_{-1} b_{-2} \ldots b_{-m})_r \quad (2.3)$$

is given by

$$(N)_r = b_{n-1}r^{n-1} + b_{n-2}r^{n-2} + \cdots + b_1 r^1 + b_0 r^0 \\ + b_{-1}r^{-1} + b_{-2}r^{-2} + \cdots + b_{-m}r^{-m}$$

Rewriting this equation more compactly, we have

$$(N)_r = \sum_{i=-m}^{n-1} b_i r^i \quad (2.4)$$

(Since computers can only store a finite number of digits, we ignore infinite expansions.) Now b_{-m} is the least significant digit. In the binary number system, $r = 2$ and b_i is either 0 or 1 for every i. We will refer to a binary number whose value is determined by Equation (2.4) or (2.2) as a **straight** binary number.

Conversion between Bases

Base r to Base 10 conversion. The conversion from any base to the base 10 system is easily accomplished by using Equation (2.2) or (2.4). We simply sum the terms of the polynominal representing the base r number to obtain its decimal equivalent.

Example 2.1

Convert $(110101.1101)_2$ to a decimal number.

$$\begin{aligned}(110101.1101)_2 &= 1 \times 2^5 + 1 \times 2^4 + 0 \times 2^3 + 1 \times 2^2 + 0 \times 2^1 + 1 \times 2^0 \\ &\quad + 1 \times 2^{-1} + 1 \times 2^{-2} + 0 \times 2^{-3} + 1 \times 2^{-4} \\ &= (32)_{10} + (16)_{10} + (0)_{10} + (4)_{10} + (0)_{10} + (1)_{10} \\ &\quad + (0.5)_{10} + (0.25)_{10} + (0)_{10} + (0.0625)_{10} \\ &= (53.8125)_{10}\end{aligned}$$

Example 2.2

Convert $(73.452)_8$ to a decimal number.

$$(73.452)_8 = 7 \times 8^1 + 3 \times 8^0 + 4 \times 8^{-1} + 5 \times 8^{-2} + 2 \times 8^{-3}$$
$$= (56)_{10} + (3)_{10} + (0.5)_{10} + (0.078125)_{10} + (0.0039063)_{10}$$
$$= (59.5820313)_{10}$$

Base r to Base t conversion. There are various ways of converting numbers from one base system to another. Probably the simplest and most straightforward method is that of **repeated divisions** for integers and **repeated multiplications** for fractions. To convert a mixed integer-fraction number, we split the process: Convert the integer part first by using repeated divisions and then the fractional part by repeated multiplications. Since conversions between numbers represented in the octal, hexadecimal, and binary systems can be accomplished without resorting to repeated divisions and multiplications, we defer discussing these conversions to the following section.

Let us first consider the conversion of a base r integer $(N)_r$ to its equivalent $(M)_t$ in base t. The conversion is accomplished by repeatedly dividing N by t. The remainder after each step is one digit of the required base t number, and the quotient is again divided by t. The remainder after the first division by t is the least significant digit of $(M)_t$, and the last remainder is the most significant digit of $(M)_t$. The following example illustrates this procedure.

Example 2.3

Convert $(15247)_{10}$ to a hexadecimal number.

$15247 \div 16 = 952 \quad$ remainder $= (15)_{10} = (F)_{16}$

$952 \div 16 = 59 \quad$ remainder $= (8)_{10} = (8)_{16}$

$59 \div 16 = 3 \quad$ remainder $= (11)_{10} = (B)_{16}$

$3 \div 16 = 0 \quad$ remainder $= (3)_{10} = (3)_{16}$

Hence, $(15247)_{10} = (3B8F)_{16}$.

To convert a base r fraction $(.F)_r$ to its equivalent $(.E)_t$ in base t, we repeatedly multiply $(.F)$ by t. The integer part after each step is one digit of the required base t fraction, and the remaining fraction is again multiplied by t. The integer resulting from the first multiplication by t is the most significant digit of $(.E)_t$, and the last integer is the least significant digit of $(.E)_t$. The following example illustrates this procedure.

Example 2.4

Convert $(0.761)_{10}$ to a binary number.

$0.761 \times 2 = 1.522 \quad$ integer part $= 1$

$0.522 \times 2 = 1.044 \quad$ integer part $= 1$

$0.044 \times 2 = 0.088 \quad$ integer part $= 0$

$$0.088 \times 2 = 0.176 \quad \text{integer part} = 0$$
$$0.176 \times 2 = 0.352 \quad \text{integer part} = 0$$
$$0.352 \times 2 = 0.704 \quad \text{integer part} = 0$$
$$0.704 \times 2 = 1.408 \quad \text{integer part} = 1$$
$$0.408 \times 2 = 0.816 \quad \text{integer part} = 0$$
$$0.816 \times 2 = 1.632 \quad \text{integer part} = 1$$
$$0.632 \times 2 = 1.264 \quad \text{integer part} = 1$$
$$\vdots \qquad\qquad\qquad \vdots$$

Hence, $(0.761)_{10} = (.1100001011 \ldots)_2$.

As seen in Example 2.4, the process of converting a fraction might not terminate. In other words, it may not be possible to represent the fraction exactly in the new base with a *finite* number of digits. The number of digits retained after the radix point depends on how precise we want the conversion to be. If we terminate the process in Example 2.4 after the first two significant fractional bits, the resulting binary fraction would be $(.11)_2$, which equals $(0.75)_{10}$. This represents an error of about 1.4% from the actual fraction $(0.761)_{10}$. If we terminate the process after ten bits, the resulting binary fraction would be $(.1100001011)_2$ $[= (0.7607422)_{10}]$, and the error would be about 0.03% from the required $(0.761)_{10}$. Obviously, the more bits we generate, the more precise the resulting binary fraction is. However, a more precise fraction takes longer to generate and requires a larger amount of storage.

Binary, octal, and hexadecimal conversions. Since $8 \; (= 2^3)$ and $16 \; (= 2^4)$ are both powers of 2, conversions between the binary, octal, and hexadecimal number systems are quite simple. In particular, these relations imply that each octal digit can be binary-coded by three bits, as shown in Table 2.1, while each hexadecimal

TABLE 2.1 BINARY-CODED OCTAL NUMBERS

Decimal	Octal	Binary
0	0	000
1	1	001
2	2	010
3	3	011
4	4	100
5	5	101
6	6	110
7	7	111

TABLE 2.2 BINARY-CODED HEXA-DECIMAL NUMBERS

Decimal	Hexadecimal	Binary
0	0	0000
1	1	0001
2	2	0010
3	3	0011
4	4	0100
5	5	0101
6	6	0110
7	7	0111
8	8	1000
9	9	1001
10	A	1010
11	B	1011
12	C	1100
13	D	1101
14	E	1110
15	F	1111

digit can be binary-coded by four bits, as shown in Table 2.2. For reference, these tables also include the equivalent decimal numbers.

To convert from *binary to octal*, we partition the binary number, starting from the radix point, into groups of three bits each. The octal digit corresponding to each group is then assigned using Table 2.1. To convert from *octal to binary*, we reverse the process. Each octal digit is assigned a group of three bits using Table 2.1, and the equivalent binary number is obtained by concatenating these groups.

Example 2.5

Convert $(1101000101.01011)_2$ to octal.

Starting from the radix point, we partition the integer and fractional parts and then use Table 2.1 to assign the corresponding octal digits:

$$\underbrace{1}_{1}\ \underbrace{101}_{5}\ \underbrace{000}_{0}\ \underbrace{101}_{5}.\ \underbrace{010}_{2}\ \underbrace{11}_{6}$$

The equivalent octal number is 1505.26. Notice that the leftmost group (of the integer part) contains only one bit and the rightmost group (of the fractional part) contains only two bits. However, to qualify for the octal representation, each group must contain three bits. To "fill in" the groups, we append *leading* zeros to the integer part and *trailing* zeros to the fractional part. Adding leading or trailing zeros does not change the value of the number and serves only to facilitate the conversion.

Binary to hexadecimal conversions are as easily obtained. Starting from the radix point, we partition the binary number into groups of four bits (one nibble) each. Using Table 2.2, each nibble is assigned its corresponding hexadecimal digit. To convert from *hexadecimal to binary*, we simply reverse the process.

Example 2.6

Convert $(11101110001011001)_2$ to hexadecimal.
Grouping the binary number into nibbles and using Table 2.2:

$$\underbrace{1}_{1} \quad \underbrace{1101}_{D} \quad \underbrace{1100}_{C} \quad \underbrace{0101}_{5} \quad \underbrace{1001}_{9}$$

Hence the equivalent hexadecimal number is 1DC59.

Binary-coded Decimal (BCD) Representation

The **binary-coded decimal (BCD)** representation is a compromise between the decimal and binary number systems. In BCD, we use four bits (a nibble) to represent each of the decimal digits 0 through 9. To represent a decimal number beyond 9, we need two or more decimal digits, and, correspondingly, its BCD representation requires two or more nibbles. Table 2.3 shows the binary and BCD equivalents of decimals 0 through 15. Note that a nibble can represent 16 numbers but the BCD system uses only ten of them. It should be understood that BCD is just a code in binary as opposed to a straight binary number, which represents the actual value.

TABLE 2.3 DECIMAL, BINARY, AND BCD RELATIONSHIPS

Decimal	Binary	BCD
0	0000	0000
1	0001	0001
2	0010	0010
3	0011	0011
4	0100	0100
5	0101	0101
6	0110	0110
7	0111	0111
8	1000	1000
9	1001	1001
10	1010	0001 0000
11	1011	0001 0001
12	1100	0001 0010
13	1101	0001 0011
14	1110	0001 0100
15	1111	0001 0101

Decimal to BCD conversions. To find the BCD representation of a decimal number, each decimal digit is independently represented by its corresponding binary nibble.

Example 2.7

Convert $(3729)_{10}$ to BCD.
Using Table 2.3, each decimal digit is represented by its corresponding BCD nibble, resulting in the BCD number:

$$\underbrace{3}_{0011} \quad \underbrace{7}_{0111} \quad \underbrace{2}_{0010} \quad \underbrace{9}_{1001}$$

Note that this conversion is much simpler than the conversion of $(3729)_{10}$ to binary. To convert $(3729)_{10}$ to binary, we have to resort to repeated divisions to get 111010010001. Example 2.7 also points out the inefficiency of the BCD representation. The binary representation of $(3729)_{10}$ requires 12 bits, whereas the BCD equivalent contains 16. Indeed, the larger the decimal number is, the more wasteful its BCD representation becomes. Nevertheless, the convenience of using the BCD system often makes up for its inefficiency.

BCD to decimal conversion. Converting a BCD number to its decimal equivalent is just as easily accomplished. Starting from the radix point, we partition the binary pattern into groups of four bits each. Each group is then converted to its corresponding decimal number using Table 2.3.

Example 2.8

Convert $(1001001101010001)_{BCD}$ to decimal.
Since the given number is an integer, we start from the least significant bit, partition the number into 4-bit groups, and then assign to each of them the corresponding decimal number:

$$\underbrace{1001}_{9} \quad \underbrace{0011}_{3} \quad \underbrace{0101}_{5} \quad \underbrace{0001}_{1}$$

Hence the equivalent decimal number is 9351.

Note that if the BCD number in Example 2.8 had been mistakenly interpreted as a binary number, the resulting decimal number would have been 37713. Again, Example 2.8 demonstrates the inefficiency involved in using the BCD system. A 16-bit BCD number can represent up to four decimal digits (decimal numbers up to 9999), whereas a 16-bit binary number can represent up to five decimal digits (decimal numbers up to 65,535).

BCD to binary conversion. To convert BCD to binary, and vice versa, it is easiest to make an intermediate conversion to the decimal equivalent.

Example 2.9

Convert $(100101000001)_{BCD}$ to binary.
Converted to decimal, this BCD number becomes $(941)_{10}$. Then, using repeated divisions, we get the binary equivalent 1110101101.

Example 2.10

Convert $(101110101101)_2$ to BCD.
Converted to decimal, this binary number becomes $(2989)_{10}$. Then, using Table 2.3, the BCD equivalent is 0010 1001 1000 1001.

BCD to hexadecimal conversion. BCD to hexadecimal conversion (as well as to other bases), and vice versa, is best done by first converting either number to decimal.

Example 2.11

(a) Convert $(3F6)_{16}$ to BCD.
Converting $(3F6)_{16}$ to decimal yields $(1014)_{10}$. The equivalent BCD number is then 1 0000 0001 0100. (Note that we have dropped the first three leading zeros of the leftmost nibble.)

(b) Convert $(11100101110101)_{BCD}$ to hexadecimal.
The decimal equivalent of this number is 3975. Converting to hexadecimal, we get F87.

2.3 FIXED-POINT NUMBER REPRESENTATION

Numbers used in scientific calculations are designated by a **sign,** by the **magnitude** of the number, and by the **position** of the radix point. The position of the radix point is required to represent fractions, integers, or mixed integer-fraction numbers. There are two ways of specifying the position of the radix point: by giving it a **fixed** position or by using the **floating-point** representation. The difference between these two representations has to do with the range of numbers that can be accommodated by a computer having a given word length. Floating-point number representation is considered in Section 2.4.

Two positions for the radix point are common: (1) radix point to the extreme left, making the number a fraction that is strictly less than 1, and (2) radix point to the extreme right, making the number an integer. In either case, the radix point is not actually present in the computer; rather, its position is implied by the fact that the number is *predefined* as an integer or as a fraction. Therefore, in integer arithmetic, the numbers are lined up to the right as if there were a radix point at the extreme right. In fraction arithmetic, the numbers (regardless of their length) are lined up to the left as if there were a radix point at the extreme left.

Note, however, that these two conventions are essentially equivalent and that it is rather easy to convert between integers and fractions. This conversion process is referred to as **shifting.** Shifting the radix point of a base r number k places to the right is equivalent to multiplying the number by r^k; shifting the radix point k places to the left has the effect of multiplying the number by r^{-k}. Thus any base r, n-digit integer can be considered as a fraction multiplied by a constant factor r^n, and any m-digit fraction in base r can be considered as an integer multiplied by a constant factor r^{-m}. But shifting is not limited to integer-fraction conversions. For example, when we multiply or divide, intermediate steps require that numbers be shifted to the left or to the right.

Sign Notations

To carry out arithmetic operations, we have to specify a number as either positive or negative. Since the computer cannot recognize the conventional sign labels + and −, we have to introduce a **code** to represent signed numbers. The sign convention commonly employed is to reserve the leftmost digit position for the **sign digit.**

For **positive** fixed-point numbers, the sign digit is 0 and the remaining digits display the *true magnitude* of the number. Let $(N)_r$ be a number in base r with an integer part of n digits (including the sign digit) and a fractional part of m digits. Then the positive number $(N)_r \geq 0$ is represented by the digit string

$$(N)_r = (\mathbf{0}b_{n-2} \ldots b_1 b_0 . b_{-1} b_{-2} \ldots b_{-m})_r \tag{2.5}$$

and its magnitude equals

$$\sum_{i=-m}^{n-2} b_i r^i \tag{2.6}$$

Three different notations are commonly used to represent a negative fixed-point number: sign-magnitude, $(r-1)$'s complement, and r's complement. To introduce them, let $(\overline{N})_r$ be the negative version of the positive number $(N)_r$ defined in (2.5). In either representation, the value of the sign digit is $r-1$. To emphasize that the leftmost digit *always* represents the sign of the number, we set it in **boldface.**

Sign-magnitude representation. In the sign-magnitude representation, the magnitude of the negative number equals that of the positive number, and they differ only in the sign digit. Thus

$$(\overline{N})_r = (\mathbf{(r-1)}b_{n-2} \ldots b_1 b_0 . b_{-1} b_{-2} \ldots b_{-m})_r \tag{2.7}$$

where the digits $b_{n-2}, \ldots, b_1, b_0, b_{-1}, b_{-2}, \ldots, b_{-m}$ represent the true magnitude of the negative number.

Example 2.12

(a) The sign-magnitude representation of $(+687)_{10}$, which is a positive number whose magnitude is $(687)_{10}$, is the 4-digit string $(\mathbf{0}687)_{10}$. Since $r-1=9$, the sign-magnitude representation of $(-687)_{10}$ is $(\mathbf{9}687)_{10}$.

(b) The sign-magnitude representation of $(+1101.011)_2$ is $(\mathbf{0}1101.011)_2$, and the sign-magnitude representation of $(-1101.011)_2$ is $(\mathbf{1}1101.011)_2$.

$(r-1)$'s complement representation. The $(r-1)$'s complement of $(N)_r$ is defined as

$$(\overline{N})_r = r^n - r^{-m} - (N)_r \tag{2.8}$$

Sec. 2.3 Fixed-Point Number Representation

If we represent $(\overline{N})_r$ by the digit string

$$(\overline{N})_r = ((r-1)\bar{b}_{n-2} \ldots \bar{b}_1\bar{b}_0.\bar{b}_{-1}\bar{b}_{-2} \ldots \bar{b}_{-m})_r \qquad (2.9)$$

each digit is given by

$$\bar{b}_i = r - 1 - b_i, \quad \text{for every } i \qquad (2.10)$$

Equation (2.10) tells us that the $(r-1)$'s complement is obtained by subtracting each digit from $r-1$. Since $r=2$ in the binary system, the application of Equation (2.10) to generate the 1's complement is quite simple: In the given number, *the zeros are changed to ones and the ones to zeros to obtain its 1's complement.*

Example 2.13

(a) The 9's complement of $(04857.43)_{10}$ is obtained from Equation (2.8) with $n = 5$ and $m = 2$:

$$(\overline{N})_r = r^n - r^{-m} - (N)_r = (10^5 - 10^{-2} - 04857.43)_{10}$$
$$= 99999.99 - 04857.43$$
$$= 95142.56$$

You can verify that the same result can be obtained by using Equation (2.10).

(b) The 9's complement of $(0.2731)_{10}$ is obtained from Equation (2.8) with $n = 1$ and $m = 4$:

$$(\overline{N})_r = r^n - r^{-m} - (N)_r = (10 - 10^{-4} - 0.2731)_{10}$$
$$= 9.9999 - 0.2731$$
$$= 9.7268$$

(c) The 7's complement of $(0374)_8$ is given by

$$(\overline{N})_r = r^n - r^{-m} - (N)_r = (10^4 - 1 - 0374)_8$$
$$= 7777 - 0374$$
$$= 7403$$

(d) The 15's complement of $(04B7)_{16}$ is given by

$$(\overline{N})_r = r^n - r^{-m} - (N)_r = (10^4 - 1 - 04B7)_{16}$$
$$= FFFF - 04B7$$
$$= FB48$$

(e) To find the 1's complement of $(01101.101)_2$, we can use Equation (2.8) with $n = 5$ and $m = 3$. In this case, however, it is simpler to obtain the 1's complement using the procedure outlined following Equation (2.10). Hence, if we change all zeros to ones and all ones to zeros, we obtain

$$(\overline{N})_2 = 10010.010$$

r's complement representation. The r's complement of $(N)_r$ is defined as

$$(\overline{N})_r = r^n - (N)_r \qquad (2.11)$$

From Equation (2.11) we see that to find the r's complement of a number, we leave all the least significant zeros unchanged, subtract the first nonzero least significant digit from r, and then subtract all the other digits from $r - 1$. Since $r = 2$ in the binary system, the application of Equation (2.11) to generate the 2's complement can be stated as follows: *Starting with the least significant bit in the given number, leave all zeros and the first one unchanged and then replace ones by zeros and zeros by ones in all the remaining bits.*

The r's complement can also be obtained from the $(r - 1)$'s complement. By comparing Equations (2.8) and (2.11), we see that adding r^{-m} to the $(r - 1)$'s complement results in the r's complement.

$$(N)_{r\text{complement}} = (N)_{(r-1)\text{complement}} + r^{-m} \tag{2.12}$$

The following example illustrates these ideas.

Example 2.14

(a) The 10's complement of $(04857.43)_{10}$ is obtained from Equation (2.11) with $n = 5$:

$$(\overline{N})_r = r^n - (N)_r = (10^5 - 04857.43)_{10}$$
$$= 100000 - 04857.43$$
$$= 95142.57$$

We can also obtain this result from the 9's complement of the given number, which was derived in Example 2.13(a). Since $m = 2$, we have

$$95142.56 + 10^{-2} = 95142.57$$

(b) The 10's complement of $(0.2731)_{10}$ is obtained from Equation (2.11) with $n = 1$:

$$(\overline{N})_r = r^n - (N)_r = (10 - 0.2731)_{10}$$
$$= 9.7269$$

Since $m = 4$, this result can also be obtained by adding 10^{-4} to the 9's complement derived in Example 2.13(b).

(c) The 8's complement of $(0374)_8$ is given by

$$(\overline{N})_r = r^n - (N)_r = (10^4 - 0374)_8$$
$$= (10000 - 0374)_8$$
$$= 7404$$

(d) The 16's complement of $(04B7)_{16}$ can be obtained by adding 16^{-0} (since $m = 0$) to the 15's complement derived in Example 2.13(d). Hence

$$FB48 + 1 = FB49$$

(e) To find the 2's complement of $(01101.101)_2$ we can use the procedure outlined following Equation (2.11). We leave the least significant bit unchanged (note that there are no least significant zeros) and then replace all zeros by ones and all ones by zeros. Hence

$$(\overline{N})_2 = (10010.011)$$

Sec. 2.3 Fixed-Point Number Representation

TABLE 2.4 FIXED-POINT REPRESENTATION OF $(\pm 9)_{10}$

Fixed-point representation	+9	−9
Sign-magnitude	00001001	10001001
1's complement	00001001	11110110
2's complement	00001001	11110111

Comparison of the three notations. Consider a fixed-point number with true magnitude $(9)_{10} = (1001)_2$. We want to represent its positive and negative versions in the three sign notations using 8 bits (a byte).

The fixed-point binary byte representation for $(\pm 9)_{10}$ is given in Table 2.4. The binary representation of $(+9)_{10}$ is the same in all three notations. (Note that we added leading zeros to fill up the byte.)

Since $r = 2$, the value of the sign bit of $(-9)_{10}$ in all three notations is $r - 1 = 1$. To obtain the sign-magnitude representation of $(-9)_{10}$ we simply set the sign bit to 1, leaving the remaining bits unchanged [see Equation (2.7)]. To obtain the 1's complement, we use the procedure outlined following Equation (2.10). The 2's complement is obtained by using the procedure outlined following Equation (2.11).

Signed Binary Numbers

Consider the sequence of binary numbers 0000 through 1111, which correspond to the decimal numbers 0 through 15. These *same* binary values can be used to represent signed numbers from decimal +7 to −8, as shown in Table 2.5. Several issues arise from the representation of signed binary numbers. To illustrate them, we are going to use the 4-bit numbers shown in Table 2.5; however, a generalization to any number of bits is straightforward.

Note that all the fixed-point numbers in Table 2.5 have unique representations *except* the zeros in the sign-magnitude and 1's complement notations. We see that *positive* and *negative* zeros have *different* representations in these two notations, while in the 2's complement convention there is a *unique* zero. The reason for this is very simple. A positive zero is represented by 0000 in any of the three notations. (Remember that the leftmost bit is the sign bit.) Since $r = 2$, the sign-magnitude representation of a negative zero is 1000 in accordance with Equation (2.7). To obtain the 1's complement representation of a negative zero, we use the procedure outlined following Equation (2.10), which results in 1111. The 2's complement representation of a negative zero is obtained using the procedure outlined following Equation (2.11), which results in 0000.

The largest positive 4-bit binary number equals decimal +7. No binary equivalent of decimal +8 exists if we use only four bits to represent signed binary numbers. Indeed, if we use the conventional binary notation and assign 1000 to represent 8, then in *signed* binary number notation, the 1 in the sign bit position indicates that this number should be regarded as a negative number.

The smallest negative 4-bit binary number equals decimal −8 in the 2's complement notation. It has no positive counterpart since both +0 and −0 in 2's complement have the same representation (0000) and occupy one of the positive numbers'

TABLE 2.5 FOUR-BIT SIGNED BINARY NUMBER REPRESENTATIONS

Decimal	1's Complement	2's Complement	Sign-Magnitude
+7	0111	0111	0111
+6	0110	0110	0110
+5	0101	0101	0101
+4	0100	0100	0100
+3	0011	0011	0011
+2	0010	0010	0010
+1	0001	0001	0001
+0	0000	0000	0000
−0	1111	0000	1000
−1	1110	1111	1001
−2	1101	1110	1010
−3	1100	1101	1011
−4	1011	1100	1100
−5	1010	1011	1101
−6	1001	1010	1110
−7	1000	1001	1111
−8	impossible	1000	impossible

bit patterns, leaving one fewer for the remaining positive numbers. In the 1's complement notation, −0 occupies one of the negative numbers' bit patterns, leaving one fewer for the remaining negative numbers. Therefore, the smallest negative 4-bit binary number in 1's complement equals decimal −7. In the sign-magnitude representation, the magnitude of the smallest negative number must equal that of the largest positive number. Since decimal +7 is the largest positive number, the smallest negative sign-magnitude number is decimal −7.

Range of signed binary numbers. We can generalize the preceding observations to establish the **range** of fixed-point, signed binary integer numbers. For an n-bit number, the largest positive integer that can be represented by n bits, including the sign bit, determines the **upper bound.** Since the largest positive integer in all three representations is $(01 \ldots 1)_2$, the upper bound is equal to $(2^{n-1} - 1)_{10}$. The **lower bound** is determined by the smallest negative number. It is $(11 \ldots 1)_2 = -(2^{n-1} - 1)_{10}$ for sign-magnitude numbers and $(10 \ldots 0)_2 = -(2^{n-1} - 1)_{10}$ for 1's complement numbers. Since the zero is uniquely represented in 2's complement, the lower bound in this case is $(10 \ldots 0)_2 = -(2^{n-1})_{10}$.

Example 2.15

What is the range of signed binary numbers represented by a byte of data?
Since $n = 8$, the upper bound is $(2^7 - 1)_{10} = +127$. In sign-magnitude and 1's complement notations, the lower bound is $-(2^7 - 1)_{10} = -127$. In 2's complement, the most negative number that can be represented is $-(2^7)_{10} = -128$.

Sec. 2.3 Fixed-Point Number Representation

Whenever we exceed the range of signed numbers, an **overflow** occurs. As will be seen later in this section, this means that the result of an arithmetic operation appears wrong because we have tried to exceed the allowed range of binary values.

Signed binary-coded numbers. The sign bit convention is also applicable if we use other binary-coded representations. Consider, for example, the number $(EC)_{16} = (1110\ 1100)_2$. If this number is interpreted as an unsigned binary number, it is equivalent to $(236)_{10}$. Interpreted as a signed binary number, the binary pattern represents a negative number since the sign bit is 1. Hence it is equivalent to $(-108)_{10}$ in sign-magnitude representation, $(-19)_{10}$ in 1's complement notation, and $(-20)_{10}$ in 2's complement.

We are not as fortunate, however, when we deal with BCD numbers. Consider, for example, decimal $+5$. Its BCD (as well as binary) representation is 0101. The sign-magnitude, 1's, 2's complement representations of this number are 1101, 1010, and 1011, respectively, and *none is a valid BCD code*. To handle signed BCD numbers we must use either the 10's or 9's complement code. In other words, the hardware generating signed BCD numbers must subtract each BCD digit from either $(10)_{10}$ or $(9)_{10}$. To represent the sign, we must append an extra digit. The coding commonly used for this sign digit is $(0000)_2\ [= (0)_{10}]$ for positive numbers and for zero, and $(1001)_2\ [= (9)_{10}]$ for negative numbers. (Remember, four bits are necessary for even one sign digit.)

Consider, for example, 3-digit BCD numbers with a fourth digit appended to indicate the sign. Using sign-magnitude notation, $(+45)_{10}$ is coded as $(0045)_{10} = (\mathbf{0000}\ 0000\ 0100\ 0101)_{BCD}$, and $(-45)_{10}$ is coded as $(9045)_{10} = (\mathbf{1001}\ 0000\ 0100\ 0101)_{BCD}$. The range of 3-digit numbers, coded as 2-byte sign-magnitude BCD numbers, is from $(-999)_{10}$ to $(+999)_{10}$.

To find the 10's complement code of $(-45)_{10}$, $(45)_{10}$ must be subtracted from 10^4 [recall Equation (2.11) and remember that the signed numbers in the example have four digits, one of which is the sign digit]. Hence $10^4 - 45 = (9955)_{10}$, and $(-45)_{10}$ is coded as $(\mathbf{1001}\ 1001\ 0101\ 0101)_{BCD}$. The range of numbers in the 10's complement, 2-byte BCD representation is from $(1001\ 0000\ 0000\ 0000)_{BCD} = -(1000)_{10}$ to $(0000\ 1001\ 1001\ 1001)_{BCD} = (+999)_{10}$. To obtain the 9's complement, subtract 1 from the 10's complement representation [see Equation (2.12)] to get $(9954)_{10} = (\mathbf{1001}\ 1001\ 0101\ 0100)_{BCD}$.

Fixed-Point Arithmetic

Data in digital computers consists of binary numbers and other binary-coded information that is operated on to achieve some computational result. Computer arithmetic differs from real arithmetic in the fundamental issue of number precision. Only *finite-precision* computations can be performed, whereas real arithmetic may produce results of *arbitrary precision* with no restriction on length. Therefore, digital arithmetic can be considered as approximating real arithmetic, subject to appropriate rounding mechanisms.

Addition. Addition is a *binary operation* on the augend and addend digit pairs with their column value positions aligned. We begin by adding the two least significant digits. If the column sum exceeds the largest symbol value (of the number system used), we carry one base value to the next column and reduce the present column sum by one base value to obtain the particular sum digit.

This procedure applies to any base system. In the following example we assume that the numbers are unsigned. We will see later how to handle signed numbers.

Example 2.16

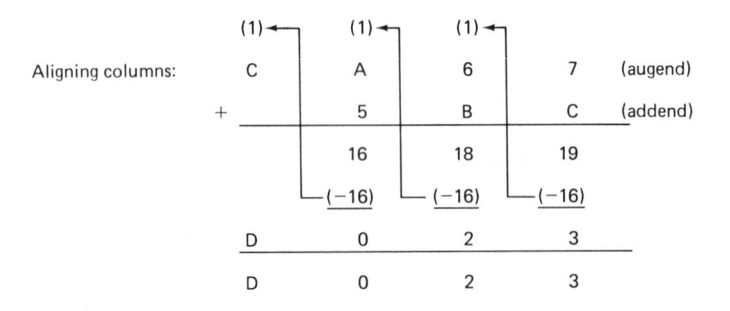

Add $(CA67)_{16}$ and $(5BC)_{16}$.

```
                        (1)◄─┐   (1)◄─┐   (1)◄─┐
   Aligning columns:   C     │  A     │  6     │  7    (augend)
                   +         │  5     │  B     │  C    (addend)
                       ──────┼────────┼────────┼────
                       16    │  18    │  19    │
                       (−16)─┘  (−16)─┘  (−16)─┘
                       ─────────────────────────────
                       D        0        2        3
                       D        0        2        3
```

Subtraction. Subtraction is a *binary operation* on the minuend and subtrahend digit pairs with their column value positions aligned. We begin by subtracting the two least significant digits. If the subtrahend exceeds the minuend, we borrow one base unit from the next column, add it to the minuend, and carry out the subtraction to obtain the particular difference digit. In the next-column subtraction, the borrowed base unit is subtracted from the minuend and the process continues.

Example 2.17

Subtract $(59)_{10}$ from $(75)_{10}$.

```
                                 ┌─►(+10)
   Aligning columns:     7       │  5      (minuend)
                         (−1)────┘
                     −   5          9      (subtrahend)
                         ──────────────
                         1          6
```

The same rules apply to any base system, but in general, subtraction is more complicated to implement than addition. Assume that we want to subtract 75 from 59. This is accomplished by reversing their order, subtracting the number with the smaller magnitude from the larger, and using the sign of the larger number for the sign of the result: $59 - 75 = -(75 - 59) = -16$.

Notice that here, too, we have assumed that the numbers are unsigned. However, in everyday arithmetic calculations we use signed numbers represented in sign-magnitude notation. When we operate on two sign-magnitude numbers, we must first *compare* their signs. If the two signs are the same, we *add* the two magnitudes, and

Sec. 2.3 Fixed-Point Number Representation

the sign of the result is the same as the signs of the two numbers. If the two signs differ, we *compare* the two magnitudes, *subtract* the smaller from the larger, and determine the sign of the result by the sign of the larger number. The following example illustrates these processes.

Example 2.18

$$+21 + (+45) = +(21 + 45) = +66$$
$$-21 + (-45) = -(21 + 45) = -66$$
$$+21 + (-45) = -(45 - 21) = -24$$
$$-21 + (+45) = +(45 - 21) = +24$$

To implement these processes, we are required to make a long sequence of decisions: compare, add, subtract, and determine sign. These processes can be implemented in hardware or software but are more complex than necessary. Instead, fixed-point addition and subtraction can be simplified if we use the r's or $(r-1)$'s complement representation, as shown in the following section.

Addition and Subtraction Using Complements

r's complement arithmetic. If the numbers are represented in r's complement notation, the key is Equation (2.11), which can be rewritten as

$$(N)_r + (\overline{N})_r = r^n \qquad (2.13)$$

and reinterpreted to say that when two numbers sum to 0 with a carry of 1 (which we *ignore*), the numbers are **radix complements** of each other.

To *add* two numbers in r's complement, add their corresponding digits (*including* the sign digits) and *ignore* any carry out of the leftmost digit. This carry is referred to as **end carry.** The sum thus obtained is also represented in r's complement.

The following example illustrates the addition of positive, negative, and oppositely signed binary numbers represented in 2's complement. (The leftmost bit represents the sign and is set in **boldface.**)

Example 2.19

The numbers in parentheses are the decimal equivalents of the binary numbers.

```
              001110  (+14)                        110010  (-14)
           +  001100  (+12)                     +  110100  (-12)
              011010  (+26)         end carry  ⟶1 100110  (-26)

              001110  (+14)                        110010  (-14)
           +  110100  (-12)                     +  001100  (+12)
  end carry ⟶1 000010  (+ 2)                        111110  (- 2)

              110100  (-12)                        001100  (+12)
           +  001110  (+14)                     +  110010  (-14)
  end carry ⟶1 000010  (+ 2)                        111110  (- 2)
```

The following example demonstrates that addition of signed numbers must be handled carefully.

Example 2.20

(a) Add $(9D)_{16}$ and $(A4)_{16}$, both represented in 16's complement.

$$\begin{array}{r} 9D \\ + A4 \\ \hline (1)\,41 \end{array}$$

Notice that both augend and addend are negative numbers. (To see this, convert the hexadecimal numbers to binary.) However, their sum turned out to be a positive number, which cannot be correct. The reason for this is that we exceeded the range of negative 2-digit hexadecimal numbers, and an overflow has occurred. To see this, note that the most negative number that can be represented in signed notation by two hexadecimal digits is $-(128)_{10}$. To find the decimal equivalents of $(9D)_{16}$ and $(A4)_{16}$, first find their 16's complements, $(63)_{16}$ and $(5C)_{16}$, respectively. Their decimal equivalents are -99 and -92, and their sum is -191, which is out of range.

(b) Add $(00111001)_2$ and $(01001011)_2$, both represented in 2's complement.

$$\begin{array}{r} 00111001 \\ + \,01001011 \\ \hline 10000100 \end{array}$$

The augend and addend are positive numbers, but their sum is a negative number, which is obviously incorrect. Again, we exceeded the range of positive 8-bit binary numbers, and an overflow has occurred.

Since digital arithmetic involves numbers of finite length, an overflow can occur whenever we exceed the range of signed numbers, as shown in Example 2.20. When the signs of the two numbers to be added are opposite, an overflow cannot occur. If the signs of the two numbers to be added are the same, an overflow may occur, depending on the magnitudes of the two numbers, and can be detected by examining the sign of the result. If the sign of the result is opposite the signs of the operands, an overflow has occurred, and the result is incorrect. The computer must therefore check for an overflow and provide an indication if one has occurred.

To *subtract* two numbers in r's complement, add the minuend to the r's complement of the subtrahend. If there is an end carry out of the sign digit, ignore it. The difference thus obtained is also represented in r's complement.

The following example illustrates the subtraction of positive, negative, and oppositely signed binary numbers represented in 2's complement.

Example 2.21

The numbers in parentheses are the decimal equivalents of the binary numbers.

$$\begin{array}{rl} 001110 & (+14) \\ -001100 & (+12) \end{array} \longrightarrow \begin{array}{l} 001110 \\ +110100 \quad \text{(2's complement of subtrahend)} \\ \hline \text{end carry} \nearrow 1\,000010 \quad (+2) \end{array}$$

$$\begin{array}{rl} 001100 & (+12) \\ -001110 & (+14) \end{array} \longrightarrow \begin{array}{l} 001100 \\ +110010 \quad \text{(2's complement of subtrahend)} \\ \hline 111110 \quad (-2) \end{array}$$

Sec. 2.3 Fixed-Point Number Representation

```
  001110  (+14)  ⟶         001110
 -110100  (-12)  ⟶        +001100   (2's complement of subtrahend)
                           011010   (+26)

  110010  (-14)  ⟶         110010
 -001100  (+12)  ⟶        +110100   (2's complement of subtrahend)
                 end carry ↙1 100110 (-26)

  110010  (-14)  ⟶         110010
 -110100  (-12)  ⟶        +001100   (2's complement of subtrahend)
                           111110   (-2)

  110100  (-12)  ⟶         110100
 -110010  (-14)  ⟶        +001110   (2's complement of subtrahend)
                 end carry ↙1 000010 (+2)
```

Subtracting oppositely signed numbers may produce a result that exceeds the range of r's complement numbers so that an overflow occurs. Consider the subtraction of 10110101 (decimal -75) from 00111001 (decimal $+57$). If we add the minuend to the 2's complement of the subtrahend, we get 10000100, which is obviously incorrect. Since the upper bound on the range of positive 8-bit binary numbers is $(127)_{10}$, the correct result, $(132)_{10}$, exceeds the range, and an overflow has occurred. As we can see, a subtraction overflow, like an addition overflow (see Example 2.20), can be detected by examining the most significant bit of the result.

$(r - 1)$'s Complement arithmetic. We can also add and subtract numbers represented in $(r - 1)$'s complement notation. The key here is Equation (2.8).

To *add* two numbers in $(r - 1)$'s complement, add their corresponding digits (including the sign digits). If there is a carry-out of the leftmost digit, increment the sum by 1 and ignore the end carry. An alternative way of describing this process is the following: If there is an end carry, add it to the result. This process is referred to as **end-around carry.** The sum thus obtained is represented in $(r - 1)$'s complement.

The following example illustrates the addition of positive, negative, and oppositely signed binary numbers represented in 1's complement. (The leftmost bit represents the sign and is set in **boldface.**)

Example 2.22

The numbers in parentheses are the decimal equivalents of the binary numbers.

```
   001110  (+14)                       110001  (-14)
  +001100  (+12)                      +110011  (-12)
   011010  (+26)         end carry ↙1 100100
                                    +       ↘1   (end-around carry)
                                      100101  (-26)

              001110  (+14)             110001  (-14)
             +110011  (-12)            +001100  (+12)
end carry ↙1 000001                     111101  (-2)
           +       ↘1  (end-around carry)
             000010  (+2)
```

```
          110011  (−12)              001100  (+12)
         +001110  (+14)             +110001  (−14)
end carry ↙1 000001                  111101  (− 2)

         +      ↖1   (end-around carry)
          000010  (+ 2)
```

To *subtract* in $(r-1)$'s complement, add the $(r-1)$'s complement of the subtrahend to the minuend. If an end carry is obtained, add it to the result (end-around carry). The difference obtained is also represented in $(r-1)$'s complement.

The following example illustrates the subtraction of positive, negative, and oppositely-signed binary numbers represented in 1's complement.

Example 2.23

The numbers in parentheses are the decimal equivalents of the binary numbers.

```
  001110  (+14)  ⟶              001110
 −001100  (+12)  ⟶             +110011   (1's complement of subtrahend)
                    end carry ↙1 000001

                              +      ↖1   (end-around carry)
                               000010  (+ 2)


  001100  (+12)  ⟶              001100
 −001110  (+14)  ⟶             +110001   (1's complement of subtrahend)
                                 111101  (− 2)


  001110  (+14)  ⟶              001110
 −110011  (−12)  ⟶             +001100   (1's complement of subtrahend)
                                 011010  (+26)


  110001  (−14)  ⟶              110001
 −001100  (+12)  ⟶             +110011   (1's complement of subtrahend)
                    end carry ↙1 100100

                              +      ↖1   (end-around carry)
                               100101  (−26)


  110001  (−14)  ⟶              110001
 −110011  (−12)  ⟶             +001100   (1's complement of subtrahend)
                                 111101  (− 2)


  110011  (−12)  ⟶              110011
 −110001  (−14)  ⟶             +001110   (1's complement of subtrahend)
                    end carry ↙1 000001

                              +      ↖1   (end-around carry)
                               000010  (+ 2)
```

Addition and subtraction with numbers in $(r-1)$'s complement notation may result in an overflow if we exceed the range of $(r-1)$'s complement representation.

Sec. 2.3   Fixed-Point Number Representation

As when the numbers are in r's complement, an overflow may occur when we add two numbers with the same sign or subtract two numbers with opposite signs. In either case, we detect the overflow by monitoring the most significant digit of the result.

Multiplication and Division

Let us conclude this section by considering multiplication and division of fixed-point signed numbers. Multiplication and division with binary numbers are the same as with decimal numbers but simpler. We will restrict our discussion to binary numbers.

Multiplication is a repeated process of *left-shift* and *add* operations. Starting with the least significant bit (*lsb*) of the multiplier, if it is 1, the multiplicand is copied to form the first partial product. If it is 0, an all-zero sequence forms the first partial product. Next, the second bit of the multiplier is examined. If it is 1, the second partial product is a copy of the multiplier, *shifted* one place to the left relative to the first one. If it is 0, an all-zero sequence forms the second partial product. This process continues until all the bits of the multiplier have been exhausted. All the partial products are then summed to form the final product. The sign of the product is determined from the signs of the multiplicand and multiplier. If they are the same, the product is positive; if not, the product is negative.

Consider the following example. The signs of the numbers in this example are assumed to be the same and have been omitted.

Example 2.24

	11001	Multiplicand
×	01101	Multiplier
	11001	Multiplier *lsb* = 1; copy multiplicand.
	00000	Multiplier bit = 0; an all-zero sequence shifted to the left.
partial products	11001	Multiplier bit = 1; copy multiplicand and shift left.
	11001	Multiplier bit = 1; copy multiplicand and shift left.
	00000	Multiplier bit = 0; an all-zero sequence shifted to the left.
	101000101	Add all partial products to form final product.

Division is a repeated process of *compare*, *right-shift*, and *subtract* operations. Subtraction is usually carried out by using the 2's complement representation. Assume that the dividend X is n bits long and that the divisor Y is m bits long. Let X_m denote the m most significant bits of X, $m \leq n$. The division process starts by comparing Y with X_m. If $Y > X_m$, we compare Y with X_{m+1}, and continue doing so until $X_{m+i} \geq Y$. At this point, we enter 1 in the most significant bit (*msb*) of the quotient Q. Y is then right-shifted i places and subtracted from X_{m+i}. The $m + i + 1$ *msb* of X is appended to the partial remainder. If the partial remainder is greater than Y, the next *msb* of Q is 1, and Y is shifted right one place and subtracted from the partial remainder. Otherwise, the initial process is repeated, with zeros placed in the appropriate bits of Q. This process continues until all the n bits of X have been exhausted, at which point we obtain the last remainder. The sign of the quotient is determined from the signs of the dividend and divisor. If they are the same, the quotient is positive; otherwise, the quotient is negative.

Consider the following example. The signs of the numbers in this example are assumed to be the same and have been omitted.

Example 2.25

Dividend: X = 0110110110
Divisor: Y = 10001
Quotient: Q = 11001
(a) Compare 5 most significant bits
of X with Y: X < Y.   01101
(b) 6 bits of X: X > Y;   011011
shift right Y and subtract;   − 10001
enter *msb* of Q = 1.   01010
(c) Partial remainder > Y;   010100
shift right Y and subtract;   − 10001
enter 1 in Q.   00011
(d) Partial remainder < Y;   000111
shift right; enter 0 in Q.
(e) Partial remainder < Y;   001111
shift right; enter 0 in Q.
(f) Partial remainder > Y;   011110
shift right Y and subtract;   − 10001
enter 1 in Q.   01101   (last remainder)

Note that the division operation may result in a quotient with an overflow. An overflow can occur in several situations, but certainly if the divisor is zero.

2.4 FLOATING-POINT NUMBER REPRESENTATION

The range of fixed-point numbers in the computer is limited by the word length. For example, in a computer having a word length of 48 bits, the range of fixed-point, sign-magnitude integers is restricted to $\pm(2^{47} - 1)$, or approximately $\pm 10^{14}$. For many scientific and engineering applications, this range is inadequate. To afford a much wider range, we use the **floating-point representation** to express real numbers.

The floating-point representation has to do with the way in which the position of the radix point is specified. This is in contrast to the fixed-point notation, where the radix point is always fixed in one position; either at the extreme right, in which case the number is treated as an integer, or at the extreme left, in which case the number is considered a fraction.

To represent a real number a in floating-point, we use the notation $a = (m, e)$, where

$$a = m \times r^e \qquad (2.14)$$

Here, r is the **radix,** m is the **mantissa,** and e is the **exponent** which designates the position of the radix point. Both m and e are fixed-point numbers, represented in sign-magnitude, r's complement, or $(r - 1)$'s complement format, with m usually being a

Sec. 2.4   Floating-Point Number Representation

fraction and e an integer. For e, there is yet a fourth representation, referred to as a **biased exponent**, which will be described later when we consider floating-point arithmetic operations.

To illustrate the wider range obtained by employing the floating-point representation, recall the example of the 48-bit word-length computer. Assuming a 36-bit fraction representation for the mantissa (including one sign bit) and a 12-bit representation for the exponent (including one sign bit), the range of floating-point numbers that this computer can handle is $\pm(1 - 2^{-35})2^k$, $k = 2^{11} - 1$, or approximately $\pm 10^{615}$.

Example 2.26

Represent the following numbers in floating-point notation.

(a) $(45.382)_{10} \longrightarrow 0.45382 \times 10^2 \equiv (0.45382, 2)$
(b) $(-21.35)_8 \longrightarrow -2135.0 \times 8^{-2} \equiv (-2135.0, -2)$
(c) $(11010.101001)_2 \longrightarrow 0.11010101001 \times 2^5 \equiv (0.11010101001, 5)$

To appreciate how floating-point numbers are actually represented in the computer, consider, for example, the number $(-21.35)_8$. It is represented in binary-coded form as

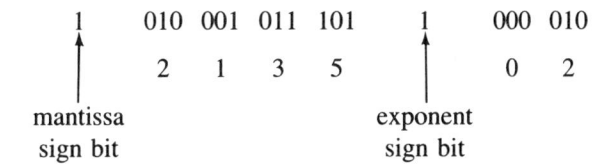

```
  1    010 001 011 101    1    000 010
        2   1   3   5          0   2
  ↑                        ↑
mantissa                exponent
sign bit                sign bit
```

Recall that the sign bit of a negative number is 1 and that of a positive number is 0. We assumed that the exponent is allocated two digits. The radix point of the mantissa is always assumed, and in this case it is to the extreme left.

Consider again Example 2.26(a). The floating-point representation of $(45.382)_{10}$ given there is 0.45382×10^2. But this number can also be represented as $45382. \times 10^{-3}$, 0.0045382×10^4, and so on. A floating-point number is said to be **normalized** if the most significant position of the mantissa contains a nonzero digit; otherwise, it is said to be **unnormalized.** Hence 0.45382×10^2 and 45382.0×10^{-3} are normalized and 0.0045382×10^4 is unnormalized.

The normalization process eliminates all the leading zeros from the mantissa. Since the mantissa length determines the precision of the floating-point number, under normalization it contains the maximum possible number of significant digits. This is particularly true since the mantissa and the exponent are each assigned a fixed number of digit positions in the computer. Thus with five digit positions being assigned to the mantissa, $0.25473 \times 10^2 = 25.473$ is normalized, whereas $0.00254 \times 10^4 = 25.4$ is unnormalized, and the two fractional least significant digits, 7 and 3, are lost. The only exception to the normalization process is zero, which cannot be normalized because its floating-point representation does not contain any nonzero digit.

If the mantissa contains k leading zeros, normalizing the floating-point number involves **shifting** the mantissa k places to the left and decreasing the value of the exponent by k. Of course, under normalization, the actual value of the number does not change. For this reason, the notation (m, e) is called a floating-point representation of the number a, with a itself being called a **floating-point number.**

The magnitude of the normalized mantissa m can have values in the range $1/r \le |m| < 1$. For binary numbers, $r = 2$ and the range becomes $0.5 \le |m| < 1$. The representation of a floating-point zero is the only exception.

Example 2.27

Consider the floating-point decimal number 0.024×10^3. Normalizing it we have 0.24×10^2. The BCD representation of the mantissa (excluding the sign bit) is 0010 0100. Notice that although the BCD representation contains two leading zeros, the mantissa is normalized. This is because the binary pattern represents a decimal number and not a binary number.

Floating-Point Arithmetic

Floating-point arithmetic operations are more complicated than those with fixed-point numbers, take more time to execute, and require more complex hardware to implement. In most computers, arithmetic operations are carried out with normalized floating-point numbers. Therefore, all the numbers must be *pre*normalized before they can be manipulated. Also, after every intermediate computation step, a *post*normalization procedure must be applied to ensure the integrity of the normalized form. In the following discussion, we assume normalized floating-point numbers and fractional mantissas.

The addition and subtraction of floating-point numbers require that the operands be **scaled** before the arithmetic operations are carried out so that they have *equal* exponents. Since the numbers are assumed to be initially normalized, scaling implies that the smaller number has to be shifted to the right until its exponent equals that of the larger number.

Addition (or subtraction) is then carried out by adding the two mantissas (or subtracting the mantissa of the subtrahend from that of the minuend), leaving the exponents untouched. When two normalized numbers are added, the result may contain an **overflow** digit. Correcting the overflow is accomplished by shifting the sum mantissa once to the right, and incrementing the exponent value by 1. When two normalized numbers are subtracted, the result may contain some leading zeros and thus have an **underflow.** To restore normalization, it is necessary to shift the mantissa to the left and decrease the exponent value until a nonzero digit appears in the most significant position.

Example 2.28

(a) Addition:

$$\begin{array}{r} 0.63524 \times 10^3 \\ +0.63215 \times 10^3 \\ \hline 1.26739 \times 10^3 \end{array}$$

To represent the sum mantissa as a fraction, the overflow can be corrected by shifting the sum once to the right and incrementing the exponent valued by 1; thus 0.126739×10^4.

(b) Subtraction:

$$\begin{array}{r} 0.63524 \times 10^3 \\ -0.63215 \times 10^3 \\ \hline 0.00309 \times 10^3 \end{array}$$

To restore normalization, the underflow can be corrected by shifting the difference twice to the left and decrementing the exponent valued by 2; thus 0.309×10^1.

Sec. 2.4   Floating-Point Number Representation   45

Example 2.29

Add the following two binary numbers:

$$\begin{array}{r} 0.10100 \times 2^2 \xrightarrow{\text{scale}} 0.01010 \times 2^3 \\ +0.11000 \times 2^3 \longrightarrow \underline{0.11000 \times 2^3} \\ 1.00010 \times 2^3 \end{array}$$

Correcting for the overflow, the sum is 0.10001×2^4.

No scaling is required for multiplication and division of floating-point numbers. To multiply two floating-point numbers, the exponents of the operands are summed and their mantissas multiplied. To divide, the exponent of the divisor is subtracted from that of the dividend and their mantissas divided. With the mantissas assumed to be fractions, the multiplication result may be unnormalized and should be restored to normalized form. The division result may overflow and, if so, should also be corrected.

Example 2.30

(a) $(0.253 \times 10^2) \times (0.124 \times 10^3) = (0.253) \times (0.124) \times 10^{2+3}$

$$= 0.031 \times 10^5 \xrightarrow{\text{normalize}} 0.31 \times 10^4$$

(b) $\dfrac{0.253 \times 10^2}{0.124 \times 10^3} = \dfrac{0.253}{0.124} \times 10^{2-3}$

$$= 2.040 \times 10^{-1} \xrightarrow{\text{overflow}} 0.204 \times 10^0$$

As was mentioned earlier, the exponent can be represented in the computer in either sign-magnitude, $(r-1)$'s complement, r's complement, or as a **biased** exponent. When adding or subtracting two floating-point numbers, first their exponents have to be compared and equalized. The comparison operation can be simplified if we can do without the signs of the exponents. One way to bypass the sign is to remove the sign bit and to convert all the exponents to positive integers by adding a positive constant, called the **bias** (b), to each exponent. A common choice of this bias constant has a magnitude that equals that of the most negative exponent. Hence the most negative exponent is represented as a zero.

Consider a floating-point binary number with an m-bit exponent. The range of this exponent in 2's complement notation is from -2^{m-1} to $2^{m-1}-1$. Choosing the bias constant b to have a magnitude that equals that of the most negative exponent, $b = 2^{m-1}$, and adding it to each exponent, all the exponents can be converted to positive integers in the range 0 to $2^m - 1$. Of course, the *actual* (unbiased) exponents can be easily retrieved from the biased exponents by using the following relation:

$$e_{\text{actual}} = e_{\text{biased}} - b \tag{2.15}$$

For example, 10-bit exponents range from $-2^9 = -(512)_{10}$ to $2^9 - 1 = (511)_{10}$. Adding the bias constant, $b = 2^9 = (512)_{10}$, to each exponent, they can be represented as positive numbers in the range 0 to $2^{10} - 1 = (1023)_{10}$. The positive exponents range from $2^9 = (512)_{10}$ to $2^{10} - 1 = (1023)_{10}$, and subtracting b [Equation (2.15)] would give the positive values of the actual positive exponents. The negative exponents are represented in the range $2^9 - 1 = (511)_{10}$ to 0, and subtracting b would give the negative values of the actual negative exponents.

As we have seen, the operations performed with the mantissas are the same as those for fixed-point numbers. The operations performed with the exponents are *compare* and *increment* (for equalizing the exponents for addition and subtraction), *add* and *subtract* (for multiplication and division), and *decrement* and *increment* (to normalize the result).

Consider a floating-point binary number representation having an n-bit normalized mantissa (including the sign bit) and an m-bit exponent (including the sign bit). Recall that the magnitude of the mantissa can assume values that are greater than or equal to 0.5 and less than 1, with the exception of zero. Then, the range of positive floating-point numbers, a^+, is

$$0.5 \times 2^{-k} \leq a^+ \leq (1 - 2^{-(n-1)}) \times 2^{k-1} \qquad (2.16)$$

and that of negative floating-point numbers, a^-, is

$$-(1 - 2^{-(n-1)}) \times 2^{k-1} \leq a^- \leq -0.5 \times 2^{-k} \qquad (2.17)$$

where $k = 2^{m-1}$.

Finally, whereas the exponent displays the *order of magnitude* of the floating-point number, the mantissa length determines the *precision* of the floating-point number. So far we have actually assumed **single-precision** formats for our floating-point number representations in the computer: Each number occupies a single word, with some bits allocated to the mantissa and the remaining bits occupied by the exponent. To increase the number of significant bits for better accuracy or a wider range, **multiple-precision** formats can be used. For example, recall the 64-bit word-length computer and assume that the mantissa is allocated 48 bits and that the exponent occupies the remaining 16 bits. In **double precision** we use two 64-bit words for each floating-point number. The exponent can still occupy 16 bits, but the accuracy can be increased to $48 + 64 = 112$ bits for the mantissa. Alternatively, we can redistribute the bits between the mantissa and the exponent, achieving both better accuracy and a wider range. As we see, there is a trade-off between the two field lengths.

2.5 BINARY CODES

We have already encountered some numeric codes. We interpreted binary patterns as representing binary, decimal, octal, hexadecimal, BCD, sign-magnitude, or 1's or 2's complement numbers. Now we shall consider some additional numeric codes as well as nonnumeric, instruction, and error-detecting codes.

Binary codes can be established for any set of discrete elements. If the set contains 2^m discrete elements, a minimum of m bits is required to code them. Note, however, that there is no maximum number of bits that may be used for a binary code.

Sec. 2.5 Binary Codes

Decimal Codes

In BCD code, each decimal digit is encoded as a straight 4-bit binary number. This is also called the **8421 code** because successive values of powers of 2 (2^3, 2^2, 2^1, and 2^0) are used to convert the binary bit pattern to its equivalent decimal digit. Since each bit is multiplied by a corresponding weight and the sum of the weighted bits gives the decimal digit, the BCD code is referred to as a **weighted code.**

A large number of other codes can be formulated by permuting four bits to represent the ten decimal digits. Some examples of the more common 4-bit decimal codes are shown in Table 2.6. Note that some of the code weights can be positive or negative. Note also that some codes (the 2421 code, for example) use similar weights for different bit positions. Thus the representations of some decimal digits are not unique in these codes.

To obtain the decimal equivalent of a weighted code word, we multiply each bit by its respective weight. For example, the code word 1101 in the positively weighted code 2421 is equivalent to: $1 \times 2 + 1 \times 4 + 0 \times 2 + 1 \times 1 = (7)_{10}$, while 1011 in the $84(-2)(-1)$ code is equivalent to $1 \times 8 + 0 \times 4 + 1 \times (-2) + 1 \times (-1) = (5)_{10}$. Note that some code words may be valid under one coding scheme but invalid under another. For example, 1101 is valid in the 2421 code but invalid in the $84(-2)(-1)$ code. Some code words, like 1011, are valid under both schemes. Since we are using only 10 of the 16 code words possible with four bits, six code words are always invalid with any decimal coding scheme.

Other sets of weights are possible. We can construct 4-bit decimal codes using the sets (6, 3, 2, 1), (6, 4, 2, -3), (4, 2, 2, 1), (7, 4, 2, 1), or (5, 2, 1, 1), to cite but a few examples. Nevertheless, codes do not have to be weighted. Table 2.6 shows an example of an **unweighted code,** the **excess-3 code.** Here, each decimal digit is encoded by adding $(3)_{10} = (0011)_2$ to its BCD equivalent and obtaining the binary code in 8421 form. For example, decimal 8 is encoded as 1011, which is decimal 11 (= 8 + 3) in the 8421 code.

One disadvantage of using the BCD code is the difficulty of computing its 9's

TABLE 2.6 EXAMPLES OF 4-BIT DECIMAL CODES

Decimal Digit	BCD 8421	2421	84 (−2) (−1)	Excess-3
0	0000	0000	00 0 0	0011
1	0001	0001	01 1 1	0100
2	0010	0010	01 1 0	0101
3	0011	0011	01 0 1	0110
4	0100	0100	01 0 0	0111
5	0101	1011	10 1 1	1000
6	0110	1100	10 1 0	1001
7	0111	1101	10 0 1	1010
8	1000	1110	10 0 0	1011
9	1001	1111	11 1 1	1100

TABLE 2.7 EXAMPLES OF DECIMAL CODES WITH MORE THAN 4 BITS

Decimal Digit	Biquinary 5043210	2-out-of-5
0	0100001	00011
1	0100010	00101
2	0100100	00110
3	0101000	01001
4	0110000	01010
5	1000001	01100
6	1000010	10001
7	1000100	10010
8	1001000	10100
9	1010000	11000

complement. In contrast, the 2421, 84(−2)(−1), and excess-3 codes have a **self-complementing** property, whereby the 9's complement of any decimal digit is obtained by interchanging the ones and zeros in its binary code. To be self-complementing, the code must be *symmetrical about the center*. This means that for a weighted code, the sum of the weights must be equal to 9, whereas for an unweighted code, the binary sum of the code words of the decimal digit and its 9's complement must be equal to the code word of 9. You can easily verify that except for the BCD code, the codes listed in Table 2.6 satisfy these conditions, and we encourage you to show that the weighted codes (5, 2, 1, 1), (4, 2, 2, 1), and (6, 4, 2, −3) are also self-complementing. However, since similar weights result in nonunique code words, we must verify that the generated set of code words is indeed self-complementing.

We mentioned earlier that four bits is the minimum number required to encode the ten decimal digits. Nevertheless, sometimes it is expedient to use more than four bits. Two such examples are shown in Table 2.7. The **biquinary** code is a 7-bit weighted code, and the **2-out-of-5** code is a 5-bit unweighted code. Both are characterized by having only two 1's in each code word. These codes are useful for error detection, as will be explained in a subsequent section.

Gray code. Many practical applications require codes in which successive code words differ in only one bit. These codes are referred to as **cyclic codes,** of which the **Gray code** is an important member. Table 2.8 shows an example of a 4-bit Gray code. As can be seen, each binary code differs from either its successor or its predecessor by a change of only one bit, from 1 to 0 or from 0 to 1. The code shown in Table 2.8 is not the only possible cyclic code; many other codes with similar characteristics can be devised.

The Gray code is often used in situations where other binary codes might produce erroneous or ambiguous results during transitions from one code word to another, in which more than one bit of the code is changing. Consider, for example, using the 8421 code and requiring a transition from 0111 to 1000. Such transition requires that all four bits change simultaneously. Depending on the logic circuit that generates the bits, there may

Sec. 2.5 Binary Codes

TABLE 2.8 FOUR-BIT GRAY CODE

Decimal	Gray code
0	0000
1	0001
2	0011
3	0010
4	0110
5	0111
6	0101
7	0100
8	1100
9	1101
10	1111
11	1110
12	1010
13	1011
14	1001
15	1000

be a significant difference in the transition times of the different bits. For example, if the most significant bit changes faster than the rest, then in going from 0111 to 1000, we will momentarily obtain the (erroneous) code word 1111. The occurrence of this code word, albeit brief, can produce an erroneous operation in a circuit whose inputs are these bits. A situation like this is referred to as a **race.** However, using the Gray code eliminates this problem, since a change in only one bit occurs per transition, and any race between the bits will have no impact on the result.

The Gray code belongs to a class of codes called **reflected codes,** a name that refers to the method used to derive it. As shown in Figure 2–1, an n-bit code is generated by

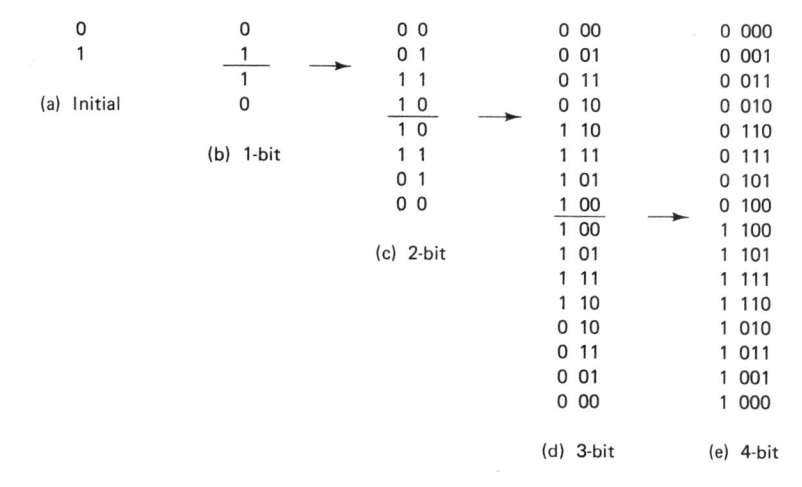

```
    0             0           0 0          0 00         0 000
    1             1           0 1          0 01         0 001
                  ─           ─ ─          ─ ──         ─ ───
                  1           1 1          0 11         0 011
(a) Initial       0           1 0          0 10         0 010
                              ───          ─ ──         ─ ───
              (b) 1-bit       1 0          1 10         0 110
                              1 1          1 11         0 111
                              0 1          1 01         0 101
                              0 0          1 00         0 100
                                           ────         ─ ───
                          (c) 2-bit        1 00         1 100
                                           1 01         1 101
                                           1 11         1 111
                                           1 10         1 110
                                           0 10         1 010
                                           0 11         1 011
                                           0 01         1 001
                                           0 00         1 000

                                         (d) 3-bit    (e) 4-bit
```

Figure 2–1 Construction of the Gray code

reflecting the $(n - 1)$-bit code. At first, the bits 0 and 1 are written in a column [part (a)]. A reflecting line is then drawn below the 1 and the column is reflected about it [part (b)]. Two zeros are added above the reflecting line and two ones are added below it, as shown in the top part of Figure 2–1(c). Another reflecting line is drawn [part (c)], and the process continues, as shown in parts (d) and (e). This process can be continued to obtain any desired number of combinations.

Alphanumeric Codes

Many applications use data that includes not only numbers but also letters of the alphabet and other special characters. Such data is called **alphanumeric** data and may be represented by numeric codes. When numbers are included in the data, they are also represented by special codes.

An **alphanumeric character set** typically includes the 26 letters of the alphabet (possibly providing for both upper- and lower-case letters), the ten decimal digits, and a number of special symbols such as +, =, *, $, ;, and !. The two most common alphanumeric codes are **ASCII** (American Standard Code for Information Interchange), shown in Table 2.9, and **EBCDIC** (Extended Binary Coded Decimal Interchange Code), shown in Table 2.10. ASCII is a 7-bit code and EBCDIC is an 8-bit code. Since many computers handle 8-bit (1-byte) codes more efficiently, an 8-bit version, called **ASCII-8** (or **USASCII-8**), has also been developed.

As we can see from these tables, some special codes are also provided in addition to the alphanumeric character set. These reserved codes are used as communication signals in applications where data transfers take place between computers that are connected through communication lines. For example, LF (line feed) and CR (carriage return) are used in conjunction with a printer; BEL is used to activate a bell; ACK (acknowledge), NAK (negative acknowledge), and DLE (data link escape) are exchanged signals over the communication lines.

Any code can be read from the tables in either binary or hexadecimal format. Hexadecimal is used only for shorthand; the data is handled in binary in the computer. To find the code corresponding to any character, locate its position in the appropriate table, read across the row to find the most significant hexadecimal digit (or binary nibble), and then read its column to find the least significant hexadecimal digit (or binary nibble). To find the character associated with a binary or hexadecimal code, we do the opposite. We use the most significant digit to locate the character's row and the least significant digit to locate its column. (Notice that although ASCII is a 7-bit code, Table 2.9 depicts it in *byte* form by adding a leading zero to the most significant digit.)

Example 2.31

Find the hexadecimal and binary codes for lower-case k in the two alphanumeric coding schemes.

ASCII: Locating k in Table 2.9, its row value is $(6)_{16} = (0110)_2$ and its column value is $(B)_{16} = (1011)_2$. Hence the ASCII code for k is $(6B)_{16}$ or $(01101011)_2$.

EBCDIC: Using Table 2.10, the EBCDIC code for k is $(92)_{16}$ or $(10010010)_2$.

TABLE 2.9 ASCII CODE

			Least significant digit (or nibble)														
Binary		0000	0001	0010	0011	0100	0101	0110	0111	1000	1001	1010	1011	1100	1101	1110	1111
	Hex.	0	1	2	3	4	5	6	7	8	9	A	B	C	D	E	F
0000	0	NUL	SOH	STX	ETX	EOT	ENQ	ACK	BEL	BS	HT	LF	VT	FF	CR	SO	SI
0001	1	DLE	DC1	DC2	DC3	DC4	NAK	SYN	ETB	CAN	EM	SUB	ESC	FS	GS	RS	US
0010	2	SP	!	"	#	$	%	&	'	(	)	*	+	,	-	.	/
0011	3	0	1	2	3	4	5	6	7	8	9	:	;	<	=	>	?
0100	4	@	A	B	C	D	E	F	G	H	I	J	K	L	M	N	O
0101	5	P	Q	R	S	T	U	V	W	X	Y	Z	[	\	]	^	_
0110	6	`	a	b	c	d	e	f	g	h	i	j	k	l	m	n	o
0111	7	p	q	r	s	t	u	v	w	x	y	z	{			}	~	DEL

Most significant digit (or nibble)

TABLE 2.10 EBCDIC CODE

Binary	Hex.	0000 0	0001 1	0010 2	0011 3	0100 4	0101 5	0110 6	0111 7	1000 8	1001 9	1011 A	1011 B	1100 C	1101 D	1110 E	1111 F
0000	0	NUL	SOH	STX	ETX	PF	HT	LC	DEL			SMM	VT	FF	CR	SO	SI
0001	1	DLE	DC1	DC2	TM	RES	NL	BS	IL	CAN	EM	CC	CU1	IFS	IGS	IRS	IUS
0010	2	DS	SOS	FS		BYP	LF	ETB	ESC			SM	CU2		ENQ	ACK	BEL
0011	3			SYN		PN	RS	UC	EOT				CU3	DC4	NAK		SUB
0100	4	SP										¢	.	<	(	+	|
0101	5	&										!	$	·	)	;	?
0110	6	—	/									|	,	%	_	>	¨
0111	7											:	#	@	'	=	''
1000	8		a	b	c	d	e	f	g	h	i						
1001	9		j	k	l	m	n	o	p	q	r						
1010	A			s	t	u	v	w	x	y	z						
1011	B																
1100	C		A	B	C	D	E	F	G	H	I						
1101	D		J	K	L	M	N	O	P	Q	R						
1110	E			S	T	U	V	W	X	Y	Z						
1111	F	0	1	2	3	4	5	6	7	8	9						

Most significant digit (or nibble)

Least significant digit (or nibble)

Sec. 2.5   Binary Codes   53

TABLE 2.11 CHARACTER STRING CODES FOR EXAMPLE 2.33

Character String	ASCII	EBCDIC
COMPUTER	43 4F 4D 50 55 54 45 52	C3 D6 D4 D7 E4 E3 C5 D9
$Integer	24 49 6E 74 65 67 65 72	5B C9 95 A3 85 87 85 99
04/12/84	30 34 2F 31 32 2F 38 34	F0 F4 61 F1 F2 61 F8 F4

Example 2.32

Find the character represented by $(01011011)_2$ [or, equivalently, by $(5B)_{16}$] in the two alphanumeric coding schemes.

ASCII: The character is located in Table 2.9 at the intersection of the $(5)_{16}$ row and the $(B)_{16}$ column and is the symbol [.
EBCDIC: Using Table 2.10, the symbol is $.

Example 2.33

ASCII and EBCDIC codes for some character strings are shown in Table 2.11. We left spaces between the bytes to make the codes more readable; however, such spaces do not exist in actual data communication. Note that the numerals shown in the table (04, 12, and 84) have codes that are different from their usual BCD representations.

Error Detection Codes

Digital data is typically prepared on an input device (such as a keyboard) and then sent over some communication link and read by a computer. The computer, in turn, manipulates the data and then may be required to send the results over a communication link to an output device (such as a display).

The process of transferring digital information is subject to error. Although modern equipment is designed to reduce errors, even relatively infrequent errors can cause serious problems. It is therefore essential to detect errors whenever possible. If errors occur infrequently, retransmission of the data can be attempted. However, in modern digital communication systems, this is not considered efficient; retransmission of data for every detected error is liable to be quite costly. For this reason, techniques have been developed to enable the correction of detected errors. Employing these techniques usually implies a more complex system. The optimal solution, therefore, lies somewhere between the two approaches—between using a simple and relatively cheap system that does not correct detected errors and using a sophisticated and expensive system capable of correcting many errors. In this section we will consider error-detecting codes only.

An **error-detecting code** is a binary code that detects digital errors during data transmission. One of the most widely used schemes for error detection is the **parity** method. It entails the addition of an extra bit, the **parity bit,** to a binary message that is being transferred from one location to another. In the following discussion, we append the parity bit to the binary message in the leftmost position.

The parity bit can designate either even or odd parity. In the **even-parity** method, the parity bit is set to 1 so that the *total number* of ones in the binary message (including the parity bit) is an *even number*; otherwise, it is set to 0. For example, assume that we want to transmit the EBCDIC character $, whose binary code is 01011011. Since it contains an odd number of ones, the parity bit is set to 1 to make the total number of ones an even number. The code that will actually be transmitted is 101011011. For the EBCDIC character C, the code that will be transmitted is 011000011. The **odd-parity** method is used in exactly the same way except that the parity bit is set to 1 so that the *total number* of ones (including the parity bit) is an *odd number*.

Regardless of whether we use even or odd parity, the parity bit becomes an integral part of the code. Consider Figure 2-2, which shows a block diagram of a digital data transmission system that uses parity checking. At the sending end, the binary message is supplied first to a **parity generator,** which produces the appropriate parity bit. The message, including the parity bit, is then transmitted over the communication link to its destination. At the receiving end, the incoming message is applied to a **parity detector,** which verifies the integrity of the parity information. If the number of ones in the received message matches the generated parity, the message is considered correct and the parity detector issues an "OK" signal that enables the data receiver. Otherwise, the message is declared incorrect and the parity detector issues an "ERROR" signal that can be used to request retransmission.

The parity method is limited in that it can only detect errors in the message but cannot detect which bit is in error. Furthermore, regardless of whether we use even or odd parity, the parity method can only detect an *odd* number of errors; an *even* number of errors cannot be detected. More elaborate schemes exist that not only check for multiple errors but also detect where the errors are and correct them.

Another example of an error-detecting code is the 2-out-of-5 code shown in Table 2.7. This code is constructed such that each decimal number is represented by a binary code word in which two bits are 1 and all the others are 0. Therefore, if a digit arriving at the receiver has three ones, an error will be indicated and the digit will be rejected as incorrect. The 2-out-of-5 code is capable of detecting any error involving a change of one or more bits that causes the number of ones to differ from two. However, there are occasions when two simultaneous bit changes may occur and a different digit, also having two ones, is produced and accepted, with the code failing to detect the error. For example, if the number 4, represented by the code 01010, is transmitted incorrectly and the least significant bit changes to 1 giving 01011, the error will be immediately detected. However,

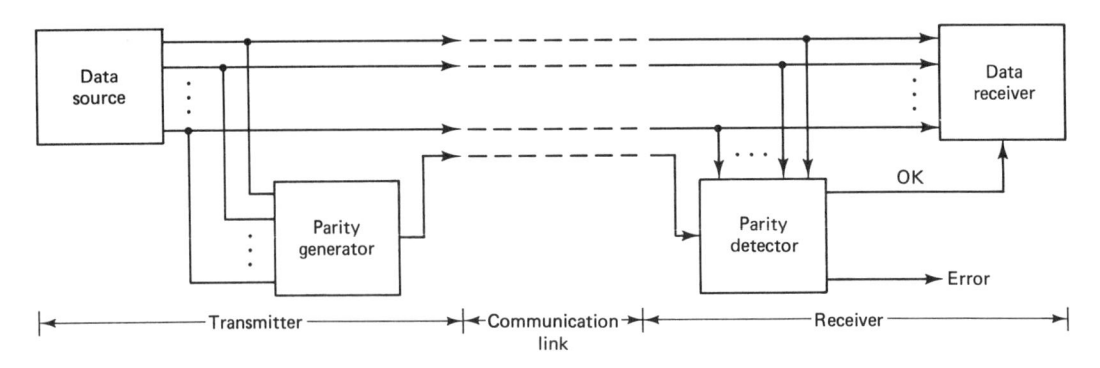

Figure 2-2 Digital data transmission using parity checking

Sec. 2.6   Interpretation of Binary Data

if the second least significant bit is also affected at the same time, the resulting code word 01001, representing decimal 3, will be accepted with the errors undetected.

The biquinary code shown in Table 2.7 is yet another example of a code with error-detecting properties. Structured like the 2-out-of-5 code, the biquinary code can be similarly employed for error detection but will also fail if two bits change simultaneously and produce a valid code word.

Instruction Codes

Apart from data representation, binary codes are also used to formulate control instructions within the computer. These are referred to as instruction codes. An **instruction code** is a group of bits that tells the computer to perform a specific operation. The instruction code is usually divided into parts, each having its own particular interpretation. The most basic part of an instruction code is the operation code. An **operation code** (or **opcode**) is a group of bits that define such operations as ADD, SUBTRACT, SHIFT, and COMPLEMENT. It is the instruction's *verb* that tells the computer what to do. The other parts of the instruction consist of one or more operands. An **operand** is the name used for the instruction's object and may be data or an address that tells where the data is.

To execute the instructions formulated for a computer, they must be binary-coded. Consider, for example, the operations LOAD and STORE. To load is to copy a number from a memory location into a register, and to store is to copy a number from a register into a memory location. (Memory and registers will be discussed in Chapter 3.) For example, Motorola's 6800 micoprocessor uses the hexadecimal opcode 86 for *LOAD register A with a value*. The same microprocessor uses the hexadecimal opcode B7 for *STORE the contents of register A in a memory location*. (Note that we use the hexadecimal notation only as a convenient shorthand representation; in the computer, opcodes are represented in binary form.) Instructions containing these opcodes can be, for example, 86 F2 (in hexadecimal), which means *LOAD register A with the value F2*, or B7 00F2, which translates into *STORE the value in register A in memory location 00F2*. F2 is internally represented in the microprocessor as its binary value, 11110010.

2.6 INTERPRETATION OF BINARY DATA

It is appropriate to conclude the discussion of binary representations by reflecting on the interpretation of binary data. As we realize by now, binary data can have various meanings, depending on the context in which it is used. To illustrate the various interpretations, let us consider the data byte 10010101. Any of the following interpretations is valid for this byte:

1. An unsigned binary number equivalent to decimal 149, octal 225, or hexadecimal 95
2. An unsigned binary number (equivalent to decimal 21) with even parity
3. A sign-magnitude representation of $-(21)_{10}$
4. A 1's complement representation of $-(106)_{10}$

5. A 2's complement representation of $-(107)_{10}$
6. An unsigned BCD number, equivalent to $(95)_{10}$
7. A sign-magnitude BCD number, equivalent to $-(5)_{10}$
8. ASCII for the character NAK, with even parity
9. An opcode in the instruction set of Motorola's 6800 microprocessor that performs the logical AND between the content of register A and the content of memory location M
10. Excess-3 coded decimal 62
11. Gray coded decimal 226

You may wonder how a computer decides which of these interpretations a given binary data might have. It does not. It is the computer designer who decides on the meanings of the binary data within the system.

PROBLEMS

1. Convert the following numbers to decimal:
   (a) $(101011)_2$, $(11011.1101)_2$, $(.01101)_2$
   (b) $(476)_8$, $(365.27)_8$, $(.7105)_8$
   (c) $(F23A)_{16}$, $(7A41.C8)_{16}$, $(.FD21)_{16}$
   (d) $(121.201)_3$, $(1302.12)_4$, $(.354)_6$, $(298)_{12}$
2. Convert the decimal number 427.5 to base 3, base 6, base 8, and base 16.
3. Convert the following numbers from the given base to the bases indicated:
   (a) $(11010.110)_2$ to decimal, octal, and hexadecimal
   (b) $(3DA9.DD)_{16}$ to decimal, octal, and binary
   (c) $(478.12)_{10}$ to binary, octal, and hexadecimal
   (d) $(372.16)_8$ to binary, decimal, and hexadecimal
4. Convert the following numbers to BCD:
   (a) $(47.28)_{10}$
   (b) $(362)_8$
   (c) $(7AF.2C)_{16}$
5. Convert the BCD code 11101011001.10011 to binary, decimal, and hexadecimal.
6. Convert the following numbers to BCD:
   (a) $(10110111011)_2$
   (b) $(1986)_{10}$
   (c) $(72AF1)_{16}$
7. Convert $(11010111011)_2$ to octal and hexadecimal.
8. Obtain the 16's and 15's complements of **027A**, **F8B6**, and **07AF.4C**.
9. Obtain the 10's and 9's complements of the decimal numbers **01398**, **9239.72**, and **9471**.
10. Obtain the 8's and 7's complements of the octal numbers **0361**, **043.216**, and **756**.
11. Obtain the 2's and 1's complements of the binary numbers **01101101**, **1010111.1100**, and **10101101011**.
12. Obtain the 10's complement of [**(11)**197]$_{12}$ and **(0BA45)**$_{16}$.

Chap. 2   Problems   57

13. Use the 10's and 9's complements to perform the indicated subtractions with decimal numbers (assume positive numbers):
    (a) 375 − 42
    (b) 725 − 1956
    (c) 7240 − 471

14. Use the 2's and 1's complements to perform the indicated subtractions with binary numbers (assume positive numbers):
    (a) 11010 − 1101
    (b) 101 − 11001
    (c) 11010 − 10000

15. Add the following positive numbers:
    (a) $(45B7)_{16} + (15)_{16}$
    (b) $(10111)_2 + (101)_2$
    (c) $(925)_{10} + (634)_8$

16. The positive and negative versions of a signed fixed-point number with true magnitude $A = (547)_{10}$ are stored in 16-bit words. List their sign-magnitude, 1's complement, and 2's complement binary fixed-point representations.

17. What are the integer ranges of sign-magnitude, 1's complement, and 2's complement representations in a fixed-point binary arithmetic system having word length of (a) 16 bits and (b) 64 bits?

18. Give the indicated multiplication of the following positive binary numbers:
    (a) 110101 × 1011
    (b) 1101101 × 1101

19. Give the indicated division of the following positive binary numbers:
    (a) 11010101/11011
    (b) 010111101/1001

20. Represent the following numbers in floating-point notation:
    (a) $(525.347)_{10}$
    (b) $(7AB.F5)_{16}$
    (c) $(101011.101101)_2$
    (d) $(-54.571)_8$

21. Normalize the following floating-point decimal numbers:
    (a) -1023.74×10^{-3}
    (b) 4.159×10^4

22. A binary floating-point number has 6 bits for a biased exponent. The constant used for the bias is 32.
    (a) List the biased representation in binary of all exponents from +31 to −32.
    (b) When adding two biased exponents, what do you have to do to obtain a biased-exponent sum?
    (c) When subtracting two biased exponents, what do you have to do to obtain a biased-exponent difference?

23. Perform the indicated arithmetic operation and write the result in normalized form:
    (a) $0.7845 \times 10^2 + 0.4467 \times 10^2$
    (b) $0.7845 \times 10^2 - 0.7521 \times 10^2$
    (c) $0.11010 \times 10^3 + 0.01110 \times 10^4$

24. Perform the indicated arithmetic operation and write the result in normalized form:
    (a) $(0.125 \times 10^2) \times (0.024 \times 10^4)$
    (b) $(0.675 \times 10^2)/(0.075 \times 10^4)$

25. A computer has the following floating-point representation: *Mantissa*: 16 bits (15 bits plus sign bit), normalized. Negative mantissas are in 1's complement. *Exponent*: 8 bits, biased and represented in base 16; the bias is 128. Show the sign bit, mantissa, and exponent representations for the following decimal numbers:
    (a) 1.5
    (b) +0.75; −0.75
    (c) 24.25

26. Using the floating-point format of Problem 25, compute the decimal values that are equivalent to the following octal representations:
    (a) 76777600
    (b) 03000177
    (c) 30000203

27. Represent the decimal number 729 in the BCD, excess-3, and 2421 codes.

28. Using the following weighted codes, construct the binary codes for the decimal digits so that they will be self-complementing:
    (a) 642(−3)
    (b) 4221
    (c) 5211

29. Find the hexadecimal and binary codes for the following:
    (a) ASCII U
    (b) EBCDIC $

30. Write the ASCII and EBCDIC hexadecimal codes for the following character strings:
    (a) base 2
    (b) Architecture
    (c) 03/24/86

31. Generate odd- and even-parity codes for the following messages:
    (a) Binary 10111010
    (b) Decimal 8 in 84(−2)(−1) code
    (c) ASCII %
    (d) Hexadecimal A4F, with each character assumed to be sent separately

32. Why is it impossible to detect an even number of errors when using either even-parity or odd-parity code?

CHAPTER 3

Logic Design Principles and Devices

3.1 BOOLEAN ALGEBRA

Computers manipulate *discrete elements* of information represented by physical qualities called **signals.** The signals are usually restricted to two possible values and are said to be *binary*. As we saw in Chapter 2, two levels are enough because any desired message, no matter how complex, can be coded in the binary system using strings of the symbols 0 and 1. Therefore, two-state devices like switches, diodes, magnetic cores, and transistors can be used to process information because the two states (on versus off, conducting versus nonconducting, positively magnetized versus negatively magnetized, high potential versus low potential) can represent the two binary symbols 0 and 1.

Claude Shannon showed in 1938 how to analyze and design digital logic circuits by using algebraic expressions involving variables that can take on only two values. He based his approach on the concept of *Boolean algebra*, developed originally by the nineteenth-century mathematician George Boole. Boole was interested in discovering the laws governing the working of the human mind. What Shannon observed was that these same laws govern the behavior of digital circuits. The guiding principle behind Shannon's approach is this: Reduce the problem of digital circuit design and analysis to the study of expressions in a Boolean algebra.

We begin our discussion of Shannon's system by listing a basic formulation of the fundamental axioms of Boolean algebra. We then focus in Section 3.2 on a Boolean algebra whose domain is the set of elements {0, 1}. This two-valued Boolean algebra, called **switching algebra,** is very useful since Boolean expressions generated by binary variables can be implemented with logic circuits that use binary devices.

A **Boolean algebra** is an algebraic structure consisting of a set of elements B together with two *binary* operations $\{+\}$ and $\{\cdot\}$ and a *unary* operation $\{^-\}$, such that the following axioms hold:

1. The set B contains at least two elements a, b such that $a \neq b$.
2. **Closure properties** of binary operations:
   For every $a, b \in B$,
   (a) $a + b \in B$
   (b) $a \cdot b \in B$
3. **Commutative laws:**
   For every $a, b \in B$,
   (a) $a + b = b + a$
   (b) $a \cdot b = b \cdot a$
4. Existence of **identities:**
   (a) There exists an identity element with respect to $\{+\}$, designated by 0, such that $a + 0 = a$, for every $a \in B$.
   (b) There exists an identity element with respect to $\{\cdot\}$, designated by 1, such that $a \cdot 1 = a$, for every $a \in B$.
5. **Distributive laws:**
   For every $a, b, c \in B$,
   (a) $a + (b \cdot c) = (a + b) \cdot (a + c)$
   (b) $a \cdot (b + c) = (a \cdot b) + (a \cdot c)$
6. Existence of **complement:**
   For each $a \in B$, there exists an element $\bar{a} \in B$ (the **complement** of a) such that
   (a) $a + \bar{a} = 1$
   (b) $a \cdot \bar{a} = 0$
7. **Associative laws:**
   For every $a, b, c \in B$,
   (a) $a + (b + c) = (a + b) + c$
   (b) $a \cdot (b \cdot c) = (a \cdot b) \cdot c$

Note that the associative laws can be derived from the other axioms.

Operator priorities in Boolean algebra are such that an expression inside parentheses must be evaluated before all other operations. The next operation that holds precedence is the complement $\{^-\}$, then the $\{\cdot\}$, and finally the $\{+\}$. When parentheses are not used, $\{\cdot\}$ operations are performed before $\{+\}$ operations. Also, the $\{\cdot\}$ symbol may be omitted, in which case ab is understood to mean $a \cdot b$.

Note that the axioms are arranged in pairs. Each statement can be obtained from the other by interchanging the $\{+\}$ and $\{\cdot\}$ operations and the identity elements 0 and 1. This is called the **principle of duality** and is illustrated as follows:

$$a + (b \cdot c) = (a + b) \cdot (a + c)$$
$$a \cdot (b + c) = (a \cdot b) + (a \cdot c)$$

Therefore, any algebraic expression (theorem) deducible from the axioms has a **dual** that is also true.

Table 3.1 lists a variety of important identities of Boolean algebra. They are listed in dual pairs, designated by (a) and (b). We can use the identities to prove other identities or to manipulate Boolean algebraic expressions into other forms.

TABLE 3.1 SOME IMPORTANT IDENTITIES OF BOOLEAN ALGEBRA

(1a) $x + 0 = x$	(1b) $x \cdot 1 = x$	Axiom 4
(2a) $x(y + z) = xy + xz$	(2b) $x + yz = (x + y)(x + z)$	Distributivity
(3a) $x + \bar{x} = 1$	(3b) $x\bar{x} = 0$	Axiom 6
(4a) $x + x = x$	(4b) $xx = x$	Idempotency
(5a) $x + 1 = 1$	(5b) $x \cdot 0 = 0$	
(6a) $x + xy = x$	(6b) $x(x + y) = x$	Absorption
(7a) $(x + \bar{y})y = xy$	(7b) $x\bar{y} + y = x + y$	
(8a) $(x + y)(x + \bar{y}) = x$	(8b) $xy + x\bar{y} = x$	Logical adjacency
(9a) $(x + y)(\bar{x} + z)(y + z) = (x + y)(\bar{x} + z)$	(9b) $xy + \bar{x}z + yz = xy + \bar{x}z$	Consensus
(10a) $\overline{x_1 + x_2 + \cdots + x_n} = \bar{x}_1 \bar{x}_2 \cdots \bar{x}_n$		DeMorgan's laws
(10b) $\overline{(x_1 x_2 \cdots x_n)} = \bar{x}_1 + \bar{x}_2 + \cdots + \bar{x}_n$		
(11a) $f(x_1, x_2, \ldots, x_n) = x_i f(x_1, x_2, \ldots, x_{i-1}, 1, x_{i+1}, \ldots, x_n)$		Shannon's expansion
$\quad + \bar{x}_i f(x_1, x_2, \ldots, x_{i-1}, 0, x_{i+1}, \ldots, x_n)$		theorems
(11b) $f(x_1, x_2, \ldots, x_n) = [x_i + f(x_1, x_2, \ldots, x_{i-1}, 0, x_{i+1}, \ldots, x_n)]$		
$\quad \cdot [\bar{x}_i + f(x_1, x_2, \ldots, x_{i-1}, 1, x_{i+1}, \ldots, x_n)]$		

The simplest example of a Boolean algebra consists of only two elements, 0 and 1, defined to satisfy

$$1 + 1 = 1 \cdot 1 = 1 + 0 = 0 + 1 = 1$$
$$0 + 0 = 0 \cdot 0 = 1 \cdot 0 = 0 \cdot 1 = 0$$
$$\bar{1} = 0$$
$$\bar{0} = 1$$

It can be easily shown that all the axioms are satisfied for this case. This algebra is often referred to as **two-valued** Boolean algebra or **switching algebra.**

3.2 BOOLEAN FUNCTIONS

The operations of switching algebra are defined in Table 3.2. The $\{+\}$, $\{\cdot\}$, and $\{^-\}$ operations are commonly referred to as OR, AND, and NOT, respectively. Each of these (and other) operations can be implemented by a physical device called a **gate,** enabling us to implement Boolean expressions in the form of logic circuits.

TABLE 3.2 DEFINITION OF OPERATIONS IN A BOOLEAN ALGEBRA OVER TWO VALUES

$\{+\}$	0	1		$\{\cdot\}$	0	1		$\{^-\}$	
0	0	1		0	0	0		0	1
1	1	1		1	0	1		1	0
OR operator				AND operator				NOT operator	

Let $\{x_{n-1}, \ldots, x_1, x_0\}$ be a set of symbols, called **variables.** A **Boolean (algebraic) expression** in $\{x_{n-1}, \ldots, x_1, x_0\}$ is an expression formed with the variables, the constants 0 and 1, the binary operators AND and OR, and the unary operator NOT. In other words, we can obtain Boolean expressions by applying the following two rules any finite number of times:

1. The constants 0 and 1 and the Boolean variables $\{x_{n-1}, \ldots, x_1, x_0\}$ are Boolean expressions in $\{x_{n-1}, \ldots, x_1, x_0\}$.
2. Moreover, if E_1 and E_2 are Boolean expressions in $\{x_{n-1}, \ldots, x_1, x_0\}$, then so are $\bar{E}_1$, $\bar{E}_2$, $E_1 + E_2$, and $E_1 E_2$.

For example, by this definition, the expressions

Sec. 3.2 Boolean Functions

$$F_1 = \overline{x_1 x_2 + (x_1 + x_3)}$$
$$F_2 = x_1 x_2 + \bar{x}_1 x_3 + x_1 \bar{x}_3$$
$$F_3 = \bar{x}_1 x_2 (x_3 + \bar{x}_2 x_1) + \bar{x}_2 x_3$$

are all Boolean expressions in x_1, x_2, and x_3. The foregoing definition of a Boolean expression is an example of a **recursive** (or **inductive**) definition. Rule 1 gives us the basic step; it points to some definite objects that are Boolean expressions. Rule 2 describes how to build more complex expressions from existing expressions. (Many constructs in computer science, including elements of many programming languages, are defined recursively.)

But now comes a crucial observation: Just as polynomial expressions in ordinary algebra may be regarded as functions, so may Boolean algebraic expressions be regarded as **Boolean** (or **switching**) **functions.** For example, let B and B^n denote, respectively, the set $\{0, 1\}$ and the set of 2^n possible n-tuples (words of length n) of zeros and ones. Then, for a Boolean expression F in the variables $\{x_{n-1}, \ldots, x_1, x_0\}$, the value of F at $(b_{n-1}, \ldots, b_1, b_0) \in B^n$ is an element of B obtained by assigning each value b_i to the corresponding variable x_i. Since a Boolean variable can take on only one of the two values 0 or 1, a Boolean (switching) function is just a function that accepts an n-tuple of zeros and ones and produces either 0 or 1 as its value at the n-tuple. Any switching function is therefore completely determined by the list of its functional values at these 2^n n-tuples. Consequently, there are 2^{2^n} such switching functions.

Definition 3.1. A **literal**, designated as x^*, is either the Boolean variable x or its complement $\bar{x}$.

Definition 3.2. A Boolean expression generated by $x_{n-1}, \ldots, x_1, x_0$ over B in the form of a *product* (conjunction) of n distinct literals is called a **minterm.** If the expression is in the form of a *sum* (disjunction) of n distinct literals, it is called a **maxterm.**

In general, 2^n minterms (maxterms) are generated by n binary variables in B. To characterize the structure of a minterm (maxterm), let $(K)_{10}$ denote the decimal equivalent of the Kth binary combination $(k_{n-1}, \ldots, k_1, k_0)_2$ of the n variables; hence $K = 0, 1, 2, \ldots, 2^n - 1$. If we let $m_K = x^*_{n-1} \ldots x^*_1 x^*_0$ denote the Kth minterm, then

$$x^*_i = \bar{x}_i \quad \text{if } k_i = 0$$
$$ = x_i \quad \text{if } k_i = 1$$

Similarly, if we let $M_K = x^*_{n-1} + \cdots + x^*_1 + x^*_0$ denote the Kth maxterm, then

$$x^*_i = x_i \quad \text{if } k_i = 0$$
$$ = \bar{x}_i \quad \text{if } k_i = 1$$

Therefore, each binary combination of the n variables *uniquely* determines a minterm (maxterm). The converse is also true: Each minterm (maxterm) is associated with only one binary combination. But since there is a one-to-one correspondence between the binary combinations and their decimal equivalents, there is a one-to-one correspondence between each decimal and a minterm (maxterm).

The value of any minterm is 1 *if and only if* the variables assume the values of its corresponding binary combination; it is 0 for any other combination. Similarly, the value of any maxterm is 0 *if and only if* the variables assume the values of its corresponding binary combination; it is 1 for any other combination. Therefore, for the *same* binary combination, the corresponding minterm and maxterm are complements of each other. For example, with three variables ($n = 3$), $m_6 = 1$ ($M_6 = 0$) if and only if $x = 1$, $y = 1$, and $z = 0$, and $m_6 = 0$ ($M_6 = 1$) for any other combination. These properties hold true for any number of variables and can be summarized as follows:

$$m_i m_j = 0 \quad \text{if } i \neq j$$
$$= m_i \quad \text{if } i = j$$
$$M_i + M_j = 1 \quad \text{if } i \neq j$$
$$= M_i \quad \text{if } i = j$$
$$m_i = \overline{M_i} \text{ and } \overline{m_i} = M_i \quad \text{for every } i$$

We can now use these concepts to derive the two *canonical forms* for expressing any Boolean function.

Theorem 3.1. Every Boolean function of n variables, $f(x_{n-1}, \ldots, x_1, x_0)$ can be written in either of the following forms:

(a) **Canonical sum-of-products:**

$$f(x_{n-1}, \ldots, x_1, x_0) = \sum_{K=0}^{2^n - 1} \alpha_K m_K \tag{3.1}$$

(b) **Canonical product-of-sums:**

$$f(x_{n-1}, \ldots, x_1, x_0) = \prod_{K=0}^{2^n - 1} (\beta_K + M_K) \tag{3.2}$$

The coefficients α_K and β_K each can assume a value of either 1 or 0. If $f = 1$ for the Kth minterm or maxterm, these coefficients will be 1; otherwise, they will be 0. In other words,

$$\alpha_K = \beta_K = f(k_{n-1}, \ldots, k_1, k_0) \tag{3.3}$$

The canonical sum-of-products, abbreviated as canonical SOP, is a sum (OR) of minterms. (Sometimes, the canonical SOP is called the *minterm form* or the *disjunctive normal form*.) Likewise, the canonical product-of-sums, abbreviated as canonical POS, is a product (AND) of maxterms. (The canonical POS is also called the *maxterm form* or the *conjunctive normal form*.)

Example 3.1

Consider the following truth table of a three-variable Boolean expression $f(a, b, c)$:

a	b	c	f
0	0	0	0
0	0	1	1
0	1	0	0
0	1	1	0
1	0	0	1
1	0	1	1
1	1	0	1
1	1	1	1

The canonical SOP form of f is

$$f(a, b, c) = 0(\overline{abc}) + 1(\overline{ab}c) + 0(\overline{a}b\overline{c}) + 0(\overline{a}bc)$$
$$+ 1(a\overline{bc}) + 1(a\overline{b}c) + 1(ab\overline{c}) + 1(abc)$$

$$= \overline{ab}c + a\overline{bc} + a\overline{b}c + ab\overline{c} + abc$$

As we see in Example 3.1, the canonical SOP form is indeed the sum (OR) of the five minterms corresponding to those binary combinations of a, b, and c for which $f = 1$. Since there is a one-to-one correspondence between the minterms and their decimal equivalents, we can use a shorthand notation and express f as

$$f(a, b, c) = \Sigma m(1, 4, 5, 6, 7) \qquad (3.4)$$

The symbol Σm in Equation (3.4) stands for "the logical sum (OR) of the minterms indicated by the decimals." Likewise, since f can also be expressed as a product (AND) of those maxterms that correspond to values of a, b, and c for which $f = 0$, we may represent f as

$$f(a, b, c) = \Pi M(0, 2, 3) \qquad (3.5)$$

The symbol ΠM in Equation (3.5) stands for "the logical product (AND) of the maxterms indicated by the decimals." Note that there is no ambiguity in using either one of these formats to express any Boolean function.

3.3 LOGIC DESIGN EXAMPLE

Let us consider the design of a circuit that drives a seven-segment display, a device used to display the decimal digits. Figure 3–1(a) shows the seven segments labeled with letters from *a* through *g*. Each segment can be illuminated (turned on) separately so that by appropriately selecting segments, we can display the decimal digits 0 through 9 as shown in Figure 3–1(b).

Our problem, therefore, is to design a logic circuit that will turn on the correct segments in response to a binary-coded decimal (BCD) input (see Section 2.2). Since a BCD code is represented by four binary variables (bits), the circuit will have four

Figure 3-1 Seven-segment logic circuit design

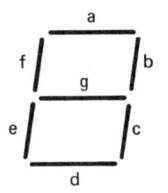

(a) Segment identification

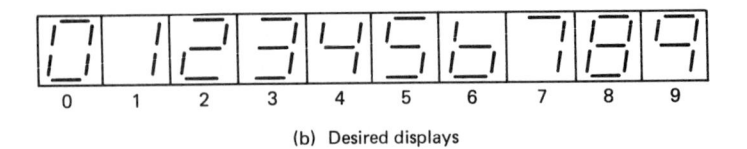

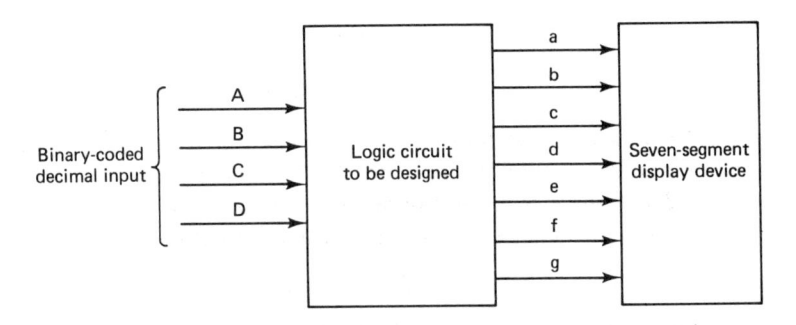

(b) Desired displays

(c) Circuit block diagram

Decimal Displayed	Inputs				Outputs						
	A	B	C	D	a	b	c	d	e	f	g
0	0	0	0	0	1	1	1	1	1	1	0
1	0	0	0	1	0	1	1	0	0	0	0
2	0	0	1	0	1	1	0	1	1	0	1
3	0	0	1	1	1	1	1	1	0	0	1
4	0	1	0	0	0	1	1	0	0	1	1
5	0	1	0	1	1	0	1	1	0	1	1
6	0	1	1	0	0	0	1	1	1	1	1
7	0	1	1	1	1	1	1	0	0	0	0
8	1	0	0	0	1	1	1	1	1	1	1
9	1	0	0	1	1	1	1	0	0	1	1

(d) Truth table

inputs, one for each bit. With seven segments, the circuit must have seven outputs, each of which will switch the corresponding segment on or off. The required circuit block diagram is shown in Figure 3–1(c).

We can tabulate the outputs for each *valid* binary combination of the inputs,

Sec. 3.4 Simplification of Boolean Functions

as shown in the truth table of Figure 3–1(d). Notice that the truth table is actually incomplete. With four input variables, we can generate 16 combinations, and the complete truth table should therefore have contained 16 rows. Since only ten combinations are actually required to specify our problem, we can assume that the binary combinations corresponding to decimals 10 through 15 will never occur, so no corresponding output will ever be generated. In the complete truth table, this can be indicated by placing X's in the output columns opposite the corresponding input rows. The X's, referred to as **don't-cares,** can be either 0 or 1, and it makes no difference which value each of them takes since the corresponding input combination is assumed never to occur. Hence, their omission from the table in Figure 3–1(d) implies ''don't care.''

Having represented the operation of the circuit in truth table form, we can now obtain the Boolean functions that govern its behavior. Consider, for example, segment d, which should be on ($d = 1$) when displaying the digit 0, 2, 3, 5, 6, or 8. Expressing these conditions in canonical SOP form, we obtain from the truth table

$$d = \Sigma m(0, 2, 3, 5, 6, 8)$$

Similar expressions can also be obtained for the remaining outputs. We can also express the output functions in the alternative canonical POS form. For example, d expressed in this form would be given by

$$d = \Pi M(1, 4, 7, 9)$$

By substituting the corresponding minterms or maxterms for the decimals, each output can be implemented (as a function of the four input variables) using AND, OR, and NOT gates. We leave it to you to supply the implementation of the seven-segment display circuit.

3.4 SIMPLIFICATION OF BOOLEAN FUNCTIONS

Space and cost reductions are important considerations in the design of digital systems and can be achieved by minimizing the number of literals and logic devices used to implement the system. In this section, we discuss a minimization technique via the simplification of Boolean functions.

Our purpose in minimizing a switching function f is to find an expression g that is equivalent to f but minimizes some cost criterion. We can approach this problem by manipulating f algebraically (using the identities of Table 3.1) or by using the **Karnaugh map** (**K-map** for short) technique. The K-map is actually a rearrangement of a truth table. For example, Figure 3–2(a) shows a K-map of four variables. The number inside each **cell** represents the decimal equivalent of the binary combination that specifies the minterm (maxterm). The brackets labeled A, B, C, and D indicate the regions where these variables are *true*. For example, $C = 0$ in all the cells in the top half of the map, and $C = 1$ in all the cells in the bottom half. Figure 3–2(b) shows the binary value assignments to each of the rows and columns of the K-map. We can now insert any function of four variables into the map by placing the functional values (1 and 0) in the appropriate cells. For example, Figure 3–2(c) shows the K-map representation of the function $f = \overline{ABCD} + ABCD$.

68 Logic Design Principles and Devices Chap. 3

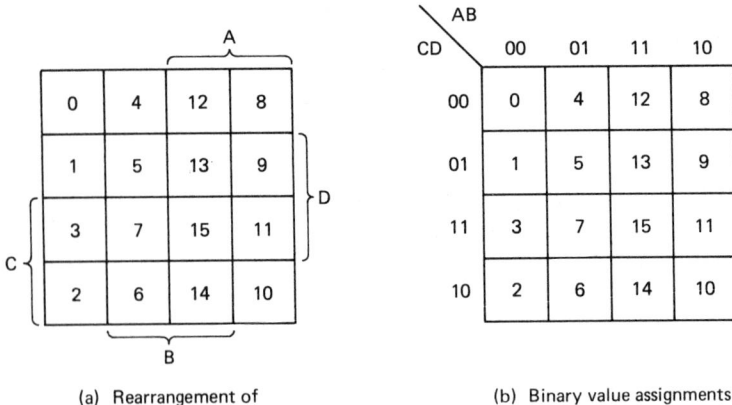

(a) Rearrangement of truth table

(b) Binary value assignments and minterm (maxterm) numbers

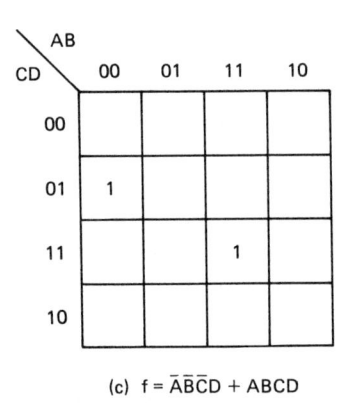

(c) $f = \overline{A}\overline{B}CD + ABCD$

Figure 3–2 Four-variable K-map

To understand how minimization is accomplished with K-maps, let us consider the following procedure.

Definition 3.3. Two cells are said to be **adjacent** if their corresponding binary combinations differ by only one bit.

In Figure 3–2(b), cell $(11)_{10}$ (corresponding to binary 1011) and cell $(15)_{10}$ (corresponding to binary 1111) are adjacent since their binary combinations differ by only one bit. Cell 9 (1001) is adjacent to cell 11 but not to cell 15, since cells 9 and 15 differ by two bits. Note that the adjacency property carries through the K-map boundaries: Cells 0, 1, 3, and 2 are adjacent to cells 8, 9, 11, and 10, respectively, and cells 0, 4, 12, and 8 are adjacent to cells 2, 6, 14, and 10, respectively. Based on the adjacency property, we can draw the following conclusion: *Every n-variable minterm (maxterm) has n other minterms (maxterms) adjacent to it.*

Definition 3.4. A set of 2^m cells, each one of them being adjacent to m cells in the set, is called a **cover**.

Sec. 3.4   Simplification of Boolean Functions

Consider, for example, four variables ($n = 4$). If the cover contains only a single cell ($m = 4$), all four variables define it; that is, the cover corresponds to a minterm or a maxterm. If the cover contains two cells ($m = 2$), they are adjacent by definition. Thus, since cells 11 and 15 are adjacent, we can OR their corresponding minterms ($A\bar{B}CD$ and $ABCD$, respectively) to obtain the product term ACD. Hence grouping two adjacent four-variable cells eliminates one variable, resulting in a product term with one less literal. In the context of a four-variable map, consider the implications of m being 3 and 4; you will reach the following general conclusion: *With n variables, each cover of 2^m cells can be expressed by a product term (a sum term) containing* (n − m) *literals.*

Since the grouping of cells under covers implies a reduction in the number of literals, we can conclude that any Boolean function can be expressed by summing (ORing) the products corresponding to the covers required to cover all the cells for which the function has a value of 1. (Of course, any Boolean function can also be expressed by multiplying—ANDing—the sums corresponding to the covers required to cover all the cells for which the function has a value of 0.) Therefore, to *minimize* a Boolean function, all that we have to do is group as many 1 (or 0) cells as possible under each cover and try to obtain as few covers as possible.

Example 3.2

Consider the minimization of $f(A, B, C, D) = \Sigma m(2, 3, 4, 7, 10, 11, 12, 15)$. Its K-map and the resulting covers are shown in Figure 3–3. Thus the minimal expression for f is

$$f = B\overline{CD} + \bar{B}C + CD$$

In the minimization process, we can take advantage of don't-care combinations (see Section 3.3). To illustrate this, recall the seven-segment display design problem considered in Section 3.3. The K-map in Figure 3–4 shows the function corresponding to segment d, with the input don't-care combinations (corresponding to decimals 10 through 15) marked by X's. Figure 3–4 also shows the minimal Boolean function for segment d. Compare this expression to the one that would have been obtained had we not used the don't-cares.

The K-map can be extended to five and six variables. Beyond that, the usefulness of the K-map approach to simplifying Boolean functions is greatly diminished. How-

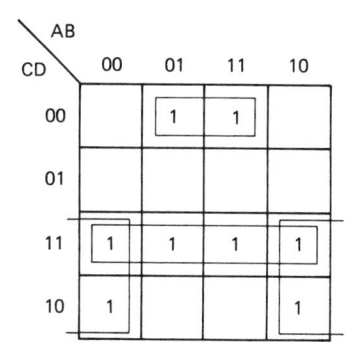

Figure 3–3 K-map for Example 3.2

$$d = C\overline{D} + \overline{B}C + \overline{B}\overline{D} + B\overline{C}D$$

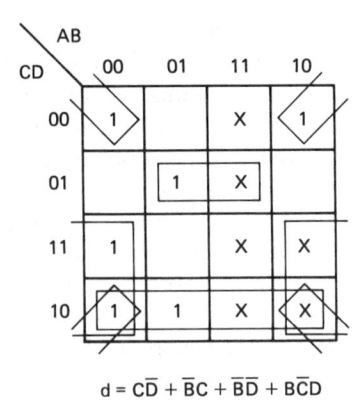

Figure 3-4 Segment d minimization using don't-cares

ever, other methods are available to handle the minimization of Boolean functions. Although these methods do not employ a graphical representation, they can be converted to computer algorithms to facilitate the minimization Boolean functions of any number of variables [see Langholz, Kandel, & Mott (1988)].

3.5 SEQUENTIAL LOGIC CIRCUITS

A **combinational logic circuit** is one whose outputs at any instant of time are functions only of the inputs at that time. In practice, this statement is not absolutely true because every physical device introduces a **propagation time delay,** albeit small, in the signal path between its inputs and outputs. Therefore, in a combinational logic circuit, the output at time t is actually a function of the inputs at time $t - t_{pd}$, where t_{pd} denotes the signal propagation time delay. The circuit we designed in Section 3.3 is a combinational circuit.

By contrast, a **sequential logic circuit** is one whose outputs at time t are functions not only of the inputs at time t but also of the inputs' past history. Therefore, a sequential circuit is characterized by having **memory.** A model of a sequential logic circuit is shown in Figure 3-5. The circuit consists of a combinational circuit and a memory. The memory outputs are fed back into the combinational part and enable the sequential circuit to operate not only as a function of the present inputs but also as a function of past inputs. The memory part is usually implemented with flip-flops (see Section 3.7), which serve as information storage devices.

The timing of the signals in the circuit determines two types of sequential circuits: synchronous and asynchronous. In a **synchronous** sequential circuit, the operation of the circuit is synchronized with the occurrence of clock pulses generated by a **clock pulse generator,** as shown in Figure 3-5. The clock pulses are input to the memory devices so that they change state only in response to the arrival of a pulse and only once for each pulse occurrence. Consequently, the outputs of a synchronous circuit can change even though its inputs remain unchanged.

By contrast, the operation of an **asynchronous** sequential circuit depends *only* on the order in which the inputs change and can be affected at any instant of time. Since we use unclocked memory devices (also called latches), the correct operation

Sec. 3.5 Sequential Logic Circuits

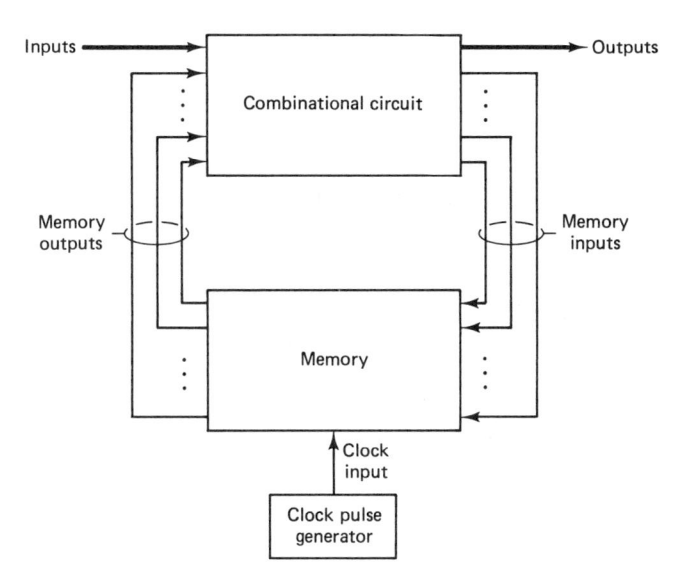

Figure 3-5 Model of a sequential logic circuit

of an asynchronous circuit depends critically on the timing of the inputs. In particular, the circuit must have a chance to settle down (become stable) from the last input change; otherwise, the circuit may operate improperly.

We will restrict our discussion to synchronous sequential circuits. For a detailed discussion of sequential circuits in general, and asynchronous circuits in particular, see Langholz et al. (1988).

The operation of a sequential circuit is often best described by using a **state diagram** or a **state table.** The state diagram and state table are completely equivalent in that they fully characterize the functions of the circuit. The state diagram represents the functions of the circuit graphically, and the state table is well suited for the systematic design of the circuit. States are represented in the state diagram by circles (vertices) labeled by (state) names. The vertices are connected by directed branches that indicate the transitions from one state to another. Each branch is labeled with the input values that cause the transition and the corresponding output values.

To illustrate the construction of a state diagram, consider the problem of binary serial addition. To add two binary numbers serially, we start with the least significant pair of bits and then successively add two corresponding bits at a time (see Section 2.3). At any stage, the addition of a pair of bits is dependent on whether or not a carry was generated from the previous stage **(carry-in)** and may result in a generated carry **(carry-out).** Figure 3–6(a) shows the truth table of a 2-bit binary adder. It has two inputs, I_1 and I_2, and two outputs, *sum* and *carry*. We show only the carry-out signal but take the carry-in into consideration in the state diagram in Figure 3–6(b).

The state diagram consists of two states, labeled Q_1 and Q_2, and depicts the various possible transitions between them. Each branch is labeled using the format I_1; I_2/*sum*;*carry* (the semicolons do not appear in the figure). Some of the branches carry multiple labels indicating that more than one input condition may cause a transition.

I_1	I_2	Sum	Carry
0	0	0	0
0	1	1	0
1	0	1	0
1	1	0	1

(a) 2-bit binary addition table

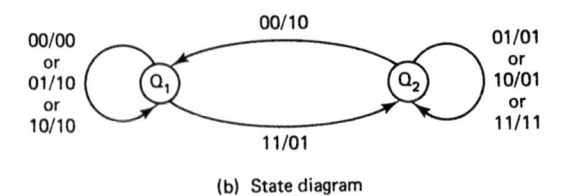

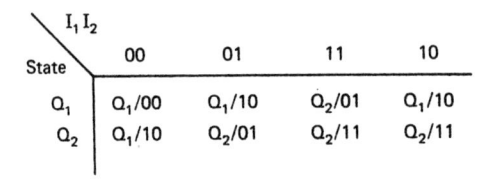

(b) State diagram

State \ $I_1 I_2$	00	01	11	10
Q_1	$Q_1/00$	$Q_1/10$	$Q_2/01$	$Q_1/10$
Q_2	$Q_1/10$	$Q_2/01$	$Q_2/11$	$Q_2/11$

(c) State table

Figure 3–6 Binary serial adder

Let us assume that carry-in is 0 and that the circuit is in state Q_1. If $I_1 I_2$ is either 00, 01, or 10, carry-out is 0 and the transition is from Q_1 to itself. If, however, $I_1 I_2 = 11$, carry-out = 1 and a transition from Q_1 to Q_2 takes place. Therefore, Q_1 can be designated the "carry = 0" state, and Q_2 is the "carry = 1" state. When the circuit is in state Q_2 (implying that carry-in = 1), if $I_1 I_2$ is either 01, 10, or 11, carry-out is 1 and Q_2 makes a transition to itself. If $I_1 I_2 = 00$, adding carry-in = 1 to the inputs results in a carry-out = 0, and Q_2 makes a transition to Q_1.

The process described by the state diagram can be reformulated in tabular form. Figure 3–6(c) shows the state table of the binary serial adder and is self-explanatory.

3.6 COMBINATIONAL LOGIC COMPONENTS

Integrated circuit (IC) technology has advanced rapidly in recent years, and digital devices can now be manufactured to provide higher speeds, lower power consumption, smaller size, and lower cost than ever before. The computer system designer has a wealth of building blocks from which to choose, from simple gates through single-chip microprocessors.

In an integrated circuit, all components are placed on a small, thin silicon semiconductor sheet. Referred to as a **chip,** the circuit is integrated because the components and wiring are all an integral part of the chip and cannot be separated from each other. The different sizes of integration of IC chips are usually defined in

Sec. 3.6 Combinational Logic Components

terms of the number of gates that they contain. Customarily, IC chips are classified in one of four categories:

1. A **small-scale integration (SSI)** device contains fewer than 10 gates. These ICs usually contain several gates or flip-flops in one package.
2. A **medium-scale integration (MSI)** device contains 10 to 100 gates. These ICs provide elementary logic functions such as registers, counters, and decoders.
3. A **large-scale integration (LSI)** device contains 100 to 10,000 gates. Examples of LSI ICs are large memories, microprocessors, and calculator chips.
4. A **very large scale integration (VLSI)** device contains more than 10,000 gates. In fact, with the technologies available today, a piece of silicon of about 5 millimeters square can contain over 100,000 gates. LSI is now giving way to VLSI in many phases of digital design, including large memories and microcomputing devices.

Standard Gates

Figure 3-7 shows some commonly used standard logic gates. The graphic symbols, referred to as **distinctive-shape symbols,** correspond to ANSI/IEEE Standard No. 91-1973. Recently, however, a new standard of graphic symbols for logic functions has emerged (ANSI/IEEE Standard No. 91-1984). The new standard is a very powerful symbolic language to describe the relationship between each input and each output of a digital circuit, without showing the internal construction of the circuit explicitly. Since the new standard is fairly complex, we use the distinctive-shape symbols throughout the book and provide a brief overview of the new standard in the appendix.

In Figure 3-7, the small circle at the output of a gate indicates a complement (NOT) operation. The NOT gate itself is often called an **inverter** since it inverts (complements) the binary signal at its input. By contrast, the transfer gate does not operate on the input variable and produces at the output the same value of the input. The transfer gate is used mostly as a buffer in digital circuits to increase the fan-out of a signal source.

In Figure 3-7, except for the single input gates, all the other gates have two inputs. However, since the binary operators AND, OR, XOR, equivalence, NAND, and NOR can be extended to multiple variables, the corresponding gates can also be extended to multiple inputs. The only limiting factor is technological and is dictated by the IC package pin-count constraints. As far as the graphic symbols are concerned, we modify each simply by adding the appropriate number of extra input lines.

If the outputs of two or more gates are directly connected together, the operation of the circuit may be indeterminate. There are, however, numerous applications that require two or more outputs of gates (or devices) to be tied together on a common line called a **bus.** One type of logic used to implement bus connections is called a **tristate** logic. Two of the states are the logic levels 0 and 1, and the third state is the condition of disconnecting the output leads from the gate. Thus tristate gates can be used to multiplex a number of signals.

Tristate logic gates are fabricated with a tristate output state and include an

Function	Graphic Symbol	Truth Table
AND	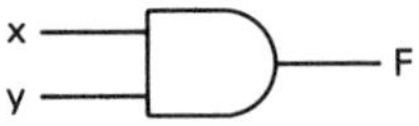 x, y → F	x y | F 0 0 | 0 0 1 | 0 1 0 | 0 1 1 | 1
OR	 x, y → F	x y | F 0 0 | 0 0 1 | 1 1 0 | 1 1 1 | 1
Inverter (NOT)	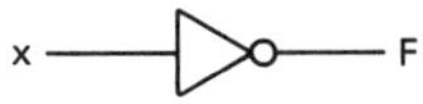 x → F	x | F 0 | 1 1 | 0
Buffer (Transfer)	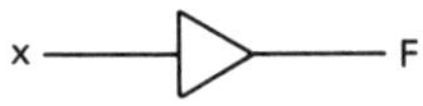 x → F	x | F 0 | 0 1 | 1
NAND (Not AND)	 x, y → F	x y | F 0 0 | 1 0 1 | 1 1 0 | 1 1 1 | 0
NOR (Not OR)	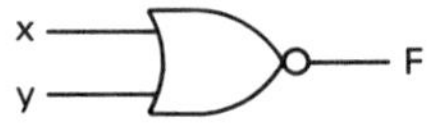 x, y → F	x y | F 0 0 | 1 0 1 | 0 1 0 | 0 1 1 | 0
Exclusive OR (XOR)	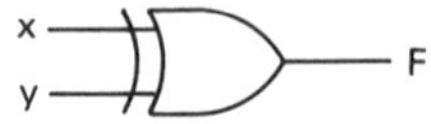 x, y → F	x y | F 0 0 | 0 0 1 | 1 1 0 | 1 1 1 | 0
Equivalence (Exclusive NOR)	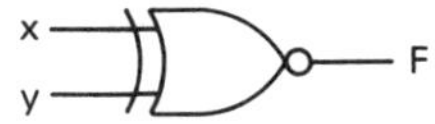 x, y → F	x y | F 0 0 | 1 0 1 | 0 1 0 | 0 1 1 | 1

Figure 3-7 Standard digital logic gates

additional control (or enable) input line. When the control line is in one logic state, say 1, the gate functions normally. But when the control line is in the other logic state, the output is, in effect, disconnected from the gate.

Sec. 3.6 Combinational Logic Components

MSI and LSI Combinational Devices

Decoder. A **decoder** is a combinational circuit that detects the occurrence of discrete binary patterns at its inputs and produces a *unique* output corresponding to each of the detected codes. If there are n input variables, the decoder will have up to 2^n outputs. To produce a unique, mutually exclusive output for each of the possible input combinations, each of the outputs must correspond to an input minterm (or maxterm). Figure 3–8 shows an example of a 2 × 4 decoder.

Encoder. While the decoder uniquely identifies (decodes) any particular input code, the opposite function, called **encoding,** is performed by the **encoder.** Figure 3–9 shows a block diagram of an encoder having k input lines and n output lines. Only one input can be activated at any given time, and the encoder produces a unique n-bit output code depending on that input.

An example of an octal-to-binary (8 × 3) encoder is shown in Figure 3–10. Note that if, for one reason or another, the assumption that only one input is activated at any given time does not hold, the encoder produces a "garbage" code. This situation can be circumvented if we assign priorities to the inputs, resulting in a **priority encoder.** An example of a priority assignment scheme is one that assigns higher priority to an input with a higher subscript. Hence, in an 8 × 3 encoder, I_7 will have the highest priority and I_0 the lowest.

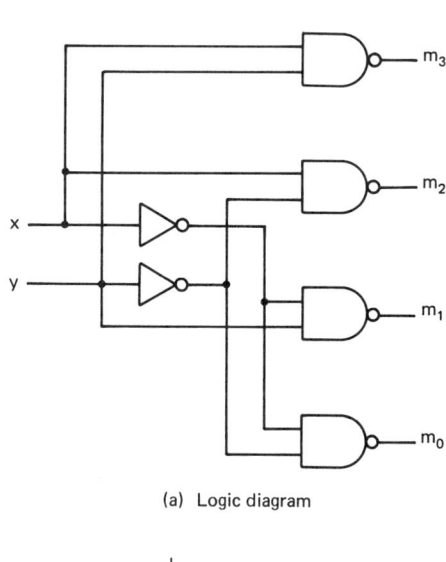

(a) Logic diagram

x	y	m_0	m_1	m_2	m_3
0	0	0	1	1	1
0	1	1	0	1	1
1	0	1	1	0	1
1	1	1	1	1	0

(b) Truth table

Figure 3–8 2 × 4 decoder

Figure 3-9 Encoder

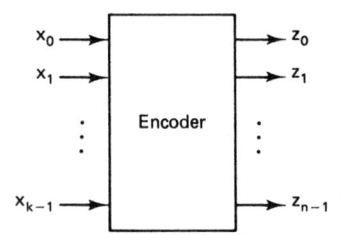

Figure 3-9 Encoder

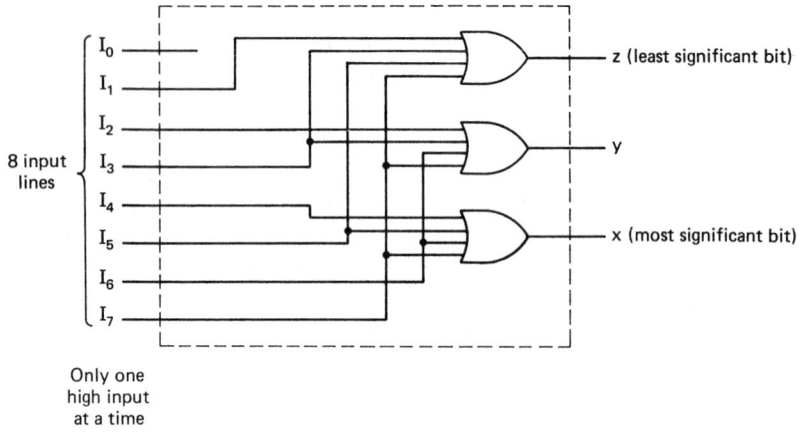

(a) Logic diagram

I_0	I_1	I_2	I_3	I_4	I_5	I_6	I_7	x	y	z
1	0	0	0	0	0	0	0	0	0	0
0	1	0	0	0	0	0	0	0	0	1
0	0	1	0	0	0	0	0	0	1	0
0	0	0	1	0	0	0	0	0	1	1
0	0	0	0	1	0	0	0	1	0	0
0	0	0	0	0	1	0	0	1	0	1
0	0	0	0	0	0	1	0	1	1	0
0	0	0	0	0	0	0	1	1	1	1

Other input not allowed

(b) Truth table

Figure 3-10 Octal-to-binary encoder

Multiplexer. A **multiplexer (MUX)** (or **data selector**) is a logic circuit that selects binary information from one of 2^n input lines and transfers it to a single output line. To select which input line will be routed to the output, the multiplexer has *n* **selection** (control) **lines.** The size of the multiplexer is therefore specified by the number of inputs, which in turn implies the number of control lines. Thus the multiplexer is a $2^n \times 1$ device.

Figure 3-11 shows an example of a 4 × 1 multiplexer. Part (a) depicts the

Sec. 3.6   Combinational Logic Components   77

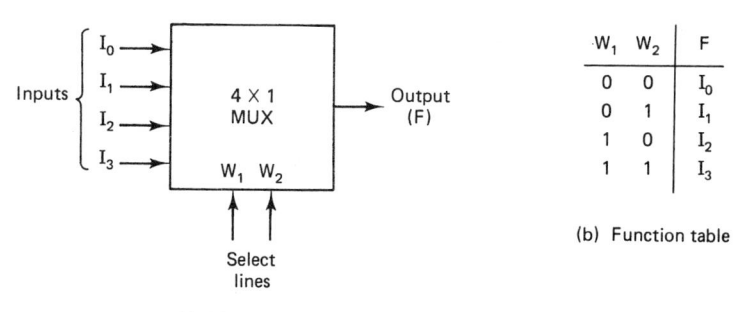

(a) Block diagram

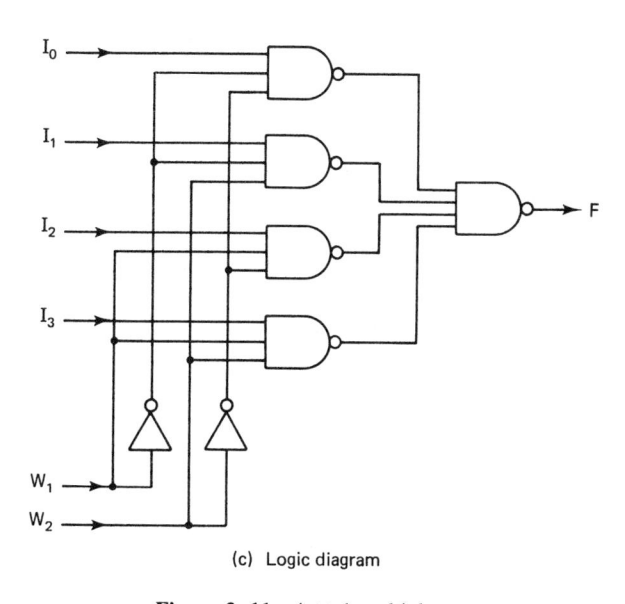

(b) Function table

W_1	W_2	F
0	0	I_0
0	1	I_1
1	0	I_2
1	1	I_3

(c) Logic diagram

Figure 3–11   4 × 1 multiplexer

multiplexer block diagram, and parts (b) and (c) show its functional table and an implementation, respectively. The two selection lines, W_1 and W_2, determine which input will have a direct path to the output. Referring to Figure 3–11(b), it is clear that

$$F = \sum_{i=0}^{3} m_i I_i$$

where each m_i is the minterm corresponding to the selection variables. In general, we can write the multiplexer logic function as

$$F = \sum_{i=0}^{2^n-1} m_i I_i$$

Multiplexers have numerous and varied applications, including data selection, data routing, operation selection, parallel-to-serial conversion, and waveform generation. Multiplexers are also very useful for implementing logic functions. In fact, *any* logic function of n variables can be implemented using a $2^n \times 1$ multiplexer, as illustrated in the following example.

Example 3.3

Consider the three-variable function F defined by the truth table in Figure 3–12. The table can be rearranged, as shown, by factoring out the variables x_1 and x_2. Note that for each evaluation of x_1 and x_2, the output F corresponds to one of four terms: 0, 1, x_3, or $\bar{x}_3$. Using these terms as inputs to a 4×1 multiplexer, with x_1 and x_2 as the two selection variables, the output of the multiplexer will correspond to the function F.

Usually, multiplexers have an additional **enable (E)** input that controls (enables or disables) the operation of the unit. The enable input can be used to connect two or more multiplexers to obtain a multiplexer with a larger number of inputs. An example of such a connection is shown in Figure 3–13(a), where two 4×1 multiplexers are connected to form an 8×1 multiplexer. In this configuration, the enable control line acts like an additional selection line. When enable = 0, the top multiplexer is enabled and the bottom one disabled. As the bit combinations of EW_1W_0 range from 000 to 011, one of the inputs from the top multiplexer is selected. When enable = 1, the bottom multiplexer is enabled and the top one disabled. As the bit combinations of EW_1W_0 range from 100 to 111, one of the inputs of the bottom multiplexer is selected. Accordingly, we label these inputs as I_4, I_5, I_6, and I_7.

Some IC chips enclose two or more multiplexers and therefore have multiple

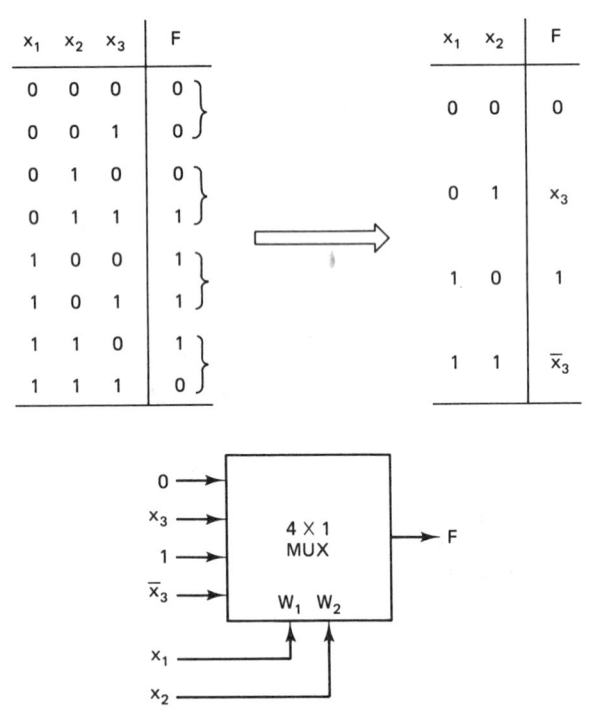

Figure 3–12 Multiplexer implementation of a logic function

Sec. 3.6   Combinational Logic Components   79

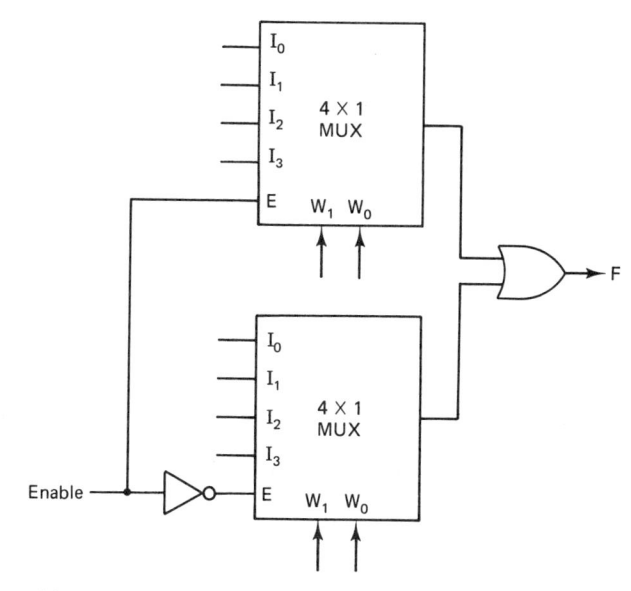

(a) Two 4 × 1 multiplexers connected to form an 8 × 1 multiplexer

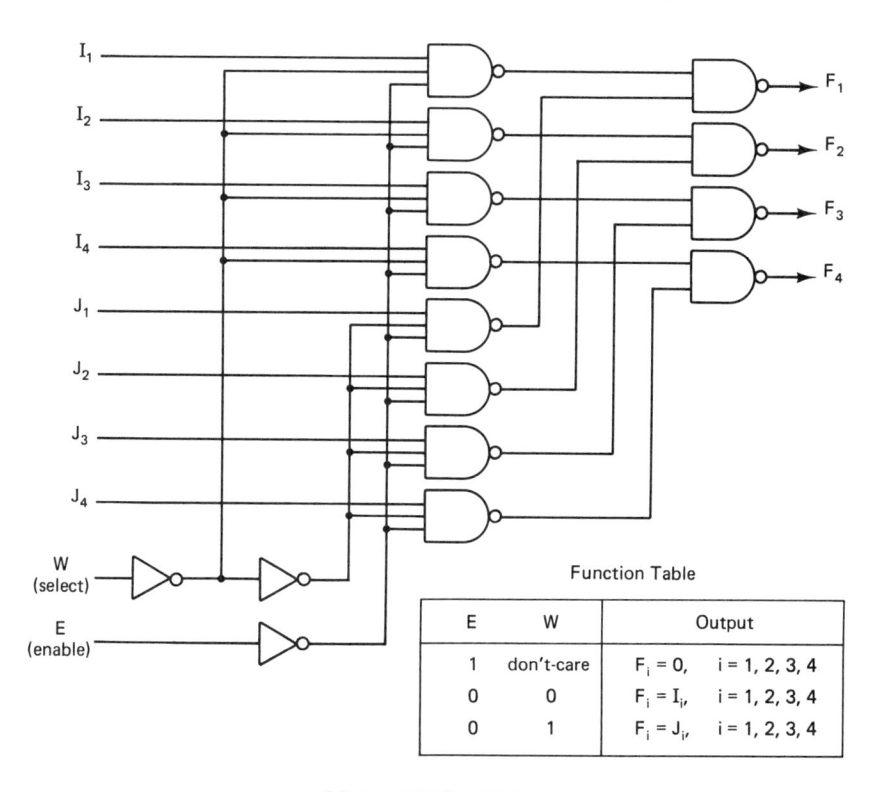

E	W	Output	
1	don't-care	$F_i = 0,$	$i = 1, 2, 3, 4$
0	0	$F_i = I_i,$	$i = 1, 2, 3, 4$
0	1	$F_i = J_i,$	$i = 1, 2, 3, 4$

(b) Quad 2 × 1 multiplexer

Figure 3-13 Multiplexers with enable input

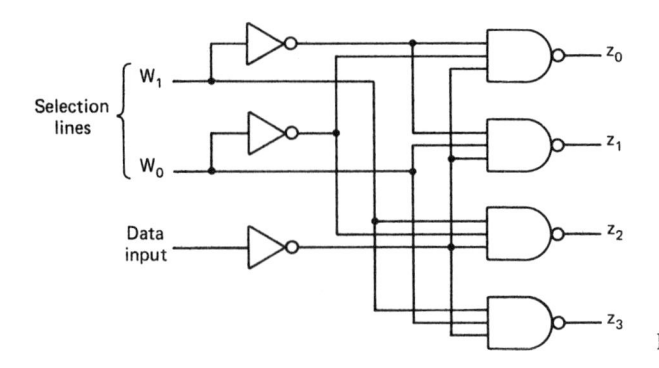

Figure 3-14 1 × 4 demultiplexer

outputs. Figure 3-13(b) shows the circuit logic diagram for four 2 × 1 multiplexers (a quad 2 × 1 MUX) enclosed within one IC package. This unit is used to select one of two input channels. That is, when $E = 0$, F_i can be selected to be equal to either I_i or J_i ($i = 1, 2, 3, 4$) according to whether W is 0 or 1, respectively. If $E = 1$, the multiplexers are disabled.

Demultiplexer. A multiplexer takes several inputs and transmits one of them to the output. A **demultiplexer** (or **data distributor**) performs the reverse operation: It takes a single input and distributes it over several outputs. An example of a 1 × 4 demultiplexer is shown in Figure 3-14.

Demultiplexers are used in many applications, such as routing a clock signal to various destinations. Also, multiplexing and demultiplexing are often used together in systems where digital data are transmitted serially over relatively long distances (see Chapter 12).

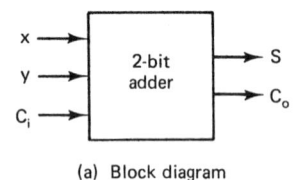

(a) Block diagram

x	y	C_i	S	C_o
0	0	0	0	0
0	0	1	1	0
0	1	0	1	0
0	1	1	0	1
1	0	0	1	0
1	0	1	0	1
1	1	0	0	1
1	1	1	1	1

$$S = x \oplus y \oplus C_i$$
$$C_o = xy + C_i(x + y)$$

(b) Truth table

Figure 3-15 Two-bit binary adder

Sec. 3.6 Combinational Logic Components

Figure 3–16 Two-bit binary subtractor

(a) Block diagram

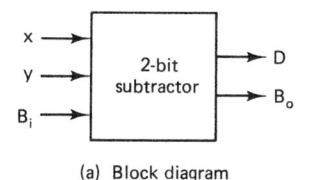

x	y	B_i	D	B_o
0	0	0	0	0
0	0	1	1	1
0	1	0	1	1
0	1	1	0	1
1	0	0	1	0
1	0	1	0	0
1	1	0	0	0
1	1	1	1	1

$D = x \oplus y \oplus B_i$
$B_o = \bar{x}y + B_i(\bar{x} + y)$

(b) Truth table

Adder/Subtractor. A block diagram of a 2-bit **parallel binary adder** is shown in Figure 3–15(a). The three inputs x, y, and C_i represent the two bits to be added and the carry from a previous, lower significant stage, respectively. The two outputs represent the sum (S) and the resulting carry (C_o). Figure 3–15(b) gives the truth table of the adder and the Boolean expressions for S and C_o.

Figure 3–16(a) shows a block diagram of a 2-bit **parallel binary subtractor.** The three inputs x, y, and B_i represent the minuend, subtrahend, and a previous borrow, respectively. The two outputs, D and B_o, designate the difference and output borrow, respectively. Figure 3–16(b) shows the truth table of the subtractor and the Boolean expressions for D and B_o.

We can construct an *n*-bit parallel binary adder (subtractor) by cascading *n* 2-bit binary adders (subtractors). For example, Figure 3–17 shows a cascade connection of four 2-bit binary adders, resulting in a 4-bit parallel binary adder. The two binary numbers are represented by the bits $x_3x_2x_1x_0$ and $y_3y_2y_1y_0$, where x_3 and y_3 are the most significant bits. The sum is represented by the $S_3S_2S_1S_0$ with S_3 being the

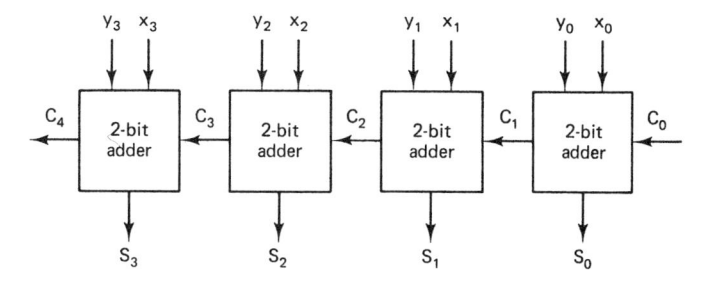

Figure 3–17 Four-bit parallel binary adder

3.7 SEQUENTIAL LOGIC COMPONENTS

Flip-Flops

A **flip-flop (FF)** is a digital device capable of storing a single bit. It has two stable states and can stay in either one indefinitely until directed by an input signal to change state. Usually, a flip-flop has two complementary outputs, designated Q and $\overline{Q}$; when $Q = 1$, the flip-flop is *set* and if $Q = 0$, the flip-flop is *reset*. Thus the two possible operating states of a flip-flop are (1) $Q = 0$, $\overline{Q} = 1$, and (2) $Q = 1$, $\overline{Q} = 0$.

A flip-flop has a control (triggering) input, called the **clock (C)** input, that enables the switchings between the two states to be synchronized with the occurrence of a clock pulse. The flip-flop can change state either at the *positive* edge or at the *negative* edge of a clock pulse. This synchronization technique is referred to as **edge-triggering.** In the following sections we introduce the most common types of flip-flops: the SR, D, JK, and T flip-flops.

SR Flip-Flop. The graphic symbol of an SR flip-flop is shown in Figure 3–18(a). The triangle, called a **dynamic indicator,** indicates that the device responds only to an input clock (C) transition from low (binary 0) to high (binary 1). Appending a small circle to the C input, as in Figure 3–18(b), indicates that the flip-flop responds to an input clock transition from high to low. In either case, the flip-flop is edge-triggered, meaning that the flip-flop is sensitive to its S and R input signals either at the positive edge or at the negative edge of the clock pulse. Hence parts (a) and (b) respectively depict the graphic symbols of a positive and a negative edge-triggered SR flip-flop.

Figure 3–19 provides the operational details of a positive edge-triggered SR flip-flop. In the **characteristics table** in part (a), the Q column denotes the **present**

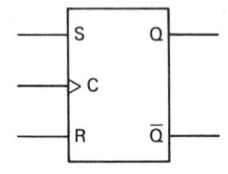

(a) Positive edge-triggered flip-flop

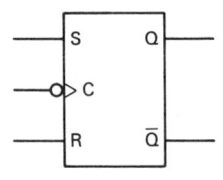

(b) Negative edge-triggered flip-flop

Figure 3–18 SR flip-flop graphic symbols

Sec. 3.7   Sequential Logic Components   83

S	R	Q	Q(t + 1)
0	0	0	0
0	0	1	1
0	1	0	0
0	1	1	0
1	0	0	1
1	0	1	1
1	1	0	} indeterminate
1	1	1	

S	R	Q(t + 1)
0	0	Q(t)
0	1	0
1	0	1
1	1	} indeterminate

Q(t)	Q(t + 1)	S	R
0	0	0	X
0	1	1	0
1	0	0	1
1	1	X	0

(a) Characteristic table   (b) Reduced characteristic table   (c) Excitation table

Figure 3–19   *SR* flip-flop operation

state of the flip-flop and the $Q(t + 1)$ column designates its **next state.** The S, R, and Q values are assumed present *prior* to the application of the next clock pulse, and the next state is attained on the leading edge of the next clock pulse. Since the clock pulse input is implicit to the operation of the flip-flop, there is no need to provide a special column for C. The operation of the flip-flop is *triggered* (enabled) only when C makes a transition from 0 to 1. Consequently, the S and R inputs are referred to as **synchronous inputs** because data on these inputs can be transferred to the flip-flop's outputs only on the triggering edge of the clock pulse. Note, however, that the next state of the *SR* flip-flop is *indeterminate* when $S = R = 1$ and Q is either 0 or 1. Hence to operate the *SR* flip-flop properly, the S and R inputs must not be 1 simultaneously.

The characteristic table can be reduced to the equivalent table shown in Figure 3–19(b). From either characteristic table we can obtain the **characteristic equation** of the positive edge-triggered *SR* flip-flop:

$$Q(t + 1) = \overline{R}Q + S \qquad (SR = 0)$$

Note that the condition $SR = 0$ is part of the characteristic equation.

To determine how to achieve a transfer between a given present state and a desired next state, we can use the **excitation table** shown in Figure 3–19(c). Given the present state $Q(t)$ and the desired next state $Q(t + 1)$, the table lists the **excitation values** required at the synchronous inputs *prior* to the application (at time $t + 1$) of the next clock pulse.

D Flip-Flop.   The positive edge-triggered *D* flip-flop, shown in Figure 3–20(a), has a single synchronous input (D) and can be implemented by modifying an *SR* flip-flop as shown in part (b). The remainder of the figure shows the full and reduced characteristic tables and the excitation table of the *D* flip-flop. These can be easily derived by substituting $S = \overline{R}$ into the characteristic table of the *SR* flip-flop [Figure 3–19(a)]. Correspondingly, the characteristic equation of the D flip-flop is given by

$$Q(t + 1) = D$$

The *D* flip-flop is useful when a single bit is to be stored. As seen from Figure 3–20(d), if $D = 0$, the flip-flop resets on the next clock pulse and sets if $D = 1$.

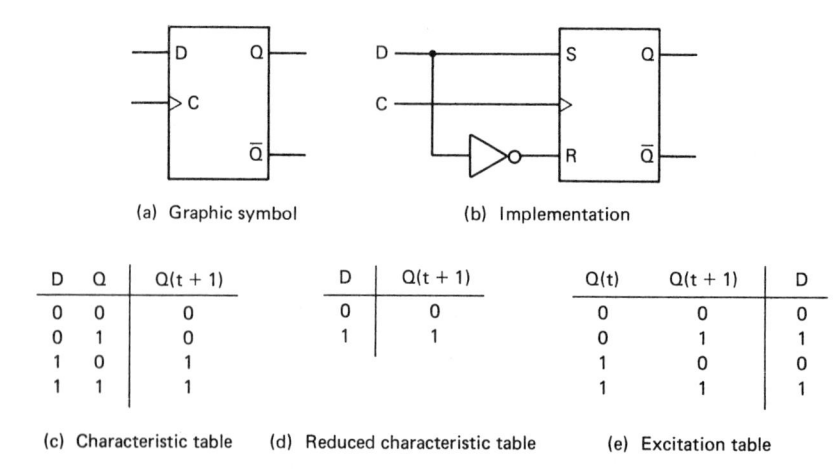

Figure 3–20 D flip-flop

(a) Graphic symbol

(b) Implementation

(c) Characteristic table

D	Q	Q(t + 1)
0	0	0
0	1	0
1	0	1
1	1	1

(d) Reduced characteristic table

D	Q(t + 1)
0	0
1	1

(e) Excitation table

Q(t)	Q(t + 1)	D
0	0	0
0	1	1
1	0	0
1	1	1

Hence, the *D* flip-flop latches onto the data at the *D* input, but only in synchronization with the triggering edge of the clock pulse.

JK Flip-Flop. The positive edge-triggered *JK* flip-flop in Figure 3–21(a) can be implemented by modifying the *SR* flip-flop as shown in part (b). Observing the characteristic table of the *JK* flip-flop [part (c) or (d)], we see that the indeterminate states of the *SR* flip-flop are now defined. In fact, the *JK* flip-flop operates exactly like the *SR* flip-flop as long as *JK* = 0. When *J* = *K* = 1, the flip-flop *complements*

(a) Graphic symbol

(b) Implementation

(c) Characteristic table

J	K	Q	Q(t + 1)
0	0	0	0
0	0	1	1
0	1	0	0
0	1	1	0
1	0	0	1
1	0	1	1
1	1	0	1
1	1	1	0

(d) Reduced characteristic table

J	K	Q(t + 1)
0	0	Q(t)
0	1	0
1	0	1
1	1	$\overline{Q(t)}$

(e) Excitation table

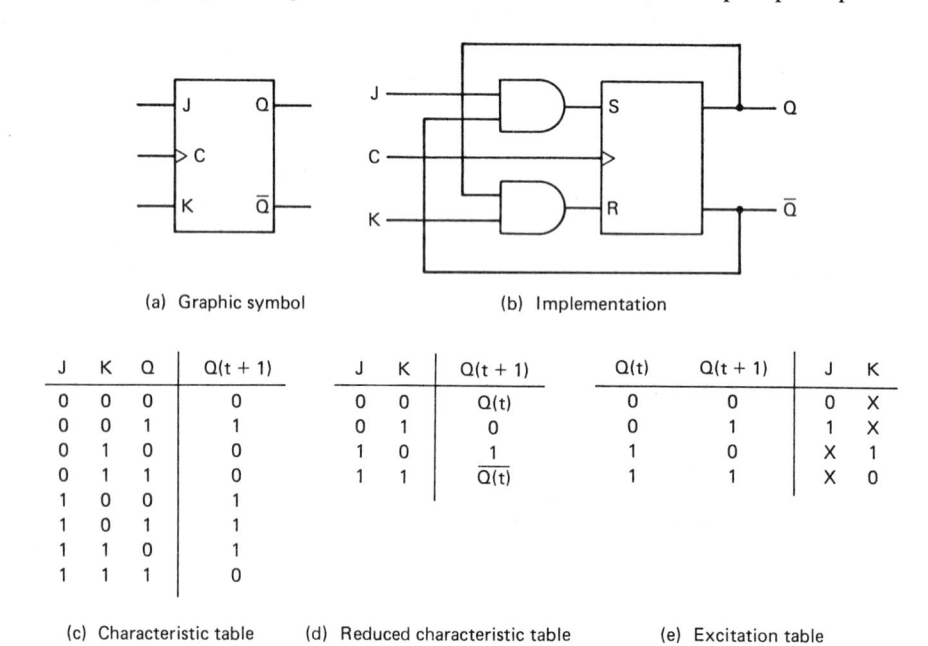

Q(t)	Q(t + 1)	J	K
0	0	0	X
0	1	1	X
1	0	X	1
1	1	X	0

Figure 3–21 *JK* flip-flop

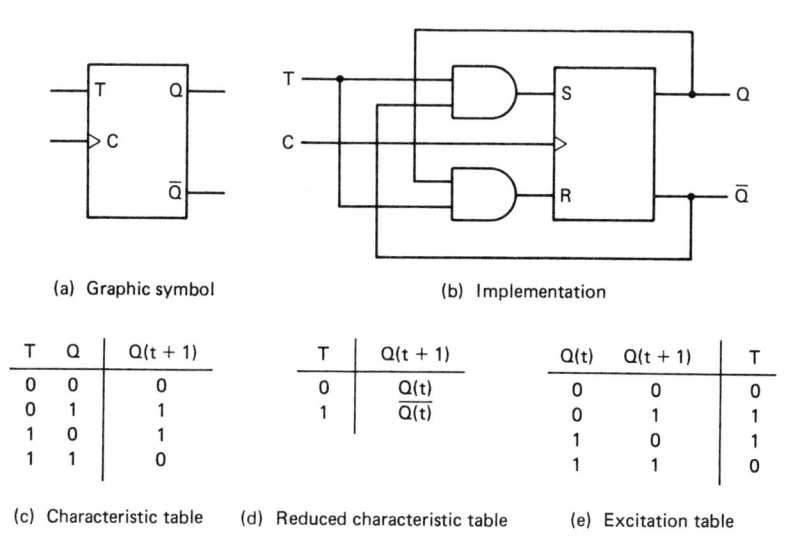

Figure 3-22 T flip-flop

(a) Graphic symbol
(b) Implementation
(c) Characteristic table
(d) Reduced characteristic table
(e) Excitation table

(*toggles*, or changes state) on *every* clock pulse. From the characteristic table we obtain the characteristic equation of the *JK* flip-flop:

$$Q(t+1) = \overline{K}Q + J\overline{Q}$$

Because the *JK* flip-flop outperforms the *SR* flip-flop, the *SR* flip-flop is no longer manufactured as an off-the-shelf device.

T Flip-Flop. The graphic symbol of a positive edge-triggered *T* flip-flop, shown in Figure 3-22(a), can be derived from the *SR* flip-flop as in part (b). (Alternatively, we can connect together the *J* and *K* inputs of a *JK* flip-flop.) From the characteristic table [part (c) or (d)], we see that a *T* flip-flop complements on every clock pulse provided that $T = 1$; hence the designation *T* (for *toggle*) flip-flop. The characteristic equation of the *T* flip-flop is given by

$$Q(t+1) = \overline{T}Q + T\overline{Q}$$
$$= T \oplus Q$$

MSI and LSI Sequential Devices

Registers. A **register** is a digital circuit commonly used to store binary information in the computer. It consists of a collection of binary storage **cells**, each implemented with a flip-flop. The number of cells determines the *length* of the register and therefore the length of the binary word stored in the register. Thus an *n*-bit register contains *n* flip-flops and can store *n* bits. Since *n* bits give rise to 2^n different binary combinations, each of the distinct *n*-tuples stored in an *n*-bit register corresponds to a *distinct state* of the register. Therefore, each register state can be associated with a unique item of information

Two operations, WRITE and READ, are associated with a register. To **write** (or **load**) information into the register, each information bit is input to one of the flip-flops; to **read** the contents of a register, we simply access (sample) the Q outputs of all the flip-flops. Since the READ and WRITE operations are applied to all the cells simultaneously, the register is commonly referred to as a **parallel register.**

Figure 3–23 shows an example of a 3-bit parallel register implemented with positive edge-triggered *SR* flip-flops. The clock pulse (*CP*) input, common to all the flip-flops, controls the loading of new data into the register. Therefore, when the CP input goes from 0 to 1, the information present on the input lines transfers to the flip-flops. For example, if $I_2 = 1$, A_2 will be 1 on the next positive-going transition of *CP*; if $I_2 = 0$, A_2 will be 0 on the next transition of *CP* from 0 to 1. If *CP* is kept 0, the content of the register cannot be changed.

Shift Registers. A **shift register** not only stores but also processes the data stored in it. A shift register consists of flip-flops connected such that the output of one flip-flop feeds the input of the next flip-flop. The clock inputs of all the flip-flops are connected to a common clock pulse source.

Figure 3–24 shows an example of a 4-bit shift register implemented with negative edge-triggered *JK* flip-flops. The flip-flops are cascaded so that the Q output ($\overline{Q}$ output) of each flip-flop is connected to the *J* input (*K* input) of the following flip-flop. The operation of the shift register is controlled by shift pulses through the shift control line. On the negative edge of the shift pulse, each flip-flop will pass the data stored in it to the flip-flop on its right, with FF_1 accepting the data from the input line and FF_4 acting as the output stage.

The shift register in Figure 3–24 is called a **serial-in, serial-out (SISO)** shift register. However, we can also configure a shift register with parallel load and access the information serially or in parallel, or load it serially and access the information

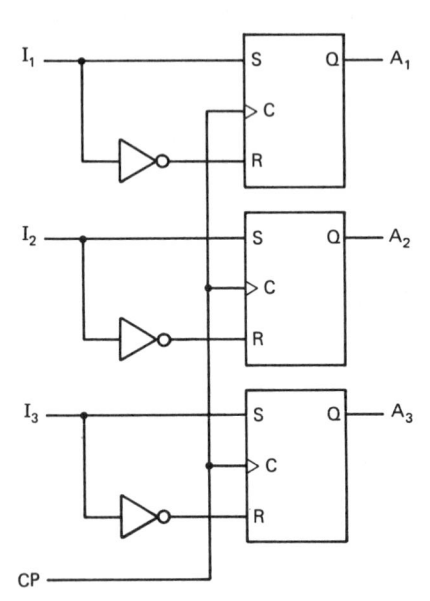

Figure 3–23 Three-bit parallel register

Sec. 3.7　Sequential Logic Components

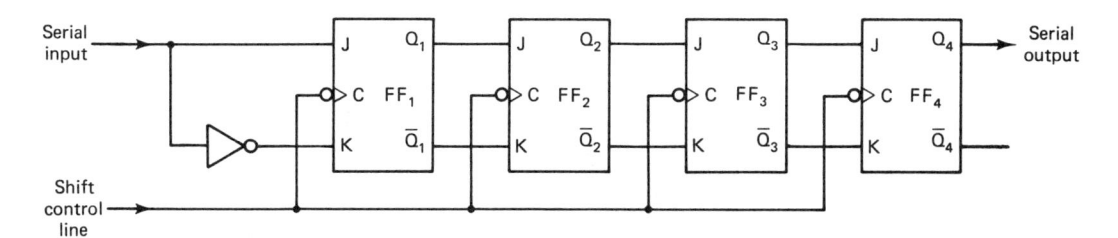

Figure 3-24 Four-bit shift register

in parallel by reading the Q outputs of all the flip-flops simultaneously. Moreover, the shift register can be configured to shift left rather than shift right as depicted in Figure 3-24; in fact, with two shift control lines, the same shift register can shift the data either left or right. It should be noted that any parallel-out register can also operate in a serial-out mode and that any parallel-load register can also operate in a serial-in mode.

It is also clear that the clock input can be used for timing and that "control inputs" can be used to specify the action that is to occur. This separation of timing and action is important in the design of complex systems. For example, Figure 3-25 shows a 4-bit **bidirectional** shift register with parallel load. The data in this shift register can also be input serially and output serially or in parallel.

If we were to connect the output Q_4 of the shift register in Figure 3-24 to the input line of another 4-bit shift register and join their shift control lines, then after four shift pulses, the content of the first register would have been transferred to the second register. But shifting data for the purpose of transferring it to another storage location is only one form of data manipulation. For example, shift registers are also used in fixed-point arithmetic operations. Recalling our discussion in Section 2.3, shifting right by one bit position is equivalent to dividing the content of the shift register by 2, whereas shifting left by one bit position is tantamount to multiplying the content of the shift register by 2.

Counters.　A **counter** is a sequential circuit that follows a prescribed sequence of distinct states under the control of input clock pulses. Consider Figure 3-26(a), which shows the logic diagram of a 4-bit binary counter implemented with negative edge-triggered *JK* flip-flops. The external count pulses are applied to the clock input of the left-hand flip-flop (A_0), and the outputs of this and subsequent flip-flops are each connected to the clock input (*C*) of the following flip-flop. Since the *J* and *K* inputs of all the flip-flops are connected to 1, each flip-flop will toggle (complement, or change state) on the transition from 1 to 0 at its clock input. (Other flip-flop types can be used; all that is required is that they operate in a complementing mode.)

To understand how the counter operates, refer to the timing diagram of Figure 3-26(b) and assume that the counter is cleared (each flip-flop is reset to 0) prior to the application of the count pulses. When the count sequence commences, A_0 complements on the trailing edge of the first input pulse as indicated by the arrow in Figure 3-26(b). Since A_0 makes a transition from 0 to 1, flip-flop A_1 will not change state. Hence the present content of the counter is $A_3A_2A_1A_0 = (0001)_2 = (1)_{10}$,

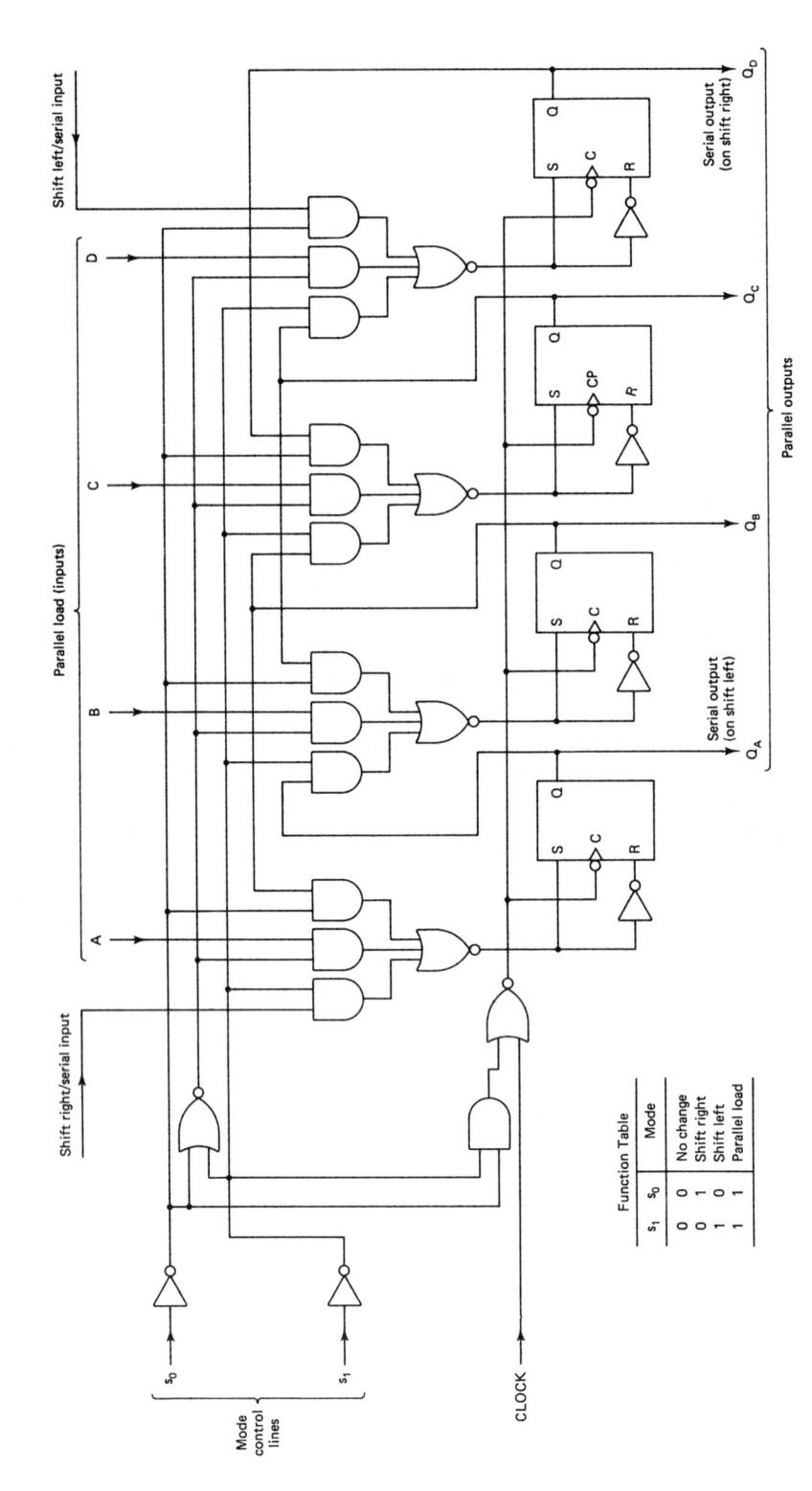

Figure 3-25 Four-bit bidirectional shift register with parallel load

Sec. 3.7 Sequential Logic Components

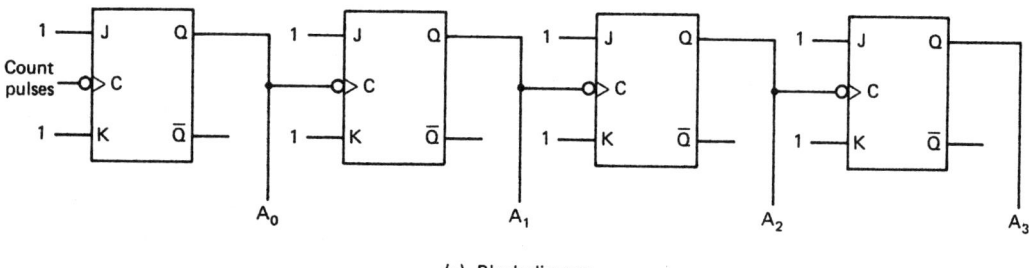

(a) Block diagram

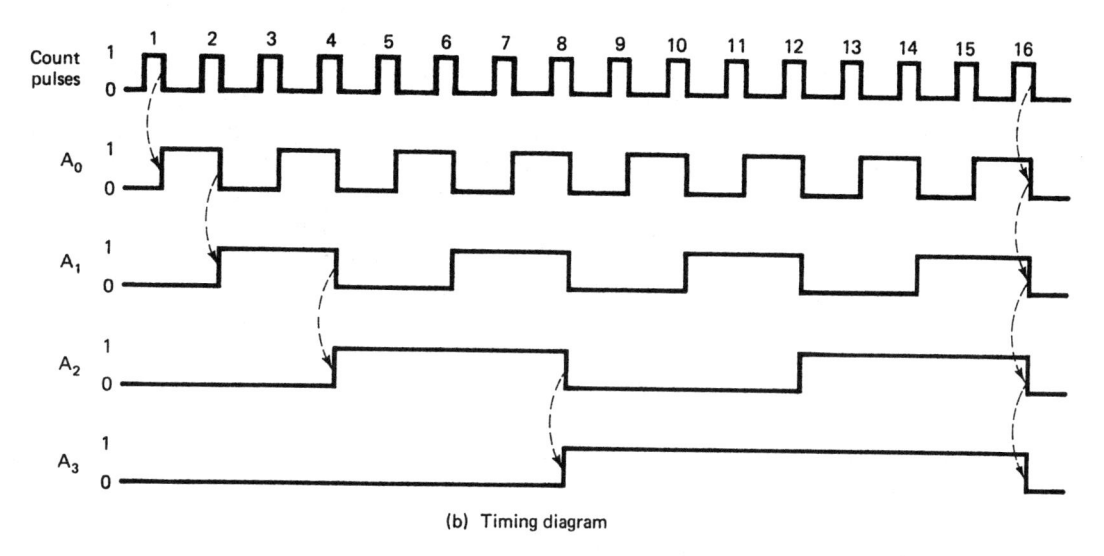

(b) Timing diagram

Figure 3-26 Four-bit binary counter

indicating a count of one pulse. Flip-flop A_0 will complement again on the trailing edge of the second clock pulse. The transition of A_0 from 1 to 0 causes A_1 to change state [as indicated by the arrow in Figure 3-26(b)], and the content of the counter after the second pulse becomes $A_3A_2A_1A_0 = (0010)_2 = (2)_{10}$. This process continues in a similar fashion with the count being incremented by 1 on the application of every input pulse. When 15 pulses have been received, the count is $A_3A_2A_1A_0 = (1111)_2 = (15)_{10}$. On the application of the sixteenth pulse, A_0 is reset, sequentially causing A_1, A_2, and A_3 to reset. Hence the counter is cleared and ready to receive the next train of 16 pulses.

Since the binary counter in Figure 3-26 has a capacity of 4 bits, it is referred to as a **modulo-16 counter.** If we increase the number of flip-flops, the count capacity of the counter will increase correspondingly. In general, to implement a modulo-M binary counter requires $\log_2 M$ flip-flops.

From the timing diagram, we see that the least significant flip-flop A_0 changes state on each count pulse and goes from 1 to 0 on the triggering edge of every second pulse. Therefore, the frequency of the output signal of the least significant flip-flop is exactly half the frequency of the count pulses. Whenever A_0 goes from 1 to 0, A_1

changes state so that A_1 goes from 1 to 0 on the triggering edge of every fourth pulse. The frequency of the output of this flip-flop is therefore exactly one-fourth the frequency of the count pulses. Similarly, A_2 goes from 1 to 0 on the triggering edge of every eighth pulse, or at one-eighth the frequency of the count pulses, and A_3 goes from 1 to 0 on the triggering edge of every sixteenth pulse, or at one-sixteenth the frequency of the count pulses. Hence starting with the least significant flip-flop, *each stage of the counter divides* the input frequency by 2. The output of the last flip-flop in Figure 3–26 divides the frequency of the count pulses by 16. In general, the output from the most significant flip-flop in a modulo-M counter divides the input frequency by M. Therefore, a modulo-M counter is also called a **divide-by-M counter.**

Counters are classified according to the way in which they are clocked. For example, in the binary counter of Figure 3–26, each flip-flop stage following the least significant one is triggered by the output of the previous stage. Thus the count pulse signal *ripples* (propagates) through the counter flip-flops from the least significant flip-flop to the most significant, and the counter is called a **ripple counter.** Furthermore, since the flip-flops are not clocked simultaneously, they do not change state at exactly the same time and therefore they operate asynchronously. Consequently, the ripple count is also called an **asynchronous counter.**

In another counting method, known as **synchronous** counting, all the flip-flops are synchronized (that is, the clock input is common to all the flip-flops) so that they can change state simultaneously. Counters constructed in this way are called **synchronous counters.**

The counter in Figure 3–26 counts *upward* from zero and is therefore called an **up counter.** However, if we access the $\overline{Q}$ outputs of the flip-flops rather than the Q outputs (as we did), the counter will be counting *downward* from some maximum count to zero. That is, the count will be decremented on each count pulse input, resulting in a **down counter.** In fact, with a single control line and an additional logic circuit, the counter can be configured to function as an up-down counter.

3.8 MEMORY DEVICES

Programmable Arrays

Read-Only Memory. A $2^n \times m$ **read-only memory (ROM)** is an LSI circuit chip containing an $n \times 2^n$ decoder connected to an **array** of m OR gates, as shown in the block diagram of Figure 3–27. Each combination of the input variables is called an **address.** With n input variables, the number of distinct addresses is 2^n. Each combination on the output lines is called a **word,** and the number of output lines determines the **word length.** Since there are 2^n distinct addresses, there are 2^n distinct output words. The number of bits ($2^n \times m$) that a ROM contains is referred to as the **capacity** of the ROM and completely specifies it. For example, a 4096-bit ROM may be organized as 2048 words of 2 bits each, meaning that it has 2 output lines and requires 11 input lines to specify $2^{11} = 2048$ words. The same ROM can be organized also as 1024 words of 4 bits each, requiring 4 output lines and 10 input lines, or as 512 words of 8 bits each with 8 outputs and 9 inputs.

Sec. 3.8 Memory Devices

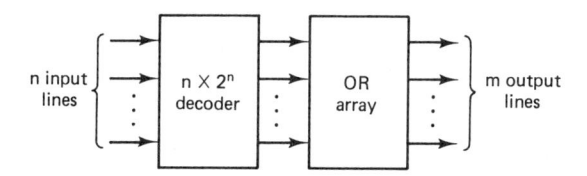

Figure 3-27 Basic ROM structure

All the 2^n outputs of the decoder in Figure 3-27 are connected through **fusible links** to each OR gate; therefore, the number of links is $2^n \times m$. When we specify a truth table for the ROM, the binary information is embedded in the ROM by "blowing" those links that are not part of the required interconnection pattern. The process of opening links is referred to as **programming** of the ROM. Hence we refer to a ROM as a **programmable array** in which the OR array is programmable. Once a ROM has been programmed, the interconnection pattern cannot be changed, and the information content of the ROM can only be read upon application of a given address; hence the term *read-only*. Consequently, the information stored in the ROM will not be lost even when power is turned off or interrupted. A memory device having this feature is called **nonvolatile.**

Three basic types of ROMs are available commercially: mask-programmable ROM, programmable ROM (PROM), and erasable PROM (EPROM). **Mask-programmable ROMs** are custom-made by the device manufacturer to specifications (a truth table) submitted by the customer. The binary information is permanently stored in the ROM at the time of manufacture by a special process called **masking.** But since masking is expensive, mask-programmable ROMs are economically feasible only if large quantities (typically 1000 or more) of the same ROM are produced. For small quantities, it is more economical to use a **programmable ROM (PROM).** PROMS are typically manufactured with all the fusible links present and can be programmed by the user by means of a special device called a **PROM programmer.**

But programming a ROM or a PROM is an irreversible process. Each time the information stored has to be changed, a new device must be produced. In contrast, the third type of ROM, the **erasable PROM (EPROM),** is reprogrammable and enables the user to modify the stored data. EPROMS are programmed with a PROM programmer and are available in two types distinguished by the method used for erasure. In one EPROM type, the data is erased by placing the device under a special ultraviolet light source for some time. In the other EPROM type, called **electrically alterable ROM (EAROM),** the data are erased through the application of special electrical signals.

Programmable Logic Array. The ROM uses a decoder to generate minterms corresponding to input addresses. However, if many input addresses do not occur, using a ROM can be wasteful because not all interconnection patterns are used. In such cases, it is more economical to use another LSI device, called a **programmable logic array (PLA),** shown in block diagram form in Figure 3-28.

A PLA performs the same functions as a ROM but differs from it in that the PLA does not generate all the minterms of the input variables. Rather, the decoder of the ROM is replaced in the PLA by an AND (gate) array that can be programmed to produce only selected product terms. This difference eliminates the inefficient

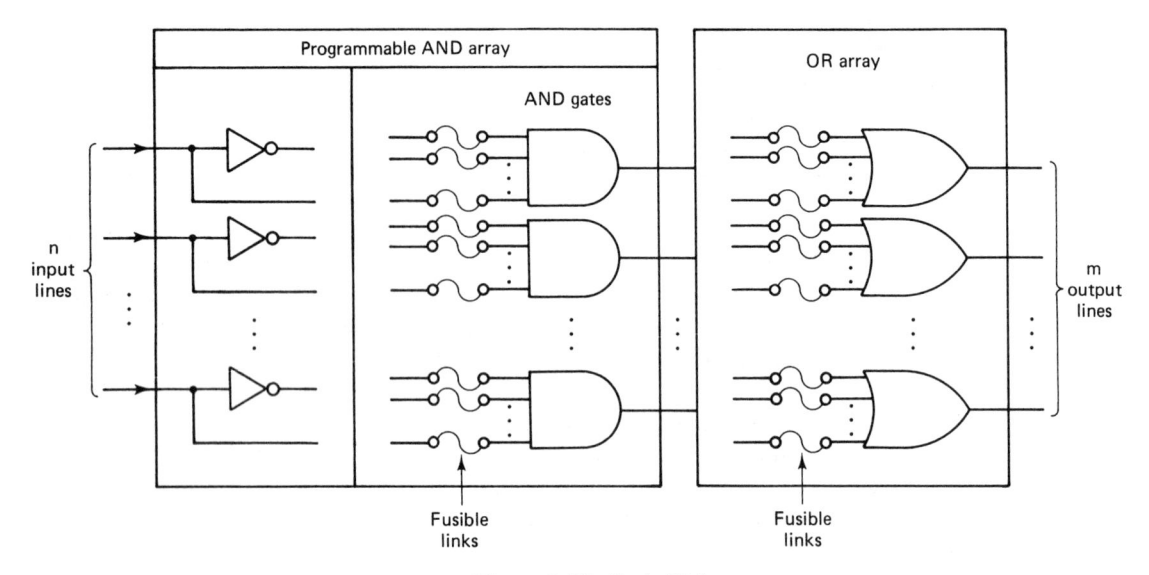

Figure 3-28 Basic PLA structure

storage of unused minterms required in a ROM. The OR array in both devices plays the same basic role: Certain product terms are ORed together.

As shown in Figure 3-28, both the AND and OR arrays of the PLA are programmable. To program the AND array, fusible links are inserted between all the n inputs and their complements and each of the AND gates. To program the OR array, links are also provided between the outputs of the AND gates and each of the OR gates. Hence, if the PLA consists of n inputs, p product terms, and m outputs, it requires p AND gates, m OR gates, and a total of $2np + pm$ fusible links. Some PLAs also come with programmable output inverters to generate either complemented or uncomplemented outputs. In this case, each output line is connected to an inverter having a link placed across it. If we leave the link intact, the inverter is bypassed and the PLA output is uncomplemented; with the link broken, the inverter is enabled and generates the complemented output. This arrangement calls for an additional set of m programmable links.

The size of a PLA is specified by the number of inputs, the number of product terms generated by the AND array, and the number of outputs. Commercially available PLAs typically have 16 inputs, 48 product terms, and 8 outputs, and the outputs may be complemented or uncomplemented. In contrast, a ROM with 16 inputs generates 2^{16} minterms, but if at most 48 product terms are needed, then $2^{16} - 48$ words of the ROM would be unused. This inefficiency points out one of the major drawbacks to ROM implementation. Typically, a PLA can accommodate many more input variables than a ROM without stretching the storage capacity of the chip. In contrast, the capacity of a ROM *doubles* with the addition of each new input variable.

There are two basic types of PLAs: **mask-programmable PLA** and **field-programmable PLA (FPLA)**. With a mask-programmable PLA, the customer submits a PLA program table describing the output functions to be implemented, and

Sec. 3.8 Memory Devices

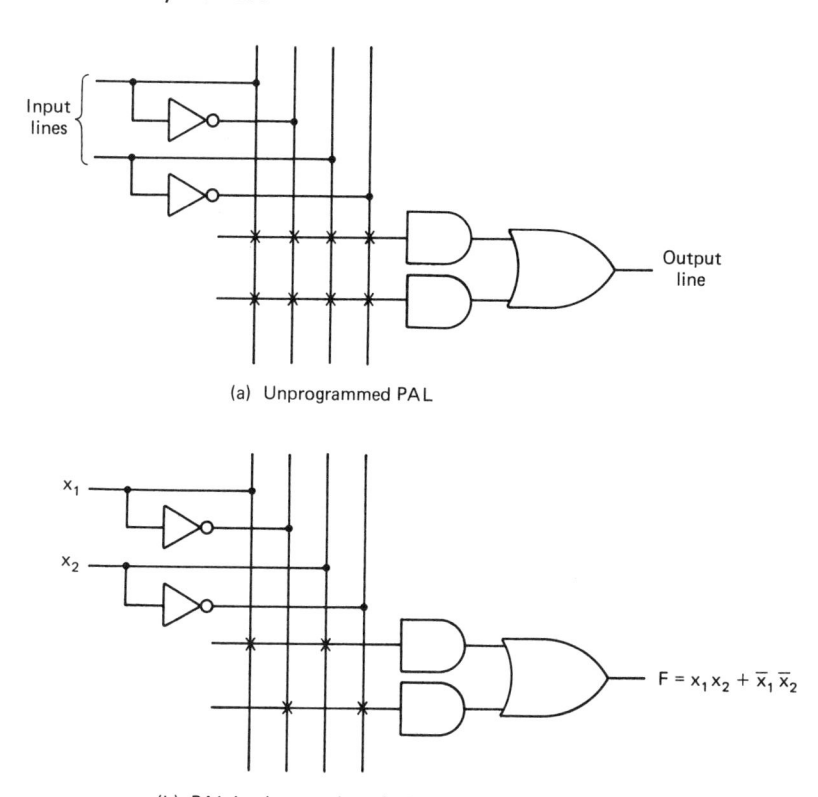

(a) Unprogrammed PAL

(b) PAL implementation of a logic function

Figure 3-29 Basic PAL structure

the manufacturer uses the table to program the PLA with the desired interconnection patterns. An FPLA, like a PROM, can be programmed in the field by the user.

Programmable Array Logic. The **progammable array logic (PAL)** is a special case of the PLA of Figure 3-28 in which the AND array is programmable and the OR array is fixed. (In some PAL types, the OR array is replaced by a NOR array.) Since only the AND array is programmable, the PAL is less expensive and easier to program than the more general PLA.

Erasable array logic is now available. It should also be noted that software exists for transforming logic equations directly into array logic devices.

Figure 3-29(a) shows a portion of an unprogrammed PAL. The accepted notation is to use an X to represent an intact link. Although one common line is shown in part (a) for each AND gate, it represents four fusible link inputs to the gate. When the PAL is programmed, the appropriate links are selectively "blown" to leave the desired connections to the AND gate inputs. As an example, we use this PAL in part (b) to implement the function $F = x_1 x_2 + \bar{x}_1 \bar{x}_2$.

The PAL allows the designer to specify the nature of the product terms, but the ways in which the product terms may be formed into sums is fixed in the chip.

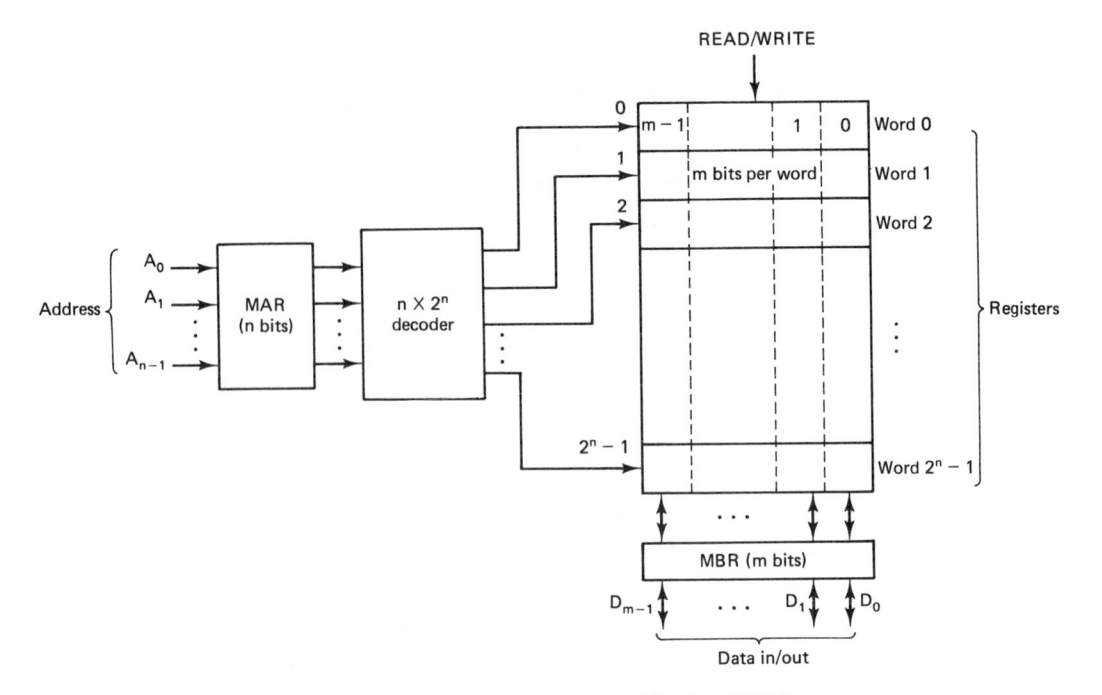

Figure 3–30 Organization of an RWM

Unlike the PLA, product terms (AND gates) in a PAL implementation cannot be shared among two or more OR gates. For a given type of PAL, the number of product terms feeding each OR gate is fixed and limited.

Since the OR array is fixed, the size of the PAL is determined not only by the number of inputs, product terms, and outputs but also by the number of inputs per OR gate. Typical PAL integrated circuits are available with 10 to 35 inputs, 1 to 30 outputs, and 2 to 20 inputs per OR gate.

Random-Access Memory

Programmable arrays are storage devices in which a *fixed* set of binary information is embedded into the unit and cannot be changed in real time during the system operation. A different type of memory, called **read/write memory (RWM),** is required if the information must be changed during system operation. Data is stored in and retrieved from an RWM by processes called **writing** and **reading,** respectively.

Figure 3–30 shows a block diagram of an RWM unit. To access a memory word, we specify its address in binary form. If the number of words is N and if we were to access each memory register *directly,* the number of required address lines would be very large, even for a relatively small N. Therefore, to keep the number of address lines manageable, we use a register-decoder combination. The register, called the **memory address register (MAR),** is used to specify the address of the memory word selected. Hence the combination of an n-bit MAR and an $n \times 2^n$ decoder can specify up to 2^n memory words.

To transfer information to and from memory registers, we use a register called the **memory buffer register (MBR)**. The length of the MBR is equal to the memory width. Reading from or writing to a memory word is controlled by the READ/WRITE line. To *read* the memory, the address of the memory word is placed in the MAR, the READ/WRITE line is set to 1, and a copy of the content of the addressed word is then brought into the MBR by the memory logic circuit. To *write* a word into memory, the data is placed in the MBR, the address of the location into which the data is to be written is loaded into the MAR, and the READ/WRITE line is set to 0. The memory logic unit then transfers the content of the MBR into the addressed location.

The operating speed of a memory unit is measured in terms of its **access time,** the amount of time required to perform a READ operation (or a WRITE operation). If the access time is the same for each address in memory, the memory is called a **random-access memory (RAM)**. [In fact, the term *RAM* is commonly used (albeit incorrectly) to denote a random-access RWM.] In other words, the actual physical location of a memory word has no effect on how long it takes to read from or write to that location. For example, programmable arrays are (*read-only*) random-access memory devices.

RWMs implemented with semiconductor integrated circuits lose the information stored in them when power is interrupted or removed. Such a memory is called a **volatile** memory. In contrast, we have seen that programmable arrays are nonvolatile because of the way in which they are constructed. Other nonvolatile memory devices, such as magnetic tapes, disks, and diskettes, will be discussed in Chapter 7.

We distinguish between two types of semiconductor random-access RWMs: dynamic and static. A **dynamic memory** incorporates a storage medium, such as a capacitor, which loses its information content over a period of time and must therefore be repeatedly refreshed to ensure data retention. In most dynamic RAMs, the refresh is performed when a memory cell is read. A **static memory** stores the information in flip-flops and maintains it without requiring any refreshing or restoring of data.

Computer-aided design (CAD) and computer-aided manufacturing (CAM) together with expert systems have proved to be powerful tools for coping with design problems of logic circuits, especially in VLSI. An expert system is a computer program that is developed from extensive interviews with experts in a particular field. It usually contains a knowledge base and a decision-making mechanism. Typical use of such a system in a CAD/CAM environment produces successful applications in the design of complex logic circuits under constraints that require not only intelligence but a large amount of expertise. These autonomous design and manufacturing systems represent advanced technology in logic design today.

PROBLEMS

1. Prove the following identities (by algebraic manipulation or by using truth tables):
   (a) $a \oplus b \oplus c = \bar{a}\bar{b}c + a\bar{b}\bar{c} + \bar{a}bc + ab\bar{c}$ (Note: $a \oplus b = \bar{a}b + a\bar{b}$)
   (b) $x_1\bar{x}_2 + \bar{x}_2 x_3 + x_3\bar{x}_1 = x_1\bar{x}_2 + \bar{x}_1 x_3$

2. Find the complement of the following functions by applying DeMorgan's laws:
   (a) $f_1(x, y, z) = \bar{x}y\bar{z} + \bar{x}\bar{y}z$
   (b) $f_2(x, y) = xy + \bar{x}\bar{y}$
   (c) $f_3(x, y, z) = x\bar{y}\bar{z} + xyz$
   (d) $f_4(x, y, z, w) = (y\bar{z} + \bar{x}w)(x\bar{y} + \bar{w}z)$
3. Let f_1 and f_2 be two Boolean functions. Show that $f_1 + f_2$ contains the sum of all the minterms of both f_1 and f_2 and that $f_1 f_2$ contains the minterms common to both f_1 and f_2.
4. Simplify the Boolean functions in Problem 2 and implement each one using AND, OR, and NOT gates.
5. Express the following functions in canonical SOP and POS forms:
   (a) $f_1(x, y, y) = (xy + z)(y + xz)$
   (b) $f_2(x, y, z) = (\bar{x} + y)(\bar{y} + z)$
   (c) $f_3(x, y, z) = 1$
6. Show that the sum of all minterms of a Boolean function with three variables is 1 and the product of all maxterms of a Boolean function with three variables is 0.
7. Show that the complement of the XOR (exclusive OR: $a \oplus b = \bar{a}b + a\bar{b}$) operation is equal to its dual.
8. A **majority gate** is a digital circuit whose output is 1 if the majority of its inputs are 1; otherwise, the output is 0. Obtain the simplified Boolean function of a three-input majority gate.
9. Consider the following truth table.

x	y	z	F
0	0	0	0
0	0	1	0
0	1	0	0
0	1	1	1
1	0	0	0
1	0	1	1
1	1	0	1
1	1	1	0

Express F in the canonical SOP form and the canonical POS form.

10. Let $f = \Sigma m(1, 3, 9, 11, 12, 13)$.
    (a) Express $\bar{f}$ in the canonical SOP form.
    (b) Obtain simplified expressions for both f and $\bar{f}$.
11. Write the output function of an 8×1 multiplexer with selection (control) inputs A, B, and D.
12. Using the multiplexer of Problem 11, implement the following function:

$$f(A, B, C, D) = \Sigma m(1, 3, 4, 7, 9, 10, 12, 14)$$

13. Find the dual functions of the following Boolean functions:
    (a) $f = [(AB + \overline{CD} + \bar{E})(\bar{A} + BC) + (\overline{DE} + B)](C + \bar{E})$
    (b) $f = (\bar{A} + B0 + 1)[(\overline{AB} + C)D] + \overline{AB}$
    (c) $f = [A\bar{B}(C + DE) \, 0] + AC(1 + CD + \overline{BE})$

Chap. 3   Problems

Note: In Problems 14–16, $\Sigma_d m$ denotes don't-care minterms and $\Pi_d M$ denotes don't-care maxterms.

14. Find a minimum sum-of-products for each of the following expressions:
    (a) $\Sigma m(0, 1, 2, 3, 7, 8, 9, 10, 11, 12, 13)$
    (b) $\Sigma m(2, 4, 6, 10) + \Sigma_d m(1, 3, 5, 7, 8, 9, 12, 13)$
    (c) $\Sigma m(1, 4, 5, 6, 13, 14, 15) + \Sigma_d m(8, 9)$

15. Find a minimum sum-of-products for each of the following functions:
    (a) $f(a, b, c) = \Pi M(2, 3, 4)$
    (b) $f(a, b, c) = \Sigma m(1, 6) + \Sigma_d m(0, 3, 5)$

16. Find a minimum sum-of-products and a minimum product-of-sums expression for each of the following functions:
    (a) $f(A, B, C, D) = B\bar{C}\bar{D} + \bar{B}C\bar{D} + CD + ABC$
    (b) $f(A, B, C, D) = \Sigma m(4, 8, 13, 15) + \Sigma_d m(1, 7, 9, 12, 14)$
    (c) $f(a, b, c, d) = \Sigma m(2, 3, 5, 7, 8, 10, 12, 15)$
    (d) $f(a, b, c, d) = \Sigma m(2, 4, 5, 8, 10, 11, 13, 15) + \Sigma_d m(0, 3, 6)$

17. Two 2-bit numbers $A = a_1 a_0$ and $B = b_1 b_0$ are to be compared by a four-variable function $f(a_1, a_0, b_1, b_0)$. The function f is to have the value 1 whenever $v(A) \leq v(B)$ [$v(X) = x_1 2^1 + x_0 2^0$ where X is any 2-bit number]. Assume that the variables A and B are such that $|v(A) - v(B)| \leq 2$. Implement f using as few gates as possible.

18. A code in which consecutive numbers are represented by binary patterns that differ in only one bit position is called a Gray code (see Section 2.5). Here is a truth table for a 3-bit Gray-to-binary decoder.

| 3-Bit Gray Code (inputs) ||| Binary Code (outputs) |||
x_1	x_2	x_3	f_1	f_2	f_3
0	0	0	0	0	0
0	0	1	0	0	1
0	1	1	0	1	0
0	1	0	0	1	1
1	1	0	1	0	0
1	1	1	1	0	1
1	0	1	1	1	0
1	0	0	1	1	1

The conversion circuit is shown below. Implement the three functions f_1, f_2, f_3, using NAND gates only.

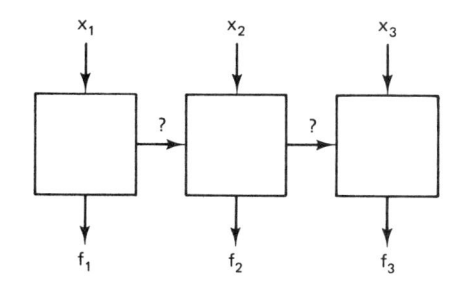

19. A sequential circuit has two inputs and one output. If the total number of ones received is greater than 4 and at least 3 pairs of inputs have occurred, then the output should be 1, coincident with the circuit reset. Derive a state table for this circuit. An example input set and the corresponding output follows.

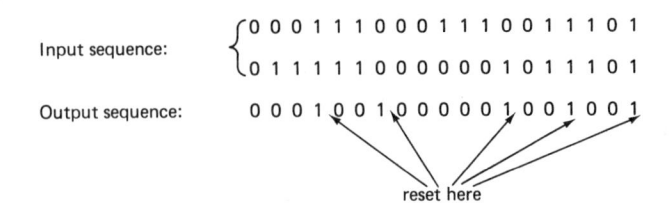

Input sequence: $\begin{cases} 0\ 0\ 0\ 1\ 1\ 1\ 0\ 0\ 0\ 1\ 1\ 1\ 0\ 0\ 1\ 1\ 1\ 0\ 1 \\ 0\ 1\ 1\ 1\ 1\ 1\ 0\ 0\ 0\ 0\ 0\ 0\ 1\ 0\ 1\ 1\ 1\ 0\ 1 \end{cases}$

Output sequence: $\ \ \ \ 0\ 0\ 0\ 1\ 0\ 0\ 1\ 0\ 0\ 0\ 0\ 0\ 1\ 0\ 0\ 1\ 0\ 0\ 1$

reset here

20. A sequential circuit has one input x and two outputs y and z. The bits yz represent a 2-bit binary number equal to the number of ones that have been received as inputs. The circuit resets when the total number of ones received is 3 or when the total number of zeros received is 3. Draw up the state diagram and table for the circuit.

21. The content of a 4-bit shift register is initially 1101. The serial input is 101101, and the register is shifted six times to the right. What is the content of the register after each shift?

22. Construct a 3-bit up-down ripple counter using negative edge-triggered JK flip-flops.

23. A read/write memory unit has a capacity of 8192 words of 32 bits per word.
    (a) How many flip-flops are needed for the memory address register (MAR)? How many for the memory buffer register (MBR)?
    (b) How many words will the memory unit contain if the MAR has 15 bits?

24. (a) What is the bit capacity of a memory unit that has 512 addresses and can store 8 bits at each address?
    (b) How many address bits are required for a 512 × 4 memory?
    (c) What is the total capacity of a memory unit with 10 address lines and four output lines?

CHAPTER 4

Basic Computer Organization

4.1 SYSTEM COMPONENTS

A stored-program **digital computer** is a system that manipulates and processes information according to ordered sets of instructions. The system is constructed from hardware modules such as registers, arithmetic and logic elements, control units, memory units and input/output (I/O) units. The ordered sets of instructions form machine **programs.** They define both the sequence and the pattern of data movement and data transformation within the hardware modules.

The computer can be separated into three major parts: the **central processing unit (CPU),** the **input/output (I/O) unit,** and the **memory unit.** The basic organization of a computer is shown in the block diagram of Figure 4–1. The CPU controls the sequencing of all information exchanges within the computer and with the outside world via the I/O unit. The memory unit consists of a large number of locations that store both the program and the data currently being used by the CPU. The three units are interconnected through various buses. A **bus** is simply a set of wires—a physical path—that serves to interconnect the registers and functional units associated with each module. Information is exchanged between the modules via the buses.

Buses as well as the functions associated with each of the units, will be discussed

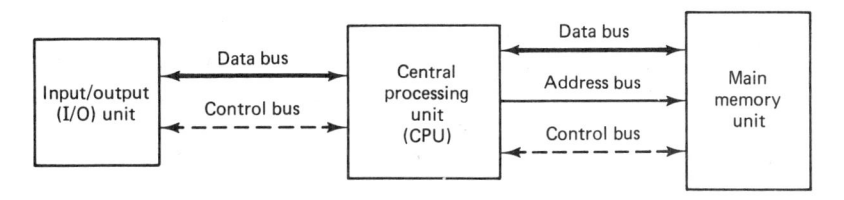

Figure 4–1 Basic components of a digital computer

in detail in Chapters 5, 6, and 7. Before studying the complexities of each particular unit in a computer, however, we will look at a complete, albeit very simple, computer system as a whole. We begin by discussing micro-operations that describe a system's implementation.

4.2 MICRO-OPERATIONS

The internal organization of a computer is determined primarily by the set of instructions that it can execute. An **instruction** is a convention used by the computer (1) to define operations such as *add*, *store*, *load*, and *jump*, and (2) to determine the location of the data on which the operation is to be performed. The set of all instructions, called the **instruction set,** encompasses a variety of arithmetic and logical operations, data transfer operations, I/O operations, and control operations. Combinations of these instructions, grouped together, form a machine program.

Instruction sets vary from computer to computer, as do instruction formats. Typically, however, a computer instruction is a binary code divided into a number of **fields.** The operation field, called the **opcode,** specifies the operation to be performed. This operation is executed on some collection of data, called the **operands,** which is either part of the instruction or is stored in registers or memory. If an operand is stored in a register or memory, the instruction must specify the location in an **address** field. The way in which operands are chosen during program execution is dependent on the **addressing mode** field of the instruction. For example, the format of an instruction might be as follows:

18	15 14	12 11 10	9 0
OP	REG NO	MODE	ADDR

In this case, 4 bits are used to specify the opcode of the instruction, giving a total of 16 possible instructions; one of eight registers is specified as one operand by the next 3 bits; 2 bits are used to specify the addressing mode to be used for the second operand; and 10 bits are available to specify the actual memory address of the second operand. More details about general types of instructions and addressing modes will be given in Chapter 5.

To execute the instructions stored in memory, each one is **fetched** (copied from memory by the CPU), placed in a register, and executed. However, an instruction is a complex entity whose execution cannot be performed during a single clock period. In fact, it takes more than one clock period to fetch the instruction. Therefore, the CPU generates sequences of functions that fetch the instruction, interpret its binary code, and carry it out. These functions are referred to as **micro-operations** (micro-ops), or sometimes as **microinstructions.** A micro-operation is a low-level operation that can be performed during one clock period. The sequences of micro-operations are referred to as **CPU cycles.** The most common cycles are the **fetch, address translation, execute,** and **interrupt** cycles. These will be discussed further in Section 4.3.

Sec. 4.2   Micro-Operations   101

Since micro-operations cause data to be transferred between registers, they can be described using a **register transfer language.** There is no one standard for this language, although most versions are very similar. We describe here the register transfer language that we shall use to define micro-operations.

Register Transfer Language

An n-bit **register** is a group of n flip-flops capable of storing n bits of binary information. In addition to the flip-flops, a register has gates that perform and/or control certain logic operations, such as LOAD, TRANSFER, and SHIFT. When to perform these operations depends on the clock, as will be seen later in this chapter.

The register transfer language presented here shall simply be referred to as RTL. To introduce the notation of RTL, assume that we want to transfer the content of register A to register B. In RTL this operation is denoted by

$$B \leftarrow (A) \qquad (4.1)$$

where (A) designates the content of register A. The transfer operation, $\leftarrow$, implies bit-pair transfers between registers A and B. Letting X_i represent the ith bit of register X, we can also write operation (4.1) as

$$B_i \leftarrow (A_i), \quad \text{for } i = 0, 1, \ldots, n - 1 \qquad (4.2)$$

where n is the size in bits of registers A and B. In both of these register transfer operations, the content of register A is not changed and the previous content of B is lost. (Notice that this has the same effect as assignment statements in high-level programming languages.)

In addition to transferring entire registers [operation (4.1)] or individual bits of registers [operation (4.2)], it is also possible to transfer parts of registers called **fields.** A field of a register is denoted by using brackets. The only restriction here is that the size of the field or register to the left of the arrow must be the same as to the right. An example of this type of transfer is

$$PC \leftarrow (IR[AD]) \qquad (4.3)$$

In this example, the AD field of the IR register is transferred to the PC register. Hence, the AD field must be the same size as the entire PC register. When parts of a register without a name must be transferred, they can be referenced by a range of bit locations. For example, in the operation

$$R1[0..3] \leftarrow (X) \qquad (4.4)$$

the content of register X is transferred to bits 0 through 3 of register R1. This implies that X is 4 bits long.

It is also possible to have constants on the right side of the arrow. Hence

$$L \leftarrow 5 \qquad (4.5)$$

stores the value 5 in register L. Notice that it would make no sense to have (5) on the right side of operation (4.5). It would also make no sense to say

$$L_1 \leftarrow 5 \qquad (4.6)$$

since the value 5 cannot be stored in one bit.

Using RTL, we can describe a variety of arithmetic and logic micro-operations. Consider, for example, the arithmetic ADD micro-op specified by

$$A3 \leftarrow (A1) + (A2) \qquad (4.7)$$

This operation means the contents of registers A1 and A2 are added, using a binary adder circuit, and the sum is transferred into register A3. Recall that addition may result in an overflow. To store the overflow, a 1-bit register could be used in conjunction with A3. Using V as the overflow register, operation (4.7) could be rewritten as

$$VA3 \leftarrow (A1) + (A2) \qquad (4.8)$$

In addition to the ADD micro-op, some other arithmetic operations that can be represented are

$A \leftarrow (A) + 1$	; increment the content of A by 1
$A \leftarrow (A) - 1$	; decrement the content of A by 1
$A \leftarrow (\overline{A})$	; derive the 1's complement of A
$A \leftarrow (A) + (\overline{B}) + 1$	; perform $A - B$ by adding the 2's complement of B to A

As shown in these examples, comments (when included) follow a semicolon. Notice also that only simple arithmetic operations are included in these examples. Remember that these register transfer operations represent micro-operations. So even though the syntax of, say, a multiplication operation is straightforward, the semantics imply that the CPU can carry out the multiplication in one clock period. Since this is usually not the case, we do not include the more complex arithmetic operations in our RTL.

We can, however, describe logical operations on one or more registers. For example,

$$C \leftarrow (A) \text{ OR } (B) \qquad (4.9)$$

means that the logic OR of the contents of registers A and B is transferred to register C. Similarly, the logic AND operation looks like this:

$$C \leftarrow (A) \text{ AND } (B) \qquad (4.10)$$

Shift register transfer operations can also be easily described. In a shift register (see Section 3.7), the content of each cell is shifted to the adjacent cell—right in a shift-right register, left in a shift-left register. What happens at the end cells depends on whether a circular shift or a serial shift is being done. We can describe a serial shift left of a 4-bit register A, with input from a 1-bit register B, as follows:

$$\text{lost} \leftarrow (A_3)$$
$$A_3 \leftarrow (A_2)$$
$$A_2 \leftarrow (A_1)$$
$$A_1 \leftarrow (A_0)$$
$$A_0 \leftarrow (B)$$

Sec. 4.2 Micro-Operations

RTL can also be used to describe data transfers to and from memory words. Each memory word is actually a register named by its memory address. In RTL, we represent the main memory unit of a computer as M and reference the ith word in the memory as M[i]. Therefore, a **memory read** can be specified with the RTL statement

$$B \leftarrow (M[A]) \qquad (4.11)$$

and a **memory write** with the RTL statement

$$M[A] \leftarrow (B) \qquad (4.12)$$

In both operations, (4.11) and (4.12), the memory word addressed by the value in register A is transferred to or from the B register in the CPU. In some computers, A and B can be general registers or even constants, while in others, A and B are special-purpose registers.

It is sometimes necessary to signify that a register transfer takes place only on certain conditions. This is done in one of two ways: by using **logical condition** statements or by defining **control conditions.** Logical condition statements are simple IF-THEN statements. For example, the operation

$$\text{IF } (V) > (W) \text{ THEN } Q \leftarrow 0 \qquad (4.13)$$

sets register Q to 0 only if the value in register V is greater than the value in register W. Notice that the logical condition statement is only defined for IF-THEN and not for ELSE.

Control conditions are another way of specifying conditional operations. With this method, the conditions are logical functions of binary variables that control the enable inputs of registers. These functions are specified to the left of the register transfer operation and are followed by a colon. As an example, consider the register transfer depicted in Figure 4–2. This transfer is described by the following RTL statement:

$$t_0(c_1 + c_2): X \leftarrow (Y) \qquad (4.14)$$

This means that the content of Y is transferred to X only when t_0 is 1 and either c_1 or c_2 is also 1. To signify that a transfer should take place when a certain condition is 0, the prime symbol (') is used. So if the condition in the RTL statement of Equation (4.14) was $t_0'(c_1 + c_2)$:, the transfer would take place only when t_0 is 0 and either c_1 or c_2 is 1.

We have defined the basic concepts of RTL. Next we shall see more examples of RTL statements as we use them to describe a specific system.

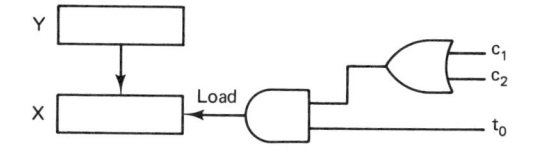

Figure 4–2 Register transfer governed by a control function

4.3 A SIMPLE COMPUTER EXAMPLE

In this section, we go through the detailed design of the architecture for a very simple computer. The computer we use is based on the Simplified Instructional Computer (SIC) presented in Beck (1985). There, the SIC is defined by its memory size, word size, registers, data formats, instruction formats, addressing modes, instruction set, and input/output provisions. Based on this information, it is possible to determine an architecture design for the SIC. It is, of course, possible to have other designs that support the SIC as defined; however, one is enough for this text. We shall first describe the structure of the SIC (slightly modified from Beck's definition) and then look at the design details.

SIC Machine Structure

The SIC machine consists of a CPU, a memory unit, and at least one I/O device. The CPU consists of 13 special-purpose registers. The purpose and size (in bits) of the registers are given in Table 4.1. The *accumulator* register, **A,** is used for all arithmetic and logic operations. In these kinds of instructions, A is always one of the operands, and the result is always stored back in A. The *index* register, **X,** is used to compute the memory address of certain operands depending on the instruction's addressing mode. The memory address of the next instruction of the program is kept in the *program counter* register, **PC.** The *linkage* register, **L,** facilitates the use of subroutines. When a subroutine is called, it is necessary to remember the current PC so that execution can continue from this point on when the subroutine is finished. We shall see how this is done when we look at the instruction set. The *instruction register*, **IR,** stores the current memory instruction that is being executed. The *status word* register, **SW,** has a number of fields that store information relative to the current

TABLE 4.1 REGISTER SET FOR THE SIC

Register	Size (bits)	Name	Intended use
A	24	Accumulator	Main calculational register
X	15	Index register	Indexed addressing
PC	15	Program counter	Contains address of next instruction
L	15	Linkage register	Stores return address for subroutines
IR	24	Instruction register	Stores current instruction
MBR	24	Memory buffer register	For input to or output from memory
MAR	15	Memory address register	Address of memory for all reads/writes
SW	11	Status word	Contains status information relative to previous instruction
C	2	Counter	Generates timing signals, t_0, t_1, t_2, t_3
INT	1	Interrupt flag	Signals that an interrupt has occurred
F	1	Fetch cycle flag	Specifies the fetch cycle
E	1	Execute cycle flag	Specifies the execute cycle
S	1	Start/stop flag	Enables C

Sec. 4.3 A Simple Computer Example

operation as well as the current program. The information stored in SW is used by both the programmer and the CPU to make decisions based on previous results.

Access to and from the memory unit is via the **MAR** and **MBR** registers only. On a *write*, the data in the MBR is written to the memory word referenced by the MAR:

$$M[MAR] \leftarrow (MBR)$$

On a *read*, the data is read from the memory word referenced by the MAR and is stored in the MBR:

$$MBR \leftarrow (M[MAR])$$

The memory unit is a RAM made up of 2^{15} words, and the size of each word is 24 bits. This implies that registers that are used for memory addresses are 15 bits long (PC, L, X, and MAR) and those that store complete words of memory are 24 bits long (A, IR, and MBR). The size of SW is related to the number of fields it contains and the number of bits required by each field. As we shall see, 11 bits suffice for our version of the SIC.

For simplicity, we shall assume that the access time of the memory unit is less than one clock period. (Note that this is usually *not* the case.) Also, because the memory unit is an asynchronous RAM, the address lines from the MAR as well as the data lines from the MBR must be held steady for the duration of the memory access. Figure 4–3 shows the registers and memory unit of the SIC. More details about how these registers work, as well as a description of the other registers in Table 4.1, will be given in the discussions that follow.

Input to and output from the CPU (not including transfers to or from memory) are accomplished 1 byte at a time. The information is transferred between the rightmost 8 bits of the A register and the I/O device. Each device on the machine is represented by an 8-bit code that is specified as the operand in I/O-related instructions.

Data for the SIC consist of either integers or characters. (There is no floating-

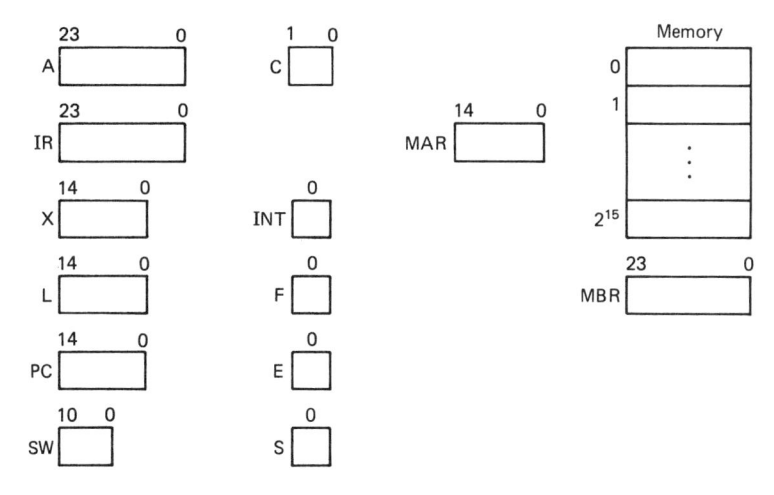

Figure 4–3 Register set and memory for the SIC

point hardware on this machine.) Integers are stored as 24-bit numbers, with negative values stored in their 2's complement representations. Characters are represented by their 8-bit ASCII code.

The format of instructions for the SIC is

```
 23      16 15  14              0
┌─────────┬─────┬────────────────┐
│   OP    │ IX  │       AD       │
└─────────┴─────┴────────────────┘
```

where OP is the 8-bit opcode specifying the operation to be performed, IX is the index flag indicating the addressing mode to be used, and AD is the 15-bit memory address of the operand. If the IX bit of an instruction is 0, the operand is stored in M[AD]. This is called **direct addressing**. If the IX bit is 1, the operand is stored in M[AD + (X)]. That is, the index register is used to offset the address specified in the instruction. This is called **indexed addressing**. Notice that the instruction specifies only one operand. For arithmetic and logic operations, the second operand is implicitly the value of the A register, and the result of the operation is always stored back in A.

Instruction Set for the SIC

The 21 instructions available on the SIC are given in Table 4.2. In this table, m represents the memory address of the operand and (m) represents the value stored at

TABLE 4.2 SIC INSTRUCTION SET

Instruction	Mnemonic	Opcode	Effect
Add	ADD m	00	A ← (A) + (m)
And	AND m	01	A ← (A) AND (m)
Compare	COMP m	02	(A):(m); CC ← result
Jump	J m	03	PC ← m
Jump Equal	JEQ m	04	PC ← m if CC set to =
Jump Greater Than	JGT m	05	PC ← m if CC set to >
Jump Less Than	JLT m	06	PC ← m if CC set to <
Jump Subroutine	JSUB m	07	L ← (PC); PC ← m
Load A	LDA m	08	A ← (m)
Load L	LDL m	09	L ← (m)
Load X	LDX m	0A	X ← (m)
Or	OR m	0B	A ← (A) OR (m)
Read Device	RD m	0C	A[0..7] ← byte from device (m)
Return Subroutine	RSUB	0D	PC ← (L)
Store A	STA m	0E	m ← (A)
Store L	STL m	0F	m ← (L)
Store SW	STSW m	10	m ← (SW)
Store X	STX m	11	m ← (X)
Subtract	SUB m	12	A ← (A) − (m)
Test Device	TD m	13	Test device (m); CC ← result
Write Device	WD m	14	Device (m) ← (A[0..7])
Interrupt Return	IRT	15	PC ← (M[0]); SW[MASK] ← 0

Sec. 4.3 A Simple Computer Example

this memory address. The opcodes for the instructions are given in hexadecimal notation.

JSUB and **RSUB** are the two instructions related to subroutines. JSUB saves the current PC in L and then jumps to the subroutine by storing the operand in the PC. RSUB returns from the subroutine by jumping to the location specified by L.

The **TD** instruction is used to test an I/O device before attempting to read from or write to it. The result of the test is stored in the *condition code*, **CC** field, of the SW. This field is 2 bits long and is used to represent one of three values: $<$, $=$, and $>$. When the TD instruction is executed, the value of the CC field is set according to the following code:

$<$ implies that the device is ready.
$=$ implies that the device is busy and cannot be used at the moment.
$>$ implies that the device is not operational.

This field is then used by the jump instructions as determined by the program. An example of how these instructions might be used by a programmer is given in the code shown in Table 4.3. In this routine, device X is continually tested until it is either ready or is found to be not operational. In the latter case, the program causes a jump to an error subroutine. If the device becomes ready, the program reads a byte of data from device X and then ends.

TABLE 4.3 SAMPLE CODE TO READ 1 BYTE FROM DEVICE X

TEST	TD	"X"
	JEQ	TEST
	JGT	ERROR
	RD	"X"
	J	END
ERROR	JSUB	EROUTINE
END	STOP	

In addition to the TD instruction, the **COMP** instruction also sets the CC field. The value stored in the CC field after a COMP reflects the relation between A and the instruction operand.

The **IRT** instruction is used by the interrupt handler to cause a jump back to where the CPU was before the interrupt occurred. When an interrupt occurs, the CPU saves the current PC in memory at address 0. To return from an interrupt, the content of this memory address must be loaded back into the PC. As described later, the interrupt mask is also cleared at this time. This instruction is intended only for interrupt handler (system) software and may not be published or accessible in the end-user assembly language.

The rest of the instructions are for arithmetic and logic operations, transfers of control (jumps), loading registers, storing registers, or reading from and writing to I/O devices. Although other instructions would be desirable for a general-purpose computer, these are enough to get a basic picture of how all the parts of a computer work together.

Timing and Control

Programs are executed by the CPU one instruction at a time. In order for the CPU to execute an instruction in memory, it must first fetch the instruction and then execute it. During the execution of the instruction, it is possible that an *interrupt* will occur. An interrupt is a signal to the CPU that some event has occurred. Examples of interrupts include "I/O completed," "program tried to divide by zero," and "time expired." When an interrupt occurs, it is necessary for the CPU to notice the signal and to transfer control to an *interrupt handler* program. The CPU coordinates its three tasks by setting up cycles: the **fetch cycle,** the **execute cycle,** and the **interrupt cycle.** (An address translation cycle is not necessary in this machine.) In each cycle, a number of micro-operations are performed to carry out the necessary task.

For things to work out right, the micro-operations of each cycle must be performed in a specific order. One way of preserving the correct order is to use a sequence counter to control which micro-operation is executed when. The 2-bit sequence counter, **C,** can be used to generate four timing signals: t_0, t_1, t_2, and t_3. This is done by having C increment on each clock pulse. (Since it has only 2 bits, it will increment back to 00 after 11.) The **S** flag is used to control when C increments. When S is 1, C increments on every clock pulse; when S is 0, C does not change. (S is determined by a manual switch located on the computer console.) Consider the setup in Figure 4–4. Using three of the timing signals as the *load* input to the registers causes the registers to be loaded in a specific order: the MBR first, then L, and then the PC. This sequence of micro-operations can also be described by the register transfer statements of Table 4.4.

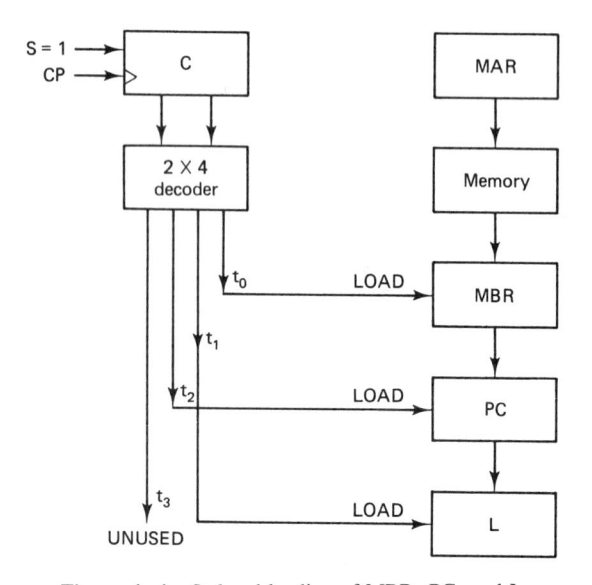

Figure 4–4 Ordered loading of MBR, PC, and L

Sec. 4.3   A Simple Computer Example

TABLE 4.4   REGISTER TRANSFER STATEMENTS FOR FIGURE 4-4

t_0:	MBR ← (M[MAR])
t_1:	L ← (PC)
t_2:	PC ← (MBR[AD])

Using the same principle of sequencing control, it is possible to set up the fetch, execute, and interrupt cycles. However, if we use the same timing signals for each cycle, micro-operations from different cycles will be executed at the same time. To prevent this, the CPU must keep track of which cycle is the current one. This is the function of the F and E flag registers. Table 4.5 relates the values of F and E to the CPU cycles. Since we only have three cycles, the combination of E = F = 1 is not used. It can be seen that, when F = 1 and E = 0 (FE'), the CPU is in the fetch cycle. As we shall see, the largest number of timing signals needed by any of the cycles is four. This means that the sequence counter, C, must be designed to generate four timing signals. But this also implies that even if a cycle does not need all four clock periods, the next one cannot start until the next t_0. A resulting design principle, therefore, is to minimize the number of timing signals needed by any cycle but also to have close to the same number in each cycle. Let us now look at each of the cycles in detail.

TABLE 4.5   CPU CYCLES

F	E	Cycle
1	0	fetch
0	1	execute
0	0	interrupt
1	1	(not used)

Fetch cycle.   The main function of the fetch cycle is to get a copy of the next instruction from memory into the CPU, ready for execution. The PC register contains the memory address of the next instruction, so the first task is to load this value into the MAR. Memory can then be read, resulting in the memory word being stored in the MBR. This word is then transferred into the IR (instructioin register) for future decoding. Because of the simple addressing of this computer, the memory address of the operand can also be determined at this time rather than in a separate address translation cycle. If the index field, IX, is equal to 1, the X register is first added to the address field of the instruction. The MAR can then be set up with the correct operand address. For the PC to be pointing to the right memory word on the next time through the fetch cycle, it is necessary to increment it sometime during this cycle after it has been used. This way the PC will also contain the correct value when a JSUB instruction is executed. If it turns out that the instruction is a general jump-type instruction, the PC will be reset to the correct value during the execute cycle. The last thing that must be done in this cycle is to set up the cycle flags for the

TABLE 4.6 REGISTER TRANSFER STATEMENTS OF THE FETCH CYCLE

$FE't_0$:	MAR ← (PC)
$FE't_1$:	MBR ← (M[MAR]); PC ← (PC) + 1
$FE't_2$:	IR ← (MBR)
$FE't_3$:	IF IR[IX] = 1 THEN MAR ← (IR[AD]) + (X)
$FE't_3$:	IF IR[IX] = 0 THEN MAR ← (IR[AD])
$FE't_3$:	F ← 0; E ← 1

execute cycle. This is done by turning the F flag off and setting the E flag. The corresponding register transfer statements for the fetch cycle are given in Table 4.6.

Each statement in Table 4.6 is done only on the condition that FE' is true and on a particular timing signal. Notice, however, that some of the statements are actually done on the same timing signal, in particular, t_3. This implies that these three statements can all be executed at the same time. There is no problem with this as long as the statements do not have to be executed in a particular order. Figure 4–5 shows the interconnections of the registers and memory for the fetch cycle.

Interrupt cycle. When an interrupt occurs, some action must be taken. Depending on the particular interrupt, this could take quite a few instructions. It is also possible that the action for an interrupt will be changed at some later time. What this means to the CPU is that the instructions for handling the interrupt are stored in memory somewhere. These instructions make up a program called the **interrupt handler.** Therefore, the function of the interrupt cycle is to save the current PC in a special place and jump to the interrupt handler code. This code will then be fetched and executed one instruction at a time. On the last instruction, the interrupt handler will cause a jump back to the PC value that was saved. The important concept here is that *the interrupt cycle does not service the interrupt*; it only causes control to be passed to a special program that will interpret and service the interrupt. We will assume that the interrupt handler code begins at M[1] and the current PC is saved in memory at M[0].

In the SIC machine, the SW register contains two fields relative to interrupts: an 8-bit field, ICODE, and a 1-bit field, MASK. Along with the 2-bit condition code field, CC, the format of the SW is

10	9	8	7		0
CC		MASK		ICODE	

The interrupt code field, ICODE, is automatically set to a value that indicates the cause of the interrupt (the error type, a device needing I/O, system startup, etc.). It is set by the device causing the interrupt and interpreted by the interrupt handler. The MASK field controls whether interrupts are allowed. This is used in this simple machine to prevent nested interrupts. In other words, we do not have to worry about an interrupt occurring while another one is still being handled. In more sophisticated machines, nested interrupts are usually allowed according to interrupt priority. In addition to the SW register, the INT register is also involved in interrupts. This

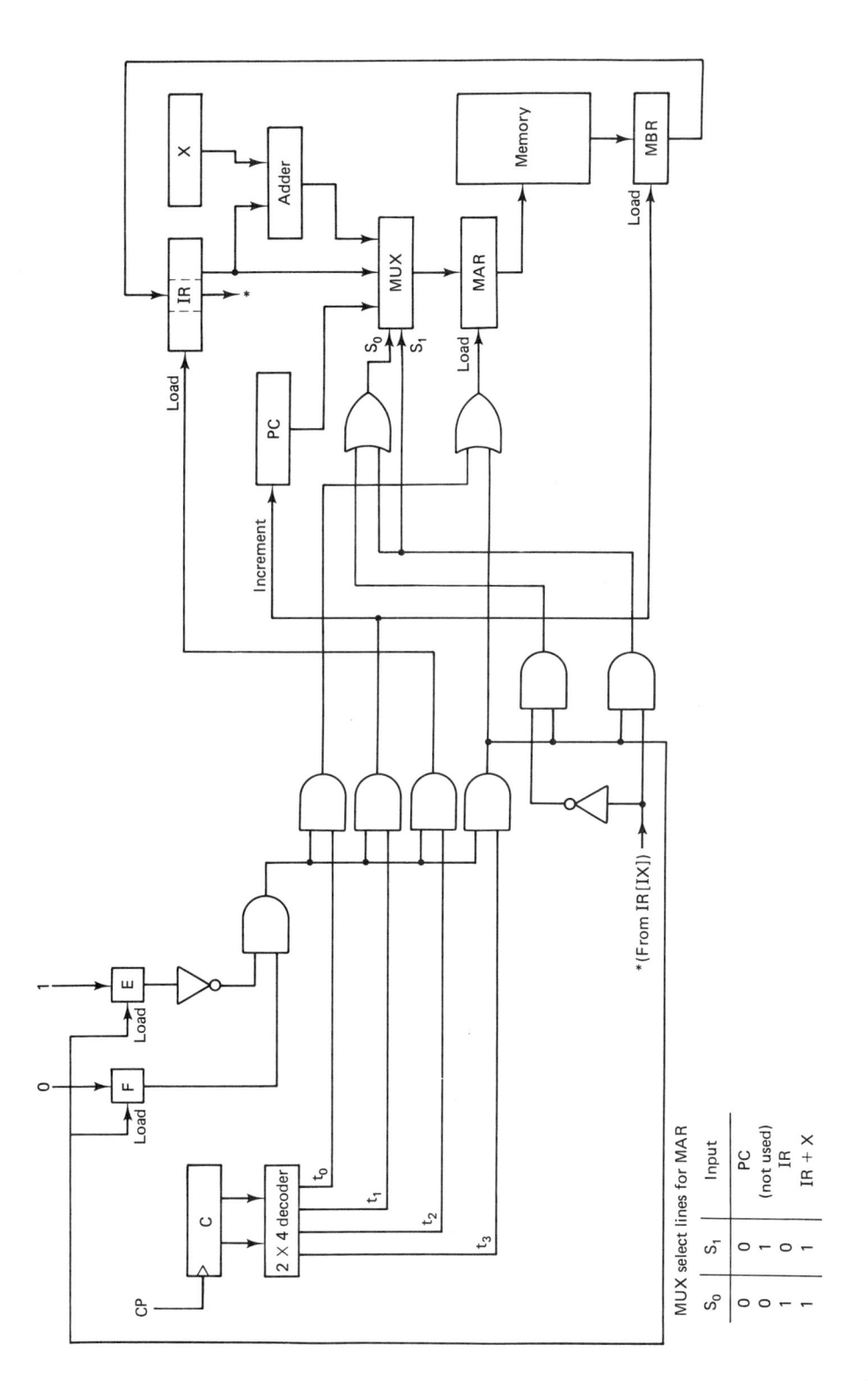

Figure 4-5 Register transfers for the fetch cycle

1-bit register is used to signal the CPU that an interrupt has occurred. It can be set by any of the I/O devices for I/O-related interrupts or by the CPU itself for program- and timer-related interrupts. Once the CPU recognizes the signal, it clears the INT flag. (Interrupts will be discussed further in Chapter 6.)

We can now look at the interrupt cycle in detail. In this cycle, both the F and E flags are equal to 0. The register transfer statements are given in Table 4.7. Notice that on t_0, the interrupt flag, INT, is cleared and the interrupt mask, SW[MASK], is set. If another interrupt were to occur at this time, INT would be set again, but SW[MASK] would prevent this new interrupt from interrupting the current interrupt. When the interrupt handler routine is finished servicing the interrupt, it reenables all interrupts by clearing SW[MASK]. (This is done with the IRT instruction by the interrupt handler routine.) Also notice that it is only necessary to set F to 1 for the fetch cycle since E is already 0.

TABLE 4.7 REGISTER TRANSFER STATEMENTS OF THE INTERRUPT CYCLE

$F'E't_0$:	MBR[AD] ← (PC), INT ← 0, SW[MASK] ← 1
$F'E't_1$:	MAR ← 0, PC ← 1
$F'E't_2$:	M[MAR] ← (MBR)
$F'E't_3$:	F ← 1

Execute cycle. The execute cycle is different from the fetch and interrupt cycles in that it is unique for every instruction. The only thing all the execute cycles have in common is that on the last timing signal, t_3, the F and E flags are set up for either the fetch cycle or the interrupt cycle. The interrupt mask, SW[MASK], must be tested to see if interrupts are enabled. (If they are, SW[MASK] will be 0.) If they are enabled and an interrupt has occurred, F and E should both be cleared for the interrupt cycle; otherwise, F should be set and E should be cleared so that the fetch cycle is next. So, if (NOT SW[MASK] AND INT) is true, F and E should be cleared. But since F is already 0 in this cycle, it is more efficient to always clear E and then set F only if the interrupt cycle is *not* necessary. The interrupt cycle is not necessary whenever SW[MASK] is 1 or when the INT flag is 0. Hence all execute cycles include the following transfer statement:

$$F'Et_3: E \leftarrow 0; \text{IF (SW[MASK] OR NOT (INT)) THEN } F \leftarrow 1 \qquad (4.15)$$

Now, if the controlling conditions for the execute cycles include only the F and E flags and the timing signal, every instruction would be executed on every execute cycle. Obviously, this is not what we want. During the execute cycle, we want to execute only the instruction that is stored in the IR. The CPU ensures this by using the instruction's opcode (the OP field of the IR) as part of the control condition. Since opcodes are unique for each instruction, one and only one instruction will be executed during a given execute cycle. For simplicity, we shall let p_i represent opcode i in the control conditions of the execute cycles. (The opcodes for each instruction can be found in Table 4.2.)

Let us consider the execute cycle for a particular instruction. For the arithmetic

Sec. 4.3 A Simple Computer Example

ADD instruction (opcode = 0), the execute cycle is shown in Table 4.8. Recall that at the end of the fetch cycle, the MAR was set up with the operand's memory address. Thus in this execute cycle, a memory read is initiated right away on t_0. The transfer statement done on t_1 causes the actual addition to take place. At time t_3, the next cycle is determined by using the transfer statement of Equation (4.15). Since nothing else needs to be done, t_2 is an idle timing signal. As will be discussed in Chapter 6, such an idle cycle could be used for *cycle stealing*. It is important to realize that no matter how many timing signals are necessary for the particular instruction being executed, changing the F and E flags can be done only on the last signal. In our example, only one timing signal is necessary for the instruction. Yet if F and E were changed on either t_1 or t_2, the fetch or interrupt cycle would start to execute right in the middle. This, of course, would cause havoc in the system.

For some instructions, a memory read is not necessary. For example, consider the two instructions J and LDL. For the J instruction, we want to store the memory address of the operand in the PC, while for the LDL instruction, we want to store the value in memory specified by the operand address. In other words, we do a memory read to get the necessary value for the LDL instruction but not for the J instruction. The execute cycles for these two instructions are as given in Table 4.9.

As some other examples, the execute cycles for the JSUB and RSUB instructions are given in Table 4.10. (JSUB was the instruction of Figure 4–4 and Table 4.4.) The execute cycles for the other instructions can be derived from the information given in Table 4.2.

Functional Units

The only other components that the CPU needs to execute the instructions are the combinational circuits for doing the arithmetic and logic operations of the computer.

TABLE 4.8 EXECUTE CYCLE FOR THE ADD INSTRUCTION

$p_0F'Et_0$:	MBR ← (M[MAR])
$p_0F'Et_1$:	A ← (A) + (MBR)
$p_0F'Et_2$:	
$p_0F'Et_3$:	E ← 0; IF (SW[MASK] OR NOT (INT)) THEN F ← 1

TABLE 4.9 EXECUTE CYCLES FOR THE J AND LDL INSTRUCTIONS

J instruction (opcode = 3)	$p_3F'Et_0$:	PC ← (IR[AD])
	$p_3F'Et_1$:	
	$p_3F'Et_2$:	
	$p_3F'Et_3$:	E ← 0; IF (SW[MASK] OR NOT (INT)) THEN F ← 1
LDL instruction (opcode = 9)	$p_9F'Et_0$:	MBR ← (M[MAR])
	$p_9F'Et_1$:	L ← (MBR[AD])
	$p_9F'Et_2$:	
	$p_9F'Et_3$:	E ← 0; IF (SW[MASK] OR NOT (INT)) THEN F ← 1

TABLE 4.10 EXECUTE CYCLES FOR THE JSUB AND RSUB INSTRUCTIONS

JSUB instruction (opcode = 7)	$p_7F'Et_0$:	MBR ← (M[MAR])
	$p_7F'Et_1$:	L ← (PC)
	$p_7F'Et_2$:	PC ← (MBR[AD])
	$p_7F'Et_3$:	E ← 0; IF (SW[MASK] OR NOT (INT)) THEN F ← 1
RSUB instruction (opcode = D)	$p_DF'Et_0$:	PC ← (L)
	$p_DF'Et_1$:	
	$p_DF'Et_2$:	
	$p_DF'Et_3$:	E ← 0; IF (SW[MASK] OR NOT (INT)) THEN F ← 1

These circuits are called **functional units.** The functional units of the SIC are as follows:

1. Two **binary adders:** one for the indexed address mode and one for the ADD and SUB operations
2. A **logic COMPARE** unit for the COMP operation
3. A **logic AND** unit for the AND operation
4. A **logic OR** unit for the OR operation

Except for the address mode adder, the inputs to each of these functional units are from the A register and the MBR, and the output is directed back to A. The input and output of the address mode adder can be seen in Figure 4–5.

System Startup

Every computer has to have some way of getting things started when it is powered up. This usually includes initializing certain registers and then executing special instructions that take care of the rest of the initialization. These special instructions are either resident in a particular part of memory or are automatically read into memory from a specific I/O device.

For the SIC machine, powering up the system causes S and F to be set to 1; E and C to be cleared; SW[ICODE] to be set to "startup"; and the PC to be set to 1. This causes the CPU immediately to start executing the resident interrupt handler routine, which proceeds to interpret the startup interrupt. In addition to system power-up, it is also desirable to be able to reset the system without turning it off and then on again. This can be done on the SIC using a manual **start/stop switch.** Moving this mechanical flip-flop to 1 causes the system to go through the power-up routine. Moving the switch to 0 just clears S, thereby stopping the counter and hence stopping the entire machine.

4.4 EXECUTION TRACE OF AN SIC INSTRUCTION

Having defined the CPU cycles, the timing and control mechanism, and the functional units of the SIC, we have actually defined how the registers and units of the computer are interconnected and how data is transferred between them. In this section, we shall

Sec. 4.4   Execution Trace of a SIC Instruction   115

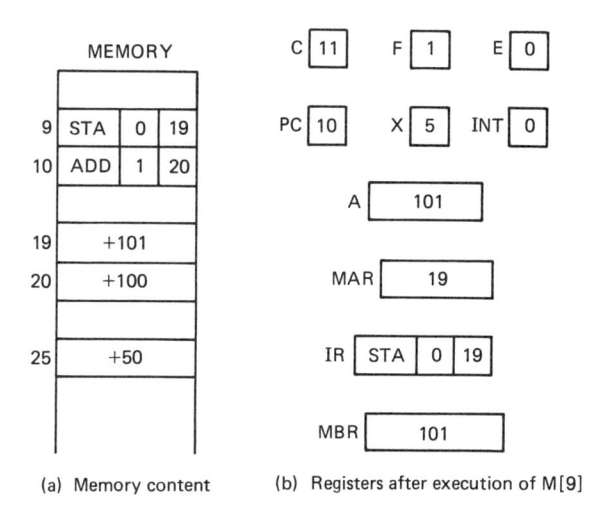

```
          MEMORY              C  11        F  1       E  0

      9 | STA | 0 | 19 |     PC  10       X  5      INT  0
     10 | ADD | 1 | 20 |
                              A     101
     19 |    +101    |
     20 |    +100    |        MAR    19

     25 |    +50     |        IR  | STA | 0 | 19 |

                              MBR    101
```

(a) Memory content   (b) Registers after execution of M[9]

Figure 4–6   Initial memory and register contents

trace an instruction through its entire fetch and execute cycle as an example of how the SIC works.

To start things off, assume that the content of the memory unit is as shown in Figure 4–6(a). We are going to trace through the execution of the instruction currently stored in M[10]. We assume that the previous instruction, M[9], has just been executed and hence the contents of the CPU registers are as shown in Figure 4–6(b). Notice that the F and E flags have already been set up for the next fetch cycle, but the C counter has not yet gone back to 00.

Execution without Interrupt

The trace of the instruction in M[10] is depicted in the sequence of "snapshots" of Figure 4–7, where each snapshot represents the state of the system right after C has been incremented. The registers that have changed since the previous snapshot are highlighted in bold.

When the counter goes to 00, the first timing signal, t_0, of the fetch cycle will be generated. Based on the fetch cycle instructions given in Table 4.6, the following actions are taken. At time t_0, the contents of the PC are transferred to the MAR [Figure 4–7(a)]. At time t_1, the memory word specified by the MAR is read into the MBR and the PC is incremented [part (b)]. On the third timing signal, t_2, the contents of the MBR are copied into the IR [part (c)]. The transfers occurring on the last timing signal of the fetch cycle, t_3, depend on the value of the IX field of the IR. Since this value is 1, the value of the AD field of the IR is added to the value of the X register and stored in the MAR. In addition to this, the F flag is cleared and the E flag is set. These transfers are depicted in Figure 4–7(d). As the C counter goes back to 00, the F and E flags force the CPU to enter an execute cycle. The particular execute cycle used is governed by the opcode currently in the OP field of the IR. In this case, the ADD execute cycle shown earlier in Table 4.8 is used. Thus on this

Figure 4-7 Register contents during execution without interrupt

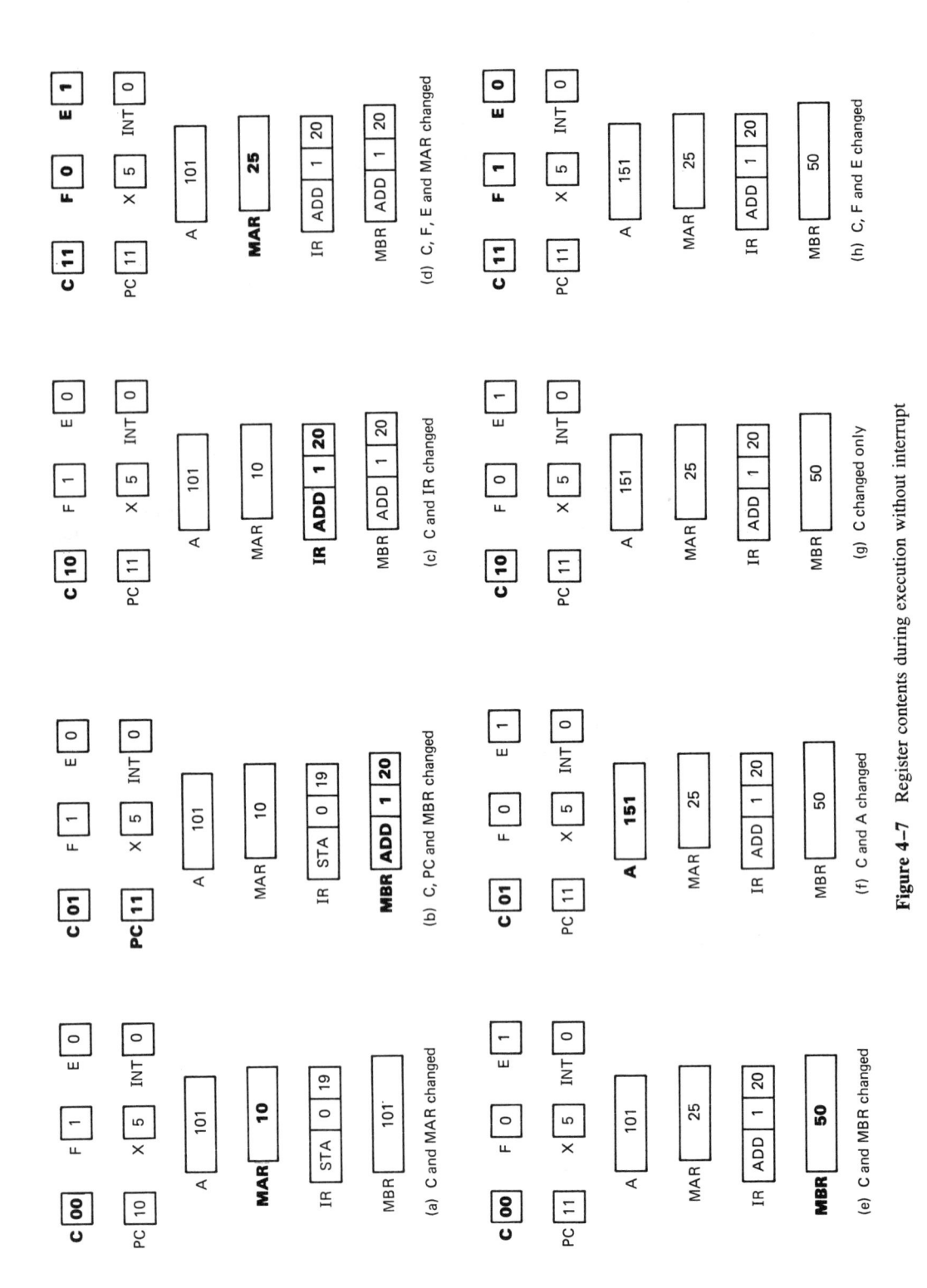

t_0 signal, the contents of the memory word specified by the MAR, M[25], are copied into the MBR [part (e)]. At time t_1, the value of the MBR is added to and stored in A. Since M[25] contains 50, the value of A becomes 151 [part (f)]. No actions are taken on timing signal t_2 other than the automatic increment of C [part (g)]. In this first example, no interrupts occurred during either the fetch or execute cycle. Thus in Figure 4–7(h), F and E are set up for the next fetch cycle.

Execution with Interrupt

Let us assume now that sometime during either the fetch or execute cycle of Figure 4–7, an interrupt occurs. We pick up the trace of the instruction in M[10] at t_2, F = 0, and E = 1 [Figure 4–7(g) in the previous example], but with INT = 1 and SW[MASK] = 0. Figure 4–8(a) reflects this new state. This time on the last timing signal of the ADD execute cycle, t_3, (NOT SW[MASK] AND INT) is true, so the conditon of the IF statement becomes false. As a result, only E is changed [Figure 4–8(b)].

When C increments to 00, the E and F flags direct the CPU to the interrupt cycle (depicted in Table 4.7). On the first timing signal of this cycle, t_0, three transfers take place: The contents of the PC are transferred to the AD field of the MBR, the INT flag is cleared, and the MASK field of the SW is set [part (c)]. At time t_1, the PC is set to 1 and the MAR is cleared [part (d)]. Then on the third timing signal, t_2, the MBR is written to memory at address 0 [part (e)]. The last action of this cycle is to set up F and E for the fetch cycle. This is done by setting F to 1 as shown in Figure 4–8(f).

As can be seen by these two examples, whether an interrupt occurs or not, at the end of the complete instruction cycle the CPU is ready to begin work on the next instruction. Exactly which instruction is next depends on what happened during the previous execute cycle and if the interrupt cycle was executed. This is irrelevant to the CPU, however, which just goes ahead and fetches the instruction referenced by the PC. Review Figures 4–7 and 4–8 for a more comprehensive understanding of how the SIC works.

118 Basic Computer Organization Chap. 4

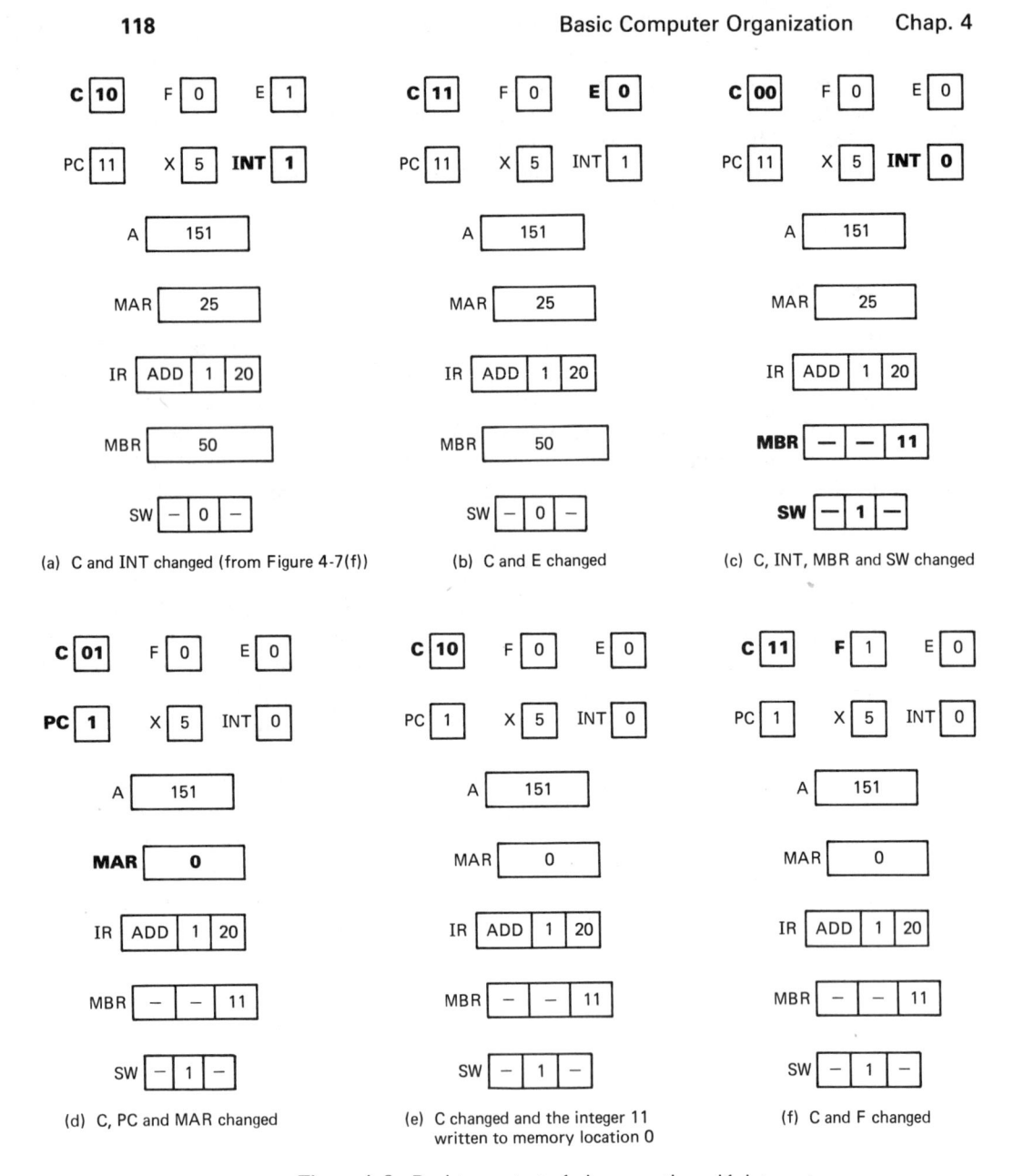

(a) C and INT changed (from Figure 4-7(f))

C [10] F [0] E [1]
PC [11] X [5] INT [1]
A [151]
MAR [25]
IR [ADD | 1 | 20]
MBR [50]
SW [− | 0 | −]

(b) C and E changed

C [11] F [0] E [0]
PC [11] X [5] INT [1]
A [151]
MAR [25]
IR [ADD | 1 | 20]
MBR [50]
SW [− | 0 | −]

(c) C, INT, MBR and SW changed

C [00] F [0] E [0]
PC [11] X [5] INT [0]
A [151]
MAR [25]
IR [ADD | 1 | 20]
MBR [− | − | 11]
SW [− | 1 | −]

(d) C, PC and MAR changed

C [01] F [0] E [0]
PC [1] X [5] INT [0]
A [151]
MAR [0]
IR [ADD | 1 | 20]
MBR [− | − | 11]
SW [− | 1 | −]

(e) C changed and the integer 11 written to memory location 0

C [10] F [0] E [0]
PC [1] X [5] INT [0]
A [151]
MAR [0]
IR [ADD | 1 | 20]
MBR [− | − | 11]
SW [− | 1 | −]

(f) C and F changed

C [11] F [1] E [0]
PC [1] X [5] INT [0]
A [151]
MAR [0]
IR [ADD | 1 | 20]
MBR [− | − | 11]
SW [− | 1 | −]

Figure 4–8 Register contents during execution with interrupt

PROBLEMS

1. Define the following terms:
   - (a) CPU
   - (b) micro-operation
   - (c) register transfer language
   - (d) control condition
   - (e) fetch cycle
   - (f) address translation cycle
   - (g) execute cycle
   - (h) interrupt cycle
   - (i) interrupt handler
   - (j) functional unit

2. Give the RTL statements that describe these diagrams.

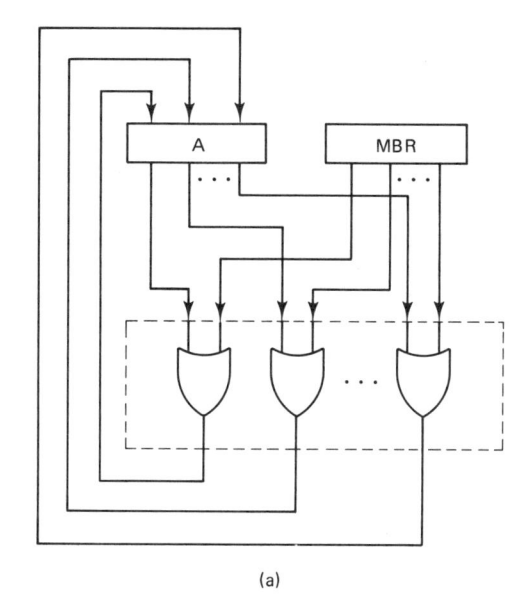

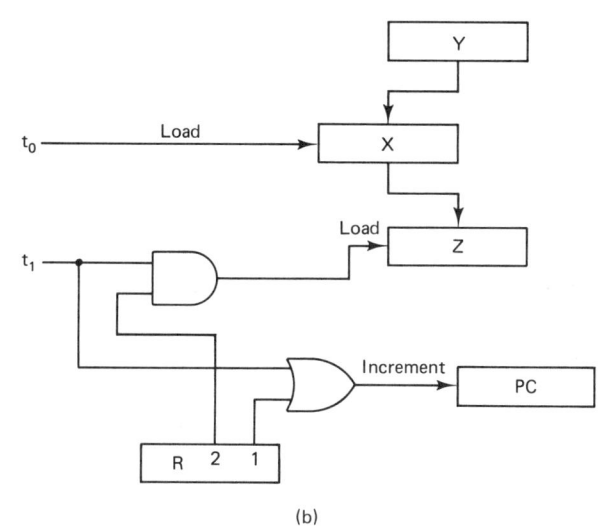

(a)

(b)

3. Draw diagrams like those in Problem 2 for the following RTL statements:
   (a) $F'Et_1$: MAR $\leftarrow$ 0, PC $\leftarrow$ 1
       $F'E't_2$: M[MAR] $\leftarrow$ (MBR)
   (b) t_0: (X):(Y)
       t_1: IF SW[CC] = 0 THEN Z $\leftarrow$ (Y)
       t_2: PC $\leftarrow$ (Z)
4. Using RTL statements, describe a circular shift right for a 5-bit register, S.
5. Assume a set of registers having these values:
       register A = 10
       register B = 0
       register C = 5
   What are the values of the registers after the following RTL statements have been executed?
       t_0: A $\leftarrow$ (A) + (C)
       Bt_1: C $\leftarrow$ 100
       t_2: B $\leftarrow$ (B) + 1
       t_3: IF C = 100 THEN A $\leftarrow$ (B)
6. Consider a computer that provides four addressing modes, has a 2^{10}-word memory, includes 16 instructions, and uses an accumulator for all arithmetic and logic instructions. Describe an instruction format that could be used by this computer.
7. What would be different in your answer for Problem 6 if the computer did not use an accumulator for the arithmetic and logic operations?
8. Consider a computer system in which each instruction takes up two words of memory. Assuming the two words are contiguous in memory, what are the implications of this format in terms of the fetch and execute cycles?
9. Give the RTL statements with control conditions for the execute cycle of the following SIC instructions:
   (a) AND *m*
   (b) JLT *m*
   (c) LDA *m*
   (d) STX *m*
   (e) RD *m*
10. Explain what the following SIC code does.

    ```
    SUB1 LDA  ZERO
    LOOP TD   10
         JGT  ERROR
         JEQ  LOOP
         RD   10
         COMP ZERO
         JEQ  EXIT
         STA  BUFFER
    EXIT RSUB
    ```

11. As in Figures 4–7 and 4–8, trace each of the following:
    (a) The execution without interrupt of a JSUB instruction
    (b) The execution with interrupt of an RSUB instruction

CHAPTER 5

The Central Processing Unit (CPU)

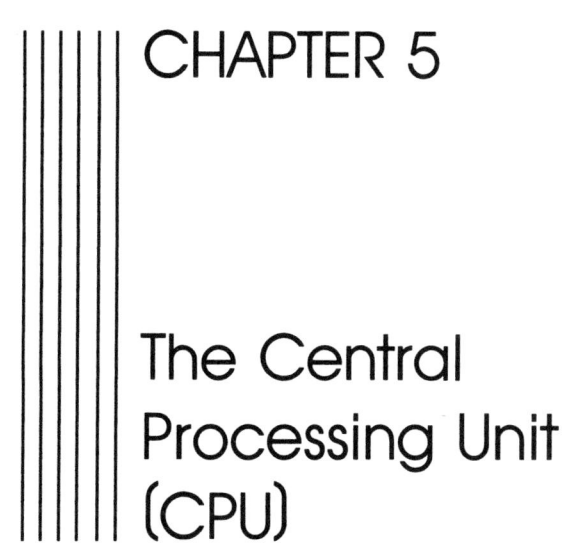

5.1 FUNDAMENTAL PARTS OF A COMPUTER

The concept of having a program stored in the memory of a computer is generally attributed to John von Neumann. In the early 1950s, he and his colleagues at the Institute for Advanced Study at Princeton developed what is now called the von Neumann machine. The basic architecture of this machine is still the frame of reference for the modern general-purpose digital computer. Figure 4–1, reproduced for convenience in Figure 5–1, shows the three fundamental parts of a von Neumann–type machine.

The program is stored in the **main memory unit,** which interfaces with the **input/output (I/O)** devices through the **central processing unit (CPU).** The CPU reads from or writes to memory by first sending the address of the word to the memory unit over the *address bus* and then either receiving or sending the data via the *data bus*. Data is exchanged between the CPU and the I/O unit also using the data bus. These operations are synchronized over the two control buses by control signals sent by the CPU and acknowledgment and interrupt signals received by the CPU.

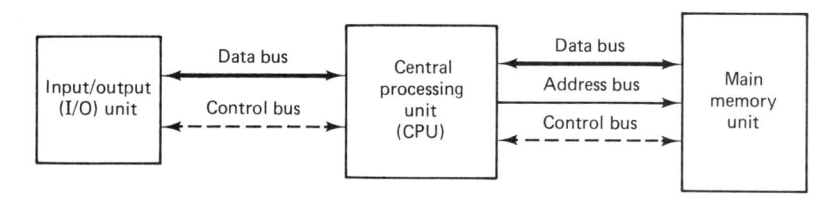

Figure 5–1 A von Neumann–type machine

The execution of the stored program is logically performed as follows:

1. The CPU fetches the next instruction from memory.
2. The CPU decodes the instruction.
3. Depending on the instruction, the CPU issues control signals to fetch another operand if necessary and then to carry out one of the following actions:
   (a) Perform an arithmetic or logic operation
   (b) Store a result in memory
   (c) Read a result from or write a result to an I/O device.
4. The CPU returns to step 1 and continues processing until the program is terminated.

This chapter deals with the organization of the CPU. I/O and memory are discussed in the following two chapters.

Every CPU is built to execute a specific set of **micro-operations.** Certain sequences of these operations, called **machine instructions,** are used to program the computer. The CPU executes each machine instruction in turn by executing the appropriate sequence of micro-operations. The subset of micro-operations selected for the execution of a particular instruction is based on the interpretation of the instruction and is determined during the design of the computer.

The CPU is made up of three major parts: the **register set,** the **arithmetic and logic unit (ALU),** and the **control logic unit (CLU).** The register set stores intermediate information necessary for executing individual instructions or sets of instructions (programs). The ALU uses the values stored in the register set to perform arithmetic and logic operations. The CLU controls the system in two ways:

1. By directing transfers to and from registers both to and from memory, the ALU, and other registers
2. By instructing the ALU as to which operation to perform

In general, the three parts of the CPU are connected as shown in Figure 5–2. Depending on the design and capabilities of a computer, each of the parts of the CPU will vary in complexity. In the following sections, we look at each part separately and then discuss some general interconnection configurations of all the parts together.

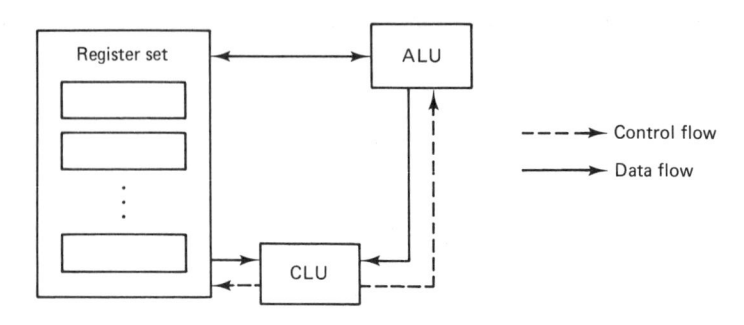

Figure 5–2 Central processing unit block diagram

5.2 THE REGISTER SET

The registers of a computer are collectively known as the **register set.** Some of the registers may be of the same type, while others may be different. For example, a computer may have several general-purpose registers with parallel load and then some separate shift registers for serial transfers. The possible combinations, as well as the number of registers, vary from computer to computer. Some registers, however, are common to almost all general-purpose computers.

Program Counter Register

One common register is the **program counter (PC).** This register stores the memory address of the next instruction to be executed. Since the execution of a program usually proceeds sequentially, the address of the next instruction is 1 higher than the address of the current instruction. (Note that we are assuming one-word instructions for now.) Therefore, we want the PC to be able to facilitate the register transfer:

$$PC \leftarrow (PC) + 1 \qquad (5.1)$$

If a jump or branch instruction is executed, the next instruction to be executed is stored at the address specified in the branch instruction. In this case, we want to load the PC directly with the new address:

$$PC \leftarrow \text{address part of branch instruction} \qquad (5.2)$$

Based on Equations (5.1) and (5.2), we see that the PC register is a binary counter with parallel load (see Section 3.7).

Instruction Register

To execute an instruction in memory that the PC is pointing to, the CPU initiates a sequence of one or more computer transfers. The actual sequence depends on the design of the CPU and the particular instruction being executed. It is possible that the operation to be performed requires one or more memory transfers. In this case, it is necessary to keep a copy of the instruction in a special register called the **instruction register (IR).** Prior to execution, an instruction is first fetched from memory and stored in the IR, and then the PC is incremented so that it is pointing to the next instruction. The register transfer sequence for this process is as follows:

$$\begin{aligned} IR &\leftarrow M[PC] \\ PC &\leftarrow (PC) + 1 \end{aligned} \qquad (5.3)$$

where M[PC] denotes the content of the memory location pointed to by the PC. Once the instruction is stored in the IR, it can be decoded by the control logic unit (CLU) and the necessary micro-operations can be activated for its execution.

General-Purpose Registers

The number of other registers in the register set varies widely. There are usually a number of general-purpose registers for storing intermediate values during the execution of instructions. Many computers contain a **program status word (PSW)** register that stores information about the condition of the CPU during an execute cycle. Typically, the PSW will include status bits from the last arithmetic operation such as overflow, carry, and sign (see Section 5.4) and permission bits for interrupts (see Section 6.2) that are allowed to occur. This register, along with the PC, can then be used to store the state of a running program when an outside interrupt needs to be serviced. After the interrupt, the CPU can continue to execute the program from where it left off.

Of the general registers, at least one serves as a **memory address register (MAR)** and at least one serves as a **memory buffer register (MBR).** The basic computer of Chapter 4 uses the MAR and MBR exclusively for referencing the memory, although it is possible to use more than one register for each of these functions.

If instead of general-purpose registers a computer has one processor register for executing instructions, this register is called the **accumulator (ACC).** This kind of setup restricts the power and versatility of the possible instruction set but simplifies the logic circuit of the control logic unit by allowing one of the operands of logic and arithmetic instructions to be always implied. When one ACC is used, it is usually a very specialized register. Sometimes a computer will have general-purpose registers but will also use one as a *pseudo-ACC* to allow implied addressing for certain instructions.

In addition to some combinations of the registers just discussed, all computers have a number of **flag registers,** which are used to control the flow of execution in the CLU and ALU. The number and exact use of these registers is particular to a given computer. Some of these registers were already mentioned in Chapter 4.

The Intel 8085 Register Set

Let us consider the register set of a simple CPU, the Intel 8085 microprocessor. (When the entire CPU is contained on one IC chip, it is called a microprocessor; see Chapter 11.) The 8085 is a 40-pin chip that processes 8 bits of data in parallel at a time. Addressing is done using 16-bit addresses for memory as well as I/O.

Figure 5–3(a) shows the register set for the Intel 8085 microprocessor. In this CPU, the A register serves as an 8-bit accumulator. The CPU also includes a program counter (PC), a stack pointer (SP), a flag register, and six 8-bit addressing registers. (The SP is used in conjunction with a memory stack as explained in Section 7.2.) As shown in Figure 5–3(b), the 8-bit registers are usually used in pairs. The A register, together with the flag register, forms the program status word (PSW). The three other pairs are used for addressing purposes, the H pair being the most commonly used. These pairs may be referenced together or separately, resulting in a wide variety of available instructions.

```
    FLAG              A (8-bit)              B (8-bit)    C (8-bit)
  ┌─┬─┬─┬──┬─┬─┬─┬─┐                         D (8-bit)    E (8-bit)
  │S│Z│X│AC│X│P│X│C│                         H (8-bit)    L (8-bit)
  └─┴─┴─┴──┴─┴─┴─┴─┘── Carry
                    ── Parity                   PC (16-bit)
                    ── Aux. carry
                    ── Zero                     SP (16-bit)
                    ── Sign
```

(a) Internal registers

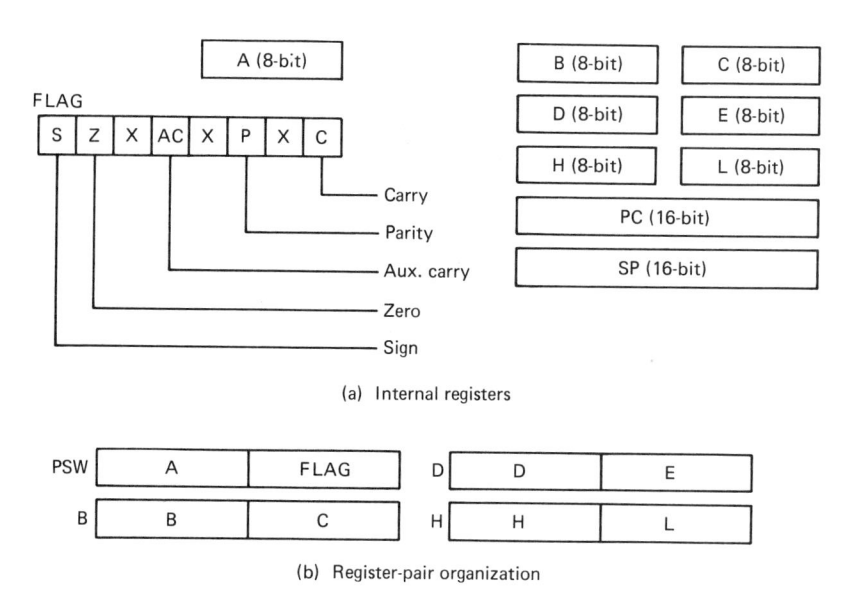

```
  PSW │    A    │  FLAG  │    D │  D  │  E
    B │    B    │    C   │    H │  H  │  L
```

(b) Register-pair organization

Figure 5–3 Register set of the Intel 8085 microprocessor

5.3 INSTRUCTION FORMATS

The internal organization of the computer is defined by the instructions that it can execute. An instruction is a convention used by the computer to define operations such as ADD, STORE, LOAD, MOVE, and BRANCH and to determine the location of the data on which the operation is to be performed. The set of all instructions, called the **instruction set,** includes a variety of arithmetic and logical operations, data transfer instructions, I/O instructions, and control instructions. Grouped together by a programmer, the instructions form a program that defines the sequence and pattern of data movement and transformation.

As was previously discussed in Chapter 4, a computer instruction is a binary code divided into a number of **fields.** The operation field, or **opcode,** specifies the operation to be performed. This operation is executed on some data, **operands,** which may be part of the instruction or stored in registers or in main memory, and whose locations are specified by the **address** field of the instruction. The way to interpret the operand field is specified by the **addressing mode.** Depending on the addressing mode and the particular operation, actual operands may be implied, may be constants, or may be stored in some other location. The length of computer instructions is not fixed. An instruction may be one or more words long, thus requiring one or more memory words to be fetched.

Address Formats

Binary codings of instructions vary from one computer to another, and each computer has its own particular instruction code format. In one of the earliest computers, each

| OPCODE | A_0 | A_1 | A_2 | A_3 |

Figure 5–4 Four-address format

instruction was comprised of an opcode and four address fields. Figure 5–4 shows such a **four-address format,** where

A_0 = address of the first operand
A_1 = address of the second operand
A_2 = address where the result of the operation is to be stored
A_3 = address of the next instruction

Since the computer usually executes instructions sequentially, we can code the algorithms in a sequential manner and therefore eliminate the need for A_3. If we assume that the memory word length is fixed, we could use the bits specifying A_3 for the other remaining addresses and be able to use a larger memory space without increasing the size of the memory word. This format, known as a **three-address format,** is shown in Figure 5–5, where

A_0 = address of the first operand
A_1 = address of the second operand
A_2 = address of the result

Consider a computer having a word length of 42 bits and a memory space of 512 words. If we assign 6 bits to the opcode (implying $2^6 = 64$ possible operations), then in the four-address format, 9 bits are left for each of the four addresses (since $2^9 = 512$ addresses of memory). Keeping the opcode the same at 6 bits leaves 36 bits for the addresses of the three-address format, or 12 bits per address. We can therefore address up to $2^{12} = 4096$ memory locations. Thus by decreasing the number of addresses in the instruction format, we can increase the size of addressable memory if the word length remains the same.

Another format, known as the **two-address format,** eliminates both the A_2 and A_3 addresses. It is the most common in commercial computers and, depending on the particular system, uses either the accumulator, A_0, or A_1 for the results. Consider again the example using a 42-bit word length with 6 bits assigned to the opcode. We can now use 18 bits $[(42 - 6)/2]$ per address and thus address a memory space of $2^{18} = 262,144$ words.

The simplest way, however, to organize a computer is to have a single CPU register and an instruction code with only two parts. This format, known as the **single-address format,** is shown in Figure 5–6. The accumulator now performs a double function: It is usually the implied address for the second operand as well as the location where the result is stored. With a 42-bit word length and reserving 6 bits for the

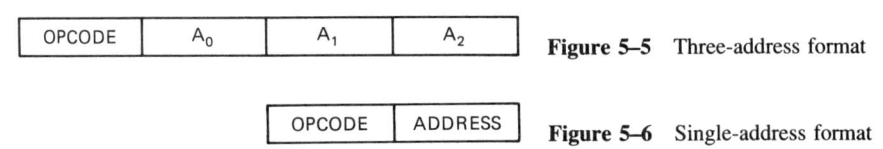

| OPCODE | A_0 | A_1 | A_2 |

Figure 5–5 Three-address format

| OPCODE | ADDRESS |

Figure 5–6 Single-address format

Sec. 5.3 Instruction Formats

opcode, we now have 2^{36} (approximately 7×10^{10}) possible addressable words of memory. Even if we reduced the word length, the single-address format would still permit an addressing capability of a very large memory space. Note, however, that while this may seem desirable, it can be done only at the expense of dramatically increasing the size of the instruction set and, correspondingly, the size of the programs.

Addressing Modes

A variety of **addressing modes** can be used to determine an address from which to fetch an operand. Some of these techniques increase the speed of instruction execution by decreasing the number of references to main memory and increasing the number of references to high-speed registers. The addressing mode specifies a rule for interpreting or modifying the address field of the instruction before the operand is actually referenced.

Some common addressing modes are listed in Table 5.1 and diagrammed in Figure 5-7, where, for simplicity, just the address field of the instruction register (IR) is defined. In the **implied mode,** the operands are specified implicitly in the definition of the instruction. For example, an ADD instruction in a single-address format implies the address of the second operand as the accumulator. The instruction CLEAR ACC is an implied-mode instruction because the operand (which is 0) is implied in the definition of the instruction and need not be stated explicity.

A particular organization that uses implied addressing is known as the **pushdown stack,** discussed in detail in Section 7.2. A stack memory is a portion of main memory, of no fixed size, set aside for subroutine operations or for handling exceptional conditions such as interrupts. All instructions have their implied operands in either the top register or in the top two registers of the stack. The result of any operation is returned to the stack and becomes the top register. When an operand is required, it is fetched from its location in memory and placed on top of the stack, thereby pushing down the contents of all the other registers in the stack.

The **immediate addressing mode,** shown in Figure 5-7(a), indicates that the

TABLE 5.1 COMMON ADDRESSING MODES

Mode	Value of operand	Sample transfer*
Implied	No operand in instruction	—
Immediate	Constant in operand field	OPR ← number
Direct	Memory at address	OPR ← M[ad]
Indirect	Memory at address of address	OPR ← M(M[ad])
Register	Register	OPR ← (R1)
Register-indirect	Memory at address of register	OPR ← M[R1]
Autoincrement	Register; increment register	OPR ← (R1) R1 ← (R1) + 1
Relative	Memory location of PC plus address	OPR ← M[PC + ad]
Index	Memory location of index register (XR) plus address	OPR ← M[XR + ad]

* OPR represents a register for storing the operand to be used when the instruction is executed.

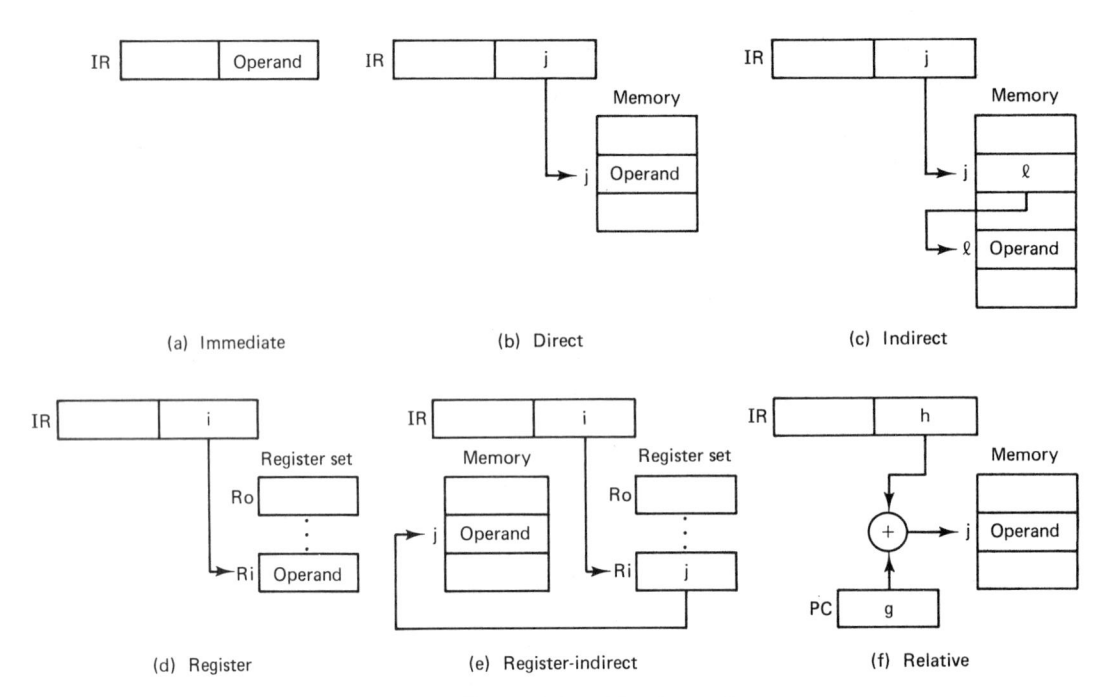

Figure 5-7 Addressing modes

actual operand is stored in the address field of the instruction. This mode is commonly used whenever constants are involved in the program or when the operand is short and we want, for example, to specify the number of places to shift a register in a SHIFT instruction. Since no memory access is needed, we call this mode immediate addressing.

In all the other addressing modes, the actual operand is not stored in the address field. Rather, some value is specified and is used to determine the location of the operand. Let us now consider these modes in three different situations: when the address field specifies a memory address, when it specifies a processor register, and when it specifies an operand for computing the effective address.

Address field specifies a memory address. The two modes in this category are the direct and indirect addressing modes. In the **direct mode,** shown in Figure 5-7(b), the operand is stored in memory at the address given in the address field of the instruction. In **indirect addressing** [Figure 5-7(c)], the address field of the instruction does not contain the operand but contains another address of where we can find the operand. This technique requires two fetches from memory to obtain the operand. Indirect addressing can be nested; that is, it can go on for more than one level.

It is customary to use one bit (I) in the instruction code to distinguish between an indirect and a direct addressing mode; for example, I = 0 for direct addressing and I = 1 for indirect addressing. To illustrate this, consider the instruction code where

Sec. 5.3 Instruction Formats

$$I = 0$$
$$\text{OPCODE} = 100$$
$$\text{ADDRESS} = 0001000$$

Since $I = 0$, the addressing mode is direct and the operand is in location 8. If, however, the instruction code is

$$I = 1$$
$$\text{OPCODE} = 100$$
$$\text{ADDRESS} = 0001000$$

we find the address of the operand in location 8. If location 8 reads

$$I = 0$$
$$\text{OPCODE} = 100$$
$$\text{ADDRESS} = 0001011$$

the operand is in location 11.

Address field specifies a processor register. With the **register addressing mode,** the operand of the instruction is stored in one of the processor registers. The address field contains a value identifying the register as shown in Figure 5–7(d). Therefore, a k-bit address field can specify any one of 2^k registers.

When the addressing mode is **register-indirect** [Figure 5–7(e)], the operand is stored in memory and the register identified in the address field contains the memory address of the operand. Although this is similar in principle to the indirect addressing mode, it requires less space to specify a register than to specify a memory address (due to the large difference in the number of registers compared to the number of memory words).

An **autoincrement** or **autodecrement mode** can be used with either register or register-indirect addressing. Table 5.1 describes autoincrement with register addressing, a mode most commonly used for counter or index variables. (In particular, this mode is often used with respect to stack pointers, discussed in Chapter 7.)

Address field used to compute effective address. This third category includes the relative, index, base, augmented, and block addressing modes. In the **relative addressing mode,** shown in Figure 5–7(f), the value of the address field is added to the program counter (PC) to give the memory address of the actual operand. The **index addressing mode** is basically the same, except that an *index register* is used instead of the PC to determine the memory address. Some computers have several index registers, and, therefore, the particular one to be used with a given instruction must be specified as part of the instruction. The **effective address** is obtained by adding the content of the specified index register to the direct address:

Effective address = (index register) + direct address

The index register is usually loaded with a number that is modified during a loop of instructions. Thus each time an instruction using the index register is executed, it will have a different effective address for the operands. The modification of the content of the index register is done by special instructions that operate on it. Here are some examples of these instructions:

1. Load index register with the content of address A.
2. Load index register immediately.
3. Store the content of the index register at address A.
4. Increment or decrement the index register by the amount A.
5. Jump to address A if the content of the index register is negative.

There are several ways of performing a loop and testing it using indexing. The particular method is a function of the design of the instructions that are used to modify the index register and the method of testing the content of the index register. Some computers test for zero content; others test for positive content.

When the index register contains a base address, the direct address in the instruction code is called the **displacement** (or **offset**) since it indicates the number of words displaced from the origin at which the operand is located. In this case, the index addressing mode is sometimes referred to as the **base addressing mode.** Since

$$\text{Effective address} = \text{direct address} + \text{(base register)}$$

we can address a large main memory space using only a small number of direct addresses in an instruction format. For example, if the computer has a 24-bit word length with 12 bits assigned for direct addressing, the computer can directly address $2^{12} = 4096$ words. To extend the addressing capability of this computer, consider a 24-bit base (index) register. By using the base register appropriately, a memory space of up to 2^{24} (approximately 16×10^6) locations can be addressed.

Another concept embedded in base addressing is the ability to **relocate** the program anywhere in main memory. If the programmer writes all the direct addresses relative to an origin address, 0, say, the program can be displaced by any amount by loading the base register with the new origin of the program, thereby shifting the program to another set of contiguous addresses in memory. Although this permits the instructions to be relocatable, it makes no provision for the data to be relocatable. If a second base register is used to address the data and all references to the data are written relative to the origin address 0, a contiguous block of operands can be shifted to any location in main memory by loading the origin of the block of addresses into the second base register. Since all references to the operands are written as if they started at address 0, the base register displaces the address referred to by the program to the proper location where the operands have been relocated.

Augmented addressing is similar to base addressing, but instead of adding the content of a special register to the direct address to obtain the effective address, the direct address is *concatenated* with the content of the register to obtain the effective address. Thus

$$\text{Effective address} = \text{(augmented address register) direct address}$$

Augmented addressing also provides the means of relocating a block of instructions or data. The word in the augmented address register is sometimes called a **page** number, while the direct address is called the "word within a page." This concept will be discussed further in Chapter 7.

The **block addressing** mode uses the address to specify the first word in a block of data. The blocks can be of variable length, where the length is specified as part of the instruction, or the instruction can indicate the length of the block by pointing to the first and last addresses of the block. Another method of specifying the length of the block is to have a special character, called an **end-of-block** character. The computer keeps fetching a block of information starting with the first address until it reaches the end-of-block character. If the blocks are of fixed length, only the address of the first word of the block needs to be specified. **Block access** is used extensively to address data stored in auxiliary storage devices such as magnetic drums, disks, and tapes.

This section has covered the most common addressing modes. It is possible for a computer to use other modes and/or combinations of the common modes. In all these cases, the IR should have the capacity for parallel load, as well as the capability of transferring any one of its specific fields to wherever it is needed.

5.4 ARITHMETIC AND LOGIC UNIT (ALU)

In the basic computer in Chapter 4, all arithmetic and logic operations were assumed to be performed on the ACC. To execute an operation in this kind of organization between any general registers or memory words, the operation has to be broken down into a sequence of micro-operations that load, manipulate, and store the ACC register.

Example 5.1

Given a single-accumulator computer, the sequence of micro-operations necessary to execute R1 ← (R2) + (R3) is as follows:

ACC ← 0	Clear ACC.
ACC ← (ACC) + (R2)	Add R2 to ACC.
ACC ← (ACC) + (R3)	Add R3 to ACC.
R1 ← (ACC)	Store ACC in R1.

The advantage of this type of system is that the design of the computer is relatively simple and straightforward. The obvious disadvantage is the amount of time necessary to perform an operation. In Example 5.1, it would take four clock pulses to execute the simple ADD operation. If the computer has a separate logic circuit for performing addition, the ADD operation can be executed in one clock pulse. Figure 5–8 depicts a setup capable of executing R1 ← (R2) + (R3) in one clock pulse.

The idea of one general adder capable of adding any two registers together and storing the result in any other register is the underlying principle of the **arithmetic and logic unit (ALU)**. We will want this same capability for other operations as well. We define the ALU, then, as a unit that contains the circuit for performing a set of arithmetic and logic micro-operations. An example of a dual-function ALU is

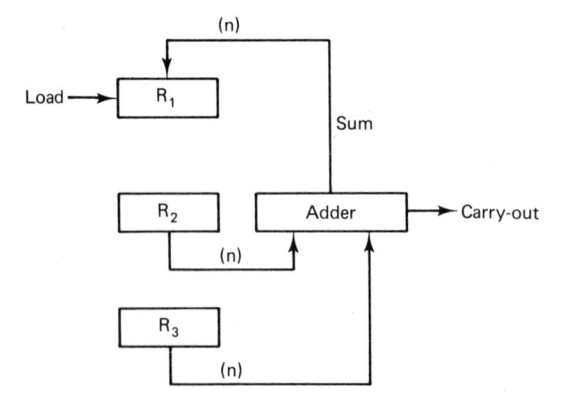

Figure 5-8 Setup for executing R1 ← (R2) + (R3)

shown in Figure 5-9. The n input lines of A and B are connected to the function blocks f_1 and f_2, and the n output lines of these blocks are connected to n multiplexers (MUX). Depending on the particular micro-operation that is to be performed, the selection lines will be set to choose the appropriate function output lines for the n

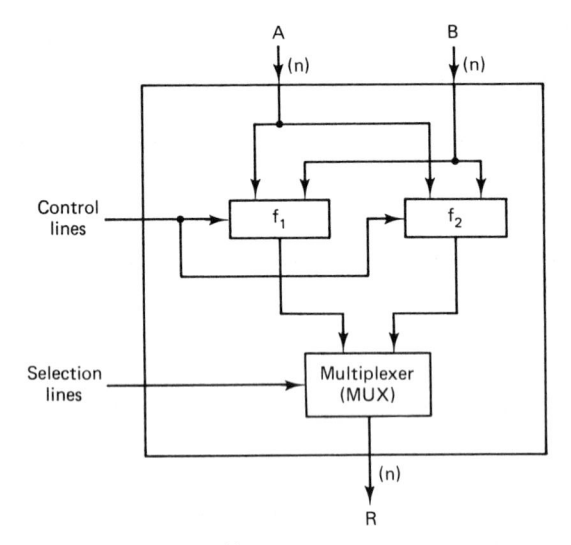

(a) Internal organization

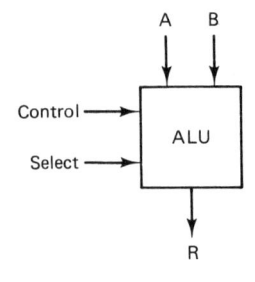

(b) Block diagram

Figure 5-9 Dual-function ALU

Sec. 5.4 Arithmetic and Logic Unit (ALU)

lines of R, the result of the ALU operation. The number of selection lines necessary depends on the number of functions in the ALU.

In this section we will study the ALU for two n-bit inputs, A and B, and a single n-bit output, R. In Section 5.6, we will consider a configuration for allowing any general register to supply the inputs and/or receive the outputs. Our design goal for the ALU will be to include the logic necessary for all the micro-operations we want to handle, with a minimum amount of circuitry. Let us start off by looking at the arithmetic functions of the ALU.

Arithmetic Functions of an ALU

Data types and representations. As was discussed in Chapter 2, there are different types of numbers, and for each of these different types, there are different ways of representing the numbers in computer systems. The different types of data usually include integer, floating-point (real), and binary-coded decimal. In general, data is represented in either sign-magnitude, 1's complement, or 2's complement notation. The logic of an ALU for a particular operation, therefore, is a function of both the kind of numbers being processed and how they are represented. Thus if integers are represented in sign-magnitude notation, addition is done by first checking the sign bit and then adding or subtracting the numbers, depending on their relative magnitudes. For example, summing $2 + 3$ can be done directly, but summing $2 + (-3)$ is processed as $-(3 - 2)$. In contrast, if the numbers are represented in 2's complement notation, they are simply added as is.

In the following sections we will discuss the logic necessary for the ALU to perform addition, subtraction, multiplication, and division on different types and representations of numbers. Later, in Section 5.5, we will present a detailed description of the control logic for adding and multiplying fixed-point numbers and for BCD addition.

Addition and subtraction. Consider the binary parallel adder of Figure 3–17 in Chapter 3, whose schematic block diagram is shown in Figure 5–10. When the carry-in Z is 0, the parallel adder performs the micro-operation $S \leftarrow X + Y$. However, if Z is 1 and Y is 0, the micro-operation performed is $S \leftarrow X + 1$. By complementing Y when $Z = 1$, the micro-operation performed by the parallel adder is $S \leftarrow X + \overline{Y} + 1$, which is actually $S \leftarrow X - Y$ when a 2's complement number representation is being used. The point of this is that we can generate different micro-operations just by varying the inputs to the parallel adder. Table 5.2 shows the possible input combinations and the resulting micro-operations that can be executed by a parallel adder.

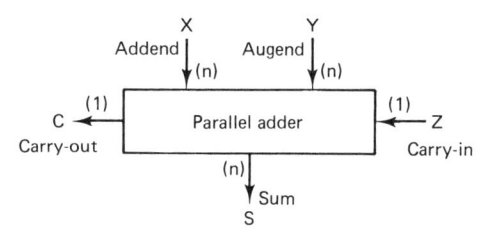

Figure 5–10 Block diagram of an n-bit binary parallel adder

TABLE 5.2 POSSIBLE ARITHMETIC MICRO-OPERATIONS OF A PARALLEL ADDER

X	Y	Z	Micro-operation	Comment
A	B	0	$S \leftarrow A + B$	Addition
A	B	1	$S \leftarrow A + B + 1$	Addition with carry
A	$\overline{B}$	0	$S \leftarrow A + \overline{B}$	A plus 1's complement of B
A	$\overline{B}$	1	$S \leftarrow A + \overline{B} + 1$	A plus 2's complement of B
A	all zeros	0	$S \leftarrow A$	Transfer A
A	all zeros	1	$S \leftarrow A + 1$	Increment A
A	all ones	0	$S \leftarrow A - 1$	Decrement A
A	all ones	1	$S \leftarrow A$	Transfer A

For the ALU, it is easy enough to change the value of the carry-in input between 0 and 1 by using a single control line. However, to generate the required four values for Y [either passing B directly onto the parallel adder ($Y = B$), complementing its value ($Y = \overline{B}$), Y = all zeros, or Y = all ones], we let B first pass through a **conversion element (CE)** before it is input to the parallel adder, as indicated in Figure 5–11. The conversion element requires two selection lines (s_1 and s_0) to choose one of the four possible outputs. For example, Figure 5–12 shows a logic circuit implementation of a 3-bit conversion element together with its associated function table.

Multiplication and division. In Section 2.3 of Chapter 2, we presented algorithms for multiplication and division. These operations are comparatively more complex than either addition or subtraction; however, they are basically made up of additions or subtractions. The multiplication algorithm goes through a sequence of adds and shifts, while the division algorithm performs a sequence of subtracts and shifts.

At this point, it may be asked whether or not we should construct a separate functional unit in the ALU for the multiplication and division operations. Since the ALU executes a number of micro-operations, the longest execution time necessary for any one of them is going to determine the **cycle time** for all the micro-operations. An ALU with just a parallel adder and a conversion element for one of the inputs (as in Figure 5–11) can execute any operation in a relatively short time. Depending on the word length, this time ranges from 50 to 100 nanoseconds (ns). However, if we try to include multiplication and division in the ALU, the cycle time will have

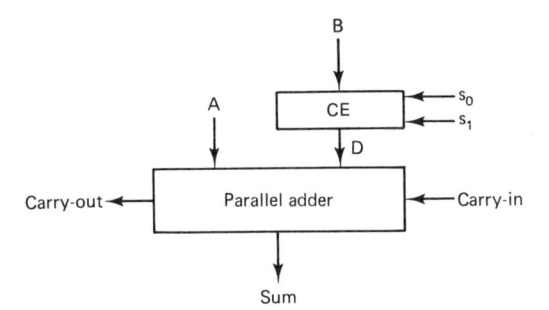

Figure 5–11 A conversion element (CE) on the B input to a binary parallel adder

Sec. 5.4 Arithmetic and Logic Unit (ALU)

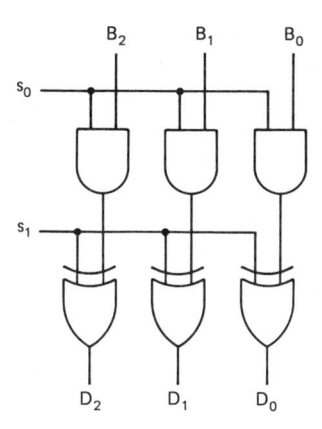

Function Table

Selection Lines		CE Outputs
s_1	s_0	($i = 0, 1, 2$)
0	0	$D_i = 0$
0	1	$D_i = B_i$
1	0	$D_i = 1$
1	1	$D_i = \overline{B_i}$

Figure 5–12 Logic circuit of a 3-bit conversion element

to increase accordingly, and it will take just as long to add two numbers as it will to multiply them. For example, assume that it takes 50 ns to add two numbers using a parallel adder and that we want to multiply two 10-bit numbers. It will then take more than 500 ns (50 ns × 10 bits) to execute the necessary adds and shifts to do the multiplication. Hence implementing this operation directly in the ALU implies that the cycle time must be greater than 500 ns and therefore *all* the arithmetic microoperations will take this long to execute. This seems an unnecessary burden to put on such simple operations as $A \leftarrow B$ or $A \leftarrow A + 1$.

One alternative to this is to have variable-length cycles. This is possible, but it is not very common. Another alternative is to keep the ALU (as far as arithmetic functions go) as it is in Figure 5–11 and to implement multiplication and division operations by having the control logic unit initiate the necessary adds, subtracts, and shifts. This means that multiply and divide would not be considered micro-operations, but it would also allow the cycle time to be kept constant and relatively small for the ALU. Since the shorter cycle time is definitely favorable, the multiply and divide operations are not included directly in the ALU. Rather, they are implemented in the CLU, or in special-purpose multiply/divide integrated circuits whose hardware implementation will be discussed in Section 5.5.

Condition bits. It is often necessary to determine certain relationships that exist between the two inputs to the ALU, in addition to the result of the particular operation. For example, it is important to know if an ADD operation resulted in an overflow or if there was an end carry from the operation when multiplying two numbers or adding sign-magnitude numbers. This information is determined at the same time that the operation is being executed and stored in what are called **condition bits (flags)** for later evaluation. These condition bits are generally considered to be a part of the program status word register (PSW) discussed earlier in Section 5.2. For example, Figure 5–13 shows a diagram of a circuit that tests for four common conditions related to 2's complement numbers:

1. **Overflow (OF):** Set when the carry-in to the last bit (C_3) and the carry-out of the last bit (C_4) are not the same.
2. **End carry (EC):** Equal to the carry-out of the last bit (C_4).
3. **Sign (S):** Equal to the sign bit of the result.
4. **Zero (Z):** Set when the result (excluding the sign bit) is 0.

In the sign-magnitude case, only bits 0, 1, and 2 would actually be added, since bit 3 is the sign bit. Hence the EC flag is related to the C_3 carry and the OF flag is set equal to the EC flag. Overflow for the 1's complement case is similar to 2's complement, with one exception (considered in Problem 11 at the end of this chapter).

Logic Functions of an ALU

Compared to the arithmetic functions, the logic functions of the ALU are much simpler. For any logic operation that we wish to implement, it is necessary only to include n of the specific logic gates for that operation (one for each input bit pair). For example, Figure 5–14 shows the logic circuit needed to implement the exclusive OR (XOR) operation for 3-bit inputs. The simplicity of the logic functions is due to the fact that no carry-borrow lateral signals are necessary as in the arithmetic functions. All logic operations are strictly executed on a single bit position using no information from previous bit positions nor sending any information to later bit positions.

An ALU can be set up to handle any number of logic micro-operations. The four basic logic operations included are usually AND, OR, NOR, and XOR. All other logic operations not explicitly included can then be derived from these four

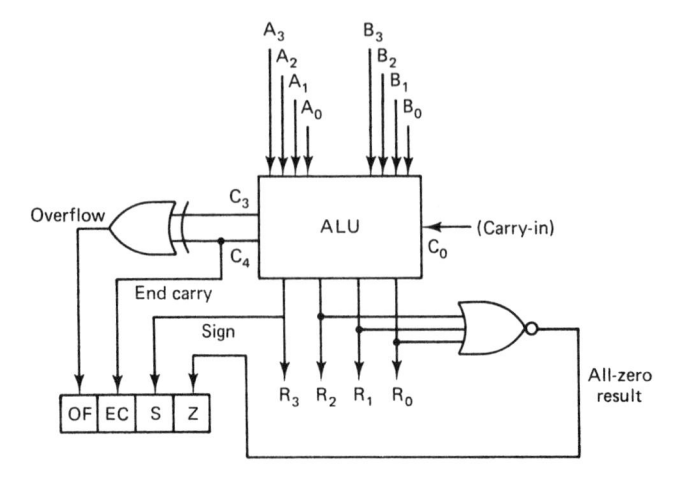

Figure 5–13 Logic diagrams for condition bits

Sec. 5.4 Arithmetic and Logic Unit (ALU)

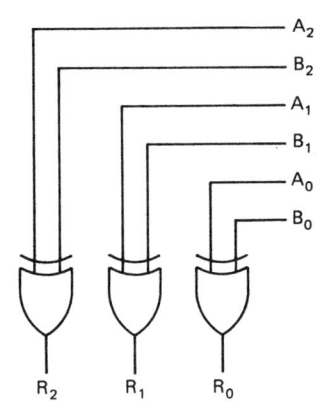

Figure 5-14 Exclusive OR operation on 3-bit inputs

basic operations. Figure 5–15 shows a realization of the four basic logic operations to be included in the ALU. The n inputs of A and B are connected in pairs to the gates of each logic operation, and the selection lines for the MUXs choose one of the operations. This logic unit is considered part of the ALU, just like the binary parallel adder. As far as the cycle time of the logic part of the ALU is concerned, it will always be less than that of the adder.

Shifter

Consider again the multiplication and division algorithms of Chapter 2. We have seen how the ALU can be used for the addition and subtraction parts, but what about the shifts? One way to implement these shifts is to load the result from the ALU (after the add or subtract) into a bidirectional shift register with parallel load (see Section 3.7), and then, on the next clock pulse, the appropriate shift can be executed. There are two main reasons, however, why this implementation is not used. First, since we do not really need to store intermediate results, using a register is an unnecessary

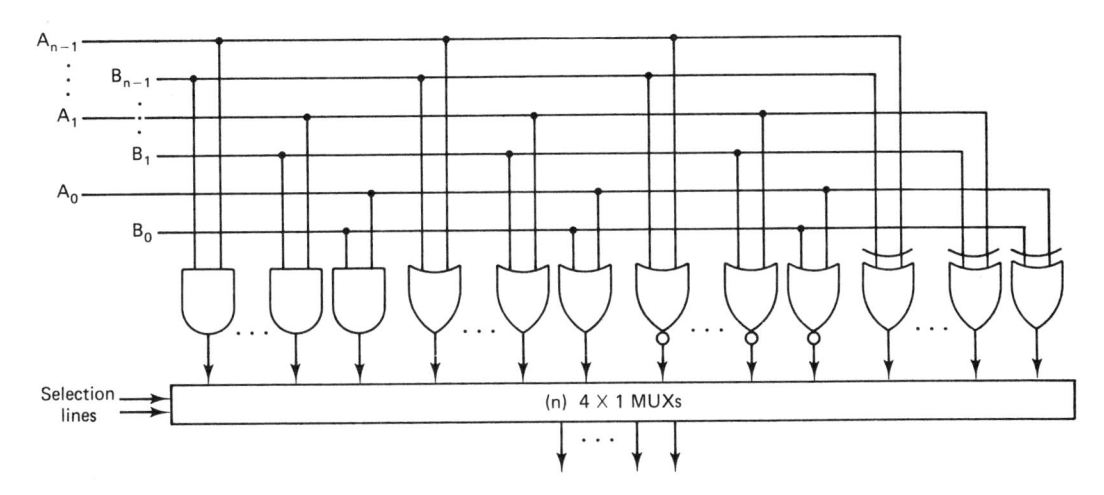

Figure 5-15 Logic unit for the four basic logic operations

expense. Second, by using a register, we are forced into using two clock pulses for each shift: one for the load and one for the shift.

We can get around these problems by implementing a combinational shifter circuit, known as a **position scaler,** shown in Figure 5–16. When the shift control is 1, the left-hand AND gates in Figure 5–16(a) are enabled while the right-hand AND gates are disabled. The insert bit passes on to the most significant bit of Z (Z_{n-1}), and each bit of A shifts one bit position to the right of Z, with the least significant bit of A (A_0) being discarded. A similar shift to the left occurs when the shift control equals 0. Notice that this is different from a shift register in that the outputs will not be shifted further and further to the right (or left) depending on how long the shift control is set (or cleared). Rather, the outputs will remain constant as long as the inputs do. As soon as the inputs change, the outputs will also change after two or three gate delays.

Since we want to perform shifts together with arithmetic or logic functions, as in multiplication or string packing, it will be more efficient to set up the shifter outside the ALU, as shown in Figure 5–17. In this way, we can add two numbers and shift

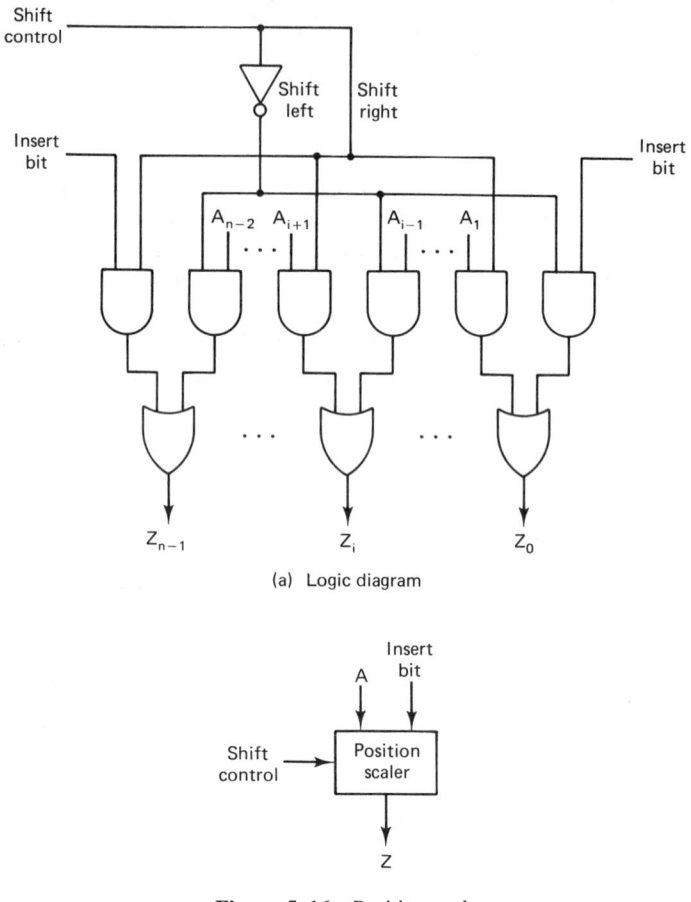

(a) Logic diagram

Figure 5–16 Position scaler

Sec. 5.5 Control Logic Unit (CLU)

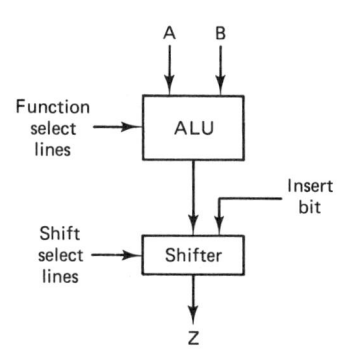

Figure 5-17 ALU-shifter configuration

the result all in one step rather than passing the result back around to the ALU input and then setting up the ALU to shift the number. To use the shifter in such a setup, it must be possible for the results of the ALU to pass through the shifter unchanged. We must therefore modify the position scaler to include a "no-shift" control. The block diagram for the complete shifter is shown in Figure 5-18. The actual design of the logic circuit is left as an exercise. In the following sections and in general, references to a computer's ALU imply the shifter as well.

5.5 CONTROL LOGIC UNIT (CLU)

Based on the particular register set, the functions included in the ALU, and the interconnections between them, a computer is able to implement a number of distinct micro-operations. We say that the organization of a computer is defined by its set of micro-operations. Also associated with each computer is a set of machine instructions that are used to program the computer. Within the computer, each of these instructions is made up of a certain sequence of micro-operations. The **control logic unit (CLU)** of the computer inputs information about the instructions and outputs the necessary control lines to activate the appropriate micro-operations.

Example 5.2

Using the same operations as in Example 5.1, suppose that a computer has an instruction of the form ADD i,j,k, which means add register j to register k and store the sum in

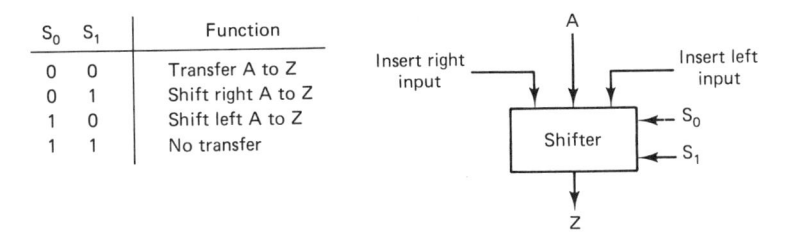

S_0	S_1	Function
0	0	Transfer A to Z
0	1	Shift right A to Z
1	0	Shift left A to Z
1	1	No transfer

Figure 5-18 Block diagram of a complete shifter

register i [$Ri \leftarrow (Rj) + (Rk)$]. If the computer is a single-ACC system, this instruction will be broken down into a sequence of micro-operations such as

$$ACC \leftarrow 0$$
$$ACC \leftarrow (ACC) + (Rj)$$
$$ACC \leftarrow (ACC) + (Rk)$$
$$Ri \leftarrow (ACC)$$

Now, let $i = 1$, $j = 2$, and $k = 3$, and let the ADD operation be coded as 101. Figure 5–19 shows a possible configuration of the CLU for this one instruction. Each P_i is a control line, only one of which is 1 at a time, that enables the distinct micro-operations. P_0 causes the ACC to be cleared. P_1 selects R2 and P_2 selects R3 from the MUX to be added to the ACC. The sum output of the adder is always sent back to the ACC but is loaded only on either P_1 or P_2. In this example, the parallel adder is designed to add the inputs that are available on the clock pulse. This way the sum, which is loaded back into the ACC, will not be input again during this micro-operation. Alternatively, two clock pulses could be used for the addition steps: one to add and one to load. P_3 is connected to the load input of R1, whose data input is connected from the ACC. To ensure that the events occur in the correct order, the **sequence counter (SC)**, together with the 2 × 4 decoder, generates the timing signals t_0 through t_3 on successive applications of clock pulses. These timing signals control all P_i and force the correct sequence to be followed.

Example 5.2 is just a small sample of the control signals generated by the CLU. Not only must each separate instruction be handled, but the control signals to fetch

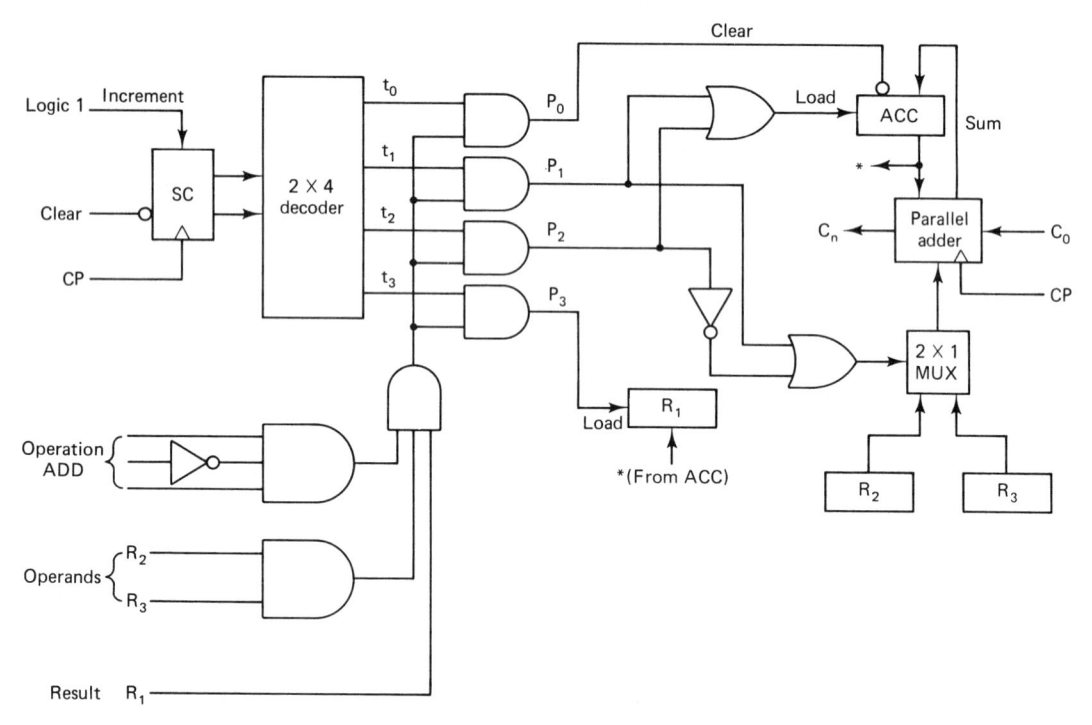

Figure 5–19 Control lines for $R1 \leftarrow (R2) + (R3)$

Sec. 5.5   Control Logic Unit (CLU)   141

the instruction and operands from memory, to handle interrupts, and to process I/O must all be generated by the CLU. Let us look at the CLU in terms of the arithmetic processor and a decimal arithmetic unit.

Arithmetic Processor

As we have seen in Chapter 4, a computer works on cycles. Usually there are a fetch cycle, an effective address computation cycle, an execute cycle, and an interrupt cycle. The number of timing signals in each cycle will vary from computer to computer and even within one machine. We can consider the CLU as made up of an **instruction processor (IP)** and an **arithmetic processor (AP)**. The IP controls the fetch, address computation, and interrupt cycles, and the AP controls the execution cycles of the arithmetic and logical operations.

Fixed-point arithmetic. In Chapter 2, the basic procedures for fixed-point arithmetic operations were outlined. We shall now consider them in terms of the register transfer statements executed by the CLU to actually perform the operations. In our discussion, we shall make the following assumptions:

1. The operands are in registers A and B.
2. The sign bits of A and B are in A_s and B_s, respectively.
3. Register E is used to hold the end carry for addition or end borrow for subtraction.
4. The codes for the operations are as follows:

$$c_0 = \text{ADD}$$
$$c_1 = \text{SUBTRACT}$$
$$c_2 = \text{MULTIPLY}$$
$$c_3 = \text{DIVIDE}$$

5. SC is a sequence counter that, together with a decoder, generates timing signals t_0 through t_n.
6. OF is the overflow condition bit.
7. The content of register I is 1 when an operation is being executed by the AP and is reset to 0 at the end of the execution.

Consider addition and subtraction of numbers represented in 2's complement notation. Recall that the 2's complement of a number x is $\bar{x} + 1$. As explained in Section 2.3, to add two fixed-point numbers, we add their corresponding bits and ignore any carry-out of the leftmost bit. To subtract, we add the 2's complement of the subtrahend to the minuend. The actual operation performed, however, is dependent on the signs of the operands, as follows:

1. If the operation is ADD and the signs are the same, add A and B.
2. If the operation is ADD and the signs are different, subtract B from A.

3. If the operation is SUBTRACT and the signs are the same, subtract B from A.
4. If the operation is SUBTRACT and the signs are different, add A and B.

Table 5.3 shows the corresponding register transfer statements necessary to perform the ADD and SUBTRACT operations such that the sum is in register A. The SC is set to control the flow of execution of the statements and is initially reset to 0. For an ADD operation, the augend is in A and the addend is in B, whereas for a SUBTRACT operation, the minuend is in A and the subtrahend is in B. If the signs are identical for an ADD operation or different for a SUBTRACT operation, the magnitudes are added in step 1. However, if the signs are different for an ADD operation or identical for a SUBTRACT operation, the magnitudes are subtracted in step 2 by adding the 2's complement of B to A. Steps 1 and 2 are thus mutually exclusive and can be executed on the same timing signal.

TABLE 5.3 REGISTER TRANSFER STATEMENTS FOR ADD AND SUBTRACT OF FIXED-POINT NUMBERS IN 2'S COMPLEMENT REPRESENTATION

1. $I(\bar{x}c_0 + xc_1)t_0$:	$EA \leftarrow (A) + (B)$,	$SC \leftarrow (SC) + 1$
2. $I(xc_0 + \bar{x}c_1)t_0$:	$EA \leftarrow (A) + (\bar{B}) + 1, OF \leftarrow 0$,	$SC \leftarrow 0010$
3. $I(c_0 + c_1)t_1$:	$OF \leftarrow (E)$,	$SC \leftarrow 0, I \leftarrow 0$
4. $IE(c_0 + c_1)t_2$:	IF $A = 0$, THEN $A_s \leftarrow 0$,	$SC \leftarrow 0, I \leftarrow 0$
5. $\overline{IE}(c_0 + c_1)t_2$:	$A \leftarrow (\bar{A})$,	$SC \leftarrow (SC) + 1$
6. $I(c_0 + c_1)t_3$:	$A \leftarrow (A) + 1, A_s \leftarrow (\bar{A_s})$,	$SC \leftarrow 0, I \leftarrow 0$

Note: $x = A_s \oplus B_s$.

In step 1, the addition may result in an overflow. The value of the E register would be 1 in this case and 0 otherwise. Regardless of whether or not there is an overflow, the sign of the result is the same as the sign of the original value in A. Therefore, if there was no overflow, the answer in A is correct as is; if there was an overflow, the OF bit is set in step 3. In step 2, the OF bit is automatically reset to 0 since subtraction of like-sign operands and addition of different-sign operands can never result in an overflow. In these cases, however, the resulting sign is the same as the sign of the larger operand. By definition of 2's complement addition and subtraction, the value of E represents the resulting sign. If the result is negative and the magnitude is zero, step 4 ensures that the result is returned as a positive zero. If the result is positive, it is converted in steps 5 and 6 to its positive representation. Hence steps 4 and 5 are also mutually exclusive and can be executed on the same timing signal. (Notice that t_i is not always generated in sequence.)

If the numbers are represented in 1's complement instead of 2's complement, the procedure for ADD and SUBTRACT is very similar to that shown in Table 5.3 (see Problem 11 at the end of this chapter, related to overflow detection). However, if the numbers are in sign-magnitude notation, the procedure is much longer, since all combinations of signs and relative magnitudes of the operands must be considered. Yet for multiplication and division operations, it is much simpler to work with numbers represented in sign-magnitude notation. We will therefore assume sign-magnitude representation in the following discussion of the multiplication operation. Since the division operation is very similar, we will not cover it here. Algorithms for division and multiplication of numbers in 2's complement notation can be found, for example, in Mano (1982).

The basic procedure for the multiplication operation is to multiply the magnitudes of the operands and determine the sign of the product by taking the exclusive OR of the signs of the operands. The procedure described in Example 2.24 in Section 2.3 presents the general idea of how the magnitudes are multiplied. However, instead of forming all the partial products and then adding them together, a better approach is to have a partial sum computed as the partial products are formed. Hence on each iteration, the partial sum is shifted and the multiplicand is added if the multiplier bit is 1 or ignored if the multiplier bit is 0. The number of iterations necessary is determined by the number of bits in the operands, excluding the sign bit. Since the multiplication of two n-bit numbers can result in a $(2n + 1)$-bit number, the product is stored in a 1-bit carry-out register and two n-bit registers.

The register transfer statements for the MULTIPLY operation are shown in Table 5.4. Register C is used as the iteration counter. Registers A and B hold the multiplier and multiplicand, respectively. Register E stores the carry-out, and registers E, X, and A (EXA) are used for the product of A and B. The bit A_0 is the least significant bit of the multiplier.

TABLE 5.4 REGISTER TRANSFER STATEMENTS FOR MULTIPLY OF FIXED-POINT NUMBERS IN SIGN-MAGNITUDE REPRESENTATION

1. $I(c_2)t_0$: $X_s \leftarrow (A_s) \oplus (B_s)$, $X \leftarrow 0$, $C \leftarrow n$, $SC \leftarrow (SC) + 1$
2. $I(A_0c_2)t_1$: $EX \leftarrow (X) + (B)$
3. $I(c_2)t_1$: $C \leftarrow (C) - 1$, $SC \leftarrow (SC) + 1$
4. $I(c_2)t_2$: $shr\{EXA\}$; IF $C \neq 0$, THEN $SC \leftarrow 0001$;
    IF $C = 0$, THEN $SC \leftarrow 0$, $I \leftarrow 0$

Note: shr = shift right.

The algorithm starts by determining the sign of the result, X_s, and clearing X, which will be used for the partial products. The iteration counter, C, is set to n, the number of bits of each of the operands excluding the sign bit. In step 2, B is added to EX only if the least significant bit of A is 1. On the same timing signal (step 3), the iteration counter is decremented. On the next timing signal (step 4), EXA is shifted to the right so that the previous A_1 becomes A_0, the least significant bit that is used in step 2. (The sign bits are not involved in the shift.) If the multiplication process is not complete ($C \neq 0$), control returns to steps 2 and 3. When $C = 0$, the process is terminated with the result in EXA, and SC and I are cleared for the next operation.

Floating-point arithmetic. The algorithms for floating-point arithmetic are more complex than those for fixed-point numbers but use these same algorithms for actually adding and multiplying different parts of the numbers. Recall from Chapter 2 that floating-point numbers are made up of a sign bit, a mantissa, and an exponent. The basic algorithm for addition and subtraction is as follows:

1. Check for zeros.
2. Align the mantissas.
3. Add or subtract the mantissas.
4. Normalize the result.

The first step avoids any unnecessary work if either operand is zero. The mantissas are aligned by shifting one of the exponents right or left in order to keep as many significant digits as possible. The actual addition or subtraction algorithm depends on how the numbers are represented, as discussed in the previous subsection on fixed-point arithmetic. At the end, the result is normalized to be consistent with the other numbers in the system.

Similarly, the multiplication algorithm can be described as follows:

1. Check for zeros.
2. Add the exponents.
3. Multiply the mantissas.
4. Normalize the product.

In this case, either one of the operands being zero implies that the product is zero and the process is terminated. Otherwise, the exponents are added and the mantissas are multiplied, again according to how they are represented in the system. As before, the final result is normalized.

For the division of floating-point numbers, the steps are a little different. In this case, the dividend is aligned before subtracting the exponents. This way, divide overflow is avoided, and as an added bonus, the quotient will always be normalized. The steps for the division algorithm are the following:

1. Check for zeros.
2. Align the dividend.
3. Subtract the exponents.
4. Divide the mantissas.

Here, the check for zeros is used to save work and also to prevent dividing by zero.

All these fixed-point and floating-point operations may be included in the CPU as any other instruction, or they may be packaged on individual IC chips. In the latter case, after the CLU decodes the particular operation and sets up the operands, it will enable the chip rather than activate the individual micro-operations directly.

Decimal Arithmetic Unit

In some applications, the amount of arithmetic that is necessary compared to the amount of I/O that occurs is very small. In a general-purpose computer, it is worthwhile, in fact imperative for speed and efficiency, that decimal input values be

Sec. 5.5 Control Logic Unit (CLU)

converted to binary for all internal computations. Only when a number is to be output to an I/O device must it be converted back to decimal. In a calculator, by contrast, for each I/O operation, just a small amount of arithmetic is done. Therefore, it is actually faster to do the arithmetic in decimal and eliminate the conversions to and from binary. Note that by decimal we mean some binary-coded representation of the decimal digits, such as BCD or excess-3.

The basic component for arithmetic in any radix is an adder. Let us therefore consider an adder for two BCD digits. The logic circuit for a BCD adder can be derived by examining the characteristics of the digits themselves. First we must recognize that the maximum sum of two BCD digits plus a possible input carry is $9 + 9 + 1 = 19$. Now, the BCD representation of decimals 0 through 9 is the same as their binary representation. However, when the sum is greater than 9, it must be represented as a single digit (0–9) and a carry (1).

Consider now the difference between the BCD sums and carries and the equivalent binary sums and carries for decimals 10 through 19 as shown in Table 5.5. We can see that for decimal numbers 10 through 19, each BCD sum and carry is equal to the binary sum and carry plus 0110 (decimal 6). This implies that the BCD adder can be made up of a 4-bit binary parallel adder that adds two BCD digits and, when the result is greater than binary 1001 (decimal 9), binary 0110 (decimal 6) is added to the sum by means of another 4-bit binary adder.

TABLE 5.5 BCD VALUES COMPARED WITH BINARY VALUES FOR DECIMALS 10–19

Carry	BCD Sum S_3	S_2	S_1	S_0	Carry	Binary Sum X_3	X_2	X_1	X_0	Decimal Value
1	0	0	0	0	0	1	0	1	0	10
1	0	0	0	1	0	1	0	1	1	11
1	0	0	1	0	0	1	1	0	0	12
1	0	0	1	1	0	1	1	0	1	13
1	0	1	0	0	0	1	1	1	0	14
1	0	1	0	1	0	1	1	1	1	15
1	0	1	1	0	1	0	0	0	0	16
1	0	1	1	1	1	0	0	0	1	17
1	1	0	0	0	1	0	0	1	0	18
1	1	0	0	1	1	0	0	1	1	19

Figure 5–20 shows a block diagram of a two-digit BCD adder based on this scheme. If the sum is greater than 9, the output from the $[X > 9]$ component will be 1, causing 0110 to be added to the previous sum; otherwise, just 0000 would be added. The logic circuit for the $[X > 9]$ component is shown in Figure 5–21, and its derivation, based on the entries in Table 5.5, is left as an exercise. To construct an n-digit BCD parallel adder, n BCD adders are cascaded together as illustrated in Figure 5–22, similar to the construction on an n-bit binary parallel adder.

Example 5.3

Consider the addition of the two 3-digit BCD numbers 917 and 265. Figure 5–23 shows the inputs and outputs of a 3-digit BCD adder for this operation.

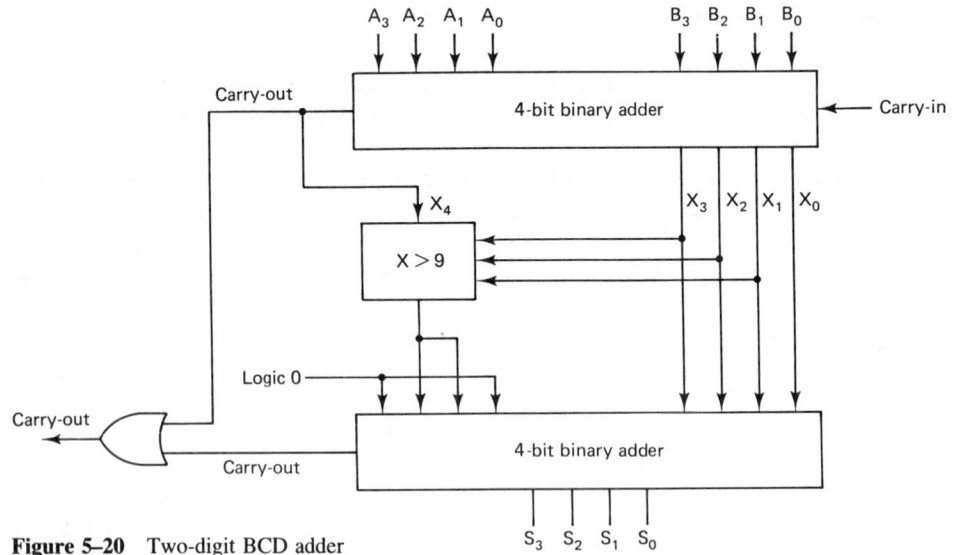

Figure 5-20 Two-digit BCD adder

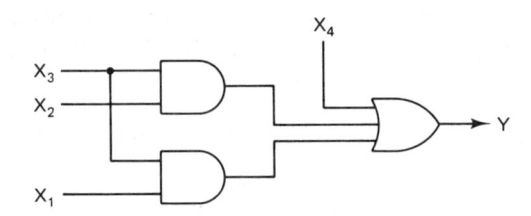

Figure 5-21 Logic circuit of the $[X > 9]$ component

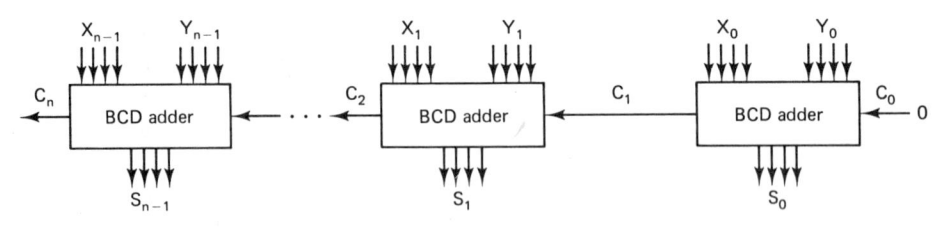

Figure 5-22 N-digit BCD parallel adder

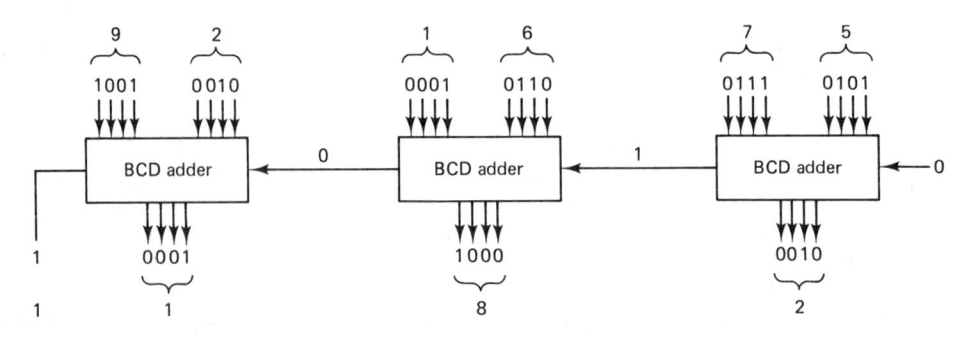

Figure 5-23 BCD addition of 917 and 265

146

Sec. 5.6   CPU Configuration

The logic circuit of a complete decimal arithmetic unit is analogous to the arithmetic portion of the ALU (see Figure 5–11). The differences are: (1) An n-digit BCD parallel adder is used instead of an n-bit binary parallel adder, and (2) the complement part of the conversion element takes the 9's complement of the input rather than the 1's complement.

The 9's complement for a BCD digit can be defined by the following Boolean functions:

$$c_0 = \overline{D_0}$$
$$c_1 = D_1$$
$$c_2 = \overline{D_2}D_1 + D_2\overline{D_1}$$
$$c_3 = \overline{D_3}\,\overline{D_2}\,\overline{D_1}$$

where D_0 through D_3 are the bits representing the BCD digit and c_0 through c_3 are the bits representing its 9's complement BCD digit. To see why this is true, recall the definition of the $(r - 1)$'s complement of a number in radix r (Section 2.3): It is the number obtained by subtracting each digit of the number from $(r - 1)$. Therefore, the 9's complement of 0 (0000) is 9 (1001), and the 9's complement of 1 (0001) is 8 (1000), and so on. Using Table 2.3, which gives the BCD representation of the digits 0–9, these functions can be verified by inspection.

5.6 CPU CONFIGURATION

The components of the CPU may be configured in various ways, depending primarily on the number of internal data buses used. We will present two example configurations.

Single-Bus Organization

One way to connect all the components of the CPU is to use a single internal bus as shown in Figure 5–24. (Do not confuse this bus with the external buses that are necessary for communications with the memory and I/O devices. These will be discussed in Chapter 11.) Since there is only one data bus, only one transfer can take place at any time. It is therefore necessary to make some special hardware provisions. The Y and Z registers shown in Figure 5–24 are examples of this. The ALU needs both its inputs simultaneously. With just a single data bus, one of the operands is stored in Y and then the other can be on the bus. While the ALU is computing the result, the input must be held constant on the bus. Therefore, the result is temporarily stored in Z until the operation is completed and is then transferred on the bus to wherever it should be stored.

In the same respect, the CLU needs information from the special-purpose registers simultaneously to generate the correct control functions. For this reason, these registers are connected directly to the CLU in addition to being connected to the data bus for general communications.

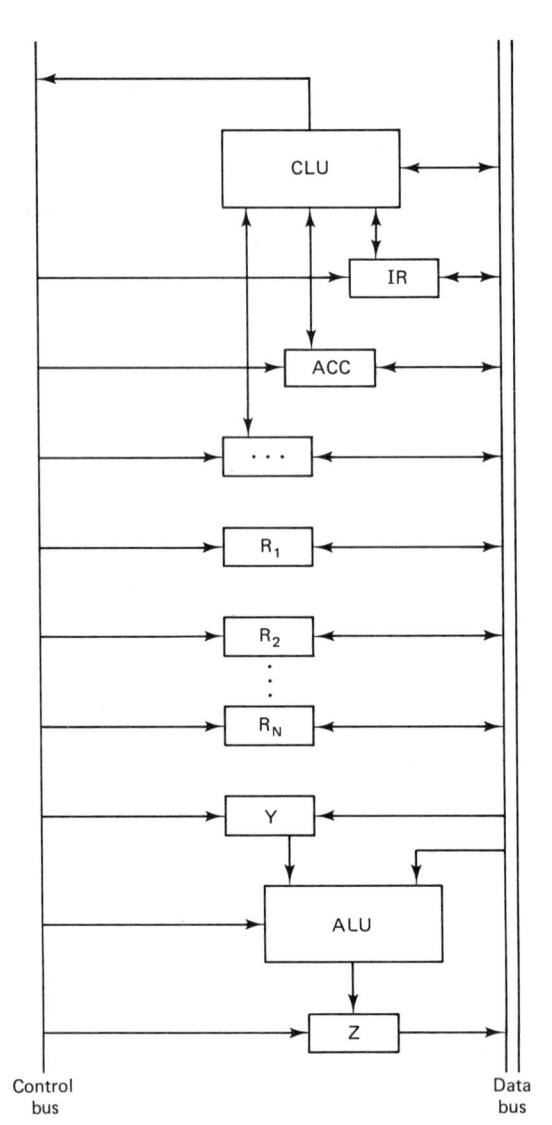

Figure 5-24 Single internal CPU data bus organization

Triple-Bus Organization

Using three internal data buses, as shown in Figure 5–25, alleviates some of the restrictions imposed by the single-bus configuration. In this case, separate buses can be used for the two inputs to the ALU as well as for the output from the ALU. If the registers of the register set are edge-triggered, it is even possible to execute an R1 ← (R2) + (R3) type of micro-operation on one timing signal.

Sec. 5.7   Reduced Instruction Set Computers (RISC)

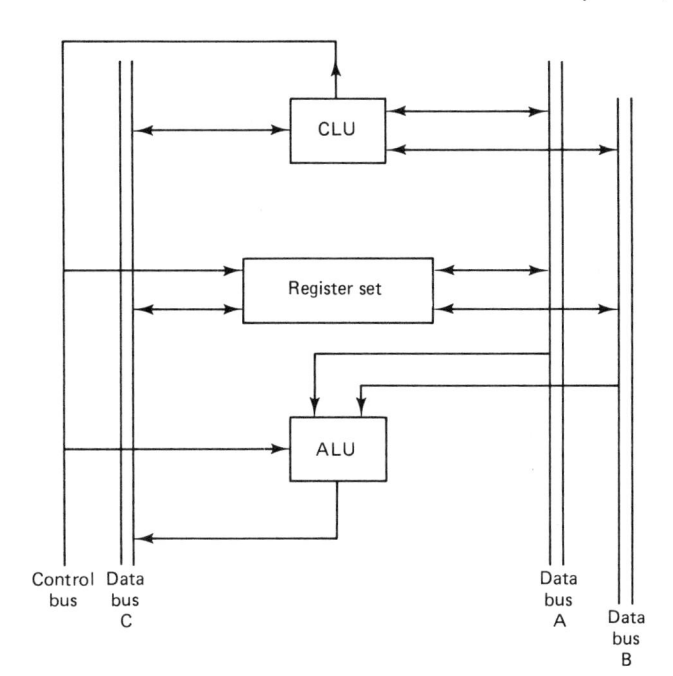

Figure 5–25   Triple internal CPU data bus organization

5.7 REDUCED INSTRUCTION SET COMPUTERS (RISC)

As the hardware component of computers has evolved over the years, so has the design of the languages used to program computers. Today's high-level programming languages are very powerful and complex compared to FORTRAN, the first high-level language (HLL). In response to this evolution, computer architects have tried to design computers that provide more and more higher-level operations and instructions in the hardware to correspond more closely to language constructs in HLLs. An example of this is the CASE hardware instruction of the VAX-11 computers. A Pascal compiler for this computer can generate this instruction to match directly a CASE statement in a Pascal program. This makes the job of the compiler writer much easier and also facilitates a very efficient code since CASE is built into the hardware. The drawback to this strategy, however, is that the increased size and complexity of the hardware instruction set results in increased design time, increased design errors, and inconsistent implementations of the hardware (Patterson & Sequin, 1981).

The traditional computer design as described has been termed a **complex instruction set computer (CISC).** A different approach is to design a **reduced instruction set computer (RISC).** A RISC system offers a very small and simple instruction set where the instructions generally execute in one cycle, a large number of general-purpose registers, and pipelined execution (see Chapter 9 for a detailed discussion on pipelining). Besides improving the design of the hardware, it is argued by RISC researchers that the smaller instruction set is easier to exploit by compiler writers. With a complex instruction set, the compiler must find cases that match a given construct exactly. In addition, optimizing the generated code is much simpler with less complicated instructions. Having a large number of registers decreases the need to access memory and, hence, increases the speed of execution of the program. These registers, logically grouped into sets called **windows,** are used primarily during procedure calls and returns.

At this point, it cannot be said which of the two architectural approaches is better. Although the RISC architecture appears to be the solution to some design problems, it is unknown for which applications and implementations this type of computer will work as claimed. Whether RISC, CISC or some future approach is the best way to support HLLs remains to be seen. It is known, however, that research in this area has helped focus attention on some important issues in computer architecture. What will probably emerge is an architecture that is a combination of the two, making use of the best of both worlds.

For a more in-depth description of the RISC organization by one of the original researchers, see Patterson (1985). Colwell et al. (1985) provide a good discussion of the pros and cons of both RISC and CISC organizations.

5.8 SUMMARY

In this chapter we have studied the CPU of a typical von Neumann computer. Although the CPU for every computer is different, all adhere to some common principles. The program to be executed is stored in memory. The CPU must retrieve an instruction of the program, execute it, and continue this cycle until the program is completed. To facilitate I/O and more sophisticated programming (such as multiprogramming), the CPU must also be able to handle interrupts.

The CPU is made up of three basic parts: the CLU (control logic unit), the ALU (arithmetic and logic unit), and the register set. The details of these parts are specific to individual computers. They depend on the micro-operations available in the hardware and the instruction set available for the software, and they are connected via data buses and control buses. Again, the specific configuration is dependent on the particular computer.

PROBLEMS

1. Define the following terms:
   (a) register set   (f) IR
   (b) ALU   (g) ACC
   (c) CLU   (h) PSW
   (d) CPU   (i) cycle time of ALU
   (e) PC   (j) position scaler
2. Give an advantage and a disadvantage for letting the IR serve as the MBR in a CPU.
3. A computer has a word length of 32 bits and a total of 16 operations. How many words of memory can be addressed by the operands in each instance?

(a) A four-address format is used.
(b) A three-address format is used.
(c) A two-address format is used.
(d) A single-address format is used.

4. Based on the register and memory contents specified, what is the value of the operand for each of the following?
   (a) Register address mode; address in instruction = 2
   (b) Register-indirect address mode; address in instruction = 1
   (c) Autodecrement address mode; address in instruction = 2
   (d) Relative address mode; address in instruction = 3

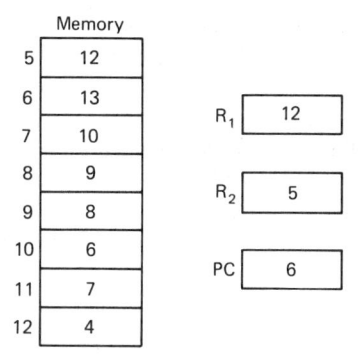

```
        Memory
    5 |  12 |
    6 |  13 |         R₁ | 12 |
    7 |  10 |
    8 |   9 |
                      R₂ |  5 |
    9 |   8 |
   10 |   6 |
                      PC |  6 |
   11 |   7 |
   12 |   4 |
```

5. Consider a relative-indirect addressing mode that is a combination of the relative and indirect addressing modes. Let the memory contents be as shown in Problem 4. If the address field of an instruction has the value 5 and the address mode is relative-indirect, what is the value of the operand?

6. How are the relative, index, base, and augmented addressing modes alike, and how are they different?

7. Give the register transfer statements necessary to execute R1 ← (R2)*[(R3) − (R4)] for each of these systems:
   (a) A single-accumulator system
   (b) A system with an ALU that can perform an operation on any two registers and store the result in any register

8. With respect to the conversion element of Figures 5–11 and 5–12, answer the following:
   (a) Why are four different values of the B input desirable?
   (b) Show how $s_0 = 0$ and $s_1 = 1$ result in $D = 1$ for $B = 101$.
   (c) Show how $s_0 = 1$ and $s_1 = 1$ result in $D = \overline{B}$ for $B = 101$.

9. Determine the value of R and the four condition bits specified in Figure 5–13 for each of the following arithmetic operations (assume 4-bit words represented in 2's complement notation):
   (a) 0110 + 0011
   (b) 1101 − 0001
   (c) 1011 + 0011
   (d) 0101 − 1010

10. Repeat Problem 9 assuming that the numbers are represented in sign-magnitude notation. (*Note*: The EC and OF flags are determined differently than shown in Figure 5–13.)

11. Add 10110 to 11001, assuming that the numbers are represented in 1's complement notation.

(a) Show that the overflow detection logic of Figure 5–13 does not work in this case.
(b) Determine the logic that would be necessary to detect overflow.

12. Why is the cycle time of the logic part of the ALU always less than that of the adder?
13. Draw the logic diagram for the complete shifter shown in Figure 5–18. (*Hint*: See Figure 5–16.)
14. In Figure 5–19, the sequence counter (SC) generates the timing signals in the order t_0, t_1, t_2, t_3. Describe what would happen if the timing signals were generated in the order t_2, t_0, t_3, t_1.
15. Consider the register transfer statements for the ADD and SUBTRACT operations of Table 5.3.
    (a) Draw a flowchart of the statements.
    (b) If the conditions of step 1 are true, the operation is completed without checking the sign of A. Why is checking unnecessary?
16. Consider the register transfer statements for the MULTIPLY operation of Table 5.4.
    (a) Draw a flowchart of the statements.
    (b) Let A = 1 01011 and B = 0 10101. Show every step of the execution of A * B.
17. Using the entries of Table 5.5, derive a logic equation for an [$X > 9$] component as shown in Figure 5–21. (Show that the logic equation represents all binary codes of entries greater than 9.)
18. In the single-CPU data bus organization shown in Figure 5–24, two intermediate storage registers, Y and Z, are necessary. If two data buses are used, which, if either, of Y and Z is necessary? Why?

CHAPTER 6

Input/Output Processing

6.1 THE INPUT/OUTPUT SYSTEM

The CPU fetches instructions and data from main memory, processes them, and stores the results back in main memory. However, if these results are to be useful, the computer must have the means and capabilities to communicate with its environment (the user). This is done through another major unit of the computer, the **input/output (I/O) system,** whose function is to transfer information between the CPU or main memory and the outside world.

The I/O system consists of **I/O devices** (also referred to as **peripherals**), **device controllers** through which I/O devices communicate with the CPU or main memory in a well-defined manner **(protocol),** and **software** intended for I/O operations and servicing. In dealing with the I/O system, it is important to realize three points:

1. The CPU and I/O devices cannot usually be synchronized. Therefore, I/O operations must be coordinated.
2. In general, I/O devices are much slower than the CPU. Therefore, I/O devices usually communicate *asynchronously* with the CPU.
3. The CPU handles machine language information while I/O devices usually carry information that is user (human)-oriented. Therefore, data must be encoded and decoded (formatted).

The overall control of I/O operations is always exercised by the CPU to a lesser or greater extent. The process of transferring information between the CPU and a peripheral consists of four steps:

1. Selecting an I/O device and checking that it is ready, or responding to it
2. Initiating the transfer and coordinating the timing of I/O operations
3. Transferring the information
4. Terminating the transfer

From the standpoint of both hardware and software, I/O poses some of the most difficult problems in designing and using computer systems. Many of these problems stem from the fact that I/O requires communication between devices of radically different characteristics. Many I/O devices are at least partly mechanical and are several orders of magnitude slower than typical electronic devices. We can classify I/O devices into three groups:

1. Devices that input information to the computer, such as keyboard, digitizer, optical scanner, analog-to-digital converter, light pen, voice input unit, and touch panel
2. Devices that display (output) the information sent from the computer, such as video display unit (VDU), plotter, graphics terminal, printer, digital-to-analog converter, and voice output unit
3. Devices that serve for both input and output, such as disk, diskette, magnetic tape, and cassette

This list of I/O devices is by no means exhaustive. New devices are being produced all the time, and the number of products available is overwhelming. But I/O devices also vary within each group. Some devices are machine-dependent, involving a specialized I/O implementation approach; other devices, such as terminals, vary considerably in their characteristics and optional capabilities.

Rather than introduce all the various I/O devices or consider how I/O is implemented in any particular computer, we choose to discuss in this chapter some characteristics common to all I/O systems. I/O operations fall into three basic modes, distinguished by the extent of CPU involvement in executing them. These modes, programmed I/O, interrupt I/O, and direct memory access (DMA), are discussed in Section 6.2. The basic mechanisms for *data transfer* under these three accessing schemes are considered in Section 6.3. To support I/O communications with the CPU and memory, devices have to be connected to one or more system buses. The process of making one device compatible with another for the purpose of communication, often referred to as *interfacing*, is the subject of Section 6.4. In many computer systems, I/O processing functions are delegated away from the CPU by using special-purpose or general-purpose *front-end I/O processors*. I/O processors are discussed in Section 6.5.

6.2 I/O ACCESSING

Many approaches to I/O organization are evident in computer systems, but most fall into one of two basic types: memory-mapped I/O, in which I/O devices are connected as **virtual** memory locations, or I/O-mapped I/O, in which I/O ports are independent of the main memory. In a **memory-mapped I/O** organization, input/output ports are hard-wired to the address bus. Each input device is treated as a section of memory that is providing data to the data bus, and each output device is treated as a section of memory having some data written into it. In other words, I/O ports occupy specific locations in the address space and are accessed as if they were memory locations. As a result, all memory reference instructions in the instruction set of the computer can also reference I/O ports. Thus memory-mapped I/O procedures do not require special instructions. An instruction for fetching or storing data at a particular memory address becomes an I/O instruction if the address is that of an I/O port. Since memory-mapped I/O makes no distinction between memory registers and I/O devices, the address space is shared between them and therefore the memory space available for programs and data is reduced.

In contrast, in an **I/O-mapped I/O** organization, input/output ports are *independent* of the memory and therefore require no direct reference to memory addresses. The CPU issues special signals that differentiate between I/O operations and memory operations. Information transfer is done under program control, using special INPUT and OUTPUT instructions to transfer data to and from peripheral devices. Thus I/O instructions activate the read/write control lines of the I/O port to transfer data between the addressed I/O port and the CPU, whereas memory reference instructions activate the memory read/write control lines for transferring data between the addressed memory location and the CPU. Notice that by separating the memory and I/O address spaces, an I/O device and a main memory location can have the same address. Therefore, up to the full address space of the computer can be used for specifying I/O devices or memory locations rather than sharing the space between them as in a memory-mapped I/O organization.

Both approaches have advantages and disadvantages. I/O-mapped I/O is usually the faster and more efficient of the two. However, the disadvantage of this method is that only a limited number of instructions can be used for I/O operations, as opposed to the memory-mapped I/O method, where all memory reference instructions can be used. Memory-mapped I/O is simpler and cheaper to implement and is more flexible in operation (though usually slower) than I/O-mapped I/O.

In either approach, I/O operations can be classified into three basic modes, depending on where the transfer control is located. These modes, programmed I/O, interrupt I/O, and direct memory access (DMA), will be discussed individually.

Programmed I/O

Programmed I/O is a method whereby the CPU controls the entire I/O transaction by executing a sequence of I/O instructions (a program). The program initiates, directs, and terminates the I/O operations. Programmed I/O is the most straightforward method to implement and requires a relatively small amount of special I/O hardware.

Basically, the hardware involved in an I/O transfer consists of a status register, a buffer register, a data counter, and a buffer pointer. The **status register** contains the current status of the I/O device and of the data to be transferred. The status bits of the I/O device indicate, for example, whether the device is ready to transfer data and whether the data is to be input to or output from memory, as well as error indications such as parity error or device power off. The status bits of the data indicate, for example, whether the data consists of a single character or a string of characters. The **buffer register** is used to hold the data temporarily. The buffer register holds the data received from the CPU until the I/O device is ready to accept it or holds the data received from the I/O device until the CPU is ready to accept it. The **data counter** is loaded with the number of characters to be transferred. Once a character has been transferred, the data counter is decremented and tested for zero. A zero count in the data counter indicates that the transfer of the I/O character string has been completed. The **buffer pointer** points to the memory location into which a character is to be written or from which it is to be read. Similar to the data counter, the pointer is updated after the transfer of each character.

Figure 6-1 shows a flowchart of a typical programmed I/O transaction. As can be seen, programmed I/O can be time consuming and rather inefficient in terms of CPU utilization. For example, the CPU might be spending a great deal of time checking the status of an I/O device to determine if the device requires service, or it might be just waiting for a device to be ready.

Communication among the CPU, memory, and I/O devices in a programmed I/O computer is done on a common bus, with I/O addressing being either memory-

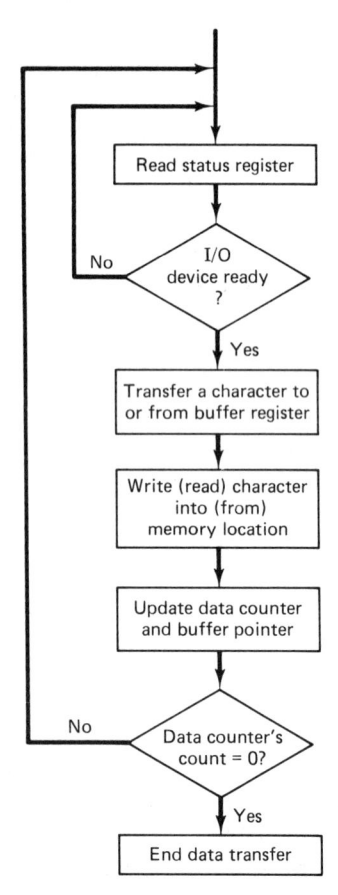

Figure 6-1 Programmed I/O flowchart

mapped or I/O-mapped. Since I/O transactions are under the direct control of the CPU, every data transfer operation involving an I/O device requires the execution of some instructions by the CPU. For example, to transfer a data character from an I/O device to a main memory location, the CPU executes an INPUT instruction to transfer the word from the device to a CPU register and then a MOVE instruction to store the word in the memory location.

Interrupt I/O

In contrast to programmed I/O, **interrupt I/O** is a *demand-driven* technique. The CPU reacts only when a device issues a request for service. This request, called an **interrupt,** represents a demand, which can sometimes be preemptive. Interrupt I/O capability frees the CPU from having to spend time checking the status of the devices to determine if they require service. The basic idea is that the CPU responds to stimuli generated by any device (or condition) requiring its attention, rather than stays on the lookout for such requests.

Interrupts can be generated by means other than I/O devices. For example, *hardware interrupts* are generated by hardware devices such as timers to indicate that certain timing conditions have been met, a memory unit to indicate a memory error, and the power supply unit to indicate power failure. *Software interrupts* are generated by the CPU to indicate arithmetic overflows, illegal opcodes or data, or division by zero. Interrupts may also occur if a user program attempts to execute system-type instructions that are not permitted in the user mode.

Under programmed I/O, the CPU is idle while waiting to input or output data. The reason for this is that the time when the next I/O character will be ready is unpredictable. Sometimes these idle periods can be quite long. For example, if a VDU terminal takes 10 milliseconds to display a character while the CPU requires 10 microseconds for the actual data transfer, only 0.1% of the CPU time is actually used. By contrast, interrupt I/O facilities allow the CPU to use the idle periods to execute a program, deferring the control of I/O transactions until the I/O device is ready.

Figure 6–2 shows a flowchart of a typical interrupt I/O routine. When an I/O device sends an interrupt signal, the instruction currently being executed by the CPU is completed, and the CPU branches out of the program and accesses a subroutine, called the **interrupt service routine,** specifically written to handle interrupt calls. However, prior to branching out of the main program, the CPU acts, either by a special instruction or automatically, to preserve the integrity of some important parameters so that it can return to the main program at the point of exit once the interrupt service routine has been terminated. The parameters pertain mostly to the CPU status and consist of the content of the program counter (the return address) and the program status word (PSW) register (see Chapter 5). In addition, the contents of CPU registers that will be used by the interrupt service routine are stored so that they can be restored before returning to the program that was interrupted. As we see in Figure 6–2, the status and buffer registers, data counter, and buffer pointer function are as under programmed I/O. When the last character has been transferred, the interrupt service routine sets a software ''done'' flag. By examining this flag, the CPU can determine the status of the I/O transfer.

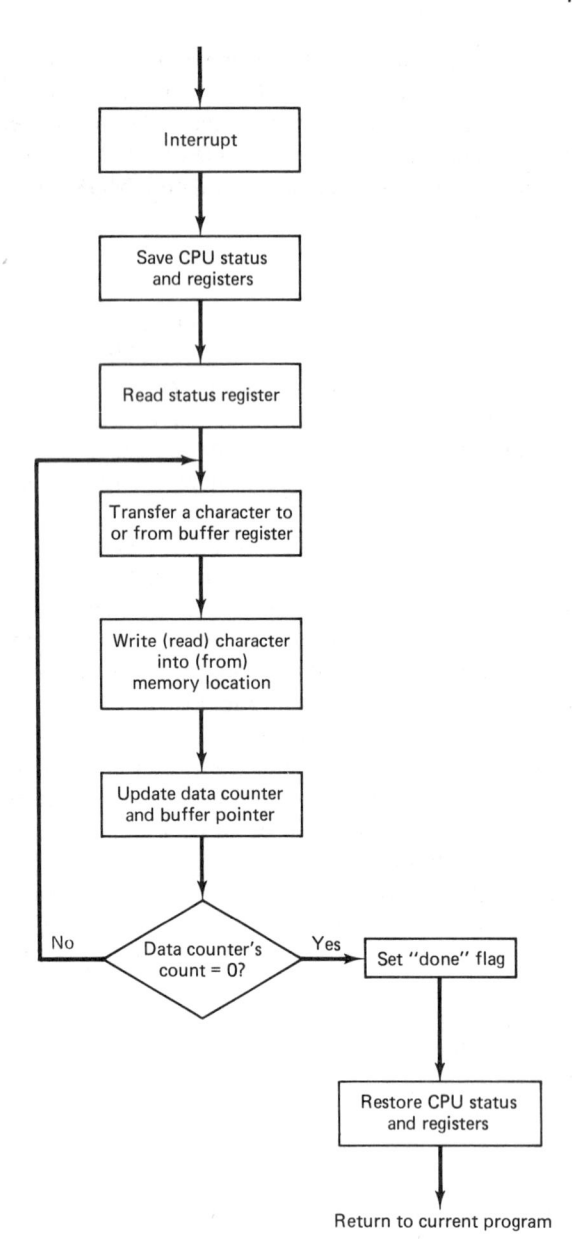

```
                    ┌─────────────┐
                    │  Interrupt  │
                    └──────┬──────┘
                           │
                    ┌──────▼──────┐
                    │Save CPU status│
                    │ and registers │
                    └──────┬──────┘
                           │
                    ┌──────▼──────┐
                    │Read status register│
                    └──────┬──────┘
                           │
                ┌──────────▼──────────┐
                │Transfer a character to│
                │or from buffer register│
                └──────────┬──────────┘
                           │
                ┌──────────▼──────────┐
                │ Write (read) character│
                │      into (from)     │
                │    memory location   │
                └──────────┬──────────┘
                           │
                ┌──────────▼──────────┐
                │  Update data counter │
                │  and buffer pointer  │
                └──────────┬──────────┘
                           │
                   ┌───────▼───────┐
              No   │Data counter's │  Yes    ┌──────────────┐
         ◄─────────│  count = 0?   │────────►│Set "done" flag│
                   └───────────────┘         └──────┬───────┘
                                                    │
                                          ┌─────────▼─────────┐
                                          │ Restore CPU status│
                                          │   and registers   │
                                          └─────────┬─────────┘
                                                    │
                                          Return to current program
```

Figure 6–2 Interrupt I/O flowchart

There are two basic types of interrupts: maskable or nonmaskable. A **maskable interrupt** is an interrupt that can be temporarily disabled by a special interrupt disable instruction. The user can designate portions of the program that should not be interrupted by beginning each portion with an *interrupt disable* instruction and terminating it with an *interrupt enable* instruction. A **nonmaskable interrupt** is an interrupt that cannot be disabled by software instructions. When a nonmaskable interrupt occurs, the program currently running is interrupted and the CPU turns to a predetermined location in memory that contains the first instruction of the interrupt service routine. A nonmaskable interrupt takes precedence over any maskable interrupt, even if one is in progress, and is usually intended for exceptional events such as memory error detection or imminent loss of power.

A computer system usually contains more than one device that can request a program interrupt. The CPU must be able to determine which device, if any, has issued a request and to act on it. To accomplish this, basically two types of methods are used to implement interrupt systems: the polled-interrupt scheme and the vectored-interrupt scheme.

Polling. In the simplest version of a **polled-interrupt** scheme, the interrupt lines of all the devices that can cause an interrupt are connected (via an OR gate) to a single **interrupt request (INTR)** control line. Each device is associated with a **status bit** that is set if the device requests CPU service. If interrupts are enabled by the CPU, then upon sensing an INTR signal, the CPU will complete the current instruction and branch to a predetermined memory location where a **polling routine** begins. This routine will cause the CPU successively to check the status bit of every device that can cause an interrupt. If a set status bit is found, the polling routine will branch to a memory location where the interrupt service routine for the specific device begins.

Figure 6–3 shows a flowchart of the polling procedure. As we can see, the polling is done in some predetermined order, which implies a priority setting for servicing interrupting devices. This way, the polling procedure also provides a built-in conflict resolution mechanism when two or more devices request an interrupt simultaneously. The interrupting device that is first in the polling order will be serviced first, then the next interrupting device in the polling order will be serviced, and so on. For example, the assigned priorities in Figure 6–3 are such that device 1 has the highest priority and device N has the lowest. Hence, if device x is interrupting the CPU simultaneously with device y, and $x < y$, device x will be serviced first.

Vectored Interrupt. The process of polling the various devices by the polling routine is clearly time consuming. If the number of devices is large, timing issues become critical, and the alternative vectored-interrupt scheme is preferable. In the **vectored-interrupt** method, each interrupting device is directly identifiable and is associated with its own interrupt service routine. Once an interrupt request is acknowledged by the CPU, the device supplies the CPU, over the data bus, with a special code called the **interrupt vector.** The interrupt vector usually represents the starting address of the device service routine. The supplied address is determined by hardware that selects one of the interrupting devices according to some priority scheme. Vectored-interrupt priority schemes will be considered shortly.

The CPU cannot always respond immediately to an interrupt request, for one of a number of reasons—for example, the CPU may have to complete the execution of the current instruction, there is an interrupt masking, the interrupt priority is lower than that of the currently running program, or the CPU requires the use of the bus. As a result, the interrupting device must wait until the CPU is ready to handle the request. To achieve this coordination, the CPU uses an **interrupt acknowledge**

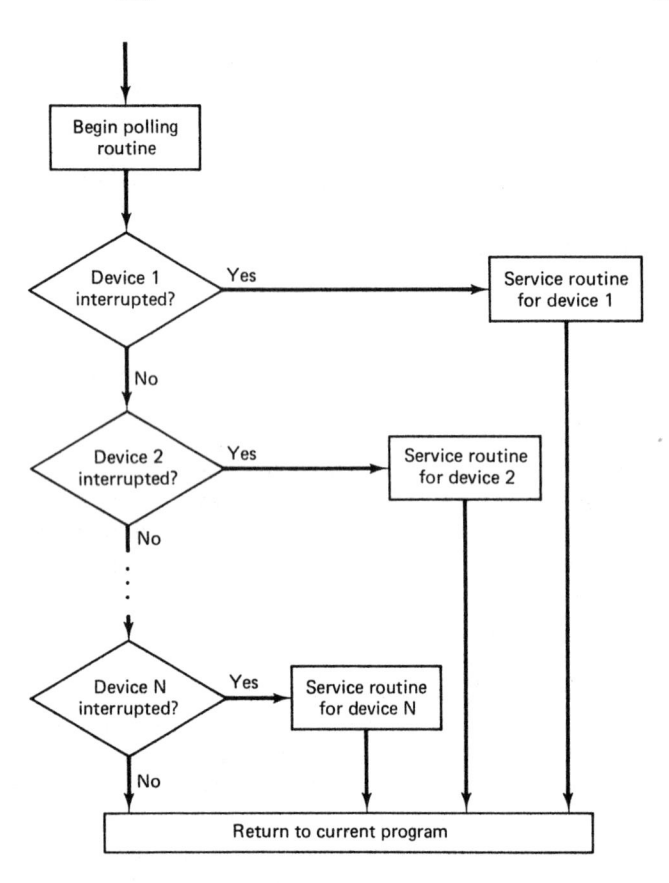

```
                    ┌──────────────┐
                    │ Begin polling│
                    │   routine    │
                    └──────┬───────┘
                           │
                        ╱     ╲      Yes         ┌──────────────┐
                    ╱ Device 1 ╲────────────────▶│Service routine│
                    ╲interrupted?╱                │ for device 1 │
                        ╲     ╱                   └──────┬───────┘
                           │ No
                           │
                        ╱     ╲      Yes         ┌──────────────┐
                    ╱ Device 2 ╲────────────────▶│Service routine│
                    ╲interrupted?╱                │ for device 2 │
                        ╲     ╱                   └──────┬───────┘
                           │ No
                           ⋮
                           │
                        ╱     ╲      Yes         ┌──────────────┐
                    ╱ Device N ╲────────────────▶│Service routine│
                    ╲interrupted?╱                │ for device N │
                        ╲     ╱                   └──────┬───────┘
                           │ No
                           ▼
                ┌─────────────────────────────┐
                │  Return to current program  │
                └─────────────────────────────┘
```

Figure 6–3 Polling flowchart

(INTA) control line. When the CPU is ready, it sets the INTA line and thus enables the device controller to place the interrupt vector on the bus.

One way to identify interrupting devices is to connect each one to a separate INTR line. In this approach, a device requiring CPU service sets its INTR line and waits for the CPU to acknowledge the request. When the CPU sets the INTA line, the device places its interrupt vector on the bus, causing the CPU to branch to the memory address indicated by the interrupt vector. To establish device priorities, we can use a *priority encoder*. (We will discuss shortly a vectored-interrupt method using a priority encoder.)

The problem with using separate INTR lines is that with many devices, the number of INTR lines required may be prohibitive. To circumvent this problem, we can use the **daisy chain** scheme shown in Figure 6–4. The position of a device in the chain indicates its assigned priority. It is customary to assign the highest priority to the device located nearest to the CPU and the lowest priority to the device located farthest from the CPU. For example, the configuration shown in Figure 6–4 implies that device 1 has the highest priority and device N the lowest.

The interrupt control line (INTR) in Figure 6–4, derived by ORing the devices' own INTR lines, is common to all the devices, whereas the interrupt acknowledge line (INTA) is *daisy-chained* among them. To see how this scheme works, assume

Sec. 6.2   I/O Accessing   161

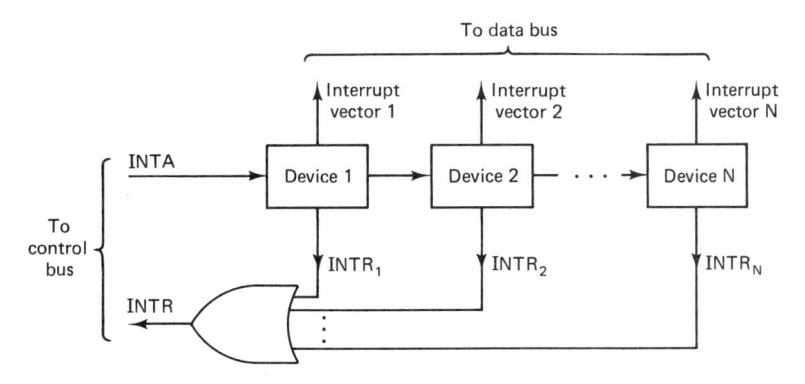

Figure 6–4   Daisy chain priority scheme

that more than one device, say a and b ($a < b < N$), requests an interrupt simultaneously. Each device sets its own INTR line (INTR$_a$ and INTR$_b$, respectively), causing the common INTR line to set. When the CPU is ready, it acknowledges the interrupt request by setting the INTA line. The INTA signal now propagates down the chain until it is blocked by the first device that requested the interrupt. Since none of the higher-priority devices, 1, 2, . . . , $a - 1$, has requested an interrupt, each will pass the INTA signal to its successor down the chain. When device a receives the INTA signal, it "keeps" the signal, preventing it from proceeding down the chain, and continues to hold the INTR$_a$ line activated while placing its interrupt vector on the bus. (In Problem 5 at the end of this chapter we ask you to design a logic circuit to implement the daisy chain priority scheme.) After being serviced, device a resets the INTR$_a$ line and "frees" INTA. The INTA signal can then continue to propagate down the chain until it reaches the next interrupt-requesting device, device b, whose INTR$_b$ line is still set. Device b is then serviced similarly to device a. When device b has been serviced, the CPU will reset the INTA line since no other device requested an interrupt.

Rather than implement a daisy chain priority scheme, we can use a **priority encoder** to produce the interrupt vector of the highest-priority device that requests an interrupt. This method is shown schematically in Figure 6–5. Usually, priorities are assigned such that a higher priority is given to an input with a higher subscript number over one with a lower subscript number. Thus, in Figure 6–5, device N (INTR$_N$) has the highest priority and device 1 (INTR$_1$) the lowest. In Problem 7, we ask you to design a priority encoder.

Figure 6–5 also shows an added feature, the **mask register,** which is usually included in any interrupt I/O scheme. The cells of the mask register, marked 1, 2, . . . , N, correspond to devices 1 through N. When a cell is set, the corresponding device is unmasked; otherwise, the device is masked. The interrupt request line of each device is ANDed with the corresponding *mask bit* and is input to the priority encoder. Thus if a device is masked, it is prevented from interrupting the CPU. In addition, the outputs of all the AND gates are ORed to form the single INTR line to the CPU.

Let us assume that more than one unmasked device, say a and b ($a < b < N$), requests an interrupt simultaneously. The CPU acknowledges the interrupt by setting

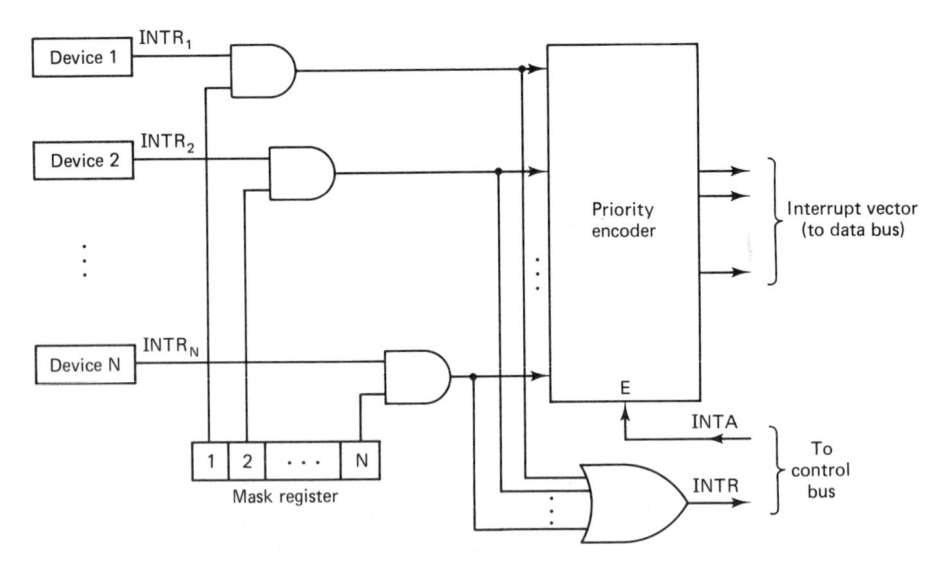

Figure 6-5 Priority encoder resolution of interrupts

the INTA line, which in turn enables the priority encoder. Hence the priority encoder outputs the interrupt vector corresponding to the higher-priority device, device b. After being serviced, device b resets $INTR_b$, and the next device in the priority order, device a, takes control. Once all the interrupting devices have been serviced, the CPU resets the INTA line.

It is possible to combine the priority encoder scheme and the daisy chain method. In this combination, devices are combined into priority groups and are daisy-chained within each group. The priority groups are selected by a priority encoder, and devices within each priority group are serviced in an order determined by their position along the daisy chain.

Direct Memory Access (DMA)

Communication between the CPU or main memory and external devices in both programmed I/O and interrupt I/O always occurs under the supervision and control of the CPU. An interrupt I/O system greatly improves the *throughput* of a computer over that obtained under programmed I/O (at the expense of additional hardware). However, both methods are often inadequate when high-speed peripheral devices, such as disks or magnetic tapes, must transfer large amounts of data in short periods of time. In these cases, data can be transferred *directly* between memory and the device. Since the CPU is essentially bypassed in this process, this I/O accessing scheme is called **direct memory access (DMA).** The DMA method involves a kind of time sharing of main memory between the I/O device and the CPU-run program and can be implemented with most computers.

The CPU is required to initialize the DMA channel, but once a DMA operation is initiated, the block transfer of data is controlled entirely by the **DMA controller** and is performed without program (CPU) intervention. In fact, the data transfer after

Sec. 6.2 I/O Accessing

the initialization stage is completely transparent to the main program. Consequently, the DMA method drastically reduces the CPU overhead resulting from I/O transactions and can allow for data transfer rates that correspond to the cycle time of main memory.

An I/O device can transfer a large block of data under DMA in one continuous operation, called **DMA block transfer.** In this scheme, both the CPU and the DMA controller try to access main memory through the **memory address register (MAR)** and **memory buffer register (MBR).** This process can be implemented using a dual-port main memory, with one port serving the CPU and the other serving the DMA controller. However, since dual-port memories are rather expensive, an alternative scheme, called **cycle stealing,** is implemented in many computers. Cycle stealing requires only a single-port memory for which the CPU and I/O device compete on an independent asynchronous basis.

In cycle stealing, a memory cycle is assigned to the DMA device for the transfer of data. During this cycle, the CPU is prevented from accessing the memory and is referred to as *floating*. The I/O device can transfer only several data words at a time before returning control of the data bus to the CPU. Hence the term *cycle stealing*, which implies that DMA transfer cycles interleave arbitrarily with CPU cycles. Note that cycle stealing is possible because not all CPU cycles require the bus; as long as the currently running program does not require memory accesses, the CPU can continue to execute the program while it turns control of the bus to the DMA controller. In fact, if the DMA operation is synchronized with a CPU execution cycle, the throughput of the system would be unaffected by the DMA process since the CPU does not usually require the bus during an execution cycle.

If both the CPU and the DMA controller attempt to access memory at the same time, priority will be given to the I/O device, and the CPU will have to wait. This is because I/O is a time-dependent operation, and some I/O devices, such as a disk or tape, cannot be stopped since there is the risk of losing information if the device is not serviced within a certain time. Therefore, if an I/O device connected via DMA is fast enough, it can steal several consecutive memory cycles, thus preventing the CPU from accessing the memory for several cycles. At any other time, the CPU will be able to access the memory in between each DMA transfer cycle.

Sometimes there are enough "free cycles" that the DMA interface can be designed to use the bus cycles only when the CPU is not using the system bus. This is termed **transparent DMA.**

DMA Controller. DMA accessing is controlled by a **DMA controller (DMAC),** which can be either dedicated to a single device or shared among several I/O devices. DMACs are currently available on single integrated-circuit (IC) chips, and some chips can even supervise DMA transfers involving several I/O devices, each possibly with a different accessing priority to memory. For example, Motorola's 68450 DMAC provides four independent DMA channels that can transfer data in blocks or words at rates of up to 4 megabytes per second.

Figure 6-6 shows in schematic form the major elements of a DMAC configured for cycle stealing DMA data transfers. The interrupt request and acknowledge lines (INTR and INTA, respectively) are used by the CPU in the initialization process of the DMAC and for signaling the termination of a block transfer. With these control

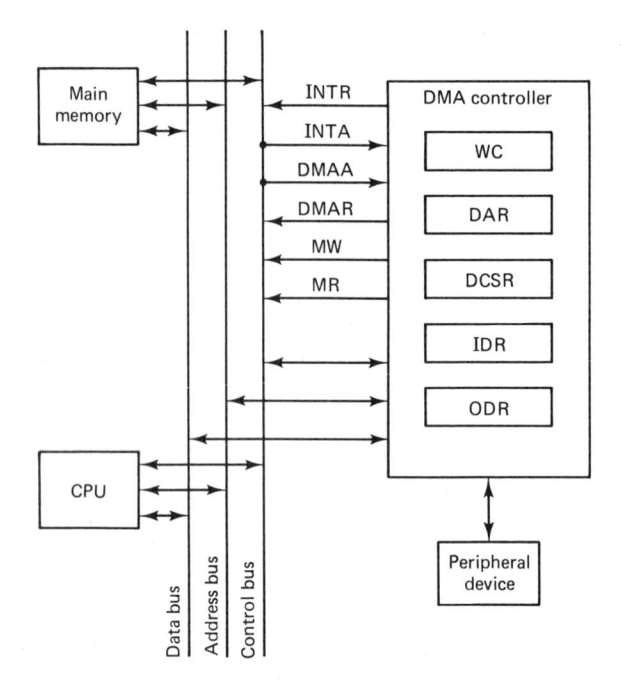

Figure 6-6 DMA controller

lines, the DMAC functions like any other device under interrupt I/O. The **memory write (MW)** and **memory read (MR)** lines control the direction of data flow to and from main memory, respectively. To effect a DMA data transfer, the DMAC issues a **DMA request (DMAR).** At the end of any current transaction involving the bus, the CPU grants this request by activating the **DMA acknowledge (DMAA)** control line. Setting the DMAA line signals the requesting device that the CPU has released control of the bus and that data can now be transferred directly to memory. The logic circuit that generates the device interrupt vector is part of the DMAC but is not shown in Figure 6-6.

The DMAC contains five registers. The **DMA address register (DAR)** holds the address of the next word to be transferred and is automatically *incremented* after each word transfer. The **word counter (WC)** specifies the number of words that remain to be transferred and is automatically *decremented* after each word transfer. The WC is continuously tested for zero. A zero count indicates that the entire transfer has been completed, at which point the DMAC interrupts the CPU. Two registers are associated with memory reads and memory writes: the **output data register (ODR),** which receives data from memory, and the **input data register (IDR),** which holds data to be written into memory. The **control/status register (DCSR)** controls the DMAC and indicates its status and that of the I/O devices attached to the DMAC. Typically, the DCSR bit pattern includes a *device enable* flag to activate the DMA process, a *done/ready* flag to indicate that the WC has reached zero, an *interrupt enable* flag, *error* bits, and several device *status* bits.

In the initialization phase, the WC, the DAR, and the DCSR are initialized by the CPU. The DMAC issues a DMAR signal. If memory read is intended (MR set), the ODR must be empty, and if memory write is intended (MW set), the IDR must have data ready for transfer. Upon setting DMAA, the CPU transfers control of the

Sec. 6.3 Data Transfer

bus to the DMAC. Data transfer then takes place and is terminated when the WC reaches zero.

6.3 DATA TRANSFER

All computers implement one or any combination of the three accessing techniques discussed in Section 6.2. However, the particular implementation in any one computer may vary, even to the extent that it may not be possible to map the implementation exactly into any one of these schemes. Nevertheless, since we are concerned only with the basic principles of device accessing methods, let us now consider the processes involved with each of the three schemes in effecting data transfers.

Data Transfer Formats

There are two basic formats for data transfer: parallel data transmission and serial data transmission. Most computers use both. **Parallel data transfer** is the simpler of the two and involves sending a data word of a certain length, usually referred to as a **character,** in parallel over a number of lines (communication links). In other words, all the bits of the character are sent simultaneously within the time frame allotted for the transmission. For example, if the character is 8 bits long, eight communication links will be required to transmit it in parallel.

The **serial data transfer** process is more complicated. Here, data is sent *sequentially* over a single communication line. To send the data serially, the transmitter and receiver must divide the time frame allotted for the transmission of a character into subintervals so that each bit will be sent and received during one of the subintervals. For example, a character that is 8 bits long will occupy eight subintervals. Note that since data is transferred in parallel to and from the CPU and memory, the interface unit (see Section 6.4) of a device that communicates in a serial mode must include circuits for *parallel-to-serial* and *serial-to-parallel* data conversions. Thus when the device inputs (receives) a character, the CPU-generated parallel data word is first converted into a serial bit stream. Similarly, when the device outputs (sends) data, the serial stream of bits entering the CPU is first converted into characters.

It is clear that a parallel data transfer is advantageous over serial transfer since it permits higher data transfer rates. However, the disadvantage of a parallel transfer is that it requires more communication links than the serial transfer. Thus serial communication is usually selected over large distances. However, if data transfer rates are of prime importance, parallel transmission may be required. For example, terminals usually access the computer in a serial data transfer mode since these devices have low data transfer rates. By contrast, a disk, which is a high-transfer-rate device, is invariably located in close proximity to the computer and accesses the computer in a parallel data transfer mode.

Data Transfer Modes

The number of communication lines usually exceeds the number of the transmitted character bits in a parallel data transfer and is more than the single link required for a serial transfer. In either case, the additional lines are control lines that are used by the transmitter to signal to the receiver when data is ready to be read and by the receiver to signal to the transmitter that the data has been read.

The signaling process in both parallel and serial data transfers can be either synchronous or asynchronous. In a **synchronous** data transfer, the control lines are used to synchronize the timing of all the events that take place within a specified time period. The CPU can supply data to or receive data from an external device without prior communication other than the address of the device. Figure 6–7(a) shows the timing of synchronous data transfers, which are controlled by the CPU. To write data to a device, the CPU places the address of the device on the address bus and then places the data on the data bus. The CPU raises the *write* control line to 1, and the device must read the data at that time. By the time the *write* line goes

(a) Synchronous data transfer

(b) Asynchronous data transfer

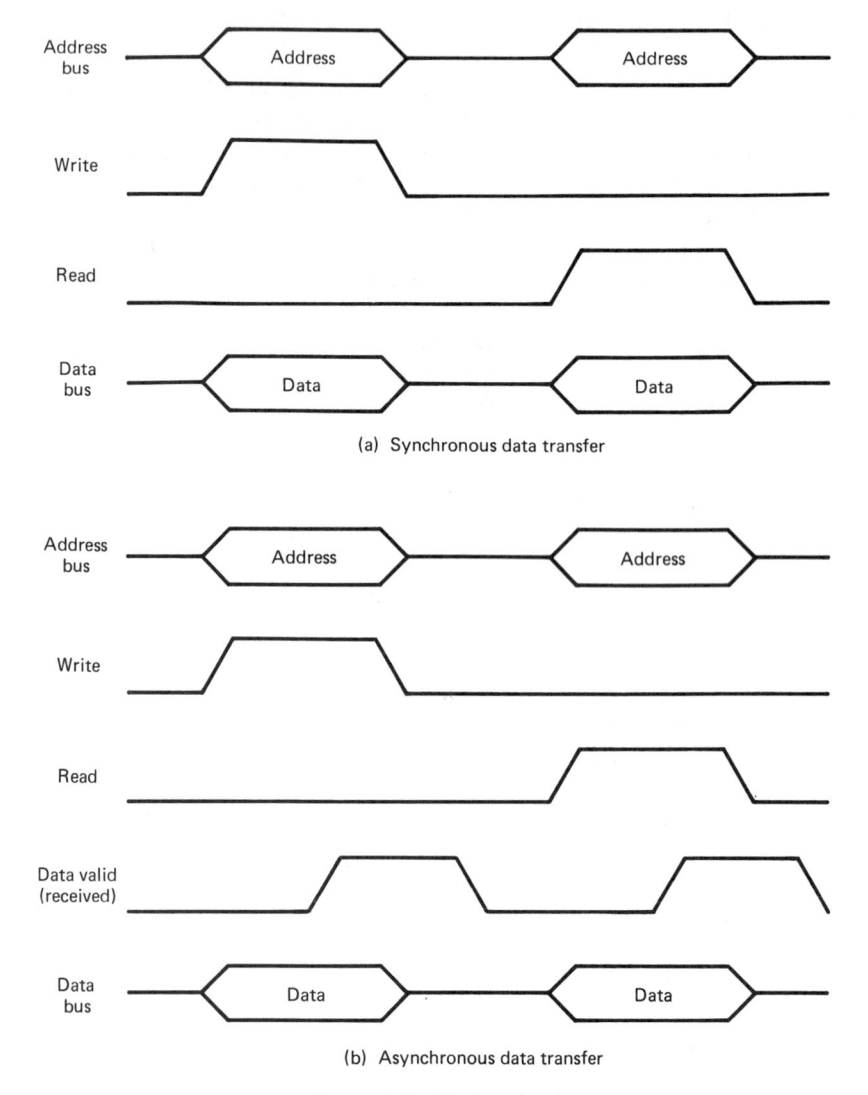

Figure 6–7 Timing signals

Sec. 6.3 Data Transfer

back to 0, the device must have already read the data. Similarly, to read data from a device, the CPU places the address of the device on the address bus and raises the *read* control line to 1. The selected device must place the data on the data bus at once and keep it there while the *read* line is at 1.

Note that in a synchronous data transfer, the device must respond during a fixed time period dictated by the CPU. In other words, all devices must be able to respond at the same speed. However, since I/O devices vary in their speed of operation, this requirement poses a problem. We can solve the problem by adjusting the durations of the *read* and *write* signals to accommodate devices with different response times or by operating all devices at the speed of the slowest one. It is clear, however, that both alternatives are undesirable.

The problem can be solved by using an **asynchronous** data transfer technique. This mode involves a back-and-forth process of passing control signals between the transmitter and the receiver. This process, called **handshaking,** ensures reliable data transfers between the transmitter and the receiver. The handshake lines between the CPU and the peripheral control the data transfer by providing communication in the form of request and acknowledge signals.

Figure 6–7 (b) shows the timing of asynchronous data transfers. To write in an asynchronous data transfer mode, the CPU places the address of the selected device on the address bus and the data on the data bus. The CPU then raises the *write* control line to 1. The device reads the data and raises to 1 the *data valid* (*received*) control line. The CPU must keep the address and data on the buses until it receives the *data valid* signal. After receiving this signal, the CPU removes the address and data from the buses and lowers the *write* line to 0. This allows the device also to lower to 0 the *data valid* (*received*) line.

A similar process is followed when the CPU reads data from a device in an asynchronous data transfer mode. The selected device places the data on the data bus and places a 1 on the *data valid* (*received*) line to indicate to the CPU that the data is on the bus and can be read. Once the CPU receives this signal, it reads the data and lowers the *read* line. This allows the device to lower the *data valid* (*received*) line.

As we can see, the handshaking process forces the CPU to wait in order to accommodate devices that differ in the speed with which they can read or prepare the data. It is a highly flexible and reliable scheme because it relies on active participation of both sender and receiver to complete a data transfer operation. If one party is not functioning, the data transfer will not be completed, and a **timeout** mechanism will be activated. The timeout is implemented by an internal counter that is activated by the handshaking signal and counts time. If the return handshake signal is not detected within a given time period, an error occurs and the timeout signal is used to interrupt the CPU to execute an appropriate error-handling routine.

Other examples of handshaking signals produced by the handshaking logic circuit are the interrupt acknowledge (INTA) and interrupt request (INTR). The INTA signal is issued when the receiver has accepted an INTR signal from the transmitter. INTA indicates that the receiver is ready to input data from the data bus, and the transmitter recognizes it by placing the data on the data bus.

Synchronous data transfer operations may yield higher transfer rates and require fewer control lines but impose speed and compatibility constraints on the peripheral devices. Asynchronous data transfer operations usually yield lower transfer rates and require a larger number of control lines but allow the use of peripherals with varying speeds in the same system.

Principles of Data Transfer Operations

Let us now focus on the basic mechanisms for data transfer under the three accessing methods discussed in Section 6.2. The simplest and most straightforward scheme is the programmed I/O. It can be implemented by as few as two I/O instructions, although additional instructions are sometimes provided. Thus under *programmed I/O*, these steps are taken:

1. The CPU checks the device status flag periodically to determine if the device is ready to begin data transfer.
2. If the device is ready, the CPU issues a *read* or *write* signal, and the data transfer takes place. If in *input* mode, an IN instruction causes a data word to be transferred from the I/O port into a CPU register; the CPU then moves the data word into the proper memory location. If in *output* mode, a data word from memory is placed in a CPU register and transferred, under an OUT instruction, to the I/O port.
3. The CPU waits for an indication from the I/O device that the data transfer operation is completed.

The following steps must be taken for carrying out an *interrupt I/O* process originated by one or more I/O devices:

1. The I/O device issues an INTR signal.
2. The CPU checks if the interrupting device is masked. If it is unmasked, the CPU checks the device interrupt priority position against the priority of the program currently running and the priorities of other devices that simultaneously request an interrupt.
3. If the device has the right priority, the CPU sends an INTA signal and fetches the device interrupt vector.
4. The CPU stores in memory the status of the currently running program (the content of the program status word register) and its return address (the content of the program counter). Usually, the CPU pushes this information into the stack memory (see Section 7.2).
5. The CPU jumps to the device interrupt service routine and executes it.
6. The CPU retrieves (pops) the PSW and PC from the stack memory and returns to the main program.

As we see, the interrupt I/O process makes use of three routines: an interrupt service routine, a PUSH routine for saving the PSW and PC in the stack, and a POP routine for retrieving the PSW and PC from the stack.

Sec. 6.4   Device Interfacing   169

To effect a *DMA operation*, the DMA controller (DMAC) must first be initialized, usually under an INTR/INTA handshaking process:

1. The word counter (WC) is loaded with the number of words to be transferred.
2. The DMA address register (DAR) is loaded with the starting address of the memory block into which (or from which) data is to be transferred.
3. The control/status register (DCSR) is loaded with a suitable control/status bit pattern.

These three registers are usually addressed by the CPU as output devices. After initializing the DMAC, the DMA process proceeds as follows:

4. A DMA request (DMAR) is issued after ensuring that the input data register (IDR) has data ready for transfer in a memory write mode or that the output data register (ODR) is empty in a memory read mode. For example, in an input transfer (memory write), the DMAC starts the device, acquires the data word, and stores it in the IDR. This word is then transferred into the memory location addressed by the DAR; that is

$$MAR \leftarrow (DAR)$$

$$MBR \leftarrow (IDR)$$

   These transfers are done using the address and data buses.
5. Upon receiving a DMA acknowledge (DMAA) signal, the data transfer follows:
   (a) The WC is decremented and the DAR is incremented after each data word transfer.
   (b) The WC is repeatedly tested for zero.
   (c) If the content of the WC is zero, the DMAC issues an INTR, signaling the termination of the DMA process. The CPU then jumps to the interrupt service routine and executes it accordingly.

6.4 DEVICE INTERFACING

The characteristics of the wide variety of peripheral devices that can be supported by a computer system vary radically. To communicate with the CPU, these devices require interface and control hardware and software to connect them to the buses. The **device controller** handles the device commands and status, while the **interface** usually refers to the hardware required to connect the device and its control circuits to the appropriate bus. These two terms are sometimes lumped together or used interchangeably.

The basic function of an interface is to synchronize the data transfer between the CPU and the peripheral. When data is input, the interface receives the data at the rate produced by the peripheral and then transfers it through the bus to the CPU whenever it is available. When data is output, the interface receives the data from the bus and then transfers it to the peripheral at the rate at which it can be accepted. In either case, the interface provides buffer storage for the data.

The interface unit can be viewed as consisting of two parts. One part is *device dependent* and serves the peripheral, and the other is *device independent*, used to connect the interface unit to the system bus. In many cases, we can use standard interface units, adhering to standard protocols and connectors. However, for special applications, the user may be required to provide interfaces and protocols. In general, the interface must perform some combination of the following functions:

1. Make peripheral status available to the CPU.
2. Have interrupt and/or DMA capabilities.
3. Signal the CPU when an operation is completed and/or if an error has occurred during an operation.
4. Transfer CPU instructions to the device.
5. Provide buffer storage for data sent to the device from the computer and from the device to the computer.
6. Check the parity of the data (see Section 2.5) and issue an error message if the data is in error. Some interfaces are also capable of error correction.
7. Decode the input data sent from the device to the computer into appropriate machine language (bit) patterns and encode the output bit patterns sent from the computer to the device into appropriate characters.
8. Provide special facilities, if required by the specific I/O device, such as:
   (a) Parallel-to-serial and serial-to-parallel data conversions
   (b) Display on the VDU screen of the character just typed at the keyboard (*echoing*)
   (c) Special keyboard characters such as *backspace*, *delete*, and *rubout*.

The availability of numerous LSI and VLSI I/O interface support chips makes the design of an interface significantly simpler. The design usually involves using an LSI interface chip and adding to it some necessary external logic circuits. Since the wide variety of peripheral devices is reflected in the details of their associated interfaces, we shall concentrate on the general structure of a device interface.

Structure of a Device Interface

The major elements of a general device interface, capable of both input and output functions, are shown in the block diagram of Figure 6–8. If the particular peripheral is an input-only or output-only device or is incapable of DMA, some of the building blocks shown will not be included in the device interface.

Associated with each of the three buses shown in Figure 6–8 are bus receivers (or transceivers) and bus driver/buffers. A **bus receiver** is a register that holds the input data for as long as required. A **transceiver** is a circuit used with *bidirectional* buses that can function either in a transmitting mode or in a receiving mode. A bus **driver/buffer** is required to place information on the bus. Since a bus may be driven by more than one source, a bus driver/buffer is a *tristate* device. (As mentioned in

Sec. 6.4   Device Interfacing   171

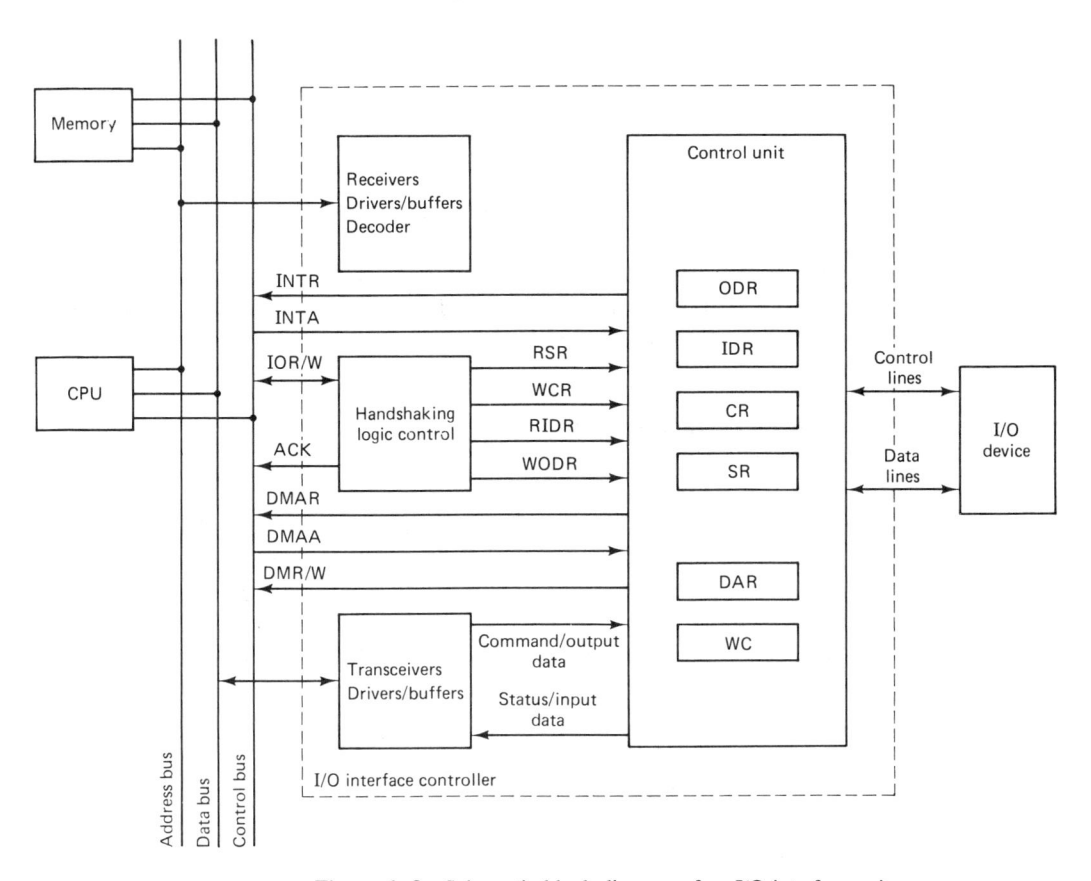

Figure 6–8   Schematic block diagram of an I/O interface unit

Chapter 3, a tristate device is a gate that can be in any one of three possible states: 0, 1, or floating. When the output of the device is floating, the gate is, in effect, disconnected from the bus.)

The address bus interface also includes a **decoder** to determine which register is addressed by the current I/O instruction. The control bus is represented by several control lines: the handshaking signals [INTR, INTA, and acknowledge (ACK)], I/O read/write (IOR/W), and the DMA signals [DMAR, DMAA, and DMA memory read/write (DMR/W)].

The DMA portion in Figure 6–8 is self-explanatory in view of our discussion of DMA accessing in Section 6.2. The **control unit** contains four registers. The **control register (CR)** is used to buffer the various commands and other information to the peripheral device. The logic associated with the CR controls the flow of data between the peripheral and the data bus. The **status register (SR)** stores the current status of the device and also provides error messages. Sometimes the CR and SR share the same I/O address and are jointly referred to as the **status/control register.** The other two registers, the IDR and ODR, serve as data buffers for input and output operations, respectively.

In an input mode, the peripheral sends a data word, which is stored in the IDR.

The *data ready* flag in the SR is set, and if the *interrupt enable* flag in the CR is also set, an INTR signal is sent to the CPU to allow it to input under interrupt I/O. To output, a data word is sent and stored in the ODR and is then forwarded to the peripheral device whenever the control unit detects (in the SR) that the device is ready to accept it.

To sequence these operations, the **handshaking logic unit** supplies the control unit with four signals. Two signals, the **write control register (WCR)** and the **read status register (RSR),** are associated with the CR and SR, respectively. The other two signals, the **read input data register (RIDR)** and the **write output data register (WODR),** control the IDR and ODR, respectively.

6.5 SYSTEM-RESIDENT I/O PROCESSORS

The DMA accessing scheme reduces CPU overhead in dealing with I/O operations and allows some concurrency in CPU-I/O operations. This idea can be further extended by delegating more I/O work away from the CPU and into a separate, more powerful I/O controller. Rather than having each I/O interface communicate with the CPU, one or more such I/O controllers can be assigned the task of communicating directly with I/O devices. Hence, unlike a DMAC, these I/O controllers can service peripherals directly and eliminate this task from the CPU. Since the CPU is the most costly element in large computers and CPU use is therefore of prime importance, this idea gave rise to special-purpose I/O controllers, which are called **I/O channels.** Fast I/O devices, such as magnetic tapes or disks, can use such a channel only one at a time. However, relatively slow devices, such as terminals, can be *clustered*, with one I/O channel controlling all of them.

With the continued decrease in hardware costs, this trend can be carried to its logical conclusion. Instead of having a special-purpose I/O channel, we can have a general-purpose computer serving as an independent **I/O processor (IOP).** Many medium and large computers have one or more minicomputers or microcomputers serving as **front ends** that handle every aspect of I/O. These IOPs operate in parallel with the main CPU and enable it to remain free to work almost exclusively on computations and user programs without being bothered by I/O tasks.

I/O processors usually contain a number of DMA channels, have their own CPUs and instruction sets, and execute their programs in parallel with the main CPU. In most cases, they are initialized by the main CPU and then communicate with it only when they have completed their tasks. In some large computers, the IOPs and the main CPU form a **multiprocessor** configuration where each processor is independent of all the others and can initiate an operation.

An IOP can support many peripheral devices via a specifically designated I/O bus. The device controllers are usually microprocessor-based and are programmed to handle specific terminals and peripherals. The controllers support the communication between the IOP and the peripherals attached to it and interface with the IOP as described in Section 6.4. Communication between the IOP and main memory is accomplished by DMA as described in Section 6.2. CPU-IOP communication varies from one computer to another and depends on the level of intelligence included in

Sec. 6.5   System-Resident I/O Processors   173

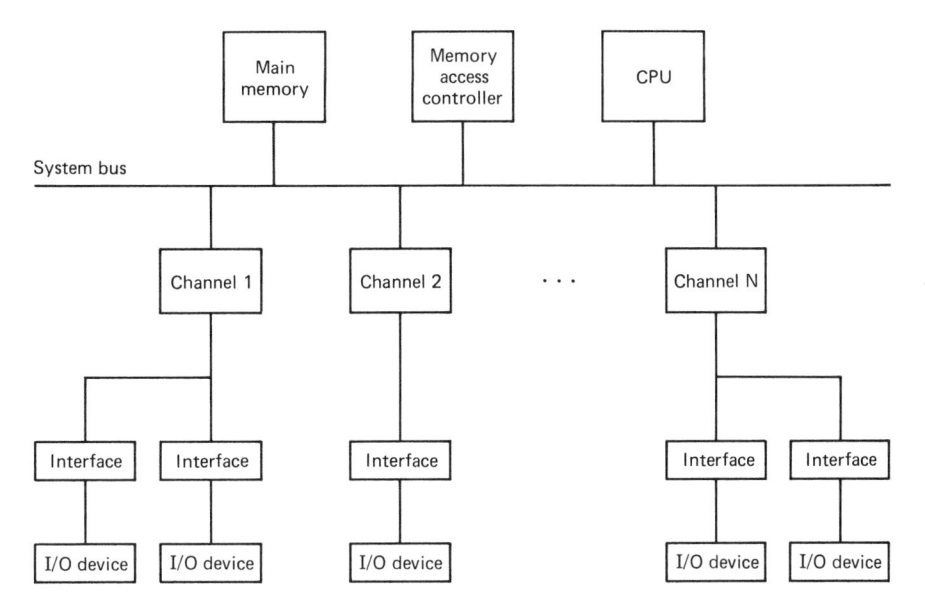

Figure 6-9 Hierarchical organization of I/O using channels

the system. The principles of CPU-IOP communication are considered later in this section. But let us begin our discussion by considering I/O channels first, since they can serve as a useful introduction to the more advanced topic of IOPs.

I/O Channels

An I/O channel is a controller more sophisticated than a DMA facility but one that nevertheless performs I/O operations in a DMA mode. An I/O channel is a special-purpose processor of limited capability that is configured to interface several I/O devices to memory, as opposed to a DMAC, which is usually connected to a single device. In addition, the channel can perform extensive error detection and correction, code conversions, and data formatting.

Using I/O channels, the I/O system can be hierarchically organized as shown in Figure 6-9. Each channel is a special-purpose computer that has an instruction set that is restricted to I/O operations and operates on a cycle-stealing basis. A high-speed I/O device usually communicates with an I/O channel via a dedicated interface, whereas low-speed devices can share an interface. The memory access controller coordinates the accessing of main memory by the CPU and the I/O channels. The I/O channel communicates with the CPU as a DMA facility and communicates with I/O devices as though it were a CPU. Therefore, the channel must perform the following tasks:

1. Select a particular device for I/O transfer and check its status.
2. Give commands (execute programs) to implement I/O operations.
3. Define storage areas in main memory into (and from) which data block transfers will take place.

4. Provide data formatting and coding facilities.
5. Control end-of-transfer activities.

Since I/O devices differ widely in their data transmission rates, channels are basically classified into two types: multiplexer channels, which are further divided into byte and block multiplexers, and selector channels. **Multiplexer channels** are used to connect a number of slow and medium-speed devices and operate them simultaneously by **interleaving** (multiplexing) their transmissions. For example, consider a terminal, a relatively slow device. Assume that it can transfer 100 characters per second (or one character every 10 milliseconds), where a character typically consists of a byte (8 bits) of data, control, and status bits. Assume further that it takes the channel 50 microseconds to process and store each character. In a multiplexing process, the channel can handle up to 200 such terminals in rotation (since $200 \times 50 = 10$ milliseconds) and get back to the first terminal before it has another character to transmit.

The mode of operation described in this example is called **character interleaving** (or **byte interleaving**). Each I/O device is logically connected to the channel for the time required to transfer one byte of data. The channel is divided into several subchannels that carry I/O information simultaneously. If device A sends the string $a_0 a_1 a_2 \ldots$, device B sends the string $b_0 b_1 b_2 \ldots$, and device C sends the string $c_0 c_1 c_2 \ldots$, the resulting string out of the channel would be $a_0 b_0 c_0 a_1 b_1 c_1 a_2 b_2 c_2 \ldots$.

Each subchannel contains a byte buffer, a device identification register, and a control/status register. Since a multiplexer channel is intended to support a large number of I/O devices simultaneously, the subchannels can share byte counters and memory address registers that are usually kept in fixed main memory locations. If the time required by a device exceeds the time allocated for its logical connection to the channel, then using a **timeout** mechanism, the channel automatically reverts to a **burst mode** in which it maintains the logical connection until the device completes all its requested transfers.

Selector channels are dedicated to high-speed devices, such as magnetic tapes and disks, that cannot be multiplexed with other devices. These devices can keep a channel busy because of their high data transfer rates. Although several such devices can be connected to each selector channel, the channel can select only one I/O device at any given time and remains dedicated to it until the device completes its operation. The principle of operation of a selector channel is similar to that of a multiplexer channel in burst mode, except that selector channels support data rates that are an order of magnitude higher than those supported by byte multiplexers. The hardware organization of a channel selector is similar to that of a DMA controller. It contains a byte counter that specifies the number of remaining bytes to be transferred, a memory address register (MAR) that specifies the next memory location to or from which data is to be transferred, a device address register, a memory buffer register (MBR), and a control/status register. Since many I/O devices are byte oriented, whereas the selector channel is capable of transferring larger words, the channel may also include a word assembly/disassembly mechanism.

A **block multiplexer channel** is a combination of the two previously described channel configurations. It operates as a high-speed multiplexer channel in burst mode, interleaving blocks rather than bytes of data. Block multiplexer channels are intended mainly to service devices, such as disks or magnetic tapes, whose startup operations (e.g., moving the read/write head to a specified track or searching for a record) are relatively time consuming and cannot be used for data transfers. Hence, rather than using a selector channel and tying up the entire channel capacity doing nothing, a block multiplexer can service other devices during those dead times, reverting to the burst operation when the record is found.

Multiprocessor Configurations

The process of off-loading the CPU from I/O responsibilities can be carried to its logical conclusion by assigning I/O tasks to a general-purpose, independent IOP rather than using special-purpose channels. The continued decrease in hardware cost certainly supports this trend, and IOP configurations differ only in the degree of independence allowed to them. Some computer systems already operate in multiprocessor configurations where IOPs are completely independent, and it seems that this approach will prevail more in the future.

The simplest interconnection scheme is probably the **common bus** organization shown in Figure 6–10. The common bus is time-shared by all the processors, and only one processor can access the memory at any given time. The other processors are either involved with their internal operations or wait for the bus. To access the memory, a processor must establish first that the bus is available and then begin transfer operations only when it is granted control of the bus. When more than one processor competes for the bus simultaneously, the **bus controller** resolves such contentions using a **bus arbitration** scheme that determines priorities among the contending processors. The priority resolution schemes are the same as those discussed in Section 6.2. Bus arbitration can be serial, in which case the processors are daisy-chained, or parallel, using priority encoding. The two schemes can be also combined, with the processors combined into priority groups that are selected by a priority encoder. Within each group, the processors are daisy-chained and are serviced in an order determined by their position along the chain.

We can generalize the common bus into a **dual-bus** multiprocessor (multicomputer, in fact) organization, which is shown in Figure 6–11. Each computer is connected through a system bus controller to the common system bus. The system bus is time-shared, and only one computer at a time can interact with any of the common resources. Intercomputer communication is carried out on the system bus through the

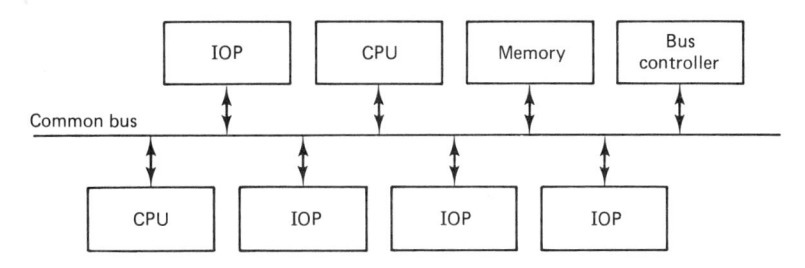

Figure 6–10 Multiprocessor common bus organization

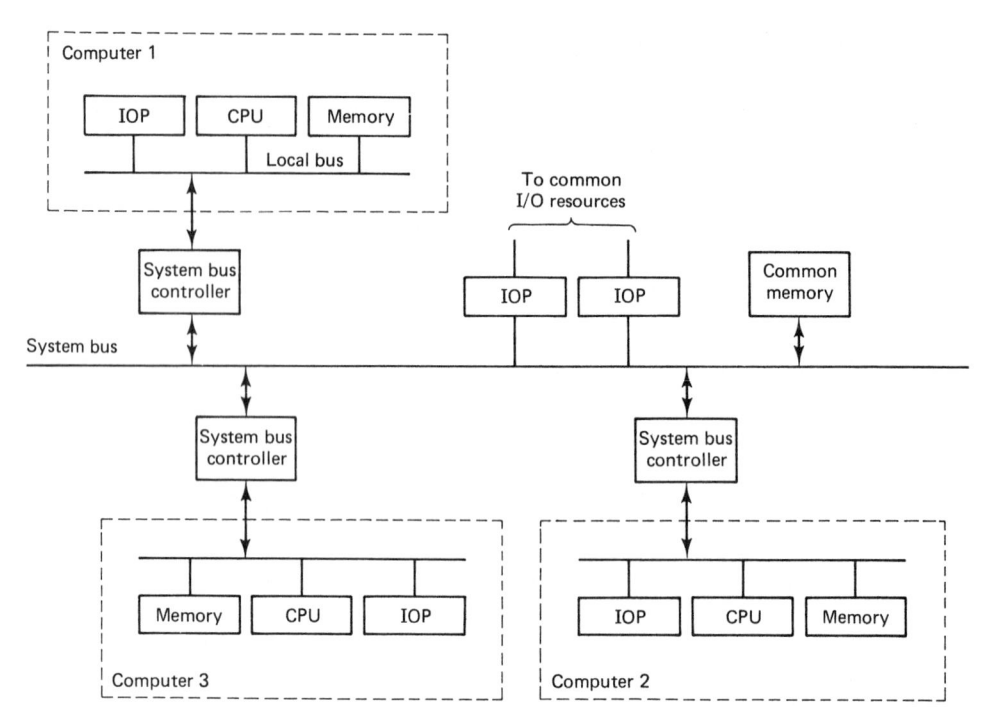

Figure 6-11 Multicomputer interconnection

common memory. Intracomputer communication is done via the local bus of each computer. Contentions for the system bus can be resolved as in the common bus organization. It is clear that in the dual-bus interconnection scheme, the throughput of the system and of each computer is greater than that afforded by the common bus organization.

The **switching (crossbar) matrix** interconnection scheme shown in Figure 6-12 is clearly different from and more complex than the two preceding configurations. The system shown consists of M memory modules, K CPUs, and N IOPs (in general, $K \neq N$ and $K + N \neq M$). The memory and processor buses are interconnected through a switching (crossbar) matrix. A switch, denoted in Figure 6-12 by a small square with an $\times$ inside it, is activated when a processor places on the bus the address of a memory module. When activated, each switch establishes a connection between the processor and the memory module whose buses intersect with the switch. Although the switching matrix supports simultaneous transfers to and from *all* memory modules, each switch can resolve contentions for the same memory module using a predetermined priority scheme.

We can do without the switching matrix if we use **multiport memories** as shown in Figure 6-13 but pay the price of requiring more expensive memory modules and complex memory control circuits. Each processor bus shown in Figure 6-13 carries the control, address, and data lines necessary to communicate with its assigned port in each memory module. Each memory module includes a contention resolution mechanism that uses some predetermined priority scheme.

Sec. 6.5 System-Resident I/O Processors

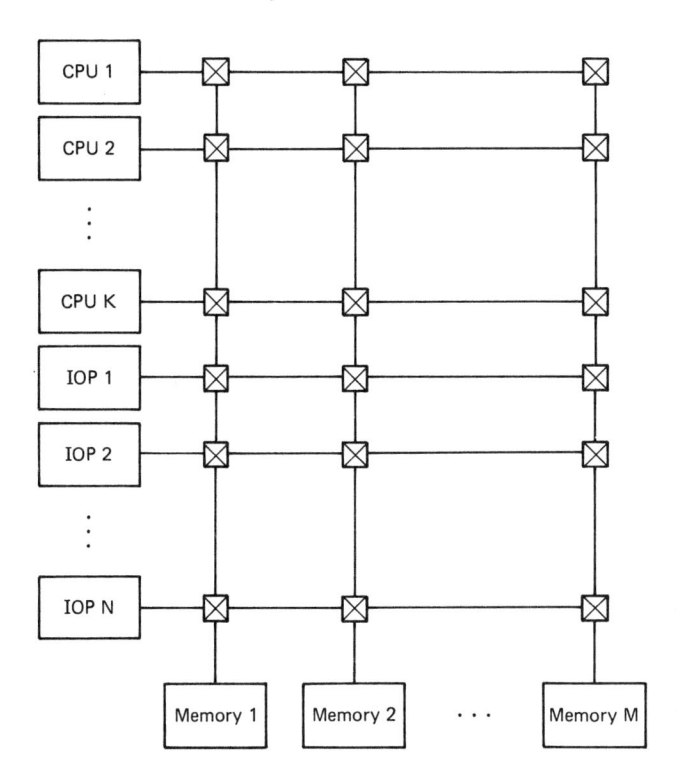

Figure 6-12 Switching matrix multiprocessor interconnection

Multiprocessor interconnection schemes can be categorized as loosely coupled or tightly coupled. **Loosely coupled** systems, discussed in Chapter 12, are characterized by multicomputer interconnection accomplished over remote communication links such as dedicated lines, telephone lines, or radio or microwave links. In contrast, all the multiprocessor interconnection schemes discussed so far in this chapter are **tightly coupled.** Such systems use a common shared resource, called a **mailbox,** for interprocessor communication. The mailbox can be a portion of common memory, or it can be a mass storage unit connected to a common (shared) IOP. Each processor can use the mailbox to leave messages for other processors or share with them system programs that are stored in the mailbox. Each processor can check the mailbox periodically for messages left for it by the other processors. However, this procedure is time consuming since it depends on the mailbox polling rate. Therefore, in an alternative scheme that is commonly used, the message sending processor initiates an interprocessor interrupt to inform the intended message-receiving processor that a new message has been inserted for it in the mailbox.

I/O Processor (IOP)

The IOP can be an autonomous processor, and the system can be organized in any of the four multiprocessor configurations discussed earlier. If not completely independent, the IOP requires some CPU assistance in the initiation of operations and in making decisions regarding I/O activities. The IOP is a general-purpose computer

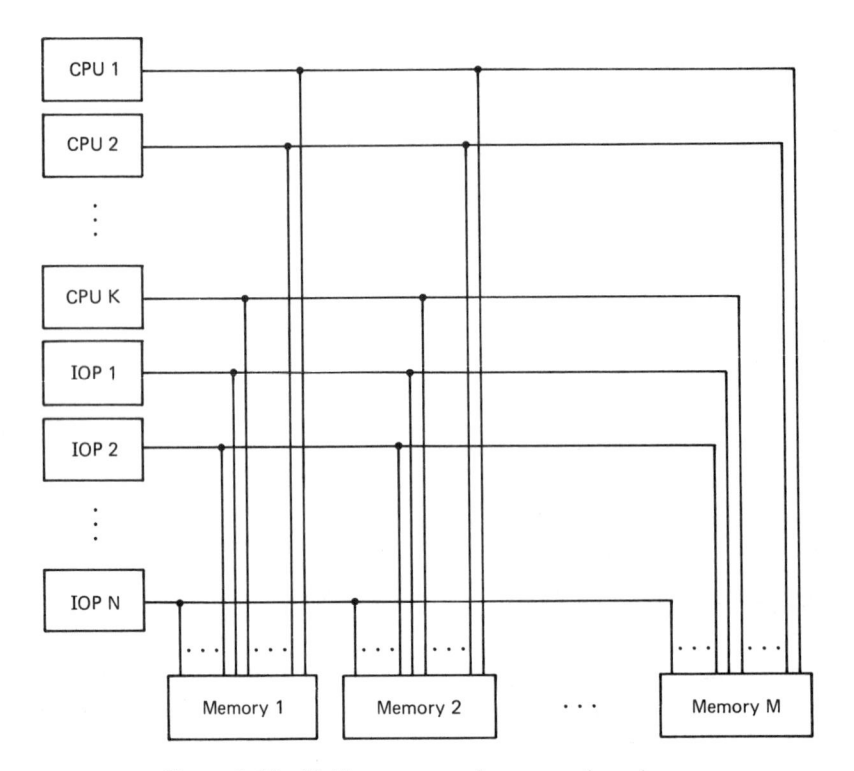

Figure 6-13 Multiport memory interconnection scheme

that communicates with main memory via a DMA facility over the system bus and with I/O devices over one or more I/O buses.

Examples of two I/O bus structures are shown in Figure 6-14. In the **single shared bus** organization (of which several can be configured), each IOP controls a fixed number of I/O devices. In the **switching matrix bus** structure, each device can be controlled by any IOP. The principle of operation of the switching matrix is similar to that of the crossbar matrix explained in conjunction with Figure 6-12.

The CPU has only a limited set of I/O instructions that allow it to initiate, test, and terminate an I/O operation. Typically, **CPU I/O instructions** are of the type START I/O, STATUS I/O, and STOP I/O. In addition to the opcode, a CPU I/O instruction contains a device address field that points to the particular I/O device intended for the transaction and a memory address field that points to the memory location into which the IOP transfers information in response to the CPU instruction.

The execution of all I/O data transfer instructions is the responsibility of the IOP. **IOP instructions** are also referred to as **commands** to distinguish them from CPU instructions. They are used in IOP I/O programs that reside in main memory and are fetched by the IOP when given an address specified by a CPU START I/O instruction. The IOP commands can be classifed into three basic types:

1. *Data transfer instructions* for input (read), for output (write), and for reading status information.

Sec. 6.5 System-Resident I/O Processors

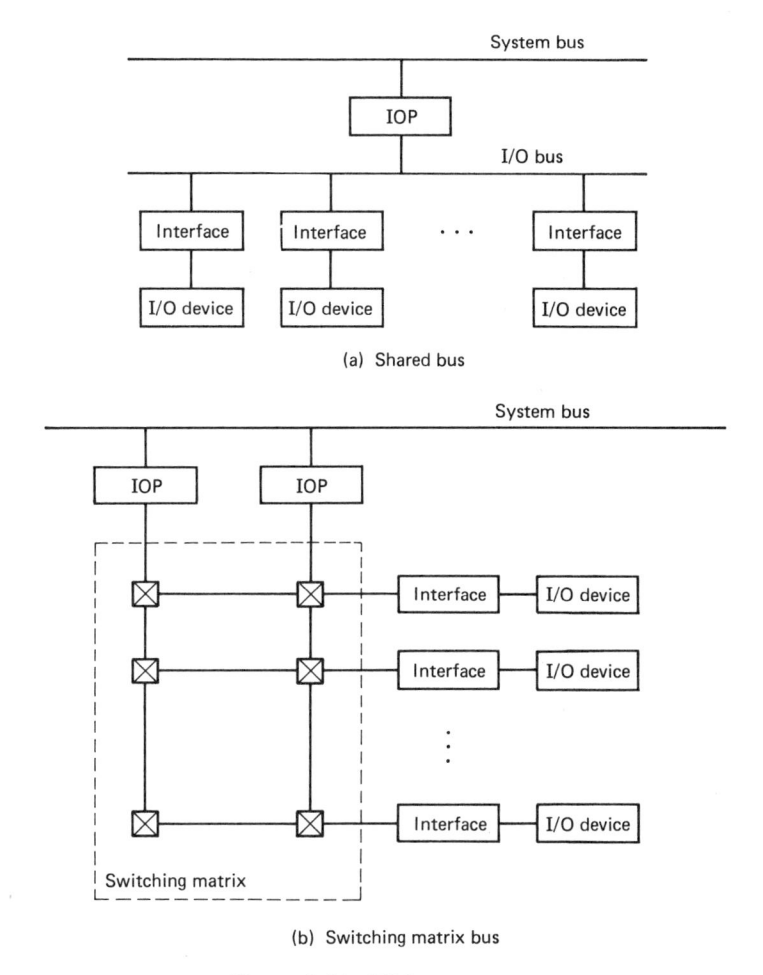

Figure 6–14 I/O bus structures

2. *General-purpose instructions* such as arithmetic, logical, and branch instructions. These instructions are used for several tasks:
   (a) To facilitate jumps within I/O programs
   (b) To evaluate complex addresses
   (c) To provide assembly/disassembly facilities, code conversions, parallel-to-serial and serial-to-parallel conversions, parity checking/generation, data formatting, and handshaking signals
   (d) To establish device priorities.
3. *Control instructions* to handle special I/O device functions other than those involved in data transfers. Here are some examples of such instructions:
   (a) Move read/write head, move backward, locate record address, and rewind for a magnetic tape device.
   (b) Print line for a line printer.
   (c) Move read/write head, locate track, and search a record for a disk.

The typical format of an IOP command consists of a number of fields:

1. An *opcode* field specifying the type of the required data transfer operation
2. A *memory address* field specifying the initial address of the memory block assigned for the transfer
3. A *word count* field specifying the number of words to be transferred (the length of the memory block)
4. A *control* field intended for special I/O device functions and specified based on the particular requirements of the I/O device
5. A *status* field used for communication purposes or for bookkeeping. Typically, this field contains a flag for generating an interrupt request by the IOP, a flag for instructing the IOP to make the status word available to the CPU, and a flag that can be used for command chaining (indicating to the IOP that the current command is not the last but is followed by another).

CPU-IOP communication may differ from one computer system to another. Typically, however, the communication process is of the handshaking type and uses a mailbox where the processors can leave messages to one another. When an IOP requires CPU service, it issues an interrupt request (INTR). Having received an interrupt acknowledge (INTA) from the CPU, the IOP then takes control over the system bus on a cycle-stealing basis and uses its DMA facility for data transfer. Prior to the execution of an I/O sequence, the CPU sends a STATUS I/O instruction to the IOP. The IOP places the device address, indicated in the device address field of the CPU instruction, on the I/O bus, and the addressed I/O device responds by transferring its status word to the IOP. In addition, the IOP responds to a CPU STATUS I/O instruction by placing its own status word in the memory location whose address was specified in that instruction. The IOP status word consists of a number of flags such as *IOP busy/ready*, *I/O device busy/ready*, *I/O device connected/disconnected*, error bits, and data transfer completed bits.

If the I/O device is ready, the CPU sends a START I/O instruction to the IOP. The memory address contained in this instruction points the IOP to the memory location where it can find the beginning of the relevant I/O program. The IOP then starts executing the program and frees the CPU to handle other tasks concurrently.

The CPU can halt this process by issuing a STOP I/O instruction. Otherwise, the data transfer operation continues until the IOP interrupts the CPU. When this happens, the CPU responds with a STATUS I/O instruction and causes the IOP to place its status word in the memory location whose address is specified in this instruction. The CPU checks the status word for error messages or for an indication that the data transfer operation has been successfully completed. If successfully completed, the CPU terminates the I/O transaction.

6.6 SUMMARY

The basic principles of I/O processing presented in this chapter have been simplified and occasionally idealized, with many details omitted. The reason for this is that we wanted to avoid discussing any particular computer I/O organization or any specific

I/O device. Of all the areas of computer organization, I/O processing varies most from one computer to another, and many of its functions depend on the particular I/O device. The hardware implementation of each of these functions is probably unique and specialized for each system.

PROBLEMS

1. How do programmed I/O, interrupt I/O, and DMA transfer differ?
2. An instruction code of a computer has a 6-bit address field. How many I/O devices can be attached to the computer?
3. What is the basic advantage of a system with priority interrupt over one without priority interrupt?
4. Consider the process of reading a character from a keyboard and then writing it to an output device. Both the keyboard and output device are polled.
   (a) Draw a flowchart for the input operation.
   (b) Draw a flowchart for the output operation.
5. Design the logic circuit associated with each I/O device to implement the daisy chain priority scheme shown in Figure 6–4. Include in your design a provision that when the interrupting device is acknowledged, it is enabled and produces its interrupt vector onto the data bus.
6. Can a priority interrupt system function without a mask register (see Figure 6–5)?
7. Four I/O devices are capable of interrupting the CPU. Each has its own interrupt request (INTR) line. Design a priority encoder that will enable the CPU to determine which interrupting device should be serviced when two or more requests are received simultaneously. Label the four interrupt lines I_0, I_1, I_2, and I_3, and assume a priority assignment scheme such that the highest priority corresponds to the highest subscript number.
8. Assign interrupt priorities to the following events:
   (a) Power failure   (c) Clock
   (b) I/O character read (d) Memory error
9. An interface has two handshake lines: an input line designated LD (load data) and an output line labeled ACK (acknowledge). When LD = 0, data is loaded from an I/O device into an interface register. ACK = 1 indicates that the interface has accepted the data. The CPU sets an I/O read line to transfer the data from the interface register into a CPU register. After receiving the I/O read signal, ACK returns to 0.
   (a) Draw a block diagram of the relevant connections between the CPU, the interface, and the I/O device.
   (b) Indicate the handshaking process on a timing diagram.
10. An I/O device transfers characters at the rate of 1200 characters per second. When enabled, the device moves a character into a buffer register and sets a DONE bit that can be tested by the program handling the device. The program is a loop containing two instructions, each of which takes 1.5 microseconds to execute. How many times will the CPU go around the loop waiting for the DONE bit to be set?
11. A DMA controller transfers characters to a single-port memory on a cycle-stealing basis. It is connected to a terminal that transmits 1200 characters per second. The CPU fetches instructions and data on the average of once every 1.5 microseconds. By how much will the CPU be slowed down because of the DMA controller?

12. A disk contains a number of sectors, each capable of storing 256 characters. It takes 0.75 milliseconds to read a sector. The CPU is interrupted for each character and takes 2.5 microseconds to process each interrupt.
    (a) How often will the CPU be interrupted?
    (b) What percentage of time will the CPU spend handling I/O?
13. Repeat Problem 12 with the I/O technique changed to DMA.
14. Data characters (8 bits per character) are transmitted over a 4800 bits per second serial line. How many characters per second can be transmitted in each of the following modes?
    (a) Asynchronously, with one start bit and one stop bit appended as header and trailer, respectively, to each data character
    (b) Asynchronously, with one start bit and two stop bits
    (c) Synchronously
15. A computer has two selector channels and one multiplexer channel (see Figure 6–9). Each selector channel supports two disks and two magnetic tapes. The multiplexer channel supports three printers and 12 VDU terminals. What is the maximum aggregate I/O transfer rate, given the following device transfer rates (in kilobytes per second): magnetic tape, 250; disk, 900; printer, 8.6; VDU, 0.85.
16. Design a bus controller (arbiter) for a multiprocessor common bus organization (see Figure 6–10) in accordance with the following specifications:
    (a) Assume that there are two CPUs and two IOPs.
    (b) Each processor has a bus request (BR) line and a bus acknowledge (BA) line.
    (c) A bus busy (BB) line indicates the status of the common bus.
    (d) Bus access is granted by priority.

CHAPTER 7

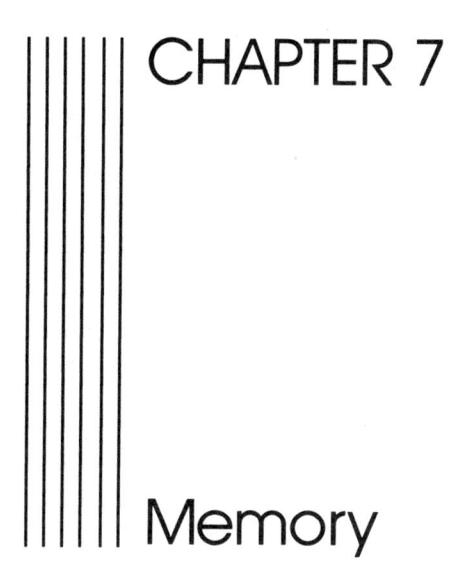

Memory

7.1 ASPECTS OF COMPUTER STORAGE

The **memory** of a digital computer is composed of a variety of devices that store the instructions and data required for its operation. Modern computers can support very large physical memory spaces and provide effective mechanisms to manage them. They also distinguish between the logical address space and the physical memory space,* have the necessary hardware support to map one space to the other, and efficiently handle large logical address spaces through dynamic storage allocation mechanisms.

The most important parameters of a memory system are these:

1. *Capacity*: The maximum number of units of data that it can store
2. *Access time*: The time taken to access the data
3. *Data transfer rate*: The number of bits per second at which data can be read
4. *Cycle time*: A measure of how often a memory can be accessed
5. *Cost*: Usually expressed in terms of dollars per bit

The memory can be divided into two major groups: main memory and auxiliary memory. **Main memory** is the central resource of a computer system that must be dynamically allocated to users, programs, and processes. It stores data and programs that are to be executed by the CPU and is therefore characterized by being directly accessible to the CPU instruction set. Since program instructions and data must be transferred to the CPU for execution, the execution time of any program is dependent

---

* All addresses generated by a program are considered logical addresses, whereas those applied to memory (or I/O devices) are considered physical addresses.

183

on the speed of the **memory transfer cycles.** The faster the main memory, the faster the computer. To facilitate this fast-access requirement, main memory is organized in many ways, characterized by a speed-cost trade-off that corresponds to the amount of additional hardware needed to meet the fast-access requirement.

If main memory is large, information processing can be faster, since most of the information required is immediately available, as opposed to being in slower auxiliary memory. However, it is important to realize that a large memory is inherently slower than a smaller memory, and, therefore, the speed of the main memory usually constitutes a processing speed limitation (bottleneck) for the computer. To illustrate this point, consider the RAM organization shown in Figure 3-30 in Chapter 3. To access a memory location, the content of the MAR has to be decoded. Now refer to the logic diagram in Figure 3-8 showing a 2 × 4 decoder. Note that two levels of logic gates must be traversed from the inputs to the outputs of the decoder. Each **logic level** introduces a propagation time delay. Since larger memories are implemented using memory modules (chips), the address decoding circuits require additional logic levels, thus increasing the propagation time delay in accessing a memory location.

The principal technology used in modern computers to implement main memory is semiconductor integrated circuits (ICs). Most semiconductor memories are **volatile**—if power is lost, the entire content of the memory is lost. In terms of the mechanism used to store and retrieve data, main memory can be classified as either **random-access memory (RAM)** or **content-addressable memory (CAM).** RAMs are accessed through addresses and can be of two types: read/write or read-only memory* (see Section 3.8). They are characterized by the fact that any addressable location can be accessed at random and requires an equal amount of access time irrespective of where the location is physically in the memory. A CAM, by contrast, is based on accessing by content rather than address and is discussed in Section 7.4.

Programs and data not immediately needed by the computer are stored in a less expensive and slower **auxiliary memory.** An auxiliary memory system is a **nonvolatile** storage device; when power is interrupted or removed, its content remains intact. This memory, also referred to as **secondary memory,** is usually composed of a variety of devices that are classified in terms of the mechanism used to store or retrieve data as either **sequential-access memory (SAM)** or **direct-access memory (DAM).** Magnetic tape is the most common SAM device, and magnetic disks and drums are the most popular DAM devices. These terms will be explained in Section 7.6.

7.2 STACK MEMORY

One type of memory that is included in most computers today is **stack memory.** This is a versatile data structure that is used for return-address storage and parameter passing in subroutine call and return, address and data manipulations, and arithmetic operations. Conceptually, a stack is analogous to dishes stored in a cabinet. When a

---

* It is common usage, however, to refer to RAM when meaning read/write memory and ROM when meaning read-only memory.

Sec. 7.2 Stack Memory

dish is needed, the top one of the pile is removed (**"popped"**). When a dish is returned to the cabinet, it is placed (**"pushed"**) on top of the dishes already there.

Although a stack can be successfully implemented by software, the evaluation of arithmetic expressions and the processing of procedures or functions and their returns are most efficiently handled by hardware-implemented stacks. In some cases, the stack is such a major part of the memory that the computer is called a **stack computer.** The best-known examples are the Burroughs B5500, B6500, B6700 general-purpose computers and the Hewlett-Packard HP3000 minicomputer. The stack of the HP3000 is discussed later in this section.

A stack is an ordered set of storage elements in which data insertions and removals are always made at one end, called the **top** of the stack. This implies that the *last* data element inserted into the stack will be the *first* to be removed. Therefore, stacks are referred to as **last-in, first-out,** or **LIFO,** data structures. The operations of insertion and removal of data into and from a stack are called **push** and **pop,** respectively. In addition to these operations, two Boolean functions (flags), *FULL*(*stack*) and *EMPTY*(*stack*), are commonly associated with a stack. These functions, also called *stack overflow* and *stack underflow*, are used to prevent trying to push an element onto a full stack and to ensure a nonempty stack before popping an element. Therefore, a **stack overflow** occurs when trying to add an element to a full stack, and a **stack underflow** occurs when trying to remove an element from an empty stack.

Hardware Implementation

Register-based implementation. Let us consider the hardware organization of a K-element stack with n bits stored in each element. The stack can be implemented by connecting together K n-bit parallel-transfer registers as shown in Figure 7–1(a). On the PUSH signal, the ith register loads the content of the $i - 1$ register, and the top register (register 0) loads the input data. On the POP signal, the ith register loads the content of the $i + 1$ register while the output data of the stack comes from the top register. Also on a POP signal, the register at the bottom of the stack (register $K - 1$) is filled with garbage.

The logic control circuit associated with each of the stack registers is shown in Figure 7–1(b). To be able to choose between the $i + 1$ and the $i - 1$ inputs, it is necessary to include a 2×1 multiplexer for each register. The *FULL*(*stack*) and *EMPTY*(*stack*) flags are usually provided by maintaining a counter [not shown in Figure 7–1(a)] and testing it for K count and 0 count, respectively. On a PUSH signal, the counter is incremented, and on a POP signal, the counter is decremented.

Another possible implementation of the stack is to use n K-bit bidirectional shift registers. Conceptually, the registers can be thought of as "lying on their sides," as shown in Figure 7–2. In this case, the PUSH and POP signals are actually the directional shift controls. On a PUSH signal, the serial input is supplied by the input data to the stack, and all the n registers are shifted to the left by 1 bit. The bits output from the left side of the registers are ignored. On the POP signal, all the registers shift right 1 bit, causing the serial output of the registers to be the data out of the stack. The serial input to the left of the registers is treated as garbage.

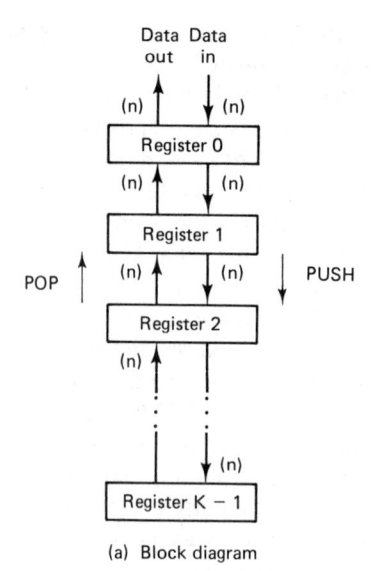

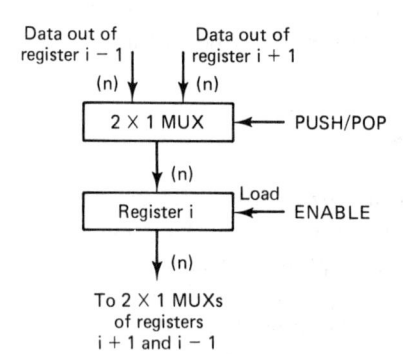

Figure 7-1 Parallel-transfer register stack

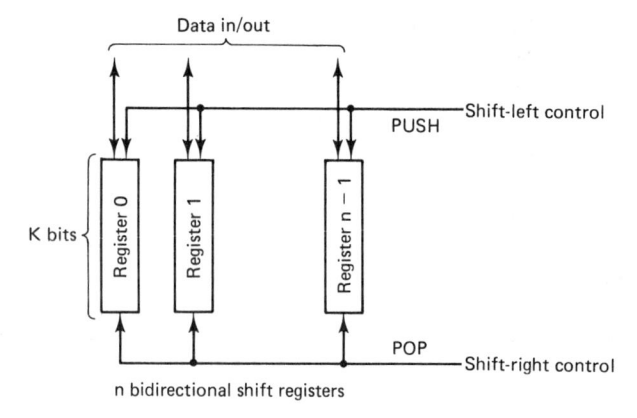

Figure 7-2 Shift register stack

Sec. 7.2   Stack Memory   187

Although both schemes can execute the PUSH and POP operations very quickly, the cost of the necessary hardware may be prohibitive. For this reason, neither of these implementations is very common. As an alternative, a RAM-based stack implementation is often used.

RAM-based implementation.   When a RAM is used to implement a stack, a totally different approach is necessary. Rather than actually transfer the content of each memory word to its neighboring word for every PUSH and POP operation, which would be much too inefficient, a special register, called the **stack pointer (SP),** is used to hold the address of the top of the stack. Hence, when data is to be stored in or removed from the stack, the RAM is accessed only by the address in the SP, which is incremented or decremented accordingly. The following example illustrates this approach.

Example 7.1

Consider the stack shown in Figure 7–3(a). It contains four elements, and the SP is pointing to the top of the stack, memory word 12, which contains the value 35. On the POP operation of Figure 7–3(b), the value in location 12 is output from the stack and the top of the stack is lowered to location 13; hence the value in the SP is now 13. Notice that the value 35 is not physically removed from location 12. Since the top of the stack is now 13, any data stored in locations 10, 11, or 12 is considered garbage. When a PUSH occurs, as shown in Figure 7–3(c), the SP is decremented by 1, and the value to be stored in the stack, in this case 19, is written to the memory word addressed by the SP. Any previous information stored in this location, 35 in this case, is overwritten.

When a RAM is used to implement a stack, it is irrelevant whether the stack grows up or down as long as the stack pointer is correctly maintained. In Example 7.1, the address stored in the SP was decremented when information was pushed onto the stack and incremented when information was popped out from the stack. In this case, the stack is said to grow in a direction toward lower memory. If the stack is designed to grow in a direction toward higher memory, the SP will have to be

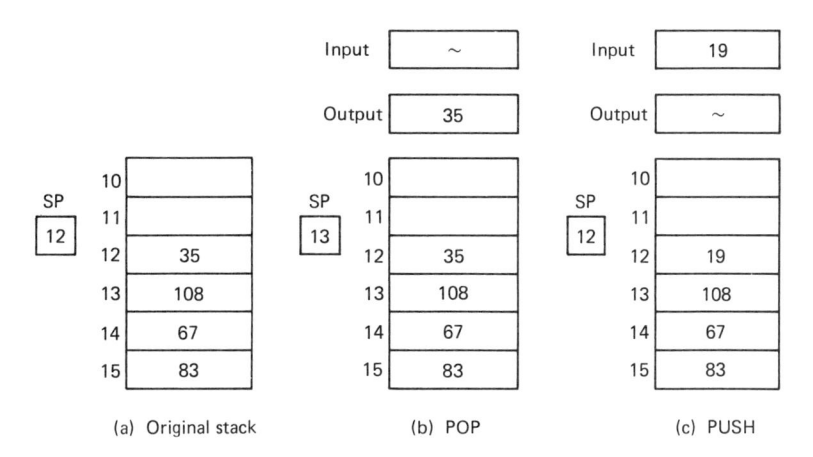

Figure 7–3 Operations on a RAM stack

incremented on a PUSH operation and decremented on a POP operation. In either case, it is important that the SP be maintained (changed) at the correct time.

Example 7.2

Consider a RAM stack that starts at address 0 and grows towards higher memory (opposite from Figure 7–3), and assume that the POP and PUSH operations interface with an outside register R1. The sequences of micro-operations that implement the POP and PUSH operations are as follows:

```
        POP                PUSH
    R1 ← M[SP]         SP ← (SP) + 1
    SP ← (SP) − 1      M[SP] ← (R1)
```

After a POP operation, the stack would be considered empty if the SP is 0 and would be considered full if the SP is equal to the largest address of the RAM stack.

It is not necessary to use a separate RAM unit to implement a RAM-based stack. Usually, a portion of main memory is set aside for use as a stack. In this case, it is necessary to define the stack *base* address and the stack *limit* address. Two registers, the **stack base (SB) register** and the **stack limit (SL) register,** are used for this purpose. Figure 7–4 shows a diagram of a stack that is included in a k-word main memory. The stack can be accessed only through the SP register. The SB and SL registers define the stack boundaries, and the address pointed to by the SP is always within the base and limit addresses. The *EMPTY(stack)* and *FULL(stack)* flags are obtained by comparing the SP to the SB and SL registers, respectively.

The HP3000 Stack

In some computers, fast-access registers are connected to an efficient RAM stack in order to store the top elements of the stack. Since these elements are used much more frequently than the others, the use of fast registers considerably reduces the access time for storing and retrieving the data. An example of such a computer is the HP3000 16-bit minicomputer. Its stack is primarily a part of main memory but also includes

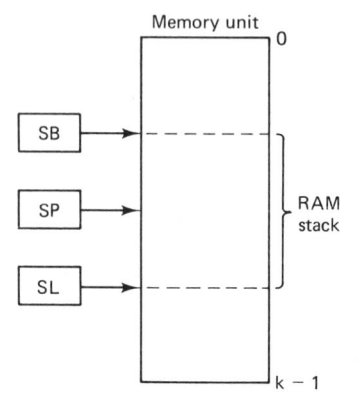

Figure 7–4 Stack within main memory

Sec. 7.3   Modular Memory

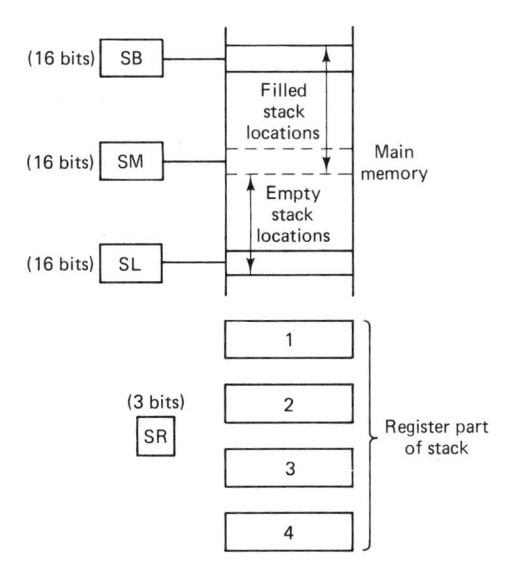

Figure 7-5 Stack structure of the HP3000

four hardware registers for storing the top of the stack elements. This structure is diagrammed in Figure 7–5.

The SM register points to the top of the stack that is stored in memory. This, however, is not necessarily the *true* top of the stack because up to four other elements may be in the register part of the stack. The SR register is a 3-bit register that is used to specify whether zero, one, two, three, or four of the stack elements are in the registers. For a programmer using the stack, the SP register is still defined as the stack pointer. However, the hardware is designed to evaluate this value as a function of the SM and SR registers and reference the correct element accordingly. When the program is not dealing directly with the stack, the hardware will still set up the register part of the stack and update the SM and SR registers as necessary. Then, for subsequent manipulations of the stack, the top elements will be in the registers. Since the number of memory references is reduced by using this approach, operations on the stack are faster.

7.3 MODULAR MEMORY

Computers execute programs by fetching instructions from memory and transferring data to and from memory. One way to speed up program execution time is to decrease memory access time by allowing more than one read or write operation to occur simultaneously. Using a RAM for simultaneous reads or writes is precluded since its input and address lines must be held steady for the *entire* memory cycle (see Section 3.8). To get around this restriction, the RAM can be separated into different modules, each with its own memory address register (MAR) and memory buffer register (MBR). As long as the reads or writes are done on different modules, they can be executed together. Modular memories are very useful in systems with pipeline processors and array processors, which are discussed in detail in Chapters 9 and 10.

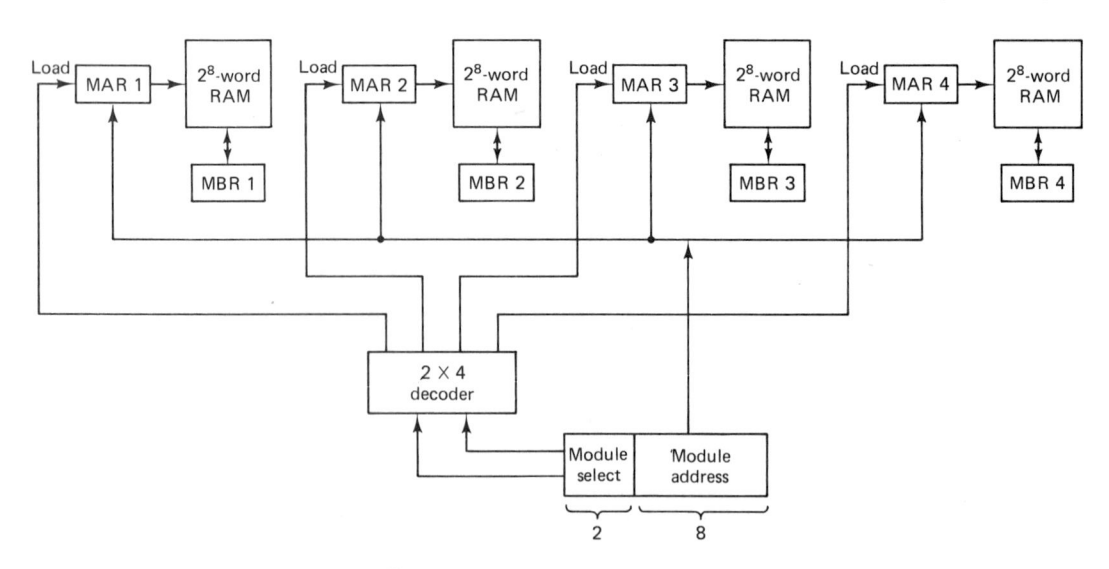

Figure 7-6 Modular memory by module address

There are two basic ways to set up modular memory. In one approach, the high-order bits of the address are used to specify a memory module, while the low-order bits select a word in that module. Figure 7-6 shows an example of a 2^{10}-word memory composed of four 2^8-word modules. Since there are four modules, the 2 high-order bits are used to select a module. The remaining address bits, 8 in this case, are used to specify the addresses of memory locations within the selected module. When a memory is set up in this way, consecutive memory words are stored in the same module. Since a program is usually executed in sequential order, only one module will be kept busy, allowing devices with direct memory access (DMA) capabilities (see Section 6.2) to use the other modules.

In the second approach to setting up a modular memory, the low-order bits are used to select a module, and the high-order bits serve to address locations within the module (just the opposite from the first approach). This organization, shown in Figure 7-7, is called **memory interleaving.** In this setup, the consecutive instruction words (memory locations) are in separate modules and can be fetched at the *same* time. This is a very effective way to speed up execution time when processing a sequential program segment. Rather than fetching one instruction, executing that instruction, and then fetching the next one, the computer can actually "look ahead" and fetch the next instruction while executing the current one. If a branch instruction is executed, the look-ahead instructions cannot be used, but no extra time is wasted in the prefetches.

Although memory interleaving results in overall faster execution times, the first method is more flexible. If k bits are used for module selection, there must be *exactly* 2^k modules in the memory interleaving setup. Otherwise, there will be "holes" of no information in the main memory address space. With the first method, by contrast, as many as 2^k modules can be referenced, but not all have to be included. If fewer than 2^k modules are used and memory expansion is necessary, it is relatively easy to add modules.

Sec. 7.4 Associative Memory

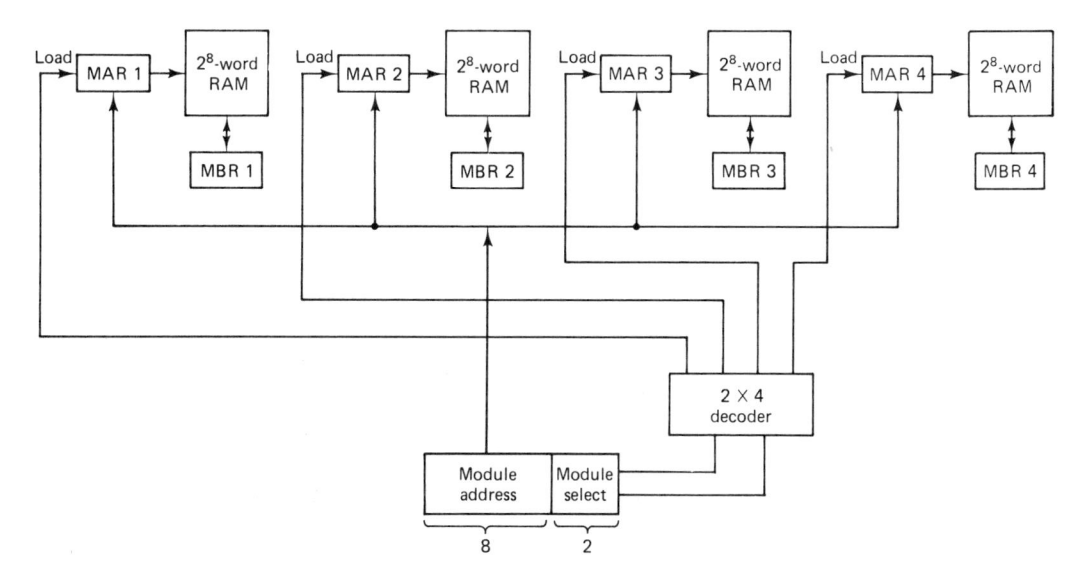

Figure 7-7 Modular memory interleaved by address module

7.4 ASSOCIATIVE MEMORY

RAMS and ROMs were introduced in Section 3.8. Both types of memories have one thing in common: They are accessed through addresses. Given an address, the memory returns the content of that address. In contrast, a totally different memory organization, called a **content-addressable memory (CAM)** or an **associative memory,** is based on accessing by content rather than address. Given a data (value), the memory is searched for any location that contains that value.

In an associative memory, all memory locations are searched *simultaneously* and *in parallel* on the basis of data content to see whether any one contains the desired value. Any location that has the desired value sends a signal to indicate that the value was found. Since associative memories perform parallel searches by data, they are much faster than RAMs for searching a memory. In certain applications, such as table lookup operations, they can be a very useful alternative memory organization. However, as we will see shortly, associative memories are more expensive than RAMs because of the extra logic circuitry needed for matching and selection.

An initial block diagram of an associative memory is shown in Figure 7-8. The memory consists of the traditional input and output lines but also includes an **argument register (A)** and a **match register (M).** The size of A is the same as the memory word length. The size of M is equal to the number of words in the memory, with each bit of M corresponding to a memory word. The data pattern to be read from or written to memory is stored in the argument register. (This is analogous to the address register for a RAM; see Section 3.8.) If the data in the argument register *matches* the data in any of the words of the memory, then the corresponding bit in the match register is set. (Matches made on the basis of equality are the most common, although other criteria could be used.) This register is then used in determining which word(s) to read or which word(s) to write, as will be discussed shortly. However, for the

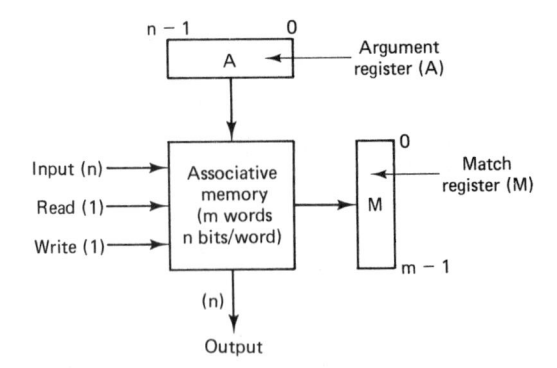

Figure 7-8 Initial diagram of an associative memory

time being, let us ignore the read and write controls and the I/O lines and concentrate on the logic for the parallel search.

Figure 7-9 shows the basic relation of the argument register to the individual words of the memory. Each memory word is compared in the **match logic (ML)** circuit to the one stored in the argument register A. If a match is found, the output of the *i*th ML circuit sets the corresponding bit in M. Although *m* ML circuits are necessary for an *m*-word memory, they are all identical. Therefore, to obtain the logic diagram of an ML circuit, let us consider one word of memory, W_i. Let A_j and W_{ij} denote the *j*th bits of A and W_i, respectively. To express logically the condition $A_j = W_{ij}$, we use the equivalence function:

$$x_j = A_j W_{ij} + \overline{A_j}\overline{W_{ij}} \qquad (7.1)$$

Hence $x_j = 1$ only if the pair of bits in position *j* are equal (i.e., if both are ones or both are zeros). Now, we want ML_i to set M_i only if *every* bit of A is equal to its corresponding bit of W_i. That is, $M_i = 1$ (i.e., $A = W_i$) only if $x_j = 1$ for every $j, j = 0, 1, \ldots, n - 1$, where *n* is the number of bits in the word. This condition calls for an AND operation of all x_j, namely:

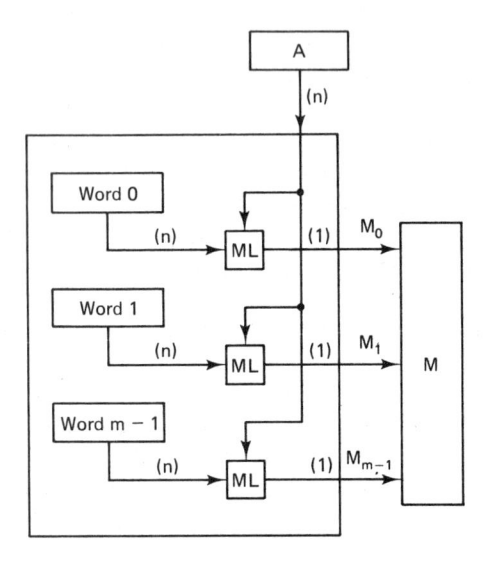

$$(A = W_i) = x_0 x_1 \ldots x_{n-1} \qquad (7.2)$$

Figure 7-9 Relation of argument register to memory words (ML = match logic)

Sec. 7.4 Associative Memory

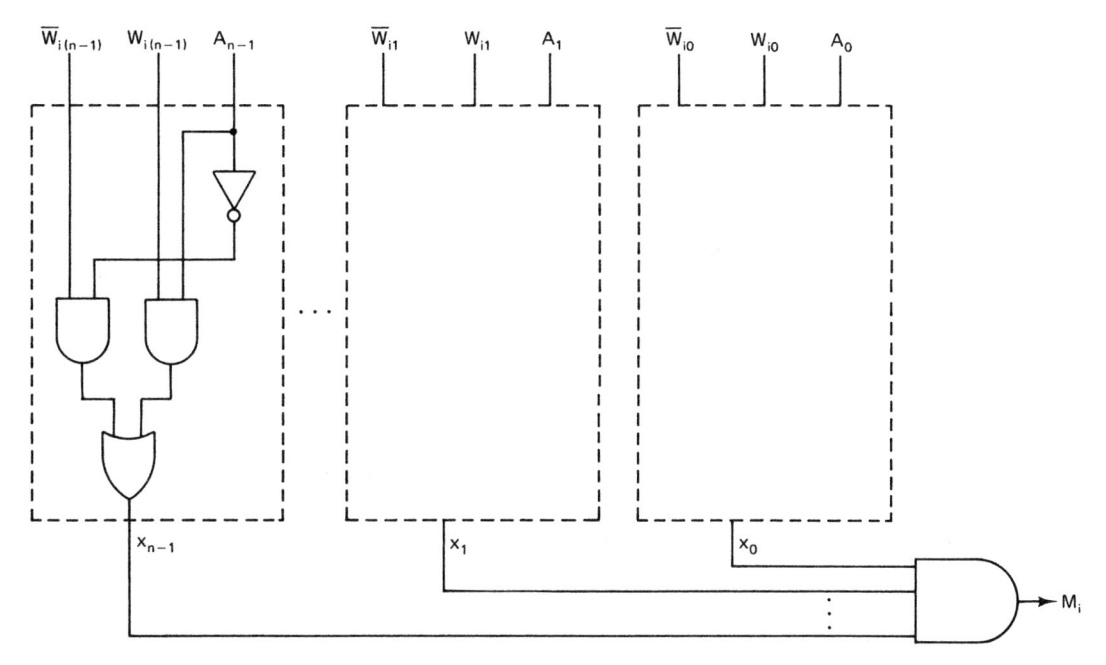

Figure 7–10 Match logic (ML) circuit

If the value of this expression is 1, then $M_i = 1$; otherwise, $M_i = 0$. The logic block diagram corresponding to Equations (7.1) and (7.2) is shown in Figure 7–10.

Key Register

In general, we want to search an associative memory only according to a certain field of bits rather than the entire word. To facilitate this, the memory includes a **key register (K)** that defines which bits in the words should be matched against the argument register (A). The content of the key register is interpreted such that $K_j = 1$ means to match bit j of each word to bit j of A, and $K_j = 0$ means to automatically consider bit j of every word as a match with bit j of A. Figure 7–11 shows the modified version of Figure 7–8 after including the key register, and the following example illustrates this procedure.

Example 7.3

Consider the following 3-word memory:

$$W_0 = 110010101$$
$$W_1 = 101010101$$
$$W_2 = 110011001$$

If K = 000011111 and A = 110010101, only the five least significant bits of each memory word will be compared to the corresponding bits of A. Hence W_0 and W_1 match A, but W_2 does not; therefore, M is 011.

194   Memory   Chap. 7

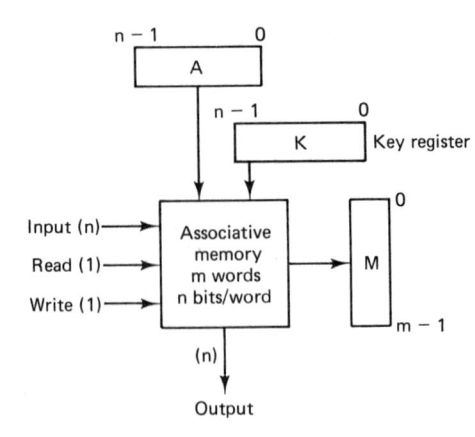

Figure 7–11 Complete block diagram of an associative memory

To include the key register in the logic expressions that were derived before, notice that no match is required between W_{ij} and A_j when $K_j = 0$. Hence only Equation (7.1) has to be modified to include this condition:

$$x_j = A_j W_{ij} + \overline{A}_j \overline{W}_{ij} + \overline{K}_j \tag{7.3}$$

Figure 7–12 shows the modified logic block diagram of Figure 7–10 after including the key register.

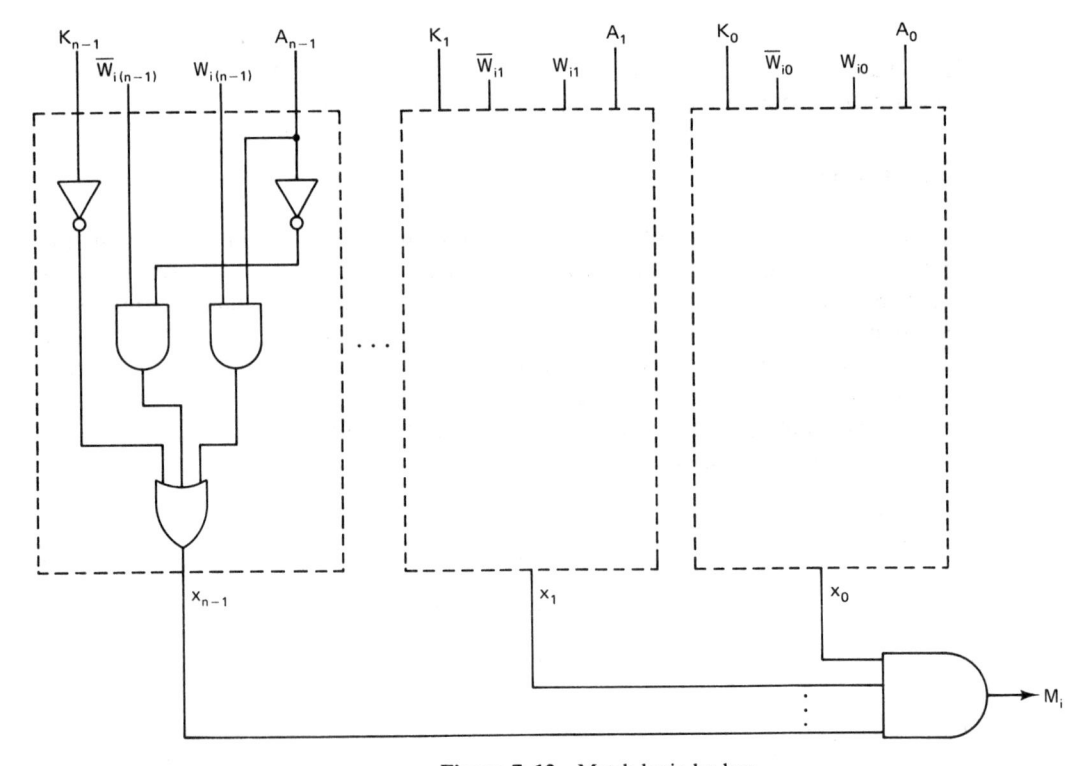

Figure 7–12 Match logic by key

Sec. 7.4   Associative Memory   195

Reading and Writing

To consider reading and writing in an associative memory, let us look at one bit of a word. The corresponding logic circuit is shown in Figure 7–13 for bit j of word i. Depending on what is stored in the memory, there are two possible outcomes of a read. If more than one word matches the argument (by the key), some means of reading the matched words in sequence is necessary. This can be done by scanning the match register one bit at a time and setting the read control line for any word whose match bit is 1. If at most only one word, the ith word say, can match the argument, then it is possible to connect the output of M_i directly to the read control line for the ith word. In this case, if an all zero word is not allowed, an all zero output can imply that no match was found.

When writing to an associative memory, the match bits can also be connected to the write control lines to fill up the memory initially. Very often, a **tag register** is kept in addition to the other registers. It contains one bit for each word of memory and is used to mark free or used words. For example, if the word is free, the corresponding tag bit is set; if the word is used, the corresponding tag bit is reset.

In general, associative memories are very fast for certain applications. One such application is studied in the next section. However, it must be remembered that they are also much more expensive than comparable RAMs and are, therefore, not yet feasible as the main memory unit of a computer.

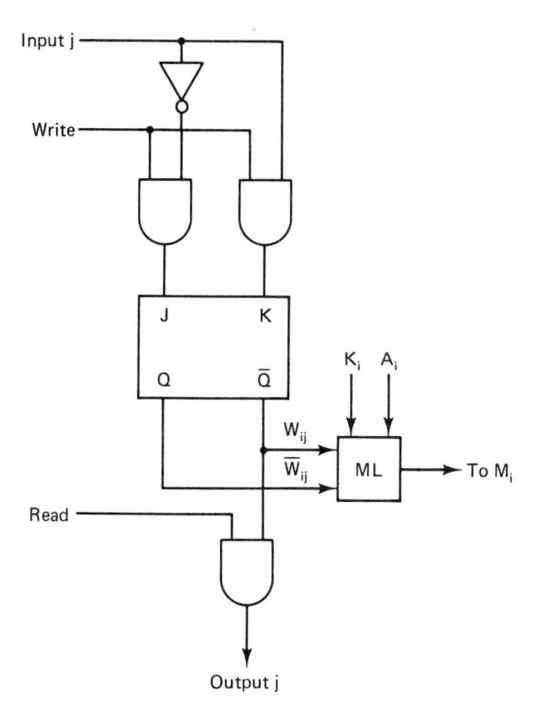

Figure 7–13 Logic of one bit of one word of an associative memory

7.5 CACHE MEMORY

The analysis of a large number of computer programs has shown that during a program's execution, memory references tend to occur in very localized patterns. Consider, for example, a block of contiguous memory locations. If this block consists of straight code, then execution will proceed sequentially through the block. If the code represents a loop, then the execution of the block will be repeated a number of times. If the block represents a data array, then it is likely that the block will often be used, not necessarily in a sequential order, but at least as a whole. This characteristic of programs is referred to as the **locality of reference principle.**

When a program is stored in main memory, the access time for fetching a memory word is a function of the capacity (size) of the memory and not a function of the size of a local block. Therefore, to make use of the locality of reference principle, a small high-speed memory can be used to hold just the active blocks of code or data. Then, rather than fetch the word at the next location from the main memory, it could be fetched much more quickly from this special memory.

This small high-speed memory is called a **cache** memory and is implemented in many computers as shown in the block diagram of Figure 7–14. The cache can be viewed as a buffer memory for the main memory. Although the cache uses information stored in main memory, it does not interface directly with it. What is stored in the cache and also replaced back into main memory is done under the direction of the CPU. For a cache to be effective, it must be faster than the main memory. There are four possible ways to decrease the access time of a memory reference:

1. *Small RAM*. With RAM, the access time is a function of the number of words in the memory (refer to the discussion in Section 7.1). Just implementing the cache as a small RAM compared to the main memory would make it faster than main memory.
2. *Associative memory*. If the cache is implemented as an associative memory, the access time is a function of the word length. In general, the word length of main memory is much smaller than the number of words in the memory. Because of this difference, associative memories are almost always faster than typical-size RAM main memories.
3. *Semiconductor memory*. Semiconductor memories are usually categorized into two types: bipolar and MOS (metal-oxide semiconductor). In general, MOS memories are used in main memories because of their low cost. Bipolar memories are faster (and, of course, more expensive) and are often used for the smaller cache memory of a computer.

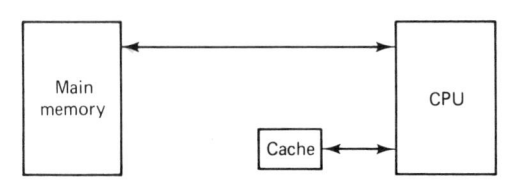

Figure 7–14 Interface of CPU, cache, and main memory

4. *Combinations*. In most computers, cache memories are made up of a combination of the other memory types.

Even though caches are more expensive than main memory, they are feasible because of their small size and their overall effect on the execution speed of a program. In general, the access time of cache memories ranges from 50 to 100 nanoseconds, which is on the order of 5 to 10 times faster than main memories.

How a Cache Works

How a cache works is conceptually very simple. Both the main memory and the cache are divided into equal-size units called **blocks.** The cache usually contains a number of blocks of memory words. When a particular memory word is to be referenced, the CPU first searches the cache. If the word is there, a **hit** occurs, and the word is used as intended. If the word is not in the cache, a **miss** occurs, and the block of main memory containing the word is brought into the cache. Because of the locality-of-reference principle, the next words to be referenced will probably be part of that block and will therefore already be in the cache when they are needed. As it turns out, most caches in computers have a **hit ratio** (the ratio of the number of hits to the total number of hits and misses) of 85% to 95%.

When the cache is full, it becomes necessary to implement a **replacement algorithm** on a miss. This algorithm decides which block should be moved out of the cache to make room for the new block. Optimally, the block that will be replaced is the one that will not be needed again for the longest time or at all. There are a number of replacement algorithms that balance efficiency with optimal replacement.

When the memory reference is a read, the word is read directly from the cache on a hit. However, if the reference is a write, there are two ways to proceed, and the choice between them must be made as a policy decision by the computer designer. In the **write-through** method, the cache and main memory are updated simultaneously. This ensures that the correct information is available in main memory at all times so that any processor can access main memory and always be dealing with valid data. However, to implement this method, the main memory must be accessed on *every* write. Therefore, every write takes the same amount of time as a miss, and thus the efficiency of the cache is reduced.

A second way of implementing writes is to update main memory only when a word that has been modified is replaced from the cache. This **write-back** method requires keeping a flag for each word in the cache to mark words that have been changed by writes. The advantage of this method is that no matter how often a word is updated while it is in the cache, it has to be changed in main memory only when it is replaced from the cache. The disadvantage of this method is that it renders the copy of the data in main memory *inconsistent* until the modified data is written back to it.

Hardware Organizations

References made to main memory are in terms of word addresses. To be able to use a cache, there must be a way of mapping a main memory address to the appropriate

Figure 7-15 Direct-mapping cache

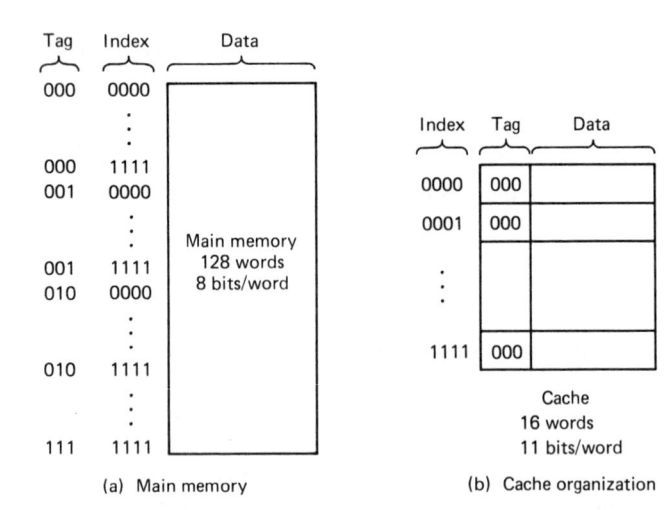

word in the cache. We can consider this mapping in terms of three hardware organizations of a cache: direct mapping, associative mapping, and set-associative mapping.

Direct mapping. Using a small RAM for a cache, the direct-mapping cache organization is shown in Figure 7–15. The main memory addresses are partitioned into two fields, the **tag** and the **index,** as shown in part (a) of the figure. The number of bits in the index corresponds to the size of the cache. For a cache of 2^k words, the k low-order bits of the main memory address are considered the index and the remaining high-order bits are considered the tag. The cache is organized as shown in part (b) of the figure. The index field serves to address the cache, and the tag field is stored as part of the word in addition to the data. The word length of the cache is therefore larger (by the number of tag bits) than that of the main memory.

When a word is referenced, the index bits of the address are used to access the cache. If the tag field *matches* the tag bits of the address, there is a hit; otherwise, there is a miss. This organization of a cache has a faster access time than the main memory RAM because it has a smaller address field. Notice that although the word length of the direct-mapping cache is larger to include the tag field, implementing each word will be more expensive, but accessing it will not be any slower.

Due to the locality-of-reference principle, we usually want to be able to store contiguous main memory locations in the cache. However, as shown in the example of Figure 7–15, these locations will have *distinct* index fields but the *same* tags. Therefore, if two words with the *same* index and *different* tags are being referenced frequently, they cannot be stored simultaneously in this type of cache. This is the main disadvantage of the direct-mapping organization and is illustrated in the following example.

Example 7.4

Assume that the main memory consists of data as shown in Figure 7–16(a). The direct mapping to a RAM cache would be as shown in Figure 7–16(b). The main memory words whose addresses are 0001010 and 0111010 have the same index but different tags and cannot both be stored in the cache simultaneously.

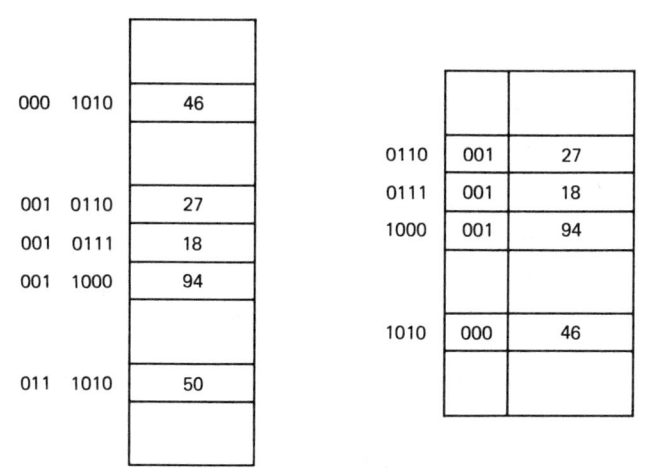

Sec. 7.5 Cache Memory

000 1010		46
001 0110		27
001 0111		18
001 1000		94
011 1010		50

(a) Main memory

0110	001	27
0111	001	18
1000	001	94
1010	000	46

(b) Cache

Figure 7–16 Example of a direct-mapping RAM cache

Associative mapping. When an associative memory is used for a cache, a different mapping is necessary. With associative mapping, the address of the main memory word and its content (the data) are stored in the cache. To reference a specific word, the address is stored in the corresponding part of the argument register (A), and the key register (K) is set up to compare just the address fields. Using the same example of main memory as in Figure 7–16(a), Figure 7–17 shows the corresponding cache for associative mapping.

For this organization, the word size of the cache is equal to the number of bits of the main memory address plus the number of data bits per word. Although the word length will affect the speed of the cache, it will still be faster than the corresponding main memory. It is also possible to store in this cache any words that have the same index and different tags.

Set-associative mapping. The set-associative mapping organization is a combination of the previous two and is shown in Figure 7–18(a). In this 16-word

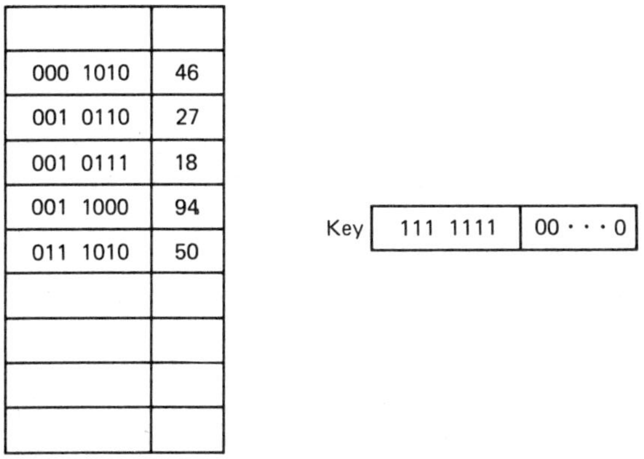

000 1010	46
001 0110	27
001 0111	18
001 1000	94
011 1010	50

Key | 111 1111 | 00 · · · 0 |

Figure 7–17 Associative-mapping cache organization

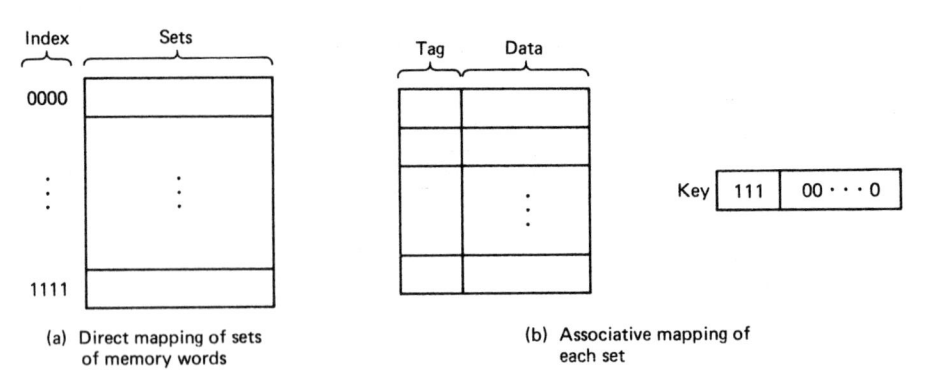

Figure 7-18 Set-associative cache organization

(a) Direct mapping of sets of memory words

(b) Associative mapping of each set

cache, each word is addressed by the index part of the main memory address, analogous to direct mapping. However, at each address of the cache, a set of main memory words, as opposed to one word, is stored. This set is actually a small associative memory containing the tag fields of the addresses and the data parts as shown in Figure 7-18(b). When a set is referenced in the cache, the tag fields of each word in the set are compared *in parallel* with the tag of the main memory address to determine if the desired word is or is not in the cache.

With this type of organization, two words with the same index and different tags can be stored in the same set. Since each word in the associative memory sets includes only the extra tag bits rather than the complete address, their access time is faster and their cost lower. The following example illustrates some of the concepts related to a cache.

Example 7.5

Consider a cache memory that is organized by a set-associative mapping and is made up of 900 sets of four memory words each. The cache takes 90 nanoseconds (ns) to access the index field of each set and 10 ns to access the tag field within the set. Let the access time of the main memory be 1000 ns. Assume that an estimated 80% of the memory references are for reads and the remaining 20% are for writes. Let the hit ratio for the read accesses be 0.90.

(a) Consider first the average access time of this system for *just* memory read cycles. Based on the read hit ratio, the access time for 90% of the time is

$$0.90 \times 100 \text{ ns} = 90 \text{ ns}$$

During the other 10% of the time, a miss occurs, taking 100 ns, and then a main memory read happens, taking 1000 ns. This means that the average access time for reads is

$$0.90 \times 100 \text{ ns} + 0.10 \times 1100 \text{ ns} = 200 \text{ ns}$$

Hence, even though a miss takes longer than a straight memory read, the average access time is much shorter due to the high read hit ratio.

(b) The average access time for both reads and writes depends on the write policy in effect. With a *write-through* procedure, every write must update the main memory word as well as the cache word. Since these can be done simultaneously, the access

Sec. 7.6 Auxiliary Memory

time of every write is 1000 ns (the given access time of a main memory write). Therefore, the *total* access time would be

$$0.80 \times 200 \text{ ns} + 0.20 \times 1000 \text{ ns} = 360 \text{ ns}$$

Notice that the higher the percentage of writes, the longer the total access time becomes. If a *write-back* procedure is used, the access time for writes is computed similarly to that for reads. Assuming a write hit ratio of 0.70, the average write access time would be 400 ns.

(c) The hit ratio of the total system is the sum of the read and write hit ratios times the percentage of reads and writes, respectively. When a *write-through* procedure is used, every write is considered a miss, so the total hit ratio reduces to

$$0.80 \times 0.90 = 0.72$$

Using a *write-back* procedure with a write hit ratio of 0.70, the total hit ratio of the system would be

$$0.80 \times 0.90 + 0.20 \times 0.70 = 0.86$$

7.6 AUXILIARY MEMORY

Of all the information that is stored in the computer, only the programs and data currently being used by the CPU need to be resident in main memory. The rest of the information, such as system programs and user files that are not being used, are kept on backup storage devices and transferred to main memory as needed. These backup, or **secondary,** storage devices are collectively referred to as **auxiliary memory.**

Magnetic Tape

Magnetic tape is one type of auxiliary memory that is used for large amounts of offline storage. It also provides the simplest means of transferring data between machines that have no direct communication link.

The tape is a thin strip of plastic, $\frac{1}{2}$ inch wide, which is coated with a magnetic recording medium. It is usually divided into 7 or 9 **tracks** along the length of the tape, as illustrated in Figure 7–19, which shows a 7-track tape. Bits are recorded as magnetic spots on each track and make up one character for every position along the tape. In addition to the character code, one bit is commonly used as a parity bit for error detection (see Section 2.5). Recording densities are commonly expressed in bytes per inch (bpi), with typical densities being 800, 1600, and 6250 bpi.

The tape is processed by a **tape drive** that has one **read/write head** for each track and is able to read or write one full character at a time. Because of the physical makeup of the tape drive, the tape must be moving at a particular speed for reading and writing. Typical speeds of magnetic tape devices range from 18.75 to 200 inches per second. When the tape is stopped, it takes some time to get it moving fast enough for a read or a write. If the tape is stopped between two characters, it would not be

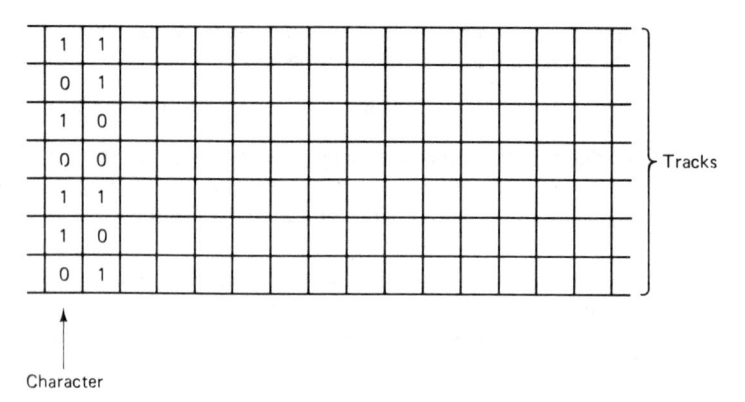

Figure 7-19 Seven-track magnetic tape

possible to move it fast enough for a read or write by the time the next character passes under the read/write head.

To circumvent this problem, characters are stored in groups called **records**. The size of the records can be either fixed or variable. The records are separated by an **interrecord gap** and an **end-of-record** character. Interrecord gaps range between 0.3 and 0.75 inch. If the records are short, most of the tape storage capacity will be wasted in interrecord gaps. Therefore, to increase tape utilization, records are constructed such that they are much longer than the required gap. A set of records forms a **file**. The files are separated by a gap (about 3 inches) and an end-of-file character. Whole records are read or written at once, and the tape is stopped only in an interrecord gap. The tape can be accelerated during the gap and be up to speed by the next record.

Magnetic tapes are **sequential-access memory (SAM)** systems. In this type of storage, data are written in the sequence in which they appear. In reading the data, each record is examined in sequence until the desired data is found. Therefore, the access time depends on the *position* of the record on the tape at the time it is requested with respect to the read/write head position along the length of the tape. Typical data rates for magnetic tape devices are 15–250 kilobytes per second.

Magnetic Disk

A magnetic disk system consists of three parts: a disk drive, a disk controller that interfaces with the CPU and/or I/O processors, and one or more disks. The disks are flat platters (often referred to as *hard disks*) coated with a thin magnetic film, usually on both sides. Several disks are stacked together on one spindle and rotate at a constant speed. (Rotation speeds range between 1200 to 3600 revolutions per minute.) These disks are collectively called a **disk pack.** The disk drive has a read/write head for each surface (except for the very top and bottom surfaces) positioned very close to the rotating surfaces. The speed of the rotating disks causes just enough air pressure to keep the heads from making physical contact with the surfaces. Since the disks rotate constantly, it is unnecessary to include gaps to allow for acceleration. A diagram of a disk pack with read/write heads is shown in Figure 7–20.

Sec. 7.6 Auxiliary Memory

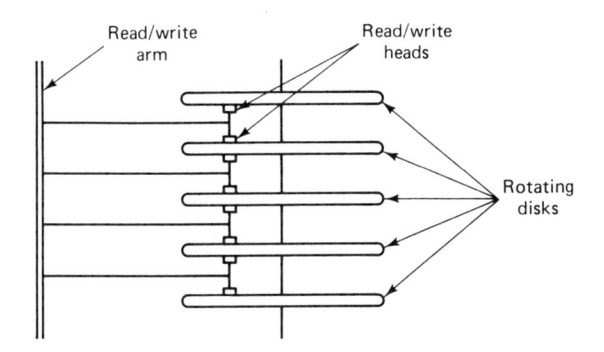

Figure 7-20 Magnetic disk pack

To write to a disk, the disk drive causes the magnetism at the point on the disk surface directly under the read/write head to change direction. To read from a disk, the head is set up to sense a change in the direction of magnetism. However, the problem with this is that the read/write head can only detect change and therefore cannot distinguish between consecutive zeros or ones. One solution to this problem is to maintain synchronization information on the disk in addition to the actual data. This information can be included by keeping a **clock** on a separate track that is read at the same time as the data. The clock signal, shown in Figure 7-21(a), is simply an alternating sequence of zeros and ones with a fixed period. Reading the clock together with the data enables the disk controller to distinguish between consecutive zeros and ones.

A different method from keeping a clock involves storing the data in a special code so that it can be read on its own. An example of this method is the **Manchester**

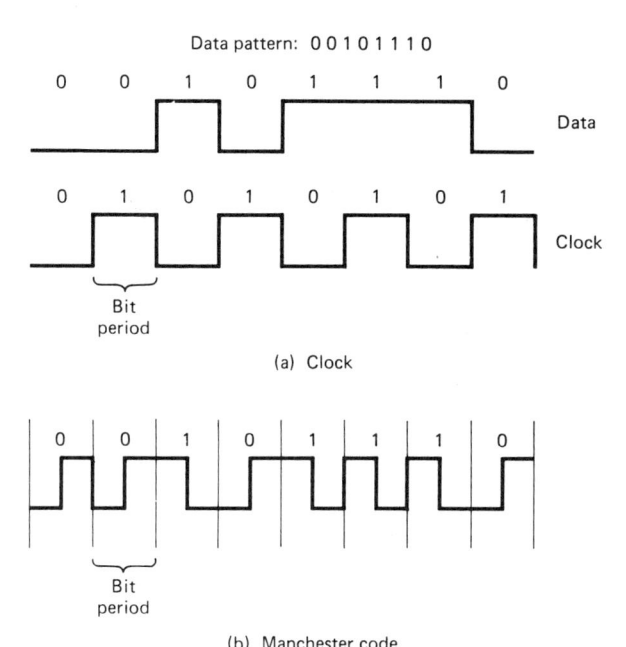

Figure 7-21 Data synchronization patterns

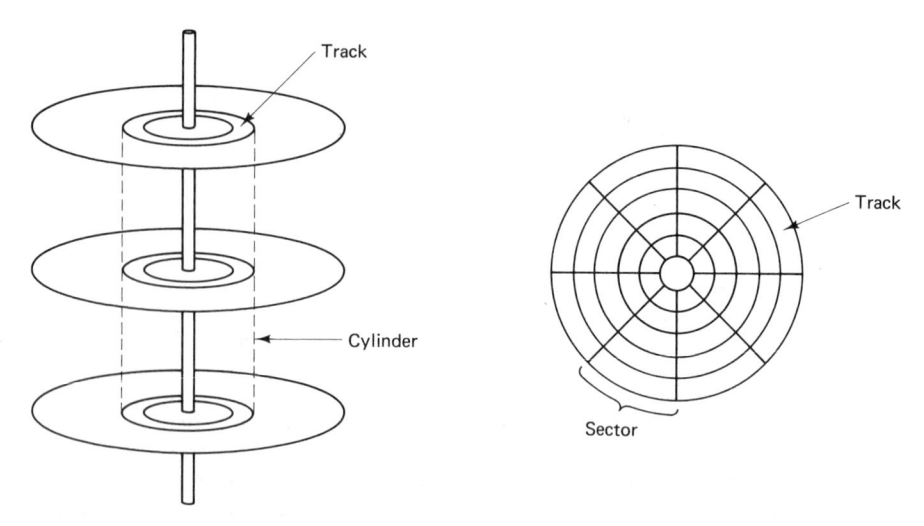

Figure 7-22 Organization of a disk

code, shown in Figure 7-21(b). At the midpoint of each bit period, a change in magnetism is forced. This way, the first half of the bit period stores the data bit, and the second half serves as the synchronization control. Although this method saves the space needed for a clock track, it results in poor bit density on the disk. However, other, more complex codes exist that provide better bit densities.

The organization of data on a disk is based on the logical divisions of the disk, as shown in Figure 7-22. Information is recorded on a number of concentric circles, called **tracks,** of which there are typically a few hundred per surface. The tracks are divided into fixed- or varying-density **sectors,** usually between 10 and 100 per track. A sector consists of a number of words, typically between 32 and 256. Some disk systems enable the number of sectors per track to be set by the program. Corresponding tracks of each surface collectively form a **cylinder.** The distance of the heads from the spindle (radial position) is called the **cylinder address.**

To transfer data between main memory and the disk, the **disk controller** must be provided with the following information: the cylinder address and surface (which together specify a unique track), the sector number where the data begins, the number of words to be transferred, the main memory address into which or from which the transfer takes place, and whether the disk is to be read from or written into. It should be noted that disk transfers always start at the beginning of a sector.

Disk systems are classified as either movable-head or fixed-head systems. In a **movable-head** system, there is only one set of read/write heads for each surface. This set is mounted on a moving arm that goes from cylinder to cylinder and can also be taken off of the disk pack completely. The access time for this system includes the time necessary to move the arm into position, called the **seek** time, and the time it takes for the data to be positioned under the read/write head, called the **latency** time. The seek time is typically 5 milliseconds between adjacent tracks and 50 milliseconds to move from the innermost cylinder to the outermost cylinder. The latency time is around 3 milliseconds on the average.

Sec. 7.6 Auxiliary Memory

In a **fixed-head** system, there is a read/write head both for every surface and for every cylinder. Although this results in a very fast access time, it precludes the use of removable disk packs. In this system, seek time does not affect access time, but latency time does. A special fixed-head disk system is the **Winchester disk** system, which is sealed and air filtered. This allows the heads to ride closer to the disk surfaces since there is a minimal amount of dust on the surfaces. The end result is a more reliable data storage medium with higher bit density capability.

Disks are **direct-access** (or **semirandom-access**) **memory (DAM)** devices. Accessing data in these devices usually requires two steps: random or direct movement of the read/write heads to the vicinity of the data, followed by a sequential access. The first step entails the positioning of the heads to the proper track; in the second step, the data on the track is accessed sequentially. Access times for hard disks range between 5 and 60 milliseconds, and data rates are 0.5 to 10 megabits per second. Floppy disks, drums, and bubble memories are also direct-access memory devices.

Floppy Disk

A floppy disk is a cheaper, smaller-capacity, and simpler version of a hard disk. It is a *flexible* (hence "floppy") plastic diskette coated with a magnetic material similar to that on hard disks but designed so that the read/write head actually rides on the surface. The clock information is contained on each track. A floppy disk (diskette) can be **single-density** or **double-density,** depending on the scheme used to code the clock. The Manchester code described earlier is an example of a single-density code. The more complex coding schemes provide for double-density storage but also require more complex disk controllers. Floppy disks are available in diameters of $3\frac{1}{2}$, $5\frac{1}{4}$, and 8 inches. They can store 250 to 1400 kilobytes of data, and the data storage density is continually being increased. Access times for floppy disks range between 150 and 300 milliseconds, and data rates are about 250 kilobits per second.

Magnetic Drum

As the name implies, this storage medium is a drum (a hollow cylinder) coated with a magnetic film. The drum is separated into concentric tracks going around its surface. Each track is associated with a fixed read/write head, and several heads may be reading or writing in parallel. Since the heads are fixed, there is no seek time. A timing track serves as a reference to identify the position of the drum. To access the data, the heads are first positioned to the proper track or tracks, and the data on these tracks is then accessed sequentially. Small drums are similar in storage capacity to disks and average 2×10^6 characters. Large drums have very large storage capacities, by comparison, of up to 9×10^9 characters.

Magnetic Bubble Memory

All the auxiliary memories discussed so far have one thing in common. They all involve *mechanical moving parts* for reading and writing data. An alternative type of memory is the magnetic bubble memory. With this memory, information is still

Figure 7-23 Direction of magnetism (arrows) in a bubble memory

stored magnetically, but the direction of magnetism is changed by electronic rather than mechanical means.

The memory itself is a thin slice of magnetic material with the direction of magnetism perpendicular to the surface of the slice. Different areas of the slice are magnetized in opposite directions, as shown in Figure 7-23. All the areas that are magnetized in one direction can be assumed to represent ones, with the other areas representing zeros. The ones areas are called **bubbles.** The recording density of bubble memories is of the order of 10^6 bits per square inch.

In the production of bubble memories, the bubbles are formed into uniform sizes. A magnetic overlay is then bonded to one side of the slice. This overlay consists of an alternating pattern of *T*'s and *I*'s, shown in Figure 7-24, called a **T-bar pattern.** A magnetic field induced on the slice causes the overlay material to be magnetized and, in turn, to attract bubbles of opposite magnetism. By rotating the magnetic field, the bubbles can be "moved" within the slice. Figure 7-25 shows how the bubbles move along the T-bar pattern. Note that it takes a 360° rotation of the magnetic field to move a bubble from one T-I cell to another. Actual generation and annihilation, as well as the replication of bubbles, are done by electric current pulses that cause local changes in the magnetic field. The T-bar patterns are set up in loops, as shown in Figure 7-26, and each loop functions like a shift register. Access time for bubble memories ranges between 400 to 900 microseconds, with shift rates (transfer rates) of the order of 100 kilobits per second.

When bubble memories were first introduced in 1966, it was thought that they would replace magnetic disks. In fact, they were often referred to as **electronic disks.** During the 1970s, nearly all the semiconductor manufacturers were involved in making bubble memories, but by 1982 only Intel was still in this business. It seems that the initial collapse of the bubble memory industry was more a result of the wrong application rather than the wrong technology. Since 1982, however, bubble memories

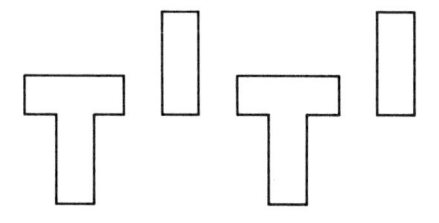

Figure 7-24 T-bar pattern of bubble memory overlay

Sec. 7.6 Auxiliary Memory

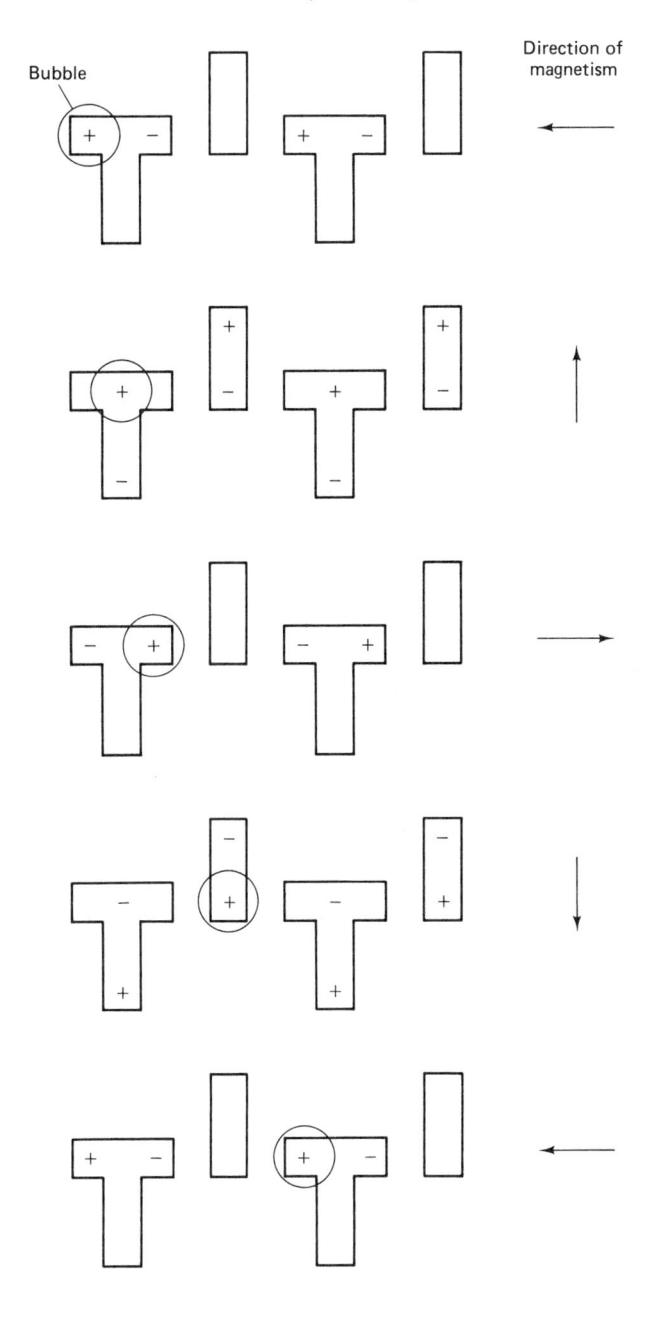

Figure 7–25 Movement of bubbles in a bubble memory

have been making a comeback. As reported in the September 1984 issue of the *IEEE Spectrum*, bubble memories are being used in applications for which magnetic disks are not suited, rather than as a replacement for magnetic disks. Basically, they are being used in two areas: (1) in environments with considerable vibrations and/or contaminants that would render magnetic media and mechanical devices useless and

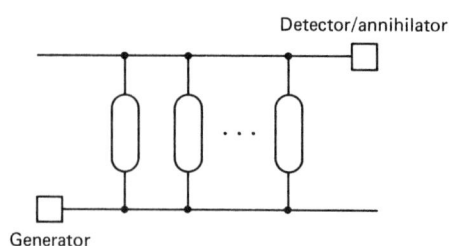

Figure 7-26 Organization of a bubble memory

(2) for applications where small size and low power consumption are important. However, it remains to be seen just how much these memories will be a part of future computer systems.

7.7 VIRTUAL MEMORY

Evolution

In the early computers, main memory units were very small and very expensive. When a program required more memory than was available, the programmer had to use an overlay process. This was done by first dividing the program into sections, called **overlays,** so that each could fit in memory. The overlays were stored on an auxiliary storage device. Special routines were written to read a particular overlay into main memory, execute that code, write it back to secondary storage, and then read in the next overlay to be executed. These overlay management routines were program dependent and had to be written by the programmer.

When the ATLAS computer system, constructed at the University of Manchester in England, was introduced in 1960, it included a technique for performing the overlay process automatically. This method is known today as **virtual memory,** and by the early 1970s it had become available on most computers. As main memories became larger and cheaper, the concept of virtual memory was expanded to facilitate **multiprogramming,** whereby parts of many programs can be in memory simultaneously and run in turn.

Principle

The underlying principle of virtual memory is the ability to address a *logical* storage space, called virtual memory, that is physically larger than the real storage space. For example, the logical storage space can be a secondary storage device and the real storage space can be main memory. Another example would be for the real storage to be a cache while the main memory serves as the virtual memory.

Whatever the combination, virtual memory requires an automatic method for mapping the *logical addresses* of a program to the *real addresses* used for the execution of the program, as seen in Figure 7-27. It also requires a method for maintaining the necessary parts of the program in the real storage space. We discuss these re-

Sec. 7.7 Virtual Memory

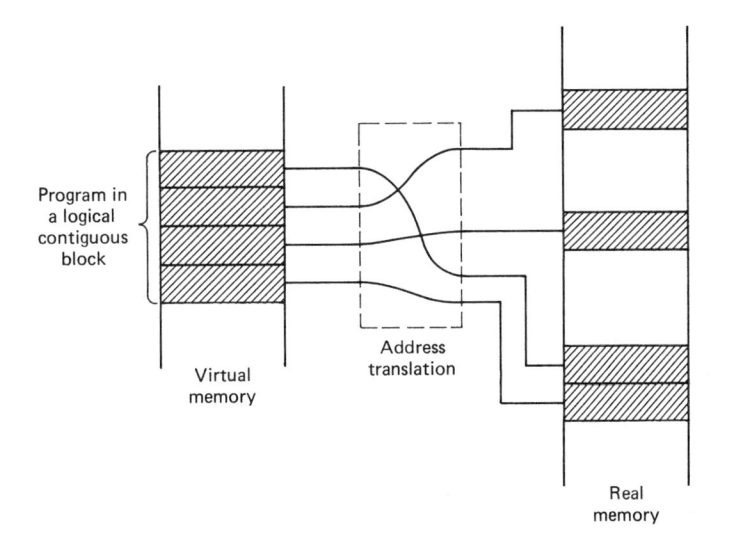

Figure 7-27 Automatic address mapping

quirements in terms of two common virtual memory implementations: paging and segmentation.

Implementation

Paging. In a paging system, the virtual memory of the program is divided into partitions called **pages.** The size of these partitions, the **page size,** is fixed by the computer and is equal to the size of the corresponding partitions in memory that are called **frames.** During the **binding** stage of a program, each logical address is set up in terms of a **page number,** p, and a **displacement** (or **offset**), d, within that page. Each new address is computed using the equations

$$p = \text{(address) DIV (page size)} \qquad (7.4)$$

$$d = \text{(address) MOD (page size)} \qquad (7.5)$$

where DIV denotes integer division and MOD is the modulo relation.

Figure 7-28 shows an example of a program before and after page binding. Notice that both the address of each program word and any reference to addresses within a program word are changed. To illustrate this, consider address 8 of program X in Figure 7-28(a). The program word in this address references address 12. After binding, address 8 becomes the logical address (2, 2) and address 12 becomes the logical address (4, 0). As seen in Figure 7-28(b), the reference to 12 in address (2, 2) has been changed to (4, 0). Furthermore, since each page will be stored in frames in memory as a unit, partial pages must be filled out to be whole pages, as in page 4 of the example in Figure 7-28(b).

Associated with each program is a hardware **page table** that maps the pages of the program to frames in real memory where the pages are stored. A logical picture

210 — Memory — Chap. 7

Program X

0	a
1	b
2	c
3	d
4	e
5	f
6	g
7	h
8	JMP 12
9	j
10	k
11	ℓ
12	m

(a) Program with contiguous addresses starting at 0

Program X

0, 0	a
0, 1	b
0, 2	c
1, 0	d
1, 1	e
1, 2	f
2, 0	g
2, 1	h
2, 2	JMP 4, 0
3, 0	j
3, 1	k
3, 2	ℓ
4, 0	m
4, 1	
4, 2	

Page size = 3

(b) Program with addresses in terms of (p, d)

Figure 7–28 Page addressing

Program X

0, 0	a
0, 1	b
0, 2	c
1, 0	d
1, 1	e
1, 2	f
2, 0	g
2, 1	h
2, 2	JMP 4, 0
3, 0	j
3, 1	k
3, 2	ℓ
4, 0	m
4, 1	
4, 2	

Page size = 3

Page Table

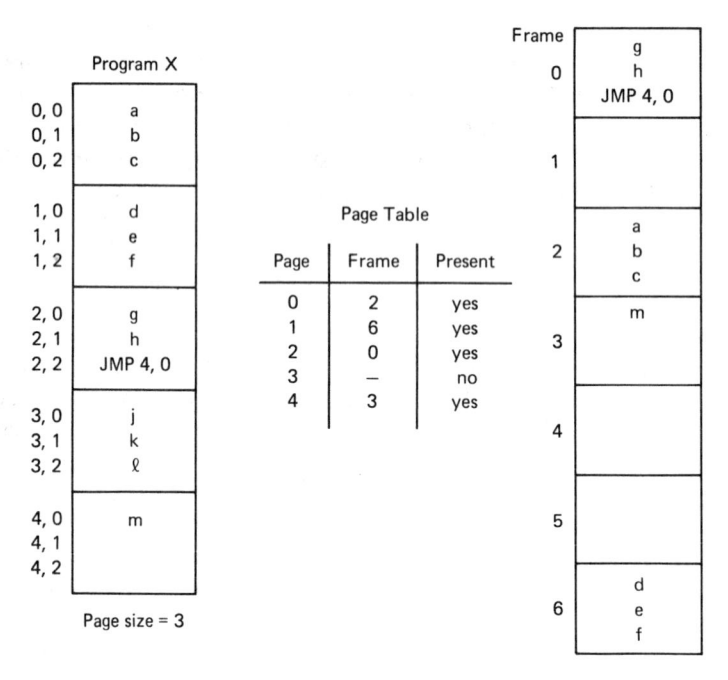

Page	Frame	Present
0	2	yes
1	6	yes
2	0	yes
3	—	no
4	3	yes

Frame

0	g, h, JMP 4, 0
1	
2	a, b, c
3	m
4	
5	
6	d, e, f

Figure 7–29 Memory allocation and page table for program X

Sec. 7.7 Virtual Memory

of a page table is shown in Figure 7-29. Hardware implementations will be discussed later. When reference is made to a program address in terms of (p, d), the page table is searched for the corresponding **frame number,** f, and then the memory access is made to location L, where

$$L = f \times \text{(page size)} + d \tag{7.6}$$

Example 7.6

Consider the JMP instruction in page 2, offset 2 of program X in Figure 7-29. To execute this instruction, the page table is referenced to determine that page 2 is stored in frame 0. Using Equation (7.6), the actual address in real memory is therefore

$$0 \times 3 + 2 = 2$$

Notice that if a referenced page is not present in memory, it must be brought into memory. Also, if there is no room in memory, a page replacement scheme is necessary. These issues will be considered later.

Segmentation. Another virtual memory implementation is known as segmentation. It is similar to paging except that programs are divided into variable-size **segments** rather than fixed-size pages. The segments are usually logical partitions of a program, such as procedures or data arrays, that are set up by a compiler or assembler. During binding, the logical addresses are defined in terms of an assigned **segment number,** s, and a **displacement** (or **offset**), d, within that segment.

Since segments vary in size, real memory is not divided into fixed-size blocks. A segment is simply stored in a block of memory that is large enough to hold it. If the segment is in real memory, the **segment table** (which is hardware implemented) maps the segment number into the starting address, called **base,** and the final address, called **limit,** of the real memory block. Figure 7-30 shows an example of a segmented program stored in memory.

Implementation of page and segment tables. In deciding how to implement a page or segment table, it is crucial to recognize that the table must be

Segment	Base	Limit	Present
0	650	825	yes
1	—	—	no
2	830	900	yes
3	200	300	yes

Segment Table

Program X:
- 0: Procedure A
- 1: Data area A
- 2: Function B
- 3: Data area B

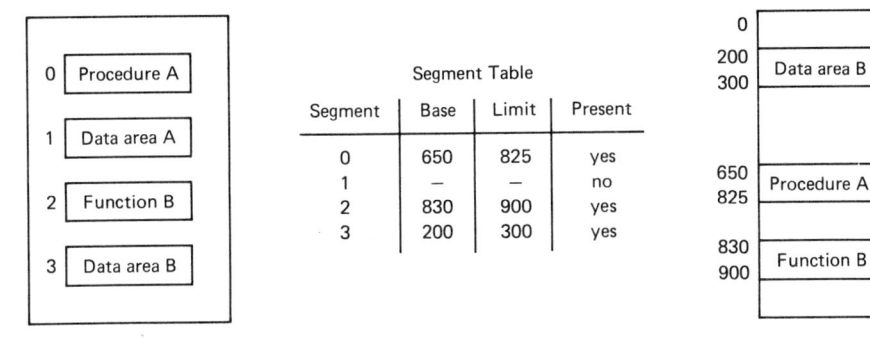

Memory:
- 0–200:
- 200–300: Data area B
- 650–825: Procedure A
- 830–900: Function B

Figure 7-30 Memory allocation and segment table for program X

212 Memory Chap. 7

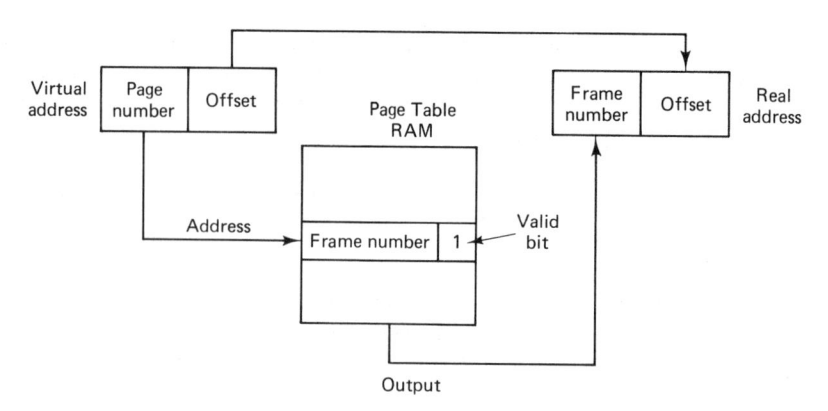

Figure 7-31 RAM implementation of a page table

referenced for *every* access to virtual memory. If the table is stored in main memory, the access time for every virtual memory reference will be at least twice that of a real memory reference. (It will be even more when the page or segment is not present in memory.) If the table is stored in registers, the access time will be much less, but the implementation costs will be rather high. In practice, page and segment tables are usually implemented in small, special-purpose cache memories whose access time is longer than that of registers but is considerably less than that of main memory.

Of the several possible hardware implementations of page and segment tables, only two are considered here. Since the implementation of both tables is essentially the same, the two implementations are discussed only in terms of page tables. Figure 7-31 shows one implementation in which the page table is a small RAM with one entry (word) for each page. The addresses correspond to the page numbers, and the content is a **valid bit,** which is 1 only when the page is in memory, and the associated frame number. When the valid bit is 0, the frame number value is considered garbage. Usually, a number of pages will not be stored in real memory and, therefore, will have valid bits of 0.

Another way to organize a page table is to store the page and frame numbers only for pages that are actually mapped to a frame. Then the number of entries in the table corresponds *exactly* to the number of pages in real memory, rather than to the total number of pages in the program. The result is a much smaller table. The table is searched for a particular page number on a page reference. If the page is found, the frame number is used; if the page is not found, it would imply that the page is not in real memory.

Since the table has to be searched for each virtual memory reference, this method is feasible only when a parallel search of all entries at once can be done. An associative memory can surely facilitate this, as shown in Figure 7-32. The page number serves as the argument to be searched on. The match bits for each word are connected directly to the read signal of each word. If there is no match, the output from the memory is considered garbage. Otherwise, there is a match, the appropriate word is output, and the frame number portion is used for the real address.

Sec. 7.7 Virtual Memory

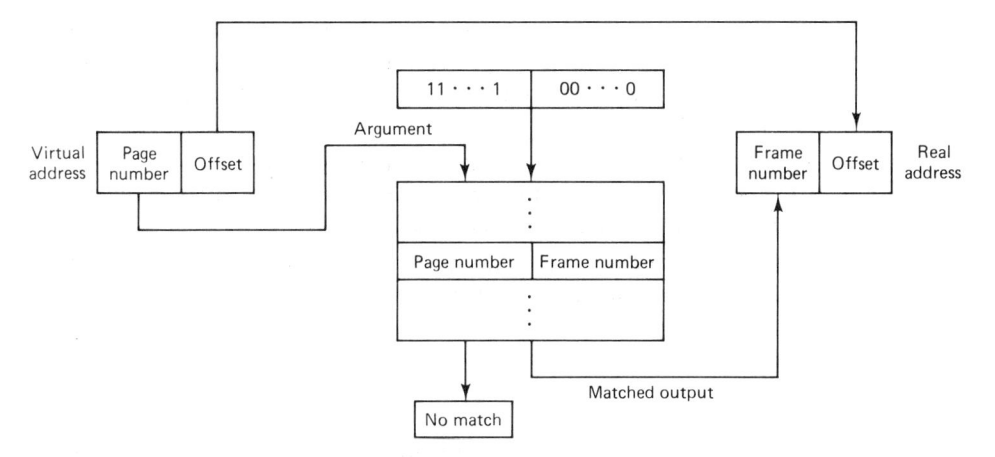

Figure 7–32 Associative memory implementation of a page table

Comparison of segmentation and paging. Some computer systems support only paging or segmentation, and some support both. Other computer systems support a combination of the two, either a **segmented-paging** implementation or a **paged-segmentation** implementation. The main advantage to using segmentation over paging is that the segments are logical entities and will thus have the same access parameters throughout. For example, data arrays are considered *nonreentrant* code; that is, they are modified when used. This means that two programs in a multiprocessing system could not share the same data array since one program might change something before the other uses it. By contrast, executable code can usually be shared because simply executing the code does not change it. Thus if a page includes even one word of a data array, the whole page has to be marked as nonreentrant and cannot be shared. With segmentation, however, it is much easier to set up entire blocks of memory that can be shared. This is quite useful for large programs that are shared by many users, such as compilers and text editors.

The main disadvantage of segmentation is the **external fragmentation** that occurs when segments are moved in and out of real memory. Since the segments are of different sizes, they will partition the memory into areas of various sizes as they are moved in and out. Hence the memory is considered fragmented. At any given time, some of the areas will contain resident segments and others will be "unused." It is usually the case that a number of the areas are too small for any segment and are therefore wasted. With paging, the amount of wasted space averages to just one-half frame per program.

Virtual Memory Management

Page and segment tables are not enough for a virtual memory to be successful. It is also necessary to manage the transfer of information to and from real memory. This management comes under the jurisdiction of the operating system. These are some of the issues involved:

1. *Real memory allocation*: maintaining a **free frame list** for paging or a **free space list** for segmentation to determine where to store pages or segments in real memory and determining how many pages or segments of a program to store in real memory
2. *Replacement strategy*: determining which page or segment to remove when real memory is full and a reference is made to a page or segment not in memory (called a page or segment **fault**) that must be brought into real memory
3. *Write policy*: determining when to update corresponding words in virtual memory when writing to words in real memory

7.8 SUMMARY

A variety of memories and memory organizations have been discussed in this chapter. They can be brought into perspective by considering the memory hierarchy diagram of Figure 7–33. At the bottom of the hierarchy are the relatively slow but inexpensive, high-capacity auxiliary memory devices. At the top is the small, high-speed cache memory. The central position of the main memory in the hierarchy allows it to communicate with both the auxiliary memory through I/O processors and also with the cache memory via the CPU.

Table 7.1 summarizes the typical size, average access time, and average cost of the different kinds of memory. It can be seen from this table that the level in the

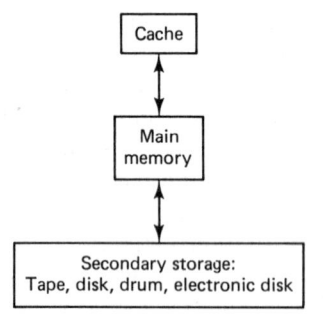

Figure 7–33 Memory hierarchy

TABLE 7.1 COMPARISON OF MEMORIES

Technology	Typical Sizes	Average Access	Cost per Bit (¢)
Cache (bipolar)	4000–16,000 bytes	0.1 microseconds	3.0
MOS main memory	8000–1 million words	0.5–1.0 microseconds	0.5
Magnetic tape	50 million bytes	1–5 seconds	0.00001
Movable-head disk	10–800 million bytes	25–60 milliseconds	0.005
Fixed-head disk	5–256 million bytes	5–15 milliseconds	0.05
Floppy disk	250–1400 kilobytes	150–300 milliseconds	0.00005
Drum	5–9000 million bytes	5–15 milliseconds	0.01
Bubble memory	1–5 million words	750 microseconds	0.02

hierarchy of a memory unit is proportional to its cost per bit. It is the responsibility of the operating system's memory management routines to maximize the utilization of all of the memory components and to provide efficient transfers of information between the various levels.

PROBLEMS

1. Define the following terms:
   - (a) stack memory
   - (b) modular memory
   - (c) interleaved memory
   - (d) associative memory
   - (e) locality of reference
   - (f) cache
   - (g) write-through policy
   - (h) write-back policy
   - (i) auxiliary memory
   - (j) bubble memory
   - (k) virtual memory

2. For the register control logic circuit of Figure 7–1(b), the load line for register i is 1 whenever the ENABLE line is 1, independent of the value of the PUSH/POP line.
   - (a) Verify that this is true.
   - (b) Explain what is loaded and how on both the PUSH and the POP signals.

3. Show the content of the stack in Figure 7–3 after the following sequences of operations:
   - (a) POP, POP, POP
   - (b) PUSH(5), PUSH(86), POP, PUSH(22)

4. What are the sequences of micro-operations for the PUSH and POP operations on a stack that grows in a direction toward lower memory?

5. For the HP3000 computer, what is the relationship of the values in SM, SB, and SL when the stack is in each of the following conditions?
   - (a) Empty
   - (b) Full
   - (c) Neither empty nor full

6. Based on Figure 7–6, specify where the memory word referenced by each of the following addresses is located:
   - (a) 0111001011
   - (b) 0011110000
   - (c) 1010101010
   - (d) 1100000001

7. Repeat Problem 6 using Figure 7–7.

8. Let the contents of an associative memory be as follows:

110010
110110
010101
001110

   What is the value of the match register (M) in each of these instances?
   - (a) K = 001110 and A = 000100
   - (b) K = 000000 and A = 101011
   - (c) K = 111111 and A = 110110
   - (d) K = 011100 and A = 110110

9. Explain why an associative memory is faster than a RAM.

10. Consider a direct-mapping cache memory of 800 words with an access time of 50 nanoseconds. Assume that the main memory has an access time of 1 microsecond, 70% of the memory requests are for reads, the average hit ratio for reads is 0.90, and the average hit ratio for writes is 0.85.
    (a) What is the average access time of this system for just memory read cycles?
    (b) What is the average access time of this system for both memory reads and writes? (Answer for both write-through and write-back policies.)
    (c) What is the hit ratio of the total system? (Answer for both write-through and write-back policies.)
11. Given the memory and cache contents shown in Figure 7–16(b), what would happen when memory word 0111010 is accessed?
12. Show the timing diagram of a Manchester code for the following data patterns:
    (a) 11001100   (c) 11111111
    (b) 10101010   (d) 00000001
13. What is the disk access time for each system where the transfer time of the data is 100 milliseconds, the seek time is 30 milliseconds, and the latency time is 4 milliseconds?
    (a) Fixed-head system
    (b) Movable-head system
    (c) Winchester system
14. Explain the orientation of the $+/-$ pairs in the T and I bars of Figure 7–25.
15. Using program X of Figure 7–28 and assuming a page size of 5 words:
    (a) Show the program with addresses in terms of (p, d).
    (b) Show a possible main memory allocation of the pages and give the associated page table.

CHAPTER 8

Microprogramming

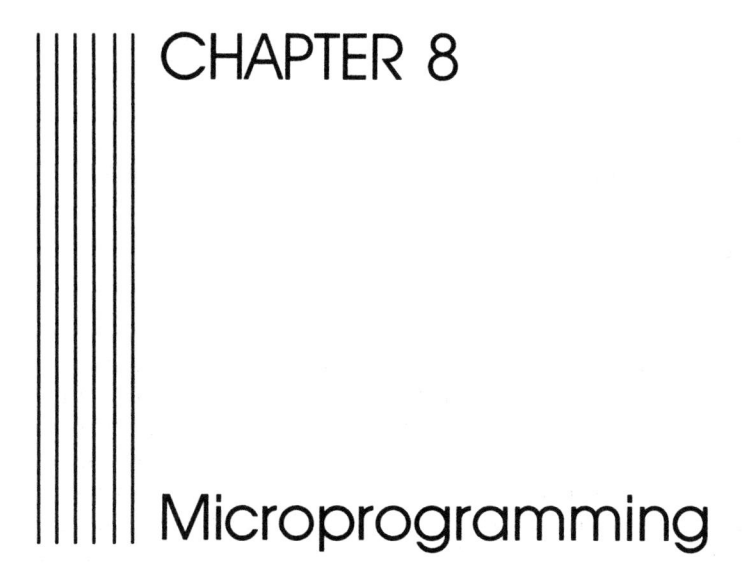

8.1 THE CONTROL LOGIC UNIT

The **control logic unit (CLU)** directs all hardware activity inside the computer. The CLU causes an instruction to be fetched from memory, decodes the instruction to determine the operation to be performed, determines the source and destination of data, and causes the movement of data and the execution of the required operation. The CLU repeats the entire process until a HALT operation is encountered in the program and executed.

The instruction codes are stored in memory together with the data. As we already know, an instruction is a complex entity whose execution cannot be accomplished during a single clock pulse. Therefore, having interpreted the binary code of the instruction, the CLU generates a sequence of control commands, called **microinstructions,** that execute the instruction. We have already seen examples of such instructions in Chapters 4 and 5. To distinguish between an instruction and a microinstruction, instructions are sometimes referred to as **macroinstructions.**

The duration of the fetch/execute cycle depends on the type of operation to be performed, the addressing mode used, and the number of operands required. Therefore, instruction cycle time may vary from one instruction to another. What the CLU does is divide each instruction cycle into a sequence of **states.** All states are identical in length, and the duration of each state is equal to the computer's clock period. A state, therefore, corresponds to the smallest unit of processing activity and defines the execution of one or more simultaneous microinstructions.

Microinstructions are low-level, primitive operations that act directly on the logic circuits of the computer. They specify functions (signals) such as these:

1. Open/close a gate from a register to a bus.
2. Transfer data along a bus.
3. Initiate control signals such as READ, WRITE, SHIFT, CLEAR, and SET.
4. Send timing signals.
5. Wait a prescribed period of time.
6. Test certain bits within a register.

There are two basic approaches to the design of a CLU: *hard-wired* (or *random logic*) design and *microprogrammed* design. In the hard-wired approach, gates, counters, and registers are interconnected to generate the control signals. Each design requires a different set of logic devices and interconnections. In the microprogrammed approach, a sequence of microinstructions, called a **microprogram,** is formed for each macroinstruction and stored in a control memory (usually a ROM) within the CLU. The required timing and control signals are then generated by executing a microprogram for each macroinstruction.

8.2 HARD-WIRED CONTROL

When an instruction is placed in the **instruction register (IR),** the CLU decodes the instruction and generates the associated sequence of microinstructions. Consider a computer that has 16 instructions so that each instruction can be encoded with a unique 4-bit opcode. (Of course, the remainder of the instruction word contains the necessary addressing information such as the registers involved, memory addresses, and offsets.) Figure 8-1 shows a possible decoder implementation for the opcode. The **mnemonics** shown are as follows:

LDR (Load a register from memory)
LDM (Load memory from a register)
ADR (Add to register)
BRU (Branch unconditionally)
BRZ (Branch on zero)

Each of the decoder outputs can be used to generate a sequence of microinstructions. These microinstructions are controlled by the timing signals and some status conditions in the system.

The address of any operand required by the opcode must be supplied to the memory address register (MAR) at the proper time. The memory unit decodes the address presented by the MAR and outputs the word stored in the addressed location via the memory buffer register (MBR). If the addressing information in the instruction is not the actual address of the operand, the CLU has to implement the steps necessary for indirect addressing, indexing, or any other available addressing mode (see Section 5.3).

Sec. 8.2 Hard-Wired Control

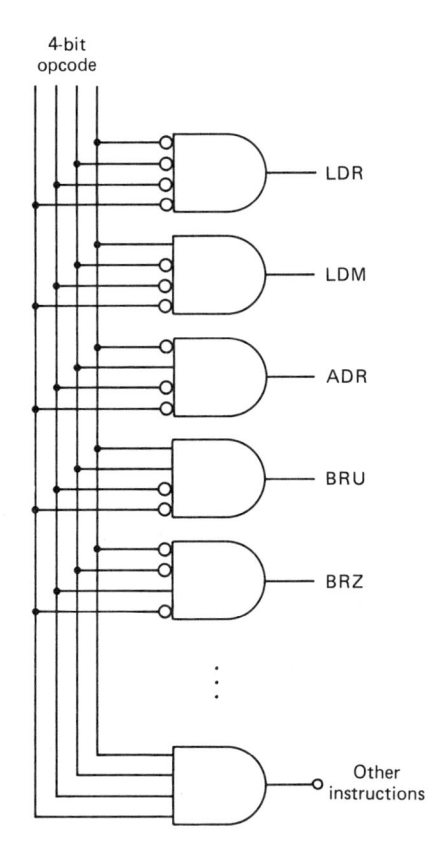

Figure 8-1 Four-bit opcode decoder

Each sequence of microinstructions is executed in a time period referred to as a **machine cycle.** The CLU divides the machine cycle into a sequence of states, $t_0, t_1, \ldots$, such that the duration of each state is equal to the computer's clock period. We can generate these timing signals using a ring counter or, as shown in Figure 8–2(a), a counter-decoder combination. This counter-decoder circuit generates an ordered sequence of four states that repeats itself every four clock pulses. The timing diagram for the circuit is shown in Figure 8–2(b).

To illustrate how the counter-decoder circuit of Figure 8–2 generates the timing signals required to execute one computer instruction, consider an ADD instruction of a single-address computer (see Chapter 5). To fetch and execute this instruction, the CLU must perform the following steps:

t_0: MAR ← (PC)   The content of the PC is sent to the MAR.

t_1: MBR ← M[MAR]   The content of the addressed memory
PC ← (PC) + 1   location is placed in the MBR and the PC is incremented.

t_2: IR ← (MBR)   The content of the MBR is sent to the IR.

t_3: MAR ← (IR[operand address])   The operand's address field of the instruction is sent from the IR to the MAR.

t_4: MBR ← M[MAR]   The operand is placed in the MBR.

t_5: ACC ← (ACC) + (MBR)   The contents of the MBR and the accumulator are added and the result placed in the accumulator.

The timing signals t_4 and t_5 are shown in parentheses in Figure 8–2(b).

As we see, the execution of the ADD instruction consists of a sequence of six states (clock pulses). In generating this sequence, we have assumed that the memory access time is on par with the other parts of the computer. However, if the memory is slower, states t_1 and t_4 would consume extra time, and the execution of the instruction would require more than six states.

Basically, a hard-wired CLU can be either synchronous or asynchronous. In a **synchronous CLU,** each operation is controlled by the clock. The clock frequency must be such that the time between two clock pulses is sufficient to allow for the completion of the slowest microinstruction. In an **asynchronous CLU,** the completion of one operation triggers the next, and, therefore, no clock is necessary. Although the design of an asynchronous CLU is more complex, it can be made to function

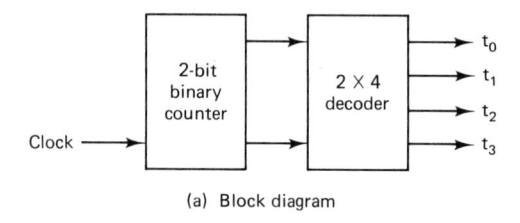

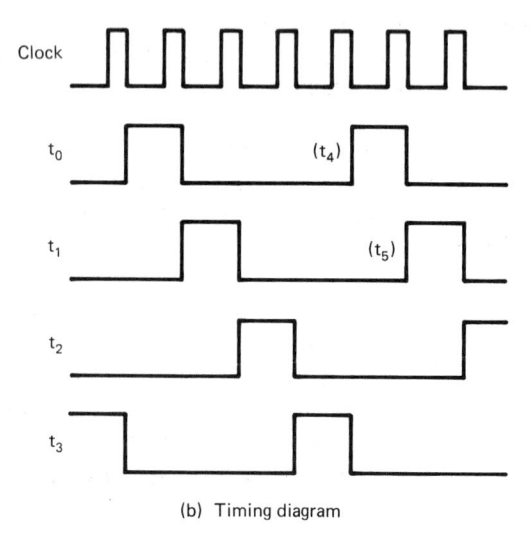

Figure 8–2 Generation of timing signals

Sec. 8.3 Microprogrammed Control

faster than a synchronous CLU. Nevertheless, with either approach, hard-wired implementation of the CLU results in an overall fast response. However, it has been largely supplanted by microprogrammed control, for reasons explored in the next section.

8.3 MICROPROGRAMMED CONTROL

The term *microprogram* was first suggested by M. V. Wilkes in the early 1950s when he proposed a novel approach to control unit design. The idea intrigued many computer scientists and engineers at the time, but it appeared to be unrealistic due to a requirement for very fast and relatively inexpensive control memory. The situation changed dramatically with the announcement of IBM's System/360 family of computers in April 1964. All but the largest models included a fast and inexpensive control memory and were microprogrammed. Since then, microprogramming has become increasingly common due to the increase in speed and the decrease in cost of control memory.

A hard-wired control logic unit requires extensive redesign of the hardware if the instruction set has to be extended or if the function of an instruction has to be changed. In contrast, in a **microprogrammed CLU,** the sequence of microinstructions (the microprogram) corresponding to each instruction in the instruction set is stored in a read-only memory (ROM) called the **control memory.** Therefore, the meaning of an instruction can be changed by changing the microprogram corresponding to that instruction, and the instruction set can be extended simply by including an additional ROM containing the corresponding microprograms. As a result, the required hardware changes in the CLU can be kept to a minimum.

As mentioned, the technique of microprogramming was first suggested in the early 1950s but was not economically feasible until reasonably priced, fast ROMs became available. The degree by which the microprograms can be changed by the user varies from one computer to another. Some do not allow any changes, some allow partial changes, and some do not have a fixed instruction set but instead allow the user to microprogram an instruction set tailored to the intended application of the computer. Consequently, a microprogrammed CLU is said to be *microprogrammable* if the control memory can be modified by the user to produce tailored macroinstructions. Otherwise, the instruction set is fixed, similar to the set of instructions in a hard-wired CLU.

Microprogrammed CLU Organization

The basic organization of a microprogrammed CLU is shown in Figure 8–3. The macroinstructions are stored in main memory and are accessed through the memory address register (MAR) and the memory buffer register (MBR). The instruction is fetched into the instruction register (IR), and the **microcontroller (sequencer)** executes the corresponding microprogram. The beginning address of the microprogram is loaded into the **control address register (CAR),** and the control memory then transfers the first microinstruction into the **control buffer register (CBR).** Fetching a microinstruction from the control memory defines a **microcycle,** during which the

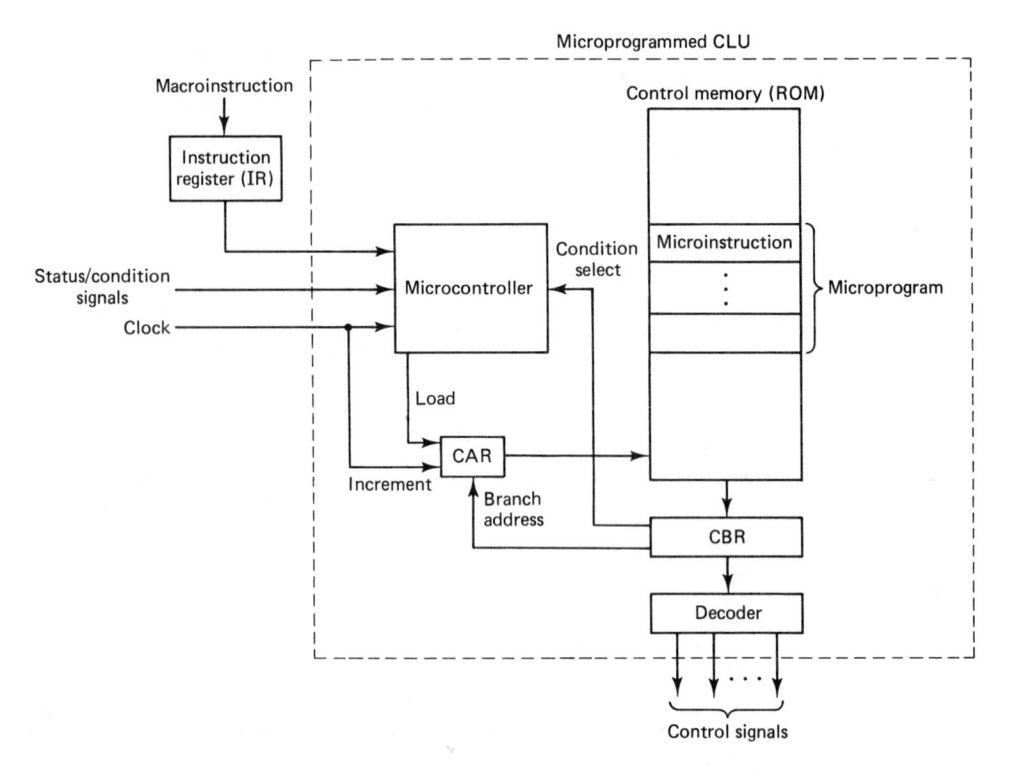

Figure 8-3 Organization of a microprogrammed CLU

microinstruction is decoded to generate the control signals required to execute it. The CAR is normally incremented by 1 at each clock pulse so that it can address the next microinstruction in sequence. Note, however, that the sequence can be altered by conditions occurring within or outside the CLU, which may cause the microcontroller to increment the CAR by more than 1. If any operands are required for a given instruction, the addressing information in the IR is decoded to furnish the operands' locations.

As we see, there is a functional resemblance between the register pair MAR and MBR and the pair CAR and CBR. The former is used to access macroinstructions, whereas the latter is used to access microinstructions. Note also that the function of the microinstruction sequencing circuit is similar to the function of the macroinstruction sequencing circuit, which uses a program counter (PC).

Microinstruction Formats

There are essentially two basic types of microinstruction formats: horizontal and vertical. In the **horizontal** microinstruction format, one bit is provided for each logic signal that can be generated by the microinstruction, as shown in Figure 8-4(a). Hence, if K distinct control signals are required, a microinstruction word length of K bits is required. To generate a particular signal, the corresponding bit in the microinstruction is set to 1; the absence of a control signal is indicated by placing a

Sec. 8.3 Microprogrammed Control

(a) Horizontal format

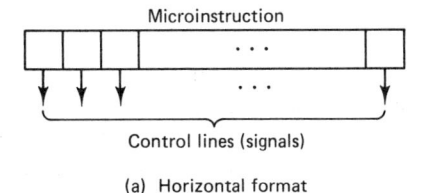

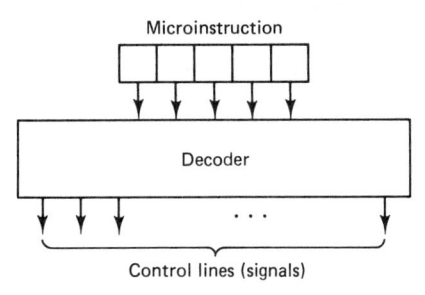

(b) Vertical format

Figure 8-4 Microinstruction formats

zero in the appropriate bit position. This approach has the advantage that as many control signals as needed can be generated concurrently, permitting a very fast operation.

Most micro-operations, however, are mutually exclusive and are never invoked simultaneously. Therefore, it is possible to divide them into groups and use a number of bits (a field) to code a set of mutually exclusive microinstructions. A decoder is then used to select the particular micro-operation to be invoked. If carried to an extreme (only one field), this coding and decoding results in a **vertical** microinstruction format, in which only one micro-operation is invoked at a time, as shown in Figure 8-4(b). A vertical microinstruction format therefore resembles a macroinstruction format and consists of a single operation code, called **micro opcode,** one or more operands, and some other fields (for conditional branches, for example).

To illustrate the difference between horizontal and vertical microinstruction formats, consider Figure 8-5, which shows an arithmetic and logic unit (ALU) with two parallel 8-bit inputs X and Y and a single parallel 8-bit output Z. The two input

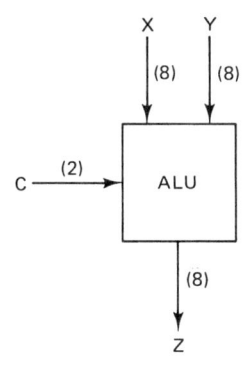

Figure 8-5 An ALU

bits labeled *C* that are used to control the operation of the ALU. The input data can be obtained from any one of six 8-bit registers R_0 through R_5 (not shown in Figure 8–5), and the output data can be written into any one of these registers. We assume that the ALU inputs and outputs remain unchanged until new data is stored in them. To access the registers, each of them is assigned a 4-bit address encoded, for example, in the excess-3 code. Thus we encode R_0 by the bit pattern 0011, R_1 by 0100, and so on, encoding R_5 by 1000.

For simplicity, let us assume that the ALU can perform only three distinct functions: no operation (NOP), add *X* and *Y* (*X* + *Y*), and subtract *Y* from *X* (*X* − *Y*). To select any one of these operations, the ALU uses the two control lines (*C*) shown in Figure 8–5. Assume, therefore, that NOP is encoded as 00, (*X* + *Y*) as 01, and (*X* − *Y*) as 10.

The sequence of micro-operations associated with the ALU consists of the following steps:

$X \leftarrow$ (Register)	Transfer the content of a register to the *X* input of the ALU.
$Y \leftarrow$ (Register)	Transfer the content of a register to the *Y* input of the ALU.
$Z \leftarrow f(X,Y)$	Select an ALU operation.
Register $\leftarrow$ (Z)	Write *Z* into a register.

If we use a horizontal microinstruction format to execute these micro-operations, the microinstruction contains 14 bits, as shown in Figure 8–6(a). Two bits are reserved for the opcode, which specifies the selected ALU operation. The 4-bit *X* field specifies the address of the register supplying the data to the *X* input, the 4-bit *Y* field specifies the register associated with the *Y* input, and the 4-bit *Z* field specifies the register into which the result of the ALU operation will be written. For example, Figure 8–6(b) shows the coded horizontal microinstruction required to execute $R_4 \leftarrow (R_1) - (R_5)$.

In contrast, a vertical format requires four microinstructions to execute the micro-operations, as shown in Figure 8–7(a). Two bits are reserved to encode each of the four steps in the sequence of micro-operations associated with the ALU. As we see, this vertical format requires 24 bits of control memory. Only 2 bits are not used, those in the microinstruction corresponding to the step "select an ALU operation." If we encode the four micro-operations "select *X*," "select *Y*," "select ALU," and "select *Z*" as 00, 01, 10, and 11, respectively, Figure 8–7(b) shows the coding required to execute $R_4 \leftarrow (R_1) - (R_5)$.

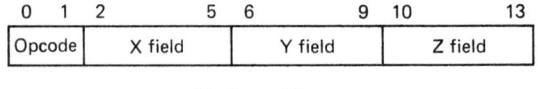

```
 0  1 2     5 6       9 10      13
┌─────┬───────┬─────────┬─────────┐
│Opcode│X field│ Y field │ Z field │
└─────┴───────┴─────────┴─────────┘
```
(a) General format

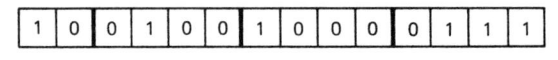

```
┌─┬─┬─┬─┬─┬─┬─┬─┬─┬─┬─┬─┬─┬─┐
│1│0│0│1│0│0│1│0│0│0│0│1│1│1│
└─┴─┴─┴─┴─┴─┴─┴─┴─┴─┴─┴─┴─┴─┘
```
(b) Microinstruction for $R_4 \leftarrow (R_1) - (R_5)$

Figure 8–6 Horizontal format for the ALU in Figure 8–5

Sec. 8.3 Mircoprogrammed Control

```
 0    1    2              5
| Select X |   Address    |

 0    1    2              5
| Select Y |   Address    |

 0    1    2    3    4    5
|Select ALU|Opcode| Unused |

 0    1    2              5
| Select Z |   Address    |
```

(a) General format

```
| 0 | 0 | 0 | 1 | 0 | 0 |

| 0 | 1 | 1 | 0 | 0 | 0 |

| 1 | 0 | 1 | 0 | X | X |

| 1 | 1 | 0 | 1 | 1 | 1 |
```

(b) Microinstruction for $R_4 \leftarrow (R_1) - (R_5)$

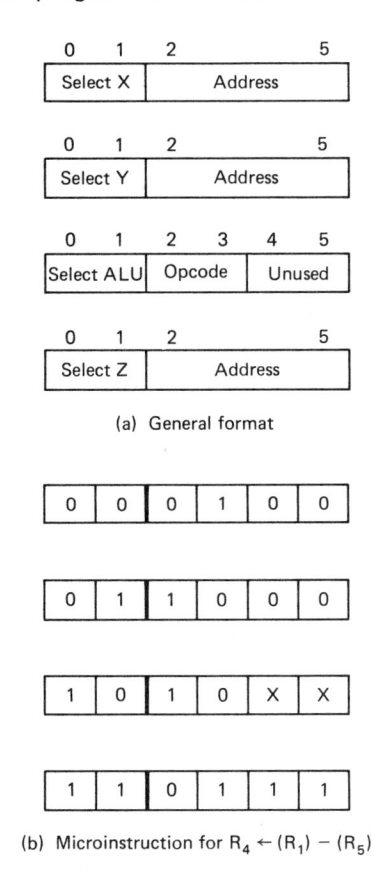

Figure 8-7 Vertical format for the ALU in Figure 8-5

It appears in this example that the horizontal format uses the control memory more efficiently than the vertical format. This is because, in this example, all the fields are used in the horizontal format. However, this may not be the case for every microprogram. For example, consider the following sequence of operations:

$$R_4 \leftarrow (R_1) - (R_5)$$
$$R_0 \leftarrow (R_4)$$
$$R_3 \leftarrow (R_1) + (R_5)$$
$$R_2 \leftarrow (R_3)$$

Note that since $(R_1) - (R_5)$ is transferred to R_4 from Z, $R_0 \leftarrow (R_4)$ simply implies that Z is also copied into R_0. A similar situation occurs with respect to the operation $R_2 \leftarrow (R_3)$.

We show in Figure 8-8(a) the four horizontal microinstructions required to execute the sequence. The microprogram uses 56 bits (4 × 14) of control memory but is quite wasteful since three fields in both the second and fourth microinstructions are not used. In contrast, the eight vertical microinstructions shown in Figure 8-8(b) require only 48 bits (8 × 6) of control memory with only 4 bits wasted.

Since vertical microinstructions resemble macroinstructions in format and operation, it is easier to write vertical microprograms than their horizontal counterparts.

| 1 | 0 | 0 | 1 | 0 | 0 | 1 | 0 | 0 | 0 | 0 | 1 | 1 | 1 | $R_4 \leftarrow (R_1) - (R_5)$

| 0 | 0 | 0 | 0 | 0 | 0 | 0 | 0 | 0 | 0 | 0 | 0 | 1 | 1 | $R_0 \leftarrow (R_4)$

| 0 | 1 | 0 | 1 | 0 | 0 | 1 | 0 | 0 | 0 | 0 | 1 | 1 | 0 | $R_3 \leftarrow (R_1) + (R_5)$

| 0 | 0 | 0 | 0 | 0 | 0 | 0 | 0 | 0 | 0 | 0 | 1 | 0 | 1 | $R_2 \leftarrow (R_3)$

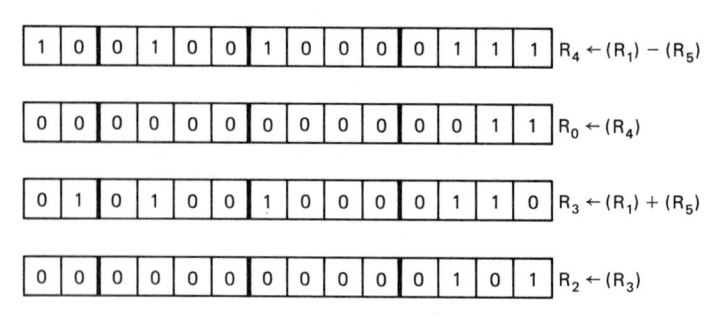

(a) Horizontal microinstruction sequence

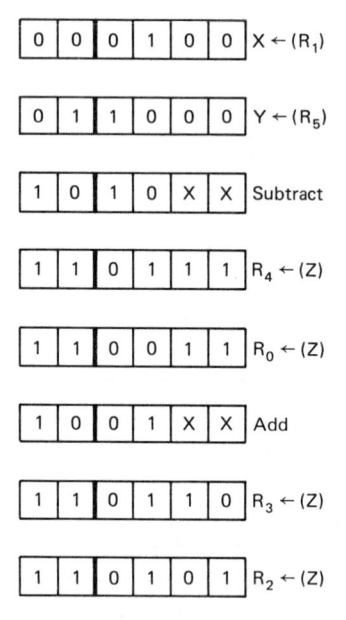

| 0 | 0 | 0 | 1 | 0 | 0 | $X \leftarrow (R_1)$

| 0 | 1 | 1 | 0 | 0 | 0 | $Y \leftarrow (R_5)$

| 1 | 0 | 1 | 0 | X | X | Subtract

| 1 | 1 | 0 | 1 | 1 | 1 | $R_4 \leftarrow (Z)$

| 1 | 1 | 0 | 0 | 1 | 1 | $R_0 \leftarrow (Z)$

| 1 | 0 | 0 | 1 | X | X | Add

| 1 | 1 | 0 | 1 | 1 | 0 | $R_3 \leftarrow (Z)$

| 1 | 1 | 0 | 1 | 0 | 1 | $R_2 \leftarrow (Z)$

(b) Vertical microinstruction sequence

Figure 8-8 Microprogram example

The vertical approach requires relatively short word lengths but requires more complex logic circuits to implement and does not take full advantage of the parallelism in the microarchitecture. Most processors employ a combination of the two approaches. The format of a microinstruction can obviously vary significantly from one design to another and depends on factors such as the chosen set of micro-operations, the trade-off between microinstruction word length and speed of operation, and the accepted degree of complexity of the microinstruction-decoding circuits.

Microinstruction Sequencing

Although it is sometimes sufficient just to fetch the next microinstruction in sequence, some mechanism is needed to allow for conditional jumps in the microprogram to

Sec. 8.4   Emulation

enable it to make decisions. Rather than set up some condition in one microinstruction and then test it in the next, conditional jumps allow microinstructions to have two possible successors and increase their execution speed. To accomplish this, two fields are provided in each microinstruction: an ADDR field, which holds the address of a potential successor to the current microinstruction, and a COND field, which determines whether the next microinstruction is fetched from (CAR) + 1 or from ADDR.

The choice of the next microinstruction is determined by the microsequencing logic circuit. The output of this circuit controls a multiplexer, which routes either (CAR) + 1 or ADDR to CAR since the address of the next microinstruction resides in CAR. Since there are only four choices concerning the next microinstruction, the COND field can be 2 bits wide, and the four choices can be indicated by setting COND as follows:

COND = 00   Do not jump; the next microinstruction is taken from (CAR) + 1.
COND = 01   Jump to ADDR under C_1.
COND = 10   Jump to ADDR under C_2.
COND = 11   Jump to ADDR unconditionally.

Here, C_1 and C_2 are two status bits that represent the conditions for the jumps. The microsequencing logic circuit combines C_1 and C_2 and the two COND bits to generate an output. Thus the control signal is 1 (routing ADDR to CAR) if COND = 01 and C_1 = 1, if COND = 10 and C_2 = 1, or if COND = 11. Otherwise, the control signal is 0, and the next microinstruction in the sequence is fetched.

8.4 EMULATION

One of the main functions of microprogrammed control is to provide a means for simple, flexible, and relatively inexpensive control of a computer. The flexibility of microprogrammed control in handling resources within a computer allows us to implement diverse classes of instructions. In a computer with a fixed set of instructions, the control memory can be a ROM. However, if we use a read/write memory (or programmable ROM) for the control memory, it is possible to alter the instruction set by writing new microprograms. This leads to the concept of emulation.

In **emulation,** a computer is microprogrammed to have exactly the same instruction set as another computer and to behave in exactly the same manner. Therefore, programs written for the emulated computer will run on the microprogrammed computer. If we have a computer with an instruction set C_1, we can now add to C_1 the instruction set C_2 of an entirely different computer. Thus programs written in the machine language of C_2 can run on C_1, and we say that C_1 *emulates* C_2.

Emulation enables us to replace obsolete equipment with more up-to-date machines without forcing the users to rewrite the bulk of their software. If the replacement computer fully emulates the original one, no software changes have to be made to run the existing programs. This is an important consideration for the users, since rewriting software is usually a costly and time-consuming task. Thus emulation facilitates transitions into new systems with minimum disruption. Emulation is easily accomplished when the machines involved have similar architectures. Nevertheless, there have also been many successes in emulating computers using machines with totally different architectures.

8.5 BIT SLICES

Microprogrammable systems can be constructed using special integrated circuits (ICs), called **bit-sliced** processors, to design the microinstruction-sequencing hardware and use it in conjunction with a wide range of data path configurations and instruction sets. That is, we can define building blocks that can be easily assembled into a computer that meets the requirements of a given application. The capabilities and the instruction set of such a computer are determined by the particular building blocks chosen, by the way they are interconnected, and by the microprogram.

The flexibility inherent in this approach can be enhanced considerably if the blocks can be used to build processors of arbitrary word lengths. This is the basis of the bit slice idea. A **bit slice** is a slice through the data path of a typical processor. The slice, consisting of only a few bits (typically 2 or 8), contains all the logic circuits required to provide ALU functions, register transfers, and control functions. The connection patterns for the circuits on the slice are established under microprogram control, while the necessary control signals are provided by other building blocks.

Take, for example, a 4-bit slice IC processor unit that contains the registers, the ALU, and the shifter for manipulating 4-bit data. If we combine two such ICs, we can construct an 8-bit processor unit. Combining four such slices, we can construct a 16-bit central processing unit as shown in Figure 8–9. The idea of bit slicing is discussed further in Section 11.8.

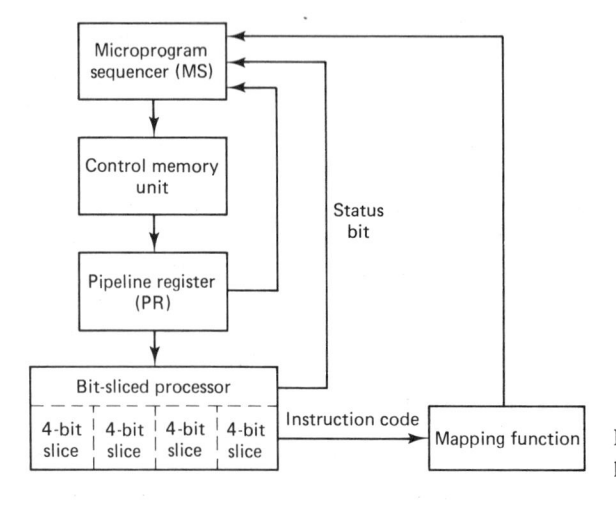

Figure 8–9 Bit-sliced central processing unit

8.6 MICROPROGRAM SUPPORT TOOLS

Let us consider some of the tools most likely to be needed by the computer designer to support the concept of microprogramming. The tools we shall examine fall into four categories: microassemblers, formatters, development and instrumentation systems, and hardware simulators.

Microassemblers

Microassemblers are software programs that allow the designer to encode a microprogram in a symbolic language (using mnemonics) and translate this representation into an absolute representation for loading into the control memory. The benefits of microassemblers are numerous:

1. Increased productivity in writing the microprogram. The microassembler enables the programmer to disregard the myriad of details concerning the specific bit representations of microinstructions and the need to lay out the microprogram in the control memory and assign absolute branch addresses.
2. A degree of independence from the hardware structure. If the microprogram is encoded symbolically, one may alter the microassembler and reassemble the symbolic microprogram.
3. Ease of change. If the programmer has to encode binary branch address values in microinstructions, the insertion of a new microinstruction would probably upset the entire microprogram and would force the programmer to alter all branch addresses. In contrast, in a symbolic language, branch addresses are represented as symbolic labels associated with microinstructions. Thus the programmer can simply insert the new microinstruction and reassemble the microprogram, causing the microassembler to reassign all the addresses.
4. Error checking. The microassembler can detect certain types of errors in the microprogram, such as branches to nonexistent microinstructions and the use of mutually exclusive or contradictory micro-operation values.
5. Cross-reference information. Most microassemblers produce a listing showing all microinstructions that reference particular symbolic values. This information is valuable during the debugging and modification cycles of the microprogram.
6. Increased readability. A symbolic representation (as opposed to a binary-coded form) of a microprogram is considerably easier to read and understand.

Microassemblers fall into two categories. The first consists of general or definition-driven microassemblers. Usually, these microassemblers have two inputs: (1) a definition of the microinstruction format and the interpretation of the symbolic values and (2) the symbolic microprogram itself. The second category of microassemblers consists of programs developed for specific microassembly language and specific microinstruction design. Usually, such microassemblers are developed for a particular computer organization, either from scratch or by using software tools available for the development of compilers or assemblers.

Formatters

Formatters are programs that facilitate the programming of PROMs (see Section 3.8), which are used to implement the control memory. Basically, a formatter takes the microprogram that has to be written into the control memory and slices it up so that it can fit into the various PROM chips that constitute the control memory.

Development Systems

This general category consists of both hardware and software tools to support microprogrammed system design. These development tools allow the programmer to store the microprogram and test data on disk files, edit them from a terminal, and simulate the control memory. Development systems also provide debugging support and emulation services for the system under development.

Hardware Simulators

Hardware simulators are programs that simulate the details of the data flows in the designed hardware. These simulators allow the designer to develop, debug, and test the microprogram logic simultaneously with the development of the hardware system.

8.7 COSTS AND BENEFITS OF MICROPROGRAMMING

Microprogrammed control offers a more structured approach to the design of the control logic unit (CLU) than does hard-wired control. Microprogrammed designs are relatively easy to change and correct, offer enhanced diagnostic capabilities, and are more reliable than hard-wired designs. Since the access time of the control memory ROM determines the CLU speed of operation, microprogrammed control may result in a slower CLU than one that is hard-wired. The reason for this is that the time taken to execute a microinstruction must also include the access time of the ROM. In contrast, any delay in a hard-wired CLU is due only to the propagation time delays through the hardware, which are relatively very small. Nevertheless, economics seems to favor hard-wired control only when the system is not too complex and requires only a few control operations.

Main memory utilization in microprogrammed computers is usually better since software that might have otherwise used main memory space is placed in the control memory. The continued improvement of ROMs (in terms of cost and in access time) will further enhance the dominant position of microprogramming. One idea in this direction is to include a third memory unit, called **nanomemory,** in addition to the main memory and the control memory. In doing so, some interesting trade-offs between horizontal and vertical microprogramming become possible.

Sec. 8.7 Costs and Benefits of Microprogramming

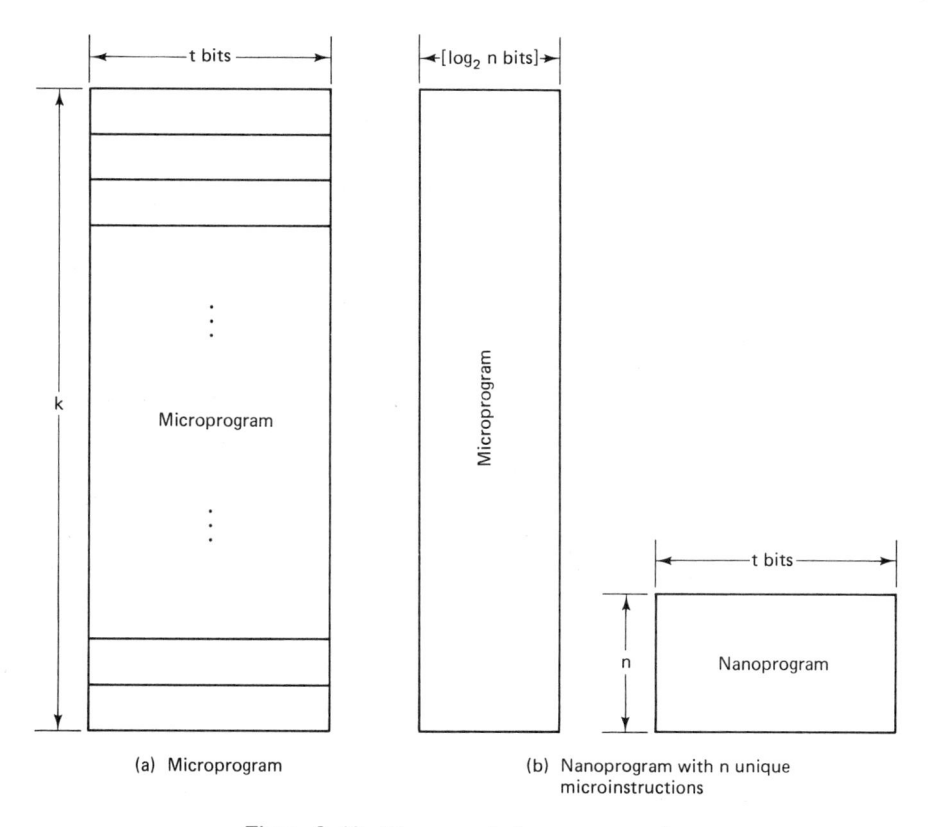

Figure 8-10 The concept of nanoprogramming

(a) Microprogram

(b) Nanoprogram with n unique microinstructions

The inclusion of a nanomemory is appropriate when many microinstructions occur several times. Consider Figure 8–10(a), which shows a microprogram consisting of k t-bit microinstructions. To store this microprogram, we need a total of kt bits of control memory. Suppose, however, that a study of the microprogram reveals that only $n \ll k$ different microinstructions are actually used. In this case, we can store these microinstructions in a special n-word, t-bit nanomemory. In other words, each microinstruction in the original program can now be replaced by the address of the nanomemory word containing that microinstruction. This way, the control memory need only be $\log_2 n$ bits wide, as shown in Figure 8–10(b), because there are only n words in the nanomemory.

To appreciate the considerable saving in control memory space resulting from this approach, suppose that the original microprogram [Figure 8–10(a)] requires a control memory of 16,384 × 128 bits but that only 256 different microinstructions occur. Thus we can use a 256 × 128–bit nanomemory to hold all the microinstructions needed, while the control memory can be reduced to a capacity of 16,384 × 8 bits. Hence we save (16,384 × 128) − (16,384 × 8) − (256 × 128) = 1,933,312 bits. Note that a computer with such *two-level* control memory will run slower than one without it because the microfetch cycle now requires two memory references: one to the control memory and one to the nanomemory. However, the performance can be improved by using additional techniques such as pipelining and multiway branching.

PROBLEMS

1. Define the following terms:
   (a) hard-wired control   (c) macroinstruction
   (b) microinstruction   (d) microprogram
2. Write the microprogram for a subtraction routine.
3. Discuss the differences between vertical and horizontal microinstructions.
4. Discuss the conditions under which it will be more feasible to use a hard-wired control than a microprogrammed control.
5. What are the address-sequencing capabilities required in a control memory?
6. Illustrate and discuss the conditional branch logic.
7. Show a block diagram for transforming a macroinstruction into a control memory address using a mapping memory (ROM or PLA).
8. Discuss the micro-operations needed for a fetch cycle routine.
9. What is the purpose of a microprogram sequencer?
10. Provide a comparison between microprograms and machine language programs.
11. Using the ALU of Figure 8–4 and the formats suggested in Figures 8–6 and 8–7, obtain the horizontal and vertical microprograms to execute the following operations:
    (a) $R_0 \leftarrow (R_1) + (R_2) + (R_3) + (R_4) + (R_5)$
    (b) $R_0 \leftarrow (R_1) + (R_2) - (R_3) - (R_4)$
    (c) $R_5 \leftarrow (R_0) + (R_5)$
12. What are the advantages of a microprogrammable bit-sliced CPU?
13. A microprogram contains 1024 words of 100 bits each, but only 120 different microinstructions are used. How many bits of control memory can be saved by using a nanomemory?

CHAPTER 9

Pipelined Computers

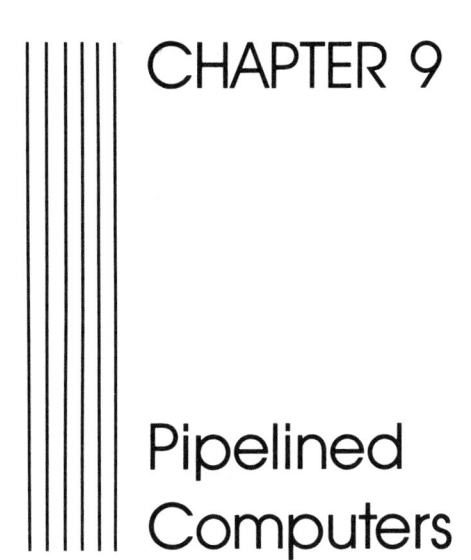

9.1 THE PIPELINE CONCEPT

In general, the efficiency of a computer system is measured in terms of both hardware speed and software facilities. This measure, referred to as **throughput,** is defined as the amount of processing that can be done in a given time interval. One technique that has led to tremendous improvement of system throughput is called **pipeline processing.** The concept of pipeline processing in a computer is analogous to an assembly line in an industrial plant. Consider the process of manufacturing cars. As a car is built, it moves along a conveyer belt of some sort past many stations. At each of these stations, some part of the construction is done on the car, which then moves to the next station. Having the car move to each station allows many cars to be on the assembly line at the same time, each at a separate station. This in turn results in finished cars coming off the line one right after the other. Without such an assembly line technique, one car could not even be started until the previous car was completely finished.

Pipeline processing in a computer is achieved by dividing a function to be performed into smaller subfunctions and designing separate hardware, called a **stage,** for each of the subfunctions. The stages are then connected together to form a single **pipeline** (or **pipe**) to perform the original function.

Example 9.1

Consider the function for the addition of two floating-point numbers (see Section 2.4) shown in Figure 9–1. It can be divided into the following three separate subfunctions:

1. Align the mantissas.
2. Add the mantissas.
3. Normalize the result.

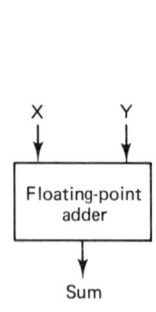

Figure 9-1 Floating-point adder

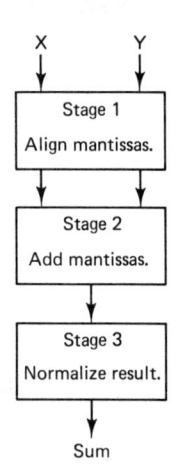

Figure 9-2 Pipeline processing of a floating-point adder

If we design a hardware stage for each of these subfunctions, we can structure the function as a three-stage pipeline as shown in Figure 9-2.

The immediate benefit of this pipelined addition process is that two new inputs can be started through the pipe as soon as the previous two pass on to stage 2. This in turn means that the sums will be available at a rate equal to the rate of input. Figure 9-3 shows schematically how a set of floating-point numbers would move through the simple pipelined adder of Figure 9-2. By the time the first pair of numbers is output from stage 3 [part (d) of the figure], the second pair has already been aligned and added and needs only to be normalized in stage 3 [part (e)]. Using the pipeline, the amount of time that elapses between the first result and the second is the amount of time necessary to normalize a number. Without a pipeline, the time between results would be the cumulative time necessary for all three subfunctions.

We define a **pipelined computer** as one with pipelined hardware components. This definition includes most computers designed today. They differ, however, in their degree of pipelining. In this chapter we discuss some of the major issues of designing and implementing pipelining in a computer.

9.2 SYNCHRONIZATION OF PIPELINES

As with any industrial assembly line, the efficiency of a pipeline can be greatly reduced by bottlenecks. A **bottleneck** occurs when processing at one station, or stage, takes proportionally longer than at other stages. Ideally, then, we want every stage in a pipe to take the *same* amount of processing time. Although it is possible to separate a function into relatively equal processing time subfunctions, the different logic of each stage makes it very difficult to generate exactly equal processing time stages. To make the time spent at each stage the same, the stages must be **synchronized.** This is usually done by inserting simple **latches** (fast registers; see Section 3.7) between the stages. Figure 9-4 shows a basic **linear** pipeline in which each

Sec. 9.2 Synchronization of Pipelines

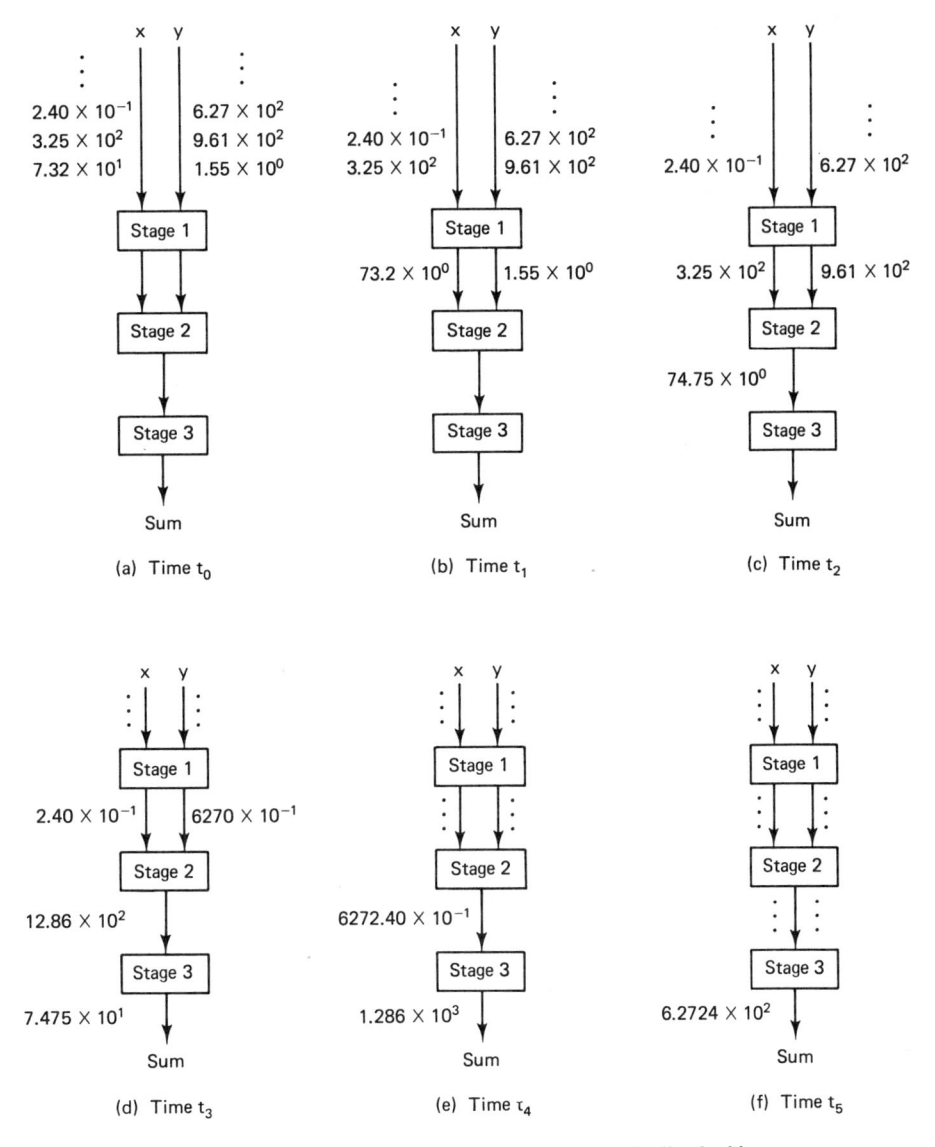

(a) Time t_0

x: 2.40×10^{-1}, 3.25×10^2, 7.32×10^1
y: 6.27×10^2, 9.61×10^2, 1.55×10^0

→ Stage 1 → Stage 2 → Stage 3 → Sum

(b) Time t_1

x: 2.40×10^{-1}, 3.25×10^2
y: 6.27×10^2, 9.61×10^2

→ Stage 1 → 73.2×10^0, 1.55×10^0 → Stage 2 → Stage 3 → Sum

(c) Time t_2

x: 2.40×10^{-1}
y: 6.27×10^2

→ Stage 1 → 3.25×10^2, 9.61×10^2 → Stage 2 → 74.75×10^0 → Stage 3 → Sum

(d) Time t_3

Stage 1 → 2.40×10^{-1}, 6270×10^{-1} → Stage 2 → 12.86×10^2 → Stage 3 → 7.475×10^1 → Sum

(e) Time t_4

Stage 1 → Stage 2 → 6272.40×10^{-1} → Stage 3 → 1.286×10^3 → Sum

(f) Time t_5

Stage 1 → Stage 2 → Stage 3 → 6.2724×10^2 → Sum

Figure 9-3 Progression of numbers through a pipelined adder

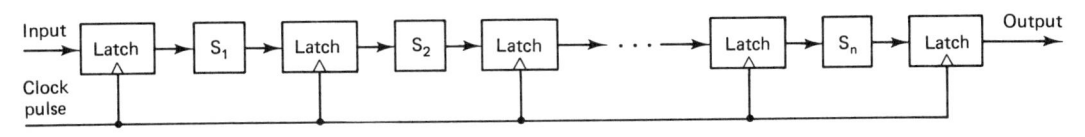

Input → Latch → S_1 → Latch → S_2 → Latch → · · · → Latch → S_n → Latch → Output

Clock pulse

Figure 9-4 Basic linear pipeline (S = stage)

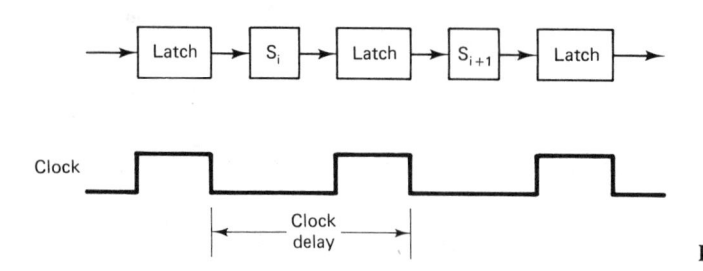

Figure 9-5 Clock period of a pipeline

stage is a purely combinational circuit separated from the next stage in the pipeline by a latch. There is also a latch at the very beginning and one at the end of the pipe to enforce synchronized input and to ensure synchronized output, respectively.

The time necessary to pass from one latch through a stage to the next latch is called the **clock delay** and is shown in Figure 9-5. Since there is only one uniform clock delay for the entire pipeline, the latches are synchronized according to the maximum processing time of the individual stages in the pipeline. Even if only one of the stages has a very long processing time, the clock delay is set for the longest processing time. Hence an efficiency-related design principle is to divide the function being pipelined into subfunctions that have hardware implementations with relatively equal processing times.

9.3 EFFICIENCY OF PIPELINES

To illustrate the overlapped operations in a linear pipeline, a **space-time diagram** is used. Figure 9-6 shows such a diagram for a three-stage pipeline. Each stage is represented on the space axis. The tasks shown in the diagram correspond to a set of inputs moving through the pipeline. The diagram shows which set of inputs, or tasks, is at which stage in the pipe on which clock delay. In the figure, the inputs are continuous, which is very efficient but is not always the case. Sometimes a new set of inputs is not immediately available or, as will be seen later, is delayed. In these cases, it is possible to have a space-time diagram such as the one in Figure 9-7. Here the second set of inputs, T_2, waits one extra clock delay before entering the pipe; the T_3 inputs enter immediately after T_2; and the T_4 inputs wait three extra clock delays before entering the pipe.

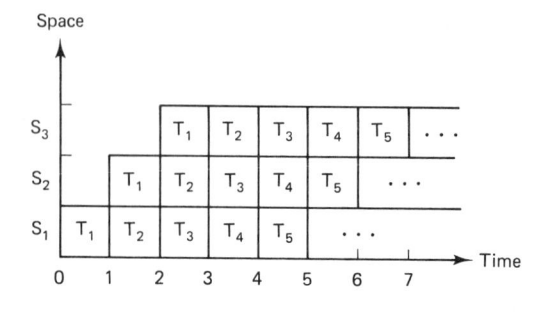

Figure 9-6 Space-time diagram for a pipeline (S = stage, T = task)

Sec. 9.3 Efficiency of Pipelines   237

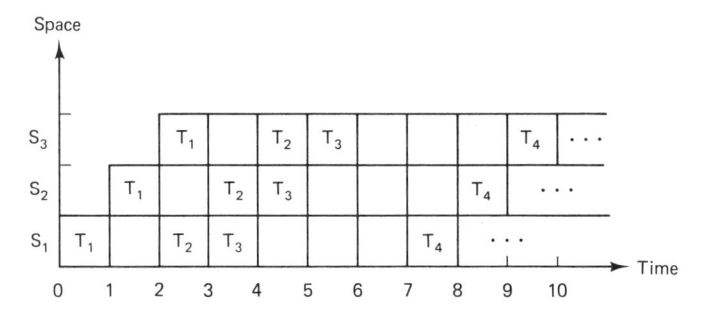

Figure 9-7 Space-time diagram with delayed inputs

By looking at the space-time diagram of a pipeline, we can determine the pipeline throughput, which is the number of results that can be completed per unit time. This rate reflects the computing power of the pipeline. To calculate the throughput, we ignore, in general, the **initial startup time** necessary to fill the pipe, that is, the time needed to get the first set of inputs all the way through the pipe. For example, consider the pipeline represented by Figure 9-6. The initial startup time of this pipeline is three clock delays. On the eighth clock delay, the fifth result is available. Therefore, the throughput is 5/(8 − 3), which equals 1. This means that after filling the pipe, one result is available every clock delay. Similarly, the throughput for the pipeline shown in Figure 9-7 is 4/(11 − 3) = 0.5. This means that, on the average, 0.5 result is available every clock delay, or one result every two clock delays. In general, the higher the throughput, the more efficient the pipeline.

In theory, a pipelined function is almost always better than a nonpipelined function. The only time it is not better is when a function cannot be separated into distinct subfunctions. In reality, however, the cost of the pipeline greatly influences when and if pipelining the function is actually better or not. This cost can be attributed, but is not limited, to the following factors:

1. The extra hardware latches necessary
2. The control necessary for scheduling the inputs (As will be seen later in the chapter, the input to a pipeline cannot always be on every clock delay.)
3. The time spent by data in the latches so as to conform to a uniform clock delay
4. The average number of inputs that will be available to make efficient use of the pipeline

The last factor, more than the others, determines the cutoff point of when pipelining is better. No matter how efficient a pipeline is, if it will be used for only one set of inputs at a time, all the overhead necessary to pipeline the function makes it slower and more expensive than if the function is not pipelined. If, however, a very large number of input sets is to be processed on a regular basis, the overhead of the pipeline is much more affordable. (A graph comparing run times for a specific pipeline example is given in Figure 9-11.)

9.4 CLASSIFICATION OF PIPELINES

Pipelines can be classified by their functions and by their configurations. Functionally, they are classified into three basic groups: arithmetic, instruction, and processor pipelining. Ramamoorthy and Li (1977) proposed three schemes for classifying pipelines according to their configurations and control strategies: unifunction or multifunction; static or dynamic; and scalar or vector.

Functional Classification

Arithmetic pipelining. Segmenting the functions of the ALU of a system comes under this category. An example of an arithmetic pipelined function is given in Section 9.7.

Instruction pipelining. In a nonpipelined computer, the CPU goes through a continuous cycle of fetch-decode-execute for all the instructions. The fetching of one instruction is not started until the previous instruction's execution is completed. To pipeline this function, consecutive instructions are fetched from memory while the previous instructions are being decoded and executed. Instruction pipelining, also called **instruction look-ahead,** fetches instructions in sequence. Hence, when an instruction causes a branch out of sequence, the pipe is emptied of all previously fetched instructions, and the branched-to instruction is fetched. Instruction pipelining is done on almost all high-performance computers today.

Example 9.2

Consider the three-stage look-ahead pipeline of Figure 9–8(a). Suppose that instruction I_2 is a branch to instruction I_k. Therefore, the pipeline must be emptied of all prefetched instructions, which, in this case, are I_3 and I_4. This is shown in the space-time diagram of Figure 9–8(b).

Processor pipelining. When the stages of a pipeline are actual processors and the latches are shared memories between the processors, the pipeline is called a

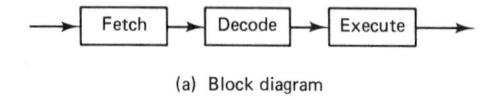

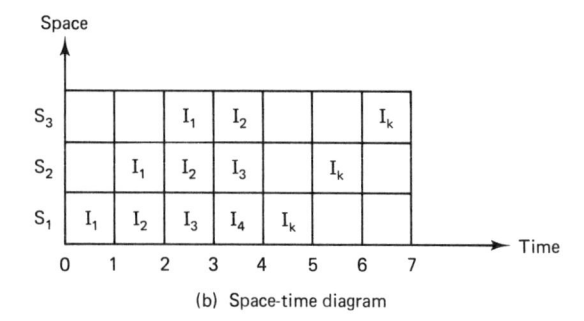

Figure 9–8 Instruction look-ahead pipeline

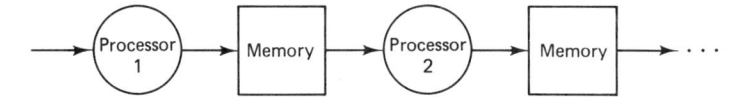

Figure 9-9 Multiprocessor pipeline

processor pipeline. In these pipelines, each processor has a specific task to perform on the data stream, as shown in Figure 9-9. The pipelining of multiple processors is a relatively new concept and, as yet, not very common.

Configurational Classification

Unifunction versus multifunction. A pipeline capable of only one basic type of operation is called a **unifunction pipeline.** For example, floating-point multiplication requires that the pipeline perform the same operation on every set of inputs. When a pipeline can perform different functions, it is called a **multifunction pipeline.** The different functions may be performed, either simultaneously or at different times, by interconnecting different subsets of stages in the pipeline. The pipeline is configured as necessary according to the values of extra control inputs.

Static versus dynamic. When instructions of the same type are to be executed simultaneously, **static pipelines** are used. These can be either unifunctional or multifunctional but may assume only one functional configuration at a time. A static multifunction pipeline works best when the function to be performed does not change frequently. Between changes, the pipeline appears to be a unifunction pipeline and repeats the same operation over and over. Before changing functions, the last set of inputs for the previous function must pass completely through the pipeline, a process referred to as *draining the pipe*. The pipeline is then configured for the new function, and the new inputs are allowed into the pipe.

With a **dynamic pipeline,** several functional configurations may exist at once. This implies that a multifunctional pipeline must be used. In this case, the configuration of the pipe is constantly changing, depending on which data for which function is in which stage for every clock delay. Dynamic pipelines require very complex control and sequencing mechanisms to configure the pipe for the particular inputs. For this reason, the actual pipelining is not under the control of the programmer. Rather, it is built into the architecture of the machine. If a pipeline in a system needs to change its function frequently, the cost of implementing a dynamic pipeline outweighs the cost of the idle time resulting from continually draining a static pipeline.

Scalar versus vector. A **scalar pipeline** processes a sequence of scalar operations on scalar operands (dealing with individual numbers as opposed to vectors) as specified by the program. An example would be an ADD operation in a FOR loop. **Vector pipelines** are designed to process vector instructions using vector operands. Computers that have vector instructions are called **vector processors** and are discussed in Chapter 10. The pipelines in the examples in this chapter could be used as scalar pipelines or as parts of vector pipelines.

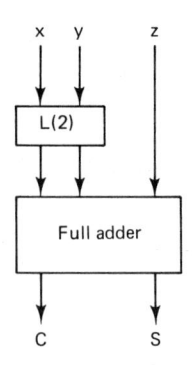

(a) Full adder stage

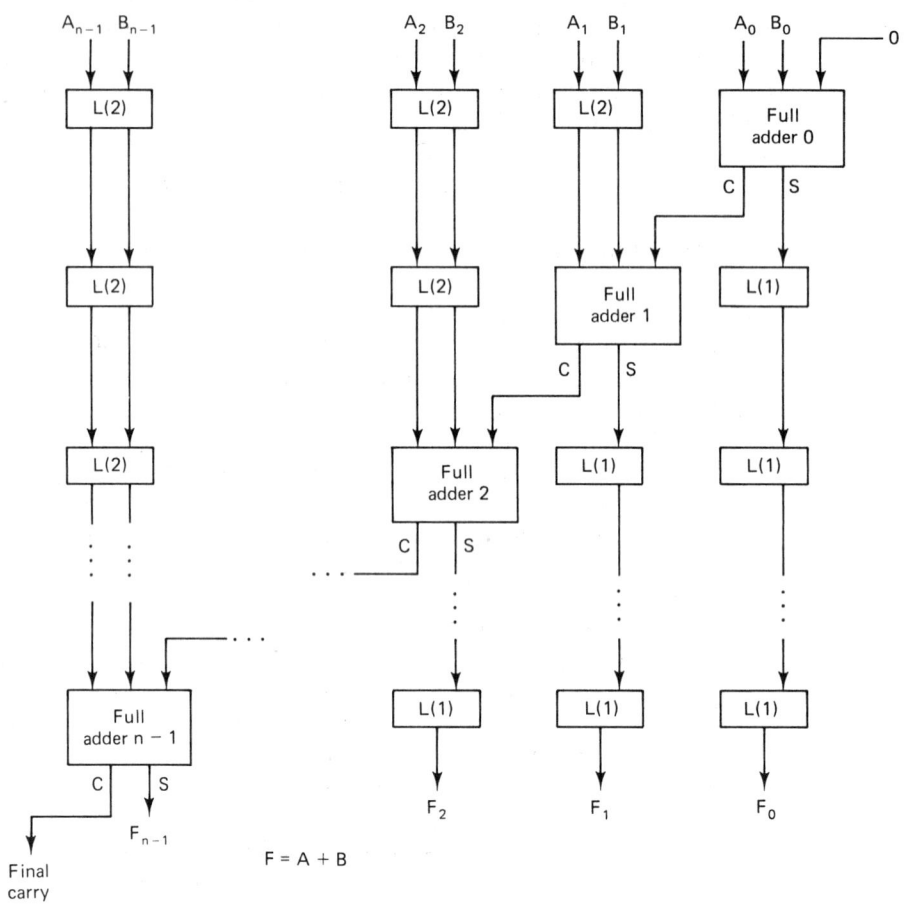

(b) N-bit parallel adder configuration

Figure 9-10 Pipelined n-bit parallel adder [$L(i)$ = i-bit latch; clock delay = time of one adder]

9.5 STAGE CASCADING

Although most pipelines are designed by partitioning a function into stages, it is possible to construct a complex pipeline out of one elementary stage. This process is known as **stage cascading.** The iterative cascading of stages can be used to construct both unifunction and multifunction pipeline units. We shall explain the concept of stage cascading by way of the following unifunction pipeline example.

Consider the full adder defined in Section 3.6. It consists of three inputs and two outputs. The inputs are the two bits to be added, x and y, and the previous carry, z. The outputs are the sum bit, S, and the generated (new) carry, C. To make the full adder into a stage, we add a 2-bit latch to inputs x and y as shown in Figure 9–10(a). Connecting a number of these stages and extra latches together, as shown in Figure 9–10(b), gives an n-bit parallel adder that works as follows:

1. On the first clock delay, A_0 and B_0 pass through adder 0, while A_1 and B_1 through A_{n-1} and B_{n-1} are loaded into the first level of latches.
2. On the second clock delay, the C output from adder 0 is available and, together with A_1 and B_1, passes through adder 1. At the same time, A_2 and B_2 through A_{n-1} and B_{n-1} pass to the second level of latches and the S output from adder 0 moves to a latch.
3. The same pattern continues for n clock delays, at which time all the F outputs are available.

The special thing about this adder is that in step 2 a new pair of A and B inputs can start moving through the pipe. As long as new pairs of numbers continue to be input, the adder will output a final result on every clock delay (after the initial n clock delays). This is the reason why this setup is considered a pipelined n-bit parallel adder.

As we already know from Section 3.6, it is possible to construct a multibit parallel adder from full adders. The approach used in that section resulted in a ripple adder. Since the least significant carry has to propagate through all the adder stages, the time it takes to add two n-bit numbers is roughly n times the time it takes to go through one full adder stage. Therefore, the time it takes to add m pairs of n-bit numbers is on the order of mn. In contrast, our pipelined parallel adder takes n times the time it takes to go through one full adder stage to produce the sum of the first pair of numbers. But after that, one sum is available every clock delay as long as the input keeps the pipe filled. This means that the time it takes to add m pairs of n-bit numbers is on the order of $m + n$.

Figure 9–11 shows a comparison of the different times for the different adders mentioned. The benefits of the pipelined adder are only realized when the savings in time outweigh the overhead of the pipeline, including the extra latches necessary. To add just one pair of n-bit numbers at a time, it would be faster and cheaper to use a fast adder (taking $m \log_2 n$ time) or even a ripple adder than to use a pipelined adder.

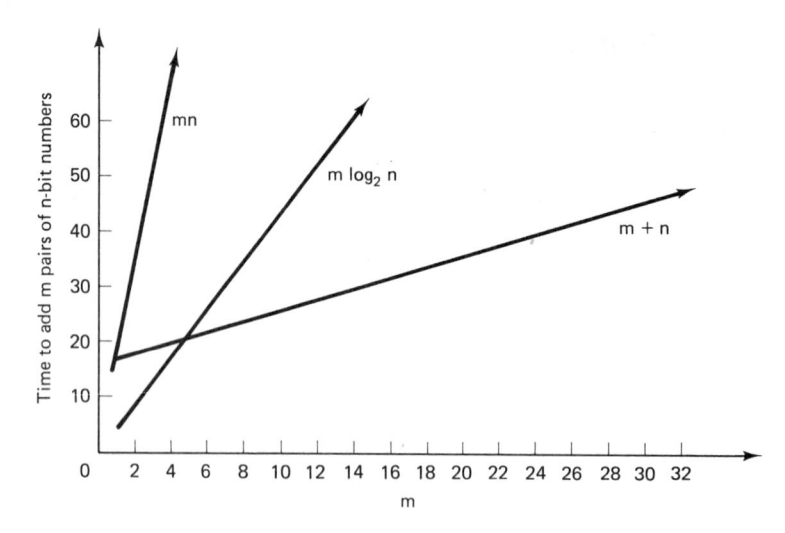

Figure 9-11 Comparison of run times of different adders

9.6 GENERAL PIPELINING PRINCIPLES

Reservation Tables

So far we have considered only simple linear pipelines as depicted in Figure 9-4. Very often, however, a pipeline has feedback and feedforward connections, as shown in Figure 9-12. For simplicity, the pipeline is drawn without the latches, although they are assumed present between all stages. A connection from one stage to an earlier stage is called a **feedback** connection, and a connection from one stage to a later stage is called a **feedforward** connection.

When dealing with a general pipeline, the order in which the stages are processed must be specified. To characterize the interconnection structure and data flow of a general pipeline, a **reservation table** is used. The table shows how the stages are successively processed for a specific function evaluation. Its rows correspond to the stages of the pipeline, and its columns represent successive clock delays. Figure 9-13 shows examples of two reservation tables representing two separate functions that could be evaluated by the pipeline of Figure 9-12. The reservation table of Figure 9-13(a) shows that the evaluation of the function requires the data to progress through the stages in the pipeline in the order $S_1, S_2, S_3, S_2, S_3, S_4$. The **evaluation time** for this function is 6 clock delays, which is the total number of time units in the reservation table. The order of the stages for the evaluation of the function of Figure 9-13(b) is S_1, S_2, S_4. Although this function uses the same pipeline as the function in part (a), its evaluation time is only 3 clock delays.

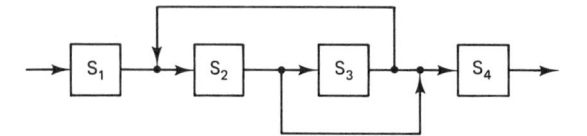

Figure 9-12 General pipeline with feedback and feedforward

Sec. 9.6   General Pipelining Principles   243

	t_0	t_1	t_2	t_3	t_4	t_5
S_1	X					
S_2		X	X			
S_3			X	X		
S_4						X

(a) 6 time unit function

	t_0	t_1	t_2
S_1	X		
S_2		X	
S_3			
S_4			X

(b) 3 time unit function

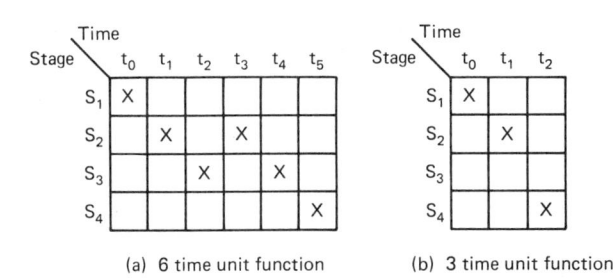

Figure 9–13   Reservation tables for the pipeline of Figure 9–12

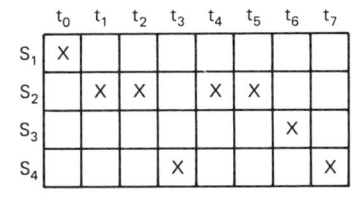

	t_0	t_1	t_2	t_3	t_4	t_5	t_6	t_7
S_1	X							
S_2		X	X		X	X		
S_3						X		
S_4				X				X

Figure 9–14   Reservation table with multiple clock delay stage

When a reservation table has more than one mark in a particular row, as shown in Figure 9–14, it means that the stage represented by that row is used more than once for the evaluation of the function. If two consecutive columns have marks in the same row, it means that the stage in question takes more clock delays than the others to process. The number of clock delays necessary for the stage is the number of consecutive marks in the row. Whenever this stage is entered in the evaluation of the function, it will take this same number of clock delays. Stage S_2 of Figure 9–14 is an example of a multiple clock delay stage.

When a reservation table has more than one mark in a column, it means that two or more stages are simultaneously processing data for the same function evaluation. Part (a) of Figure 9–15 gives an example of such a table, and part (b) shows a possible hardware implementation. Notice that this is different from the general simultaneous use of stages by different sets of inputs. The marks in the third column of Figure 9–15(a) represent the concurrent processing of the output from stage S_2, so one set of inputs will be processed by two different stages at the same time.

The hardware implementation of a reservation table is not necessarily unique. For example, the reservation table of Figure 9–14 can be implemented by either of

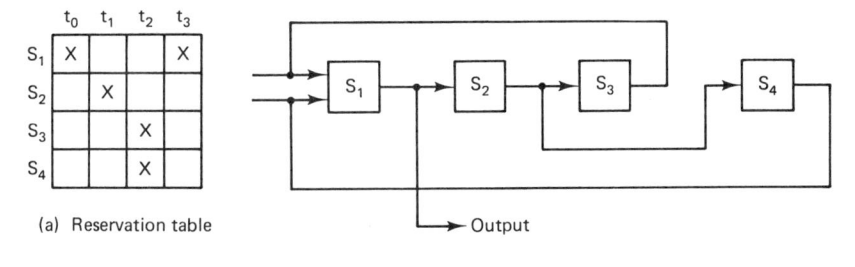

	t_0	t_1	t_2	t_3
S_1	X			X
S_2		X		
S_3			X	
S_4			X	

(a) Reservation table

(b) Hardware implementation

Figure 9–15   Pipeline with concurrent state processing

the pipelines of Figure 9–16. The circles in the figures represent multiplexers. The implementation that is actually used depends on such considerations as cost, availability of existing pipes to facilitate a new function, and need to generalize the system.

An implementation that can be configured to implement more than one function is called a **multifunction pipeline.** With a multifunction pipeline, it is necessary to include control and sequencing hardware that can be set to correspond to the reservation

(a) 4 latch implementation

(b) 9 latch implementation

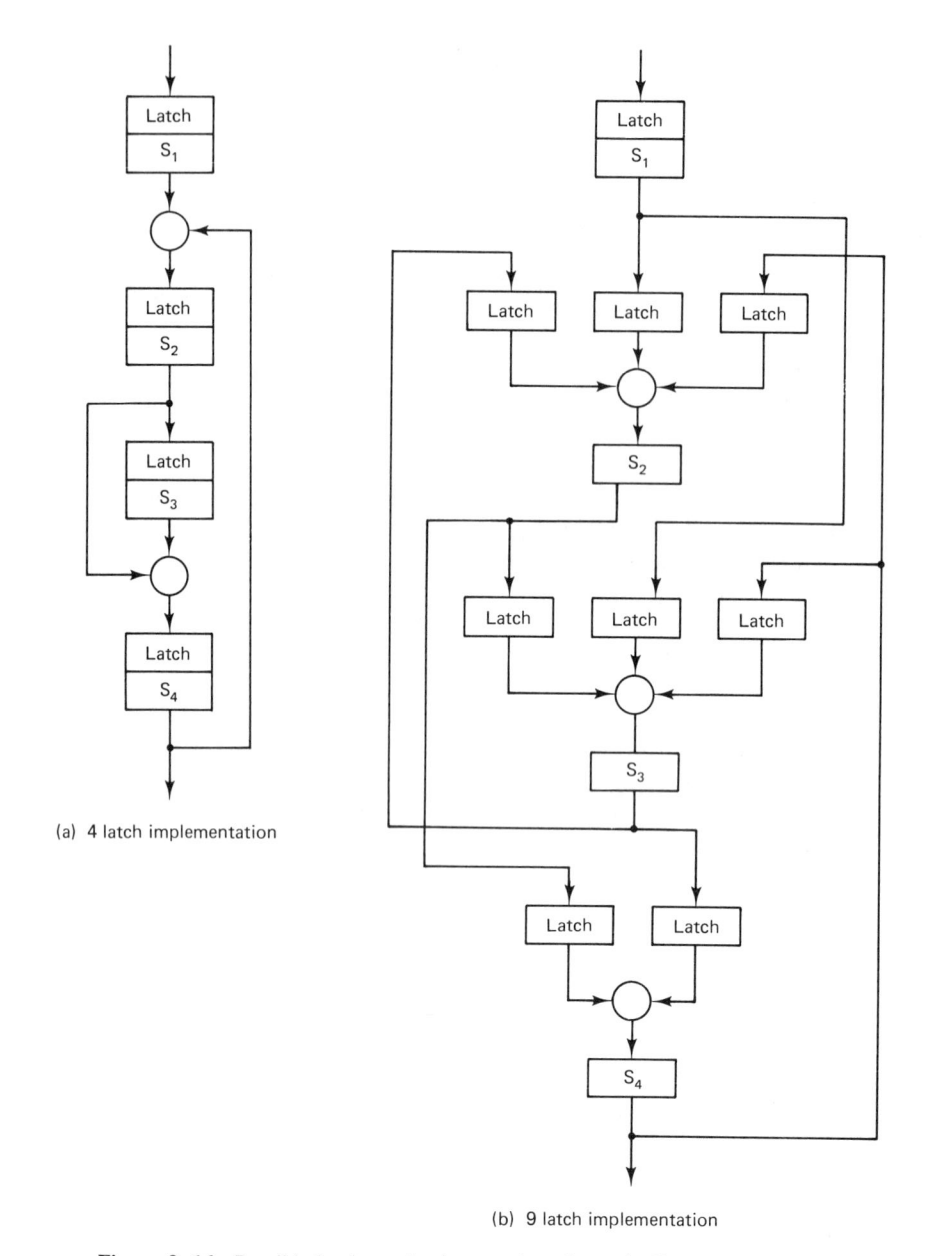

Figure 9–16 Possible hardware implementations for a pipeline corresponding to the reservation table of Figure 9–14

Sec. 9.6 General Pipelining Principles

	t_0	t_1	t_2	t_3	t_4
S_1	A				
S_2					
S_3		A		A	
S_4			A		A

(a) 5 time unit function A

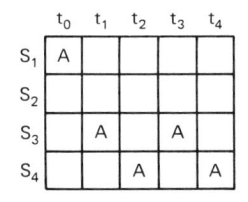

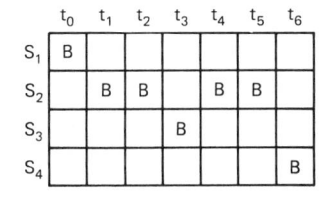

	t_0	t_1	t_2	t_3	t_4	t_5	t_6
S_1	B						
S_2			B	B		B	B
S_3					B		
S_4							B

(b) 7 time unit function B

Figure 9–17 Multifunctions for a pipeline

table of each function. For example, Figure 9–17 shows reservation tables for two different function evaluations by the pipeline of Figure 9–16(b). When a reservation table shows the functions of a multifunction pipeline, the name of the function is used as the mark in the table instead of just an X. For function A, the output from S_1 must be directed to S_3, whereas for function B, the output from S_1 must go to S_2. The multiplexers that are set depend on the function being evaluated.

Scheduling and Collision Prevention

An **initiation** of a reservation table corresponds to the start of a single function evaluation (task) that will follow the path designated by the table. When an initiation is made, the **pipeline controller** must reserve the appropriate stages of the pipeline for the data of this initiation at the relative times defined by the reservation table. If the data of two separate initiations were to enter the same stage at the same time, a **collision** would occur. Since one stage cannot compute two separate results simultaneously, collisions must be prevented by the pipeline controller.

Example 9.3

Consider the reservation table shown in Figure 9–18(a). The space-time diagram of Figure 9–18(b) represents two collision-free initiations, one at t_0 and one at t_1. The

	t_0	t_1	t_2	t_3	t_4	t_5
S_1	X			X		X
S_2		X			X	
S_3			X			

(a) Reservation table

(b) Collision-free initiations

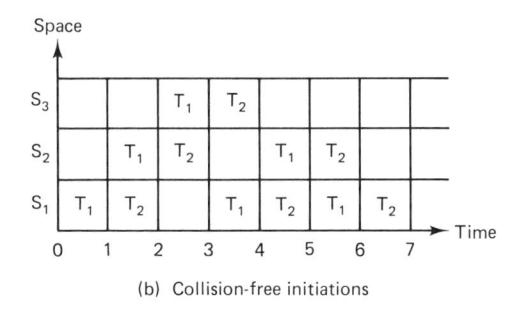

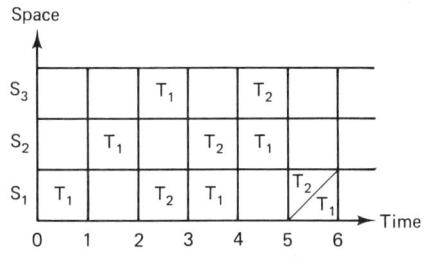

(c) Initiation resulting in a collision

Figure 9–18 Initiations for a pipeline

space-time diagram of Figure 9–18(c) shows two initiations, at t_0 and t_2, that result in a collision at t_5.

We shall present a method for determining an efficient **scheduling algorithm** that can be implemented by the pipeline controller to prevent collisions.

The number of time units between two initiations in a pipeline is called the **latency**. A sequence of latencies between successive initiations is called a **latency sequence**. When a latency sequence repeats itself, it is called a **latency cycle**. In a static, linear pipeline with no feedback or feedforward connections, as in Figure 9–4, a simple latency cycle of {1} will provide the optimal throughput of the pipeline. This means that a new initiation (as long as input remains) is started every clock delay. For the pipeline represented in Figure 9–18(a), however, a latency cycle of {1} cannot be used. If it is used, the first and second initiations would start out without any problem, but the third initiation would result in a collision at time t_5, as shown in Figure 9–19(a). A latency cycle of {1, 6}, however, would work fine for this pipeline as shown in Figure 9–19(b). In this case, the second initiation starts 1 clock delay after the first, but the third initiation does not start until 6 clock delays after the second. The cycle repeats itself so that the fourth initiation starts 1 clock delay after the third, the fifth starts 6 clock delays after the fourth, and so on.

For a pipeline-scheduling algorithm, we are interested in latency cycles that are collision-free for a continuous stream of initiations. That is, we want a latency cycle that will *never* result in a collision between any initiations currently in the pipe. One possible latency cycle that will always work is the simple cycle {n}, where n is the total number of time units in the reservation table. This, of course, reduces the pipeline's efficiency to zero over the use of a nonpipelined implementation and is very undesirable.

To determine the scheduling algorithm, we start off by generating all possible latency cycles that are collision-free. This set of cycles is based on the **forbidden set of latencies, F,** for the pipeline that contains all the possible latencies that cause collisions between two *successive* initiations. For two successive initiations, a collision will occur when the latency between them is equal to the column distance between any two X's on the same row of the reservation table.

Example 9.4

Looking back at Figure 9–18(a), the X's in row 1, columns t_0 and t_3, have a column distance of 3 between them; the X's in row 1, columns t_3 and t_5, have a column distance of 2 between them; the X's in row 1, columns t_0 and t_5, have a column distance of 5 between them; and the X's in row 2, columns t_1 and t_4, have a column distance of 3 between them. Therefore, the forbidden latency set, F, is {2, 3, 5}. As can be seen in Figure 9–18(c), the latency between the first and second initiations is 2. Since 2 is within F, there is a collision.

The **collision vector, C,** is a binary vector representation of the forbidden set of latencies. It has n bits such that starting from the least significant bit, the ith bit is 1 if i is a forbidden latency and 0 otherwise; namely,

$$C = (c_n \ldots c_2 c_1) \tag{9.1}$$

where $c_i = 1$ if i is within F and $c_i = 0$ otherwise.

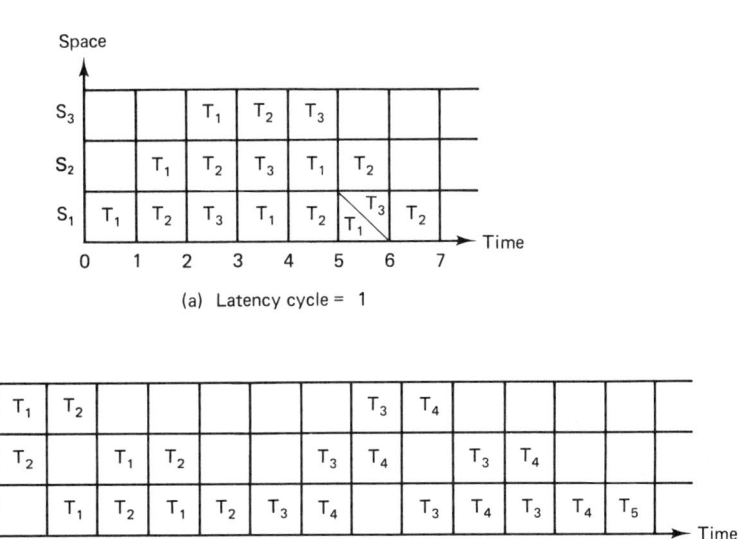

Sec. 9.6 General Pipelining Principles   247

Figure 9-19 Different latency cycles for a pipeline

(a) Latency cycle = 1

(b) Latency cycle = 1, 6

Example 9.5

For the reservation table of Figure 9-20, $F = \{2, 3, 5, 8\}$ and $C = (10010110)$. Starting with the least significant bit of C, this means that two successive initiations will not collide with each other if and only if the latency between them is 1, 4, 6, 7, or greater than or equal to 9 time units.

The collision vector, C (and the forbidden set of latencies, F), represents latencies that will cause collisions between two *successive* initiations. However, what we really want to know are the latencies that will cause collisions between *any* two initiations. To determine these latencies, observe a special property of the collision vector: The least significant bit of C represents whether or not a collision will occur between the first two consecutive initiations, that is, one right after the other. Therefore, if there is a time lapse between these two initiations (in time units), the collision vector can be shifted to the right by this number of time units in order to continue to represent

	t_0	t_1	t_2	t_3	t_4	t_5	t_6	t_7	t_8	Forbidden latencies
S_1	X			X				X		3, 5, 8
S_2		X		X		X				2, 3, 5
S_3			X				X			5
S_4					X		X			2

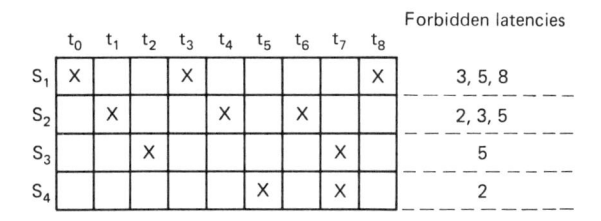

Forbidden list: $F = \{2, 3, 5, 8\}$
Collision vector: $C = (10010110)$

Figure 9-20 F and C for a reservation table

the forbidden latencies. The shifted vector then corresponds to the current position of the first initiation in the pipe with respect to the second delayed initiation.

Example 9.6

If at time t_{12}, $C = (1100101)$ and no initiations occur for two time units, then at time t_{14}, $C = (0011001)$.

Based on this property, the following procedure is used to determine the forbidden latencies for all new initiations, considering all previous initiations.

Let S be a parallel-load, shift-right register (see Section 3.7) with serial input (to the leftmost flip-flop stage) and serial output (from the rightmost flip-flop stage). The serial input is permanently connected to 0; each time that S is shifted to the right, the 0 will propagate to the next stage. Assume that S stores the current collision vector of a pipeline. Then, given some value in S, an initiation of a new task can occur at time $t + k$ only if, after shifting the S register k times, its output is 0. If the output is 1, a collision would occur, and the new task must not be initiated. On the first input to the pipe, the initial collision vector is stored in S. When a new initiation occurs at time $t + k$, the original collision vector still represents possible collisions between this initiation and successive initiations, but it does not represent possible collisions between initiations already in the pipe and successive initiations. To determine all the current forbidden latencies, the original collision vector must be bitwise ORed with the shifted collision vector, S. The resulting vector now represents the latencies for successive initiations that will or will not result in collisions. Storing this vector in the S register corresponds to saving the current state of the system.

Example 9.7

Let $C_I = (10010110)$ be the initial collision vector of the pipeline represented by Figure 9–20. Therefore, S currently stores C_I. Assume that a new initiation occurs after 4 time units. This is possible since after four shifts, S is (00001001) and its last output is 0. Bitwise ORing S with C_I gives (10011111), which becomes the new value of S. Based on this value of S, a new initiation cannot occur in the next time unit. If it did, it would not collide with its immediate predecessor, but it would collide with the initiation before that one. This was the case exemplified in Figure 9–19(a).

A **state diagram** (see Section 3.5) can be derived to characterize the successive initiations of tasks in a pipeline. Figure 9–21 shows the state diagram for the pipeline of Figure 9–20. The initial state corresponds to the initial collision vector. The other states represent collision vectors after some sequence of latencies for initiations. The states are generated by the procedure just given. Each of the transition arrows represents allowable latencies for next initiations from one state to another. The notation 9^+ in the state diagram means any latency greater than or equal to 9. Example 9.7 explains the transition labeled 4 from the initial state.

The state diagram represents, in compact form, all possible initiation sequences for a pipeline. The main objective of the scheduling algorithm is to use the sequence that will provide the *highest throughput*. The key to such an efficient scheduling algorithm is based on the analysis of cycles in the state diagram that correspond to the latency cycles mentioned earlier. A **cycle** consists of an ordered set of states and

Sec. 9.6 General Pipelining Principles

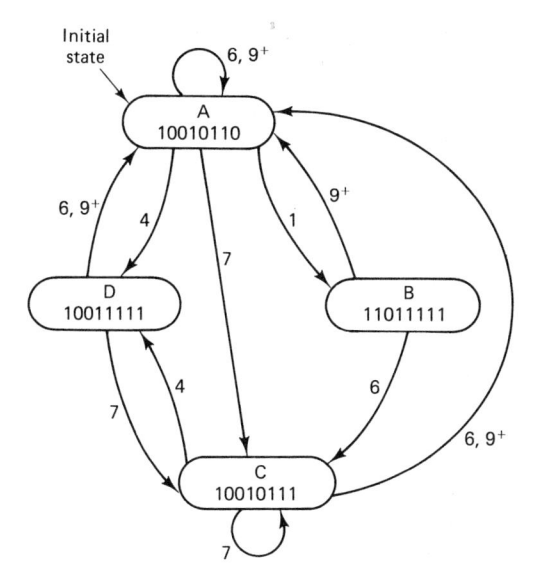

Figure 9–21 State diagram for the pipeline of Figure 9–20

their transition latencies such that from any state in the cycle, the cyclic sequence of transitions leads through the other states in the cycle and back to the starting state. The notation for cycles can be either the state labels in order or the transitions in order. If a cycle consists of nonrepeating states, it is called a **simple cycle.**

Example 9.8

In the state diagram of Figure 9–21, the ordered set $\{A, C, D\}$ forms a cycle. Starting in state A, transition 7 can be followed to state C, transition 4 can be followed to state D, and then transition 6 or 9^+ can be followed back to state A. This cycle is simple and can also be represented as $\{7, 4, 6\}$.

Note that since the states and their transitions in a particular order form the cycle, the same states may form a different cycle in a different order. For any cycle, the average latency is computed as the total latencies in the cycle over the number of states in the cycle. For example, the average latency of the cycle of states A, D, and C in Figure 9–21 is $(4 + 7 + 6)/3 = 5.667$. Notice that a cycle does not have to start with the initial state. In Figure 9–21, there is a cycle between states D and C whose average latency is $(7 + 4)/2 = 5.5$. To optimize the control strategy of the pipeline, the best latency cycle to use is the one with the **minimum average latency (MAL).** Table 9.1 shows all the simple cycles for the state diagram of Figure 9–21. The MAL for this pipeline is 4.25 time units.

Although true for the state diagram of Figure 9–21, taking the shortest latency path from each state, known as the **greedy cycle,** is not always the optimum cycle. Consider, for example, the reservation table in Figure 9–22(a). As can be seen in the state diagram of Figure 9–22(b) and the associated table of Figure 9–22(c), the cycle $\{4\}$ has a lower average latency than the greedy cycle $\{3, 8\}$. Therefore, it is more efficient in the long run to wait for the fourth latency before making the second initiation than to start it on the third latency.

TABLE 9.1 SIMPLE LATENCY CYCLES FOR THE PIPELINE OF FIGURE 9–21

Simple Cycle	Average Latency
A	6.0
A-B	5.0
A-B-C	4.33
A-B-C-D*	4.25†
A-C	6.5
A-C-D	5.667
A-D	5.0
A-D-C	5.667
C	7.0
C-D	5.5

* Greedy cycle.
† Minimum average latency.

The scheduling method presented for unifunction pipelines can be generalized to designing scheduling algorithms for multifunction pipelines. In this case, successive initiations of different functions, as well as of the same function, must be included in the state diagram. For example, in a multifunction pipeline for two functions, A and B, the latency sequences must incorporate the possibility of an initiation of function A followed by an initiation of function A, an initiation of A followed by an initiation of B, an initiation of B followed by an initiation of B, and an initiation of B followed

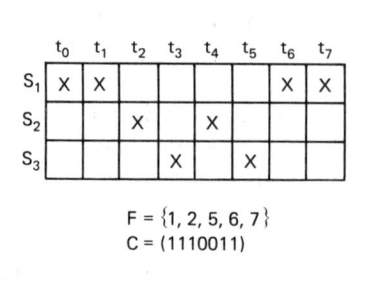

(a) Reservation table

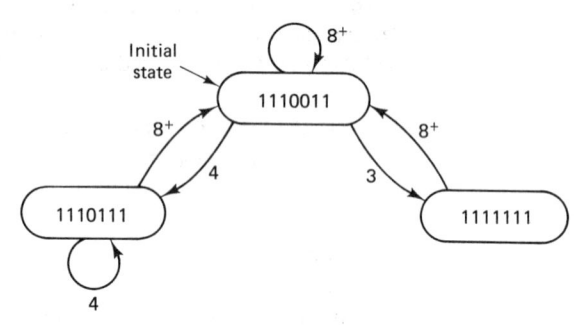

$F = \{1, 2, 5, 6, 7\}$
$C = (1110011)$

(b) State diagram

Simple Cycles	Average Latency
3, 8*	5.5
8	8
4	4†
4, 8	6

* Greedy cycle
† MAL

(c) Simple latency cycles

Figure 9–22 Pipeline in which greedy cycle does not have MAL

Sec. 9.6 General Pipelining Principles

by an initiation of A. Once the state diagram is derived, however, it becomes straightforward for the pipeline controller to ensure the desired latency cycle.

Delay Insertion for Optimum Throughput

The number of stages in a pipeline does not affect the throughput of the pipeline outside of the initial startup time. If the pipeline is a basic linear pipeline and the input is continuous, then after the initial startup, the throughput will be one result every clock delay regardless of the number of stages. In this case, the latency cycle being used is {1}. In general, we can describe the maximum possible throughput of a pipeline (after startup) as the reciprocal of the minimum average latency time:

$$\text{max throughput} = 1/\text{MAL} \qquad (9.2)$$

In some cases, it is possible to decrease the MAL by adding **noncompute delay** stages to the pipeline. Although this increases the number of stages in the pipeline, the actual throughput is better. A noncompute delay stage does not change the values of its inputs but merely stores the inputs for one clock delay. Figure 9–23 shows an example, first presented by Patel and Davidson (1976), of a reservation table whose MAL is reduced by inserting noncompute delay stages. After determining where to insert the delays, as in Figure 9–23(b), a stage is set up for each delay necessary.

	t_0	t_1	t_2	t_3	t_4	t_5
S_1	X		X			X
S_2	X	X		X		
S_3			X	X		

F = {1, 2, 3, 5}
C = (10111)

(a) Reservation table

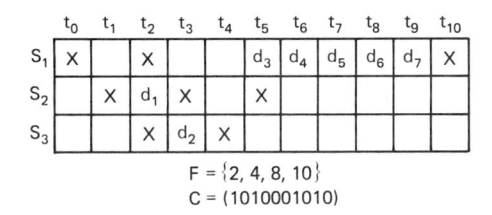

	t_0	t_1	t_2	t_3	t_4	t_5	t_6	t_7	t_8	t_9	t_{10}
S_1	X		X			d_3	d_4	d_5	d_6	d_7	X
S_2		X	d_1	X		X					
S_3			X	d_2	X						

F = {2, 4, 8, 10}
C = (1010001010)

(b) Reservation table with inserted delays

	t_0	t_1	t_2	t_3	t_4	t_5	t_6	t_7	t_8	t_9	t_{10}
S_1	X		X								X
S_2		X		X		X					
S_3			X	X							
d_1			X								
d_2				X							
d_3						X					
d_4							X				
d_5								X			
d_6									X		
d_7										X	

(c) Resulting new pipeline representation

Figure 9–23 Improved MAL with insertion of noncompute delays

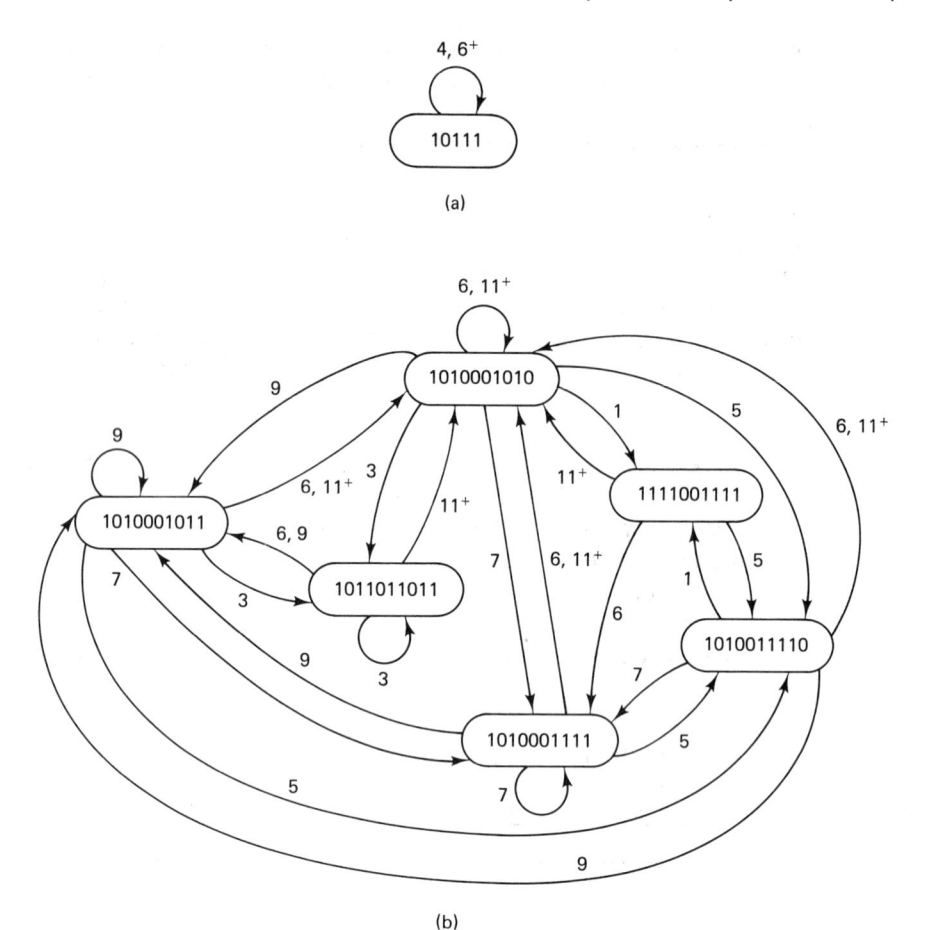

Figure 9-24 State diagrams for pipelines of Figure 9-23

Since a separate stage is used for each delay, no new forbidden latencies are introduced because of the new stages. The resulting new pipeline is represented in Figure 9-23(c). The state diagrams of Figure 9-24 show that the MAL for the pipeline has been reduced from 4 clock delays in Figure 9-24(a), which corresponds to Figure 9-23(a), to 3 clock delays in Figure 9-24(b), which corresponds to Figure 9-23(c). Each initiation will take longer in the pipe of Figure 9-23(c), but initiations can be started more often, and hence the maximum throughput can be increased from 0.25 to 0.33. The procedure used to determine where to insert the delay stages is beyond the scope of this book but can be found in Kogge (1981).

9.7 MULTIFUNCTION PIPELINE EXAMPLE

The Control Data Corporation (CDC) CYBER 205 is a highly pipelined computer. Among its arithmetic pipelines is the floating-point multiply pipeline. This is a mul-

Sec. 9.7 Multifunction Pipeline Example

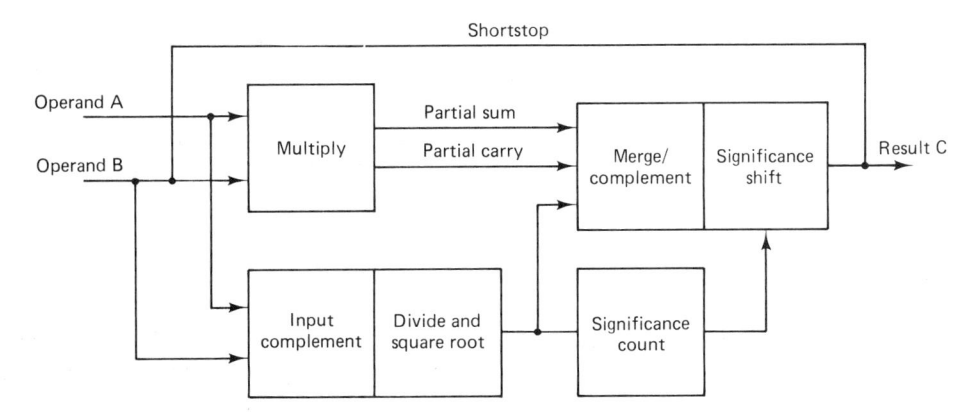

Figure 9-25 Floating-point multiply pipeline of the CYBER 205 (Courtesy of Control Data Corporation)

tifunction pipeline that performs multiplication, division, and square-root operations. The configuration of the pipeline is shown in Figure 9-25.

If operands A and B are to be multiplied, they first pass through the *multiply* stage, which generates the product of the mantissas. The *merge/complement* stage then adds the exponents. Finally, the resulting floating-point number is normalized in the *significance shift* stage.

Both division and square-root operations require the subtraction of one operand's mantissa from the other's (see the division algorithm of Section 2.3). To facilitate this, the appropriate operand is complemented in the *input complement* stage before the mantissas are divided or the square root is taken in the *divide and square root* stage. At this point, if the operation is division, the exponents are subtracted in the *merge/complement* stage and the result is normalized in the *significance shift* stage. But if the operation is that of taking the square root, only a single exponent is involved. Instead of passing through the *merge/complement* stage, the square root of the mantissa passes through the *significance count* stage. The result is then normalized, as in the other operations, in the *significance shift* stage. Figure 9-26 shows the reservation tables for these three functions.

(a) Multiply

	t_0	t_1	t_2
Multiply	M		
Input complement			
Divide and square root			
Merge/complement		M	
Significance count			
Significance shift			M

(b) Divide

	t_0	t_1	t_2	t_3
Multiply				
Input complement	D			
Divide and square root		D		
Merge/complement			D	
Significance count				
Significance shift				D

(c) Square-root

	t_0	t_1	t_2	t_3
Multiply				
Input complement	S			
Divide and square root		S		
Merge/complement				
Significance count			S	
Significance shift				S

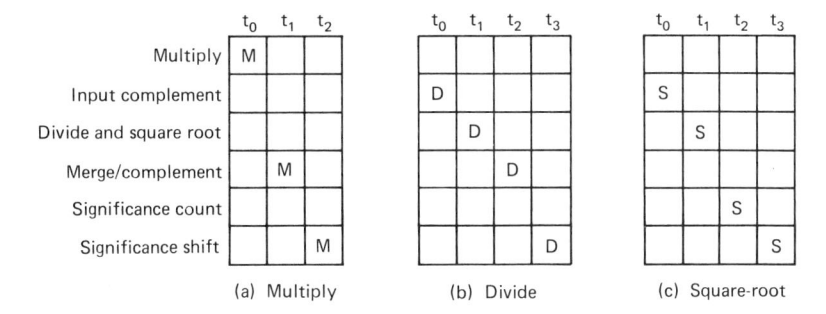

Figure 9-26 Reservation tables for the pipeline of Figure 9-25 (M = multiply, D = divide, S = square-root)

The CYBER 205 has a special *Shortstop* feedback connection, also shown in Figure 9–25. This allows the result from any function to be routed directly to the input of the other functions without having to be stored in some intermediate register first. This greatly enhances the speed of the computer when processing vector instructions such as finding the product of all the elements of a vector.

9.8 RECURRENCE PROBLEM PIPELINE

The block diagram of Figure 9–27 shows a special kind of *pipeline with feedback*. In this case, the ith output, z_i, is a function of the ith input, x_i, and m previous outputs, $z_{i-1}, z_{i-2}, \ldots, z_{i-m}$; that is:

$$z_i = f(x_i, z_{i-1}, z_{i-2}, \ldots, z_{i-m}) \qquad \text{for every } i \qquad (9.3)$$

This equation is called a **recurrence equation.** Problems associated with the pipeline described by Equation (9.3) are referred to as **recurrences.** In trying to build a pipeline with a recurrence, the potential for destroying the efficiency of the pipeline is great.

Example 9.9

Consider the pipeline of Figure 9–28(a), which contains three stages. After the initial startup time of 3 clock delays, a z_i is output on every clock delay as long as the x_i's are continuously input into the pipeline, as in Figure 9–28(b). If the pipeline is modified as in Figure 9–28(c), only one z_i is output every 3 clock delays, as in Figure 9–28(d).

As shown by Example 9.9, including the previous outputs in the inputs of the pipeline has eliminated any benefits of the pipeline. Although x_2 is available at time t_2, it cannot pass through the pipe until z_1 is available at time t_4. However, as it turns out, many kinds of recurrence problems can be rewritten as

$$z_i = f(g, z_j, z_{j-1}, \ldots, z_{j-m+1}) \qquad (9.4)$$

where $j = (i - \text{number of clock delays in the pipe})$ and g is a function only of the previous j inputs. In this case, the feedback can be incorporated into the pipeline as in Figure 9–29.

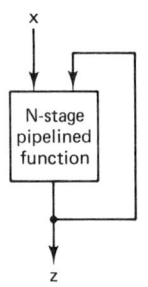

Figure 9–27 Recurrence problem

Sec. 9.8 Recurrence Problem Pipeline

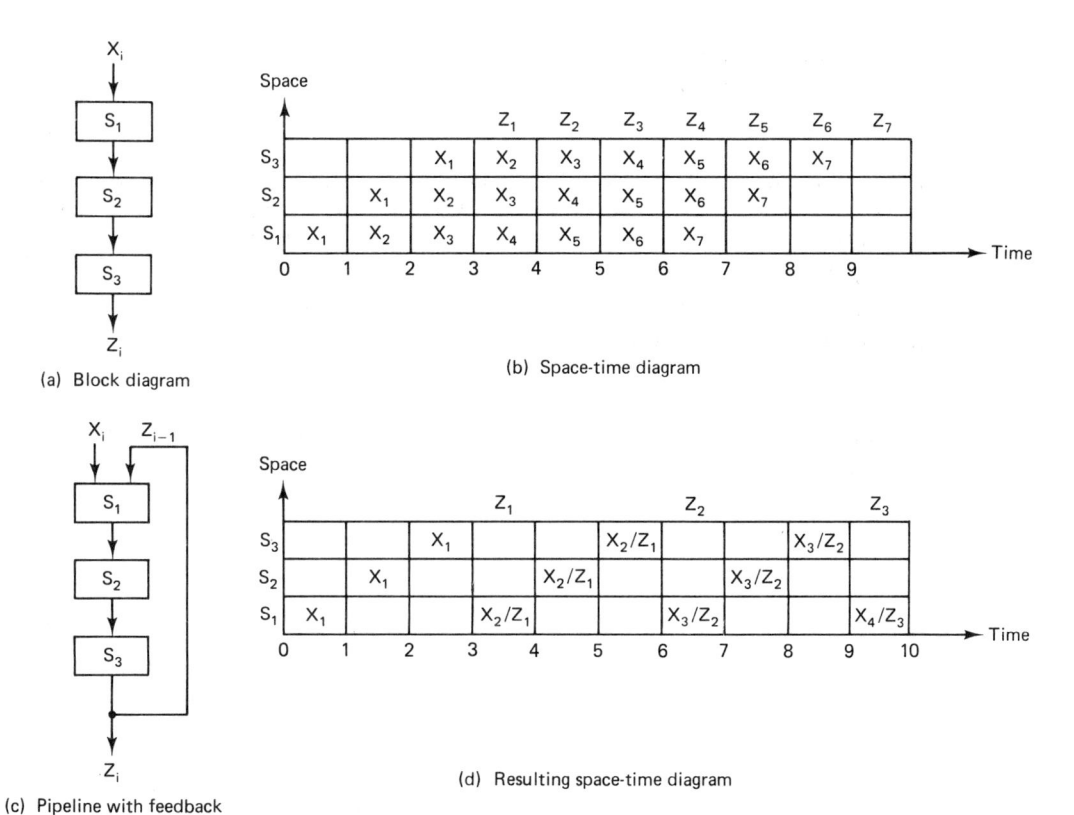

(a) Block diagram

(b) Space-time diagram

(c) Pipeline with feedback connection

(d) Resulting space-time diagram

Figure 9-28 Three-stage recurrence pipeline

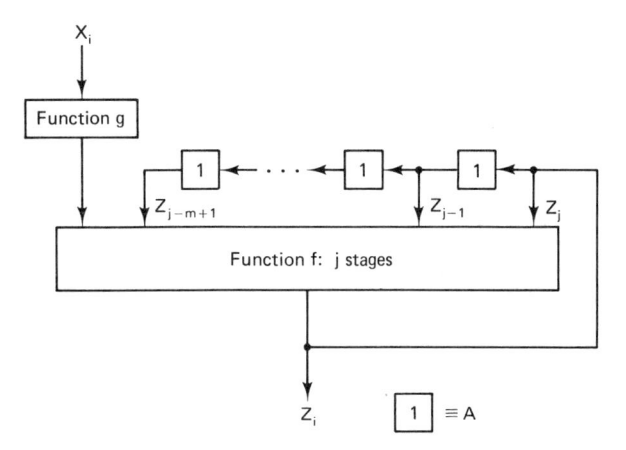

Figure 9-29 Pipeline for recurrence problem

$1 \equiv A$

Let us consider a specific recurrence problem to clarify these concepts. Assume that we want to design a pipeline to compute

$$B[I] = A[I] + B[I - 1] \qquad (9.5)$$

for two arrays A and B, where $B[0]$ is some initial value. If each element of A and B is a 4-bit number, then a 4-stage pipelined adder ADD can be used as the f function of Equation (9.4). Also, since ADD is a function of the ith A input and one of the previous B outputs, $m = 1$.

Based on the notation of Equation (9.3), let $x_i = A[I]$ and $z_i = B[I]$. Equation (9.5) can then be rewritten in terms of Equation (9.3) as

$$B[I] = \text{ADD}(A[I], B[I - 1]) \qquad (9.6)$$

Since a four-stage adder is being used for ADD, $j = i - 4$. Then, based on Equation (9.4), we can rewrite Equation (9.6) as

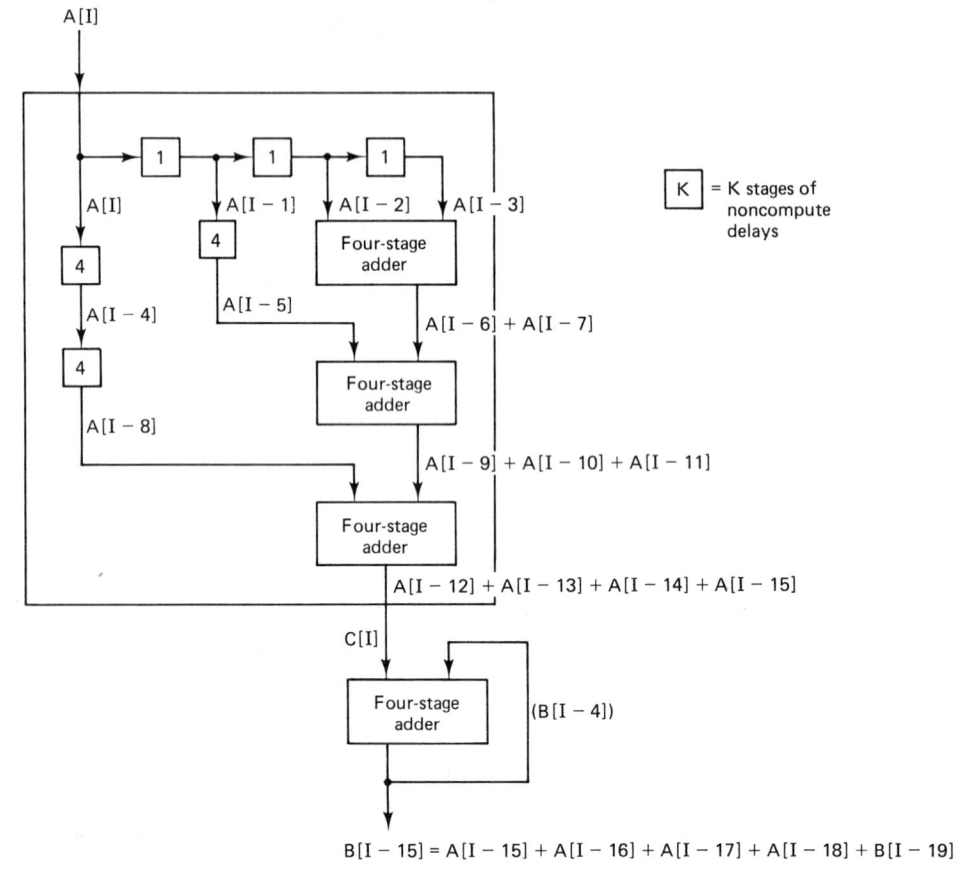

$$B[I] = \text{ADD}(C[I], B[I - 4]) \qquad (9.7)$$

Figure 9–30 Pipeline for new recurrence function

TABLE 9.2 RELATIVE COMPLEXITY OF PIPELINE CATEGORIES

Complexity (in ascending order)	Pipeline Category
1	Unifunction static scalar
2	Unifunction static vector
3	Multifunction static scalar
4	Multifunction static vector
5	Multifunction dynamic scalar
6	Multifunction dynamic vector

where $C[I] = g(A[I], A[I-1], A[I-2], A[I-3])$ and $g(w, x, y, z) = w + x + y + z$. Now $B[I]$ is equal to a function of four A terms and one $B[I-4]$ term.

Using the four-stage adder allows the new recurrence function (9.7) to be pipelined as shown in Figure 9–30. The connections in the pipeline are labeled to show the position of the A inputs relative to the ith input. Since there are no negative ith elements, the outputs are meaningless until $i = 16$. Hence the first output, $B[1]$, will not be available until $A[16]$ is being input, resulting in an initial startup time of 16 for the pipe. After the pipe is filled, however, the throughput will be 1.

9.9 SUMMARY

The concept of pipeline processing can be used in a computer to improve system throughput in a variety of ways. The three basic types of pipelining are **arithmetic, instruction,** and **processor** pipelining. The increased throughput of a system with one or more of these types of pipelining depends on the function and the cost of the pipelining. The cost of a pipeline includes the extra hardware required for latches and control mechanisms, and the nonproductive time of filling the pipeline and forcing latencies to avoid collisions.

Pipelines can be categorized on the basis of whether or not they are **unifunctional** or **multifunctional, static** or **dynamic,** and **scalar** or **vector.** In terms of implementation and scheduling, pipelines range from the very simple to the very complex. Table 9.2 lists the pipeline categories in increasing order of complexity. (Note that unifunction pipelines are never dynamic pipelines.)

PROBLEMS

1. Define the following terms relative to pipelines:
   - (a) clock delay
   - (b) initial startup time
   - (c) instruction look-ahead
   - (d) draining the pipe
   - (e) static multifunction pipeline
   - (f) stage cascading
   - (g) feedback connection
   - (h) reservation table
   - (i) collision
   - (j) latency
   - (k) MAL
   - (l) greedy cycle

2. Why are latches inserted between stages of a pipeline?
3. Consider a pipeline represented by the following reservation table.

	t_0	t_1	t_2	t_3
S_1	X			
S_2			X	
S_3				X
S_4		X		

   (a) What is the initial startup time of the pipeline?
   (b) What is the maximum throughput of the pipeline?
   (c) Show the space-time diagram of four inputs to the pipeline such that the maximum throughput is achieved.
4. Repeat Problem 3 for the following pipeline.

	t_0	t_1	t_2	t_3	t_4
S_1	X	X			
S_2					X
S_3				X	
S_4			X		

5. Why are dynamic pipelines always multifunction pipelines?
6. Consider a pipelined 4-bit parallel adder constructed by cascading stages of full adders.
   (a) Draw the configuration of this pipelined adder.
   (b) Show the progression of the following input streams through the pipeline.

A	B
1101	1011
0001	1100
0111	0101
1111	0001
0010	0110

   (c) Draw the space-time diagram for the A-B pairs of numbers.
7. Diagram two different pipelines that could be defined by the following reservation table.

	t_0	t_1	t_2	t_3	t_4	t_5
S_1	X				X	
S_2		X	X			
S_3			X			
S_4				X		
S_5						X

8. Consider the following pipeline.

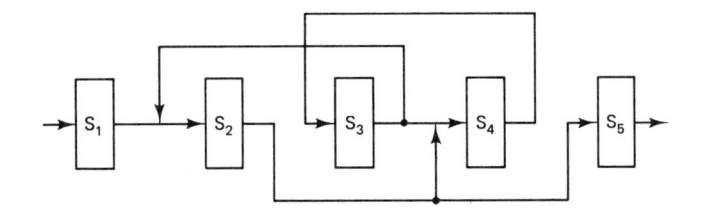

   (a) Show two different reservation tables that could be set up.
   (b) Give the evaluation time for each of the tables of part (a).
9. Using a space time-diagram for the following pipeline, show two successive initiations whose latency is < 5, and that (a) move through the pipe without a collision and (b) result in a collision.

	t_0	t_1	t_2	t_3	t_4
S_1	X		X		
S_2		X			X
S_3				X	
S_4					X

10. Based on the pipeline of Figure 9–18(a), mark whether or not the following latency cycles would be collision-free or not. Show space-time diagrams to support your answers.
    (a) {6}   (d) {1, 3}
    (b) {4}   (e) {6, 1}
    (c) {1, 6, 4} (f) {0}
11. Consider the pipeline represented by the reservation table of Problem 7.
    (a) What are the forbidden sets of latencies for this pipeline?
    (b) What is the collision vector of this pipeline?
    (c) Give the state diagram that characterizes the successive initiations of the pipeline.
    (d) List the simple cycles and their corresponding average latencies for the pipeline.
    (e) Which cycle gives the MAL for this pipeline?
    (f) What is the maximum throughput of the pipeline?
12. Repeat Problem 11 for the following pipeline.

	t_0	t_1	t_2	t_3	t_4
S_1			X	X	
S_2		X		X	X
S_3	X				
S_4		X			

CHAPTER 10

Parallel Processing

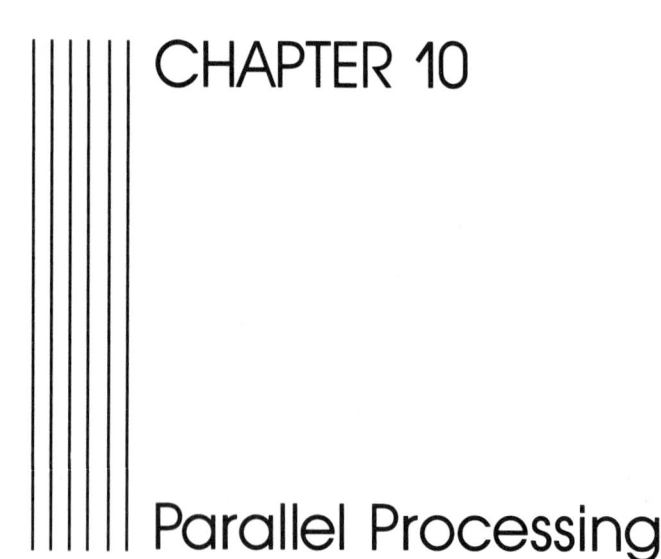

10.1 NEED FOR PARALLEL PROCESSING

Many recent advances in computer architecture are based on the concept of parallel processing. **Parallel processing** in a computer can be defined as the concurrent execution of instructions. This can be in the form of events occurring (1) during the same time interval, (2) at the same instant, or (3) in overlapped time spans, as shown in Figure 10-1. How this parallelism is actually implemented in computers is the subject of this chapter.

Fast and efficient computers are in high demand in many areas today. Many involve the numeric simulation of continuous fields. Such problems are computationally intensive and can be found in such disciplines as oceanography, astrophysics, seismology, meteorology, and atomic, nuclear, and plasma physics. The amount of "number crunching" in terms of both volume of data and number of computations, is extremely large. For example, one type of seismic exploration involves the generation of a sonic wave in the ground. The echoes from this wave are picked up by

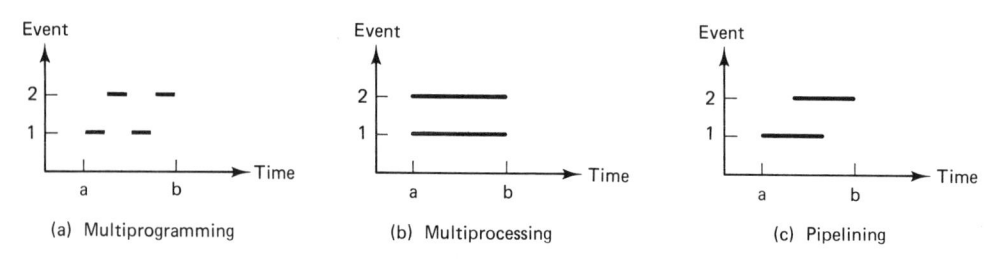

Figure 10-1 Concurrent execution of events

Sec. 10.1 Need for Parallel Processing

a few thousand geophones in the area. This data is then used to construct two-dimensional geometric cross sections of the underground strata. Typically, 3000 different time values, each from about 48 different locations, are recorded for each sonic wave. This produces between 5 and 8 million floating-point numbers per mile along a survey line.

As a result of the mathematics involved in the computer simulations of continuous fields, the computation process can be divided into a number of independent paths that can go on concurrently. Thus computers capable of parallel processing, which can exploit this inherent parallelism in simulations, are very desirable. Other areas that benefit from the use of parallel processing computers include artificial intelligence, genetic engineering, finite-element analysis for structural designs and wind tunnel experiments for aerodynamic studies, and design of electronic LSI and VLSI circuits.

10.2 PARALLEL PROCESSING TECHNIQUES

Except for those in Chapter 9, the computers studied so far have an overall architecture that can be described as **serial.** As described in Section 5.1, a serial computer consists of a main memory unit for storing data and instructions, a CPU for interpreting and executing the instructions, and I/O devices. Each operation of the computer, from the initial fetch of an instruction to its execution to storing or writing out the result, is usually performed sequentially, that is, one after the other. A **parallel** computer has the ability to overlap or perform many of these operations simultaneously.

A number of ways have been developed to introduce parallelism into the architecture of serial computers. Among them are the following:

1. *Pipelining.* As described in Chapter 9, pipelining can be considered parallelism as in Figure 10–1(c).
2. *Multiple functional units.* Rather than have one ALU in a CPU that performs all the arithmetic and logic functions, it is possible to build separate units for separate functions. It is also possible to have more than one unit for performing a particular function. Both approaches allow parallel computations to take place.
3. *Overlapping CPU and I/O operations.* In early computers, the CPU was responsible for directing all I/O operations and for executing the program instructions in memory. Having a special-purpose I/O processor (see Section 6.5) that handles all I/O operations allows the execution of other programs' instructions to proceed at the same time.
4. *Memory interleaving.* As described in Section 7.3, memory interleaving allows more than one word to be fetched from memory at a time. In conjunction with some of the other parallel techniques, this can be used to provide instructions and data at a very fast rate.
5. *Multiprogramming.* From the point of view of the computer system, multiprogramming is the type of parallelism shown in Figure 10–1(a). In this case, the events are programs that are executed sequentially in the same time interval.

6. *Multiprocessing*. Instead of having one CPU in a system, many processors working together on the same problem result in the parallelism of Figure 10–1(b) (see also Section 6.5). In this case, the events can be parts of a single program or completely separate programs. Unless the programs are written in a concurrent language, however, the former is difficult.

The architectures discussed in this chapter make use of these methods, both individually and in combinations, to effect parallelism in a computer.

10.3 SPEEDUP OF PARALLEL COMPUTERS

Consider a parallel computer with n identical processors working concurrently on a single problem. At first it seems that the problem can be solved n times faster than if a single processor system were used. Unfortunately, this is not the case. Because of reasons such as conflicts over memory access, conflicts over communication paths, and inefficient algorithms for actually implementing the concurrency of the problem, the **speedup** is much less than n.

A lower-bound estimate for the actual speedup, known as Minsky's conjecture, is $\log_2 n$. As for the upper bound, it depends on whether or not the entire program, including the I/O portion (usually sequential code), is considered. If so, $n/\ln n$ is considered to be a general upper bound (Hwang and Briggs, 1984). Table 10.1 gives some estimates of the speedup of an n-processor system for both the upper and lower bounds.

As a result of these bounds, it can be seen that adding more processors is not necessarily the best way to make a computer faster. For each added processor, there is less and less speedup and more and more complexity in managing all the processors. For this reason, efforts are made to exploit concurrency in algorithms, thereby making a better use of a small number of fast processors, rather than depending on a large number of ultimately slower processors, for program speedup. Much research is also being done to resolve some of the conflicts resulting from multiple processors in a system, which should increase the lower and upper bounds for speedup.

TABLE 10.1 ESTIMATES OF UPPER AND LOWER BOUNDS FOR SPEEDUP

Number of processors	Lower bound ($\log_2 n$)	Upper bound ($n/\ln n$)
2	1	2.89
4	2	2.89
8	3	3.85
16	4	5.77
32	5	9.23

10.4 CLASSIFICATION OF PARALLEL COMPUTER ARCHITECTURES

Parallelism in a computer can be applied at several levels, as follows:

1. *Job level*: between jobs or phases of jobs. This is the underlying principle of multiprogramming.
2. *Procedure level*: between procedures and within loops. This must be included as a feature of the language.
3. *Instruction level*: between phases of an instruction cycle, that is, fetch, decode, and execution of the instruction.
4. *Arithmetic and bit level*: between bits within arithmetic circuits. An example is the parallel adder.

Parallelism on the arithmetic and bit level is fairly standard in computers today. The current emphasis is on implementing parallelism on the other three levels. Although some implementations are done with software, we will concentrate in this chapter on hardware implementations.

There have been many attempts at classifying the designs of parallel computer architectures. None adequately separates all the designs into distinct groups. The most common classification scheme is Flynn's taxonomy. We shall discuss this scheme and two others: Shore's and Feng's.

Flynn's Classification

Michael J. Flynn (1966) introduced a scheme for classifying the architecture of a computer on the basis of how the machine relates its instructions to the data being processed. He defined a **stream** as a sequence of items, either instructions or data, executed or operated on by a processor. His classifications are as follows:

1. *SISD*: single instruction stream, single data stream
2. *SIMD*: single instruction stream, multiple data stream
3. *MISD*: multiple instruction stream, single data stream
4. *MIMD*: multiple instruction stream, multiple data stream

These organizations, shown in Figure 10–2, will be described in some detail.

SISD. An SISD computer [Figure 10–2(a)] is the conventional serial computer that was mentioned in Section 10.1, in which the instructions are executed one by one and a single instruction deals with at most one data operation. It is possible to use pipelining to speed up the processing, and most SISD computers are pipelined to some extent. The important SISD characteristic is the sequential execution of the instruction.

SIMD. In an SIMD computer [Figure 10–2(b)], a single instruction may initiate a large number of operations. These **vector instructions,** as they are called,

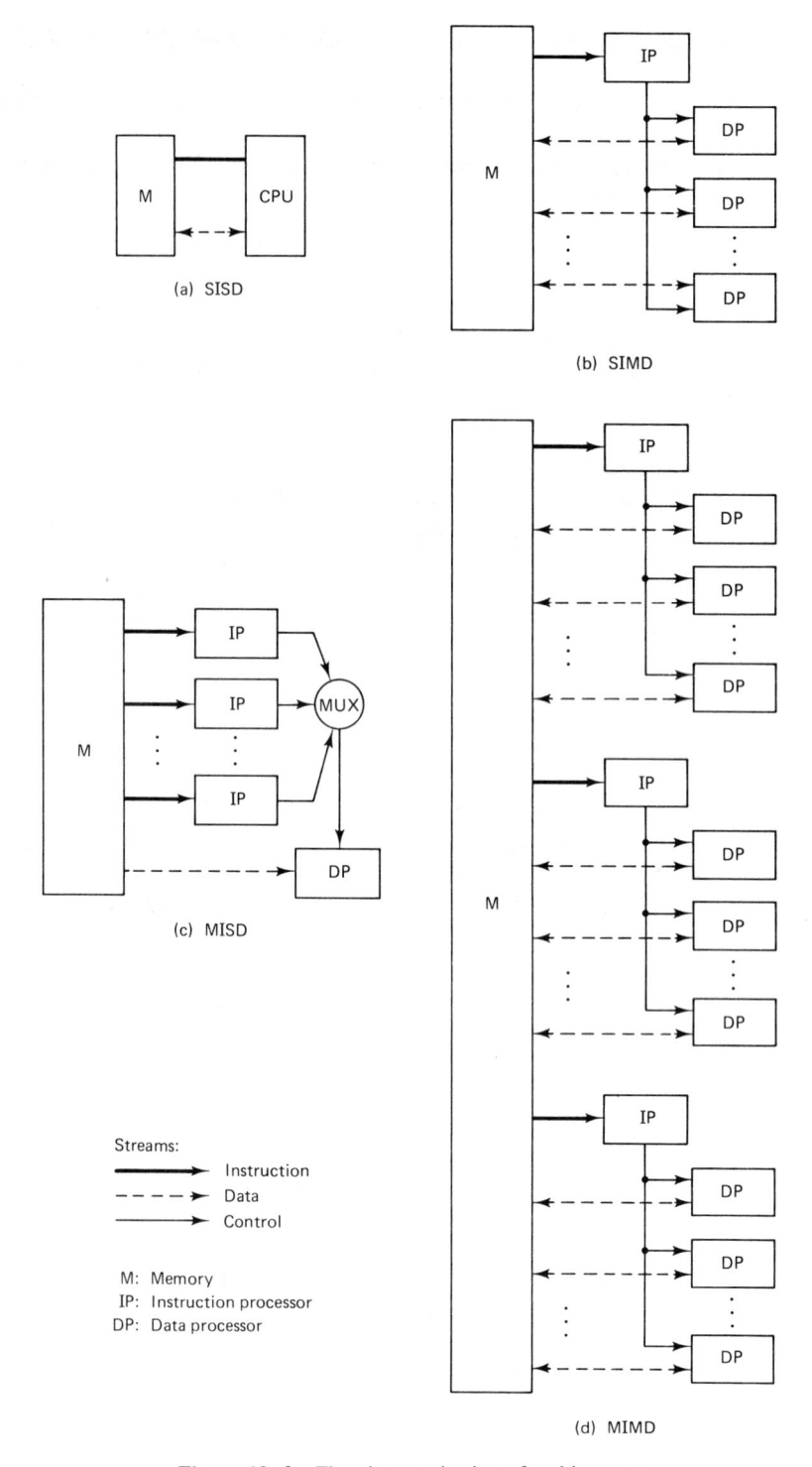

Figure 10–2 Flynn's organization of architectures

Sec. 10.4 Classification of Parallel Computer Architectures

are executed one at a time but are able to work on several data streams at once. Again, it is possible to use pipelining to speed up the processing. This class corresponds to the array processors to be discussed in Section 10.6.

MISD. The MISD class implies several instructions operating simultaneously on a single data item. The theoretical organization is shown in Figure 10–2(c), but no computer falls into this category.

MIMD. An MIMD computer [Figure 10–2(d)] is characterized by the simultaneous execution of more than one instruction, where each instruction operates on several data streams. This class includes multiprocessor systems, from linked mainframe computers to large arrays of microprocessors.

Shore's Classification

J. E. Shore's (1973) classification of computer architectures is based on the organizations of constituent parts of the computer and distinguishes six types of machines.

Machine I. In this computer, one instruction is executed at a time, and each one operates on one word at a time. The processing unit may or may not be pipelined.

Machine II. This computer also executes one instruction at a time, but it operates on a slice of one bit from each data word at a time, as opposed to all the bits of one data word. Again, pipelining is irrelevant to this classification.

Machine III. A computer in this class has two processing units that can operate on the data, one word at a time or a *bit slice* at a time. (The ith bit slice of n words is the ith bit of each of the n words, considered as a whole.) It is also known as an **orthogonal computer.**

Machine IV. This computer is characterized by a number of processing elements (processing units and memory units), all under the control of a single control logic unit (CLU). The only communication between the processing elements is through the control logic unit.

Machine V. Modifying Machine IV so that the processing elements can communicate with their nearest neighbor results in Machine V. Therefore, a processing element can reference data in its own memory area as well as the memory area of the adjacent processing element.

Machine VI. This computer, called a **logic-in-memory array,** implies a machine with the processor logic distributed through the memory. An example of such a machine is the associative array processor, which will be described in Section 10.6.

Feng's Classification

Tse-yum Feng (1972) has suggested classifying computer architectures by their degree of parallelism. The **degree of parallelism** is represented by the pair (n, m), where n is the word length and m is the bit slice length. These pairs fall into one of the following four categories:

1. When $n = 1$ and $m = 1$, there is no parallelism. The words and bits are processed one at a time. This is called **word serial/bit serial (WSBS)**.
2. When $n > 1$ and $m = 1$, the parallelism is called **word parallel/bit serial (WPBS)**. In this case, n complete bit slices are processed one at a time.
3. **Word serial/bit parallel (WSBP)** parallelism occurs when $n = 1$ and $m > 1$. Then n words are processed one at a time, but m bits of each word are processed in parallel.
4. The last category is called **word parallel/bit parallel (WPBP)** and implies a parallelism with $n > 1$ and $m > 1$. In this case, nm bits are processed simultaneously.

A schematic diagram of these categories is shown in Figure 10–3. The difference between this classification and the previous two is that by classifying computers in one of these four categories, their particular degree of parallelism, (n, m), is also specified. A more general terminology for Feng's classification is **bit-serial** processing for WSBS, **bit-slice** processing for WPBS, **word-slice** processing for WSBP, and **fully parallel** processing for WPBP.

Comparison of Classifications

Shore's Machine I classification corresponds to Flynn's SISD class, and Machines II through V can be considered subdivisions of the SIMD class. With respect to Feng's classification, Machine I is WSBP, Machine II is WPBS, and machines III through VI are WPBP.

10.5 VECTOR PROCESSING

A **vector** is an ordered set of n elements. The number of elements, n, is called the **vector length.** An operation that works on at least one vector operand is called a **vector instruction.**

Example 10.1

Let $X = (2, 5, 3)$ and $Y = (1, 6, 4)$ be two vectors, each of length 3. We can define a vector operation ADDV (A, B, C), which, for every i, adds the elements a_i and b_i of the vectors A and B and stores the sum in c_i of the vector C. Therefore, executing ADDV (X, Y, Z) would result in the vector $Z = (3, 11, 7)$. In this example, X, Y, and Z are vector operands for the vector instruction ADDV.

Sec. 10.5 Vector Processing

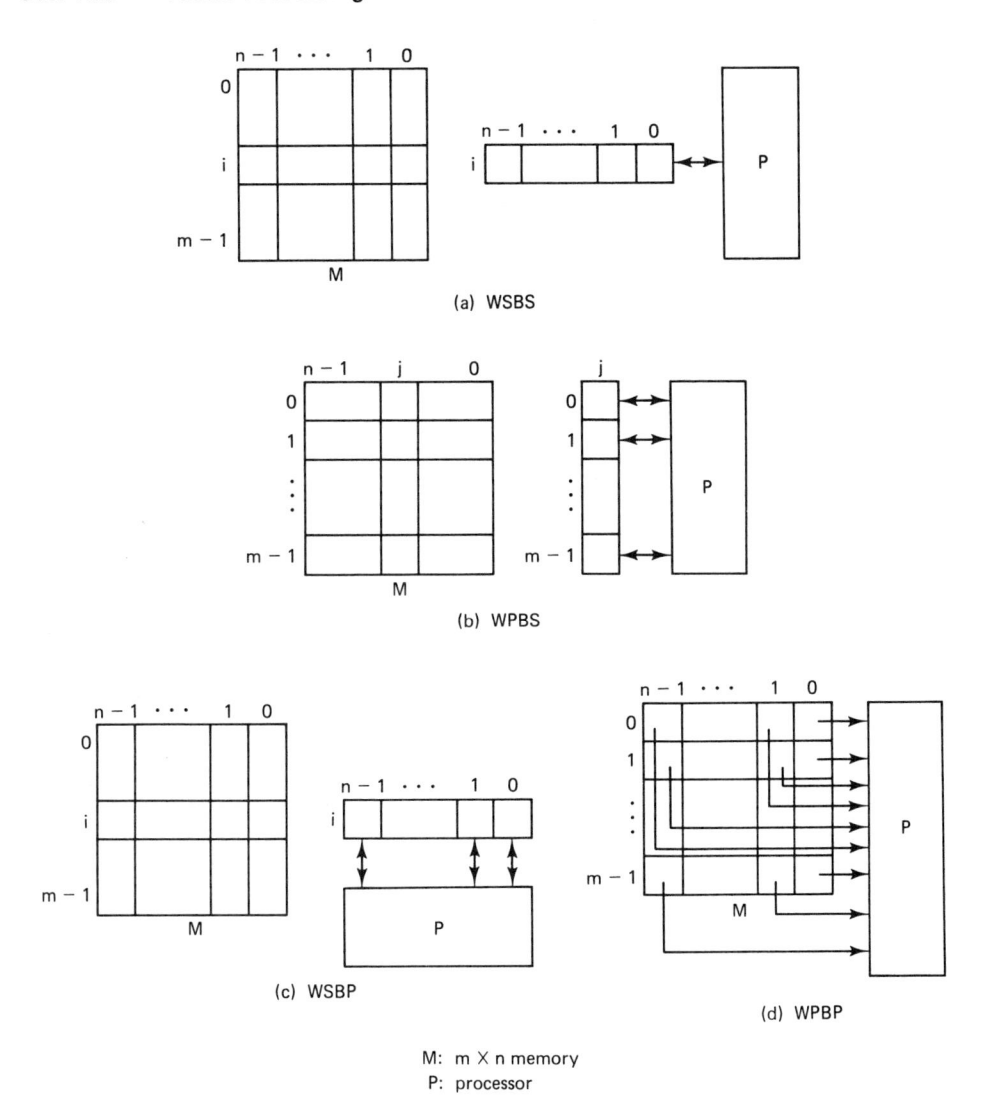

Figure 10-3 Representation of Feng's organization

(a) WSBS
(b) WPBS
(c) WSBP
(d) WPBP

M: m × n memory
P: processor

Vector instructions in a computer are executed by a **vector processor.** The instructions can be of all types: for example, integer vector operations, as in Example 10.1; Boolean vector operations; and character vector operations. One of the main advantages of vector processing is that loop control mechanisms are unnecessary. They are built into the hardware, thereby eliminating the overhead associated with programming a loop in a conventional scalar computer.

Characteristics of Vector Instructions

Any computer instruction must specify certain basic information for execution. This information must include the following, either explicitly or implicitly:

1. The operation to be performed
2. The operands to be used
3. The status to be recorded
4. The next instruction to be performed

The main difference between a scalar instruction and a vector instruction is the way in which the operands are specified. Most vector operands are stored in memory and are almost always addressed directly. In addition to specifying the addresses of the operands, a vector instruction must also specify information such as this:

1. The dimensions of the vector (A matrix is considered a two-dimensional vector in this context.)
2. The length of each dimension of the vector
3. The data type of each dimension of the vector
4. The arrangement of the vector elements in memory (The elements do not have to reside in contiguous memory locations, although this is usually the default.)

Two new concepts unique to vector processing are the **block floating-point** data format and **padding.** These concepts are not applicable to scalar processors and greatly influence the architecture of a vector processor if included. Recall that a floating-point number has four parts: the magnitude sign, the mantissa, the exponent sign, and the exponent (see Section 2.4). To represent a floating-point vector, this same information must be included for *each* element of the vector. It is usually done with four vectors, one for each part of the floating-point element. This allows each element of the vector to be individually normalized with its own exponent specifying the radix-point position. However, if one exponent is used for the entire vector, a significant amount of memory can be saved. This is the principle of block floating-point as discussed by Higbie (1976). In order to use just one exponent, it is necessary to scale the mantissas appropriately. However, if this results in a loss of the significant data for any of the elements, block floating-point should not be used. Figure 10-4 shows an example of a vector in the floating-point and block floating-point formats. As can be seen, the position of the decimal point must be explicitly specified for the mantissa elements when using the block floating-point format.

Padding refers to the automatic lengthening of a vector. This is usually done in one of two ways, for two separate purposes:

1. When a machine is built to process vectors, it can usually operate with two vectors faster than it can with one vector and one scalar. For this reason, when an operation such as ''multiply a vector by a constant'' is necessary, the constant is replicated to form a vector of the necessary length, with each element being equal to the constant. This padding of the constant vector is done by the memory control unit or as part of a pipeline, thereby requiring only one copy of the constant actually to be stored in memory.
2. Another reason for padding is to facilitate an operation on vectors of different lengths. In this case, the shorter vectors are padded with some identity constants

Sec. 10.5 Vector Processing

(a) Vector floating-point format

Sign vector: +, +, −, +
Mantissa vector (normalized): 0.3246, 0.1170, 0.3764, 0.5889
Exponent sign vector: +, −, +, +
Exponent: 1.0, 1.0, 0.0, 2.0

(b) Block floating-point format

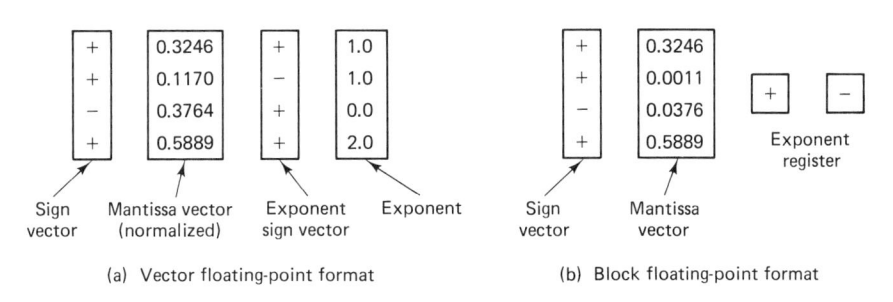

Sign vector: +, +, −, +
Mantissa vector: 0.3246, 0.0011, 0.0376, 0.5889
Exponent register: +, −

Figure 10–4 Two floating-point vector formats

for the operation. If the operation is addition, the shorter vector is padded with zeros; if the operation is multiplication, the shorter vector is padded with ones.

Typical Hardware Architectures

Many computer architectures are capable of vector processing. In general, however, vector processors feature one of two competing design approaches: parallel vector processing and pipelined vector processing. In a **parallel vector processor,** a number of **computational elements** (CEs) are used for each operation. All the CEs are under the control of one vector processor unit, and each one operates on a particular element from each of the vector operands, as shown in Figure 10–5(a). Array processor systems and multiprocessor systems, which will be described shortly, are parallel vector processors.

Rather than have separate CEs for the separate elements of the vector operands, a **pipelined vector processor** has comparatively few CEs, but each one of them is pipelined. Since vector instructions need to perform the same operation many times, they are well suited to the pipeline structures discussed in Chapter 9. Figure 10–5(b) shows the block diagram for the pipelined vector processor.

Vector Addressing Considerations

Just as there are a number of addressing modes for the serial computer (see Chapter 5), there are a variety of possible addressing modes in a vector processor. The speed of accessing an operand from memory, however, becomes much more critical to the speed of execution on a vector processor than on a serial computer. Since each element of the vector operand is a separate word, retrieving an n-element vector from a conventional RAM requires n reads. The time involved here could easily destroy any saving due to the parallel or pipelined processing of the vector. Let us therefore consider typical addressing implementations of vector processors, which can be divided into two classes: dense (regular) addressing and sparse addressing.

Dense (regular) addressing. One general characteristic of **dense,** or **regular,** addressing is that the pattern of the vector in memory is more or less known in advance. Basically, neighboring elements of a vector are stored in locations such that the addresses are contiguous or structured in some other orderly manner. The

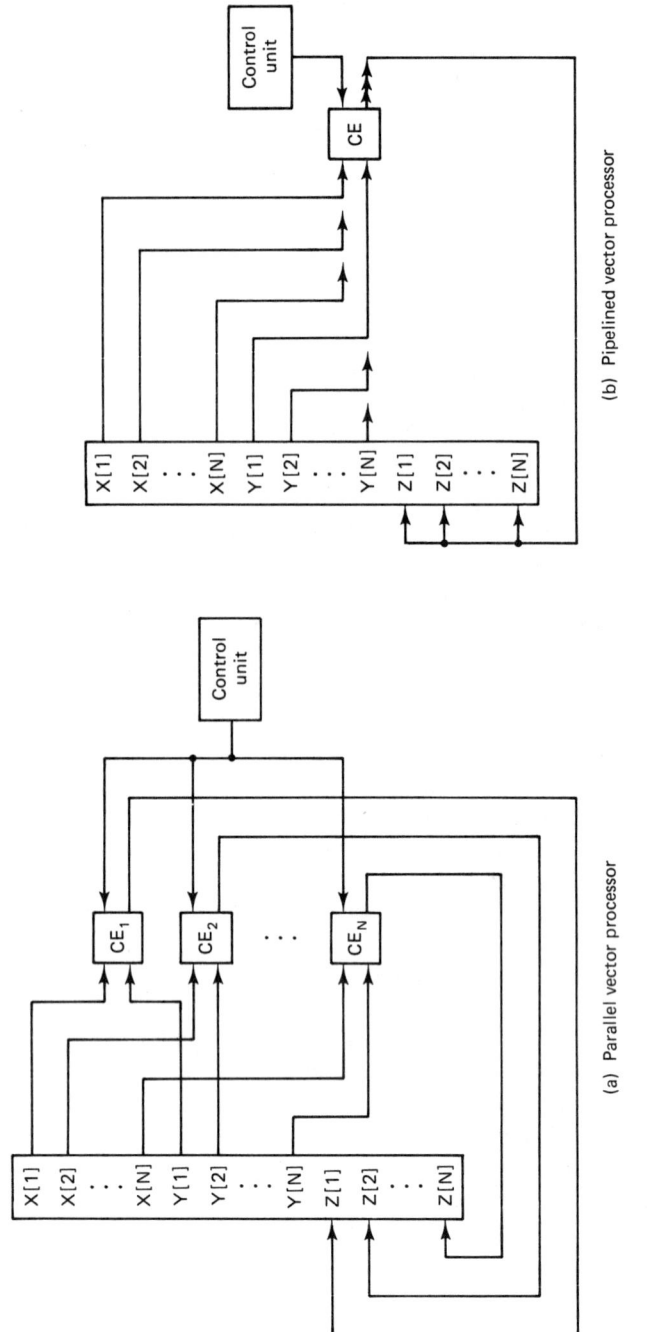

Figure 10-5 Vector processor architectures

(a) Parallel vector processor

(b) Pipelined vector processor

Sec. 10.5 Vector Processing

other general characteristic of this type of addressing is that all elements of the vector are basically stored together as a group. This will become clearer as we proceed. The three most common patterns of this type are as follows:

1. Sequential
2. Nonsequential but regular
3. Submatrix

We shall discuss each of these patterns in terms of the 4 × 3 matrix M, stored in memory as shown in Figure 10-6.

In **sequential** addressing, neighboring elements of the vector are stored in contiguous memory locations. With respect to matrix M in Figure 10-6(a), consider the vector of the second column $X = (M_{12}, M_{22}, M_{32}, M_{42})$. Looking at its location in memory [Figure 10-6(b)], we see that element $X[i + 1]$ is stored right after element $X[i]$ (for $1 \leq i < 4$). The difference in their addresses is therefore 1.

If we consider a row of matrix M, however, we find that it is not stored in one contiguous block of memory. Let Y be the vector of the second row, $Y = (M_{21}, M_{22}, M_{23})$. In this case, for an $m \times n$ matrix, the element $Y[i]$ is stored m locations away from $Y[i + 1]$. Hence, although the pattern of addresses for the vector Y is not sequential, it is **regular** and is of pattern type 2.

The third type, **submatrix,** is really just a combination of the other two. Consider the vector $Z = (M_{32}, M_{42}, M_{33}, M_{43})$, which is a submatrix of M. Part of this vector is stored sequentially and part is stored in a nonsequential but regular pattern. Nevertheless, it is still stored in a definite pattern, and the entire vector is within the group of words storing the matrix M. Therefore, it is considered one of the dense (regular) type.

In each of these three cases, the time necessary to access a vector operand is

$$M = \begin{bmatrix} M_{11} & M_{12} & M_{13} \\ M_{21} & M_{22} & M_{23} \\ M_{31} & M_{32} & M_{33} \\ M_{41} & M_{42} & M_{43} \end{bmatrix}$$

(a) 4 × 3 matrix

58	M_{11}
59	M_{21}
60	M_{31}
61	M_{41}
62	M_{12}
63	M_{22}
64	M_{32}
65	M_{42}
66	M_{13}
67	M_{23}
68	M_{33}
69	M_{43}

(b) Memory storage locations (matrix M stored in column-major order)

Figure 10-6 Matrix M storage configuration

basically dependent on the architecture and design of the memory rather than on the address computation. Typically, some combinations of the high-speed memory designs discussed in Chapter 7 are used and include *interleaved memory* and *associative memory*.

Sparse addressing. This addressing mode refers to the case where the address patterns of the vector operands must be dynamically computed. Although not as common as dense (regular) addressing, there are definite situations in which it is more suitable and also more efficient to use sparse addressing. The two common methods of this class are bit vectors and index vectors.

As the name implies, a **bit vector** is a vector in which each element consists of a single bit, either 0 or 1. This means that one word can store many elements of the vector rather than a separate word for each element. The retrieval of such a vector from memory is therefore orders of magnitude faster than the more general vectors. Bit vectors can be used in addressing by keeping track of the elements of some other vector that are to form the specific vector operand in question.

Example 10.2

Going back to Figure 10–6, suppose that the vector operand to be used in an operation is $W = (M_{11}, M_{31}, M_{32}, M_{43})$. According to the order in which the matrix is stored in memory, the bit vector $B = (101000100001)$ describes the vector W.

In cases like Example 10.2, no natural pattern can be used to address the elements of the operand vector. The address bit vector, however, can be used to derive the address computations necessary.

The second method, using an **index vector,** is similar in principle to using a bit vector. Instead of storing bits that refer to another existing vector, the addresses of the vector operand elements are stored. The stored addresses may be direct addresses or offsets from some base address.

Example 10.3

Again using the matrix M of Figure 10–6 and the vector W of Example 10.2, an index vector I can be used to describe W, where $I = (58, 60, 64, 69)$.

Although an index vector will take up more space in memory than a bit vector and will therefore require a longer time to retrieve, in some cases it is the only choice. It is probably the only efficient way of implementing table lookups or interpolation functions on a vector computer. As for storing the index vector, it can be stored so as to be addressed in one of the dense (regular) patterns. This will speed up the memory access time to some extent.

10.6 ARRAY PROCESSORS

An **array processor** is a synchronous computer with more than one processing element operating in parallel. The **processing elements (PEs),** each consisting of an ALU and registers, are all under the control of a *single* control logic unit (CLU). The ALU

Sec. 10.6 Array Processors

in a PE may or may not be pipelined. Since the PEs operate in parallel, array processors are capable of vector processing. An array processor has two distinguishing characteristics:

1. The PEs are designed as passive devices without any instruction decoding or control capabilities.
2. All the PEs perform the same function at the same time under the control of a single CLU.

Organization of Array Processors

Each PE of an array processor can be connected so as to communicate with one particular section of memory, or it can be dynamically connected to any section of memory as directed by the CLU. Basically, the two organizations of array processors are distinguished by this property of the PEs. In either case, the PE includes an ALU and any registers necessary for communication with other components in the computer. Let us now look at the two organizations in detail.

Processing elements with local memories. The configuration depicted in Figure 10–7 represents an array processor with n PEs, each with its own local memory. We consider the memory unit as divided into $n + 1$ distinct modules, one connected to each PE and one connected to the CLU. This array processor is often referred to as an SIMD computer. That is, it handles single instructions one at a time, operating on multiple data streams.

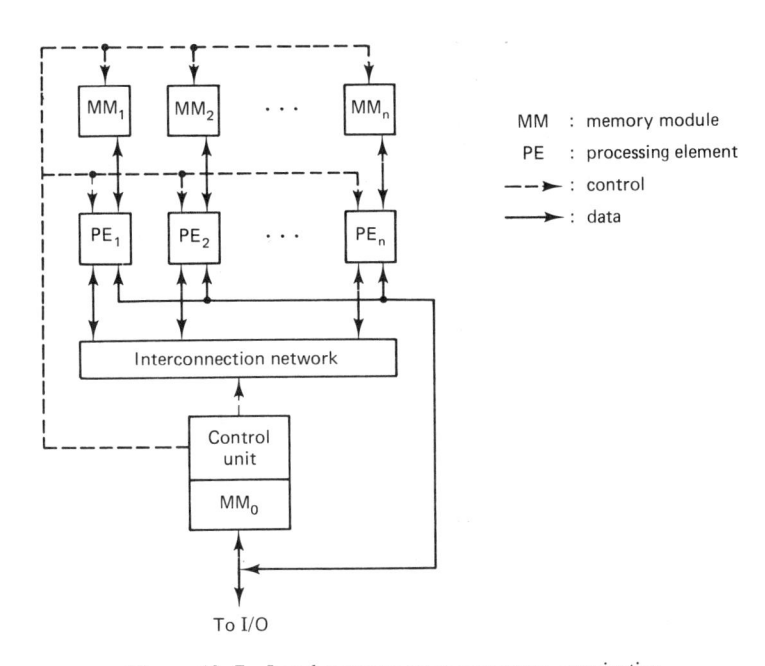

Figure 10–7 Local memory array processor organization

The memory part of the CLU contains the system and user programs. The CLU fetches instructions from this memory, decodes them, and then determines in which PE they should be executed according to the locations of the operands. Although all the PEs can operate at once, the CLU may disable some if they are not necessary for the current instruction. In this type of an array processor, each PE is hard-wired to a separate memory module. Data is passed between them only via the **interconnection network** and only as directed by the CLU. We consider the interconnection network for this type of array processor later in this section.

Processing elements with parallel memories. A different way of designing an array processor is to organize the PEs and memory so that different PEs can communicate with different memory modules (MMs). To facilitate this setup, an **alignment network** component is necessary to connect the PE and MMs. Figure 10–8 depicts this type of organization.

All the PEs and MMs are still under control of the CLU, and the CLU still has its own memory. The alignment network, also under control of the CLU, provides connections between the PEs and MMs. Because of these dynamic connections, it is possible to have a different number of MMs and PEs in one system. For example, two PEs could be connected to the same MM, or vice versa. The organization shown in Figure 10–8 shares some characteristics of multiprocessing systems, and we therefore defer our discussion of its alignment network to Section 10.7.

Array processor examples. Probably the three best-known array processors are the ILLIAC IV, the BSP (Burroughs Scientific Processor), and the MPP (Massively

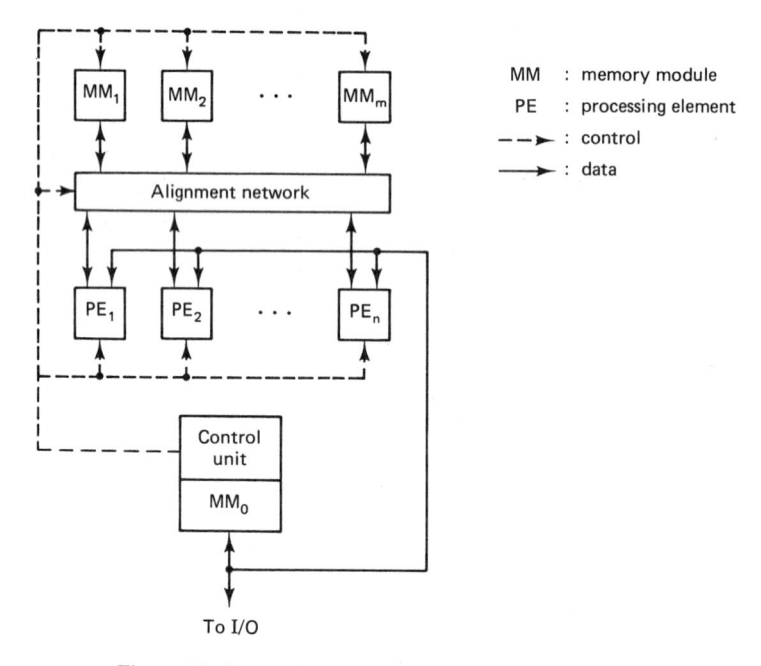

Figure 10–8 Parallel memory array processor organization

Sec. 10.6 Array Processors

Parallel Processor). The ILLIAC IV system was developed at the University of Illinois in the 1960s and then built by the Burroughs Corporation in 1972. It has 64 PEs with local memory units (as in Figure 10-7) that are connected through a *mesh* interconnection network. (Particular network types will be discussed later in this section.)

The BSP system was also built by the Burroughs Corporation as a commercial system that improved on many aspects of the ILLIAC IV. Its production suspended in 1979, this system had 16 PEs and 17 memory modules connected together (as in Figure 10-8) via a **crossbar** alignment network. Unlike the ILLIAC IV, the BSP system was extended to be a FORTRAN vectorizing machine.

The MPP system, the most recent of the three, was built in the early 1980s. It was developed at NASA's Goddard Space Flight Center primarily for processing satellite imagery. Like the ILLIAC IV, this system has PEs with local memories connected via a mesh interconnection network. Unlike the ILLIAC IV, this system has 16,384 PEs! It is a bit-slice array processor built with VLSI technology.

SIMD Interconnection Networks

The interconnection network of the SIMD array processor is basically a **data routing network** for specific registers between the PEs. For simplicity, consider one register R_i, in each PE_i, which is connected to this data routing network. The function of the interconnecting network is to take the data from *j* such registers and pass it to *k* other registers. It is not necessary that all *n* registers from the *n* PEs be connected, and, in fact, they are usually not all connected. If it is necessary to pass data between two PEs that are not connected through the network, the data can be passed through intermediate PEs that are connected. Let us look at some specific networks in this context.

Static and dynamic networks. We can divide data routing networks into two classes: static and dynamic. **Static** networks are characterized by fixed connections, whereas **dynamic** networks have variable connections that are configured as necessary.

As an example of a static network, consider the simple **ring network** shown in Figure 10-9. For this first example we also include the details of the PEs. Register R_1 is connected via a switch to register R_2, register R_2 is connected to register R_3, and so on. To pass data from PE_3 to PE_1, the data has to go from R_3 to R_4 and then to R_1.

The ring and some other examples of static networks that can be used as interconnection networks are shown in Figure 10-10. For simplicity, Figure 10-10 shows the switches only in the interconnection networks.

Dynamic networks can be further classified as single-stage or multistage. A **single-stage** dynamic network is basically an $N \times N$ switch box (a switching matrix). Figure 10-11(a) shows a schematic diagram of a 2×2 switch box with its four possible interconnection states [Figure 10-11(b)]. The hardware implementation of an $N \times N$ switch box essentially entails N demultiplexers and N multiplexers, as shown in Figure 10-11(c). The necessary connections are made by controlling the select lines of the demultiplexers to the multiplexers. If the switch is *fully connected*

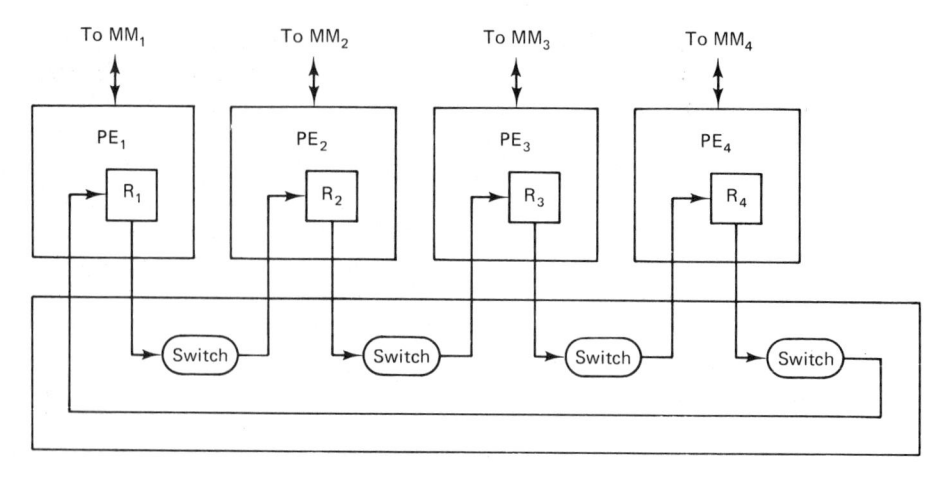

Figure 10-9 Ring structure interconnection network

(i.e., if any input can be connected to any output), as shown in Figure 10-11(c), the switch is called a **crossbar switch.** (Crossbar switches will be discussed in more detail in Section 10.7). When a switch is not fully connected, it is necessary to recirculate data items through the switch until they are passed to the appropriate output.

Example 10.4

Consider the 4 × 4 switch in Figure 10-12. If it is desirable to connect input 4 to output 2, input 4 must first pass to output 1, be circulated to input 1, and then passed to output 2.

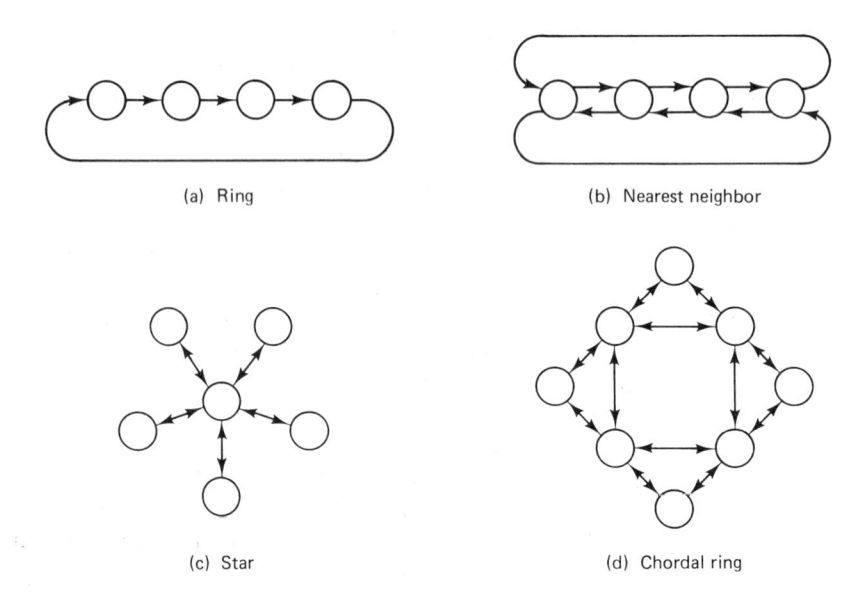

(a) Ring

(b) Nearest neighbor

(c) Star

(d) Chordal ring

Figure 10-10 Static network topologies

Sec. 10.6 Array Processors

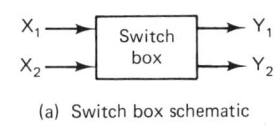

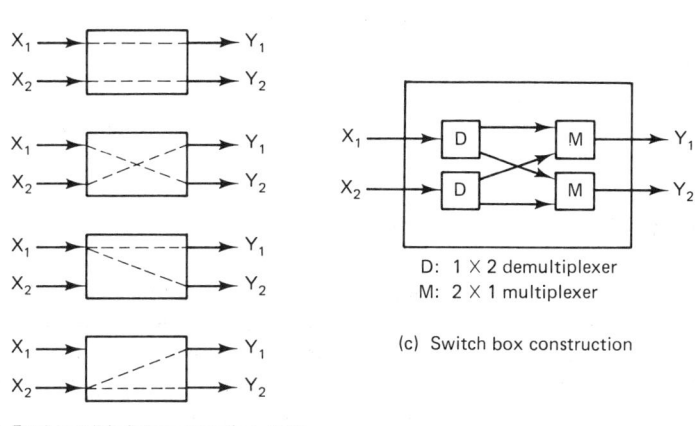

(a) Switch box schematic

(b) Four possible interconnection states

(c) Switch box construction

D: 1 × 2 demultiplexer
M: 2 × 1 multiplexer

Figure 10-11 2 × 2 switch box

Most stage interconnection networks in array processors are of this single-stage recirculating type.

A **multistage** dynamic network is made up of a number of switch boxes and is capable of connecting any input to any output without being fully connected. The switch boxes are connected in a network topology that can be rearranged to form all possible combinations. An example of such a network that is well defined is the **Benes network.** Figure 10–13 shows an 8 × 8 Benes network made up of twenty 2 × 2 switch boxes. In this network, it is possible for each of the eight inputs to be connected to any one of the outputs at a given time. For example, to connect input 1 to output 7, the path *a-g-l-p-t* can be followed through the switches, and to connect input 1 to output 3, the path *a-e-i-m-r* can be followed. The important thing here is that there is more than one possible path for a given connection. So, for instance, if the connection of input 8 to output 6 was using the path *d-h-l-p-s*, the connection of input 1 to output 7 could use the path *a-e-i-n-t* instead of the path *a-g-l-p-t*. This way, both connections could be in effect at the same time. As long as no two inputs need to be passed to the same output at the same time, all requested connections can be processed simultaneously using a multistage dynamic network. Thus the paths *a-g-l* and *b-g-l* could not be processed simultaneously, but the paths *a-g-l* and *b-g-k* could.

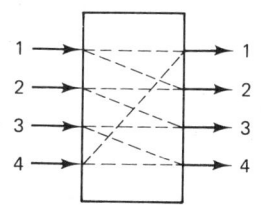

Figure 10-12 4 × 4 switch box

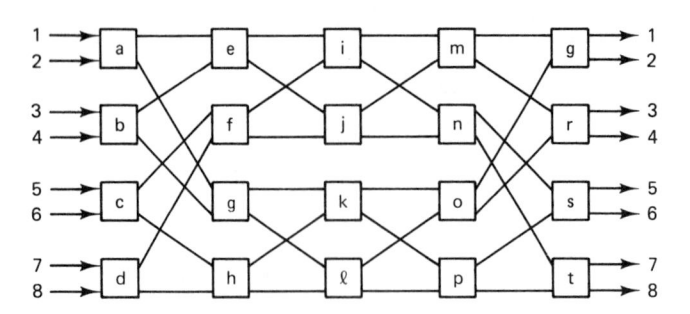

Figure 10-13 8 × 8 Benes network

Associative Array Processors

In all the parallel organizations discussed so far, we have implicitly assumed that the memory units are RAMs. This means that each word has to be accessed by specifying the word address and, more important, that only one word in a memory module can be accessed at a time. Therefore, no matter how fast data can be processed in the parallel processing units, the *actual* speed of these architectures is dependent on the speed of the RAM unit.

Another type of memory that is very well suited to parallel architectures is the **associative memory** introduced in Chapter 7. This memory differs from a RAM in that it is *content-addressable*, and the entire memory can be searched simultaneously. When an associative memory is used in an array processor, the computer is called an **associative processor.**

The major drawback of associative processors is the cost of the memory units. At present, the cost-to-performance ratio is considered too high for the commercial success of these machines. However, some associative processors have been built for military applications. The PEPE (Parallel Element Processing Ensemble) computer is an associative processor used for radar signal-processing applications. The STARAN computer, built by Goodyear Aerospace, is also considered an associative processor. The first STARAN was set up for digital image processing in 1975. Since then, more enhanced models with larger memory units and faster processing speeds have been installed.

10.7 MULTIPROCESSOR SYSTEMS

A **multiprocessor system** is one in which a group of processors *in a single computer* communicate and cooperate with one another in solving a problem. (Do not confuse this with a **multiprogramming system,** where more than one program runs on the system. Multiprogrammning is facilitated by the operating system and can be implemented on either a uniprocessor or a multiprocessor system.) The processors may communicate along direct data lines, via shared memory, or by means of some combination thereof. Our use of the phrase "in a single computer" implies that we do not consider multiple computers connected together a multiprocessor system. That type of system is more commonly referred to as a **distributed system.** More important,

Sec. 10.7 Multiprocessor Systems

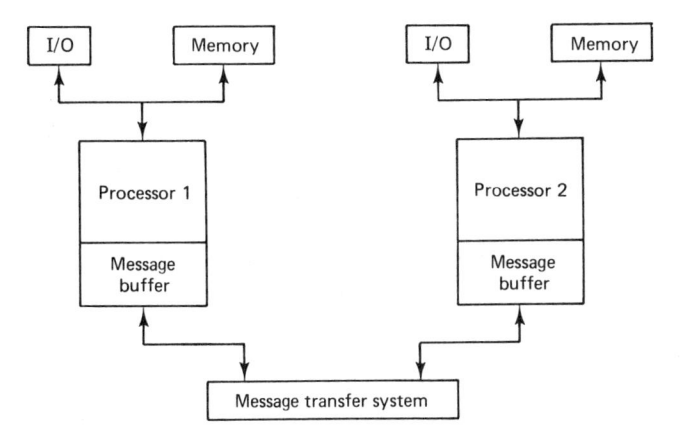

Figure 10-14 Private-memory multiprocessor system

this restriction implies that one operating system is used for all the processors in the system.

Private-Memory and Shared-Memory Systems

We can group multiprocessor systems into two broad classifications based on the type of connection between the processors. A **private-memory** multiprocessor system (sometimes called a **loosely coupled** system) refers to a configuration in which the processors have large local memories and possibly their own sets of I/O devices. The processors communicate with each other via a **message transfer system** as shown in Figure 10-14. Each processor also includes a buffer area for storing messages that arrive while one is being serviced. The message transfer system in a loosely coupled system has a definite effect on the performance of the system. It can be as simple as a shared bus or as complex as an efficient shared-memory system with built-in communication controls. The most common examples of private-memory multiprocessors are the hypercube machines. In a hypercube, the processor-memory pairs (or **nodes**) are connected in a special way such that, for an n-processor system, each node is connected directly to $\log_2 n$ other nodes and the longest path between any two nodes is $\log_2 n$. Figure 10-15 shows two examples of hypercubes: a two-dimensional hypercube in part (a) and a three-dimensional hypercube in part (b).

In the second type of multiprocessor system, referred to as a **shared-memory**

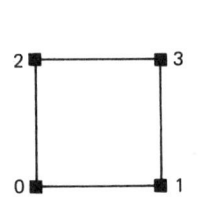

(a) Four-node, two-dimensional hypercube

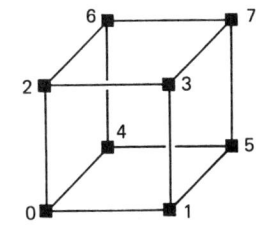

(b) Eight-node, three-dimensional hypercube

Figure 10-15 Hypercube architectures

(or **tightly coupled**) system, all the processors share one common main memory, as shown in Figure 10–16. Usually each processor has separate I/O devices and may also have separate caches. Each processor is connected to the computer's main memory via an interconnection network, as shown in Figure 10–16(a), or by using a **multiport memory,** as shown in Figure 10–16(b). Notice that in the context of multiprocessor systems, the alignment networks mentioned in Section 10.6 are referred to as interconnection networks. In the case of shared memory, the system is less flexible for expansion. There must also be a logic circuit to deal with simultaneous attempts (contentions) by two or more processors to access the shared memory. This will be discussed in the next subsection.

As for actual machines, commercial hypercubes available include the FPS T-series machines, the Intel iPSC, and the NCUBE. There are many shared memory machines, but the two most powerful are the ETA 10 and the Cray-3 supercomputers.

Multiprocessor Hardware Organizations

The advantages of multiprocessor systems are many. Among them are high reliability, increased availability of memory units and I/O devices, and increased computing

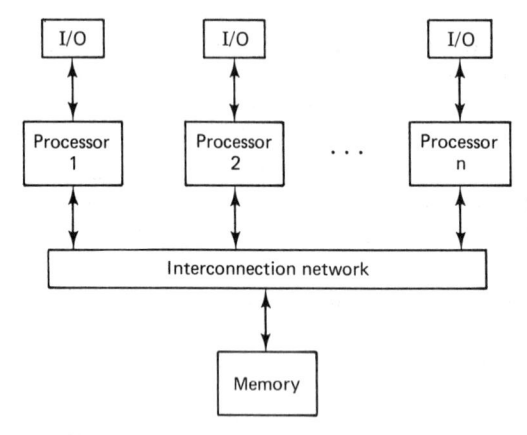

(a) Connections via an interconnection network

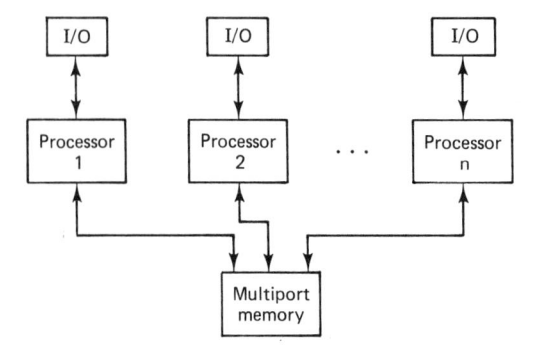

(b) Connections using multiport memory

Figure 10–16 Shared-memory multiprocessor system

power. Whether the system is loosely coupled or tightly coupled, the connections between the processors, as well as the memory units and I/O devices, determine the performance and efficiency of the entire system. The three most common organizations are common bus, crossbar switch, and multiport memories.

Common bus. The common bus, also referred to as **time-shared bus,** is the simplest connection scheme for a multiprocessor system. As shown in Figure 10-17, it is a single communication path between the functional components. The bus itself is a passive device, with transfer operations controlled by the bus interfaces within the components.

A major advantage of the common bus organization is the relative simplicity of adding or removing components. Although it is necessary for proper communication protocols for each component to know what other components are on the bus, this is handled by software and can be easily modified.

Unfortunately, the single communication path, which results in a low-cost, simple system, is also the cause of some serious problems. In particular, if the bus fails, the whole system fails. Also, as the system becomes busier, the contention for the bus causes a serious degradation in performance. Variations on this scheme, such as two unidirectional buses or multiple bidirectional buses, do not manage to overcome the disadvantages without sacrificing the simplicity of the system. In general, this type of organization is used only in small multiprocessor systems.

Crossbar switch. The concept of a crossbar switch was introduced in Section 10.6. In the context of multiprocessor systems, it implies a separate path connecting every processor to every memory unit. Since each memory unit is accessed on a different path, no blocking due to simultaneous transmissions will occur. A crossbar switch organization for a multiprocessor system is depicted in Figure 10-18. The number of processors, I/O devices, and memory units are arbitrary and do not have to be the same.

Although simultaneous transmissions to separate memory units can occur with no problem, the switch must be capable of resolving conflicts resulting from simultaneous accesses to the same memory unit. These conflicting requests are usually handled on a predetermined priority basis. As it turns out, the hardware required to implement these switches can become quite complex. Yet this complexity actually makes the interfaces at the functional components much simpler. It is also easy to remove a malfunctioning component without stopping or degrading the entire system.

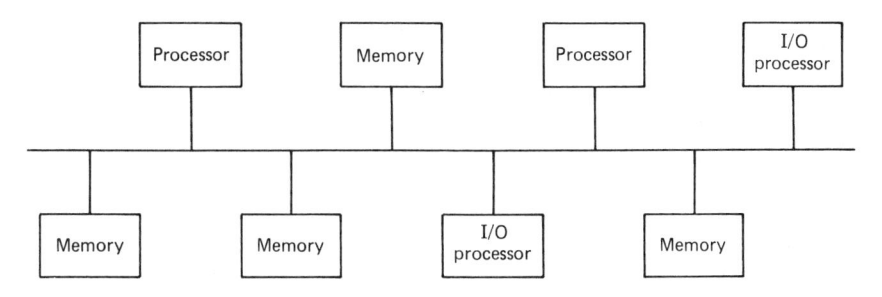

Figure 10-17 Common bus multiprocessor organization

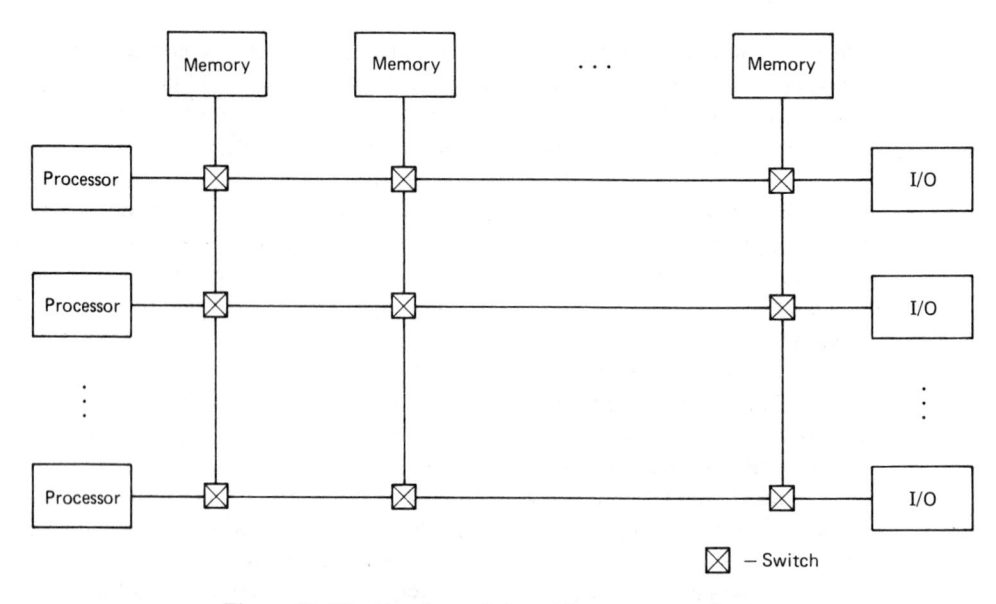

Figure 10-18 Crossbar switch multiprocessor organization

This organization is most cost effective for medium-sized systems. However, when the total number of processor-memory connections becomes large, this organization becomes very expensive.

Multiport memories. This third organization is accomplished by taking the control logic, switching logic and priority arbitration out of the crossbar switch, and putting them in the interface of each memory unit. All the other functional components then access the memory units through a specific port, as shown in Figure 10-19. One port is supplied for each functional component.

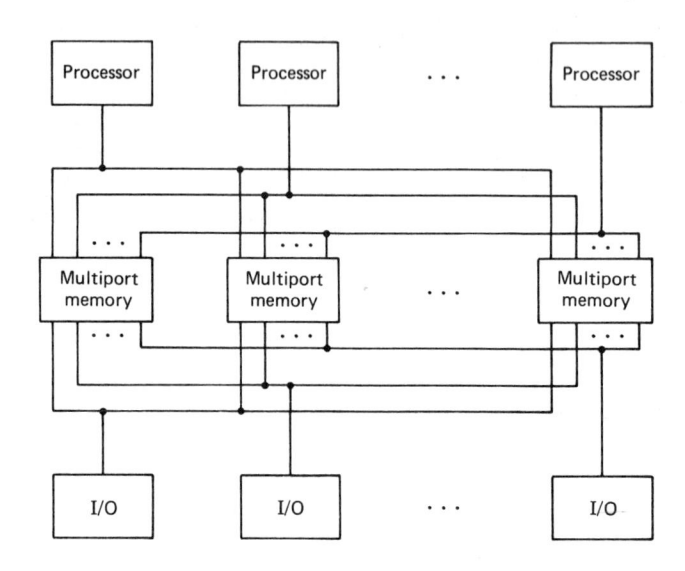

Figure 10-19 Multiport memory multiprocessor organization

Sec. 10.7 Multiprocessor Systems

As in the crossbar switch, conflicts are usually resolved according to assigned priorities. One nice feature of the multiport memory organization is that access to particular memory units can be restricted simply by not connecting the restricted component to a memory port. This is used to create private storage units, usually for security reasons.

The multiport memory organization, too, is best suited for medium-sized systems. It is mainly the unavailability of switches featuring reasonable cost and good performance that has prevented the growth of large multiprocessor systems.

Multicaches in Multiprocessor Systems

As was hinted at in the discussion of tightly coupled multiprocessor systems, separate caches may also be a part of the system. The compelling reasons for having caches are the same as those discussed in Chapter 7, and caches can also be used in loosely coupled systems. Unfortunately, the presence of private caches in a multiprocessor system, as shown in Figure 10–20, poses problems that may result in data inconsistencies. This is known as the **cache coherence** problem.

The problem of cache coherence exists only when the caches are associated with individual processors. In this case, it is possible for several copies of the same data to exist in different caches at the same time. If one processor then writes to its cache, the other caches will contain the unmodified and therefore incorrect data. A simple write-through policy will not solve the problem either, since only the main memory unit will be modified and not all the caches that contain the data.

Example 10.5

Suppose that a word X in main memory contains the value 76, and suppose that a copy of this word exists in the private caches of processors P_1, P_2, and P_3. Further assume that a write-through policy is in effect. If processor P_1 modifies its copy of word X to 85, the word X in main memory is also changed to 85. However, P_2 and P_3 are still using the value of 76, not the new value of 85, resulting in data inconsistencies.

One way of avoiding the cache coherence problem is to associate the caches with the shared memory rather than with the processors. As shown in Figure 10–21, the processors would then have to go through the interconnection network to access the cache, thereby losing a major portion of the speedup gained by using the cache

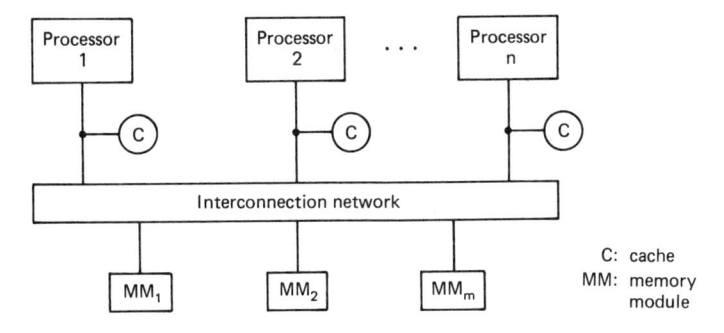

Figure 10–20 Multiprocessor system with private caches

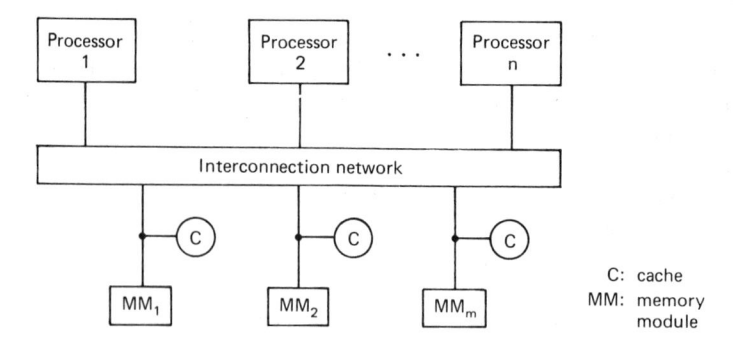

Figure 10-21 Multiprocessor system with shared caches

in the first place. Two different methods have been proposed to address the cache coherence problem: static coherence check and dynamic coherence check.

The basic concept of the **static coherence check** method is to separate the data into *shared* and *private* classes. It can then be handled in separate ways to prevent any inconsistencies. One method of dealing with separate data is to keep the shared data, which is modifiable, in main memory and store only the private data, which will be used by only one processor, in appropriate caches. Another method involves maintaining a special shared cache for the shared data and, again, storing the private data in caches.

In the **dynamic coherence check** method, multiple copies of any data are allowed. Whenever a processor modifies the data in its own cache, it must invalidate any copy of the data in the other caches. However, implementing this method results in the following disadvantages:

1. Degradation of the average hit ratio (see Section 7.5) due to data invalidation
2. Traffic between caches to enforce consistency
3. Conflicts resulting from concurrent access to the global tables used for keeping track of which caches contain which copies of the memory words
4. More write-backs due to invalidation of modified data (Usually, modified data is not written back to main memory unless there are unmodified words to replace.)

10.8 PARALLEL ORGANIZATIONS IN GENERAL

We have considered in this chapter some of the organizations used to effect parallel processing. Although there are many different kinds of parallel processors (as witnessed by the different classification schemes), they all fall into three general categories: array processors, multiprocessors, and data flow systems.

Array processor systems consist of a number of processing elements that operate in parallel under the direction of a single control unit. Each of the processing elements performs the same operation at the same time, on different data elements. **Multiprocessor** systems consist of a number of complete processors that can process data independently.

A completely different kind of parallel organization is the **data flow** architecture. In a data flow architecture, instead of a program counter determining when instructions are to be executed, instructions are automatically enabled for execution as soon as their required data operands are available. There is no control flow mechanism (program counter), and the order of instruction execution is determined completely by the data dependencies between the instructions; hence the name *data flow*. Theoretically, maximal concurrency is possible with this type of architecture, given sufficient resources (processors, memory ports, I/O devices, etc.). For a more detailed discussion of data flow systems, see Hwang and Briggs (1984) and the February 1982 issue of *IEEE Computer Magazine*.

PROBLEMS

1. Define the following terms:
   - (a) SIMD
   - (b) MIMD
   - (c) bit slice
   - (d) vector instruction
   - (e) block floating point
   - (f) padding
   - (g) dense addressing
   - (h) array processor
   - (i) interconnection network
   - (j) crossbar switch
   - (k) associative processor
   - (l) multiprocessor
   - (m) cache coherence

2. Classify each of the following types of parallelism as either (A) during the same interval [Figure 10–1(a)], (B) at the same instant [Figure 10–1(b)], or (C) in overlapped time spans [Figure 10–1(c)].
   - (a) Pipelining
   - (b) Multiple functional units
   - (c) Overlapping CPU and I/O operations
   - (d) Memory interleaving
   - (e) Multiprogramming
   - (f) Multiprocessing

3. Graph the lower bound (Minsky's conjecture) and the upper bound for the speedup of a program as a function of the number of processors from 2^0 to 2^{10}.

4. Show a block floating-point format of the following floating-point vectors:
   - (a) $(0.826 \times 10^3, -0.1530 \times 10^1, 0.2649 \times 10^2)$
   - (b) $(-0.1837 \times 10^{-2}, 0.43 \times 10^{-3}, 0.205 \times 10^{-2})$
   - (c) $(0.686 \times 10^1, -0.7060 \times 10^0, 0.111 \times 10^{-2})$

5. Let $A = (5, 234, 100, 97, 3)$ and $B = (802, 311, 65)$. Show how these vectors might be padded to increase the efficiency of the following operations:
   - (a) $A \times B$
   - (b) $A + B$
   - (c) $3 \times A$

6. Based on the matrix of Figure 10–6, state whether the following regular addressed vectors are sequential, nonsequential, or submatrix.
   - (a) $(M_{31}, M_{41}, M_{12}, M_{22})$
   - (b) $(M_{43}, M_{13}, M_{22}, M_{31})$
   - (c) (M_{23}, M_{33}, M_{43})
   - (d) $(M_{22}, M_{23}, M_{32}, M_{33}, M_{42}, M_{43})$

7. Referring to the matrix of Figure 10–6, for each of the following vectors, give the bit vector that describes its location in memory and tell whether the vector has dense or sparse addressing.
   (a) $(M_{42}, M_{32}, M_{22}, M_{12})$
   (b) (M_{12}, M_{13}, M_{11})
   (c) $(M_{11}, M_{21}, M_{31}, M_{41}, M_{43})$
   (d) $(M_{31}, M_{32}, M_{41}, M_{42})$
8. Give the index vector for the vector in Problem 7(c).
9. Draw a logic diagram for a 3 × 3 switching box.
10. Referring to the 4 × 4 recirculating switch of Figure 10–12, describe what is necessary to connect the following:
    (a) Input 3 to output 2
    (b) Input 1 to output 4
    (c) Input 2 to output 3
11. Specify paths that can be followed in the 8 × 8 Benes network of Figure 10–13 to make the following sets of *simultaneous* connections:
    (a) 1-8, 8-1
    (b) 2-5, 4-3, 7-2
    (c) 6-6, 7-1, 2-2
12. For the Benes network of Figure 10–13, explain why it is true that the paths *a-g-l* and *b-g-k* could be processed simultaneously but the paths *a-g-l* and *b-g-l* could not.
13. How do processes running on different processors communicate in each processor?
    (a) Private-memory multiprocessor
    (b) Shared-memory multiprocessor
14. Compare and contrast the performance and efficiency of a multiprocessor system where the connections between the processors are via
    (a) a common bus
    (b) a crossbar switch
    (c) multiport memories
15. Compare and contrast the cache organizations of Figures 10–20 and 10–21.
16. Classify the following machines according to Flynn's taxonomy:
    (a) BSP
    (b) CYBER 205
    (c) Intel iPSC
    (d) NCUBE
    (e) STARAN
    (f) Cray-3
    (g) ILLIAC IV
    (h) MPP
    (i) PEPE
    (j) FPS T-series

CHAPTER 11

Microcomputer Organization

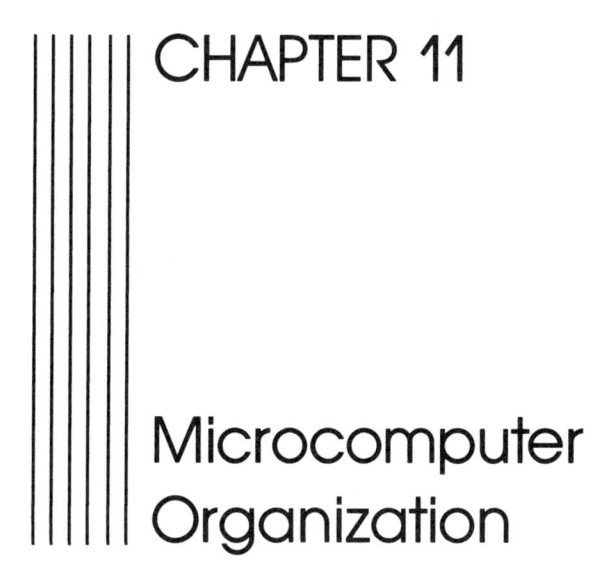

11.1 THE MICROCOMPUTER REVOLUTION

The principles of *organization* of a microcomputer are the same as for any larger computer. So you may ask, why have a chapter on microcomputer organization? For one thing, we believe that a book on computer organization warrants a chapter on microcomputer organization solely due to the tremendous impact of microelectronics technology. The advent of large-scale integration (LSI) and very large scale integration (VLSI) technologies resulted in the placement of a large variety of computer-related devices, on integrated-circuit (IC) chips, at the disposal of every system designer. Today, each one of us can use these building blocks to construct rather complex digital systems, computers, or embedded computer systems.

You can also use this chapter to review the various concepts introduced in earlier chapters. We now assemble these concepts and integrate them in the discussion of microcomputer organization.

The microcomputer revolution began with the **microprocessor,** the single-chip processor. It took three decades from the introduction of the first electronic computers before microprocessors appeared, but they benefited very much from the experience gained in the design of large computers. Many advanced organizational features that form a basic part of almost all microprocessors today were rarely incorporated in the much larger and more expensive computers of a few years ago. Let us then consider briefly the evolution of microprocessors over the past two decades.

11.2 TECHNOLOGICAL DEVELOPMENTS

The evolution of microprocessors can be divided into four generations. *First-generation microprocessors*, introduced in the early 1970s, consisted mostly of 4-bit words (e.g., Intel 4040) or 8-bit words (e.g., Intel 8080). These microprocessors were fabricated using PMOS technology and were used in simple industrial applications and consumer equipment.

Second-generation microprocessors appeared as early as 1973 and consisted of 8-bit words (e.g., Intel 8085, Zilog Z80, and Motorola 6809). These microprocessors were also fabricated in PMOS technology, but the chips were larger and of increased density (more transistors per chip). Second-generation microprocessors were capable of addressing larger memory spaces (up to 64 kilobytes) and handling more I/O devices than first-generation microprocessors. They were also characterized by faster speeds of operation, reduced speed times power products, and more powerful instruction sets. Typical applications of second-generation microprocessors included intelligent terminals, data acquisition systems, complex industrial controllers, and communication systems.

Early 1978 marked the beginning of the *third microprocessor generation* with the introduction of Intel 8086 single-chip, 16-bit microprocessor. Other manufacturers followed suit with similar microprocessors, such as Zilog Z8000 and Motorola 68000. The predominant technology used for fabricating these microprocessors is NMOS. In comparison with 8-bit microprocessors, 16-bit microprocessors are characterized by increased chip density, stronger processing capabilities, and higher speeds. Third-generation microprocessors can address very large memory spaces (up to 16 megabytes), include virtual memory features, and have more powerful interrupt-handling capabilities.

Intel's APX-432, a 32-bit processing system introduced in 1981, marked the beginning of the *fourth generation*. Latest versions of the Motorola 68000 also include 32-bit word-handling capabilities, as do National Semiconductor's NS 16032 and Texas Instruments' TI 99000. Fabricated by HMOS technology and characterized by further increases in chip density and processing speeds, fourth-generation microprocessors compete strongly with mainframes. Virtual memory addressing capabilities of spaces up to 2^{40} bytes, floating-point hardware, separation of system and user software, and a more efficient support of multiprocessor configurations are but some of the features of these microprocessors. The APX-432 is the first microprocessor to use a new bus structure that employs packet switching. (Packet switching is discussed in Section 12.6.)

Related to the development of microprocessor chips is the development of a large variety of IC *support chips*: dual-port RAMs, floating-point ROMs, intelligent peripheral controllers, cluster terminal controllers, parallel and serial interface units, direct memory access (DMA) controllers, memory management units, multiprotocol communication controllers, programmable communication interfaces, I/O controllers, and I/O processors, to mention just a few.

Although 8-bit microprocessors are still useful for many applications, they are, of course, limited relative to 16- and 32-bit microprocessors, particularly when large and complex operations are called for. Eight-bit microprocessors are also limited in their memory-addressing capabilities. A typical 8-bit microprocessor has a 16-bit address bus, so it can address only up to 65,536 (64K) bits of external memory. In addition, a large number of operations must be programmed (i.e., implemented with subroutines), resulting in greater processing times and the use of valuable memory space.

Sec. 11.3 General Overview of a Microcomputer System   289

In contrast, 16- and 32-bit microprocessors are larger and faster. They use far more hardware, available through VLSI technology, to implement a variety of functions that would otherwise have been implemented in software. Since they can process longer words, these microprocessors have increased memory-addressing capabilities as well as more addressing modes, which enable them to address millions of words directly. The microprocessors contain more registers, support larger instruction sets, and can do many more things faster and more efficiently. Clock frequencies in these microprocessors typically range between 8 and 20 MHz, in contrast with 8-bit microprocessors where clock frequencies are up to about 6 MHz. New architectures incorporated into 16- and 32-bit microprocessors speed up the fetch-execute cycle and memory-referenced operations, resulting in speed increases of some orders of magnitude. Finally, newer microprocessors typically offer memory management capabilities that allow them to be used in multitasking, multiuser computing environments.

11.3 GENERAL OVERVIEW OF A MICROCOMPUTER SYSTEM

Figure 11–1 shows a block diagram of a microcomputer system. The central processing unit is a microprocessor chip, designated MPU (microprocessor unit), connected to

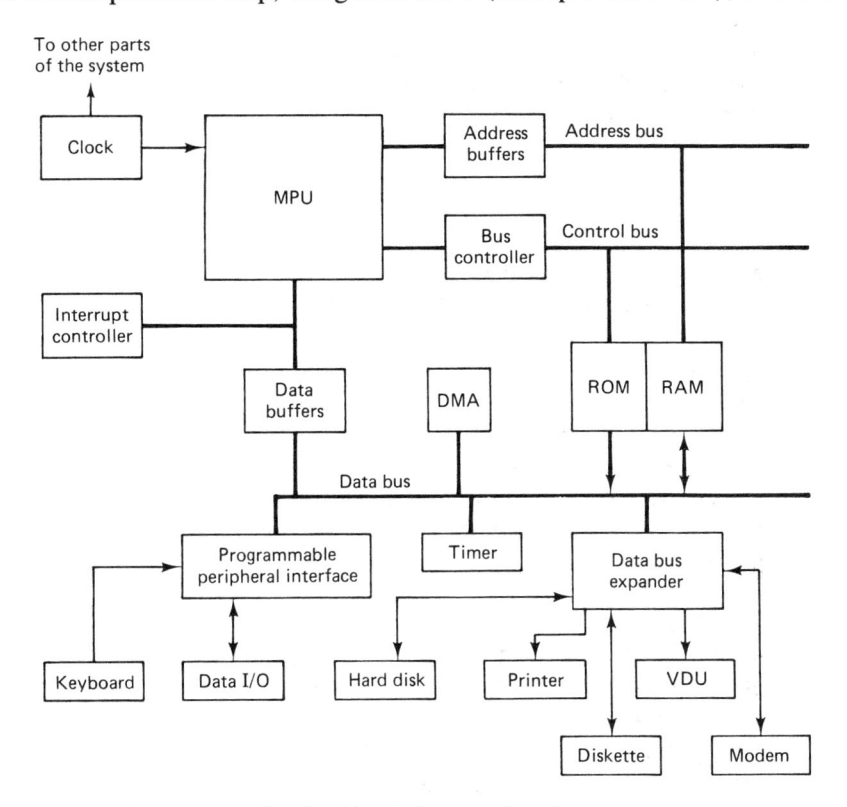

Figure 11–1 Simplified block diagram of a microcomputer system

memory and peripheral units through data, address, and control buses. Various support chips are also shown, including a clock generator, a bus controller, an interrupt controller, and a direct memory access (DMA) controller. All these components can be grouped into three distinct functional units: **microprocessing unit (MPU), memory,** and **input/output (I/O).** (Of course, the MPU is none other than the CPU.) Communication between these units is controlled by the MPU.

The MPU executes programs that are stored in memory. It manipulates the data and makes decisions based on data. It provides timing and control signals for the bus controller, the I/O, and memory. The ROM and RAM store programs and data. The RAM provides instructions and data to the MPU upon request and accepts new data from the MPU for storage. The ROM stores only system programs. The I/O unit provides communication links between the MPU and the outside world and allows the MPU to input data to or output data from external (peripheral) devices such as keyboards, printers, monitors, and disk or diskette storage units.

The MPU uses **buses** (communication paths) to communicate with the various parts of the microcomputer system. We distinguish three types of buses: the data bus, the address bus, and the control bus. The **data bus** transmits data to and from the MPU. Data in this case consists of any values stored in memory that are to be read by the MPU or values in MPU registers that are to be written into memory. The data bus is therefore *bidirectional* because the data can flow in either direction, from memory to MPU or from MPU to memory. To effect this data transfer, the MPU uses a *read/write* control line. For example, when this control line is set to 1, the MPU reads the data from the data bus, but if it is reset to 0, the MPU places (writes) data on the data bus. The **address bus** enables the MPU to select any memory location or I/O port (device) for data transfers. The address bus can be *unidirectional* because information flows in only one direction, from the MPU to memory or I/O.

In some microprocessor designs, the address and data buses are (at least partially) multiplexed (e.g., Intel 8085 and 8086). In other words, the same bus is used for either bidirectional data transfers or unidirectional address selections. Other microprocessor designs, such as Motorola 68000, use separate data and address buses.

The **control bus** contains the various control lines required to control the MPU operations (e.g., the *read/write* control line). The bus is usually bidirectional; however, some microprocessors employ a unidirectional control bus. In this latter case, some control lines go only out of the MPU while others go only into the MPU.

The program that controls the operation of a microcomputer system consists of instructions that the microprocessor can execute. The **instruction set** can be divided into groups according to the type of operations that the instructions perform. These groups include arithmetic, logical, data transfer, input/output, control, and branch instructions.

Many organizations and interconnections are possible among the internal building blocks of a microcomputer system. Particular organizations enhance the execution of one group of instructions while degrading that of others. Therefore, there is no such thing as a "best" microcomputer architecture. Rather, the best microcomputer organization is application dependent. For example, if a microcomputer is used mostly for data logging, its organization should be optimized for memory access and I/O

Sec. 11.4 Single-Chip Processing Unit (MPU)

operations. If it is used mainly for number crunching, an architecture oriented toward mathematical calculations is needed.

11.4 SINGLE-CHIP PROCESSING UNIT (MPU)

The internal organization of the MPU, like that of the CPU, consists of (1) the **register set,** (2) the **arithmetic and logic unit (ALU),** and (3) the **control logic unit (CLU).** Data transfers within the MPU are accomplished via one or more *internal* buses. The number of bits that the MPU (specifically, the ALU) can process in parallel defines the basic **word length** of the microprocessor. The MPU word is the basic addressable element in memory and therefore defines the basic data element of the microprocessor and specifies the width of the data bus. For example, the word length of a 16-bit microprocessor is 16 bits, requiring a 16-bit-wide data bus.

The information handled by the microprocessor is of two types: instructions and data (operands). The basic word length is usually independent of either the instruction or operand length. An instruction may be one, two, or more words long and can consist of none, one, two, or more operands. The microprocessor can support several data (operand) types, such as arithmetic, logical, Boolean, and alphanumeric data.

Register Set

The register set consists of general-purpose registers, of which there are usually between 8 and 32 (depending on the specific microprocessor), and special-purpose registers, each of which is dedicated to a specific function and most of which are affected directly or indirectly by program instructions. A **general-purpose register** can be used (by an instruction) as an accumulator, a source or destination data register, or an address register containing a memory pointer or an index value. In addition, a general-purpose register can be used to facilitate block moves, to permit stacking, and to enhance index addressing. Some microprocessors impose restrictions on some of the general-purpose registers. For example, some registers can be used only for memory addresses or only as data registers. Although these restrictions limit programming flexibility (if we use these registers for other functions, we must first temporarily store their contents), they enable the computer designer to incorporate more compact instruction formats.

Special-purpose registers, by contrast, are dedicated to specific functions. The **program counter (PC)** usually contains the memory address from which the next instruction word will be fetched. Most microprocessors include more than one **accumulator (ACC),** the functions of which are to hold one of the operands to be operated on by the ALU and to store the result of an ALU operation. The **instruction register (IR)** holds the instruction opcode. **Index registers** store constant values used in calculating the effective memory address in an indexed addressing mode.

Most microprocessors incorporate a special-purpose register, called the **stack register,** that points to a portion of RAM set aside for subroutine operations or for handling exceptional conditions (e.g., interrupts). The stack saves the address of the instruction that is to be executed after the subroutine is completed. Thus the next instruction fetched will be the subroutine's first, and when the microprocessor fetches the last instruction of the subroutine (which is always a *return* instruction), it replaces the content of the PC with the address of the top of the stack and thereby resumes execution of the main program. Nested subroutines can also be supported, provided that there is enough memory to store the necessary return addresses.

Most 16- and 32-bit microprocessors use **segment registers** to implement memory mapping when accessing main memory. This mechanism translates program logical addresses into physical addresses. Some microprocessors contain a **memory refresh register** that provides an automatic, transparent refresh of dynamic RAMs (see Section 3.8). Usually, the microprocessor contains a **vector interrupt register** that allows the table of interrupt vectors to reside *anywhere* in memory. In this case, all that the MPU has to do to fetch the first instruction of the interrupt service routine is *indirectly* address the memory location holding this instruction.

A number of **temporary registers,** which are not accessible to the user, are included in most microprocessors and are intended for holding immediate operands or storing temporary results of operations. For example, the **status register** holds various indications, called **flags,** provided by the microprocessor. Each flag is used to indicate the status of a particular microprocessor condition as a result of an operation. Some flags are affected directly by instructions, while the values of other flags may be examined under program control to determine the sequence of instructions to follow. Here are examples of some common flags:

1. *Sign flag*. This flag is used to indicate the sign of the result of any data manipulation or data transfer operation. It takes the value of the most significant bit (the sign bit) of the result and can be tested for positive sign (sign bit = 0) or negative sign (sign bit = 1). This flag assumes the value of the most significant bit (*msb*) of the result even when unsigned numbers are used. The microprocessor has no way of knowing if the data represents unsigned or signed numbers or nonnumeric information; it is up to the programmer to keep track of these.
2. *Carry flag*. This flag is set to 1 if an arithmetic operation, such as addition or subtraction, results in a carry or a borrow out of the *msb*; otherwise, the carry flag is reset to 0.
3. *Auxiliary carry flag*. This flag is used to reflect the status of the intermediate carry in two-digit BCD (decimal) arithmetic operations.
4. *Parity flag*. The parity flag usually indicates an odd parity of a result. If the number of ones in the result is even, the parity flag is set to 1; otherwise, the parity flag is reset to 0 (making the total number of ones odd).
5. *Interrupt flag*. This flag is used to enable or disable interrupts. When the interrupt flag is reset to 0, interrupts are enabled, and when it is set to 1, interrupts are disabled.

Some microprocessors have additional status indicators. For example, an *overflow flag* is used to indicate an overflow resulting from 2's complement arithmetic

Sec. 11.4   Single-Chip Processing Unit (MPU)

(see Section 2.3). Notice that this flag is different from the carry flag and that the two are not interchangeable. Some microprocessors include a *subtract flag* that is set to 1 for operations involving subtractions and is reset to 0 for operations involving additions.

Many 16- and 32-bit microprocessors can operate in either a **user mode** or a **system (supervisor) mode.** This two-mode process is provided to enhance the security in the system. Most user programs execute in the user mode while the operating system executes in the system mode. Most instructions execute the same in either mode, but some instructions, such as I/O instructions and interrupts, can be executed only in the system mode. Correspondingly, to indicate the current status of the processor, the status register includes a *user/system flag*.

Finally, some microprocessors have a *trap flag* that is set to generate an interrupt after the execution of each instruction. This feature enables the programmer to operate the microprocessor in a *single mode*, which is useful for program debugging.

Arithmetic and Logic Unit (ALU)

The **arithmetic and logic unit (ALU)** performs arithmetic, logical, and data manipulation operations on binary numbers. In various microprocessors, the ALU is capable of addition, subtraction, comparison, shifting, and logical operations as specified by the control logic unit (CLU). In most microprocessors, 2's complement arithmetic is used to represent negative numbers.

The ALU width corresponds to the basic word length of the MPU. The ALU requires storage registers to hold the input words (operands) and a latch (which is sometimes internal to the ALU) to hold temporary results of an ALU operation. The inputs are held in an accumulator, a temporary register, or in any general-purpose register within the MPU, or they may come from main memory. The result of an ALU operation is sent through the data bus to the accumulator, to a general-purpose register within the MPU, to a specified main memory location, or to any other destination. Since some ALU operations affect one or more flags, the result of an ALU operation carries status signals to set or reset these flags in the status register.

In general, ALU operations can be classified as either single-operand or two-operand operations. Here are some examples of common **single-operand** ALU operations:

1. INCREMENT: Increases the value of an operand by 1.
2. DECREMENT: Decreases the value of an operand by 1.
3. CLEAR: Resets an operand to 0.
4. SHIFT: Shifts an operand either to the left (using a SHIFT-LEFT instruction) or to the right (using a SHIFT-RIGHT instruction) by one or more bit positions. In most microprocessors, the bit shifted out of the operand is not lost but is shifted instead into the carry flag bit of the status register.
5. ROTATE: A modified SHIFT operation in which the carry flag and an operand form a ring (circulating) shift register. Here, too, it is possible either to ROTATE-LEFT or to ROTATE-RIGHT an operand.
6. INVERT: Complements all the bits of an operand.

Among the most common **two-operand** ALU instructions are the following:

1. ADD: Produces the binary sum of two operands. If the operation results in a carry-out of the most significant bit, the carry flag in the status register is set to 1.
2. SUBTRACT: Subtracts one operand from another. Usually, the subtrahend is expressed in 2's complement and is added to the minuend. The end carry generated by this operation is stored in the carry flag.
3. COMPARE: Determines by subtraction which of the two operands is larger. The result may be positive, negaitve, or zero and will affect the appropriate condition flags.
4. AND, OR, XOR: Operate logically on corresponding bits of the two operands.

ALU arithmetic operations in some 8-bit microprocessors are limited to binary addition and subtraction. In contrast, the more powerful 16- and 32-bit microprocessors provide for signed and unsigned arithmetic, multiplication and division, decimal arithmetic, and even floating-point arithmetic.

Control Logic Unit (CLU)

The **control logic unit (CLU)** has the dual task of synchronizing the operation of the internal units of the MPU, such as the ALU and registers, and the operation of other microcomputer modules, such as I/O ports and memories. The functions of the CLU are to fetch instructions from memory and decode them and then to generate the appropriate timing and control signals required by the MPU for executing these instructions. In its dual role, the CLU also generates timing and control signals that are sent, via the control bus, to other components of the microcomputer system and handles and responds to external signals such as interrupts.

To provide the required synchronization among all its elements, the microcomputer system incorporates a **clock pulse generator.** The timing signals provided by the clock circuits are periodic and are either **single-phase** or **multiphase.** A multiphase signal consists of multiple periodic signals synchronized with each other but usually out of phase. Figure 11-2 shows examples of single-phase and two-phase clock signals. Although some 8-bit microprocessors have used a two-phase clock implementation, almost all newer microprocessors (some 8-bit and all 16- and 32-bit microprocessors) now use a single-phase clock implementation.

The control logic unit is actually a special-purpose computer within the MPU and requires a program to guide it in the execution of instructions. In most microprocessors, the CLU is **microprogrammed.** That is, the timing and control signals required to fetch and execute an instruction are generated by executing a set of **microinstructions** (or **microcode**) resident in the **control memory,** which is usually a ROM. The microinstructions stored in the ROM form a **microprogram** that completely defines the control signals. Thus each microprocessor instruction, referred to as a **macroinstruction,** generates a sequence of microinstructions that in turn produces the necessary control and timing signals for executing that macroinstruction. Hence address generation, fetching, and microcode decoding are accomplished in a manner

Figure 11-2 Timing signals

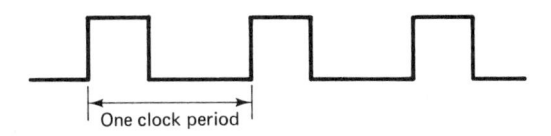

(a) Single-phase clock

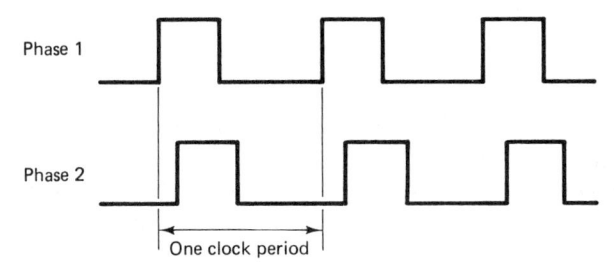

(b) Two-phase clock

similar to that for the macroinstructions. Likewise, we can include in a microprogram unconditional branches, conditional branches on status flags, and subroutine calls and returns. Typically, the various micro-operations, triggered by a macroinstruction, include such things as ALU source operand selection, ALU function, carry control, shift control, interrupt control, and data in/out control. As we already know, the use of microprogramming reduces considerably the extent of the hardware and provides a highly ordered CLU organization that can be quickly and easily modified and diagnosed.

Let us briefly review the operational sequence of a microprogrammed CLU. When a macroinstruction is fetched from memory, its opcode is used to identify the ROM starting address of the microprogram segment (**microroutine**) that implements the instruction. Having received the microroutine starting address, the ROM supplies the microinstructions sequentially. It usually transfers the microinstructions to a pipeline register (see Chapter 9) that serves as a buffer and increases both performance and speed by overlapping the execution of a microinstruction and the fetching of the next microinstruction. Once all the microinstructions in the particular microroutine have been executed, the execution of the macroinstruction is completed. When the next macroinstruction is fetched, the process is repeated.

11.5 INSTRUCTION SET

The **instruction set** includes arithmetic and logical instructions, data transfer instructions, input/output instructions, branch instructions, and control instructions. All microprocessors support most of these instruction types, but instruction sets vary from microprocessor to microprocessor, as do the instruction formats. Each microprocessor manufacturer provides the user with a listing of the various instructions that are available and their formats.

Instructions are made up by concatenating a number of bytes. The part of the instruction that specifies what it does is called the **operation code (opcode).** The part of the instruction containing the information, data, or address that is needed to complete the execution of the instruction is called an **operand.** Instructions may vary in length, but each has the same format: an opcode followed by one or more operands. Instructions requiring only one operand are called **single-operand** instructions; instructions requiring more than one operand are called **multi-operand** instructions. To locate and access an operand, the microprocessor employs one of the various **addressing modes** available to it.

Since each instruction is represented as a pattern of bits, it is possible to program the microprocessor by writing the binary code of each instruction. This is called **machine language programming.** Clearly, this process is tedious and time consuming, prone to errors, and hopeless for a large number of instructions. Usually, however, an alternative low-level programming approach, called **assembly language programming,** is used. In assembly language, each machine language instruction is denoted by a symbol, called a **mnemonic,** rather than by a bit pattern. The one-to-one translation between these symbolic instructions and their corresponding machine language codes is performed by a program called an **assembler.** There are two types of assemblers: a **self-assembler,** which runs on the microcomputer for which it generates the machine language code, and a **cross-assembler,** which runs on a computer different from the one on which the machine code that it generates would be executed.

To illustrate the difference between machine language and assembly language instructions, consider the register-to-register transfer operation B ← (A). A machine language instruction for such a transfer may be | 01 | 000 | 111 |

where the bit pattern 01 denotes the opcode, and 000 and 111 denote the address of the destination register B and the address of the source register A, respectively. The corresponding assembler language instruction would be something like this:

MOV B,A

Hence the task of the assembler would be to produce the codes 01 for the MOV (move) instruction, 000 to designate register B, and 111 to designate the source register A.

Instruction Types

Arithmetic instructions. Arithmetic instructions provide for arithmetic data manipulations. Typical instructions in this class are ADD, ADD WITH CARRY, 1'S and 2'S COMPLEMENTS, and MULTIPLY and DIVIDE. The opcode in each of these instructions is followed usually by the addresses of the source and destination registers where the operands relevant to the instruction are stored.

For example, the INCREMENT instruction will increment by 1 the content of the source register and store the result in the destination register. Likewise, the 2'S COMPLEMENT instruction will subtract the content of the source register from 2^n (where n is the word length) and place the result in the destination register.

Sec. 11.5   Instruction Set

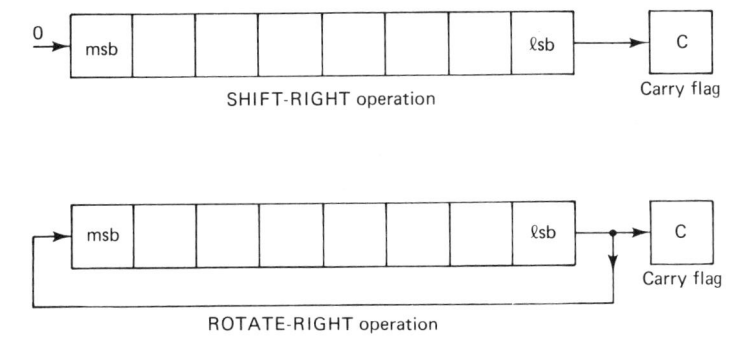

Figure 11-3   SHIFT and ROTATE operations

Logical instructions. This class of instructions provides for logical data manipulations. Typical instructions in this class are AND, OR, XOR (exclusive OR), NOT, ROTATE, SHIFT, and COMPARE. The format of these instructions is similar to that of arithmetic instructions.

For example, the AND instruction will logically AND (bit by bit) the contents of the source and destination registers and store the result in the destination register. A ROTATE-LEFT *n* BITS instruction will rotate the content of the destination register to the left by *n* bits and store the result back in the destination register. The last bit rotated will be retained in the carry flag bit of the status register. The difference between a ROTATE and SHIFT instruction is shown in Figure 11-3. The COMPARE instruction determines (by subtraction) whether the content of the destination register is greater than, equal to, or less than that of the source register and sets appropriate status flags to reflect the result.

Data transfer instructions. Data transfer instructions allow the transfer of information between two MPU registers or between a main memory location and an MPU register. These instructions include MOVE, EXCHANGE DATA, and LOAD.

Let us consider two such instructions. A MOVE DATA instruction will deposit the content of the source register into the destination register. In a LOAD REGISTER IMMEDIATE instruction, the data is part of the instruction. Thus this instruction can be used to introduce constants into the program.

Input/output instructions. This class of instructions provides for the transfer of information between the MPU and an input or output port. Typical instructions in this class involve data input and output and data bus operations during I/O.

There are basically two types of I/O operations: memory-mapped I/O, where input/output devices are connected as virtual memory locations, and I/O-mapped I/O, where input/output ports are independent of the memory. In **memory-mapped I/O,** input/output ports are hard-wired to the address bus. Each input device is treated as a section of memory that is providing data to the data bus, and each output device is treated as a section of memory having some data written into it. In other words, I/O ports are given assigned addresses and are accessed as if they were memory locations. Consequently, memory-mapped I/O procedures do not require special instructions since all memory-reference instructions in the instruction set of the microprocessor can also reference I/O ports.

In **I/O-mapped I/O** operations, there is no need to make any direct reference to memory addresses. Rather, information transfers are done under program control and are initiated by interrupt signals issued by devices requesting MPU service. If a **direct memory access (DMA)** facility is available, peripheral devices can access main memory directly, thus bypassing the MPU.

Branch instructions. Branch instructions constitute an important part of the instruction set. They provide the user with a means to alter the normal sequence of instruction execution, possibly as a result of some decision-making mechanism. Typical branch instructions are conditional and unconditional jumps, subroutine instructions, and software interrupts.

An example of a conditional jump is the JUMP-ON-CARRY instruction. If the carry flag is set, the content of the data address register is transferred to the program counter, and the remaining bytes of the instruction are interpreted as the address of the next instruction to be fetched. If the carry flag is reset, the program counter is not changed, and the instruction has no effect on the flow of the program. In unconditional jump instructions, the program counter is always changed to enable the jump.

Subroutine and software interrupt instructions enable the user to exit the main program from any particular point and then reenter at the same place or at some well-defined relative place. Exit and reenter can be accomplished with JUMP and RETURN instructions.

Control instructions. Typical instructions in this class include interrupt instructions, no operation (NOP), and HALT (or WAIT). Hard(ware) interrupts, as opposed to soft(ware) interrupts, are not caused by a program instruction but rather by a device requesting communication with the MPU. The interrupt signal from the device is applied directly to an interrupt intput of the MPU. When an interrupt occurs, the microprocessor branches out of the currently running program and accesses a subroutine specifically written to handle an interrupt call.

There are basically two types of interrupts: maskable and nonmaskable. A **maskable interrupt** can be temporarily disabled by a special INTERRUPT DISABLE instruction. The user can designate portions of the program that should not be interrupted by beginning each portion with an INTERRUPT DISABLE instruction and terminating that portion with an INTERRUPT ENABLE instruction. In contrast, a **nonmaskable interrupt** cannot be disabled by any software instruction. When a nonmaskable interrupt occurs, the currently running program is interrupted.

Since a microcomputer may contain more than one device that can request a program interrupt, the microcomputer must determine which device (if any) has issued a request and act on it. Microprocessors accomplish this in two basic ways. One is the **vectored-interrupt** scheme, in which an external logic circuit provides the microprocessor (over the data bus) with the starting address of the service subroutine associated with the interrupting device. This scheme is usually prioritized to resolve conflicts that arise when two or more devices interrupt the MPU simultaneously. The second method is the **polled-interrupt** scheme, in which all the devices send their interrupt requests on a single control line, thus activating a common interrupt service routine. This routine, in turn, successively interrogates the interrupt request status bit of each device. When the interrupting device is found, the common interrupt routine will jump to a routine that handles the device.

11.6 ADDRESSING MODES

A microcomputer is called **byte-addressable** if each byte in memory has a different address. If each word has a different address but each byte does not, the microcomputer is called **word-addressable.** For example, a byte-addressable microcomputer with a 16-bit address field has a maximal address space of 2^{16} *bytes*, as opposed to 2^{16} *words* if it were a word-addressable microcomputer.

Most microprocessors use a variety of **addressing modes.** The number of addressing modes in a microprocessor indicates the extent of the instruction set and the efficiency in handling a variety of data structures. Addressing modes were discussed in detail in Chapter 5 and are briefly reviewed here.

Although the terminology used may differ from one microprocessor manufacturer to another, the following list explains the most common addressing modes.

1. *Direct addressing*. The effective memory address where the operand is located is specified as part of the instruction, immediately following the opcode. This is the most straightforward method, very fast at accessing information in memory. However, if all memory locations are to be addressed directly, the instruction would have to consist of several words.
2. *Register addressing*. In this variant of direct addressing, the operand is located in an MPU register and the address of the register is part of the instruction.
3. *Indirect addressing*. The stated address in the address field of the instruction points to the location in which the effective address is located. If the location is an MPU register, this addressing mode is called *register indirect addressing*. Indirect addressing can be extended to several levels, called **levels of deferral,** where one location refers to another, which in turn refers to another location, and so on.
4. *Base addressing*. This approach is used primarily to reference arrays or to relocate a program within memory. The address is formed by adding the content of a memory location or register (either of which can be addressed indirectly) to a specified number called **displacement.**
5. *Indexed addressing*. The stated address in the instruction is added to the content of an *index register* to form the effective address. By using special instructions, the index register may be incremented or decremented to facilitate the sequencing through a set of consecutive or evenly spaced addresses. When the index register is automatically incremented or decremented each time it is being used, the process is called **autoindexing.**

6. *Relative addressing.* Closely related to indexed addressing, the stated address in the instruction is added to the content of the program counter to form the effective address.

7. *Immediate addressing.* The operand for the instruction is part of the instruction, and, therefore, no addressing is needed to get the information. Formally, immediate addressing is not an addressing mode.

8. *Page addressing.* If the number of main memory locations is larger than the number of locations that can be addressed *directly* by an instruction, the main memory is divided into **pages**. The size of each page is equal to the maximum number of directly addressable locations. The page is accessed using any one of the addressing modes listed here, and the effective address of the referenced memory location is the stated address relative to the beginning of the page in which the instruction appears.

Various addressing modes can be implemented using combinations of those listed. For example, in an *indirect relative addressing* mode, the stated address of the instruction would point to a location the content of which would be added to the content of the program counter to form the effective address in which the operand is located.

11.7 TIMING ISSUES

To understand how a microprocessor operates, it is essential to become familiar with the issue of system **timing**. Basically, the MPU is a **synchronous sequential circuit** (see Section 3.5) whose next state is determined by instructions, by the present state of the control logic unit (CLU), and sometimes by external events such as interrupts. As we know, a sequential circuit is comprised of a memory part and a combinational part (see Figure 3–5). The memory part in the MPU consists of various registers and flags. Changes in the contents of these registers and flags are determined by the combinational circuits in the MPU and are synchronized with occurrences of clock pulses. The combinational part performs various functions corresponding to, for example, data manipulation, data transfers between registers, status maintenance, and various decision-making processes and acts also on external signals received from memory and I/O devices.

The combinational part consists of many gate levels, which introduce significant amounts of time delays. Therefore, the clock rate is fixed so that there is sufficient time between clock pulses to accommodate these delays, as well as the time necessary for the memory part to change state.

The time required for fetching and executing an instruction is called the **instruction cycle**. It is the time consumed by the MPU to fetch the opcode of the (next) macroinstruction from memory and decode it, to fetch the rest of the instruction (operand fetching) if required, and to execute the instruction. The instruction cycle is further divided into **machine cycles**, M_1, M_2, ... A machine cycle is required each time the MPU accesses an external device, such as memory or an I/O port. Thus to execute an instruction, the MPU initiates a sequence of machine cycles. Each machine cycle is further subdivided into **clock states**, t_1, t_2, ... Although the number of clock states per machine cycle varies, each clock state has the same length, and its duration equals the clock period. Therefore, the clock state designates the smallest unit of processing activity.

To access an external device, the MPU must follow this sequence of events:

1. Send out the address of the device on the address bus.
2. Prepare the data bus by issuing a *read* (*write*) control signal causing the device to place its data word on the data bus. If an instruction is fetched, the MPU fetches its first word and increments the program counter (PC).
3. Read the data or instruction word from the data bus and place it in an internal register. If the MPU is in a write mode, the external device reads the word from the data bus.

Thus at least three clock states are required for each machine cycle. Additional states would be required, for example, when the external device is not ready, for instruction decoding, or in a machine cycle that handles interrupts.

11.8 BIT-SLICED MICROPROCESSOR

Single-chip microprocessors are limited and inflexible for some applications. For example, the word length and instruction set of the microprocessor are fixed, and its effective speed is limited. Some applications, however, require higher speeds or special instructions. For example, a realtime data acquisition system requires instructions that perform multiplication, division, and floating-point arithmetic. To use a microprocessor as a disk controller, we need instructions such as character detection and insertion and disk read and write. We can program a single-chip microprocessor to execute these special instructions, but this would invariably result in slower speeds.

To construct a very fast microprocessor, we need logic elements that have very fast switching characteristics. Integrated circuit logic families manufactured with *bipolar* technology are capable of effective speeds that are greater, by at least a factor of 4, than those provided by logic families based on MOS technologies. However, bipolar devices require relatively large amounts of power dissipation and therefore cannot be incorporated into a single-chip microprocessor design.

This problem can be circumvented by using the **bit-slice** technique to construct the microprocessor. Bit-sliced microprocessors are designed to have high performance levels that single-chip microprocessors are unable to provide. Bit-sliced microprocessors differ from conventional MOS microprocessors in that the data handling part is separated from the control function. The MPU is therefore partitioned into a set of LSI chips rather than placed on a single chip.

The control part of a bit-sliced MPU is microprogrammable and consists of a microprogram controller and memory. The data handling part consists of a number of similar processor slices that are connected in parallel. Each slice consists of a small number of bits (usually two or four) of each register and a corresponding ALU together with the logic circuits necessary to perform arithmetic and logic operations on these bits. Thus, using the bit-slice approach, the designer can implement a variety of microprocessor architectures with varying word lengths and instruction sets.

To perform a useful operation equivalent to a single machine language instruction, the MPU must go through a sequence of microinstructions. In a single-chip microprocessor, this is done by the control logic unit, whose microprogram is usually not accessible to the user. In contrast, bit-sliced microprocessors are **user microprogrammable.** The user must create the microprogram, specify the various microroutines, and have them stored in a ROM.

A typical building block of a bit-sliced microprocessor consists, for example, of a 4-bit slice containing a 4-bit ALU, a shifter (which may be part of the ALU), multiplexers, buses, registers, and flags. We can then connect such blocks in parallel to handle larger word lengths. For example, Figure 11-4 shows the connection of four 4-bit slices to form a 16-bit MPU. It is important to note two things in relation to this organization:

1. The data and address buses are built up to 16 bits from the 4 bits of each slice.
2. The microinstruction word fetched from the microprogram memory is split. One group of microinstruction bits provides the microinstruction opcode to all the slices. The other group of bits goes to the microprogram controller to determine, for example, the next microinstruction address.

It is clear that additional components are required to implement a complete microprocessor from slices. These components include a program counter, instruction register and decoder, registers to handle I/O and main memory interfacing, and possibly a stack. Various support chips are available to handle the execution of instructions, but additional logic circuits are almost always required to construct a complete microprocessor from slices. Another disadvantage of bit-sliced microprocessors is the limited availability of software support. However, these disadvantages should be contrasted with the many advantages provided by this architectural approach. Bit-sliced microprocessors offer more design flexibility than conventional microprocessors and are adaptable to new applications. Slices can be easily connected to achieve any degree of data precision at high speeds, and the designer can specify word lengths and instruction sets.

Bit-sliced Organization

A microprogrammed bit-sliced microprocessor consists of two basic modules: the control module and the data processing module. The two main elements of the **control module** are the **microprogram controller** (or **sequencer**) and the **microprogram memory.** The organization of such a CPU is shown schematically in Figure 11-5, which illustrates the relationships of these elements.

The **data processing module** includes an ALU, general-purpose registers, a program counter, a status register, an instruction register, a data register, a memory address register, and the necessary logic circuits to perform basic arithmetic and logical operations. The data processing module is controlled by microroutines, the sum total of which is referred to as a *microprogram*, which are stored in the micro-

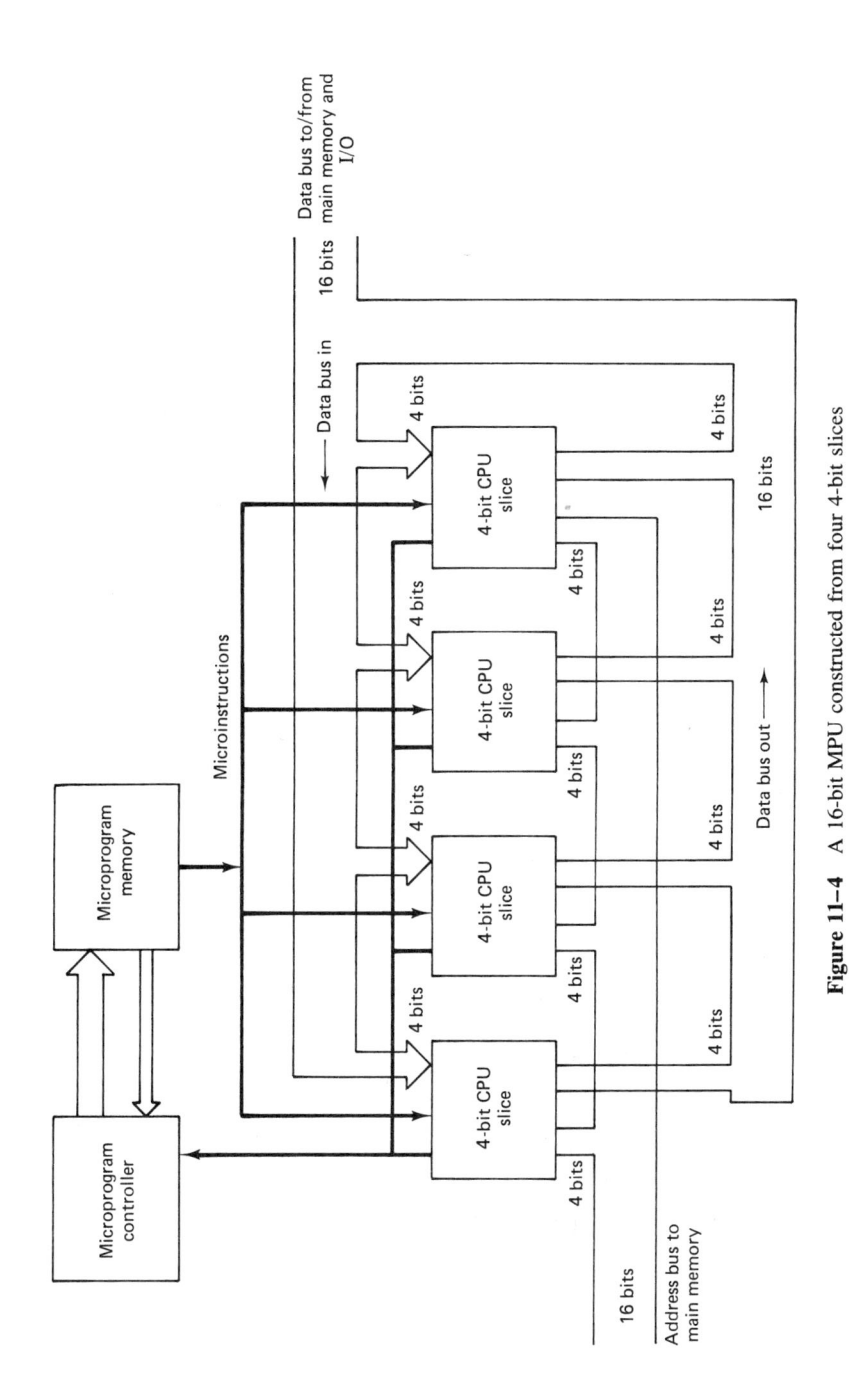

Figure 11-4 A 16-bit MPU constructed from four 4-bit slices

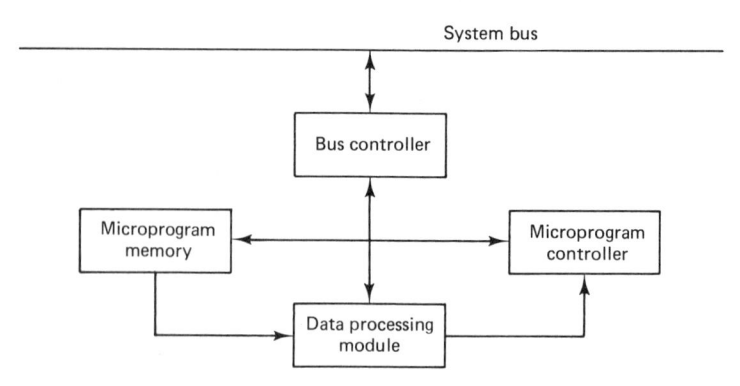

Figure 11-5 Schematic diagram of a bit-sliced CPU

program memory. To achieve high speeds, this memory is usually constructed from bipolar ROMs or PROMs.

The microprogram controller sequences the order in which the microinstructions are executed. Each microinstruction initiates actions in the data processing element and/or the **bus controller.** The microinstruction contains a number of fields that control the operation of the data processing element, provide for operations such as I/O control, and determine the next microinstruction to be executed on the basis of information derived from the opcode and control flags of the macroinstruction.

The microinstruction word fetched from the microprogram memory is split into different groups. One group is fed back to the microprogram controller. A second group controls the data processing module. The third group regulates the flow of information between the bus controller and the CPU. This procedure is called **horizontal microprogramming** and allows for several functions to be performed simultaneously within a single microinstruction cycle. However, since not all the control signals are required within the *same* microinstruction cycle, this approach is quite wasteful because each control bit is dedicated to a single cycle and is issued every microinstruction cycle whether it is required or not. In particular, this approach leads to longer microinstruction words.

An alternative approach to horizontal microprogramming is to **timeshare** the control signals that are mutually exclusive within the same microinstruction cycle and consequently reduce the number of control bits. This procedure is called **vertical microprogramming.** To illustrate the difference between the two approaches, consider a situation where seven control signals are generated in horizontal programming but only one is actually required in the same microinstruction cycle. Since the signals are mutually exclusive, we can use vertical microprogramming to generate any one of the seven control signals with only three control bits by simply using a 3×8 decoder.

PROBLEMS

1. Show schematically how the MPU uses an interrupt vector on the data bus to branch to the I/O device interrupt service routine in main memory.

2. Consider an 8-bit MPU having a 16-bit address bus. Associated with the MPU are 256 I/O ports.
   (a) Use as many 4 × 16 decoder chips—each having a chip enable (E) input—as necessary to design a circuit, in block diagram form, that will generate the 256 I/O port select signals. The circuit is to be enabled by an I/O control (IOC) line from the MPU.
   (b) How many address bits are required?
   (c) Which portion of the 16-bit address bus carries the device addresses?
3. What is the minimum number of address bits required to address a memory unit composed of two 256 × 8-bit memory chip? Show a block diagram implementation of this memory unit.
4. What is the minimum number of address bits required for addressing a memory unit composed of four 256 × 8-bit memory chips?
   (a) How many bits are allocated for the chip select function?
   (b) How many bits are allocated for the memory word address function?
   (c) Show a block diagram implementation of this memory unit.
5. How many devices can be selected with an 8-bit address using an 8 × 256 decoder? Give the hexadecimal code of the 8-bit address:
   (a) When selecting device number 1.
   (b) When selecting device number 10.
   (c) When selecting device number 65.
6. How many control signals can be generated from 9 microinstruction bits using three 3 × 8 decoders? Show a block diagram implementation.
7. Consider a 16-bit MPU whose instructions are composed of two 8-bit fields. The first byte represents the opcode, and the second byte represents the address field or an operand.
   (a) What is the maximum directly addressable memory space?
   (b) How many bits are needed for the program counter (PC) and for the instruction register (IR)?
   (c) What is the impact on the MPU speed if the microcomputer has (i) an 8-bit address bus and an 8-bit data bus, or (ii) an 8-bit address bus and a 4-bit data bus?
8. A microcomputer has 332 instructions and 16K words of main memory storage. How many bits are required for the instruction word in a single-address system (see Chapter 5)?
9. Provide a flowchart showing the operations carried out by the MPU in fetching and executing any program instruction.
10. Assume that the accumulator (ACC) contains the number $(C6)_{16}$, register B contains the number $(94)_{16}$, and the carry flag C contains 1. Both ACC and B are 8-bit registers. What are the contents of ACC and C after executing each of the following instructions?

    (a) ADD B   ACC ← (ACC) + (B)
    (b) XOR B   ACC ← (ACC) ⊕ (B)
    (c) CMA   ACC ← $\overline{(ACC)}$
    (d) RTL   Rotate ACC and C left
    (e) SUB B   ACC ← (ACC) − (B)

11. Consider an instruction called ADT that fetches an operand from memory, adds it to the accumulator, and divides the result by 2. The fractional part of the result is neglected.
    (a) How many clock states are needed to execute this instruction?
    (b) Use register transfer language (RTL; see Chapter 4) to show the sequence of microoperations required to execute this instruction during each clock state.

12. Consider two MPUs, A and B. MPU A requires 4 clock states to access memory and 2 clock states to perform an addition. MPU B requires 5 clock states to access memory and 2 clock states to perform an addition.
    (a) If MPU A is driven by a 4-MHz clock and MPU B is driven by a 6-MHz clock, what is the total time required by each microprocessor to fetch three numbers from memory, sum them, and store the result back in memory?
    (b) If MPU A is to perform the operations in part (a) in the same time taken by MPU B, what should its clock frequency be?
13. Three status bits s_0, s_1, and s_2 are used by an MPU to identify the required bus transactions as shown in the table:

s_2	s_1	s_0	Bus Cycle
0	0	0	Interrupt acknowledge (INRA)
0	0	1	I/O read (IOR)
0	1	0	I/O write (IOW)
0	1	1	Halt
1	0	0	Fetch instruction (FI)
1	0	1	Memory read (MR)
1	1	0	Memory write (MW)
1	1	1	Inactive

   (a) Design a logic circuit to decode the status information for the bus controller.
   (b) Give an example of a transaction that would require the MPU to inactivate the bus.
14. Figure 11-2(b) shows the timing signals of a two-phase clock. Design a circuit that will produce these signals when driven by a pulse source for the following duty cycles:
    (a) 25%
    (b) 50%
    (c) 75%
    Plot a timing diagram showing the relationship between phase 1, phase 2, and the pulse source for each case. (*Note*: Duty cycle refers to the percentage of time in which the signal from a pulse source is at logic 1.) (*Hint*: Use a T flip-flop.)
15. (a) Is it always necessary to poll I/O devices to exchange data with an MPU when programmed I/O is used?
    (b) If two devices are ready to be serviced at the same time, how does the MPU choose which to service first under programmed I/O with interrupt?
16. As illustrated in Figure 11-4, MPU slices can be cascaded to achieve any degree of precision for numbers upon which they operate. Cascading, however, is not the only way in which bit-sliced MPUs can be combined to perform parallel processing. Suppose that we want to process three-dimensional vectors, each 8 bits long. Using 4-bit slices as in Figure 11-4, show the interconnection of such slices to form a three-dimensional vector computation unit.
17. To time various functions, the MPU sometimes uses an interval timer. It includes a down counter (see Chapter 3) that is loaded with a number from an output port, and when the interval has elapsed (the counter reaches zero), an interrupt flag is set. When the interrupt is acknowledged, the starting address of the service routine is placed on the data bus. Assume an 8-bit bus, and design the interval timer in block diagram form.

CHAPTER 12

Computer Communication Networks

12.1 THE EVOLUTION OF COMPUTER COMMUNICATION NETWORKS

Computer communication networks are derived from a combination of computers and telecommunications. Historically, these two technologies have evolved separately, each serving a different purpose. In recent years, however, rapid developments in digital technology have made their merger possible.

The declining cost and increased computing power of digital hardware afforded by LSI and VLSI technologies have seen telecommunications evolve from noncomputerized voice-only switching systems, via a centralized uniprocessor architecture, into today's integrated, multiprocessor-based, voice/data systems. This same driving force is also behind the evolution of computer systems: from a large central computer operating in batch processing mode, via remote access, interactive, time-sharing systems, into today's **distributed processing systems** involving a variety of computing resources joined together to form a cooperating system under a decentralized control scheme.

VLSI technology is rapidly changing the economics of computer organization. Mini- and microcomputers can be used effectively for a wide range of applications. They have versatile instruction sets, extensive addressing capabilities, and software sufficient to satisfy many sophisticated users. End users are also feeling the same trend—instead of bringing work to the computer, the computer is brought to the users. Nevertheless, the migration of computing power and resources toward the end user and the distribution of processing elements have not rendered large computers obsolete. More appropriately they have served to delineate application areas where one type of system can be used more effectively than the other. Many applications, such as image processing and weather prediction, require processing powers that cannot be delivered by small computers. Likewise, some applications, such as realtime data acquisition, either cannot use a large computer or do not require one and can be executed on smaller machines.

Classification of Computer Communication Networks

A **computer communication network** can be defined as an interconnected group of independent computer systems that communicate with one another for the purpose of sharing hardware and software resources. We can classify computer networks into two categories:

1. **Long-haul** or **wide-area networks** that connect, over long distances, geographically separated and dispersed computer systems. This class can be further subdivided into three types:
   (a) Remote-access communication networks
   (b) Private communication networks
   (c) Public data communication networks
2. **Local area networks (LANs)** that connect computer systems residing in a local, geographically limited area.

Private communication networks and **remote-access networks** are restricted to a closed community of users who share common interests, and the networks usually provide more than just data communication services. For the most part, they employ packet-switching facilities and are either **resource-sharing,** like the ARPANET developed in the United States, or **mission-oriented,** like the EURONET established by the European Economic Community (EEC). ARPANET spans the United States and extends to some parts of Western Europe, while EURONET serves the EEC member countries. Though remote-access networks may not fall strictly within the definition of a computer communication network, they are the most common type of private data communication network. They provide remote terminal access over a wide geographic area to one or more host computers. Terminals communicate with the host to obtain time-sharing or remote batch services or to access large common databases. These networks use line concentrators to reduce the cost of communication lines and usually provide dial-in access so that users can access their local concentrator over telephone lines. Examples of remote-access networks are the Computer Sciences Corporation's INFONET and the Control Data Corporation's CYBERNET, both spanning the United States, Western Europe, and some other countries.

Public data networks provide common services to a wide variety of users and are operated by a common carrier, although the connected equipment may belong to many different subscribers. They span large geographic areas; however, services provided over voice telephone circuits suffer from a limited choice of data rates, unfavorable communication costs, and error rates that are too high for data communications. Nevertheless, new public networks have evolved in recent years to better serve the unique requirements of data communications. All-digital transmission services, such as the Dataphone Digital Service of AT&T, offer a choice of data rates at reasonable cost and much improved error rates. Other public networks, such as Tymnet and Telenet in the United States, provide similar improved data communication services by integrating packet-switched nodes into (leased) analog or digital common carrier circuits.

Local area networks (LANs) are contained within a limited geographic area (less than 15 miles) and are characterized by high data rates and low error rates. They typically use decentralized control schemes, and a large number of LANs use broadcast transmission. LANs interconnect a variety of otherwise independent devices, such as computers, terminals, workstations, peripherals, and telephones, over inexpensive media and incur significantly lower communication costs than those of long-haul networks. Ethernet is probably the most celebrated LAN. Developed by the Xerox Corporation in the 1970s and later upgraded in cooperation with Digital Equipment Corporation and Intel, Ethernet uses low-loss coaxial cable as transmission medium and supports data transmission rates of 10 Mbps (million bits per second) under decentralized control. Maximum station separation is 1.5 miles, and the maximum number of stations per network is 1024.

Computer Communication Issues

Computer networking involves a large variety of complex issues that are impossible to consider in a single chapter. Therefore, our discussion will be restricted to major aspects of computer networking.

A **network architecture** is a highly structured, complex logical system that delineates the physical and logical elements of the communication system and specifies the interconnections and interactions that are allowed between the various constituents of the network. To control the communication process, some conventions are required to determine *when* and *how* to communicate and *what* is communicated. These conventions, referred to as **communication protocols,** are collections of rules used to control the exchange of information between the communicating constituents of the network. A prevailing model of network architecture is discussed in Section 12.2.

A computer communication network is composed of a collection of nodes, called **switching nodes,** interconnected by **transmission channels.** The **topology** of the network is the structure defined by the internodal connection scheme. Various network topologies are discussed in Section 12.3.

In Section 12.4, we consider a number of issues related to data transmission techniques. Digital data can be transmitted in three basic modes: **simplex, half duplex,** and **full duplex.** If the transmission channel is **multipoint,** some combinations of these are also feasible. When a sender transmits data, the receiver must **synchronize** itself onto the data for proper sampling but must also be able to determine the beginning and the end of each block of data. Also, because transmission facilities are often expensive and communicating systems do not always use the full capacity of the data channel, it should be possible to share that capacity. This is done by **multiplexing,** and we discuss three schemes that are commonly used in computer communication networks: **frequency division multiplexing (FDM), time division multiplexing (TDM),** and **statistical time division multiplexing (STDM).**

The **transmission medium** carries the data between a transmitter and a receiver.

It may be a physical guide such as twisted-pair telephone wires, coaxial cables, or fiber-optic cables. Alternatively, the transmission medium can be physically unconfined, such as air, seawater, or a vacuum. Characteristics of these media are considered briefly in Section 12.5.

A major feature of a computer communication network is the architecture of the switching nodes and the type of **switching technique** employed. Computer communication networks classified in terms of the switching techniques can be categorized into two types: **switched networks** and **broadcast networks.** The switching technique employed by the former can be **circuit switching, message switching, packet switching,** or some combination or variation of them. Broadcast networks include **radio, satellite,** and **local (LAN)** networks. We discuss only switched network techniques in Section 12.6.

12.2 COMPUTER COMMUNICATION NETWORK ARCHITECTURE

A computer communication network allows for the exchange of information between **elements** (devices capable of sending or receiving information) in different **systems** (any collection of one or more elements). The elements that are connected in a system can be of different types. The communication process is controlled by conventions that are referred to as communication protocols. A **communication protocol** is a collection of rules, procedures, and techniques that are generally implemented in software. The protocol specifies **data formats,** referred to as the protocol **syntax; control formats,** called the protocol **semantics,** which include information concerning headers, trailers, data lengths, and error handling; and **timing information** for sequencing and speed matching. Data transfer is accomplished by a finite sequence of message exchanges between the communicating elements. By controlling message flows, logical communication links, which may or may not correspond to direct physical connections, are established between the communicating elements.

The network architecture is organized in the form of a **layered structure** that implies a hierarchy of network protocols and provides a convenient form of functional decomposition. To appreciate some of the concepts involved, let us now consider a prevailing network architecture model, the open system interconnection reference model.

Open System Interconnection (OSI) Reference Model

The open system interconnection (OSI) reference model for computer communication network architecture was developed by the International Standards Organization (ISO) and adopted by many other standard-making organizations as a step toward international standardization of network protocols. It provides the conceptual framework for defining standards for interconnecting heterogeneous computer systems.

Open system interconnection implies that systems can enter an exchange of information by virtue of their mutual support and use of the applicable standards; they are *open* to one another for the purpose of *interconnection*. It does not imply any particular form of system implementation, technology, or means of intercon-

Sec. 12.2 Computer Communication Network Architecture

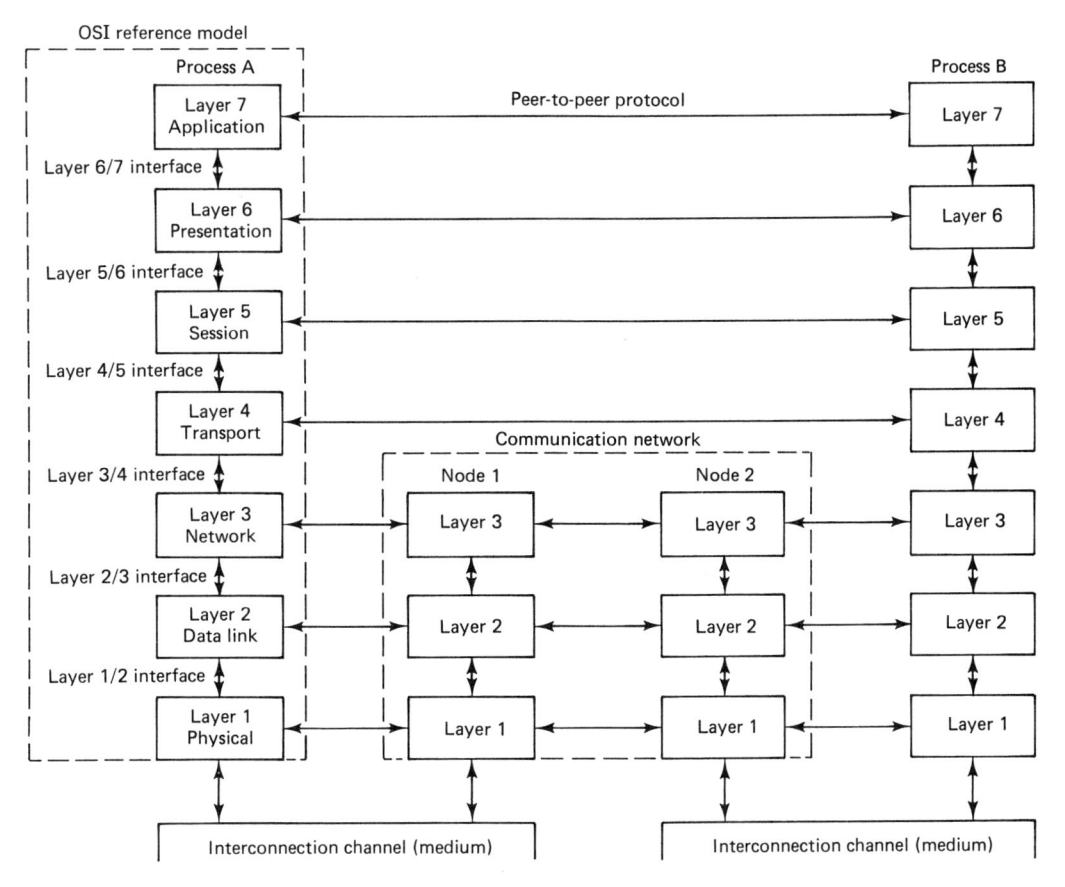

Figure 12-1 The OSI reference model and the process of communication across a channel

nection. These are left up to various vendors whose equipment should recognize and support the applicable standards.

The OSI reference model is comprised of seven layers. Figure 12-1 shows schematically the process of communication across a network between two processes, A and B. Each process is structured similarly and depicts the OSI model in its entirety. The processes can communicate either directly over the interconnection channel (transmission medium) or via one or more intermediate network nodes, as shown in Figure 12-1. The nodes are also layered but consist, in this example, of only three layers each. As will become apparent later in this section, it is not always necessary to include all seven layers.

The number of layers, the name, and the function of each layer may vary from network to network. Nevertheless, the purpose of each layer in any network is to provide some services to the layer above it. The details of how these services are actually implemented are concealed from the serviced layer. The advantage of this approach is that the seemingly unmanageable problem of element-to-element communication can be decomposed into a number of more manageable subproblems.

Corresponding layers on different systems are called **peers** and communicate using their associated **peer-to-peer protocols.** The implementation of the functions of any layers is called an **entity.** An entity can be a subroutine or a process in a multiprocessing system, or numerous identical or different entities may be associated with a layer. If the communication is between peer entities (e.g., computer to computer), the protocols are said to be **symmetric.** If the communication is between different entities (e.g., computer to terminal), the protocols are **asymmetric.** Identifying asymmetries clearly implies simpler entities for the logically inferior element. For example, the commands sent by a terminal to a computer are not the same as those sent by the computer to the terminal.

Notice that, with the possible exception of the physical layer, there is no *direct* data transfer between peer layers. To get data across to its peer layer, each layer uses **virtual communication** whereby it sends data and control information to the layer below it. This process continues until the physical layer is reached, at which point there may or may not be a direct **physical communication** between the two communicating systems. The example in Figure 12–1 shows that process A interconnects with process B via nodes 1 and 2.

A network architecture typically specifies peer protocols, indicates the functional relationships between layers, and identifies the information that has to pass between layers. It does not specify the formats of the interlayer **interfaces** (see Figure 12–1), which define the operations, called **primitives,** that each layer offers to the one above it. These are left for the equipment vendor to decide on, providing therefore some built-in flexibility, but requiring, nevertheless, strict adherence to the network architecture. The only exception is the physical-layer boundary of the equipment, which must be visible in order to facilitate physical interconnection. Let us now briefly consider the functions of each of the OSI seven layers.

Layer 1: The physical layer. The physical layer provides the means to attach the physical medium and control its use. It is concerned with the electrical characteristics of the access to the physical medium, such as voltage levels and the timing of voltage changes (1/0 mark/space ratios); the mechanical characteristics, such as connector types; and the procedural characteristics, such as sequencing of events and transmission modes (e.g., half duplex or full duplex; see Section 12.4). Examples of layer 1 standards are RS-232-C, RS-449, and IEEE 802 for LANs.

Layer 2: The data link layer. Data streams over the physical medium are prone to errors. The data link layer provides error detection and control to enhance the quality of the service provided to higher layers and to make the link reliable. It partitions raw data streams into **frames,** recognizes frame boundaries, uses handshaking (see Chapter 6) for peer communication, and retransmits destroyed frames. It is also responsible for data rate matching (flow control) to keep a transmitter from swamping the receiver. Examples of layer 2 standards are High-Level Data Link Control (HDLC), Advanced Data Communication Control (ADCC) procedures, and IEEE 802 for LANs.

Sec. 12.2 Computer Communication Network Architecture 313

Layer 3: The network layer. This layer performs network functions, such as switching (circuit, message, or packet switching; see Section 12.6) and routing information between end devices. It establishes, maintains, and terminates connections across the network and can also perform the function of an intermediate node (as shown in Figure 12–1) or that of linking two separate networks. An example of a layer 3 standard is X.25.

Layer 4: The transport layer. Since the network layer takes care of data transmission and switching technique, data transfer between transport entities is transparent. The transport layer can therefore provide the layers above it with a reliable transmission mechanism and a required quality of service. It ensures acceptable error rates and sequential delivery of data with no losses or duplications and specifies priorities and delays. An example of a layer 4 standard is Transport Protocol (TP).

Layer 5: The session layer. When two applications wish to exchange information, some agreement has to be reached on the form that the exchange will take. Layer 5 is responsible for setting up this liaison, which is called a **session,** and for managing, coordinating and sychronizing the dialogue. It also provides recovery services in case of some failure. Standardization of session protocols has not yet been resolved.

Layer 6: The presentation layer. The presentation layer ensures that the data exchanged between devices is presented to the application entities in a form that they can understand. It enables different types of equipment, using different data formats, to communicate. It manipulates and converts structured data to resolve differences in data formats and representations and provides services such as (character) code conversions, file format conversions, message compression, and data encryption. Standardization of layer 6 protocols is still an open issue.

Layer 7: The application layer. This is the highest layer defined by the model. It is concerned with directly supporting user applications, and it is up to the user to fill in its content. Applications include exchange of information between end users, application programs, or devices, and task allocation. Basically, two types of protocols are required by layer 7. The first supports user services and is particular to the specific application. The second type is more general and is intended for network services such as management functions.

Two points should be mentioned with respect to the OSI reference model. The first is that the model by itself does not guarantee interconnection. Each layer specifies the functions and services to be implemented in protocols. Some protocols are network independent, while others are dependent on the network to a greater or lesser extent. Examples of the former are the protocols associated with layers 5, 6, and 7. An example of the latter is the physical layer, which will be implemented differently if the medium is a coaxial cable or if the network is packet-switched. The second point is that the physical medium itself is not part of the model. In long-haul networks, for example, it consists of public networks, direct leased lines, and modems or other driving equipment necessary to enable end users (computers, controllers, terminals, etc.) to connect them. In LANs, the physical medium consists of cables, repeaters, and transceivers that allow user equipment to interface to the network. (A **repeater** is a device that receives data on one communication link and transmits it, bit by bit, on another link as fast as it is received. A **transceiver** is a device that combines a transmitter and a receiver.)

To illustrate the OSI principles in operation, assume that application X in process A in Figure 12–1 has a message to send to application Y in process B. X transfers the data to an application entity in the application layer of A. A **header** that contains the required information for the peer layer 7 protocol is appended to the data. The original data with the header is now passed as a unit to layer 6 of A. The presentation entity treats the whole unit as data and appends its own header. This process continues down through layer 2, which generally adds both a header and a **trailer** to the message. The layer 2 unit, called a **frame,** is then passed by the physical layer onto the communication medium.

When the frame is received by B, the reverse process occurs. As the data ascends, each layer strips the outermost header, acts on the protocol information contained, and passes the remainder up to the next layer. Note that at each stage, a layer may fragment the data unit into several parts to suit its own requirements. These fragmented data units must be reassembled by the corresponding peer layer before being passed up.

Protocol Functions

The specific functions of a particular protocol depend on the communication system and the characteristics of the communication process being implemented at any of the layers. Let us examine some of the underlying functions involved in the design of protocols.

Segmentation. The communication system at the application level handles the transfer of streams of data from one entity to another. For reasons such as error control and equitable access to shared transmission facilities, lower levels require that data streams be segmented (broken) into blocks of some maximal size. This protocol function can be referred to as segmentation. Since the segmented data has to be reassembled into data streams appropriate to the application level, the protocol must also be able to reverse the process.

Framing. Data flow over the physical link is carried out by partitioning the data stream and transmitting it as a series of frames. In addition to the data embedded in the frame (the data field), the protocol-framing mechanism provides the addresses of the source and/or destination, error-correcting codes, and headers and trailers to mark the beginning and end of each frame. This function is also referred to as **encapsulation.**

If a frame contains arbitrary data, the protocol has to ensure that some bit patterns in the data field are not mistaken for framing controls; otherwise, the frame may terminate prematurely. Various techniques have been devised to solve this problem, for example, indicating the size of the frame in the header and *bit stuffing* (the insertion of extra bits into a data stream to avoid the appearance of unintended control sequences).

Error control. Noisy communication channels can corrupt transmitted bits, but data can also incur errors or be lost while being transferred to or from memory, across a computer or network node interface, or through a failed node. All these circumstances may result in loss, damage, or duplication of data and control information, and the protocol must therefore provide error-correcting mechanisms. This is usually done by adding redundant control information to the data being transmitted. Examples of error-correcting mechanisms are the ARQ (automatic repeat request) scheme and the use of cyclic codes.

Flow control. This protocol function is required to interface the data rates of the information source to those of the destination so that the former will not swamp the latter. Flow control is also needed to deal with competing logical flows for limited network resources, in which case it is referred to as **congestion control.**

Sequencing. In some cases, the protocol is required to enable the transfer of data units to the destination in the *same order* in which they were issued by the source. Sequencing mechanisms are usually based on some sequence number indicators that are attached to each transmitted message.

Prioritization. Data and (particularly) control messages may need to be prioritized so that they can get through to the receiving entity with minimum delay. Prioritization reduces queuing delays and is important for interactive applications and for ensuring that critical network functions, such as routing messages, are not unduly delayed.

Addressing. Communicating entities must be able to identify each other at each protocol layer. The source address allows the receiver of the data to identify its origin, and a destination address is required for proper routing (delivery) of the data. The issue of addressing is in fact more complex than appears at first sight, as illustrated by the following scenarios: (1) There may be more than one network involved, so each must have its own identifier; (2) a system (e.g., computer) may be attached to a node via a shared transmission medium, in which case the interface and the node must have distinct identifiers; (3) communicating entities (e.g., programs or processes) may reside on different systems of different vendors, each system having its own identification conventions; and (4) the processes are associated with logical I/O ports, which have to be addressed.

Since it is obviously impossible to enforce uniform addressing rules, the common approach to this problem is to use a hierarchical address space. Addressing therefore involves a **name,** which specifies a service (e.g., a computer or a network); an **address,** which identifies where (e.g., a node); and a **route,** which specifies how to get there. It is important to make a distinction between names, which are logical addresses, and addresses, which are physical locations. A logical address can denote one or more physical addresses. Using logical addresses, the sender need not know the physical location of the receiver, and communicating entities can relocate without change of address.

Transmission services. A protocol may be required to provide some additional facilities, such as connection and security mechanisms. A connection is an association between the communicating entities, and the connection mechanism establishes for each of them that the other exists, can be accessed, and can support the desired data flow (which can be either simplex, half duplex, or full duplex; see Section 12.4). A security mechanism may be required, for example, to restrict access and to preserve the integrity of data.

Classification of Network Protocols

Network protocols form a cooperating hierarchy and can be classified into a number of categories (Falk, 1983):

1. **Internetworking protocols** specify the procedures for communication between constituents located on different networks.
2. **Network protocols** are transparent to the user and are intended to ensure reliable and efficient transmission of data. These protocols can be further divided as follows:
   (a) **Network management protocols,** which are associated with the establishment of internodal transmission facilities, routing, and a variety of network management services such as user billing, adding or dropping users or nodes, node failures, and network software releases and updates
   (b) **Data transfer protocols,** which are involved with supporting *datagram* and *virtual circuit* services. (These switching strategies are discussed in Section 12.6.)
3. **Network access protocols** are used by subscribers to communicate with the network nodes to which they are attached. They support international interfacing standards as well as nonstandard interfaces.
4. **End-to-end protocols** define procedures to establish end-to-end sessions. A variety of existing (or planned) protocols support terminal handling, file transfers, remote job entries, electronic mail, facsimile, graphics, packet voice, and teleconferencing.

12.3 COMPUTER COMMUNICATION NETWORK TOPOLOGIES

The **topology** of the network is the structure defined by the internodal connection scheme. The structure can be viewed as a graph whose vertices are the switching nodes and whose branches are the transmission channels. One of the most difficult aspects in communication network design is the choice of topology (Cerf, 1981), which involves many theoretical and practical problems. It is related to another

Sec. 12.3   Computer Communication Network Topologies   317

problem, that of assigning communication channel capacity for the system. To illustrate the problems involved, consider the following circular argument: Channel capacity assignment depends on the expected traffic demand and the routing method; the routing method is influenced by the choice of topology; the choice of topology depends on the traffic.

The problem is therefore one of optimization and may be stated as follows: Given the traffic matrix (which specifies the amount of required traffic between the nodes) and the cost matrix (which specifies the cost of the various channels connecting the nodes and is in turn dependent on the length and data rates capabilities of the channel), minimize a performance function (which can be the cost of capacity, in dollars per unit of capacity, say) subject to some constraints. The constraints can be **delay,** which is the time from the acceptance of a message by the network until its delivery, and **throughput,** which is the effective data transfer rate in bits per second.

As can be appreciated, this is a very complex problem. It is usually partitioned into a number of subproblems that are arranged in increasing order of complexity. Only heuristic methods have been identified thus far for solving this problem (Inose and Saito, 1978).

Network Topologies

Some possible network topologies are shown in Figure 12–2. In the **star** topology [Figure 12–2(a)], all the nodes in the network are connected to a central (switching) node. The operation of the network is totally dependent on a centralized controller. If the center fails, the communication process in the whole network must be suspended. For example, various remote-access networks and LANs are configured as a star and are centrally controlled by a circuit-switched PBX (private branch exchange) or the more modern CBX (computerized branch exchange).

The **tree** topology shown in Figure 12–2(b) may or may not have a central node. If it does have a central node, there may be more than one. By providing intermediate nodes, this topology enables the reduction of the total branch length relative to the star topology. What is actually shown in Figure 12–2(b) is a **hierachical** (tree) network with more than one center (controller) and with intermediate nodes that can act as concentrators (multiplexers). If one of the centers fails, the network can continue to be partially operational. Most remote-access networks are of this topology.

The **mesh** topology shown in Figure 12–2(c) is most common in public data communication networks and in modern private communication networks. Although the total branch length is much greater relative to the tree topology, the mesh topology is advantageous since it provides alternative routes (branches) between nodes. Tree branches can of course spring out of each or some of the nodes shown. The **fully connected** topology depicted in Figure 12–2(d) is shown only for completeness. With N nodes, it requires $N(N - 1)/2$ (full-duplex) branches and $(N - 1)$ I/O ports for each node and is therefore impractical.

The **ring** topology shown in Figure 12–2(e) is more commonly found in LANs. It may employ centralized control, with one node designated the center, or decentralized control, with all nodes having equal status. The network consists of a set of

318   Computer Communication Networks   Chap. 12

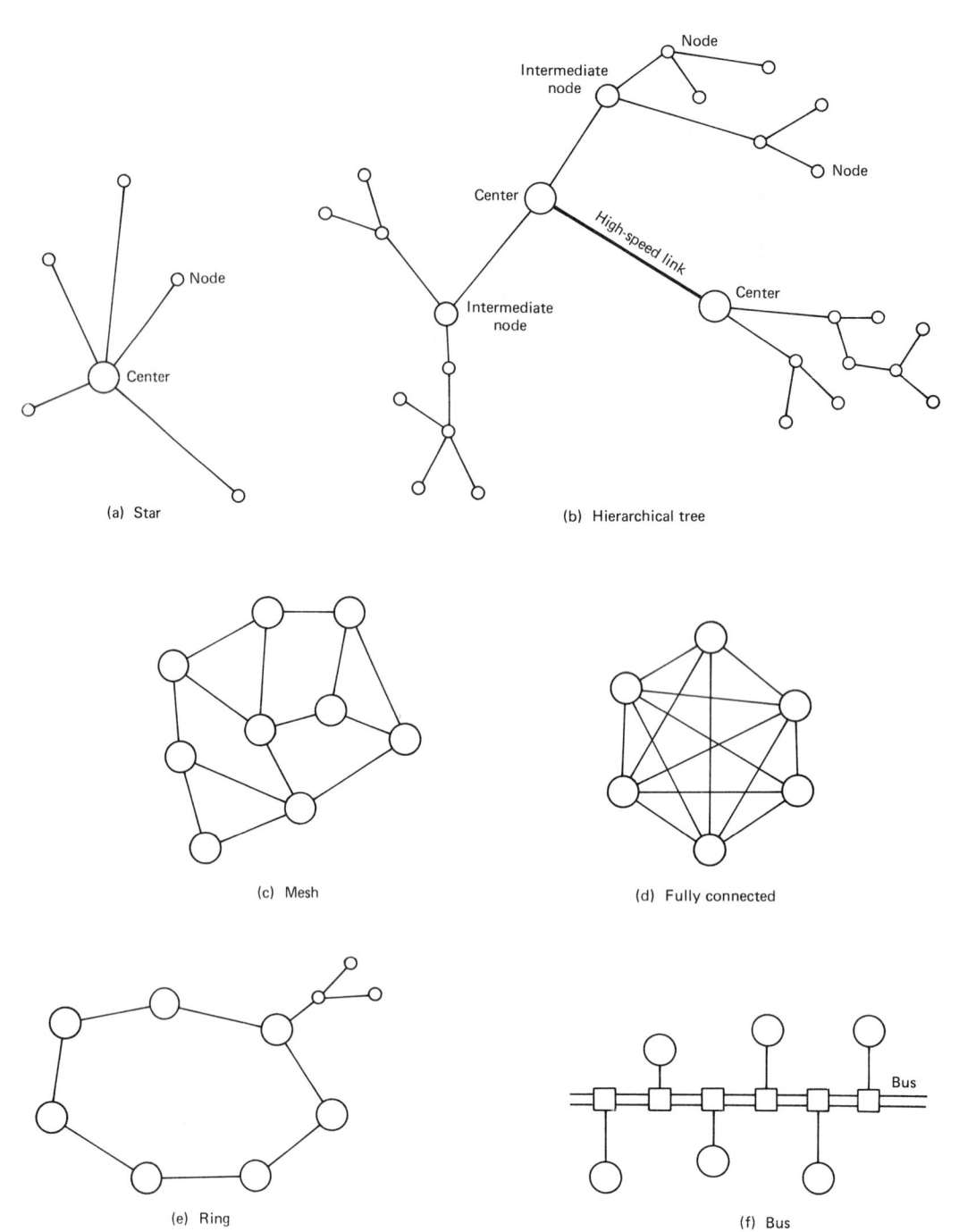

(a) Star

(b) Hierarchical tree

(c) Mesh

(d) Fully connected

(e) Ring

(f) Bus

Figure 12-2   Network topologies

repeaters joined by point-to-point links in a closed loop. Each station is attached to the network at a repeater. Data packets are **broadcast** and are circulated successively around the ring. Each node is capable of receiving incoming data, removing it for the subscribers connected to it (each node can have tree branches), or transmitting data to the next node. The three main ring access methods are **register insertion, slotted ring,** and **token ring.**

The last topology to be considered, the **bus,** is shown in Figure 12–2(f). Predominantly used in LANs, the communication network is the transmission medium, which is shared by the attached nodes, and does not require switches or repeaters. Data packets broadcast by one station can be received by all the other stations. Since the channel is shared, only one station can transmit at a time, therefore requiring some form of access control. This control can be decentralized (distributed) in the form of a protocol shared by all the attached nodes, or it can be centralized. The two most common decentralized medium access control methods are **CSMA/CD** (carrier-sense multiple access with collision detection) and the **token bus.** A centralized control scheme used in some LANs is called **centralized reservation.**

12.4 DATA TRANSMISSION TECHNIQUES

Link Topologies

Data transfer between two stations, referred to as a **point-to-point** link, can be in one of three modes: simplex, half duplex, or full duplex. A **simplex** transmission channel can transfer information in one direction only, as in radio or TV broadcasts. Since the receiver cannot communicate with the sender and the sender cannot be informed of transmission errors, a simplex channel is hardly ever used in data communications.

A **half-duplex** transmission channel is capable of bidirectional transfers, but not simultaneously. Information can be transmitted in only one direction at a time, as in radio communication systems. Two modems are required to implement a half-duplex channel. Transmitting in one direction, one modem is the sender and the other is the receiver. Having completed the transfer, transmission in the opposite direction is effected by reversing their roles; the receiving modem becomes the sender and the transmitting modem acts as the receiver. The **turnaround** time in the half-duplex mode is the time required to switch the channel from one direction to the other. A **full-duplex** transmission channel allows simultaneous, bidirectional transfers, as in telephone systems.

If there are more than two stations, the link topology is **multipoint.** In this case, the station that initiates the information exchange is usually referred to as **primary** and the others as **secondary** stations. Multipoint links can therefore be configured in three ways:

1. *Primary and secondaries half duplex.* The primary can transmit to one of the secondaries in one direction and, having completed the transfer, can receive from the secondary in the other direction.

2. *Primary full duplex, secondaries half duplex.* The primary can transmit to one of the secondaries and simultaneously receive data from another.
3. *Primary and secondaries full duplex.* The primary and one of the secondaries can transmit while they receive.

Transmission Modes

Digital data is transmitted **serially** in computer communication networks, over a *single* communication channel, in bit streams that are grouped into **frames.** To communicate intelligibly, some sort of sychronization must take place between the sender and the receiver. The receiver must know (1) when a frame begins and ends and (2) the duration of each bit, so that it can sample the channel at appropriate times to read it. Clearly, even small timing differences between the sender and the receiver can lead to errors, with the receiver eventually being out of sychronization with the sender.

Two methods are used to achieve this two-level synchronization. In one of them, referred to as **asychronous transmission,** bit streams are divided into characters of relatively small length (typically, 5 to 8 bits per character). Though timing errors can still occur, limiting character length implies a reduced probability of error. Each character is appended with two bits, called **start** and **stop bits,** as header and trailer, respectively. Although the time intervals between successive characters (successive start/stop bits) can be random, the receiver can resynchronize itself at the beginning of each character and thus reduce the effect of cumulative timing errors. Adding start/stop bits also enables the receiver to determine the beginning and end of each character. Asynchronous transmission is relatively simple to implement but incurs an **overhead** of at least 2 bits per character. For example, if the character is 8 bits long, the overhead is 2/10 = 0.2, or 20%. The overhead can be reduced by increasing the character length; however, this would result in larger cumulative timing errors.

The second synchronization scheme, referred to as **synchronous transmission,** allows the transmission of larger blocks of data. To counteract the timing differences between the sender and the receiver, the sender sends its clock information to the receiver on a separate line or embeds it in the data. To enable the receiver to identify the beginning and the end of data blocks, each block is appended with control information, called **preamble** and **postamble,** as header and trailer, respectively. Part of this control information is used for data link control purposes (e.g., error and flow control), but a special bit pattern indicates the beginning and end of each frame. Since the data field of each frame can be arbitrarily long (at least in principle), synchronous transmission overhead can be quite small.

Multiplexing

Transmission facilities are often expensive, and communicating systems do not always use the full capacity of the data channel. Therefore, significant economies can be achieved by sharing transmission facilities, a process called **multiplexing.** We shall look at the principles of the three multiplexing schemes most commonly used in computer communication networks.

Sec. 12.4 Data Transmission Techniques

Frequency division multiplexing (FDM). FDM is used when the channel bandwidth exceeds the total bandwidth required by the transmitted signals. The signals are multiplexed to share the channel bandwidth and are transmitted over it *simultaneously*. Each signal is modulated to occupy a frequency band of the channel that is not occupied by other signals. The information of the various signals is therefore contained in nonoverlapping frequency bands of the channel.

The FDM process is shown in Figure 12–3(a). Assume that there are n different signals, $x_1, x_2, \ldots x_n$, each being band-limited to ω_m Hertz. To separate these n signals in frequency, each is modulated with a subcarrier frequency, $\omega_1, \omega_2, \ldots \omega_n$, respectively. The subcarrier frequencies are chosen far enough apart that each signal spectrum is separated from all the others. This implies that each subcarrier frequency is separated from an adjacent subcarrier by at least $2\omega_m$. Therefore, if the subcarrier frequencies are properly chosen, the multiplexing operation assigns a slot in the frequency domain for each of the individual messages in modulated form. Each of the input messages modulates the appropriate subcarrier, after possibly passing through

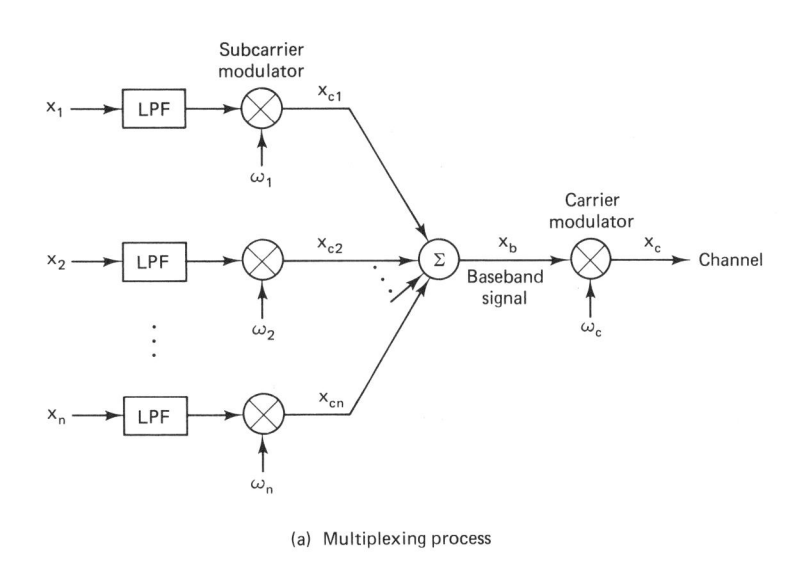

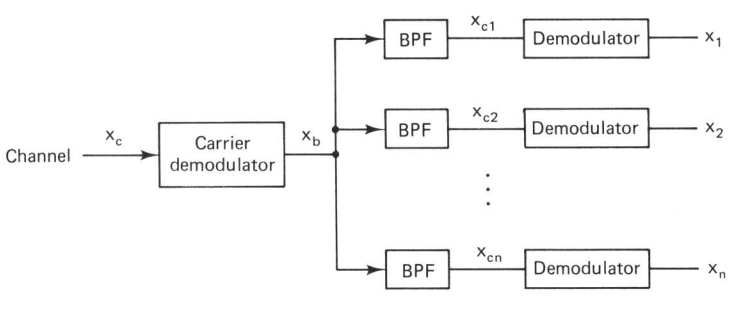

Figure 12–3 Frequency division multiplexing (FDM)

a low-pass filter (LPF) to limit its bandwidth. The resulting modulated signals, x_{c1}, x_{c2}, ... x_{cn}, are summed to produce what is called the **baseband signal** x_b. The baseband signal may then be transmitted either directly over the channel or may be used to modulate a carrier ω_c with the resulting signal x_c being transmitted.

Message recovery, or **demultiplexing,** depicted in Figure 12–3(b), is accomplished in three steps. First, a carrier demodulator reproduces the baseband signal. Then the modulated subcarriers are separated using bandpass filters (BPF). Finally, each message is individually demodulated and recovered.

Time division multiplexing (TDM). TDM is used when the channel data rate capability exceeds the total data rates of the transmitted messages. The TDM process is shown in Figure 12–4. We assume, again, that there are n signals, each prefiltered (or buffered) by a low-pass filter (LPF). At the transmitter side, the signals are sampled sequentially by a rotating switch, called a **commutator,** which extracts one sample from each input per revolution. The samples are then interleaved and sent over a single transmission channel. At the receiver side, a similar rotary switch, called a **decommutator,** separates the samples and distributes them through LPFs (or buffers) for the reconstruction of the individual messages.

If all the inputs have the same message bandwidth W, the commutator should rotate at a rate $f_s \geq 2W$, so that successive samples from any input are spaced in time by $T_s = 1/f_s \leq 1/2W$. With n input signals, the pulse-to-pulse spacing is $T_s/n = 1/nf_s$, and the pulse rate of the TDM signal is $r = nf_s \geq 2nW$.

Almost all practical TDM systems employ electronic switching to generate the multiplexed signal. Notice, however, that TDM requires synchronization between the commutator and the decommutator. This is critical in TDM since each sample must be distributed to the correct output line at the appropriate time. For this reason, TDM is also referred to as **synchronous TDM.**

Finally, let us briefly consider TDM in the context of digital signals. If the input messages have identical bit rates, multiplexing can be done on a bit-by-bit basis, called **bit interleaving** and shown in Figure 12–5(a), or on a word-by-word basis, called **word interleaving** and shown in Figure 12–5(b). If the bit rates of the incoming messages are not identical, inputs are allocated more time slots in proportion to their bit rates, as illustrated in Figure 12–6. Of the four multiplexed inputs shown in Figure

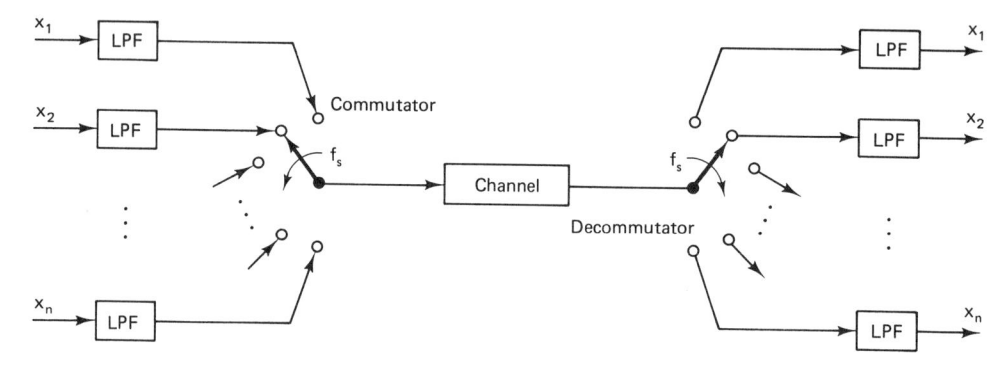

Figure 12–4 Time division multiplexing (TDM)

Sec. 12.4 Data Transmission Techniques

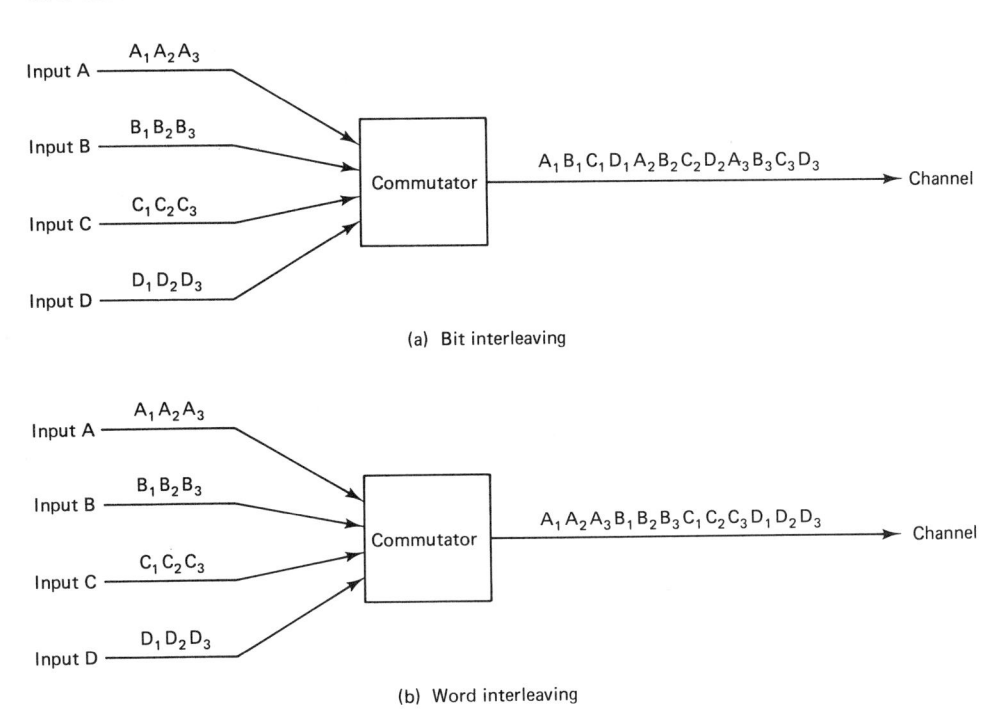

Figure 12-5 Time division multiplexing of digital signals having identical rates

12-6, three have identical bit rates (B, C, and D), while the bit rate of input A is three times higher. As can be seen, input A is allocated (proportionally) more time slots by having the commutator sample it more frequently.

Statistical time division multiplexing (STDM). Synchronous TDM allocates time slots on a fixed basis. At any given time, however, some inputs may not have data to send, resulting in wasted time slots. The STDM provides an alternative

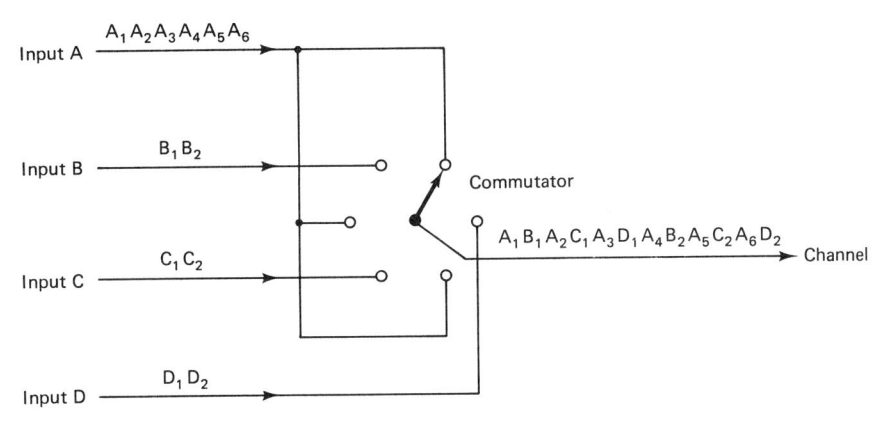

Figure 12-6 Time division multiplexing of digital signals having different rates

by *dynamically* allocating available time according to input demand. It keeps all time slots filled with data as long as there is data waiting to be sent, and it interchanges slot allocations, if necessary, to accomplish this. STDM achieves this efficiency by skipping over idle inputs, with the result that the output data rate of the multiplexed line is less than the total data rates of the inputs. Hence STDM can serve as many inputs as TDM but would require a lower-data rate line, or, using the same line, it can serve more inputs than TDM.

Each input to STDM is assigned a buffer that can hold at least several characters. A buffer control mechanism monitors the buffers and instructs the multiplexer to sample those with the highest occupancy. For identification purposes, every character or block of data to be transmitted is defined by an address attached to it by the multiplexer. Modern time division multiplexers tend to be of the STDM type. Some have added control features enabling them to operate as intelligent terminals that not only multiplex and demultiplex data but also use data.

12.5 TRANSMISSION MEDIA

The **transmission medium** is any facility that carries data from one location to another. A computer communication network can use any one or a combination of transmission media, which can be supplied by any of several vendors. The transmission medium can be a physical guide such as twisted-pair telephone wires, coaxial cables, or fiber-optic cables, or the transmission can be "wireless," using radio, microwave, or satellite channels.

Twisted pairs are most commonly used in telephone systems. They are easy to install but have relatively low noise immunity. They offer moderate data rates of up to 9.6 kbps in local loop connections, but can achieve much higher data rates when used for long-distance applications. Twisted pairs have bandwidth on the order of 200 kHz and require repeaters every 2–6 km. Coaxial cables offer better noise immunity than twisted pairs but are more difficult to install. They can accommodate high data rates of up to 500 Mbps with bandwidth on the order of 300 MHz, and they require repeater spacing at intervals of 1–10 km. Fiber-optic cables have very high noise immunity, can support data rates of up to 1 Gbps with a 1 GHz bandwidth, and require repeaters every 10–100 km.

Using radio or microwaves as the transmission medium eliminates the need for a physical connection between stations and facilitates communication over long distances. Wireless media can be used in broadcast or point-to-point links, have wideband capabilities, can be implemented quickly, and support mobile stations. However, they are subject to interference and propagation anomalies and require more elaborate measures for security. Satellite communication is a newer technique that offers some attractive advantages. Connection to the network can be as simple as pointing an antenna at the satellite. The cost of transmission is independent of the distance within the area covered by the satellite, about a quarter of the earth's surface with a single satellite. Communication can be point to point or broadcast, with high quality of transmission and very large bandwidths.

12.6 NETWORK SWITCHING TECHNIQUES

A major feature of a computer communication network is the switching technique employed. Computer communication networks can be classified as switched networks or broadcast networks. **Switched networks** are composed of a collection of switching nodes through which messages are routed from source to destination. In contrast, a **broadcast network** has no switching nodes, and its users share a common transmission medium onto which a message can be broadcast by anyone and received by everyone. We are going to address switched networks only and will discuss the principles of three switching techniques: circuit switching, message switching, and packet switching. However, before considering them, let us first examine the underlying principles of any switching technique.

The purpose of any switching strategy is to allow *end-to-end* message transfers. Any station requesting such service initiates it by notifying the switching node to which it is attached. This initialization process must at least include the destination address, which may be appended to or embedded in the message. Based on the destination address, the switching node assigns a **route** for the message. The route may be end-to-end or only partial, in which case the switching node decides on the next node that will handle the continuation of the call setup. All these decisions are based on the **routing scheme** in effect.

Since there are usually alternative paths to traverse the network from any source to any destination, the routing process is certainly not a trivial task. Routing decisions may be based on a variety of objectives, some of which may conflict. To cite but a few possibilities, the objective may be routing by the shortest (overall) path, minimum message delay, minimum communication costs, maximum throughput, or equity in using transmission resources. Thus, for example, to minimize message delay under conditions of changing loads, many control messages (overhead) would have to be exchanged between the various switching nodes on the way, resulting in reduced network throughput. By contrast, maximizing throughput may result in increased delays. Similarly, if traffic buildups result in congestion at some links, routing by shortest path may give poor results.

Each switching node contains a **routing table,** which lists all the possible routes available between it and any other node. If the table is fixed and does not vary with the traffic patterns, the routing is **static. Dynamic routing,** which is also referred to as **adaptive routing,** uses a table that changes as a function of the traffic loads and attempts to give the best route at different times. The routing tables can be updated from a central network facility, in which case the routing scheme is called **centralized,** or they can be updated by each node, resulting in a **decentralized** routing scheme. Let us now turn our attention to the three switching strategies.

Circuit Switching

Circuit switching has been used for a long time in telephone exchanges and telex services. A circuit-switched network establishes an end-to-end **dedicated circuit** (path) between the communicating entities. The path is not always a physical wire connecting the two communicating stations. Most modern circuit-switched networks use time division multiplexing (in which bit streams from different sources are interleaved; see Section 12.4).

The communication process involves three phases. In the first phase, the end-to-end circuit is set up. Then the circuit is maintained for the duration of the message transfer. Finally, after the transfer has ended, the circuit is disconnected. To set up a connection, both stations, as well as the required transmission resources, must be available at the same time *before* the exchange can begin. The setup procedure introduces a delay into the overall communication process. If acknowledgments are required, this delay is cumulative and is incurred *before* the message can be sent. All the required resources must be dedicated for the duration of the call, even if no information is being exchanged. This may be appropriate in realtime applications such as voice communications or when a continuous flow of data is involved, but is too inefficient and wasteful of channel capacity otherwise. Finally, call termination also introduces a delay.

To counteract these inefficiencies, some circuit-switched data communication networks employ very fast setup and disconnect mechanisms that often allow a switched connection to be used only for the duration of one message or for one message and an interactive response. Thereafter, the circuit is disconnected, and the resources are used to handle other messages, to be reconnected again when a second message is available. Another possible approach, in the context of digital data exchange, is that of message switching, which will be considered next.

Circuit-switched networks can be either **blocking** or **nonblocking.** If the network cannot connect two stations because all paths between them are in use, blocking occurs. A nonblocking network permits every pair of stations to be connected at once. Whereas blocking is acceptable in voice telephone networks, it is unacceptable when data transfers are involved; these require a nonblocking network configuration.

Message Switching

Interactive data transmission is often bursty and characterized by high **peak-to-average ratios (PAR).** PAR measures the ratio between the desired *peak transmission rate*, determined by the time response requirements of the station, and the *average transmission rate* during a session. For example, a complex graphics station might require a PAR of 1000, say, as opposed to 20 for a dumb terminal.

For data with high PARs, circuit switching is rather inefficient, and message switching might be more appropriate. With message switching, the end stations do not have a dedicated path between them. Rather, the data message is transmitted to the switching node, where it is stored in a queue. When it reaches the head of the queue, it is then transmitted to the next node if a link is available. This process continues until the network is traversed from source to destination. Since messages are stored in the switching node and then forwarded to the next node on the route, message switching is also referred to as **store-and-forward switching.** Any one message is treated as an entity throughout the network and is delivered via the same route.

Each message contains a header that includes the destination address, and any one message can be sent to several destinations. Prioritization can be also built into

Sec. 12.6   Network Switching Techniques

the header, allowing the switching nodes to process high-priority messages before lower-priority ones. Since messages are stored temporarily at each node, peak traffic periods can be adjusted for. For example, lower-priority messages can be held longer in the queue. The switching nodes also provide error checking and recovery services.

Message switching is actually an old idea that was, and still is, used in telegraph networks. Modern message-switched networks use computers to automate delivery procedures, resulting in networks of high capacity and efficiency. Although message-switched networks are not suited for realtime applications such as voice traffic, they are very well suited for applications such as electronic mail, computer file transfers, and query-and-response transactions. It is obvious that these networks increase the utilization of communication resources and do not require that the sender and receiver be available at the same time. Although message switching does not require a call setup, the entire message must be received at each node before it can be retransmitted. The total delay in message switching is therefore almost always much longer than that in circuit switching.

Message-switched networks are nonblocking. Messages will always be accepted, but their delivery may be delayed. In contrast to a circuit-switched network, in which a called-party-busy condition may be encountered, a message-switched network allows for a called party to be busy or temporarily out of service. The message can be routed either to another destination or stored until the intended receiver is ready to accept it.

Packet Switching

Packet switching operates on the same principles as data store and forward; however, it is distinguished from message switching by the size of the message. As we will see, it can therefore operate with higher-speed links between the switching nodes and tends to minimize delay at the expense of efficiency.

A packet-switched network divides the data traffic into blocks, called **packets,** of some given maximum length. A typical maximum length is a few thousand bits, in contrast to message switching, where much larger messages are allowed. Each packet is individually protected by an error detection mechanism and contains in its header the source and destination addresses.

As it turns out, limiting packet length has a remarkable effect on the delivery delay of the message. To illustrate this, consider Figure 12–7, which shows the timing diagram of transmitting a message from source to destination across three nodes. The source station is attached to node 1 and the destination station to node 3. As can be seen from the figure, dividing a message into two packets [part (a)] results in a longer delivery time than if it is divided into five packets [part (b)]. Packet switching can therefore use higher-speed links. Limiting packet size also affects the storage requirements in each of the switching nodes. Unlike a message switch, which requires mass storage and considerable processing capabilities, a packet switch typically requires a smaller storage capacity, which is easier to manage.

Each message is treated as a single entity throughout the network, and its delivery is handled as in message switching. However, in contrast to message switching, where the entire message is delivered via the same route, dividing it into limited-size packets

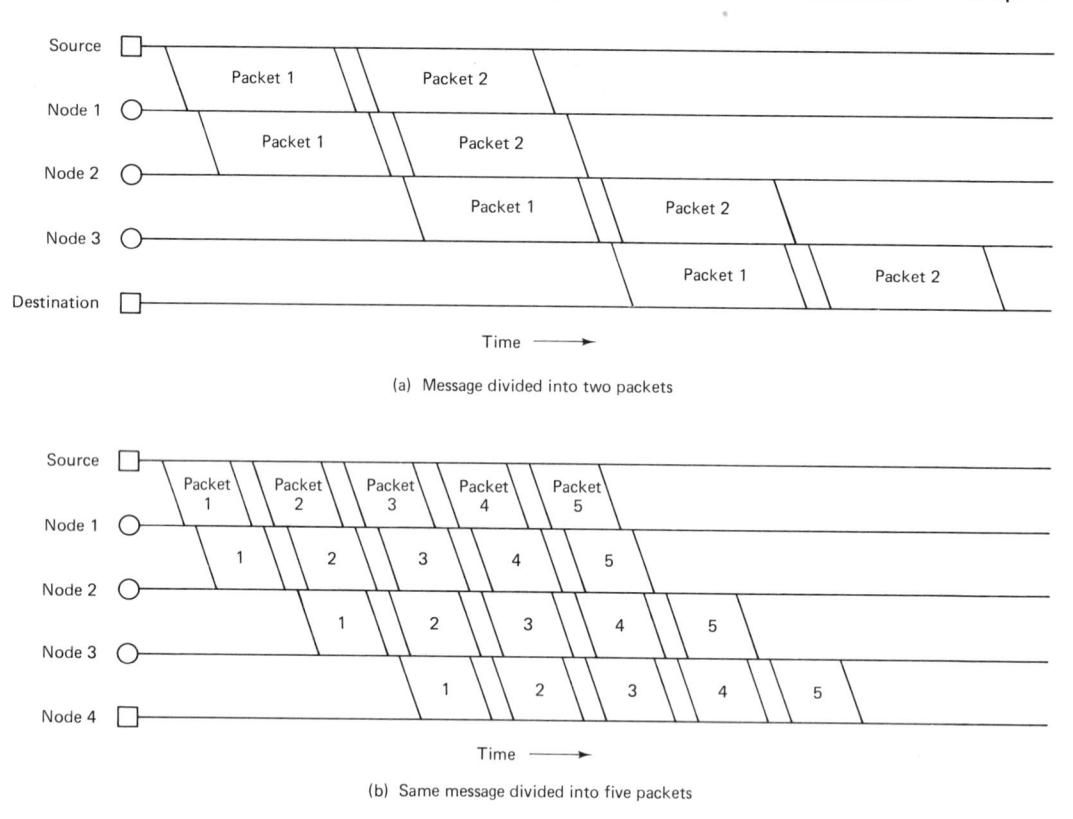

Figure 12-7 The effect of packet size on delivery delay

implies two different forwarding mechanisms (protocols) for packet switching: the datagram and the virtual circuit. In the **datagram** strategy, each packet, which is now referred to as a datagram, is independently submitted to the network and carries all the information required for its delivery to the destination. Since there is no a priori association among datagrams, each can take a different route. Hence the order in which the sender enters the datagrams into the network may differ from the order in which these same datagrams are removed from the network by the receiver. Therefore, packets may arrive at the destination out of sequence, requiring a reorganization to restore the original message. Hence each datagram must also contain a sequencing number that indicates its position within the message.

In the **virtual circuit** strategy, a logical (virtual) connection must be set up between a pair of stations wishing to communicate before data transfer can be established. This implies a call setup procedure, a data transfer phase, and a disconnect procedure. However, unlike circuit switching, where the connection is dedicated, a logical connection means that each station can have more than one virtual circuit to any other station and can have virtual circuits to more than one station. Since a logical connection is established in advance, the switching nodes are not required to make routing decisions, and the order of packet delivery matches the order of packet entry into the network.

Packets must be reassembled and, if not in sequence, must also be reorganized. These processes, implemented in software at the nodes, may be required to handle many messages simultaneously, resulting in possible deadlocks that have to be resolved. Also, there is an overhead associated with packetizing. Smaller packets can be delivered faster, but their overheads will be higher. This means that there is some optimum packet size that balances delay and efficiency.

12.7 SUMMARY

We have examined the tip of the iceberg of what is considered no less than a revolutionary development—computer communication networks. The bibliography at the end of the book includes some references that can be pursued for a deeper understanding of the technical aspects of this subject.

Some of the pertinent issues include data encoding and error detection and correction mechanisms; the design of protocols, routing schemes, switching, and broadcast strategies; timing, framing, synchronization, error, and flow control; and internetworking—the ability to interconnect various distinct networks so that any two stations on any of the constituent networks can communicate.

APPENDIX

Logic Graphic Symbols

A.1 IEEE STANDARD

This appendix provides a brief overview of the new IEEE standard of graphic symbols for logic functions.† The standard is a symbolic language to describe the relationship between each input and each output of a digital circuit without showing explicitly how the circuit is constructed internally.

The new standard promotes the use of *rectangular outline* symbols as the preferred symbols but also permits, to some extent, the use of the traditional, *distinctive-shape* symbols.

A.2 SYMBOL COMPOSITION

The general composition of a logic symbol is shown in Figure A-1. The dimensions of the rectangular outline are arbitrary. The normal direction of signal flow is from left to right, unless indicated otherwise by an arrowhead attached to the corresponding signal line. The graphic symbol is associated with one or more *qualifying symbols*, classified as (1) general qualifying symbols and (2) qualifying symbols relating to inputs and outputs.

The *general qualifier* is used to define the logic function implemented by the device and is placed near the top center of the graphic symbol as shown in Figure A-1. Examples of general qualifying symbols defined in the new standard are listed in Table A.1. The possible positions for qualifying symbols relating inputs and outputs are designated by * in Figure A-1. As seen, these qualifiers can be placed both outside

---

† *IEEE Standard Graphic Symbols for Logic Functions* (ANSI/IEEE Std 91–1984) (New York: Institute of Electrical and Electronics Engineers, 1984).

Sec. A.2 Symbol Composition

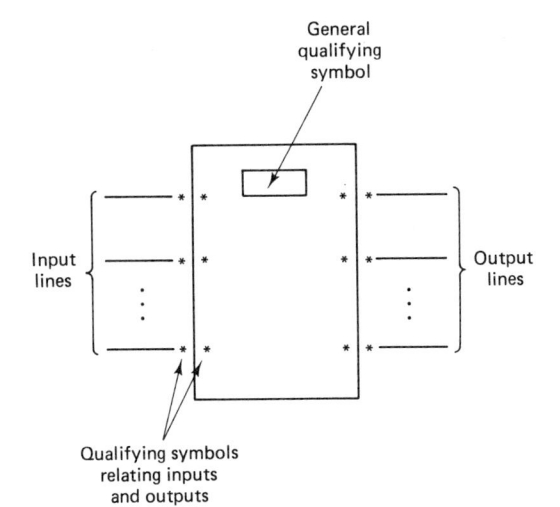

Figure A-1 General logic symbol

TABLE A.1 GENERAL QUALIFYING SYMBOLS

Symbol	Description	Comments
&	AND	
≥ 1	OR	Symbol indicates that to perform an OR function, at least one active input is needed to produce an active output.
$= 1$	XOR	
$=$	Equivalence	
1	Single input	The one input must be active.
X/Y	Code converter	For example, decimal/BCD, BCD/excess-3, and binary/seven-segment code converters.
2k	Even element	An even number of inputs must be active to produce an active output, for example, an even-parity generator.
2k + 1	Odd element	An odd number of inputs must be active to activate the output, for example, an odd-parity generator.
MUX	Multiplexer	
COMP	Comparator	
Σ	Adder	
Π	Multiplier	
SRGm	Shift register	m designates the length of the register.
CTRm	Counter	m designates the number of bits. Hence, the count sequence consists of 2^m states.
RCTRm	Ripple counter	Count sequence length $= 2^m$.
CTR DIV m	Synchronous counter	Count sequence length $= m$.
ROM	Read-only memory	
RAM	Random-access read/write memory	

and inside the outline of the graphic symbol. Examples of such qualifiers are listed in Tables A.2 and A.3.

A circuit logic diagram can be drawn more compactly by having symbol outlines abutted or embedded (i.e., shared between elements), as shown in Figure A-2. In general, a common line that is in the direction of the signal flow lines, as in part (a) of the figure, indicates that there is no functional relation between the devices sharing that line. By contrast, a common line perpendicular to the direction of the signal flow lines, as in part (b), indicates that there is at least one logical connection between the devices sharing that line. In this case, qualifying symbols can be placed on one or both sides of the common line, as shown in part (c). [Note how the internal

TABLE A.2   QUALIFYING SYMBOLS FOR INPUTS AND OUTPUTS

Symbol	Description	Comments
	Logic negation at the input	An external 0 produces an internal 1.
	Logic negation at the output	An internal 1 produces an external 0.
	Active-LOW input	Equivalent to ... in positive logic.
	Active-LOW output	Equivalent to ... in positive logic.
	Dynamic input	Input is active on the transition from (external) 0 to (external) 1.
	Dynamic input with negation	Input is active on the transition from (external) 1 to (external) 0.
	Active-LOW dynamic input	Input is active on the transition from (external) high to (external) low.
	Internal connection	A 1 on the left side produces a 1 on the right side.
	Negated internal connection	A 1 on the left side produces a 0 on the right side.

TABLE A.3 QUALIFYING SYMBOLS INSIDE THE OUTLINE

Symbol	Description	Comments
Postponed output	Postponed output	The output changes when the input initiating (causing) the change returns to its initial state, for example, a pulse-triggered (master-slave) flip-flop.
EN	Enable input	
→ m	Shift-right input	m = 1, 2, 3, etc., designates the number of bit positions that will be right-shifted when the input is activated.
← m	Shift-left input	
+m	Count-up input	m = 1, 2, 3, etc., designates the amount by which the content of the device is increased when the input is activated.
−m	Count-down input	
>	Greater-than input of a comparator	
<	Less-than input of a comparator	
=	Equal input of a comparator	
CT = m	Content-setting input	When the input is activated, the content of the element (for example, a counter or a register) will take on the value m.
J, K, T, S, R, D	Data inputs	Inputs typically associated with bistable devices or storage elements.

(a) No functional relation between devices

(b) At least one logical connection

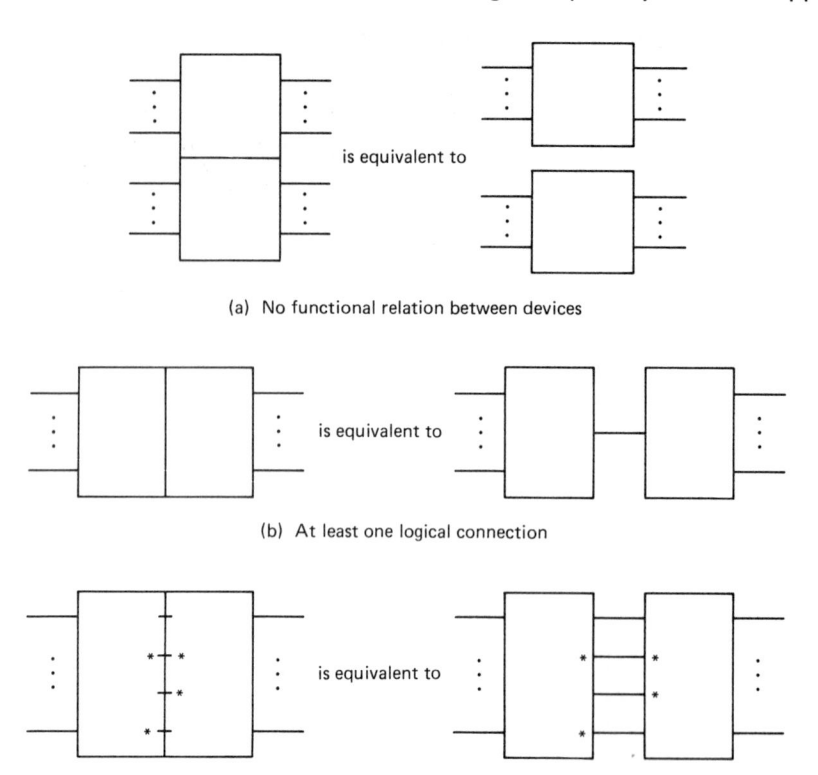

(c) Qualifying symbols for specific logical connections

Figure A–2 Embedded outlines

connection symbol (see Table A.2) is used in Figure A-2(c) to indicate the logical connections.]

If a graphic symbol depicts a number of the same devices, a single (common) general qualifier suffices to characterize the logic function implemented by all the devices. For example, the symbol shown in Figure A-3(a) defines a hex inverter, a device (integrated circuit) consisting of six inverters. Similarly, the element shown

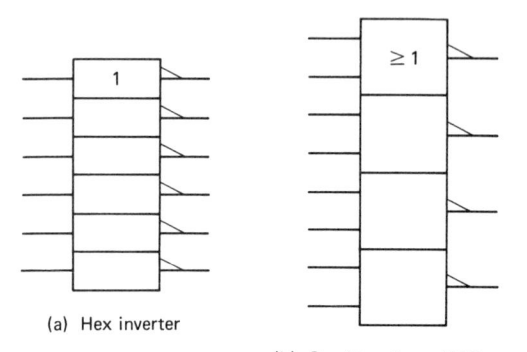

(a) Hex inverter

(b) Quad two-input NOR gates

Figure A–3 Gate configurations

Sec. A.2　Symbol Composition

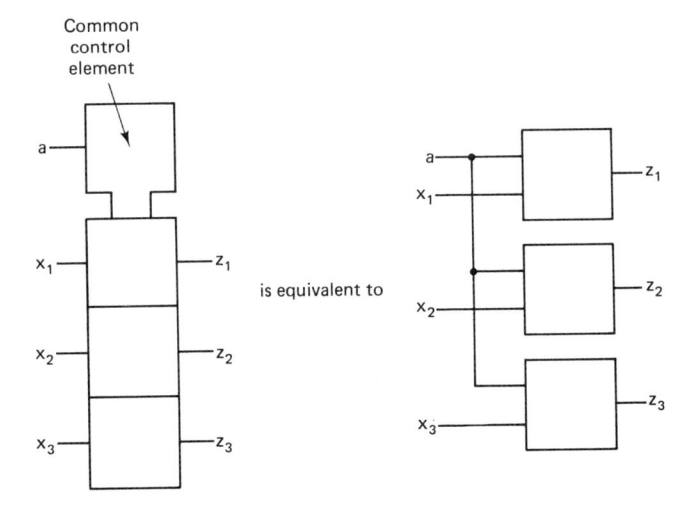

Figure A-4　Common control block

in Figure A-3(b) depicts a device consisting of 4 two-input NOR gates. In either example, the single qualifier implies that each device in the package performs the same function.

Common inputs to more than one device in a circuit can be grouped in a *common control block*, the notched block shown in Figure A-4. As seen, the input *a* affects each of the elements below the common control block. When a common input affects only some of the element below the common control block, this input must be qualified by *dependency notation* in a manner to be explained later.

We can also group common outputs into a *common output element*, as shown in Figure A-5. The common output element is designated by a double line at its top. A common output depends on all the elements above the common output block but may also depend on inputs into the common output block. Consequently, just like any other element, the logic function of the common output element must be specified by a general qualifier. In Figure A-5, the common output element implements the AND function.

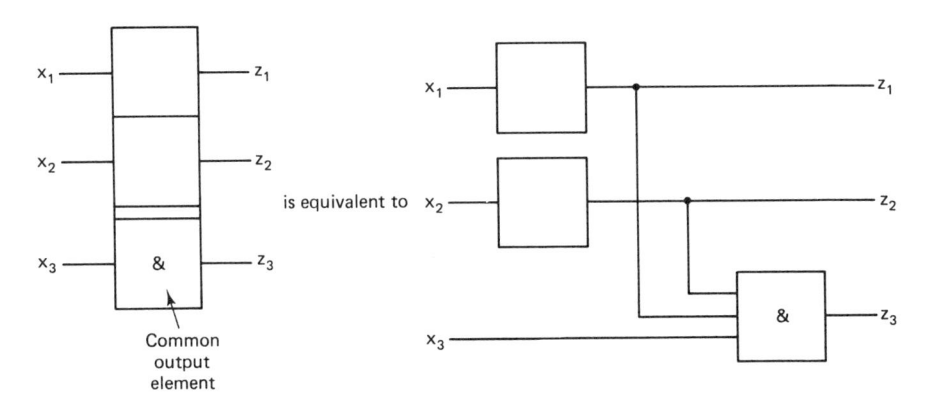

Figure A-5　Common outline element

A.3 DEPENDENCY NOTATION

Dependency notation is fundamental to the new standard. It supplements the information provided by the qualifying symbols by specifying the relationships between inputs and outputs so that the logical operation of the device can be determined entirely from the logic symbol. Of the 11 types of dependencies defined in the standard, we choose to introduce only three: G (AND), C (control), and M (mode) dependencies. These three types of dependencies will enable us to summarize the discussion of the new standard using a nontrivial example.

G (AND) Dependency

The letter *G* denotes AND dependency. In this type of dependency, any input or output designated G*m* (where *m* is an identifying number) is ANDed with any other input or output labeled with *m*. Moreover, if two inputs or outputs are designated with G*m*, they are related to each other by an OR function.

An example of G dependency is shown in Figure A-6. Since the input x_2 is labeled G1, it is ANDed with x_1 because the x_1 input is identified with the same label $m = 1$. Since the x_3 input is labeled with $\bar{1}$ [the bar indicates complement (negation)], x_3 is ANDed with the complement of x_2. Similarly, because the *internal* state of the output line is designated G2, it affects x_7 since x_7 is also labeled 2. Finally, since inputs x_4 and x_5 are designated with G3, they are first ORed and the result is then ANDed with x_6, whose label is $m = 3$.

C (Control) Dependency

Control dependency is denoted by the letter *C* and is typically associated with a clock input. In this type of dependency, if the *internal* state of any input or output designated

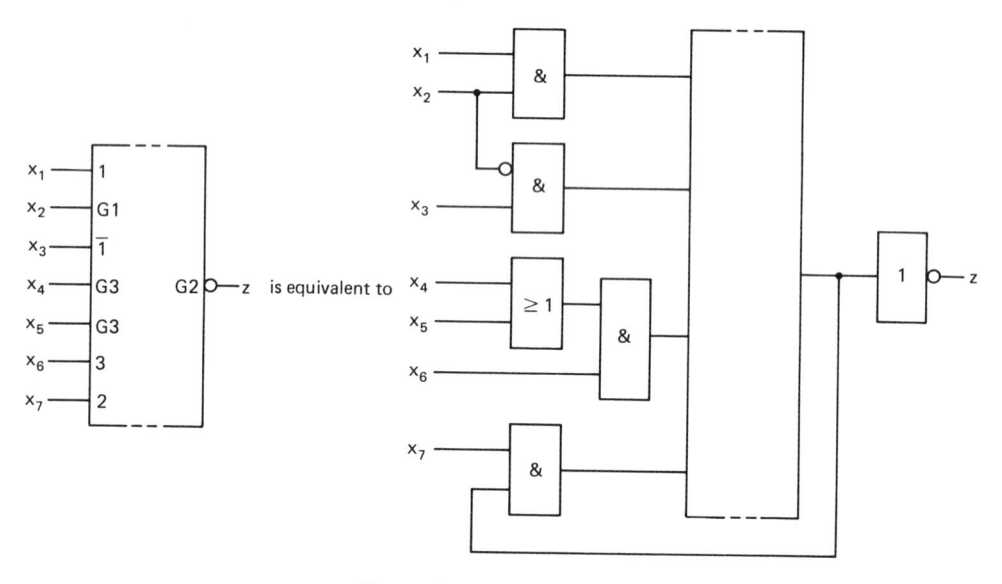

Figure A–6   G dependency

Sec. A.4   Concluding Example

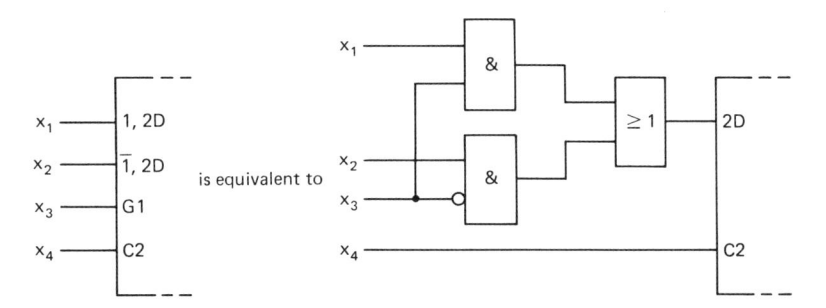

Figure A-7   C dependency

Cm is 1, any other input or output labeled m is enabled. If the internal state of a Cm input or output is 0, inputs or outputs affected by Cm are disabled and have no effect on the function of the device.

Figure A-7 shows an example of control dependency (combined with G dependency). We see that input x_3 selects which of inputs x_1 and x_2 affects the input D when x_4 becomes 1.

M (Mode) Dependency

Mode dependency is denoted by the letter M and is used to indicate how the functions of affected inputs or outputs depend on the mode of operation of the device. M dependency affects inputs similar to C dependency: When the internal state of an Mm input or output is 1, any input or output labeled m is enabled. If the internal state of the Mm input or output is 0, the affected inputs have no effect on the function of the element, and the affected outputs can be ignored.

Figure A-8 shows an example of mode dependency. When $a = 1$, mode 1 is established so that the output z will be 1 only if the content of the device (a register or a counter; see Table A.3) equals 13. If $a = 0$, the output z will be 1 only when the content of the element equals 3. (Note the $\overline{1}$ at the CT = 3 label.)

A.4 CONCLUDING EXAMPLE

Consider the device shown in Figure A-9. The general qualifier, CTR DIV 16, indicates that the device is a divide-by-16 (4-bit) synchronous counter (see Table A.1). The four elements below the common control block are identical (the label 1,5D appears

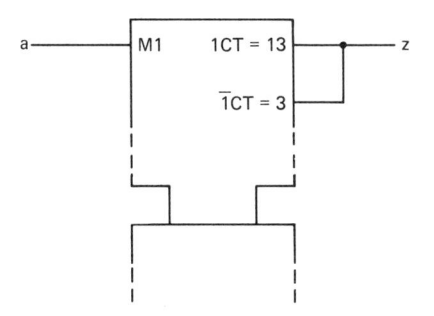

Figure A-8   M dependency

TABLE A.4 FUNCTION TABLE OF THE COUNTER IN FIGURE A-9

CL	LD	a	b	Function
low	X	X	X	Clear
high	low	X	X	Load
high	high	Either *a* or *b* low		No change
high	high	high	high	Increment count

only once) and represent the four flip-flops, which are of the D type. The four inputs to the D flip-flops and the load (LD) line into the common control block indicate the counter has a parallel load capability.

The dynamic indicator at the clock (CP) input implies that the C5 input is activated by a low-to-high transition of CP. In other words, the flip-flops are positive edge-triggered. The label /2,3,4+ following C5 means that the clock increments the counter (+ stands for count-up; see Table A.3) only when M2, G3, and G4 are high.

Since the letter *C* denotes control dependency, any input labeled with a 5 prefix is dependent on (synchronized with) the clock. For example, the label 5CT = 0 on the clear (CL) input means that the clear function is dependent on the clock; that is, it is a synchronous clear. Thus when CL is low, the counter is reset to 0 (CT = 0) on the positive-going edge of CP. Similarly, the 5D labels at the inputs of the flip-flops indicate that the flip-flops operate in synchronization with the triggering edge of the clock.

The counter has two modes of operation. When LD is low, the counter is in mode M1, in which the input data are loaded into the flip-flops on the positive-going edge of CP. (The number 1 appears in the 1,5D label.) When LD is high, the counter is in mode M2 and will be able to advance through its count sequence, provided that G3 and G4 are also high.

Finally, the qualifier 3CT = 15 means that the output *z* will be high only when G3 is high *and* the count is 15. Table A.4 summarizes the operation of the counter.

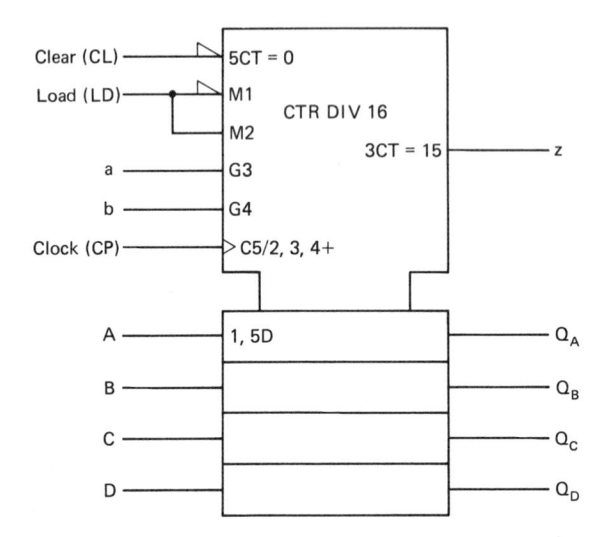

Figure A–9 Four-bit synchronous counter

Bibliography

ALEXANDRIDIS, N. A. (1984). *Microprocessor System Design Concepts.* Rockville, Md.: Computer Science Press.

BAER, J. L. (1980). *Computer Systems Architecture.* Rockville, Md.: Computer Science Press.

BANERJI, D. K., AND J. RAYMOND. (1982). *Elements of Micro-programming.* Englewood Cliffs, N.J.: Prentice-Hall.

BARTEE, T. C. (1985). *Digital Computer Fundamentals* (6th ed.). New York: McGraw-Hill.

BATCHER, K. E. (1980). "Design of a Massively Parallel Processor." *IEEE Trans. on Computers,* C-29, 836–840.

BECK, L. L. (1985). *System Software: An Introduction to Systems Programming.* Reading, Mass.: Addison-Wesley.

BLACK, U. D. (1983). *Data Communication Networks and Distributed Processing.* Reston, Va.: Reston.

BOOLE, G. (1854). *An Investigation of the Laws of Thought.* New York: Dover (reprinted 1958).

BOUKNIGHT, W. J., S. A. DENENBERG, D. E. MCINTYRE, J. M. RANDALL, A. H. SAMEH, AND D. L. SLOTNICK. (1972). "The ILLIAC IV System." *Proc. IEEE,* 60, 369–388.

CERF, V. G. (1981). "Packet Communication Technology," Chapter 1 in *Protocols and Techniques for Data Communication Networks,* ed. F. F. Kuo. Englewood Cliffs, N.J.: Prentice-Hall.

CHOU, W. (ED.). (1983). *Computer Communications, Vol. I.* Englewood Cliffs, N.J.: Prentice-Hall.

CHOU, W. (ED.). (1985). *Computer Communications, Vol. II.* Englewood Cliffs, N.J.: Prentice-Hall.

COLWELL, R. P., ET AL. (1985). "Computers, Complexity, and Controversy." *Computer,* 18, 8–19.

DAVIES, D. W., D. L. A. BARBER, W. L. PRICE, AND C. M. SOLOMONIDES. (1977). *Computer Networks and Their Protocols.* New York: Wiley.

DUBOIS, M., AND F. A. BRIGGS. (1982). "Effects of Cache Coherency in Multiprocessors." *IEEE Trans. on Computers,* C-31 (11).

ENSLOW, P. H. (1977). "Multiprocessor Organization." *Computing Surveys*, 9, 103–129.

FALK, G. (1983). "The Structure and Function of Network Protocols," Chapter 2 in *Computer Communications, Vol. 1*, ed. W. Chou. Englewood Cliffs, N.J.: Prentice-Hall.

FENG, T. Y. (1972). "Some Characteristics of Associative/Parallel Processing." *Proc. 1972 Sagamore Comp. Conf.*, Syracuse U., 5–16.

FLYNN, M. J. (1966). "Very High-Speed Computing Systems." *Proc. IEEE*, 54, 1901–1909.

GIVONE, D. D., AND R. P. ROESSER. (1980). *Microprocessors/Microcomputers: An Introduction.* New York: McGraw-Hill.

GROSLINE, G. W. (1986). *Computer Organization* (2nd ed.). Englewood Cliffs, N. J.: Prentice-Hall.

HAMACHER, V. C., Z. G. VRANESIC, AND S. G. ZAKY. (1984). *Computer Organization* (2nd ed.). New York: McGraw-Hill.

HAYES, J. P. (1978). *Computer Architecture and Organization.* New York: McGraw-Hill.

HIGBIE, L. C. (1976). "Vector Floating-Point Data Format." *IEEE Trans. on Computers*, $C\text{-}25$ (1), 25–32.

HOCKNEY, R. W., AND C. R. JESSHOPE. (1981). *Parallel Computers: Architecture, Programming, and Algorithms.* London: Adam Hilger Ltd.

HOLT, C. E. (1985). *Microcomputer Organization.* New York: Macmillan.

HWANG, K., AND F. A. BRIGGS. (1984). *Computer Architecture and Parallel Processing.* New York: McGraw-Hill.

IEEE. (1982). Special issue on data flow systems. *IEEE Computer Magazine.*

IEEE. (1984). "Whatever Happened to Magnetic Bubble Memories?" *IEEE Spectrum* (September), 22.

INOSE, H., AND T. SAITO. (1978). "Theoretical Aspects in the Analysis and Synthesis of Packet Communication Networks." *Proc. IEEE*, 66, 1409–1422.

KARNAUGH, M. (1953). "The MAP Method for Synthesis of Combinational Logic Circuits." *Trans. AIEE*, 72, 593–598.

KOGGE, P. M. (1981). *The Architecture of Pipelined Computers.* New York: McGraw-Hill.

KRUTZ, R. L. (1980). *Microprocessors and Logic Design.* New York: Wiley.

KUCK, D. J., AND R. A. STOKES. (1982). "The Burroughs Scientific Processor (BSP)." *IEEE Trans. on Computers*, $C\text{-}31$, 363–376.

KUO, F. F. (ed.). (1981). *Protocols and Techniques for Data Communication Networks.* Englewood Cliffs, N.J.: Prentice-Hall.

LANGHOLZ, G., A. KANDEL, AND J. L. MOTT. (1988). *Digital Logic Design.* Dubuque, Iowa: Brown.

LEWIS, M. H. (1983). *Logic Design and Computer Organization.* Reading, Mass.: Addison-Wesley.

LIN, W. C. (1985). *Computer Organization.* New York: Harper & Row.

MANO, M. M. (1982). *Computer System Architecture* (2nd ed.). Englewood Cliffs, N.J.: Prentice-Hall.

McNAMARA, J. E. (1971). *Technical Aspects of Data Communication.* Boston: Digital Equipment Corporation.

NEWELL, S. B. (1982). *Introduction to Microcomputing.* New York: Harper & Row.

PATEL, J. H., AND E. S. DAVIDSON. (1976). "Improving the Throughput of a Pipeline by Insertion of Delays." *IEEE/ACM 3rd Ann. Symp. Computer Arch.*, 159–163.

Bibliography

PATTERSON, D. A. (1985). "Reduced Instruction Set Computers." *Comm. of the ACM*, 28, 8–21.

PATTERSON, D. A., AND C. H. SEQUIN. (1981). "RISC I: A Reduced Instruction Set VLSI Computer." *Proc. 8th Ann. Symp. Computer Arch.*, 443–457.

RAMAMOORTHY, C. V., AND H. F. LI. (1977). "Pipeline Architecture." *Computing Surveys*, 9, 61–102.

ROONEY, V. M., AND A. R. ISMAIL. (1984). *Microprocessors and Microcomputers*. New York: Macmillan.

SCHNEIDER, G. M. (1985). *The Principles of Computer Organization*. New York: Wiley.

SHANNON, C. E. (1938). "A Symbolic Analysis of Relay and Switching Circuits." *Trans. AIEE*, 57, 713–723.

SHIVA, S. G. (1985). *Computer Design and Architecture*. Boston: Little, Brown.

SHORE, J. E. (1973). "Second Thoughts on Parallel Processing." *Comp. Elec. Eng.*, 1, 95–109.

SIEGEL, H. J. (1984). *Interconnection Networks for Large-Scale Parallel Processing*. Lexington, Mass.: Lexington Books/Heath.

STALLINGS, W. (1984). *Local Networks*. New York: Macmillan.

STALLINGS, W. (1985). *Data and Computer Communications*. New York: Macmillan.

TANENBAUM, A. S. (1981). *Computer Networks*. Englewood Cliffs, N.J.: Prentice-Hall.

TANENBAUM, A. S. (1984). *Structured Computer Organization* (2nd ed.). Englewood Cliffs, N.J.: Prentice-Hall.

TOY, W., AND B. ZEE. (1986). *Computer Hardware/Software Architecture*. Englewood Cliffs, N.J.: Prentice-Hall.

VICK, C. R., AND R. E. MERWIN. (1973). "An Architecture Description of a Parallel Processing Element." *Proc. Int. Workshop on Computer Arch.*

WILKES, M. (1951). "The Best Way to Design an Automatic Calculating Machine." *Proc. Manchester U. Computer Inaugural Conf.*

Index

A

ACC (*see* Accumulator register)
Access time, 94, 183
Accumulator register, 104, 124, 291
Adder/subtractor, 81
Addition algorithms:
    fixed-point, 35–41
    floating-point, 44
    unsigned numbers, 36
    using complements, 37
Addition overflow, 38, 41
Address, 90, 100
Address bus, 99, 121, 290
Address format, 125–27
    four-address, 126
    single-address, 126
    three-address, 126
    two-address, 126
Addressing modes, 100, 127–31, 299–300
    augmented, 130
    autodecrement, 129
    autoincrement, 129
    base register, 130, 299
    block, 131
    direct, 106, 128, 299
    immediate, 127, 300
    implied, 127
    index, 106, 129, 299
    indirect, 128, 299
    page, 300
    register, 129, 299
    register-indirect, 129, 299
    relative, 129, 300
Address space, 155
Address translation cycle, 100, 108
Algol, 12, 13
Algorithm, 1
Alignment network, 274
    crossbar, 275
Alphanumeric codes, 50–53
ALU (*see* Arithmetic and logic unit)
AND dependency, 336
AND gate, 74
AND operator, 62, 294
ANSI/IEEE standard for graphic symbols, 73, 330
APL, 12
Arbitration, 175
Argument register, 191
Arithmetic and logic unit, 131–39, 293–94
    arithmetic functions, 133–36
    logic functions, 136–39
Arithmetic micro-operations, 102, 133–34, 296
Arithmetic pipelining, 238
Arithmetic processor, 141
Array processor, 272–78
    associative, 278
    examples of, 274
    organization, 273
    processing elements, 273–74
ASCII, 22, 50–53
ASCII-8, 50
Assembler, 296
    cross-assembler, 296
    self-assembler, 296
Assembler language, 296
Associative mapping, 199
Associative memory, 191–95, 278
Associative processor, 278
Asynchronous counter, 90
Asynchronous sequential circuit, 70
Asynchronous transfer, 167
Augmented addressing, 130
Autodecrement, 129
Autoincrement, 129
Autoindexing, 299
Auxiliary carry, 292
Auxiliary memory, 184, 201–8

B

Base addressing, 130, 299
Base of a number, 22
Base register, 130
Basic, 17
Batch processing, 13
BCD (*see* Binary-coded decimal)
BCD adder, 144–47
Benes network, 277
Biased exponent, 43, 45, 58
Binary, 59
Binary adder, 81
Binary-coded decimal, 22, 27–29
    conversion to binary, 28

343

Index

Binary-coded decimal (cont.)
  conversion to decimal, 28
  conversion to hexadecimal, 29
  signed, 35
Binary codes (see Codes)
Binary counter, 87–90
  up-down, 90
Binary information, 21
Binary number, 22
  straight, 23
Binary signal, 59
Binary subtractor, 81
Biquinary code, 48
Bit, 22
  least significant, 22
  most significant, 22
Bit interleaving, 322
Bit slice, 228, 301
Bit-sliced processor, 228, 301–4
  organization, 302
Bit vector, 272
Block access, 131
Block addressing, 131
Block floating-point, 268
Blocking network, 326
Boolean algebra, 59–62
  switching, 59, 62
  two-valued, 62
Boolean expression, 62
Boolean function, 62–65
  simplification of, 67–70
Borrow, 36, 81
Branch instruction, 298
Broadcast network, 325
Bubble memory, 205–8
Buffer, 74
Buffer pointer, 156
Buffer register, 156
Bus, 1, 73, 99, 281
  address, 99, 121
  arbitration, 175
  bidirectional, 290
  common, 175, 281
  control, 99, 122
  controller, 175, 182, 304
  data, 99, 121
  dual, 175
  I/O, 178
  time-shared, 281
  unidirectional, 290
Bus receiver, 170
Byte, 22

C

Cache coherence, 283
  dynamic check, 284
  static check, 284
Cache memory, 196–201, 283

CAM (see Content-addressable memory)
Canonical forms:
  product-of-sums, 64
  sum-of-products, 64
Carry, 36
  end-around carry, 39
  end carry, 37, 136
Carry flag, 292
Central processing unit, 10, 99, 121, 289
  address formats, 125
  addressing modes, 127, 299
  arithmetic and logic unit, 131, 293
  bus organization, 147
  control logic unit, 139, 294
  instruction formats, 125
  register set, 123, 291
Character interleaving, 174
Chip, 72
Circuit switching, 188, 325–26
Circular shift, 102
Clock, 70, 203
  clock pulse generator, 70, 294
  input to flip-flop, 82
  multiphase, 294
  single-phase, 294
Clock delay, 236
Clock state, 217, 300
CLU (see Control logic unit)
Cobol, 12, 13
Codes, 46–55
  alphanumeric, 50–53
  biquinary, 48
  decimal, 47
  excess-3, 47
  Gray, 48
  Manchester, 203
  self-complementing, 48
  2-out-of-5, 48
  unweighted, 47
  weighted, 47
Collision, 245
Collision vector, 246
Combinational logic circuit, 70
  devices, 75–82
Command, 178
  types of, 178–79
Common bus, 175, 281
Communication protocols, 309
  asymmetric, 312
  classification of, 316
  peers, 312
  symmetric, 312
Compare instruction, 106, 294
Complement, 30–33, 37–42
  arithmetic operations with, 37
  operator, 60
  $(r-1)$'s, 30
  r's, 31

Computer:
  first generation, 7
  second generation, 11
  third generation, 16
  fourth generation, 18
Computer architecture, 2
  parallel computer architecture, 263
Computer communication networks, 307
Conditional branch, 298
Condition bits, 107, 135
Condition code, 107, 227
Content-addressable memory, 191–95
Control bus, 99, 127, 290
Control conditions, 103, 298
Control dependency, 336
Control logic unit, 139–47, 217, 294–95
  asynchronous, 220
  hard-wired, 218
  microprogrammed, 221, 294
  synchronous, 220
Control memory, 221, 294, 302
  formatters, 230
Conversion between bases, 23–27
  base r to base t, 24
  BCD to binary, 28
  BCD to decimal, 28
  BCD to hexadecimal, 29
  binary, octal, and hexadecimal, 25
  conversion to base-10, 23
Counter, 87–90
CPU (see Central processing unit)
CPU cycles (see Cycle)
CPU-IOP communication, 180
Crossbar:
  alignment network, 275
  switch, 176, 276, 281
CSMA/CD, 319
Cyber-205, 252–54
Cycle:
  address translation, 100, 108
  execute, 10, 100, 112
  fetch, 10, 100, 109
  greedy, 249
  in a pipeline, 248
  instruction, 10, 217, 300
  interrupt, 100, 110
  machine, 219, 300
Cycle stealing, 163
Cycle time of ALU, 134
Cyclic codes, 48
Cylinder, 204
Cylinder address, 204

D

Daisy chain, 160
DAM (see Direct-access memory)

Index

Data bus, 99, 121, 290
Data counter, 156 (*see also* Word counter)
Data distributor, 80
Datagram, 328
Data flow architecture, 285
Data routing network, 275
Data selector, 76
Data transfer, 165–69, 180
   asynchronous, 167
   handshaking, 167
   parallel, 165
   serial, 165
   synchronous, 166
Data transfer instructions, 103, 168, 297
Data transfer operations, 103, 168, 297
Data transfer rate, 183
Data types, 21, 133
Decimal arithmetic unit, 144–47
Decimal codes, 47
Decimal number, 22
Decoder, 75, 171
Degree of parallelism, 266
Delay, 70, 317
   propagation time delay, 70, 184
DeMorgan's laws, 61
Demultiplexer, 80
Demultiplexing, 80, 322
Dense addressing, 269
Device address, 180
D flip-flop, 83
Digital logic gates, 73–74
Direct-access memory, 184, 205
Direct address, 106, 128, 299
Direct mapping, 198
Direct memory access, 162–65, 298
Disk, 202–5
   fixed-head, 205
   movable-head, 204
   Winchester, 205
Disk controller, 204
Diskette (*see* Floppy disk)
Disk pack, 202
Displacement, 130, 209, 299 (*see also* Offset)
Distributed system, 278
Division algorithms:
   fixed-point, 41–42
   floating-point, 45
Division overflow, 42
DMA (*see* Direct memory access)
DMA block transfer, 163
DMA controller, 163–65
Don't-care, 67
Down counter, 90
Drum, 205
Dual bus, 175
Duality, 60

Duplex:
   full duplex, 319
   half duplex, 319
Dynamic pipeline, 239

E

EAROM, 91
EBCDIC, 22, 50–53
Edge triggered flip-flop, 82
Effective address, 129
Emulation, 227
Enable input, 78
Encoder, 75
End-around carry, 39
End carry, 37, 136
EPROM, 91
Equivalence gate, 74
Error detection code, 53–55
Evaluation time, 242
Excess-3 code, 47
Exclusive-NOR, 74
Exclusive-OR (*see* XOR)
Execute cycle, 10, 100, 112
   flag, 104
Execution trace, 114
Exponent, 42, 58
   biased, 43, 45, 58
External fragmentation, 213

F

FDM, 321–22
Fetch cycle, 10, 100, 109–10
   flag, 104
Fixed-point, 29
   arithmetic, 35–42, 141–43
   BCD representation, 35
   binary representation, 33–35
   representation, 30–35
Flag, 104, 136, 292
   auxiliary carry, 292
   carry, 292
   execute, 104
   fetch, 104
   interrupt, 104, 292
   overflow, 292
   parity, 292
   sign, 292
   subtract, 293
   trap, 293
   user/system, 293
Flag register, 124
Flip-flop, 82–85
   characteristic equation, 83

characteristic table, 82
clock, 82
D, 83
dynamic indicator, 82
edge-triggered, 82
excitation table, 83
JK, 84
SR, 82
synchronous inputs, 83
T, 85
Floating CPU, 163
Floating-point, 29, 42–46
   arithmetic, 44–46, 143–44
   double-precision, 46
   multiple-precision, 46
   normalization, 43
   representation, 42–44
   scaling, 44
   single-precision, 46
Floppy disk, 205
Flowchart, 156, 158, 181
Forbidden set of latencies, 246
Fortran, 11, 13
Four-address format, 126
Frame, 209, 314, 320
Frame number, 211
Frequency division multiplexing (*see* FDM)
Full-duplex, 319

G

Gate, 62, 73
General-purpose registers, 124, 291
Graphic symbols, 73, 330
   AND dependency, 336
   control dependency, 336
   dependency notation, 336–37
   distinctive-shape, 73
   mode dependency, 337
   qualifying symbols, 330
Gray code, 48–50
Greedy cycle, 249

H

Half-duplex, 319
Handshaking, 167
Handshaking logic unit, 172
Hardware, 1
Hardware interrupt, 157
Hard-wired, 218
Header, 314
Hexadecimal number, 22
   binary coded, 26
   conversion to binary, 27

High-level language, 11, 13, 149
Hit, 197
Hit ratio, 197, 284
Horizontal microinstruction, 222, 304
Horizontal microprogramming, 304
HP3000, 188

I

IC (*see* Integrated circuit)
Immediate mode, 127, 300
Implied mode, 127
Index addressing, 106, 129, 299
Index field, 198
Index register, 104, 129, 291, 299
Index vector, 272
Indirect address, 128, 299
Initial startup time, 237
Input data register, 164
Input-output, 2, 99, 153
   devices, 154
   instructions, 178, 297
   interface, 169
   processor, 177–80
   transfer, 165
Instruction, 100
   execution trace of, 114
   of SIC, 106
Instruction code, 55
Instruction cycle, 10, 217, 300
Instruction field, 100
Instruction format, 100
   of SIC, 106
Instruction look-ahead, 238
Instruction pipelining, 238
Instruction processor, 141
Instruction register, 104, 123, 218, 291
Instruction set, 100, 125, 295–99
   of SIC, 106
Instruction types, 296–99 (*see also* Micro–operation; Microinstruction)
   arithmetic, 296
   branch, 298
   control, 298
   data transfer, 297
   input/output, 297
   logical, 297
Integrated circuit, 14, 72
Intel 8085 register set, 124
Interconnection network, 274
   SIMD, 275
Interface:
   interlayer, 312
   I/O, 169–72
Interleaved memory, 12, 190, 261

Interleaving:
   bit, 322
   character, 174
   memory, 12, 190, 261
   word, 322
International Standards Organization, 310
Interrupt, 157, 298
   handler, 108
   maskable, 158, 298
   nonmaskable, 158, 298
   polling, 159, 299
   priority, 159
   service routine, 157
   vectored, 159–62, 298
Interrupt acknowledge, 159
Interrupt cycle, 100, 110–12
Interrupt flag, 104, 292
Interrupt I/O, 157–62
Interrupt request, 159
Interrupt vector, 159
   register, 292
Inverter gate, 73
I/O, 153 (*see also* Input-output)
I/O accessing, 154
I/O bus, 178
I/O channels, 173–75
I/O instruction, 178
I/O interface, 169
I/O-mapped I/O, 154, 298
IOP (*see* Input-output processor)
IOP instructions, 178
I/O transfer (*see* Data transfer)
IR (*see* Instruction register)
ISO, 310

J

JK flip-flop, 84
Jump instruction, 106

K

K-map, 67
Karnaugh map, 67
Key register, 193

L

LAN, 309
Large-scale integration, 6, 14, 73
   combinational devices, 75–82
   sequential devices, 85–90
Last-in first-out, 185

Latency, 246
   cycle, 246
   forbidden set of, 246
   sequence, 246
Latency time, 204
Layers:
   application, 313
   data link, 312
   network, 313
   physical, 312
   presentation, 313
   session, 313
   transport, 313
Length of a string, 22
Levels of deferral, 299
LIFO, 185
Linear pipeline, 234
Link topology, 319
   full-duplex, 319
   half-duplex, 319
   multipoint, 319
   point-to-point, 319
   simplex, 319
Lisp, 20
Literal, 63
Load instruction, 106
Local area network, 309
Locality of reference, 196
Logical address, 208
Logical conditions, 103
Logical storage, 208
Logic circuit:
   combinational, 70
   sequential, 70
Logic design, 65
Logic gates, 73–74
Logic graphic symbols, 73, 330
Logic micro-operations, 102, 136, 297
Loosely coupled system, 177, 279
LSI, 6, 14, 73
   combinational devices, 75–82
   sequential devices, 85–90

M

Machine cycle, 219, 300
Machine language, 10, 296
Macroinstruction, 217, 294
Magnetic bubble memory, 205–8
Magnetic disk, 202–5
Magnetic diskette (*see* Floppy disk)
Magnetic drum, 205
Magnetic tape, 201–2
Mailbox, 177
Main memory, 121, 183
Majority gate, 96
Manchester code, 203

Index

Mantissa, 42
Mapping:
　associative, 199
　direct, 198
　set-associative, 199
MAR (*see* Memory address register)
Mask register, 161
Match logic, 192
Match register, 191
Maxterm, 63
MBR (*see* Memory buffer register)
Medium-scale integration, 6, 14, 73
　combinational devices, 75–82
　sequential devices, 85–90
Memory:
　access time, 95, 183
　associative, 191
　auxiliary, 201
　cache, 196
　content-addressable, 184, 191
　data transfer rate, 183
　direct-access, 205
　dynamic, 95
　IC, 95, 184, 196
　modular, 189
　multiport, 176, 280, 282
　nonvolatile, 91, 184
　random-access, 94, 184
　read-only, 90–91
　read/write, 94, 184
　sequential-access, 184, 202
　stack, 184
　static, 95
　virtual, 16, 208
　volatile, 95, 184
Memory address, 92
Memory address register, 94, 104, 124, 163, 189
Memory buffer register, 95, 104, 124, 163, 189
Memory capacity, 90, 183
Memory cycle, 184
Memory hierarchy, 214
Memory interleaving, 12, 190, 261
Memory-mapped I/O, 155, 297
Memory module, 190
Memory read, 95, 103, 105, 164, 195
Memory refresh register, 292
Memory space, 126
Memory unit, 99, 122
Memory word, 90
Memory write, 95, 103, 105, 164, 195
Message switching, 188, 326–27
Message transfer system, 279
Microcode, 294
Microcomputer, 287
　byte-addressable, 299
　general overview, 289
　word-addressable, 299

Microcontroller, 221
Microinstruction, 100, 217, 294
　arithmetic, 102, 296
　branch, 298
　control conditions, 103, 298
　data transfer, 103, 297
　format, 222–26
　horizontal, 222, 304
　input/output, 297
　logic, 102, 297
　logical conditions, 103
　sequencing, 226
　shift, 102
　vertical, 223, 304
Micro-operation, 100, 122
　arithmetic, 102
　control conditions, 103
　data transfer, 103
　logic, 102
　logical conditions, 103
　shift, 102
Microprocessing unit (*see* Central processing unit; Microprocessor)
Microprocessor, 17, 287
　addressing modes, 299
　arithmetic and logic unit, 293
　bit-sliced, 228, 301
　control logic unit, 294
　first generation, 287
　fourth generation, 288
　instruction set, 295
　register set, 291
　second generation, 288
　third generation, 288
　timing, 300
Microprogram, 218, 294, 302
　assembler, 229
　controller, 302
　example of, 224
　sequencer, 221, 302
　simulator, 230
Microprogrammed control, 221
Microprogram memory, 302 (*see also* Control memory)
Microprogramming, 14, 217
　advantages, 221
　horizontal, 222, 304
　support tools, 229–30
　vertical, 223, 304
MIMD, 265
Minimum average latency, 249
Minterm, 63
MISD, 265
Miss, 197
Mnemonics, 10, 218, 296
Mode dependency, 337
Modular memory, 189–90
MPU (*see* Central processing unit)

MSI, 6, 14, 73
　combinational devices, 75–82
　sequential devices, 85–90
Multicache, 283
Multifunction pipeline, 239, 244
　example of, 252
Multiplexer, 76–80
Multiplexer channels, 174
Multiplexing:
　frequency division, 321–22
　statistical time division, 323–24
　time division, 322–23
Multiplication algorithms:
　fixed-point, 41–42
　floating-point, 45
Multiport memory, 176, 280, 282
Multiprocessing, 14, 262
Multiprocessor system, 172, 278–84
　common bus, 175, 281
　crossbar switch, 176, 276, 281
　hardware organization, 280
　multicache, 283
　multiport memory, 176, 280, 282
　private-memory, 279
　shared-memory, 279
Multiprogramming, 13, 14, 208, 261, 278
MUX (*see* Multiplexer)

N

NAND gate, 74
Nanomemory, 230
Network protocols (*see* Communication protocols)
Network topology (*see* Topology)
Nibble, 22
Nonblocking network, 326
Noncompute delay, 251
Nonvolatile, 91, 184
NOR gate, 74
Normalization, 43
NOT gate, 73, 74
Number system, 22

O

Octal number, 22
　binary coded, 25
　conversion to binary, 26
Offset, 130, 209
　page, 209
　segment, 211
Opcode (*see* Operation Code)

Open system interconnection model (see OSI)
Operand, 55, 100, 125, 296
Operand scaling, 44
Operation Code, 55, 100, 125, 178
OR gate, 74
OR operator, 62, 299
OSI, 310–14
Output data register, 164
Overflow, 35, 38, 39, 41, 42, 44, 136
Overhead, 320

P

Packet, 327
Packet switching, 327–29
Padding, 268
Page, 130, 209, 300
Page addressing, 300
Page number, 209
Page size, 209
Page table, 209
  implementation, 211
Paging, 209
PAL, 93–94
Parallel binary adder, 81–82
Parallel binary subtractor, 81–82
Parallel computer, 261
  classification of, 263–66
Parallel processing, 13, 260
Parallel register, 86
Parallel transfer, 165
Parity, 53
  even-parity, 53
  odd-parity, 54
Parity detector, 54
Parity flag, 292
Parity generator, 54
Partial product, 41
PC (see Program counter)
Peripheral, 153
Personal computer, 17
Pipeline, 233
  arithmetic, 238
  complexity of, 257
  dynamic, 239
  efficiency of, 236
  example of, 252
  instruction, 238
  linear, 234
  multifunction, 239, 244
  processor, 239
  scalar, 239
  static, 239
  synchronization of, 234
  unifunction, 239
  vector, 239

Pipeline controller, 245
Pipelined computer, 233
  example of, 252
Pipelined vector processor, 269
Pipeline processing, 233
Pipelining, 14, 15, 233, 261
  configurational classification, 239
  functional classification, 238
  principles, 242
PLA, 91–93
Polled-interrupt, 159
Polling, 159, 299
  polling routine, 159
Pop stack, 185
POS, 64
  canonical, 64
Position scalar, 138
Priority encoder, 75, 161
  design of, 181
Priority interrupt, 159–62
  daisy chain, 160
  priority encoder, 161
Processing elements:
  with local memories, 273
  with parallel memories, 274
Processor pipeline, 239
Product-of-sums (see POS)
Program, 1
Program counter, 104, 123, 291
Programmable array logic, 93–94
Programmable arrays, 90–94
Programmable logic array, 91–93
Programmed I/O, 155–57
Program status word, 104, 124
Prolog, 19
PROM, 91
Propagation time delay, 70, 184
Protocol (see Communication protocol)
Protocol classification, 316
Protocol functions:
  addressing, 315
  congestion control, 315
  encapsulation, 314
  error control, 315
  flow control, 315
  framing, 314
  prioritization, 315
  segmentation, 314
  sequencing, 315
  transmission services, 316
PSW (see Program status word)
Push-down stack, 127
Push stack, 185

R

Radix, 22, 42
Radix point, 23
RAM, 95

Random-access memory, 94–95
Range:
  of signed binary-coded numbers, 35
  of signed binary numbers, 34
Read, 86, 95, 167
Read microinstruction, 106
Read-only memory, 90–91
Read/write memory, 94
  organization of, 94
Record, 202
  end-of-record, 202
  interrecord gap, 202
Recurrence, 254–57
  equation, 254
  problem, 254
Reduced instruction set computer, 149
Register, 85, 101
Register-indirect mode, 129, 299
Register mode, 129, 299
Register set, 123, 291
  of Intel 8085, 124
  of SIC, 104
Register transfer language, 101–3
Register transfer operations, 101
Register transfer statements:
  arithmetic, 102
  control, 103
  data transfer, 103
  logic, 102
  shift, 102
Register with parallel load, 86, 88
Relative addressing, 129, 300
Remainder, 41
Replacement algorithm, 197
Reservation table, 242
  initiation of, 245
Return from interrupt, 106
Return from subroutine, 106
Ripple counter, 90
RISC, 149
ROM, 90–91
Rotate, 293
Routing, 325
  adaptive, 325
  centralized, 325
  decentralized, 325
  dynamic, 325
  static, 325
$(r-1)$'s complement representation, 30
r's complement representation, 31
RTL (see Register transfer language)

S

SAM, 184, 202
Scalar pipeline, 239

Index

Scaling, 44
Scheduling algorithm, 246
Secondary memory, 184, 201–8
Sector, 204
Seek time, 204
Segment, 211
Segmentation, 211
Segment number, 211
Segment register, 292
Segment table, 211
   implementation, 211
Selector channels, 174
Self-complementing code, 48
Sequence counter, 108, 140
Sequencer, 221, 302
Sequential-access memory, 184, 202
Sequential addressing, 271
Sequential logic circuit:
   asynchronous, 70
   devices, 85–90
   memory of, 70
   synchronous, 70, 300
Serial input, 87
Serial-in serial-out, 86
Serial transfer, 165
Set-associative mapping, 199
Seven-segment display, 65
Shift, 29, 43, 44
Shifter, 137
Shift micro-operation, 102, 293
Shift register, 86, 102
   bidirectional, 87
   SISO, 86
   with parallel load, 88
SIC computer, 104
   functional units, 113
   instruction format, 106
   instruction set, 106
   register set, 104
   startup, 114
   timing and control, 108
Signal, 59
Sign digit, 30
Signed numbers, 30–35
   addition and subtraction, 37–41
   multiplication and division, 41–42
   range of, 34
   signed binary, 33–35
   signed binary-coded, 35
Sign flag, 292
Sign-magnitude, 30
SIMD, 263
SIMD interconnection network, 275–78
   Benes, 277
   crossbar switch, 276
   dynamic, 275
   fully connected, 275
   multistage, 277
   ring, 275
   single-stage, 275
   static, 275
Simple cycle, 249
Simplex, 319
Simplified instructional computer (*see* SIC)
Single-address format, 126
SISD, 263
SISO, 86
Small-scale integration, 6, 14, 73
Software, 1, 153
Software interrupt, 157
SOP, 64
   canonical, 64
Space-time diagram, 236
Sparse addressing, 272
Special-purpose registers, 291
Speedup, 262
SR flip-flop, 82
SSI, 6, 14, 73
Stack, 184
   base register, 188
   computer, 185
   limit register, 188
   of HP3000, 188
   overflow, 185
   pointer, 187
   underflow, 185
Stack memory, 184–89
   register-based implementation, 185
   RAM-based implementation, 187
Stack register, 291
Stage, 233
Stage cascading, 241
   feedback connection, 242
   feedforward connection, 242
Start bit, 320
State diagram, 71, 248
State table, 71
Static pipeline, 239
Statistical time division multiplexing, 323–24
Status bits, 64, 156, 159
Status/control register, 64, 155, 171, 292
STDM, 323
Stop bit, 320
Store-and-forward switching, 326
Stored-program computer, 8, 99
Store instruction, 106
Straight binary number, 23
Stream, 263
Submatrix addressing, 271
Subtraction algorithms:
   fixed-point, 35–41
   floating-point, 44
   unsigned numbers, 36
   using complements, 37
Subtraction overflow, 39, 41
Sum-of-products (*see* SOP)
Supercomputer, 17, 18
Switching:
   circuit, 325
   message, 326
   packet, 327
   store-and-forward, 326
Switching algebra, 59, 62
Switching matrix, 176
Synchronous counter, 90
Synchronous inputs, 83
Synchronous sequential circuit, 70, 300
System mode, 293

T

Tag field, 198
Tag register, 195
Tape, 201–2
   drive, 201
   read/write head, 201
   track, 201
TDM, 322–23
Test instruction, 106
T flip-flop, 85
Three-format address, 126
Throughput, 233, 251, 317
Tightly coupled system, 177, 279
Time division multiplexing (*see* TDM)
Timeout, 167, 174
Time-shared bus, 281
Timing and control, 108
Timing signals, 104
Topology:
   bus, 318
   fully connected, 317
   hierarchical, 317
   mesh, 317
   ring, 317
   star, 317
   tree, 317
Track, 201, 204
Trailer, 314
Transceiver, 170, 314
Transfer gate, 73
Transmission modes:
   asynchronous, 320
   serial, 320
   synchronous, 320
Transparent DMA, 163
Tristate, 73
Two-address format, 126

U

Underflow, 44
Unifunction pipeline, 239
Unsigned numbers:
   addition, 36
   subtraction, 36

Up counter, 90
User mode, 293

V

Valid bit, 212
Vector addressing, 269–72
   dense, 269
   sequential, 271
   sparse, 272
   submatrix, 271
Vectored interrupt, 159
Vector instruction, 266
   characteristics of, 267
Vector interrupt register, 292
Vector processing, 266–72
Vector processor, 267
   computational elements, 269
   hardware architecture, 269
   pipelined, 239, 269
Vertical microinstruction, 223, 304
Vertical microprogramming, 304
Very large-scale integration, 7, 16, 73
VHSIC, 16
Virtual circuit, 328
Virtual communication, 312
Virtual memory, 16, 208–14
   implementation, 209
   management, 213
Virtual memory locations, 154
VLSI, 7, 16, 73
Volatile, 95, 184

W

Word, 90
Word counter, 164
Word interleaving, 322
Word length, 90
Write, 85, 95, 166
Write-back, 197, 284
Write microinstruction, 106
Write-through, 197

X

XOR, 74
XOR operation, 96, 299